THE AUSTRALIAN
Road Atlas

Contents

iv **IN AND AROUND THE CAPITAL CITIES**
vi Sydney & Suburbs
xii Melbourne & Suburbs
xviii Adelaide & Suburbs
xxii Perth & Suburbs
xxvi Darwin & Suburbs
xxviii Brisbane & Suburbs
xxxii Hobart & Suburbs

2 Overview Map and Map Symbols
4 Australia-wide Distance Chart
6 Inter-City Route Maps

NEW SOUTH WALES AND AUSTRALIAN CAPITAL TERRITORY

9 Location Map
10 Central Sydney
11 North Sydney
12 Sydney Suburbs
13 Central Coast
14 Sydney & Surrounds
16 Blue Mountains
18 Newcastle
19 Newcastle & Surrounds
20 Mid North Coast
21 North Coast
22 Wollongong
23 Southern Highlands
24 Central Eastern New South Wales
26 North Eastern New South Wales
28 South Western New South Wales
30 North Western New South Wales
32 Central Canberra
33 Canberra Suburbs
34 Australian Capital Territory
35 South Eastern New South Wales
36 Snowy Mountains & the South Coast

VICTORIA

38 Location Map
39 Central Melbourne
40 Melbourne Suburbs
41 Dandenong & Yarra Ranges
42 Melbourne & Surrounds
44 Mornington & Bellarine Peninsulas

46 Geelong
47 Ballarat
48 Bendigo
49 Goldfields
50 Great Ocean Road
51 Eastern Victoria
52 Southern Central Victoria
54 North Central Victoria
56 High Country
58 North Western Victoria
60 Central Western Victoria
62 South Western Victoria

SOUTH AUSTRALIA

64 Location Map
65 Central Adelaide
66 Adelaide Suburbs
67 Adelaide & Surrounds, North
68 Adelaide & Surrounds, South
69 Peninsulas & Kangaroo Island
70 Flinders Ranges
71 South Eastern South Australia
72 South Central South Australia
74 Central South Australia
76 North Eastern South Australia
78 North Western South Australia
80 South Western South Australia

WESTERN AUSTRALIA

82 Location Map
83 Central Perth
84 Perth Suburbs
85 Perth & Surrounds
86 South-West Coast
87 South Coast
88 South Western Western Australia
89 Central Western Western Australia
90 Southern Western Australia
92 Central Western Australia
94 Northern Western Australia
96 Pilbara
98 Kimberley

NORTHERN TERRITORY

100 Location Map
101 Central Darwin
102 Darwin & Surrounds
104 Top End
106 Central Northern Territory
108 Southern Northern Territory
110 The Red Centre

QUEENSLAND

112 Location Map
113 Central Brisbane
114 Brisbane Suburbs
115 Brisbane & Surrounds, South
116 Gold Coast
117 Brisbane & Surrounds, North
118 Fraser Coast
119 The Whitsunday Coast
120 Townsville to Cairns Region
121 Cairns & Surrounds
122 South Eastern Queensland
124 North Eastern Queensland
126 Far North Eastern Queensland
128 Cape York Peninsula
129 Far North Western Queensland
130 North Western Queensland
132 South Western Queensland

TASMANIA

134 Location Map
135 Tasmania Distance Chart
136 Central Hobart
137 Hobart Suburbs
138 Hobart & Surrounds
140 Southern Tasmania
142 Northern Tasmania
144 Tasmanian Highlands
145 Launceston Region

146 **INDEX OF PLACE NAMES**

Inner Urban Map Legend

Freeway, with tunnel and toll	
Highway, with tunnel	
Highway, with National Highway Route Marker	M31 · 31
Highway, with National Route Marker	A1 · 1
Highway, with Metroad Route Marker	5
Arterial road, with tunnel	
Arterial road, with State Route Marker	C141 · 26
Collector road	
Local road, vehicle track	
Railway / tram line, with station	
Ferry route	
River, creek	
Lake, reservoir	

SANDY BAY Suburb

TARONGA ZOO ⊕ Place of Interest

■ Hospital, university, college

✈ Airport

★ Lighthouse

+ Hill, mountain, peak

National park

Other reserve

Aboriginal land

Prohibited area

Maps are in a Lamberts Conformal Conic Projection
Geocentric Datum Australia, 1994 (GDA94)

IN AND AROUND
THE CAPITAL CITIES

SYDNEY & SUBURBS

YOUR GUIDE

With a population of 4 million and over 2 million international visitors each year, Sydney is widely regarded as one of the world's most beautiful cities. It is Australia's largest city and boasts great restaurants, superb architecture, cultural diversity and interesting historic sites. Set within a landscape of sweeping surf beaches, bushland, soaring cliffs and the glittering waters of Sydney Harbour, this is an irresistible destination.

CITY CENTRE

Art Gallery of New South Wales 10 G7
One of the most comprehensive collections in the country, including the largest permanent collection of Aboriginal art in the world.

Australian Museum viii G5
Australia's oldest museum, housing natural history displays and one of the world's best indigenous exhibitions.

Chinese Garden viii F5
Lakes, waterfalls, pavilions and rare exotic species.

Darling Harbour viii F5
Leisure precinct containing some of the city's major cultural and entertainment institutions.

Government House 10 F4
Set within the lush surrounds of the Royal Botanic Gardens; the magnificent state rooms, with period furnishings, may be seen on tours.

Justice and Police Museum 10 E5
Displays the history of crime and punishment in Sydney.

Powerhouse Museum viii F5
Former power station that now houses fascinating scientific, social and technological displays.

The Rocks viii G3
Historic waterside area with weekend market, galleries, cafes and craft shops.

Royal Botanic Gardens viii G4
On the site of Sydney's first farm, these magnificent gardens contain some 17 000 species.

State Library of New South Wales 10 F6
Includes the Mitchell Library, and its priceless collection of Australiana.

Sydney Aquarium 10 C7
Home to an amazing array of sea life and a living replica of the Great Barrier Reef.

Sydney Harbour Bridge 10 E1
The second-longest single-span bridge in the world. The south-east Pylon Lookout contains the Harbour Bridge Exhibition and a viewing platform.

Sydney Observatory 10 C4
Features night viewing and an astronomy museum.

Sydney Opera House 10 F3
An architectural giant of the 20th century; guided tours are available.

Sydney Tower 10 E7
The highest observation deck in the Southern Hemisphere.

Victoria Barracks 10 H12
Considered one of the best examples of Imperial military architecture in the world.

SUBURBS AND SURROUNDS

Bondi Beach ix L8
Excellent for swimming and strolling.

Centennial Park ix I8
Beautiful 220 ha of woodland, lakes, trails and gardens.

Elizabeth Bay House viii H5
Built in 1839; a museum charting the life of the upper classes in 19th-century Sydney.

Elizabeth Farm 15 K8
Incorporates the oldest European building in Australia (1793).

Ku-ring-gai Chase National Park 15 M5
A magnificent stretch of bush set around the Hawkesbury River; fishing, bushwalking and river cruises are popular.

Manly xi O5
Seaside holiday village; its beach is one of Sydney's best.

North Head xi O8
The best coastal views in Sydney.

Old Government House 15 K8
Australia's oldest public building, with the country's best collection of Colonial furniture.

Old Quarantine Station xi N7
Used to house afflicted convicts; take an evening ghost tour and enjoy the billy tea and damper afterwards.

View across Sydney Harbour

Royal National Park 15 K12
A landscape of sandstone outcrops, woodland, rainforest, cliffs and beaches.

Sydney Tramway Museum 15 J11
The largest collection of trams in the Southern Hemisphere; runs novelty tram trips.

Taronga Zoo xi J9
First opened in 1916, of particular interest is the Free Flight Birdshow.

Vaucluse House xi M11
Once the home of Blue Mountains explorer W. C. Wentworth, the house is fully furnished, with a beautiful 19th-century landscaped garden.

Visitor information

Sydney Visitor Centre The Rocks
106 George Street
(02) 9255 1788

Sydney Visitor Centre Darling Harbour
Palm Grove
(02) 9281 0788

Manly Visitor Information Centre
Manly Wharf Forecourt
(02) 9977 1088

Motoring organisation
NRMA 13 1122

Getting around

Travelling through Sydney can be daunting. The traffic is dense, the peak 'hour' lasts for several hours and some of the traffic lanes are narrow. However, with some planning, Sydney is not a difficult city to negotiate. Carefully choose a main through-route and then navigate using the route signs. Main routes are generally clearly signposted. The South Western Motorway (Route 5), the Western Motorway (Route 4), the Eastern Distributor (Route 1) and the Hills Motorway (Route 2) are all toll roads with attended toll gates.

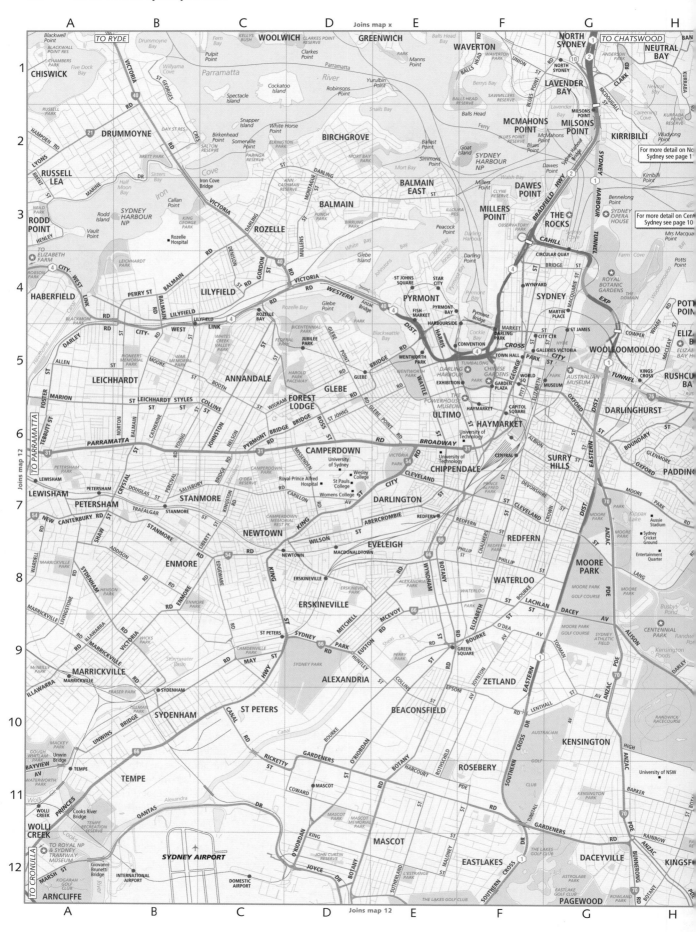

Joins map x

Joins map 12

0   1   2 km

Joins map xi

TO MANLY

MOSMAN

MIDDLE HEAD RD
RAWSON PARK

SYDNEY HARBOUR NP
GEORGES HEIGHTS OVAL

CLIFTON GARDENS

CLIFTON GARDENS

Little Sirius Cove
Sirius Cove Reserve

Georges Head

SYDNEY HARBOUR NP

SYDNEY HARBOUR NP

South Head
★ Hornby Lighthouse

Lady Bay

JACKSON

TARONGA ZOO

Chowder Bay

SYDNEY HARBOUR NP
Chowder Head

SYDNEY HARBOUR NP

Green Point
GREEN POINT RESERVE

HMAS WATSON NAVAL BASE

Taylors Bay

ATHOL WHARF RD
BRADLEYS HEAD RD

Camp Cove

WATSONS BAY

Cremorne Reserve

Robertsons Point

PORT

Bradleys Head

SYDNEY HARBOUR NATIONAL PARK

Watson Bay

ROBERTSON PARK

Gap Bluff
The Gap

GAP PARK

Manly

Ferry

Vaucluse Point

Village Point

Parsley Bay

76

CAMBRIDGE AV

Dunbar Head
Outer South Head

AV

RD

PARK

Steel Point

Shark Bay

Vaucluse Bay

PARSLEY BAY RESERVE

RD

SYDNEY HARBOUR NP

WENTWORTH

LIGHTHOUSE RESERVE

★ Macquarie Lighthouse

HERMITAGE FORESHORE RESERVE

VAUCLUSE HOUSE ☆

VAUCLUSE PARK

VAUCLUSE

CHRISTISON PARK

Shark Island

SYDNEY HARBOUR NP

Hermit Bay

Hermit Point

RD
VAUCLUSE RD

NEW   SOUTH

HOPETOUN

HEAD RD

HEAD

DIAMOND BAY RESERVE

SYDNEY HARBOUR

SYDNEY HARBOUR NP

Clarke Island

Point Piper
Felix Bay

Woollahra Point

RD

TOWNS   RD

RD

Diamond Bay

Darling Point

DARLING POINT

McKELL PARK

WYUNA RD
WOLSELEY RD

POINT PIPER

Blackburn Cove

Double Bay

Rose

Bay

DUMARESQ RESERVE

76

SOUTH   RD

RESERVE

N

STEYNE PARK

RD
RD

NEW   SOUTH

LYNE PARK

HEAD

DUDLEY PAGE RESERVE

AV

WILLIAM ST

O'SULLIVAN

DANGAR OVAL

DOVER   RD

RODNEY RESERVE

OCEAN

DOUBLE BAY

BELLEVUE

CRANBROOK SPORTSGROUND

ROYAL SYDNEY GOLF CLUB

NEWCASTLE

DOVER HEIGHTS

76
EDGECLIFF

SOUTH

VICTORIA

WOOLLAHRA GOLF CLUB

ROSE BAY

OLD

RESERVE

OCEAN

DOUBLE BAY BOWLING CLUB

WOOLLAHRA OVAL

RD

MILITARY

WOOLLAHRA

BELLEVUE HILL

ROYAL SYDNEY GOLF CLUB

MURRIVERIE

HANDY

HUGH BAMFORD RESERVE

ST
SYD

RD

COOPER PARK

RD

MILITARY

EINFELD

BELLEVUE PARK

BARRACLIFF PARK

RD

NORTH BONDI

BONDI GOLF CLUB

OXFORD

DR   OLD

SOUTH

BLAIR

RD

Bondi Junction

EBLEY ST

BONDI JUNCTION

PENVIL

DICKSON PARK

CURLEWIS

ST

WAIROA

BIRRELL

BRONTE

COUNCIL ST

WELLINGTON

BONDI BEACH

CAMPBELL PDE

BONDI GOLF CLUB

YORK

NEWLAND

QUEENS PARK

WAVERLEY PARK

BENNETT ST

BONDI

RD

BONDI BEACH ☆

Bondi Bay

RAY O'KEEFE RESERVE

QUEENS PARK RD

WAVERLEY BOWLING CLUB

ST

TAMARAMA PARK

HUNTER PARK

Ben Buckler

WAVERLEY

MURRAY

HEWLETT

TAMARAMA

Mackenzies Point

CLOVELLY

RD

ST

BRONTE

BRONTE PARK

Tamarama Bay

FRENCHMANS

RD

MACPHERSON

BRONTE

RD

Nelson Bay

ALBION

FERN

VARNA PARK

ST

AVOCA

CLOVELLY

ST

RANDWICK

GLEBE GULLY RESERVE

RD

CLOVELLY

BURNIE PARK

CLOVELLY

Beeries Cove

TASMAN   SEA

RD

RD

ARDEN

BURROWS PARK

Shark Point

COOGEE

BARDON PARK

ST

Gordons Bay

CARRINGTON

BAY

COOGEE OVAL

DUNNINGHAM RESERVE

Dolphins Point

PEROUSE

RD

Coogee Bay

BAKER PARK

RD

MOUNT

OBERON ST

GRANT RESERVE

COOGEE

BANGOR ST

ARDEN

MALABAR

BLENHEIM PARK

TRENERRY RESERVE

Wedding Cake Island

TO LA PEROUSE

SOUTH COOGEE

1
2
3
4
5
6
7
8
9
10
11
12

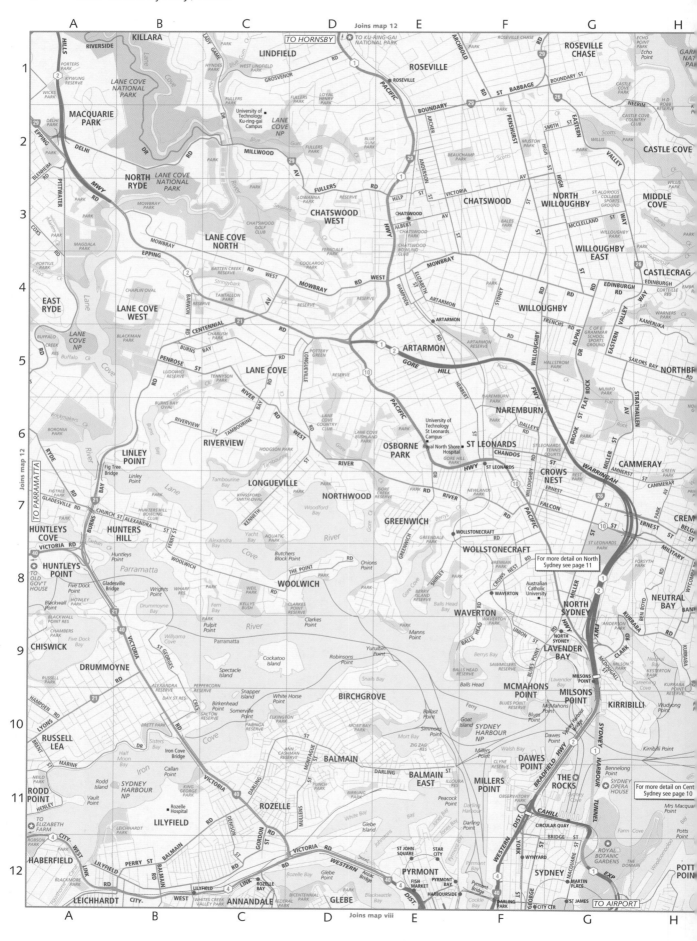

0   1   2 km

I   J   K   L   M   N   O   P

TO MONA VALE

ALLAMBIE HEIGHTS

LLARNEY HEIGHTS

GARIGAL NATIONAL PARK

GARIGAL NATIONAL PARK

WAKEHURST

GUMBOOYA RESERVE

WARRINGAH GOLF CLUB

NORTH MANLY

CORRIE RD   WILLIAM ST

BRIGHTON ST   BENNETT

JOHN FISHER RD

FLORA & RICHIE ROBERTS RESERVE

CURL CURL

Curl Curl Lagoon

Dee Why Head

1

Harbour

Yeoland Point

MANLY WAKEHURST WAR MEMORIAL PARK

MANLY DAM RESERVE

WAKEHURST GOLF CLUB

SEAFORTH OVAL

BANTRY RESERVE

Manly Reservoir

KENTWELL RD

PITTWATER

DAVID THOMAS RESERVE

MILLERS RESERVE

WARRINGAH GOLF CLUB

NOLAN ST

CAMPBELL PDE

MANLY VALE

HARBORD PARK

HARBORD

HARBORD

LAWRENCE ST

OLIVER ST

JACKA PARK

ALBERT ST   EVANS ST

CARRINGTON

McKillop PARK

Curl Curl Beach

2

H C PRESS PARK

SEAFORTH GARDEN & RECREATION

NORTH SEAFORTH

BLIGH PARK

URUNGA ST

NORTH BALGOWLAH RESERVE

WOODBINE ST

BANGAROO ST

WOODBINE

MANLY WARRINGAH WAR MEMORIAL PARK

KENNETH ST

CONDAMINE

QUIRK ST

MANLY GOLF CLUB

KEIRLE PARK

Lagoon

QUEENSCLIFF

LAGOON PARK

QUEENSCLIFF

QUEENSCLIFF

Queenscliff Bay

TASMAN

Sugarloaf Bay

Sugarloaf Point

Pickering Point

NORTH BALGOWLAH

CLONTARF ST

FRENCHS FOREST

SEAFORTH

BRIDGE

ST   CK

DEVIATION

BALGOWLAH

KENNETH ST

CONDAMINE

MANLY WEST PARK

Ck

MANLY GOLF CLUB

STEYNE

BALGOWLAH

North Steyne Beach

SEA

3

Cove

RD

PARK

BROOK

BURNT

BRIDGE

RD

BALGOWLAH GOLF CLUB

BALGOWLAH OVAL

WEEROONA RD

BALGOWLAH

PITTWATER

HURON

NORTH STEYNE PARK

RD

PARK

The Pinnacle

Powder Hulk Bay

SANGRADO PARK

PONSONBY

CRES

PDE

SYDNEY

ETHEL ST

RD

WANGANELLA ST

SOUTH

WHITE ST

LAUDERDALE AV

FAIRLIGHT

RD

SYDNEY

NORTH HARBOUR RESERVE

KANGAROO PARK

IVANHOE PARK

MANLY OVAL

TOWER HILL PARK

ST STEYNE

North Steyne

4

SEAFORTH CRES

SEAFORTH

MANLY

FISHER BAY RESERVE

NEW ST

WEST

PERONNE

BRIMBECOM PARK

North

Harbour

LAUDERDALE AV

WEST ESPLANADE EAST

ESPLANADE PARK

ASHBURNER ST

RD

Manly Beach

The Spit Bridge

Fisher Bay

Bradys Point

Sandy Bay

WELLINGS RESERVE

ESPL

DARLEY RD

Cabbage Tree Bay

Middle

Pearl Bay

SPIT RES

CLONTARF RESERVE

Parriwi Head

CLONTARF

BAREENA PARK

AV

WOODLAND

NANBAREE RESERVE

RESERVE

BALGOWLAH HEIGHTS

Manly Cove

ESPLANADE PARK

LITTLE MANLY RESERVE

MANLY

SCENIC

SYDNEY HARBOUR NATIONAL PARK

Blue Fish Point

5

BEAUTY POINT

Beauty Point

Quakers Hat

QUAKERS HAT PARK

BEATRICE

Clontarf Point

CUTLER RD

PARK

TANIA PARK

SYDNEY HARBOUR NATIONAL PARK

North

Harbour

Smedleys Point

Manly Point

Little Manly Cove

Little Manly Point

Spring Cove

NORTH HEAD

DR

MILITARY RESERVE

6

Long Bay

CLIVE PARK

ELIZABETH PARK

Fig Tree Point

Quakers Hat Bay

PARK

RD

ROSHERVILLE RESERVE

Shell

Chinamans Beach

Wy-ar-gine Point

WYARGINE RESERVE

Harbour

The Bar

Grotto Point

GROTTO POINT RESERVE

Crater Cove

The Sound

Dobroyd Head

Cannae Point

Manly

OLD QUARANTINE STATION

SYDNEY HARBOUR NATIONAL PARK

7

RNE

OURIMBAH

MACPHERSON ST

RD

AWABA

BALMORAL

THE SPIT

THE ESPLANADE

HUNTER PARK

Rocky Point

Hunters Bay

Quarantine Head

LITARY

ILITARY

MILITARY

BELMONT

MOSMAN PARK

MOSMAN BOWLING CLUB

ST

Balmoral Beach

HMAS PENGUIN NAVAL BASE

Middle Head

MIDDLE HEAD OVAL

SYDNEY HARBOUR NATIONAL PARK

NORTH HEAD

8

SHOFFORTH ST

REID PARK

AVENUE

COWLES

MOSMAN

BRADLEYS HEAD RD

RD

RAGLAN

MIDDLE HEAD

RAWSON PARK

GEORGES HEIGHTS

Obelisk Bay

JACKSON

RAGLAN

SIRIUS COVE RESERVE

Little Sirius Cove

SYDNEY HARBOUR NP

GEORGES HEIGHTS OVAL

CLIFTON GARDENS

Georges Head

South Head

Hornby Lighthouse

SYDNEY HARBOUR NP

HMAS WATSON NAVAL BASE

Lady Bay

9

RNE T

TARONGA ZOO

CLIFTON GARDENS

Chowder Bay

SYDNEY HARBOUR NP

Chowder Head

Camp Cove

Green Point

GREEN POINT RESERVE

WATSONS BAY

Little Sirius Point

Taylors Bay

CREMORNE RESERVE

Robertsons Point

ATHOL WHARF RD

Bradleys Head

SYDNEY HARBOUR NATIONAL PARK

PORT

Ferry

Vaucluse Point

Village Point

Watsons Bay

ROBERTSON RD

Gap Bluff

The Gap

GAP PARK

10

RD

Manly

SYDNEY HARBOUR

Bradleys Head

Shark Island

Steel Point

Shark Bay

Vaucluse Bay

Parsley Bay

PARK

CAMBRIDGE AV

HEAD RD

Dunbar Head

Outer South Head

11

SYDNEY HARBOUR NP

Clarke Island

HERMITAGE FORESHORE RESERVE

WENTWORTH

VAUCLUSE HOUSE

Vaucluse Bay

PARSLEY BAY RESERVE

LIGHTHOUSE RESERVE

Macquarie Lighthouse

VAUCLUSE

HOPETOUN

VAUCLUSE

NEW SOUTH HEAD RD

OLD SOUTH HEAD RD

CHRISTISON PARK

TASMAN

SEA

SYDNEY HARBOUR NP

Point Piper

Felix Point

Woollahra Point

SYDNEY HARBOUR NP

Hermit Bay

Hermit Point

Rose Bay

DIAMOND BAY RESERVE

Diamond Bay

12

ARLING POINT

Darling Point

McKELL PARK

Double Bay

WYUNA RD

POINT PIPER

ROSE BAY

TOWNS RD

TO BONDI

N

I   J   K   L   M   N   O   P

MELBOURNE & SUBURBS
YOUR GUIDE

Often described as the world's most livable city, Melbourne is a vibrant and multicultural metropolis offering great restaurants, excellent shopping and world-class sporting venues. It also boasts stunning new buildings, tree-lined boulevards and magnificent public gardens. Situated at the head of Port Phillip and centred on the north bank of the Yarra River, the city has a population of 3.4 million. Visitors will find there is always something happening in Melbourne, whether it be a lively festival or a major sporting event.

CITY CENTRE

Crown Entertainment Complex 39 B9
Shop, wine and dine or have a flutter at the casino.

Federation Square xvii K3
Shops, restaurants, the National Gallery of Victoria and the Australian Centre for the Moving Image.

Fitzroy Gardens xv L11
Beautiful gardens with Captain Cook's Cottage, the Fairy Tree and Model Tudor Village.

Koorie Heritage Centre 39 A6
An insight into Victorian Aboriginal cultural life.

Melbourne Aquarium xvii J3
The magic of marine life – over 270 species from the Southern Ocean and inland waterways.

Melbourne Cricket Ground (MCG) xvii M3
The hallowed venue for Australian rules football and cricket; contains the Australian Gallery of Sport and an Olympic Museum.

Melbourne Museum xv K9
A superb introduction to Melbourne and Australia.

Old Melbourne Gaol 39 D4
Contains chillingly macabre exhibits, including the gallows where Ned Kelly swung.

Queen Victoria Market xvii J1
A large range of fresh fish, meat, fruit, vegetables and delicatessen items along with clothing and general merchandise are on offer at this Melbourne landmark.

Royal Botanic Gardens xvii L5
Melbourne's showpiece and considered to be among the best in the world.

St Patrick's Cathedral 39 G5
Massive 19th-century bluestone building, and one of the world's best examples of Gothic Revival architecture.

State Library of Victoria 39 D5
Begun in 1854 and completed in 1913, the library holds more than one million books.

Victorian Arts Centre 39 E9
Contains three theatres, the Performing Arts Museum and the George Adams Gallery.

SUBURBS AND SURROUNDS

Dandenong Ranges 41 B8
Scenic hills and native rainforests only 50 km from the city.

Healesville Sanctuary 41 D7
The 32-ha wildlife sanctuary is world renowned, with over 200 animal and bird species.

Melbourne Cemetery xv K7
Dating back to the 1850s; explore Melbourne's history on a guided tour.

Melbourne Zoo xv I6
Great for animal lovers; see the magnificent butterfly house and walk the 'people cage' through the lions' enclosure.

Montsalvat 43 J5
An artists' colony established in the 1930s, featuring medieval-style buildings, and arts and crafts.

Museum of Modern Art at Heide 43 J5
One of Australia's most renowned art spaces, housing a collection of the great Australian artists.

Organ Pipes National Park 40 C4
An 85-ha park named after its unusual 20-m wall of basalt columns; they were formed over one million years ago from lava flow from local volcanoes.

Puffing Billy Railway 41 B9
Old-fashioned steam train with open carriages and restaurant car that travels 25 km through forest from Belgrave to Gembrook and back.

Rippon Lea Estate 43 J6
National Trust Romanesque mansion with 5 ha of beautiful English-style gardens and resident peacocks.

Melbourne city

St Kilda xvii K10
Lively beachside suburb that hosts an art and craft market on the Esplanade every Sunday; Acland Street is famous for its continental cake shops.

Scienceworks xvi C4
Interactive science and technology museum, with Planetarium, and Australia's first plane and car on display.

Studley Park Boathouse xv O9
Hire a boat or just sit by the Yarra and enjoy the Devonshire teas and bush atmosphere.

Williamstown xvi D10
Take a ferry from St Kilda to Melbourne's oldest suburb, a former maritime village with great pubs, churches and quaint cottages.

Yarra Valley 41 C6
Good scenery, excellent wineries, fine food outlets and restaurants, historic gardens and forest.

Visitor information

Melbourne Visitors Centre
Corner Swanston and Flinders streets
(03) 9658 9658

Information kiosks
Flinders Street Station and Bourke Street Mall

Victorian Tourism Information Service
13 2842
www.visitmelbourne.com.au
www.visitvictoria.com

Motoring organisation
RACV 13 1955

Getting around

The city centre is easy to explore, with its wide streets laid out in a grid system. Parking in the centre consists of mainly short-term parking meters and undercover carparks, which at peak times can be difficult to find or expensive. Outside the centre there is usually no problem finding a parking spot.

The CityLink toll road links the Tullamarine, West Gate and Monash freeways. There are no toll booths. Travellers can buy an e-TAG or a Day Pass, or pay by credit card afterwards, within 24 hours of making a journey. Call 13 2629 for details.

0   1   2 km

I   J   K   L   M   N   O   P

COBURG

ANDERSON RESERVE

MORELAND

TO EPPING

PRESTON

BRUNSWICK WEST

BRUNSWICK

THORNBURY

BRUNSWICK EAST

NORTHCOTE

PRINCES HILL

FITZROY NORTH

WESTGARTH

FAIRFIELD

PARKVILLE

MELBOURNE ZOO

CARLTON NORTH

MELBOURNE CEMETERY

CLIFTON HILL

TO MONTSALVAT & MUSEUM OF MODERN ART AT HEIDE

Royal Childrens Hospital

University of Melbourne Western Precinct

The Royal Melbourne Hospital

University of Melbourne Parkville Campus

Ormond College
St Hildas College
Queens College
Trinity College
Newman College

CARLTON

FITZROY

COLLINGWOOD

ABBOTSFORD

STUDLEY PARK BOATHOUSE

KEW

TO RINGWOOD

EASTERN FWY

YARRA BEND PARK

YARRA BEND GOLF COURSE

Melbourne Museum

Carlton Gardens

St Vincents Hospital

Queen Victoria Market

RMIT University

Melbourne Central

Flagstaff Gardens

St Vincents & Mercy Private Hospital

NORTH RICHMOND

TO HEALESVILLE SANCTUARY & YARRA VALLEY

MELBOURNE

PARLIAMENT

Fitzroy Gardens

Treasury Gardens

EAST MELBOURNE

WEST RICHMOND

HAWTHORN

For more detail on Central Melbourne see page 39

SOUTHERN CROSS

Federation Square

Flinders Street

Birrarung Marr

Melbourne Aquarium

SOUTHBANK

Alexandra Gardens
Queen Victoria Gardens

Kings Domain

TO ST KILDA

Melbourne Cricket Ground

Yarra Park

RICHMOND

Richmond Union Bowling Club

BURNLEY

I   J   K   L   M   N   O   P

1   2   3   4   5   6   7   8   9   10   11   12

0   1   2 km

I   J   K   L   Joins map xv   M   N   O   P

NORTH MELBOURNE   CARLTON   FITZROY   COLLINGWOOD   ABBOTSFORD   KEW   1

MELBOURNE   EAST MELBOURNE   2

For more detail on Central Melbourne see page 39

SOUTHBANK   HAWTHORN   3

RICHMOND   BURNLEY   4

SOUTH MELBOURNE   CREMORNE   5

ALBERT PARK   SOUTH YARRA   TOORAK   6

MIDDLE PARK   7

ALBERT PARK   PRAHRAN   8

ST KILDA WEST   WINDSOR   ARMADALE   9

ST KILDA   10

ST KILDA EAST   11

BALACLAVA   CAULFIELD NORTH   12

ELWOOD   RIPPONLEA

TO FRANKSTON

Joins map 40

I   J   K   L   M   N   O   P

ADELAIDE & SUBURBS
YOUR GUIDE

Adelaide is set on the wide curves of the River Torrens between the Mount Lofty Ranges and Gulf St Vincent. It is the only major metropolis in the world where the city's centre is completely encircled by parkland. It has a population of almost 1.1 million, but remains a friendly and open place. The city offers visitors a well-preserved history, the warmth and light of the South Australian outdoors and excellent wining and dining.

CITY CENTRE

Adelaide Casino xxi I5
Located in a beautifully restored railway station.

Adelaide Festival Centre 65 D7
One of the best performance venues in the world, with various exhibitions scattered throughout the centre.

Art Gallery of South Australia 65 E7
A superb overview of Australian art from the 18th century on.

Botanic Gardens xxi J4
Join a free tour of these beautiful, formal 16-ha gardens on the edge of the CBD.

Central Market xxi I6
Bustling market with some of the best and cheapest local produce in the country.

Light's Vision xxi I4
On Montefiore Hill, bronze statue of Colonel Light, the first surveyor-general of the city.

Migration Museum 65 E7
Housed in the former Destitute Asylum; features exhibits charting migrants' lives before, during and after their arrival.

Museum of Classical Archaeology 65 E7
Within the grounds of the University of Adelaide, this museum houses objects that date back to the third millennium BC.

Rundle Mall xxi J5
The major shopping precinct and a vibrant, cosmopolitan cafe strip.

St Peter's Cathedral 65 D5
One of Australia's finest cathedrals, built in 1869 in the Gothic Revival style.

South Australian Museum 65 E7
Features the world's largest collection of anthropological Aboriginal artefacts and a range from the Pacific Islands and Egypt.

Tandanya – National Aboriginal Cultural Institute 65 F8
Houses displays of Aboriginal culture, art, artefacts and a performance space for dance and theatre.

SUBURBS AND SURROUNDS

Adelaide Hills 67 D10
Historic villages, gardens, museums and vineyards sit among bushland and European-style farmland.

Belair National Park 67 C9
The state's oldest national park, established in 1891; includes the impressive gardens of the governor's old summer residence.

Cleland Wildlife Park xxi P10
Excellent park housing native marsupials and aviaries; night-time walks available.

Glenelg xx C11
Board a tram to this seaside resort with its old-world feel.

Haigh's Chocolates Factory xxi J7
Australia's oldest chocolate-maker. Have a look behind the scenes from the visitor centre's viewing area and take home a treat from the old-world shop's tempting array.

Henley Beach xx A4
Charming seaside town. Stop at Henley Square, set just back from the water, for a spot of live music at one of the area's restaurants, bars or cafes.

Linear Park xx F4
Lovely strip of parklands and walking paths hugging the banks of the River Torrens.

McLaren Vale wine region 67 B12
Set among rolling hectares of almond and olive groves, these 53 wineries form one of the country's top wine-producing regions.

St Peter's Cathedral and Pennington Gardens

Penfolds Magill Estate xxi O5
The first venture of one of Australia's best known winemakers. There are opportunities for cellar-door tastings and sales and the vintage cellar, dating to 1844, is still used for making shiraz.

South Australian Maritime Museum 67 B8
Re-creations of 19th-century dock life and the immigrant experience, including replicas of parts of old sailing boats.

Victor Harbor 68 F9
Popular holiday resort located on the Fleurieu Peninsula; includes a horse-drawn tram, heritage sites, penguins, dolphins and whales.

Visitor information

South Australian Visitor and Travel Centre
18 King William Street
(08) 8303 2220,
freecall 1300 655 276
www.southaustralia.com

Motoring organisation
RAA 13 1111

Getting around

Adelaide's city centre is compact and easily negotiated on foot. The Explorer Tram offers visitors the chance to tour the city's attractions at a leisurely pace and with the benefit of a recorded commentary. A fleet of Popeye motor launches cruise the River Torrens and also provide an ideal means of transport to the Adelaide Zoo. The historic Glenelg tram departs Victoria Square regularly for a return trip to Adelaide's premier seaside suburb. Car travel is recommended for touring some of the further-flung regions; the roads are excellent and navigation should not be a problem.

0 1 2 km

I J K L M N O P

TO ELIZABETH

TO HIGHBURY

1

SPECT
PROSPECT
NAILSWORTH
BROADVIEW
KLEMZIG
NEWTON
NEWTON SPORTS GROUND
COLLINSWOOD
VALE PARK
CAMPBELLTOWN
FELIXSTOW
NEWTON
A1
A10
A17
A11
River
GOLF COURSE
CAMPBELLTOWN LEISURE CENTRE
LOWER NORTH EAST RD

2

FITZROY
THORNGATE
MEDINDIE GARDENS
NOTTAGE TCE
WALKERVILLE
MARDEN
PAYNEHAM
GLYNDE
HECTORVILLE
ROSTREVOR
MAIN NORTH
LOWER
PORTRUSH RD
MONTACUTE
GLYNBURN
ST BERNARDS
ROSTREVOR RESERVE
Torrens
PATTESON SPORTS GROUND
A11

3

FITZROY
THORNGATE TCE
ROBE
MEDINDIE
GILBERTON
JOSLIN
ROYSTON PARK
PAYNEHAM
PAYNEHAM SOUTH
FIRLE
TRANMERE
MAGILL
WOODFORDE
NORTH ADELAIDE PARK
NORTHCOTE
MANN RD
PARK RD
ST PETERS PARK
PAYNEHAM OVAL
MARIAN
REID
DALY OVAL
MOULES
GLEN STUART
A10
A21
A11
A17

4

JEFFCOTT
O'CONNELL
NORTH ADELAIDE
MELBOURNE
ST PETERS
EVANDALE
MAYLANDS
TRINITY GARDENS
ST MORRIS
MAGILL
SUMMIT
TERINGIE
WELLINGTON SQUARE
BROUGHAM GARDENS
PRINCE ALFRED COLLEGE SPORTS GROUND
UNIVERSITY OF ADELAIDE SPORTS GROUND
COLLEGE PARK
STEPNEY
University of South Australia Magill Campus
NORTON SUMMIT RD
OLD NORTON SUMMIT RD
PENFOLD
THE GUMS RECREATION GROUND

5

PALMER GARDENS
KING
FROME
HACKNEY
ZOOLOGICAL GARDENS
University of South Australia
BOTANIC GARDENS
Royal Adelaide Hospital
MAGILL
BEULAH PARK
KENSINGTON PARK
KENSINGTON GARDENS
AULDANA
PENFOLDS MAGILL ESTATE
Light's Vision
ADELAIDE OVAL
PIONEER WOMENS MEMORIAL GARDENS
University of Adelaide
NORWOOD OVAL
THE PARADE
HASLAM OVAL
PARADE
ROSSLYN PARK
KENSINGTON PARK SPORTS FIELD
KENSINGTON GARDENS
SKYE
ADELAIDE CASINO
ADELAIDE
RUNDLE MALL
GRENFELL
PULTENEY
EAST TCE
RUNDLE
KENT TOWN
NORWOOD
KENSINGTON
MARRYATVILLE
LEABROOK
ERINDALE
WATTLE PARK
HALLETT
A11

6

MORPHETT
WILLIAM ST
VICTORIA SQUARE
WAKEFIELD
ADELAIDE
ADELAIDE CENTRAL MARKET
HUTT
BARTELS RD
DEQUETTEVILLE TCE
FLINDERS ST
ROSE PARK
TOORAK GARDENS
HEATHPOOL
TUSMORE
STONYFELL
FERGUSON PARK
RYMILL PARK
For more detail on Central Adelaide see page 65
St Andrew's Hospital
VICTORIA PARK RACECOURSE
DULWICH
A21
A17
TUSMORE PARK
HAZELWOOD PARK

7

SIR LEWIS COHEN AV
VEALE GARDENS
PEACOCK
UNLEY
GLEN
OSMOND RD
EASTWOOD
GREENHILL
HAZELWOOD PARK
BURNSIDE
HORSNELL GULLY
PARK LANDS
OSMOND GARDENS TCE
HAIGH'S CHOCOLATES
PARKSIDE
Glenside Hospital
GLENSIDE
LINDEN PARK
GLYNBURN
GREENHILL RECREATION PARK
A21
PORTRUSH
GREENHILL

8

AYVILLE
TRAMWAY
GLENELG
SOUTER PARK
UNLEY
UNLEY OVAL
DUTHY
FREWVILLE
GLEN OSMOND
GLENUNGA
ST GEORGES
BEAUMONT
GREENHILL
GOODWOOD
FULLARTON
PARK
GLENUNGA RESERVE
ST GEORGES RESERVE
MILLER RESERVE
DASHWOOD

9

MILLSWOOD
HYDE PARK
FISHER
MALVERN
HYDE PARK RESERVE
HEYWOOD PARK
HIGHGATE
MYRTLE BANK
FULLARTON
RIDGE PARK
GLEN OSMOND
MOUNT OSMOND
WATERFALL GULLY
RESERVE
MOUNT OSMOND GOLF COURSE
A1
A17
RD

10

KINGS PARK
UNLEY PARK
CROSS
WESTBOURNE PARK
HAWTHORN
HAWTHORN PLAYING FIELDS
BELAIR
KINGSWOOD
University of Adelaide Waite Campus
URRBRAE
CLAREMONT
AV
SOUTH
EASTERN
LEAWOOD GARDENS
CLELAND
CLELAND WILDLIFE PARK
CLELAND CONSERVATION PARK
A3
HAWTHORN
WESTBOURNE PARK OVAL
WAITE
BARKER
MOUNT
M1

11

UNLEY PARK
BATCHELOR RESERVE
TUTT
NETHERBY
MITCHAM
SPRINGFIELD
BROWN HILL CREEK
FWY
BEADE PARK
LOWER MITCHAM
TORRENS PARK
BLYTHEWOOD
OLD BELAIR
M1

12

COLONEL LIGHT GARDENS
CLAPHAM
TORRENS PARK
MITCHAM
BROWNHILL CREEK RECREATION PARK
CRAFERS WEST
ADELAIDE HILLS
TO HAHNDORF
MORTLOCK PARK
CLAPHAM
BELAIR
RANDELL RD
SPRINGBANK
PANORAMA
LYNTON
JAMES RD
BELAIR
TO BELAIR NATIONAL PARK

Joins map 66

I J K L M N O P

PERTH & SUBURBS

YOUR GUIDE

With a Mediterranean-type climate and magnificent coastal river setting, Perth is ideal for an outdoor lifestyle. Visitors will find clean surf beaches, tranquil forests and well-kept parklands – all within easy reach of the city centre. Perth is a cosmopolitan city with a population of almost 1.4 million. The Swan River winds through the suburbs, widening to lake size near the city centre, with the hills of the Darling Range forming a distant backdrop.

CITY CENTRE

Art Gallery of Western Australia 83 D5
Houses a fine collection of Australian and international works.

Barrack Street Jetty 83 C7
Board a ferry for a trip, past the exclusive waterside suburbs to Fremantle, South Perth and the Swan Valley wine region.

Kings Park xxiv E7
A 404-ha bushland reserve with landscaped gardens, walkways, lakes, a war memorial and good city views.

Northbridge xxiv F5
Lively arts precinct including the Perth Cultural Centre, the Art Gallery of Western Australia and the Perth Institute of Contemporary Arts; colourful weekend art and craft markets in the Cultural Centre Mall.

Old Mill 83 A8
Picturesque 1838 white-washed windmill; now houses an interesting collection of early colonial artefacts.

Perth Institute of Contemporary Arts (PICA) 83 D4
Sample the latest in visual and performance art.

Perth Mint 83 F6
Houses the world's largest collection of natural gold specimens; lift a gold bar and watch a gold pourer at work.

Perth Zoo xxiv F7
Set in a magnificent garden; includes a butterfly house and Australian animal exhibits.

Queens Gardens 83 G7
Site of a 19th-century brickworks; now ornamental lily ponds and garden beds.

WACA Oval xxiv G6
Famous venue for national and international cricket and Australian Rules Football matches; tours of the ground and museum Tuesday 10am.

Western Australian Museum 83 D4
Comprehensive collection including two of Perth's oldest buildings: the original Perth Gaol (1856) and an 1860s cottage.

SUBURBS AND SURROUNDS

Aquarium of Western Australia 85 B4
World-class aquarium at Hillarys Boat Harbour; houses Australia's largest underwater tunnel.

Burswood International Resort Casino xxv B7
Includes an indoor stadium, and a shimmering glass pyramid containing a tropical garden and waterfall.

Canning Vale Sunday Markets xxv C12
Western Australia's biggest undercover marketplace.

Claremont Museum xxiv C8
The former Freshwater Bay School, built in 1862 by convicts; now houses an interesting social history display.

Darling Range 85 E6
Approximately 80 000 ha of escarpment and jarrah forest in the Hills Forest area.

Fremantle Arts Centre and History Museum xxiv C11
A striking Gothic building, once a female lunatic asylum; now offers contemporary art exhibitions, Fremantle history displays, a ghost walk and a garden area with cafe.

Fremantle Prison xxiv C12
Convict-built from limestone quarried on site in the 1850s; huge, forbidding and full of history.

Lake Monger xxiv E4
See Western Australia's famous black swans and other waterbirds.

Old Swan Brewery xxv C12
Restaurant with a range of handcrafted ales from its impressive microbrewery.

Subiaco xxiv E6
A popular shopping, cafe and market area in one of Perth's oldest suburbs.

Perth city skyline

Swan Valley 85 D4
A premier wine-producing district ideal for touring, with historic attractions such as the town of Guildford.

Tranby House xxv B6
Built in 1939 and beautifully restored by the National Trust; one of the oldest and finest colonial houses in Western Australia.

University of Western Australia xxiv E7
Landscaped gardens and Mediterranean-style buildings; contains the Brendt Museum of Anthropology and the Lawrence Wilson Art Gallery.

Western Australian Maritime Museum xxiv B12
Displays include an excellent reconstruction of the 1629 Dutch wreck *Batavia*.

Visitor information

Western Australian Visitors Centre
Corner Forrest Place and Wellington Street
(08) 9483 1111, freecall 1300 361 351
www.westernaustralia.com

Fremantle Tourist Bureau
Fremantle Town Hall
Corner William and Adelaide streets
(08) 9431 7878

Motoring organisation
RAC 13 1111

Getting around

The city centre is compact and easy to explore. A free, regular bus service known as the CAT (Central Area Transit) System operates around central Perth. You can also travel free on Transperth buses and trains within the Free Transit Zone in the city centre. Transperth produces a handy tourist guide and map that shows the Free Transit Zone.

A good way to discover the city is on the Perth Tram Co. tours, which operate daily. These replicas of the city's first trams extend east to Burswood International Resort Casino and west to the University of Western Australia. On weekdays Fremantle Tram Tours operates a 'tram' tour (the vehicle is actually a bus) around the streets of historic Subiaco and out to Lake Monger.

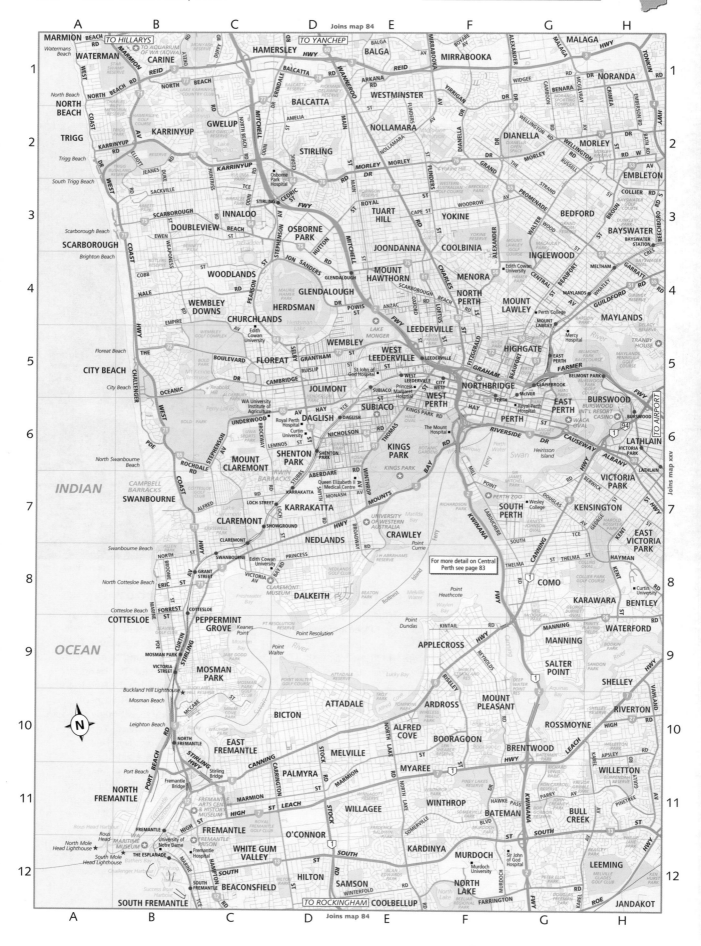

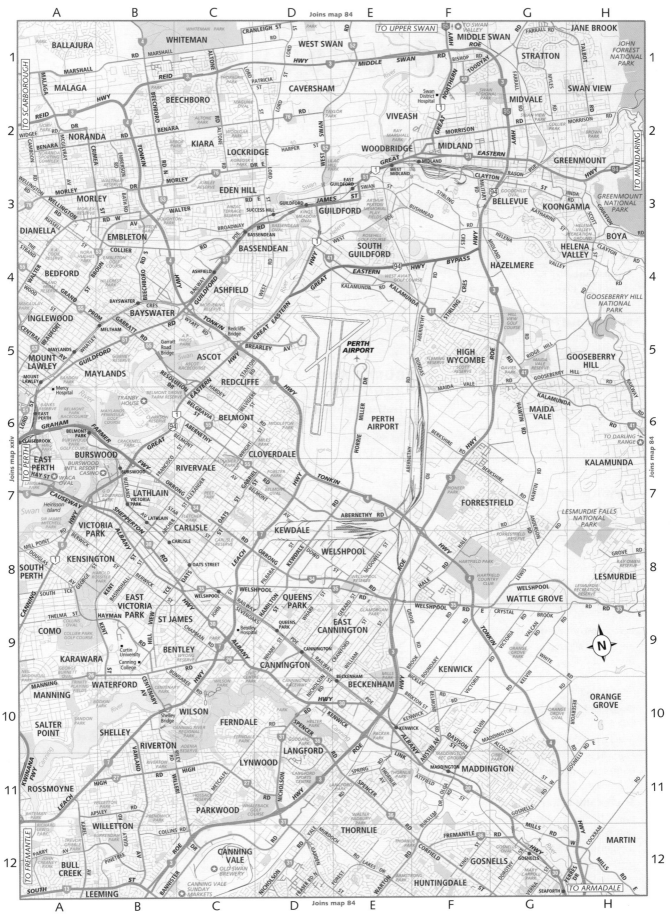

0 1 2 3 4 5 km

DARWIN & SUBURBS
YOUR GUIDE

Darwin is about the size of a large provincial town, with all the facilities you would expect of a capital city. Its climate changes from hot and dry to hot and humid later in the year. Twice rebuilt, Darwin has a spacious, ordered feel thanks to the wide streets, newish low buildings and expansive manicured lawns. But it is also a city with a magnificent tropical chaos as streets give way to mangrove estuaries, brightly coloured foliage and huge ocean tides.

CITY CENTRE

Aquascene 101 B7
Hand feed Darwin's many fish species at high tide.

Bicentennial Park xxvii B10
Take a stroll on the Esplanade; extensive trails, memorial sites and brilliant views.

Christ Church Cathedral 101 F9
Built in 1902, hit by Japanese gunfire in 1942 and destroyed by Cyclone Tracy in 1974; the new building incorporates the original porch, and an incredible altar hewn from a jarrah log that was more than 400 years old.

Darwin Botanic Gardens xxvii B9
Lush gardens that date back to a vegetable patch established in the 1870s; impressive tropical, orchid and palm collections, and a self-guided Aboriginal plant-use trail.

Mindil Beach Sunset Market xxvii B9
Live entertainment, exotic foods, art and craft, a tropical sunset and beach fireworks; Thursday nights, May to October, and Sunday nights, June to September.

Overland Telegraph Memorial 101 F10
Marks the centenary of significant Darwin events, including the completion of the Overland Telegraph.

Stokes Hill Wharf xxvii C11
Once the main port of the city and now a popular leisure area with food outlets, a pearl store, bar and restaurant.

World War II Oil Storage Tunnels 101 F10
Network of five concrete tunnels built to store oil for the navy; one tunnel is open to the public and features photographs and stories of the war years.

SUBURBS AND SURROUNDS

Australian Aviation Heritage Centre xxvii F7
Impressive list of exhibits including a massive B52 bomber and the wreckage of a Zero fighter shot down over Darwin in 1942.

Casuarina Coastal Reserve xxvii E2
Long, white sandy beach, dunes, and mangrove and monsoon vine thickets.

Crocodylus Park xxvii H6
For a safe encounter with these prehistoric monster reptiles, among other wildlife; also a research centre and museum.

Cullen Bay Marina xxvii A9
Wonderful views, waterfront dining, shops and boardwalk; departure point for sunset cruises.

Darwin Crocodile Farm 102 E4
Houses 7000 estuarine and freshwater crocodiles combined; tours and feeding displays.

East Point Military Museum xxvii A6
Artillery, war planes, archival footage of Japanese bombings and photographic collection.

Fannie Bay Gaol Museum xxvii B8
Darwin's prison from 1883 to 1979; local history displays and remnants of prison life such as old cells and gallows.

Howard Springs 102 E3
Nature reserve with a spring-fed, crocodile-free pool for swimming.

Museum and Art Gallery of the Northern Territory xxvii B8
Features one of the most significant Aboriginal art collections, and a Cyclone Tracy gallery.

Visitor information

Tourism Top End
Corner Mitchell and Knuckey streets
Darwin (08) 8936 2499
www.tourismtopend.com.au

Motoring organisation
AANT 13 1111

Getting around

Darwin is very easy to negotiate either by car or on foot. The streets are well signed and traffic is light even at peak times. The Tour Tub bus tour of the city's top sights departs daily from the north end of Smith Street Mall. Cullen Bay Marina is the departure point for cruises around Fannie Bay, Stokes Hill Wharf and Frances Bay, and for ferry trips to Mandorah on the Cox Peninsula.

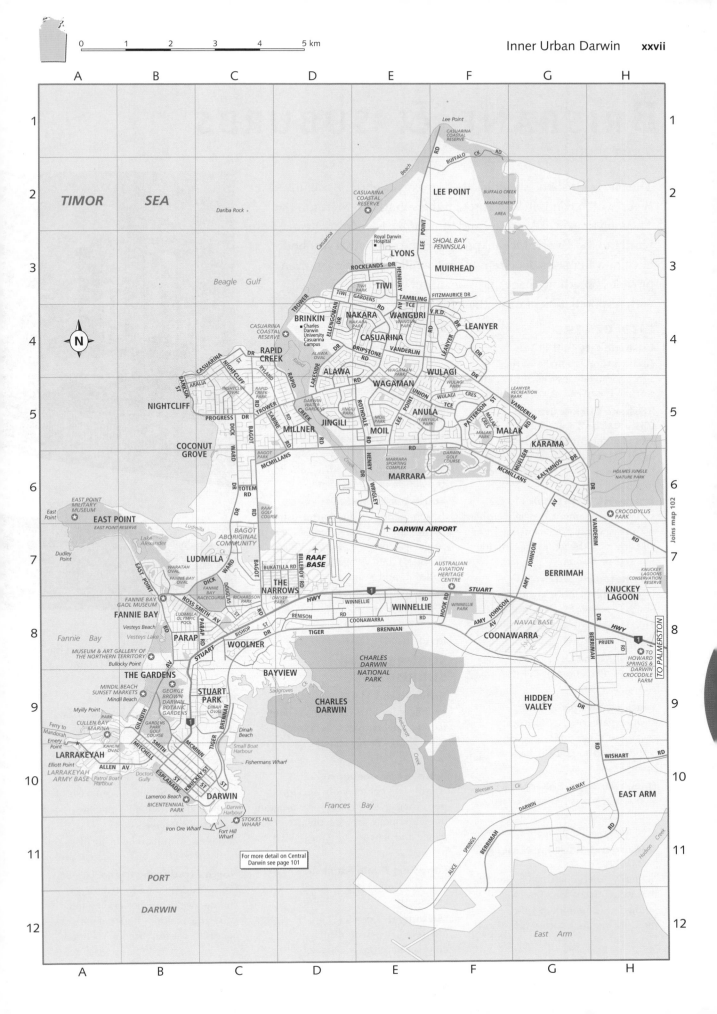

0 1 2 3 4 5 km

A B C D E F G H

1

TIMOR   SEA

Lee Point

CASUARINA
COASTAL
RESERVE

2

Dariba Rock

CASUARINA
COASTAL
RESERVE

LEE POINT

BUFFALO CK RD

BUFFALO CREEK
MANAGEMENT
AREA

3

Beagle   Gulf

Royal Darwin
Hospital

LYONS

SHOAL BAY
PENINSULA

MUIRHEAD

ROCKLANDS DR

HENBURY AV

TIWI

TAMBLING TCE

FITZMAURICE DR

TIWI
GARDENS

4

CASUARINA
COASTAL
RESERVE

Charles
Darwin
University
Casuarina
Campus

BRINKIN

NAKARA

WANGURI

V.R.D.

LEANYER

ELLENGOWAN DR

NAKARA
PARK

CASUARINA

WANGURI
PARK

LEANYER DR

DRIPSTONE RD

VANDERLIN

ALAWA
OVAL

**RAPID
CREEK**

ALAWA

WULAGI

CASUARINA ST

NIGHTCLIFF RD

RYLAND RD

LAKESIDE DR

RAPID CREEK RD

WAGAMAN
PARK

WULAGI
PARK

LEANYER
RECREATION
PARK

5

NIGHTCLIFF

BANKSIA ST

ARALIA ST

NIGHTCLIFF
OVAL

RAPID
CREEK
PARK

WAGAMAN

WULAGI TCE

VANDERLIN DR

PROGRESS DR

TROWER RD

SABINE RD

DARWIN
WATER
GARDENS

JINGILI

ROTHDALE RD

JINGILI
PARK

MOIL

LEE POINT RD

UNION

CRES

ANULA

YANYULA
PARK

PATTERSON ST

MALAK RD

MALAK

DICK WARD DR

BAGOT RD

MILLNER

MOIL
PARK

MALAK
PARK

KARAMA

6

**COCONUT
GROVE**

MCMILLANS

BAGOT
PARK

MARRARA
SPORTING
COMPLEX

DARWIN
GOLF
COURSE

MCMILLANS RD

MUELLER RD

KALYMNOS DR

TOTEM RD

MARRARA

HENRY WRIGLEY DR

HOLMES JUNGLE
NATURE PARK

VANDERIM DR

7

*East
Point*

EAST POINT
MILITARY
MUSEUM

EAST POINT RESERVE

Ludmilla

BAGOT
ABORIGINAL
COMMUNITY

RAAF GOLF
COURSE

✈ **DARWIN AIRPORT**

AUSTRALIAN
AVIATION
HERITAGE
CENTRE

BERRIMAH

AMY JOHNSON AV

CROCODYLUS
PARK

KNUCKEY
LAGOONS
CONSERVATION
RESERVE

*Dudley
Point*

EAST POINT

*Lake
Alexander*

LUDMILLA

DICK WARD DR

DOUGLAS

BAGOT RD

BUKATILLA RD

BILLEROY RD

**RAAF
BASE**

8

Fannie   Bay

FANNIE BAY
GAOL MUSEUM

WARATAH
OVAL

FANNIE BAY
OVAL

FANNIE
BAY
RACECOURSE

**THE
NARROWS**

RICHARDSON PARK

DWYER ST

HWY

WINNELLIE

WINNELLIE
PARK

STUART

KNUCKEY
LAGOON

EAST POINT RD

ROSS SMITH AV

BENISON ST

COONAWARRA RD

HOOK RD

NAVAL BASE

HWY

FANNIE BAY

PARAP

PARAP RD

BISHOP ST

WOOLNER

TIGER ST

BRENNAN

AMY JOHNSON AV

COONAWARRA

BERRIMAH RD

PRUEN RD

TO PALMERSTON

9

MUSEUM & ART GALLERY OF
THE NORTHERN TERRITORY

Bullocky Point

LUDMILLA
OLYMPIC
POOL

STUART

BAYVIEW

Sadgroves Ck

**CHARLES
DARWIN
NATIONAL
PARK**

**HIDDEN
VALLEY**

DR

THE GARDENS

MINDIL BEACH
SUNSET MARKETS

Mindil Beach

GILRUTH AV

GEORGE
BROWN
DARWIN
BOTANIC
GARDENS

**STUART
PARK**

BRENNAN

DINAH OVAL

**CHARLES
DARWIN**

Richardt Creek

Myilly Point

CULLEN BAY
MARINA

KAHLIN
OVAL

GARDENS
PARK GOLF
COURSE

SMITH ST

MCMINN

*Dinah
Beach*

10

*Ferry to
Mandorah*

*Emery
Point*

MITCHELL

TIGER ST

*Small Boat
Harbour*

WISHART RD

LARRAKEYAH

Elliott Point

LARRAKEYAH
ARMY BASE

ALLEN AV

*Patrol Boat
Harbour*

*Doctors
Gully*

ESPLANADE

KNUCKEY ST

MCMINN ST

DARWIN

Fishermans Wharf

DARWIN RD

RAILWAY

EAST ARM

Bleesers Ck

11

BICENTENNIAL
PARK

Lameroo Beach

*Darwin
Harbour*

Iron Ore Wharf

*Fort Hill
Wharf*

STOKES HILL
WHARF

Frances   Bay

For more detail on Central
Darwin see page 101

ALICE SPRINGS

BERRIMAH RD

Hudson Creek

12

PORT

DARWIN

East   Arm

A B C D E F G H

Joins map 102

BRISBANE & SUBURBS

YOUR GUIDE

The city of Brisbane straddles the lazy curves of the Brisbane River, which winds its way through the suburbs to Moreton Bay. The long fingers of Moreton and Stradbroke islands create a barrier to the Pacific Ocean, providing the city with a vast body of calm water at its doorstep. Inland, a hilly subtropical terrain provides breathing space and a beautiful backdrop for the city with its population of more than 1.6 million.

CITY CENTRE

Brisbane City Hall 113 D6
Architectural landmark of the city centre; also houses the contemporary work of the Brisbane City Gallery.

Brisbane Cricket Ground ('The Gabba') xxx H9
Home to the Australian Rules football team the Brisbane Lions; hosts international and state cricket matches.

Brunswick Street Mall 113 G2
Part of a lively inner-city neighbourhood with reasonably priced cuisine from all corners of the world; fascinating markets on Sundays.

City Botanic Gardens xxx G8
Ornamental plantings, glittering ponds, a mangrove boardwalk and broad sweeps of lawn on the banks of the Brisbane River.

Customs House 113 F4
Gallery and restaurant in historic riverside setting.

Eagle Street Pier 113 F6
Popular gathering spot with restaurants, bars and cafes; on Sundays, setting for Brisbane's largest open-air market.

Queensland Art Gallery 113 B7
Renowned artists represented from Australia and abroad; features a meditative Water Mall.

Queensland Maritime Museum 113 D11
Seafaring relics charting Queensland's maritime history from the Dutch landing at Cape York in 1606; includes dry dock with World War II frigate.

Queensland Museum 113 B7
Extensive natural history collection with endangered species display and a virtual 'trip' back 220 million years. Museum also houses Sciencentre, an interactive science experience for the whole family.

St John's Cathedral 113 F4
Gothic-style building with the only stone-vaulted ceiling in a cathedral in the Southern Hemisphere.

South Bank Parklands xxx G8
Beach, rainforest and butterfly house in the city; on Friday evenings, a magical setting for Lantern Village Market; Craft Village Market Saturday and Sunday.

Story Bridge xxx H7
The city's best-known landmark and the largest steel cantilever bridge in Australia.

SUBURBS AND SURROUNDS

Bribie Island 115 F1
Excellent for bushwalking, crabbing, fishing and boating; access from Caboolture–Bribie Island Road (via bridge).

Brisbane Powerhouse xxxi I8
A lively arts centre set in a restored powerhouse. Offers a diverse program of contemporary music, theatre, dance and artwork, and fortnightly markets.

Lone Pine Koala Sanctuary 115 D5
Visit the world's largest koala sanctuary.

Miegunyah xxx H5
Historic house with displays commemorating Queensland's pioneering women.

Mount Coot-tha Forest xxx B7
Take in the sensational views from the summit; wander through Mount Coot-tha Botanic Gardens.

Mount Glorious 115 B3
Dense forests and spectacular views; visit Walk-about Creek Wildlife Centre en route.

New Farm Park xxxi I8
Nestled on the river bend at the end of Brunswick Street; garden oasis of tropical and ornamental species.

Newstead House xxxi I5
A classic Australian homestead on the banks of the river at Breakfast Creek.

North Stradbroke Island 115 G6
Popular destination for fishing, surfing, swimming, horseriding and canoeing; includes national park; access by car ferry from Cleveland.

Victoria Bridge and the city

Ormiston House 115 F5
Former home of the founder of
Queensland's big sugar industry (open
Sunday, March to November).

Redcliffe Peninsula 115 E2
Juts out into Moreton Bay, providing
beautiful sandy beaches; swimming
is generally safe and the fishing is
excellent.

St Helena Island 115 F4
Former penal settlement, now a
national park; cruises to the island,
incorporating guided tours of historic
and Aboriginal heritage sites, depart
from Manly Boat Harbour.

XXXX Brewery xxx F7
Home to Queensland's iconic fourex
beer since 1978. For beer lovers, the
tour is a must.

Visitor information

Brisbane Visitor Information Centre
Queen Street Mall
(07) 3006 6290
www.ourbrisbane.com

Visitor Information Centre
South Bank Parklands
Allgas building, Stanley Street Plaza
(07) 3867 2051

Redlands Tourism Centre
1 Passage Street, Cleveland
(07) 3821 0057

Bayside Information Centre
66 Bay Terrace, Wynnum
(07) 3893 0589

Redcliffe Tourist Information Centre
Pelican Park, Hornibrook Esplanade
(07) 3284 3500

Motoring organisation
RACQ 13 1111

Getting around

Brisbane has well-signed roads and little
traffic congestion, yet it is not an easy
city for the first-time visitor to negotiate.
There is a crisscrossing network of major
motorways and a number of one-way
streets. Brisbane's best through-routes
are all multilane motorways with staffed
tollgates.

The Gateway Motorway also provides
excellent access to Brisbane Airport. The
transport system (bus, rail, catamaran
and ferry) is efficient, with a couple
of excellent bus routes specifically for
tourists. A boat trip on the Brisbane
River is a must, and there is a very good
commuter ferry and catamaran (CityCat)
service that stops at key destinations
around the city.

HOBART & SUBURBS
YOUR GUIDE

Hobart, Australia's second oldest and most southerly city, is situated on the broad estuary of the River Derwent under the spell of majestic Mount Wellington. A strong maritime flavour and sense of the past give Hobart an almost European air. This feeling is heightened in winter, when daytime temperatures drop to a crisp average 12 degrees Celsius. However, it is also very much an Australian city, surrounded as it is by bushland and boasting prime examples of distinctive colonial architecture.

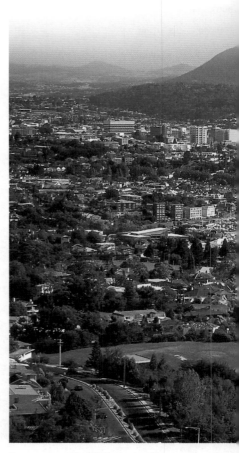

CITY CENTRE

Anglesea Barracks 136 E8
The oldest military establishment in Australia, dating back to 1846, with beautiful Georgian buildings; guided tours on Tuesday mornings.

Battery Point 1 B8
Former mariners' village; tearooms, restaurants and an antique shop around every corner.

Constitution Dock 136 E7
Historic hub of Hobart's busy waterfront; buy fresh seafood on the dock.

Maritime Museum of Tasmania 136 F7
Treasure chest of seafaring relics from when Hobart was a famous seaport.

Narryna Heritage Museum 136 F9
Colonial collection in a historic townhouse. Visitors can view everyday items used by wealthy 19th century families to see how life used to be.

Parliament House 136 F8
Originally a customs house designed by John Lee Archer and constructed by convicts in the late 1830s; visitors may inspect the restored Legislative Council Chamber.

Penitentiary Chapel Historic Site 136 E5
View the tunnels, courtrooms and solitary confinement cells; ghost tours operate most evenings.

Royal Botanical Gardens 1 B5
The state's horticultural jewel, contained within convict-built walls; includes the Botanical Discovery Centre.

St Davids Park 1 B8
A good place to rest; Hobart's first colonial burial ground was here with gravestones dating back to 1804.

Salamanca Place 136 F8
Setting for the bustling Saturday market; historic 1830s warehouses now house quality arts and crafts, cafes and restaurants.

Tasmanian Museum and Art Gallery 136 F7
Notable for its magnificent colonial landscape paintings, Aboriginal history and the convict experience.

Theatre Royal 136 F6
Australia's oldest theatre still in operation.

SUBURBS AND SURROUNDS

Cadbury Schweppes Chocolate Factory xxxiv B1
A chocolate-lover's dream come true; tours on weekdays and free samples.

Cascade Brewery 139 I5
Set in the foothills of Mount Wellington and over 150 years old; offers tours on weekdays.

D'Entrecasteaux Channel 138 G11
A leisurely drive from Hobart along the coastline of this deep-blue channel takes you through tiny towns and boutique produce farms; stunning views.

Derwent Valley 138 G4
Neat agricultural landscapes, rolling hills and historic buildings.

Kangaroo Bluff Historic Site 1 E7
The site of a fascinating old fort built in 1885 to guard against a feared Russian invasion.

Moorilla Estate xxxiv B3
Vineyard developed in 1955 that put Tasmanian cool-climate wines on the map. Taste wines, sample beer brewed on site and tour the Museum of Antiquities.

Mount Nelson Signal Station Reserve 1 B11
Enjoy sweeping views of the Derwent Valley and Storm Bay; the view from the restaurant at the summit is spectacular at night.

Mount Wellington 139 I5
Superb views of the D'Entrecasteaux Channel and the Derwent Valley, 1270 m above the city.

View across Sandy Bay towards Hobart city

Richmond 139 J3
Probably Australia's best preserved Georgian Colonial village; boasts the country's oldest bridge, built by convicts in the 1820s; the local gaol pre-dates Port Arthur.

Runnymede xxxiv E8
National Trust Georgian-style house with lovely gardens.

Tasmanian Transport Museum xxxiv B5
Contains a restored and working collection of steam engines, locomotives and railway carriages.

Wrest Point Casino 1 B9
Australia's first legal casino, opened in 1973. Features a revolving top-floor restaurant with views up the Derwent River.

Visitor information

Tasmanian Travel and Information Centre
Corner Elizabeth and Davey streets, Hobart
(03) 6230 8233
www.discovertasmania.com

Motoring organisation
RACT 13 1111

Getting around

Traffic flows freely throughout Hobart; however, be warned that many of the streets are one way. Metered street parking is readily available and the Council operates several carparks at modest rates. Metro Tasmania operates a bus service that runs frequently during business hours, with a limited evening/weekend timetable. Ferries and cruise boats leave regularly from Franklin Wharf and Brooke Street Pier at Sullivans Cove. During summer, sailing vessels run charter tours as far afield as Port Arthur and Bruny Island. There are also a number of coach tours, including a daily tour of the city and suburbs.

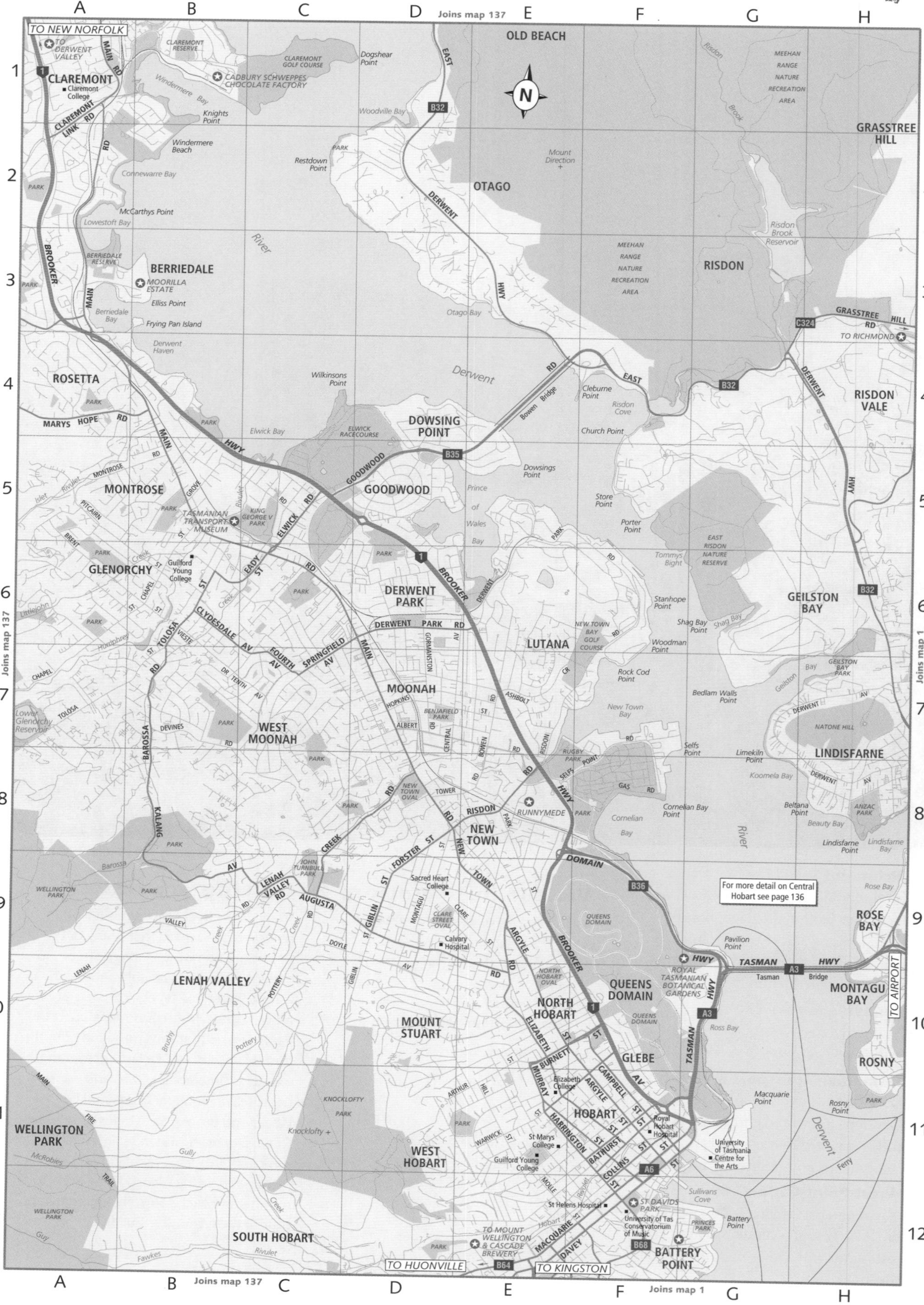

0   1   2 km

TO NEW NORFOLK

TO DERWENT VALLEY

CLAREMONT
Claremont College
CLAREMONT LINK RD
MAIN RD
BROOKER

CLAREMONT RESERVE
CADBURY SCHWEPPES CHOCOLATE FACTORY
CLAREMONT GOLF COURSE
Dogshear Point
OLD BEACH

Windermere Bay
Knights Point
Woodville Bay
EAST
B32

Windermere Beach
Connewarre Bay
Restdown Point
PARK
OTAGO
Mount Direction

McCarthys Point
Lowestoft Bay
DERWENT HWY

PARK
BERRIEDALE RESERVE
BERRIEDALE
MOORILLA ESTATE
Elliss Point
Berriedale Bay
Frying Pan Island
Derwent Haven

MEEHAN RANGE NATURE RECREATION AREA
RISDON
Risdon Brook
Risdon Brook Reservoir

GRASSTREE HILL

MAIN RD
Otago Bay
Derwent River
RD
GRASSTREE HILL RD
C324
TO RICHMOND

ROSETTA
MARYS HOPE RD
PARK
Wilkinsons Point
Derwent River
Bowen Bridge
EAST
Cleburne Point
Risdon Cove
B32
RISDON VALE

Elwick Bay
ELWICK RACECOURSE
DOWSING POINT
Church Point
DERWENT HWY

MONTROSE
PITCAIRN
GROVE
TASMANIAN TRANSPORT MUSEUM
KING GEORGE V PARK
ELWICK RD
GOODWOOD RD
GOODWOOD
B35
Dowsings Point
Prince of Wales Bay
Store Point
Porter Point
EAST RISDON NATURE RESERVE

BRENT
GLENORCHY
Guilford Young College
CLYDESDALE AV
FOURTH AV
SPRINGFIELD AV
MAIN RD
DERWENT PARK RD
DERWENT PARK
GORMANSTON RD
BROOKER HWY
Tommys Bight
Stanhope Point
Shag Bay Point
Shag Bay
GEILSTON BAY
B32

TOLOSA
CHAPEL
VIESTE
DR TENTH AV
HOPKINS
ALBERT
CENTRAL
MOONAH
NEW TOWN BAY GOLF COURSE
Woodman Point
Rock Cod Point
Bedlam Walls Point
GEILSTON BAY PARK
DERWENT

Lower Glenorchy Reservoir
BAROSSA RD
KALANG
DEVINES
PARK
WEST MOONAH
BENJAFIELD PARK
ASHBOLT
BOWEN
RISDON RD
New Town Bay
Selfs Point
Limekiln Point
NATONE HILL
LINDISFARNE

Barossa
WELLINGTON PARK
PARK
NEW TOWN OVAL
TOWER
RISDON
FORSTER ST
NEW TOWN RD
GIBLIN ST
RUGBY
SELFS POINT
GAS RD
Cornelian Bay Point
Koomela Bay
Beltana Point
ANZAC PARK
Beauty Bay

KALANG AV
LENAH VALLEY RD
JOHN TURNBULL PARK
Sacred Heart College
MONTAGU
CLARE STREET OVAL
Calvary Hospital
NEW TOWN
DOMAIN
RUNNYMEDE
Cornelian Bay
Derwent River
Lindisfarne Point
Lindisfarne Bay
ROSE BAY

Rose Bay
For more detail on Central Hobart see page 136

WELLINGTON PARK
VALLEY
AUGUSTA
DOYLE
GIBLIN ST
ARGYLE RD
BROOKER HWY
B36
QUEENS DOMAIN
Pavilion Point
TASMAN HWY
A3
Tasman Bridge
ROSE BAY

LENAH VALLEY
POTTERY
MOUNT STUART
NORTH HOBART OVAL
ELIZABETH ST
NORTH HOBART
ROYAL TASMANIAN BOTANICAL GARDENS
TASMAN HWY
A3
Tasman
Ross Bay
MONTAGU BAY

MAIN
FIRE
TRAIL
BURNETT
MURRAY ST
ARTHUR
HILL
WARWICK
Elizabeth College
CAMPBELL ST
ARGYLE ST
GLEBE
AV
Macquarie Point
ROSNY
Rosny Point
PARK

WELLINGTON PARK
McRobies
Gully
KNOCKLOFTY PARK
Knocklofty
HARRINGTON ST
BATHURST ST
St Marys College
Guilford Young College
HOBART
COLLINS ST
Royal Hobart Hospital
University of Tasmania
Centre for the Arts
A6
Sullivans Cove
Derwent River
Ferry

WELLINGTON PARK
Guy
TRAIL
Fawkes Rivulet
SOUTH HOBART
WEST HOBART
Hobart Rivulet
St Helens Hospital
TO MOUNT WELLINGTON & CASCADE BREWERY
MACQUARIE ST
DAVEY ST
University of Tas Conservatorium of Music
ST DAVIDS PARK
PRINCES PARK
Battery Point
B68
BATTERY POINT

B64

0 1 2 km

TO GAGEBROOK

Joins map xxxiv

RISDON VALE

DERWENT PARK

Store Point
Porter Point

RISDON

SUGARLOAF

EAST RISDON NATURE RESERVE

Sugarloaf Hill

PARK

CAMBRIDGE

LUTANA

Stanhope Point

Tommys Bight

Shag Bay Point

Woodman Point

GEILSTON BAY

Faggs

MEEHAN RANGE NATURE RECREATION AREA

NEW TOWN BAY GOLF COURSE

Rock Cod Point

New Town Bay

Bedlam Walls Point

GEILSTON BAY PARK

PARK

Flagstaff Gully Reservoir

Koomela Bay

NATONE HILL

LINDISFARNE

NEW TOWN

GAS

Cornelian Bay Point

Limekiln Point

Selfs Point

Beltana Point

Beauty Bay

ANZAC PARK

Lindisfarne Bay

FLAGSTAFF

Cornelian Bay

Lindisfarne Point

Shore Street Point

WARRANE

MEEHAN RANGE NATURE RECREATION AREA

RUGBY PARK

B32

Rose Bay

ROSE BAY

GORDONS HILL

Warrane Recreation Reserve

TASMAN

CAMBRIDGE

TO RICHMOND

QUEENS DOMAIN

B36

Pavilion Point

TASMAN

Gordons Hill Nature Recreation Area

CAMBRIDGE

MORNINGTON

TO AIRPORT

B33

Mackillop College

NORTH HOBART OVAL

ROYAL TASMANIAN BOTANICAL GARDENS

A3

Montagu Point

MONTAGU BAY

ROSNY PARK GOLF COURSE

ROSNY PARK

Mornington Reservoir

Waverley Flora Park

QUEENS DOMAIN

QUEENS DOMAIN

Ross Bay

Montagu Bay

ROSNY HILL NATURE RECREATION AREA

Rosny College

KNOPWOOD HILL NATURE RECREATION AREA

NORTH HOBART

GLEBE

ROSNY

BELLERIVE

Elizabeth College

Macquarie Point

Sheoak Point

CLARENCE

SOUNDY PARK

HOBART

Rosny Point

PARK

Kangaroo Bay

MORNINGTON PARK

CLARENCE

St Marys College

Royal Hobart Hospital

University of Tasmania Centre for the Arts

BELLERIVE OVAL

SOUTH

Bellerive Beach

WENTWORTH PARK

WEST HOBART

A6

St Helens Hospital

Ferry

KANGAROO BLUFF HISTORIC SITE

Kangaroo Bluff

ST DAVIDS PARK

Sullivans Cove

PRINCES PARK

Battery Point

Second Bluff

Howrah Beach

University of Tasmania Conservatorium of Music

B68

BATTERY POINT

For more detail on Central Hobart see page 136

Little Howrah Beach

ROKEBY RD

FITZROY GARDENS

Short Beach

Howrah Point

HOWRAH

A6

KING ST

B33

River

Derwent

TRANMERE

University of Tasmania Teaching & Learning

Mt Carmel College

Wrest Point WREST POINT CASINO

University of Tasmania Sandy Bay Campus

University of Tasmania Hytten Hall

Christ College

Lords Beach

B68

DYNNYRNE

University of Tasmania Horticulture

Red Chapel Beach

Nutgrove Beach

LONG BEACH RESERVE

Sandy Bay Point

SANDY BAY

Long Sandy Bay

SKYLINE RESERVE

MT NELSON

ALEXANDRA BATTERY PARK

Long Beach

Little Sandy Bay

Blinking Billy Point

Blinking Billy Beach

Derwent

C643

MOUNT NELSON

SIGNAL STATION

RESERVE

B68

Tranmere Point

TRANMERE

Mount Nelson

TRUGANINI CONSERVATION AREA

TO KINGSTON

TO D'ENTRECASTEAUX CHANNEL

ROAD ATLAS

Inter-City Route Maps

The inter-city route maps and distance charts will help you plan your route between major cities. As well, you can use the maps during your journey, since they provide information on distances between towns along the route, roadside rest areas and road conditions. The table below provides an overview of the routes mapped. The inter-city route maps can be found on pages 6–8.

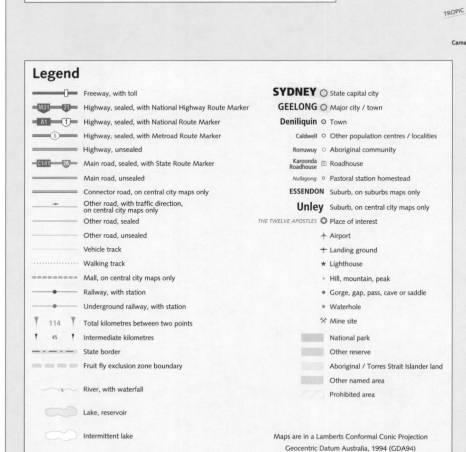

INTER CITY ROUTES	DISTANCE	TIME
Sydney–Melbourne via Hume Hwy/Fwy	881 km	12 hrs
Sydney–Melbourne via Princes Hwy/Fwy	1037 km	15 hrs
Sydney–Brisbane via New England Hwy	1001 km	14 hrs
Melbourne–Adelaide via Western & Dukes hwys	733 km	8 hrs
Melbourne–Adelaide via Princes Hwy	906 km	11 hrs
Melbourne–Brisbane via Newell Hwy	1676 km	20 hrs
Darwin–Adelaide via Stuart Hwy	3026 km	31 hrs
Adelaide–Perth via Eyre & Great Eastern hwys	2700 km	32 hrs
Adelaide–Sydney via Sturt & Hume hwys	1417 km	19 hrs
Perth–Darwin via Great Northern Hwy	4032 km	46 hrs
Sydney–Brisbane via Pacific Hwy	966 km	14 hrs
Brisbane–Darwin via Warrego Hwy	3406 km	39 hrs
Brisbane–Cairns via Bruce Hwy	1703 km	20 hrs
Hobart–Launceston via Midland Hwy	200 km	3 hrs
Hobart–Devonport via Midland & Bass hwys	286 km	4 hrs

Legend

Freeway, with toll	
Highway, sealed, with National Highway Route Marker	
Highway, sealed, with National Route Marker	
Highway, sealed, with Metroad Route Marker	
Highway, unsealed	
Main road, sealed, with State Route Marker	
Main road, unsealed	
Connector road, on central city maps only	
Other road, with traffic direction, on central city maps only	
Other road, sealed	
Other road, unsealed	
Vehicle track	
Walking track	
Mall, on central city maps only	
Railway, with station	
Underground railway, with station	
114 Total kilometres between two points	
45 Intermediate kilometres	
State border	
Fruit fly exclusion zone boundary	
River, with waterfall	
Lake, reservoir	
Intermittent lake	
Coastline, with reefs and rocks	

SYDNEY State capital city
GEELONG Major city / town
Deniliquin Town
Caldwell Other population centres / localities
Rorruwuy Aboriginal community
Karoonda Roadhouse Roadhouse
Nullagong Pastoral station homestead
ESSENDON Suburb, on suburbs maps only
Unley Suburb, on central city maps only
THE TWELVE APOSTLES Place of interest
Airport
Landing ground
Lighthouse
Hill, mountain, peak
Gorge, gap, pass, cave or saddle
Waterhole
Mine site
National park
Other reserve
Aboriginal / Torres Strait Islander land
Other named area
Prohibited area

Maps are in a Lamberts Conformal Conic Projection
Geocentric Datum Australia, 1994 (GDA94)

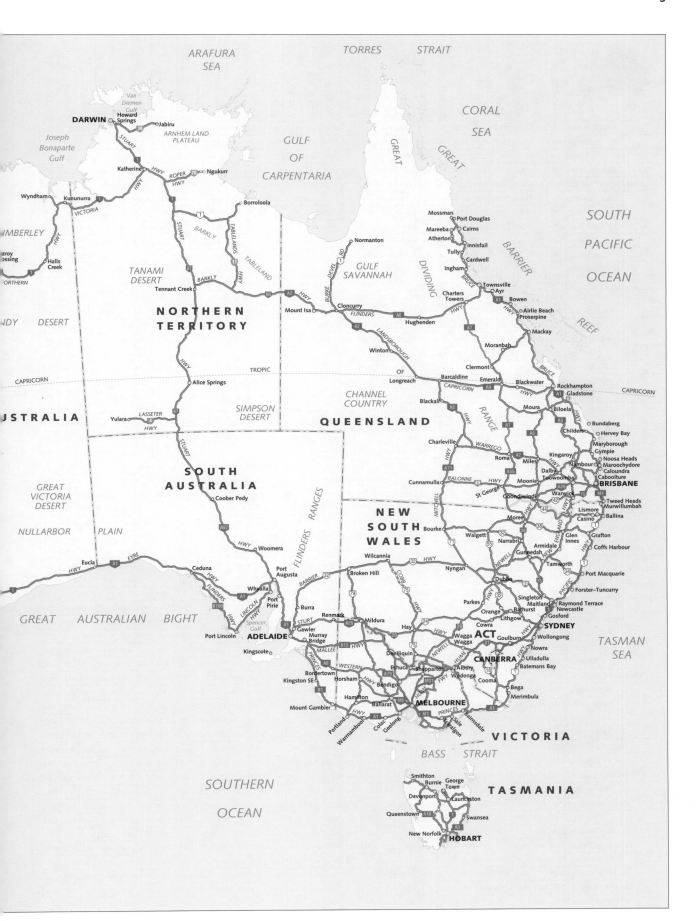

Approximate Distances AUSTRALIA

	Adelaide	Albany	Albury	Alice Springs	Ayers Rock/Yulara	Bairnsdale	Ballarat	Bathurst	Bega	Bendigo	Bordertown	Bourke	Brisbane	Broken Hill	Broome	Bunbury	Cairns	Canberra	Carnarvon	Ceduna	Charleville	Coober Pedy	Darwin	Dubbo	Esperance	Eucla	Geelong	Geraldton
Adelaide		2662	965	1537	1578	1010	625	1198	1338	640	274	1129	2048	514	4268	2887	3207	1197	3568	772	1582	847	3026	1194	2183	1267	711	3086
Albany	2662		3487	3585	3626	3672	3287	3720	4000	3302	2936	3388	4310	2773	2626	335	5466	3719	1300	1890	3841	2895	4428	3526	479	1395	3373	818
Albury	965	3487		2362	2403	336	412	466	427	313	679	779	1407	865	5093	3712	2764	348	4393	1597	1232	1672	3851	553	3008	2092	382	3911
Alice Springs	1537	3585	2362		443	2547	2162	2595	2875	2177	1811	2263	2979	1648	2731	3810	2376	2594	4114	1695	2320	690	1489	2401	3106	2190	2248	4009
Ayers Rock/Yulara	1578	3626	2403	443		2588	2203	2636	2916	2218	1852	2304	3226	1689	3174	3851	2819	2635	4532	1736	2763	731	1932	2442	3147	2231	2289	4050
Bairnsdale	1010	3672	336	2547	2588		388	802	328	423	736	1115	1743	1119	5278	3897	3100	455	4578	1782	1568	1857	4036	863	3193	2277	349	4096
Ballarat	625	3287	412	2162	2203	388		878	716	124	351	996	1747	754	4893	3512	3104	760	4193	1397	1449	1472	3651	893	2808	1892	86	3711
Bathurst	1198	3720	466	2595	2636	802	878		531	779	1180	569	1000	958	5011	3945	2416	309	4626	1830	1022	1905	3769	205	3241	2325	848	4144
Bega	1338	4000	427	2875	2916	328	716	531		751	1064	994	1399	1447	5436	4225	2910	222	4906	2110	1447	2185	4364	630	3521	2605	677	4424
Bendigo	640	3302	313	2177	2218	423	124	779	751		366	872	1623	696	4908	3527	2980	661	4208	1412	1325	1487	3666	769	2823	1907	210	3726
Bordertown	274	2936	679	1811	1852	736	351	1180	1064	366		1138	1922	788	4542	3161	3257	1071	3842	1046	1591	1121	3300	1068	2457	1541	437	3360
Bourke	1129	3388	779	2263	2304	1115	996	569	994	872	1138		922	615	4442	3613	2078	772	4294	1498	453	1573	3200	364	2909	1993	1082	3812
Brisbane	2048	4310	1407	2979	3226	1743	1747	1000	1399	1623	1922	922		1537	4648	4535	1703	1241	5216	2420	742	2495	3406	854	3831	2915	1745	4734
Broken Hill	514	2773	865	1648	1689	1119	754	958	1447	696	788	615	1537		4379	2998	2693	1097	3679	883	1068	958	3137	753	2294	1378	840	3197
Broome	4268	2626	5093	2731	3174	5278	4893	5011	5436	4908	4542	4442	4648	4379		2417	4045	5214	1451	3750	3989	3421	1870	4806	2745	3255	4979	1921
Bunbury	2887	335	3712	3810	3851	3897	3512	3945	4225	3527	3161	3613	4535	2998	2417		5691	3944	1091	2115	4066	3120	4219	3751	664	1620	3598	609
Cairns	3207	5466	2764	2376	2819	3100	3104	2416	2910	2980	3257	2078	1703	2693	4045	5691		2619	5428	3576	1625	3066	2803	2211	4987	4071	3102	5890
Canberra	1197	3719	348	2594	2635	455	760	309	222	661	1071	772	1241	1097	5214	3944	2619		4625	1829	1225	1904	3972	408	3240	2324	730	4143
Carnarvon	3568	1300	4393	4114	4532	4578	4193	4626	4906	4208	3842	4294	5216	3679	1451	1091	5428	4625		2796	4747	3801	3253	4432	1628	2301	4279	482
Ceduna	772	1890	1597	1695	1736	1782	1397	1830	2110	1412	1046	1498	2420	883	3750	2115	3576	1829	2796		1951	1005	3184	1636	1411	495	1483	2314
Charleville	1582	3841	1232	2320	2763	1568	1449	1022	1447	1325	1591	453	742	1068	3989	4066	1625	1225	4747	1951		2026	2747	817	3362	2446	1500	4265
Coober Pedy	847	2895	1672	690	731	1857	1472	1905	2185	1487	1121	1573	2495	958	3421	3120	3066	1904	3801	1005	2026		2179	1711	2416	1500	1558	3319
Darwin	3026	4428	3851	1489	1932	4036	3651	3769	4364	3666	3300	3200	3406	3137	1870	4219	2803	3972	3253	3184	2747	2179		3564	4547	3679	3737	3723
Dubbo	1194	3526	553	2401	2442	863	893	205	630	769	1068	364	854	753	4806	3751	2211	408	4432	1636	817	1711	3564		3047	2131	891	3950
Esperance	2183	479	3008	3106	3147	3193	2808	3241	3521	2823	2457	2909	3831	2294	2745	664	4987	3240	1628	1411	3362	2416	4547	3047		916	2894	1160
Eucla	1267	1395	2092	2190	2231	2277	1892	2325	2605	1907	1541	1993	2915	1378	3255	1620	4071	2324	2301	495	2446	1500	3679	2131	916		1978	1819
Geelong	711	3373	382	2248	2289	349	86	848	677	210	437	1082	1745	840	4979	3598	3102	730	4279	1483	1500	1558	3737	891	2894	1978		3797
Geraldton	3086	818	3911	4009	4050	4096	3711	4144	4424	3726	3360	3812	4734	3197	1921	609	5890	4143	482	2314	4265	3319	3723	3950	1160	1819	3797	
Grafton	1845	4177	1184	3052	3093	1397	1544	825	1069	1420	1719	808	330	1404	4975	4402	2033	911	5083	2287	1069	2362	3733	651	3698	2782	1542	4601
Horsham	433	3095	531	1970	2011	577	192	997	905	218	159	1067	1841	599	4701	3320	3145	879	4001	1205	1520	1280	3459	987	2616	1700	278	3519
Kalgoorlie–Boulder	2184	886	3009	3107	3148	3194	2809	3242	3522	2824	2458	2910	3832	2295	2338	779	4988	3241	1460	1412	3363	2417	4140	3048	407	917	2895	978
Katherine	2712	4114	3537	1175	1618	3722	3337	3455	3880	3352	2986	2886	3092	2823	1556	3905	2489	3658	2939	2870	2433	1865	314	3250	4233	3365	3423	3409
Kununurra	3224	3602	4049	1687	2130	4234	3849	3967	4392	3864	3498	3398	3604	3335	1044	3393	3001	4170	2427	3382	2945	2377	826	3762	3721	3877	3935	2897
Longreach	2098	4357	1748	1804	2247	2084	1965	1538	1963	1841	2107	969	1175	1584	3473	4582	1109	1741	4856	2467	516	2494	2231	1333	3878	2962	2016	4781
Mackay	2670	4932	2029	2451	2894	2365	2369	1681	2106	2245	2544	1544	968	2159	4120	5157	735	1884	5503	3042	1091	3141	2878	1476	4453	3537	2367	5356
Meekatharra	3055	1159	3880	3978	4019	4065	3680	4113	4393	3695	3329	3781	4703	3166	1467	950	5444	4112	627	2283	4234	3288	3269	3919	1278	1788	3766	541
Melbourne	733	3395	313	2270	2311	277	111	779	605	146	459	978	1676	842	5001	3620	3033	661	4301	1505	1431	1580	3759	822	2916	2000	72	3819
Mildura	394	2916	571	1791	1832	825	460	804	956	402	417	870	1654	294	4522	3141	2948	803	3822	1026	1323	1101	3280	800	2437	1521	546	3340
Moree	1567	3829	926	2704	2745	1262	1294	578	1003	1141	1482	441	481	1056	4608	4054	1838	781	4735	1939	702	2014	3366	373	3350	2434	1264	4253
Mount Gambier	452	3114	721	1989	2030	697	309	1187	1025	433	186	1324	2098	856	4720	3339	3402	1069	4020	1224	1777	1299	3478	1244	2635	1719	365	3538
Mount Isa	2706	4754	2383	1169	1612	2719	2600	2173	2598	2476	2742	1604	1810	2219	2838	4979	1207	2736	4221	2864	1151	1859	1596	1968	4275	3359	2651	4691
Newcastle	1553	3930	704	2805	2846	917	1116	338	589	1017	1427	768	821	1157	5111	4155	2341	431	4836	2040	1205	2115	3869	404	3451	2535	1086	4354
Perth	2700	410	3525	3623	3664	3710	3325	3758	4038	3340	2974	3426	4348	2811	2230	187	5504	3757	904	1928	3879	2933	4032	3564	738	1433	3411	422
Port Augusta	307	2355	1132	1230	1271	1317	932	1365	1645	947	581	1033	1955	418	3961	2580	3111	1364	3261	465	1486	540	2719	1171	1876	960	1018	2779
Port Hedland	3921	2025	4746	3264	3707	5100	4546	4979	5259	4561	4195	4647	5181	4032	601	1816	4578	4978	850	3149	4522	3954	2403	4785	2144	2654	4632	1320
Port Lincoln	647	2289	1472	1570	1611	1657	1272	1705	1985	1287	921	1373	2295	758	4149	2514	3451	1704	3195	399	1826	880	3059	1511	1751	894	1358	2713
Port Macquarie	1804	4136	942	3011	3052	1155	1354	565	827	1255	1665	859	584	1363	5150	4361	2287	669	5042	2246	1244	2321	3908	610	3657	2741	1324	4560
Renmark	250	2772	715	1647	1688	969	604	948	1100	546	269	1014	1798	438	4378	2997	3092	947	3678	882	1467	957	3136	944	2293	1377	690	3196
Rockhampton	2336	4598	1695	2486	2929	2031	2035	1347	1772	1911	2210	1210	634	1825	4155	4823	1069	1550	5504	2708	831	3176	2913	1142	4119	3203	2033	5022
Sydney	1414	3936	565	2811	2852	759	977	211	431	878	1288	780	966	1169	5222	4161	2479	292	4842	2046	1233	2121	3980	416	3457	2541	947	4360
Tamworth	1534	3866	893	2741	2782	1186	1233	457	858	1109	1408	589	573	1093	4880	4091	2110	700	4772	1965	974	2051	3638	340	3387	2471	1231	4290
Tennant Creek	2043	4091	2868	531	949	3053	2668	2836	3261	2683	2317	2267	2473	2154	2225	4316	1870	3039	3608	2201	1814	1196	983	2631	3612	2696	2754	4078
Toowoomba	1921	4183	1280	2852	3099	1616	1620	956	1357	1496	1795	795	127	1410	4521	4408	1705	1199	5089	2293	615	2368	3279	727	3704	2788	1618	4607
Townsville	2862	5121	2419	2061	2504	2755	2759	2071	2496	2635	2871	1733	1358	2348	3730	5346	345	2274	5113	3231	1280	2751	2488	1866	4642	3726	2757	5545
Wagga Wagga	948	3470	145	2345	2386	481	550	321	402	426	822	711	1262	848	5076	3695	2619	249	4376	1580	1164	1655	3834	408	2991	2075	527	3894
Warrnambool	649	3311	567	2186	2227	534	174	1052	862	298	383	1170	1933	829	4917	3536	3278	987	4217	1421	1623	1496	3675	1067	2832	1916	185	3735

Distances on this chart have been calculated over main roads and do not necessarily reflect the shortest route between towns.
Refer to page 135 for distance chart of Tasmania.

Approximate Distances AUSTRALIA

	Grafton	Horsham	Kalgoorlie–Boulder	Katherine	Kununurra	Longreach	Mackay	Meekatharra	Melbourne	Mildura	Moree	Mount Gambier	Mount Isa	Newcastle	Perth	Port Augusta	Port Hedland	Port Lincoln	Port Macquarie	Renmark	Rockhampton	Sydney	Tamworth	Tennant Creek	Toowoomba	Townsville	Wagga Wagga	Warrnambool
Adelaide	1845	433	2184	2712	3224	2098	2670	3055	733	394	1567	452	2706	1553	2700	307	3921	647	1804	250	2336	1414	1534	2043	1921	2862	948	649
Albany	4177	3095	886	4114	3602	4357	4932	1159	3395	2916	3829	3114	4754	3930	410	2355	2025	2289	4136	2772	4598	3936	3866	4091	4183	5121	3470	3311
Albury	1184	531	3009	3537	4049	1748	2029	3880	313	571	926	721	2383	704	3525	1132	4746	1472	942	715	1695	565	893	2868	1280	2419	145	567
Alice Springs	3052	1970	3107	1175	1687	1804	2451	3978	2270	1791	2704	1989	1169	2805	3623	1230	3264	1570	3011	1647	2486	2811	2741	531	2852	2061	2345	2186
Ayers Rock/Yulara	3093	2011	3148	1618	2130	2247	2894	4019	2311	1832	2745	2030	1612	2846	3664	1271	3707	1611	3052	1688	2929	2852	2782	949	3099	2504	2386	2227
Bairnsdale	1397	577	3194	3722	4234	2084	2365	4065	277	825	1262	697	2719	917	3710	1317	5100	1657	1155	969	2031	759	1186	3053	1616	2755	481	534
Ballarat	1544	192	2809	3337	3849	1965	2369	3680	111	460	1294	309	2600	1116	3325	932	4546	1272	1354	604	2035	977	1233	2668	1620	2759	550	174
Bathurst	825	997	3242	3455	3967	1538	1681	4113	779	804	578	1187	2173	338	3758	1365	4979	1705	565	948	1347	211	457	2836	956	2071	321	1052
Bega	1069	905	3522	3880	4392	1963	2106	4393	605	956	1003	1025	2598	589	4038	1645	5259	1985	827	1100	1772	431	858	3261	1357	2496	402	862
Bendigo	1420	218	2824	3352	3864	1841	2245	3695	146	402	1141	433	2476	1017	3340	947	4561	1287	1255	546	1911	878	1109	2683	1496	2635	426	298
Bordertown	1719	159	2458	2986	3498	2107	2544	3329	459	417	1482	186	2742	1427	2974	581	4195	921	1665	269	2210	1288	1408	2317	1795	2871	822	383
Bourke	808	1067	2910	2886	3398	969	1544	3781	978	870	441	1324	1604	768	3426	1033	4647	1373	859	1014	1210	780	589	2267	795	1733	711	1170
Brisbane	330	1841	3832	3092	3604	1175	968	4703	1676	1654	481	2098	1810	821	4348	1955	5181	2295	584	1798	634	966	573	2473	127	1358	1262	1933
Broken Hill	1404	599	2295	2823	3335	1584	2159	3166	842	294	1056	856	2219	1157	2811	418	4032	758	1363	438	1825	1169	1093	2154	1410	2348	848	829
Broome	4975	4701	2338	1556	1044	3473	4120	1467	5001	4522	4608	4720	2838	5111	2230	3961	601	4149	5150	4378	4155	5222	4880	2225	4521	3730	5076	4917
Bunbury	4402	3320	779	3905	3393	4582	5157	950	3620	3141	4054	3339	4979	4155	187	2580	1816	2514	4361	2997	4823	4161	4091	4316	4408	5346	3695	3536
Cairns	2033	3145	4988	2489	3001	1109	735	5444	3033	2948	1838	3402	1207	2341	5504	3111	4578	3451	2287	3092	1069	2479	2110	1870	1705	345	2619	3278
Canberra	911	879	3241	3658	4170	1741	1884	4112	661	803	781	1069	2736	431	3757	1364	4978	1704	669	947	1550	292	700	3039	1199	2274	249	987
Carnarvon	5083	4001	1460	2939	2427	4856	5503	627	4301	3822	4735	4020	4221	4836	904	3261	850	3195	5042	3678	5504	4842	4772	3608	5089	5113	4376	4217
Ceduna	2287	1205	1412	2870	3382	2467	3042	2283	1505	1026	1939	1224	2864	2040	1928	465	3149	399	2246	882	2708	2046	1965	2201	2293	3231	1580	1421
Charleville	1069	1520	3363	2433	2945	516	1091	4234	1431	1323	702	1777	1151	1205	3879	1486	4522	1826	1244	1467	831	1233	974	1814	615	1280	1164	1623
Coober Pedy	2362	1280	2417	1865	2377	2494	3141	3288	1580	1101	2014	1299	1859	2115	2933	540	3954	880	2321	957	3176	2121	2051	1196	2368	2751	1655	1496
Darwin	3733	3459	4140	314	826	2231	2878	3269	3759	3280	3366	3478	1596	3869	4032	2719	2403	3059	3908	3136	2913	3980	3638	983	3279	2488	3834	3675
Dubbo	651	987	3048	3250	3762	1333	1476	3919	822	800	373	1244	1968	404	3564	1171	4785	1511	610	944	1142	416	340	2631	727	1866	408	1067
Esperance	3698	2616	407	4233	3721	3878	4453	1278	2916	2437	3350	2635	4275	3451	738	1876	2144	1751	3657	2293	4119	3457	3387	3612	3704	4642	2991	2832
Eucla	2782	1700	917	3365	3877	2962	3537	1788	2000	1521	2434	1719	3359	2535	1433	960	2654	894	2741	1377	3203	2541	2471	2696	2788	3726	2075	1916
Geelong	1542	278	2895	3423	3935	2016	2367	3766	72	546	1264	365	2651	1086	3411	1018	4632	1358	1324	690	2033	947	1231	2754	1618	2757	527	185
Geraldton	4601	3519	978	3409	2897	4781	5356	541	3819	3340	4253	3538	4691	4354	422	2779	1320	2713	4560	3196	5022	4360	4290	4078	4607	5545	3894	3735
Grafton		1638	3699	3419	3931	1502	1298	4570	1473	1451	367	1895	2137	491	4215	1822	5436	2162	254	1595	964	638	311	2800	431	1688	1059	1718
Horsham	1638		2451	3145	3657	2036	2463	3322	300	305	1360	257	2671	1235	3133	740	4188	1080	1462	428	2129	1096	1327	2476	1714	2800	644	230
Kalgoorlie–Boulder	3699	2451		3826	3314	3879	4454	871	2917	2438	3351	2636	4276	3452	582	1877	1737	1811	3658	2294	4120	3458	3388	3613	3705	4643	2992	2833
Katherine	3419	3145	3826		512	1917	2564	2955	3445	2966	3052	3164	1282	3556	3718	2405	2089	2745	3594	2822	2599	3666	3324	669	2965	2174	3520	3361
Kununurra	3931	3657	3314	512		2429	3076	2443	3957	3478	3564	3676	1794	4067	3206	2917	1577	3257	4106	3334	3111	4178	3836	1181	3477	2686	4032	3873
Longreach	1502	2036	3879	1917	2429		791	4750	1947	1839	1135	2293	635	1638	4395	2002	4006	2342	1677	1983	682	1749	1407	1298	1048	764	1680	2139
Mackay	1298	2463	4454	2564	3076	791		5325	2298	2276	1103	2720	1282	1606	4970	2577	4653	2917	1552	2420	334	1744	1375	1945	970	390	1884	2543
Meekatharra	4570	3322	871	2955	2443	4750	5325		3788	3309	4222	3507	4237	4323	763	2748	866	2682	4529	3165	5524	4329	4259	3624	4576	5129	3863	3704
Melbourne	1473	300	2917	3445	3957	1947	2298	3788		548	1195	420	2582	1017	3433	1040	4823	1380	1255	692	1964	878	1162	2776	1549	2688	458	257
Mildura	1451	305	2438	2966	3478	1839	2276	3309	548		1173	562	2474	1159	2954	561	4175	901	1397	144	1942	1020	1140	2297	1527	2603	554	535
Moree	367	1360	3351	3052	3564	1135	1103	4222	1195	1173		1627	1770	503	3867	1474	5088	1814	542	1317	769	641	272	2433	354	1493	781	1449
Mount Gambier	1895	257	2636	3164	3676	2293	2720	3507	420	562	1627		2928	1425	3152	759	4373	1099	1663	455	2386	1286	1584	2495	1971	3057	901	197
Mount Isa	2137	2671	4276	1282	1794	635	1282	4237	2582	2474	1770	2928		2273	4792	2399	3371	2739	2312	2618	1317	2384	2042	663	1683	892	2315	2774
Newcastle	491	1235	3452	3556	4067	1638	1606	4323	1017	1159	503	1425	2273		3968	1575	5189	1915	249	1303	1272	158	289	2936	788	1996	605	1271
Perth	4215	3133	582	3718	3206	4395	4970	763	3433	2954	3867	3152	4792	3968		2393	1629	2327	4174	2810	4636	3974	3904	4129	4221	5159	3508	3349
Port Augusta	1822	740	1877	2405	2917	2002	2577	2748	1040	561	1474	759	2399	1575	2393		3614	340	1781	417	2243	1581	1511	1736	1828	2766	1115	956
Port Hedland	5436	4188	1737	2089	1577	4006	4653	866	4823	4175	5088	4373	3371	5189	1629	3614		3548	5395	4031	4688	5195	5125	2758	5054	4263	4729	4570
Port Lincoln	2162	1080	1811	2745	3257	2342	2917	2682	1380	901	1814	1099	2739	1915	2327	340	3548		2121	757	2583	1921	1851	2076	2168	3106	1455	1296
Port Macquarie	254	1462	3658	3594	4106	1677	1552	4529	1255	1397	542	1663	2312	249	4174	1781	5395	2121		1541	1218	396	270	2975	630	1942	843	1509
Renmark	1595	428	2294	2822	3334	1983	2420	3165	692	144	1317	455	2618	1303	2810	417	4031	757	1541		2086	1164	1284	2153	1671	2747	698	652
Rockhampton	964	2129	4120	2599	3111	682	334	5524	1964	1942	769	2386	1317	1272	4636	2243	4688	2583	1218	2086		1410	1041	1980	636	724	1550	2209
Sydney	638	1096	3458	3666	4178	1749	1744	4329	878	1020	641	1286	2384	158	3974	1581	5195	1921	396	1164	1410		427	3047	926	2134	466	1132
Tamworth	311	1327	3388	3324	3836	1407	1375	4259	1162	1140	272	1584	2042	289	3904	1511	5125	1851	270	1284	1041	427		2705	499	1765	748	1407
Tennant Creek	2800	2476	3613	669	1181	1298	1945	3624	2776	2297	2433	2495	663	2936	4129	1736	2758	2076	2975	2153	1980	3047	2705		2346	1555	2851	2692
Toowoomba	431	1714	3705	2965	3477	1048	970	4576	1549	1527	354	1971	1683	788	4221	1828	5054	2168	630	1671	636	926	499	2346		1360	1135	1794
Townsville	1688	2800	4643	2174	2686	764	390	5129	2688	2603	1493	3057	892	1996	5159	2766	4263	3106	1942	2747	724	2134	1765	1555	1360		2274	2933
Wagga Wagga	1059	644	2992	3520	4032	1680	1884	3863	458	554	781	901	2315	605	3508	1115	4729	1455	843	698	1550	466	748	2851	1135	2274		724
Warrnambool	1718	230	2833	3361	3873	2139	2543	3704	257	535	1449	197	2774	1271	3349	956	4570	1296	1509	652	2209	1132	1407	2692	1794	2933	724	

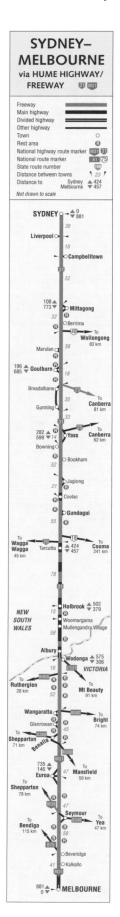

SYDNEY–MELBOURNE via HUME HIGHWAY/FREEWAY

SYDNEY–MELBOURNE via PRINCES HIGHWAY/FREEWAY

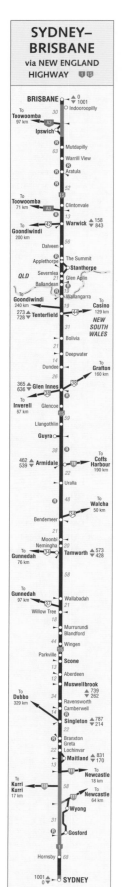

SYDNEY–BRISBANE via NEW ENGLAND HIGHWAY

MELBOURNE–ADELAIDE via WESTERN & DUKES HIGHWAYS

MELBOURNE–ADELAIDE via PRINCES HIGHWAY

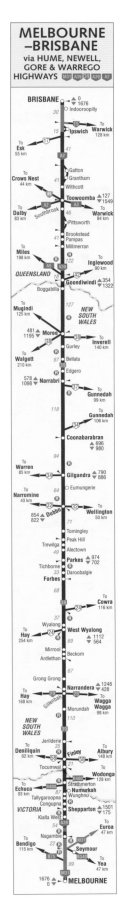

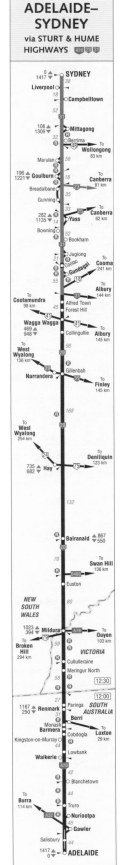

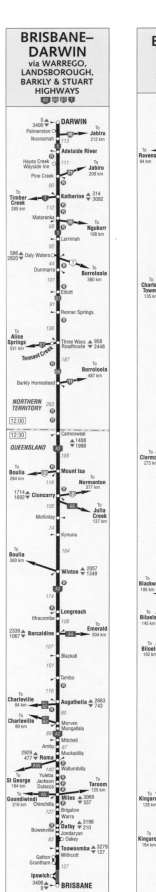

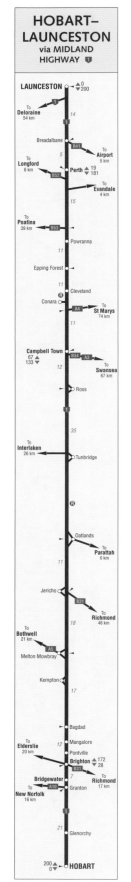

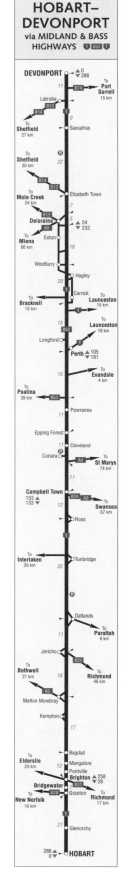

MAPS

NEW SOUTH WALES and AUSTRALIAN CAPITAL TERRITORY

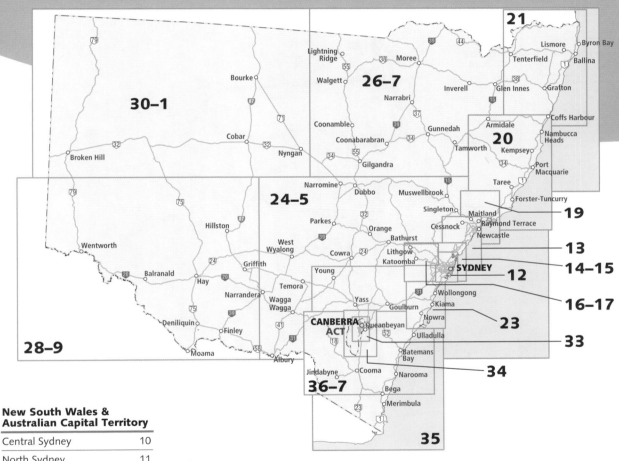

New South Wales & Australian Capital Territory

Central Sydney	10
North Sydney	11
Sydney Suburbs	12
Central Coast	13
Sydney & Surrounds	14–15
Blue Mountains	16–17
Newcastle	18
Newcastle & Surrounds	19
Mid North Coast	20
North Coast	21
Wollongong	22
Southern Highlands	23
Central Eastern New South Wales	24–5
North Eastern New South Wales	26–7
South Western New South Wales	28–9
North Western New South Wales	30–1
Central Canberra	32
Canberra Suburbs	33
Australian Capital Territory	34
South Eastern New South Wales	35
Snowy Mountains & The South Coast	36–7

INTER-CITY ROUTES	DISTANCE
Sydney–Melbourne via Hume Hwy/Fwy	881 km
Sydney–Melbourne via Princes Hwy/Fwy	1037 km
Sydney–Brisbane via New England Hwy	1001 km
Sydney–Brisbane via Pacific Hwy	966 km
Sydney–Adelaide via Hume & Sturt hwys	1417 km

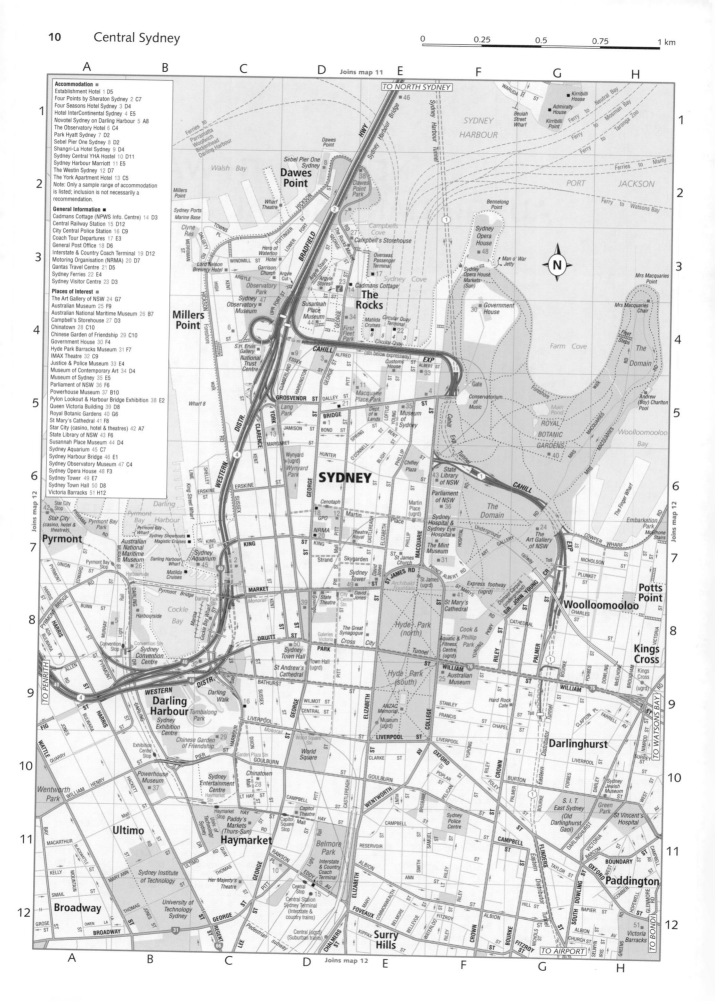

0   0.25   0.5   0.75   1 km

Accommodation ■
Establishment Hotel 1 D5
Four Points by Sheraton Sydney 2 C7
Four Seasons Hotel Sydney 3 D4
Hotel InterContinental Sydney 4 E5
Novotel Sydney on Darling Harbour 5 A8
The Observatory Hotel 6 C4
Park Hyatt Sydney 7 D2
Sebel Pier One Sydney 8 D2
Shangri-La Hotel Sydney 9 D4
Sydney Central YHA Hostel 10 D11
Sydney Harbour Marriott 11 E5
The Westin Sydney 12 D7
The York Apartment Hotel 13 C5
Note: Only a sample range of accommodation
is listed; inclusion is not necessarily a
recommendation.

General Information ■
Cadmans Cottage (NPWS Info. Centre) 14 D3
Central Railway Station 15 D12
City Central Police Station 16 C9
Coach Tour Departures 17 E3
General Post Office 18 D6
Interstate & Country Coach Terminal 19 D12
Motoring Organisation (NRMA) 20 D7
Qantas Travel Centre 21 D5
Sydney Ferries 22 E4
Sydney Visitor Centre 23 D3

Places of Interest ■
The Art Gallery of NSW 24 G7
Australian Museum 25 F9
Australian National Maritime Museum 26 B7
Campbell's Storehouse 27 D3
Chinatown 28 C10
Chinese Garden of Friendship 29 C10
Government House 30 F4
Hyde Park Barracks Museum 31 F7
IMAX Theatre 32 C9
Justice & Police Museum 33 E4
Museum of Contemporary Art 34 D4
Museum of Sydney 35 E5
Parliament of NSW 36 F6
Powerhouse Museum 37 B10
Pylon Lookout & Harbour Bridge Exhibition 38 E2
Queen Victoria Building 39 D8
Royal Botanic Gardens 40 G6
St Mary's Cathedral 41 F8
Star City (casino, hotel & theatres) 42 A7
State Library of NSW 43 F6
Susannah Place Museum 44 D4
Sydney Aquarium 45 C7
Sydney Harbour Bridge 46 E1
Sydney Observatory Museum 47 C4
Sydney Opera House 48 F3
Sydney Tower 49 E7
Sydney Town Hall 50 D8
Victoria Barracks 51 H12

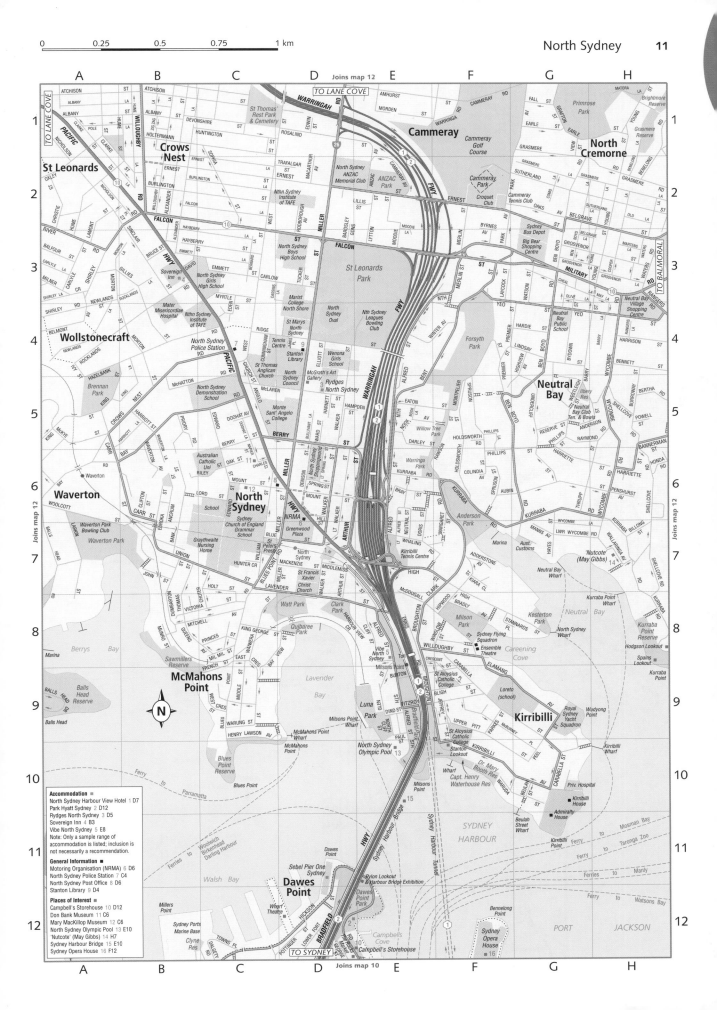

0   0.25   0.5   0.75   1 km

A   B   C   D   E   F   G   H

TO LANE COVE
WARRINGAH RD
TO LANE COVE

St Thomas' Rest Park & Cemetery

Cammeray

North Cremorne

Primrose Park

Grasmere Reserve

Brightmore Reserve

Crows Nest

St Leonards

Cammeray Golf Course

North Sydney ANZAC Memorial Club

ANZAC Park

Cammeray Tennis Club

Croquet Club

Nthn Sydney Institute of TAFE

North Sydney Boys High School

St Leonards Park

FALCON ST

Big Bear Shopping Centre

MILITARY RD

TO BALMORAL

North Sydney Girls High School

Sovereign Inn

North Sydney Oval

Nth Sydney Leagues Bowling Club

Sydney Bus Depot

WARRINGAH FWY

Wollstonecraft

Mater Misericordiae Hospital

Nthn Sydney Institute of TAFE

North Sydney Police Station

Marist College North Shore

St Marys North Sydney

Forsyth Park

Neutral Bay Public School

Neutral Bay Village Shopping Centre

Brennan Park

North Sydney Demonstration School

St Thomas Anglican Church

Stanton Library

Wenona Girls School

McGrath's Art Gallery

Rydges North Sydney

North Sydney Council

Neutral Bay

Neutral Bay Club Ten. & Bowls

Monte Sant' Angelo College

Warringa Park

BERRY ST

North Sydney Shoppingworld

Willow Tree Park

Waverton

Australian Catholic Uni North Riley

North Sydney

Sydney Church of England Grammar School

Kurraba Point

Anderson Park

'Nutcote' (May Gibbs)

Waverton Park Bowling Club

Waverton Park

Graythwaite Nursing Home

NRMA

Greenwood Plaza

Kirribilli Tennis Centre

Aust. Customs

Kurraba Point Reserve

Berrys Bay

Marina

Sawmillers Reserve

St Peters Presb

North Sydney

St Francis Xavier

Christ Church

Clark Park

Marina

Neutral Bay Wharf

North Sydney Wharf

Neutral Bay

Kurraba Point Reserve

Hodgson Lookout

Spains Lookout

Kurraba Point

Balls Head Reserve

Balls Head

McMahons Point

Watt Park

Quibaree Park

King George Park

Luna Park

Milsons Point Wharf

Sydney Flying Squadron

Ensemble Theatre

Milson Park

Kesterton Park

Careening Cove

North Sydney Wharf

Kirribilli

Royal Sydney Yacht Squadron

Wudyong Point

McMahons Point Wharf

North Sydney Olympic Pool

St Aloysius Catholic College

Stanton Lookout

Loreto (school)

Kirribilli Wharf

Blues Point Reserve

Blues Point

St Aloysius Catholic College

Kirribilli

Dr. Mary Booth Res

Capt. Henry Waterhouse Res

Kirribilli House

Priv. Hospital

Admiralty House

Beulah Street Wharf

Ferry to Parramatta

Dawes Point

Sebel Pier One Sydney

Millers Point

Dawes Point Park

SYDNEY HARBOUR

Kirribilli Point

Ferries to Mosman Bay

Ferry to Taronga Zoo

Ferries to Manly

Ferry to Watsons Bay

Sydney Harbour Bridge

Sydney Harbour Tunnel

Bennelong Point

Walsh Bay

Sydney Ports Marine Base

Wharf Theatre

Woolwich Birkenhead Darling Harbour

Clyne Res

Pylon Lookout & Harbour Bridge Exhibition

Campbells Cove

Campbell's Storehouse

Sydney Opera House

PORT JACKSON

TO SYDNEY

Joins map 10

Accommodation ■
North Sydney Harbour View Hotel 1 D7
Park Hyatt Sydney 2 D12
Rydges North Sydney 3 D5
Sovereign Inn 4 B3
Vibe North Sydney 5 E8
Note: Only a sample range of accommodation is listed; inclusion is not necessarily a recommendation.

General Information ■
Motoring Organisation (NRMA) 6 D6
North Sydney Police Station 7 C4
North Sydney Post Office 8 D6
Stanton Library 9 D4

Places of Interest ■
Campbell's Storehouse 10 D12
Don Bank Museum 11 C6
Mary MacKillop Museum 12 C6
North Sydney Olympic Pool 13 E10
'Nutcote' (May Gibbs) 14 H7
Sydney Harbour Bridge 15 E10
Sydney Opera House 16 F12

Joins map 12

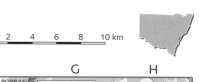

0 2 4 6 8 10 km

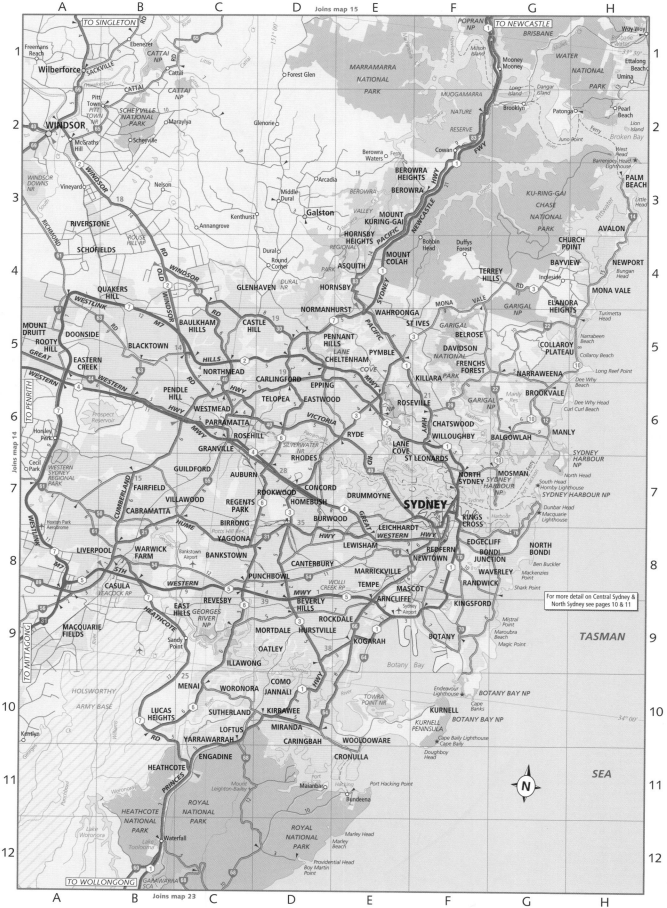

TO SINGLETON

Freemans Reach
Wilberforce
Ebenezer
CATTAI NP
Cattai
SACKVILLE
CATTAI NP
Forest Glen
MARRAMARRA NATIONAL PARK
POPRAN NP
TO NEWCASTLE
BRISBANE
Woy Woy
Brisbane Water
WATER
NATIONAL
PARK
Ettalong Beach
Umina

Pitt Town
PITT TOWN NR
SCHEYVILLE NATIONAL PARK
WINDSOR
McGraths Hill
Maraylya
Scheyville
Glenorie
Middle Dural
Arcadia
Forest Glen
MUOGAMARRA NATURE RESERVE
Mooney Mooney
Long Island
Dangar Island
Brooklyn
Patonga
Juno Point
Pearl Beach
Lion Island
Broken Bay

WINDSOR
WINDSOR DOWNS NR
Vineyard
Nelson
Kenthurst
Annangrove
Dural
Round Corner
Galston
BEROWRA VALLEY REGIONAL PARK
MOUNT KURING-GAI
HORNSBY HEIGHTS
BEROWRA HEIGHTS
BEROWRA
Cowan
Bobbin Head
Duffys Forest
West Head
Barrenjoey Head Lighthouse
PALM BEACH
KU-RING-GAI CHASE NATIONAL PARK
AVALON
CHURCH POINT

RIVERSTONE
SCHOFIELDS
ROUSE HILL RP
GLENHAVEN
DURAL NR
ASQUITH
MOUNT COLAH
HORNSBY
NORMANHURST
TERREY HILLS
Ingleside
BAYVIEW
NEWPORT
MONA VALE

QUAKERS HILL
WESTLINK
MOUNT DRUITT
DOONSIDE
ROOTY HILL
EASTERN CREEK
BLACKTOWN
NORTHMEAD
BAULKHAM HILLS
CASTLE HILL
PENNANT HILLS
CHELTENHAM
CARLINGFORD
PYMBLE
ST IVES
BELROSE
DAVIDSON
FRENCHS FOREST
GARIGAL NP
ELANORA HEIGHTS
Narrabeen Beach
Collaroy Beach
COLLAROY PLATEAU
NARRAWEENA
Long Reef Point
Dee Why Beach

GREAT WESTERN
PENDLE HILL
WESTMEAD
PARRAMATTA
TELOPEA
EPPING
EASTWOOD
ROSEVILLE
GARIGAL NP
CHATSWOOD
WILLOUGHBY
BROOKVALE
MANLY
Dee Why Head
Curl Curl Beach

Horsley Park
Cecil Park
WESTERN SYDNEY REGIONAL PARK
FAIRFIELD
GUILDFORD
ROSEHILL
GRANVILLE
AUBURN
RHODES
RYDE
CONCORD
DRUMMOYNE
LANE COVE
ST LEONARDS
NORTH SYDNEY
MOSMAN
SYDNEY HARBOUR NP
North Head
Hornby Lighthouse
SYDNEY HARBOUR NP
BALGOWLAH

CUMBERLAND
VILLAWOOD
CABRAMATTA
REGENTS PARK
BIRRONG
ROOKWOOD
HOMEBUSH
BURWOOD
LEICHHARDT
WESTERN
SYDNEY
KINGS CROSS
EDGECLIFF
BONDI JUNCTION
NORTH BONDI
WAVERLEY
Ben Buckler
South Head
Dunbar Head
Macquarie Lighthouse

WARWICK FARM
Bankstown Airport
YAGOONA
BANKSTOWN
CANTERBURY
LEWISHAM
MARRICKVILLE
TEMPE
REDFERN
NEWTOWN
RANDWICK
KINGSFORD
Mackenzies Point
Shark Point

LIVERPOOL
HUME
WESTERN
PUNCHBOWL
WOLLI CREEK RP
MASCOT
Sydney Airport
ARNCLIFFE
BOTANY
Mistral Point
Maroubra Beach
Magic Point

CASULA
Leacock RP
EAST HILLS
REVESBY
GEORGES RIVER NP
BEVERLY HILLS
ROCKDALE
HURSTVILLE
KOGARAH
Botany Bay

MACQUARIE FIELDS
Sandy Point
MORTDALE
OATLEY
ILLAWONG
Endeavour Lighthouse
BOTANY BAY NP
TOWRA POINT NR
KURNELL
Cape Banks
BOTANY BAY NP
KURNELL PENINSULA
Cape Baily Lighthouse
Cape Baily

HOLSWORTHY ARMY BASE
MENAI
WORONORA
COMO
JANNALI
SUTHERLAND
KIRRAWEE
MIRANDA
CARINGBAH
WOOLOOWARE
Doughboy Head

Kentlyn
LUCAS HEIGHTS
LOFTUS
YARRAWARRAH
ENGADINE
CRONULLA
Maianbar
Port Hacking Point
Bundeena
Marley Head
Marley Beach
SEA

HEATHCOTE
PRINCES
Mount Leighton-Bailey
Port Hacking
ROYAL NATIONAL PARK
Providential Head
Boy Martin Point

HEATHCOTE NATIONAL PARK
Lake Woronora
Waterfall
ROYAL NATIONAL PARK
Lake Toolooma
GARAWARRA SCA

TO WOLLONGONG

TASMAN

For more detail on Central Sydney & North Sydney see pages 10 & 11

N

Joins map 15
Joins map 23
Joins map 14
TO PENRITH
TO MITTAGONG

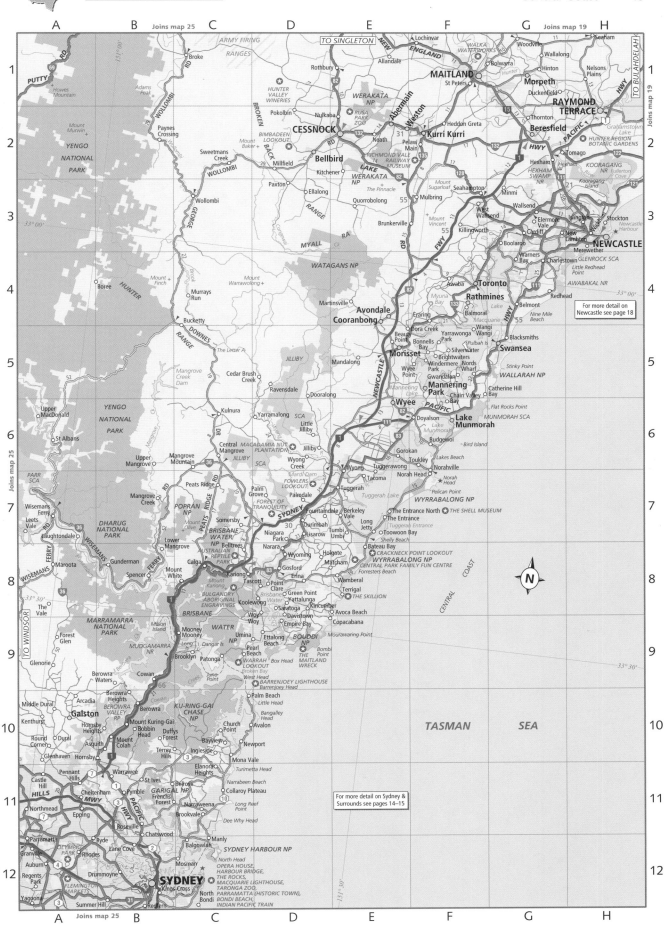

Joins map 25
Joins map 19
Joins map 25
Joins map 25

For more detail on Newcastle see page 18

For more detail on Sydney & Surrounds see pages 14–15

TASMAN SEA

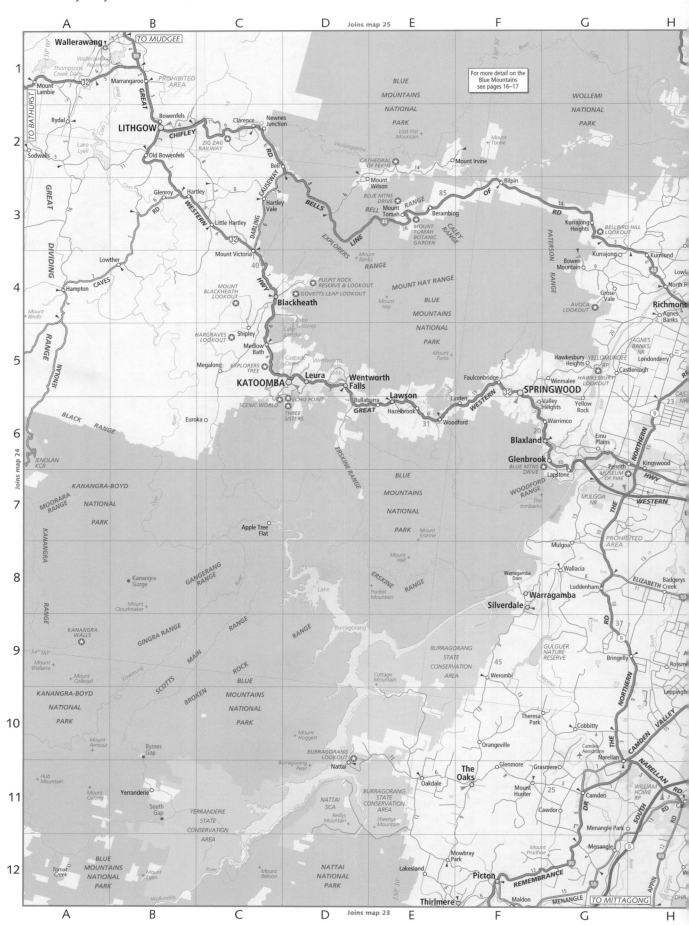

I J K L M N O P

Joins map 25   Joins map 13

TO NEWCASTLE

PARR STATE CONSERVATION AREA

YENGO NATIONAL PARK

Central Mangrove

JILLIBY

Wyong Creek

Gorokan

Mardi Dam

Wyong

Tuggerawong

Tacoma

Webbs Creek

Upper Mangrove

Mangrove Mountain

STATE

FOWLERS LOOKOUT

Palm Dale

Tuggerah

Rocky Point

Tuggerah Lake

The Entrance North

Mangrove Creek

Peats Ridge

BRISBANE WATER

CONSERVATION AREA

Fountaindale

Berkeley Vale

The Entrance

Long Jetty

THE SHELL MUSEUM

Wisemans Ferry

Leets Vale

WISEMANS

Laughtondale

DHARUG NATIONAL PARK

Lower Mangrove

Mount Olive

Somersby

POPRAN NATIONAL PARK

PEATS RIDGE

FWY

Ourimbah

Lisarow

Niagara Park

Tumbi Umbi

Toowoon Bay

KEN DUNCAN GALLERY

Bateau Bay

Sackville North

Maroota

Gunderman

Spencer

Mount White

Calga

NATIONAL

PARK

AUSTRALIAN REPTILE PARK

Belltrees

PACIFIC

Narara

Wyoming

Holgate

Matcham

Wamberal

Wamberal Point

CENTRAL PARK FAMILY FUN CTR

WAMBINA NR

WYRRABALONG NP

Colo

Ebenezer

Cattai

MARRAMARRA

Forest Glen

HENRY KENDALL COTTAGE

Kariong

Mount Kariong

Tascott

Point Clare

Gosford

Erina

GOSFORD CITY ARTS CENTRE

Green Point

Terrigal

THE SKILLION

CRACKNECK POINT LOOKOUT

Wilberforce

CATTAI NP

SCHEYVILLE

NP

Marylya

Glenorie

NATIONAL

PARK

BULGANDRY ABORIGINAL ENGRAVINGS

Koolewong

BRISBANE

Yattalunga

Saratoga

Woy Woy

Davistown

Kincumber

Avoca Beach

Copacabana

COAST

Pitt Town

McGraths Hill

Scheyville

Nelson

Middle Dural

Arcadia

Berowra Waters

Berowra Heights

WATER

Ettalong Beach

Umina

MOUNT ETTALONG LOOKOUT

Empire Bay

Tudibaring Head

Mourawaring Point

BOUDDI NP

Vineyard

Riverstone

Kenthurst

Galston

Hornsby Heights

Cowan

Berowra

BEROWRA VALLEY RP

NEWCASTLE HWY

MUOGAMARRA NATURE RESERVE

Long Island

Brooklyn

Milson Island

Mooney Mooney

Dangar Island

NP

Patonga

Pearl Beach

WARRAH LOOKOUT

Box Head

THE MAITLAND WRECK

Bombi Point

CENTRAL

Annangrove

Round Corner

Dural

Asquith

BEROWRA VALLEY RP

Mount Colah

Bobbin Head

Cowan

Lion Island

West Head

BARRENJOEY LIGHTHOUSE

Barrenjoey Head

Palm Beach

Little Head

Quakers Hill

Glenhaven

Castle Hill

Mount Kuring-Gai

Duffys Forest

KU-RING-GAI CHASE NATIONAL PARK

The Basin

Pittwater

Bangalley Head

Avalon

Schofields

Hornsby

Normanhurst

Warrawee

Terrey Hills

Church Point

Bayview

Newport

Bungan Head

WESTLINK M7

Baulkham Hills

Doonside

Blacktown

OLD WINDSOR RD

HILLS

Pennant Hills

Pymble

St Ives

GARIGAL NP

Belrose

Ingleside

Mona Vale

Turimetta Head

Eastern Creek

FEATHERDALE WILDLIFE PARK

Northmead

Carlingford

Epping

Eastwood

PACIFIC HWY

LANE COVE

MONA VALE RD

Davidson

Frenchs Forest

Elanora Heights

Narrabeen Beach

Collaroy Plateau

Collaroy Beach

WESTERN HWY

Pendle Hill

Wentworthville

Parramatta

Meadowbank

Ryde

Killara

Narraweena

Brookvale

Long Reef Point

Dee Why Beach

Prospect Reservoir

HISTORIC TOWN

PARRAMATTA OLYMPIC PARK

Rhodes

Lane Cove

Chatswood

Manly Reservoir

Dee Why Head

Curl Curl Beach

WESTERN SYDNEY RECREATION PARK

Merrylands

Granville

Auburn

Concord

St Leonards

North Sydney

Balgowlah

Manly

SYDNEY HARBOUR NP

TASMAN

Guildford

Yennora

Lidcombe

FLEMINGTON MARKETS

Croydon

OPERA HOUSE HARBOUR BRIDGE, INDIAN PACIFIC TRAIN, THE ROCKS

SYDNEY

Mosman

TARONGA ZOO

North Head

Hornby Lighthouse

Villawood

Regents Park

HUME HWY

Birrong

Summer Hill

Kings Cross

Edgecliff

Bondi Junction

North Bondi

Dunbar Head

MACQUARIE LIGHTHOUSE

SEA

Cabramatta

Warwick Farm

Bankstown Airport

Bankstown

Belmore

Canterbury

Marrickville

Redfern

Newtown

Waverley

BONDI BEACH

Ben Buckler

Mackenzies Point

Shark Point

Hoxton Park Aerodrome

Liverpool

Wiley Park

Tempe

Mascot

Randwick

Kingsford

Casula

LEACOCK RP

East Hills

Revesby

Beverly Hills

Arncliffe

Banksia

Sydney Airport

Botany

Mistral Point

Maroubra Beach

Magic Point

For more detail on Sydney Suburbs see page 12

Macquarie Fields

Sandy Point

GEORGES RIVER NP

Riverwood

Penshurst

Hurstville

Kogarah

Botany Bay

La Perouse Museum

Menai

Illawong

Como

Oatley

TOWRA POINT NR

Kurnell

Cape Banks

Woronora

Sutherland

Miranda

KURNELL PENINSULA

BOTANY BAY NP

Cape Baily

HEATHCOTE

Kirrawee

Caringbah

Cronulla

Lucas Heights

Loftus

HWY

Wooloowarе

Doughboy Head

Engadine

Yarrawarrah

Port Hacking

HOLSWORTHY ARMY BASE

Heathcote

Malabar

Bundeena

Port Hacking Point

Woronora Dam

PRINCES HWY

Mount Leighton-Bailey

The Waterrun

HEATHCOTE NP

ROYAL NATIONAL PARK

Marley Head

Waterfall

Marley Beach

Providential Head

Boy Martin Point

TO SHELLHARBOUR

I J K L M N O P

Joins map 23

1
2
3
4
5
6
7
8
9
10
11
12

33° 30'

34° 00'

151° 30'

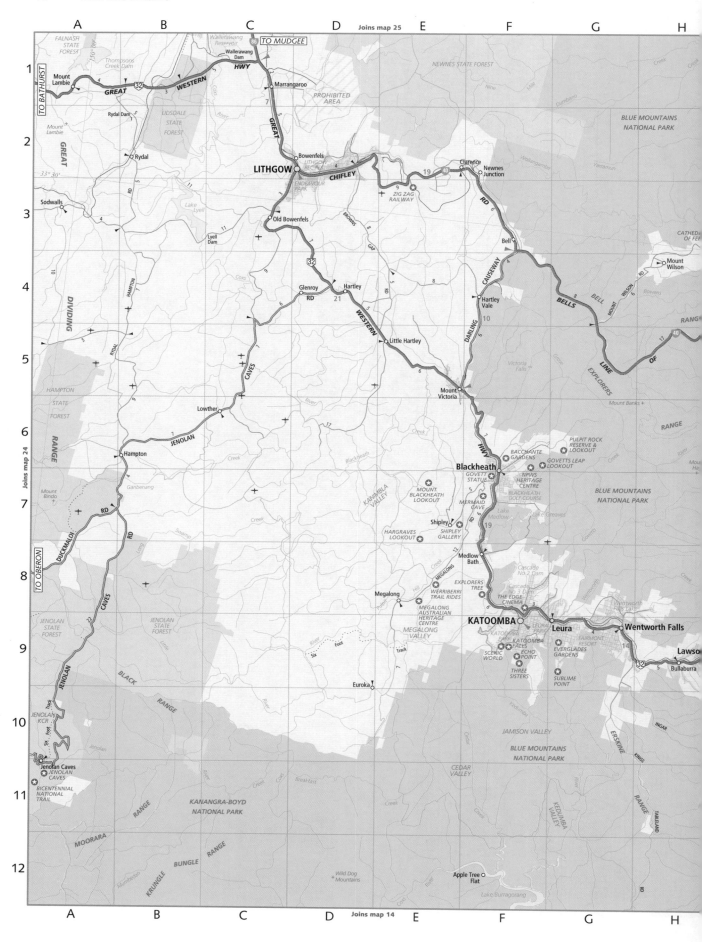

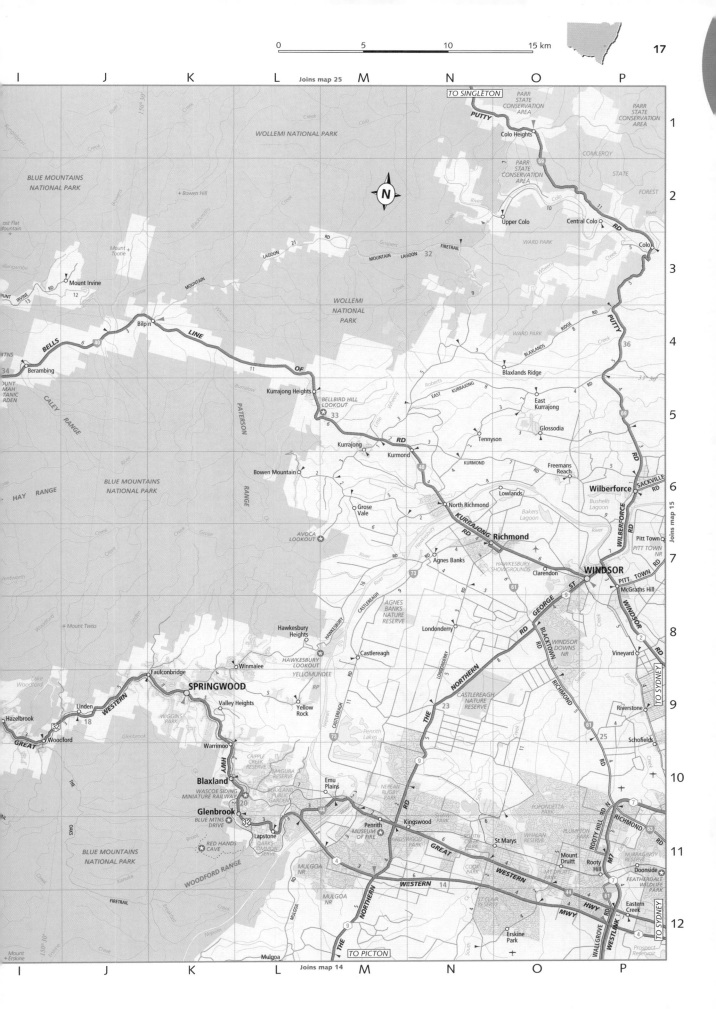

I J K L M N O P

0   5   10   15 km

1
2
3
4
5
6
7
8
9
10
11
12

TO SINGLETON

PUTTY

PARR
STATE
CONSERVATION
AREA

PARR
STATE
CONSERVATION
AREA

Colo Heights

COMLEROY

WOLLEMI NATIONAL PARK

BLUE MOUNTAINS
NATIONAL PARK

+ Bowen Hill

STATE

FOREST

Mount
Tootie

Upper Colo

Central Colo

Colo

RD

WARD PARK

MOUNTAIN   LAGOON   32

LAGOON

FIRETRAIL

Mount Irvine

WOLLEMI
NATIONAL
PARK

WARD PARK   RIDGE

PUTTY

BELLS

LINE

OF

Bilpin

Berambing

Blaxlands Ridge

BLAXLANDS

Kurrajong Heights

BELLBIRD HILL
LOOKOUT

EAST   KURRAJONG

East
Kurrajong

PATERSON

33

Kurrajong

Glossodia

Tennyson

RD

SACKVILLE

Kurmond

KURMOND

Freemans
Reach

Wilberforce

CALEY   RANGE

MOUNT
BOTANIC
GARDEN

Bowen Mountain

Lowlands

Bushells
Lagoon

HAY   RANGE

BLUE MOUNTAINS
NATIONAL PARK

RANGE

Grose
Vale

North Richmond

KURRAJONG

Richmond

Bakers
Lagoon

Pitt Town

PITT TOWN
NR

AVOCA
LOOKOUT

RD

Agnes Banks

HAWKESBURY
SHOWGROUNDS

Clarendon

WINDSOR

McGraths Hill

+ Mount Twiss

HAWKESBURY
LOOKOUT

CASTLEREAGH

AGNES
BANKS
NATURE
RESERVE

Londonderry

GEORGE   ST

Hawkesbury
Heights

Castlereagh

BLACKTOWN

WINDSOR
DOWNS
NR

Vineyard

Faulconbridge

Winmalee

YELLOMUNDEE
RP

SPRINGWOOD

Lake
Woodford

WESTERN

Linden

Valley Heights

Yellow
Rock

CASTLEREAGH

CASTLEREAGH
NATURE
RESERVE

THE

NORTHERN

RICHMOND

Riverstone

Hazelbrook

HWY

Woodford

GREAT

WIGGINS
PARK

Glenbrook

23

Schofields

Warrimoo

Penrith
Lakes

CRIPPLE
CREEK
RESERVE

THE
OAKS

Blaxland

WASCOE SIDING
MINIATURE RAILWAY

MAGURA
RESERVE

Emu
Plains

NEPEAN
RUGBY
PARK

POPONDETTA
PARK

RICHMOND

Doonside

Glenbrook

BLUE MTNS
DRIVE

BLAXLAND
PUBLIC
GARDEN

Lapstone

SHAW
PARK

PLUMPTON
PARK

NURRAGINGY
RESERVE

RED HANDS
CAVE

Penrith

PENRITH
MUSEUM
OF FIRE

Kingswood

KINGSWOOD
PARK

St Marys

SOUTH
CREEK
PARK

WHALAN
RESERVE

Mount
Druitt

MT DRUITT
PARK

Rooty
Hill

FEATHERDALE
WILDLIFE
PARK

BLUE MOUNTAINS
NATIONAL PARK

WOODFORD RANGE

MULGOA
NR

MULGOA
NR

GREAT

WESTERN

COOK
PARK

ST CLAIR
RESERVE

HWY

WALLGROVE

Eastern
Creek

MWY

WESTLINK

TO SYDNEY

FIRETRAIL

THE

NORTHERN

Erskine
Park

Mulgoa

TO PICTON

TO SYDNEY

0   0.25   0.5   0.75   1 km

TO STOCKTON BEACH

Accommodation ◼
Aloha Motor Inn 1 A9
Holiday Inn Esplanade 2 H5
Hotel Novocastrian 3 H5
Newcastle Backpackers 4 A5
Noah's on the Beach 5 H5
Radisson Central City 6 C6
Note: Only a sample range of
accommodation is listed; inclusion is
not necessarily a recommendation.

General Information ◼
City Hall 7 E5
Ferry Terminal 8 F5
Newcastle Railway Station 9 G5
Police 10 G6
Post Office 11 F5
Royal Newcastle Hosp 12 G5
Visitor Information 13 E5
Water Police 14 E5

Places of Interest ◼
Band Rotunda 15 F6
Bogey Hole (swimming pool) 16 G6
Christ Church Cathedral 17 F6
Convict Stockade 18 G5
Cooks Hill Gallery 19 D6
Customs House 20 G5
Fort Scratchley 21 H4
Historical Navigation Tower 22 E6
Hunter Street Mall 23 F5
King Edward Park 24 F7
Maritime & Military Museums 25 H4
Merewether Baths 26 B11
Newcastle Workers Club 27 D6
Obelisk 28 F6
Queens Wharf 29 F5
Regional Art Gallery 30 E6
Regional Museum 31 B5
Soldiers Baths (swimming pool) 32 H5
Supernova 33 B5
Sydney Harbour Seaplanes 34 F5
von Bertouch Galleries 35 D6
War Memorial Cultural Centre 36 E6
William IV Steamship 37 E5

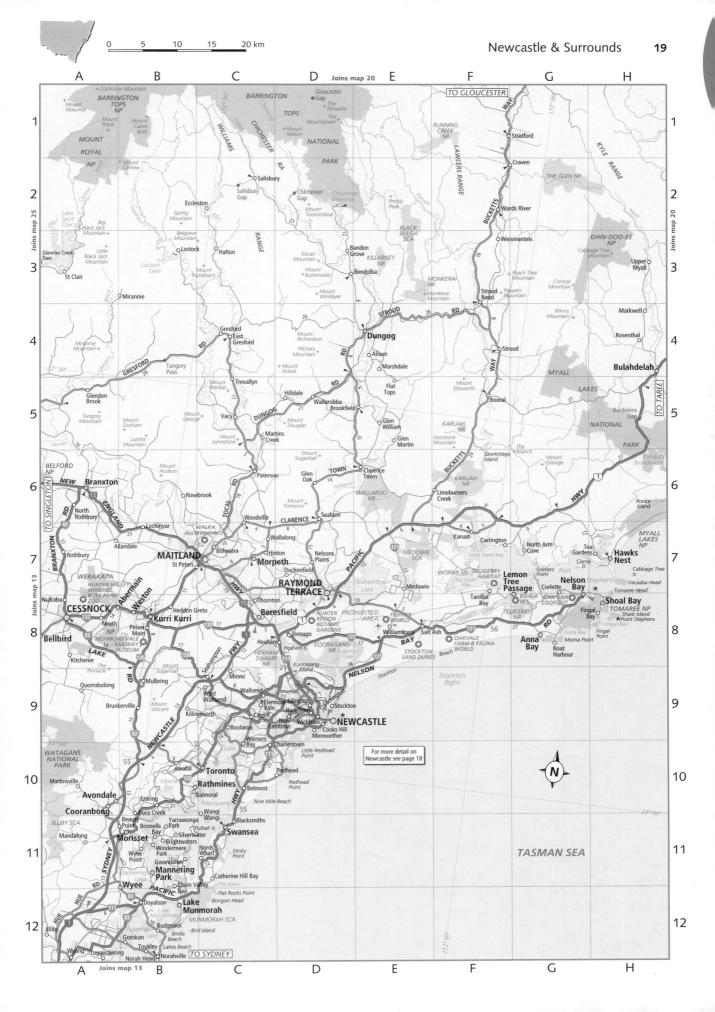

0   20   40   60 km

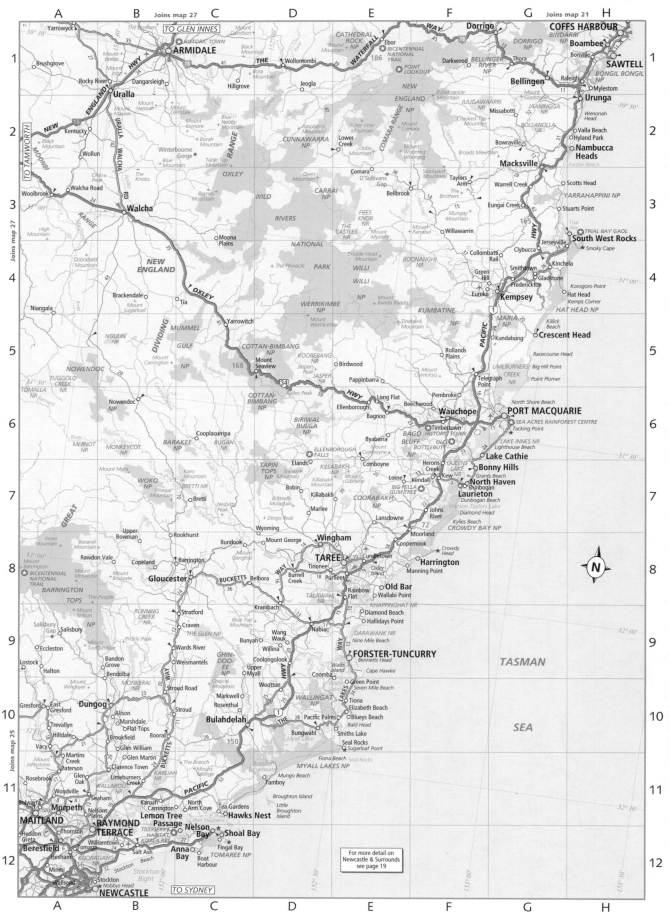

For more detail on
Newcastle & Surrounds
see page 19

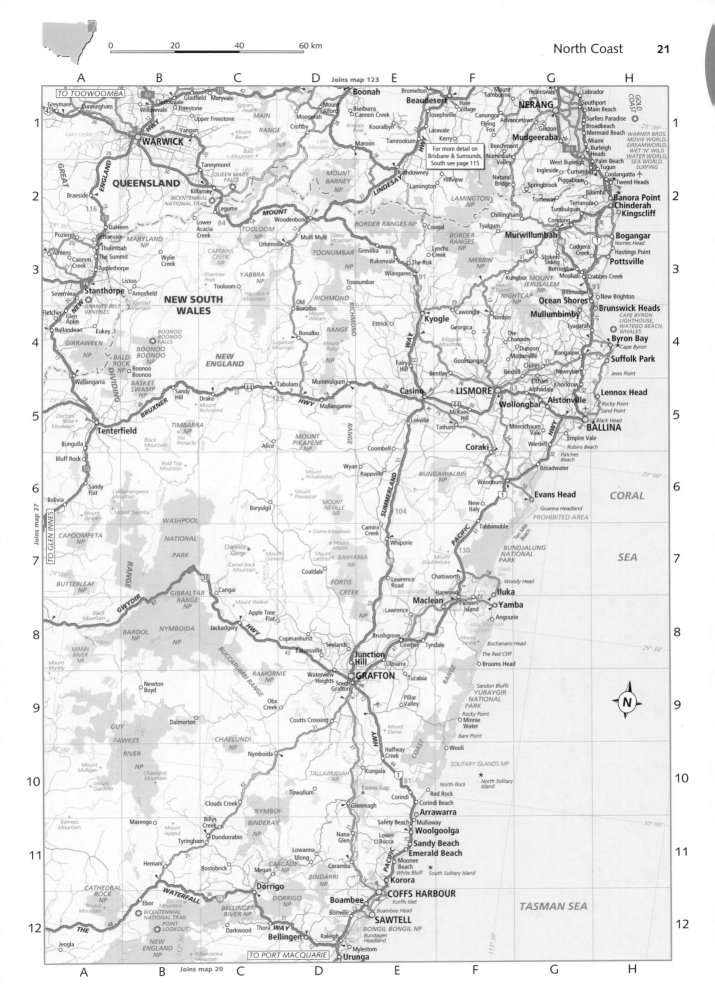

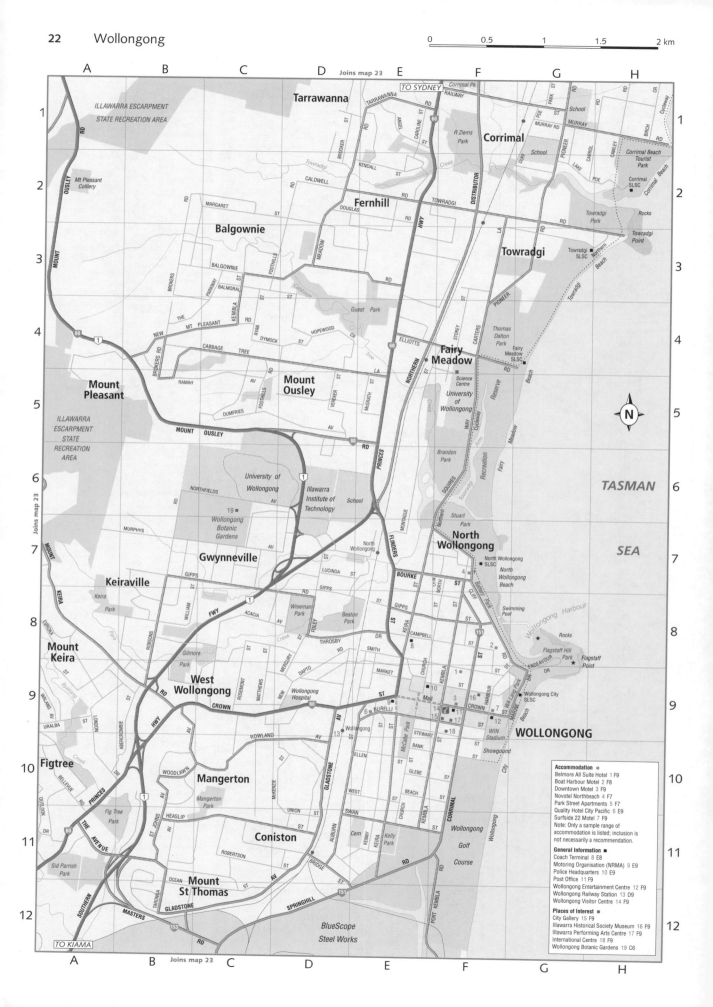

Accommodation ■
Belmore All Suite Hotel 1 F9
Boat Harbour Motel 2 F8
Downtown Motel 3 F9
Novotel Northbeach 4 F7
Park Street Apartments 5 F7
Quality Hotel City Pacific 6 E9
Surfside 22 Motel 7 F9
Note: Only a sample range of
accommodation is listed; inclusion is
not necessarily a recommendation.

General Information ■
Coach Terminal 8 E8
Motoring Organisation (NRMA) 9 E9
Police Headquarters 10 E9
Post Office 11 F9
Wollongong Entertainment Centre 12 F9
Wollongong Railway Station 13 D9
Wollongong Visitor Centre 14 F9

Places of Interest ■
City Gallery 15 F9
Illawarra Historical Society Museum 16 F9
Illawarra Performing Arts Centre 17 F9
International Centre 18 F9
Wollongong Botanic Gardens 19 C6

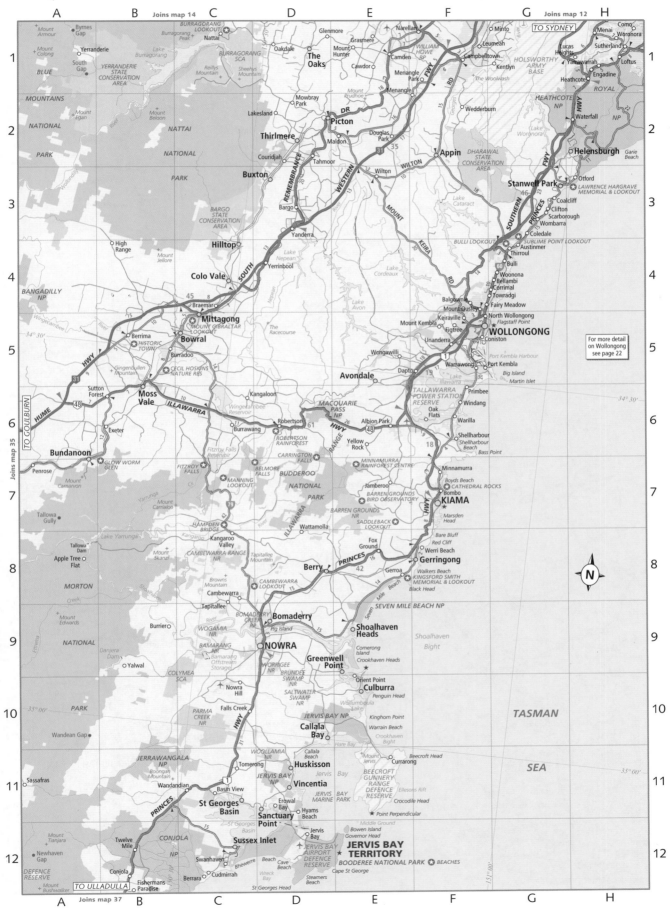

0   5   10   15   20 km

Joins map 14
Joins map 12
TO SYDNEY
Joins map 35
Joins map 37
TO GOULBURN
TO ULLADULLA

For more detail on Wollongong see page 22

Map labels (selected):

Mount Armour, Byrnes Gap, Yerranderie, Mount Colong, South Gap, BLUE MOUNTAINS NATIONAL PARK, Mount Egan, Mount Beloon, YERRANDERIE STATE CONSERVATION AREA, Reillys Mountain, Sheehys Mountain, BURRAGORANG SCA, Lake Burragorang, BURRAGORANG LOOKOUT, Nattai, NATTAI NATIONAL PARK, Glenmore, Oakdale, The Oaks, Mowbray Park, Lakesland, Picton, Mount Hunter, Grasmere, Cawdor, Camden, Menangle Park, Narellan, Minto, Leumeah, Campbelltown, Kentlyn, The Woolwash, HOLSWORTHY ARMY BASE, Como, Woronora, Menai, Lucas Heights, Yarrawarrah, Sutherland, Loftus, Engadine, Heathcote, ROYAL NP, HEATHCOTE NP, Waterfall, Garie Beach, Helensburgh, Stanwell Park, LAWRENCE HARGRAVE MEMORIAL & LOOKOUT, Coalcliff, Clifton, Scarborough, Wombarra, Coledale, SUBLIME POINT LOOKOUT, Austinmer, Thirroul, Bulli, BULLI LOOKOUT, Woonona, Bellambi, Corrimal, Towradgi, Fairy Meadow, North Wollongong, Flagstaff Point, WOLLONGONG, Coniston, Port Kembla Harbour, Big Island, Martin Islet, Thirlmere, Maldon, Douglas Park, Tahmoor, Couridjah, Appin, DHARAWAL STATE CONSERVATION AREA, Wilton, Buxton, Bargo, BARGO STATE CONSERVATION AREA, Lake Cataract, Yanderra, Mount Keira, Balgownie, Mount Ousley, Keiraville, Mount Kembla, Figtree, Unanderra, High Range, Mount Jellore, Hilltop, Lake Nepean, Yerrinbool, Lake Cordeaux, Wongawilli, Dapto, Warrawong, Port Kembla, Lake Illawarra, BANGADILLY NP, Colo Vale, Braemar, Mittagong, MOUNT GIBRALTAR LOOKOUT, Bowral, Burradoo, Berrima, HISTORIC TOWN, Gingenbullen Mountain, CECIL HOSKINS NATURE RES, Kangaloon, Avondale, TALLAWARRA POWER STATION RESERVE, Primbee, Windang, Warilla, Sutton Forest, Moss Vale, Exeter, Wingecarribee Reservoir, Robertson, Burrawang, ROBERTSON RAINFOREST, MACQUARIE PASS NP, Albion Park, Yellow Rock, Oak Flats, Shellharbour, Shellharbour Beach, Bass Point, Bundanoon, Penrose, GLOW WORM GLEN, Mount Carnarvon, FITZROY FALLS, FITZROY FALLS RESERVOIR, BELMORE FALLS, MANNING LOOKOUT, CARRINGTON FALLS, BUDDEROO NATIONAL PARK, MINNAMURRA RAINFOREST CENTRE, BARREN GROUNDS BIRD OBSERVATORY, BARREN GROUNDS NR, Minnamurra, Boyds Beach, CATHEDRAL ROCKS, Bombo, KIAMA, Tallowa Gully, Apple Tree Flat, Tallowa Dam, Mount Skanzi, MORTON NATIONAL PARK, Lake Yarrunga, HAMPDEN BRIDGE, Kangaroo Valley, CAMBEWARRA RANGE NR, Tapitallee Mountain, Wattamolla, SADDLEBACK LOOKOUT, Marsden Head, Bare Bluff, Red Cliff, Werri Beach, Gerringong, Fox Ground, Gerroa, Walkers Beach, KINGSFORD SMITH MEMORIAL & LOOKOUT, Black Head, Mount Edwards, Danjera Dam, Yalwal, Burrier, Cambewarra, CAMBEWARRA LOOKOUT, Browns Mountain, Tapitallee, WOGAMIA NR, BAMARANG NR, BAMARANG OFFSTREAM STORAGE, Berry, Bomaderry, BOMADERRY CREEK NR, Pig Island, Shoalhaven Heads, Comerong Island, Crookhaven Heads, SEVEN MILE BEACH NP, Shoalhaven Bight, NOWRA, WORRIGEE NR, BRUNDEE SWAMP NR, SALTWATER SWAMP NR, Greenwell Point, Orient Point, Culburra, Penguin Head, Crookhaven Bight, TASMAN, Wandean Gap, COLYMEA SCA, Nowra Hill, Falls Creek, PARMA CREEK NR, JERVIS BAY NP, Callala Bay, Kinghorn Point, Warrain Beach, Wollumboola Lake, Jerrawangala NP, Boongan Mountain, Wandandian, Tomerong, WOOLLAMIA NR, Basin View, JERVIS BAY NP, Huskisson, Callala Beach, Vincentia, Jervis Bay, JERVIS BAY MARINE PARK, Mount Jervis, Currarong, Beecroft Head, BEECROFT GUNNERY RANGE DEFENCE RESERVE, Ellesons Rift, Crocodile Head, SEA, Sassafras, St Georges Basin, Erowal Bay, Hyams Beach, Sanctuary Point, St Georges Basin, Point Perpendicular, Mount Tianjara, Twelve Mile, CONJOLA NP, Sussex Inlet, Bewerre, Jervis Bay, Bowen Island, Governor Head, Middle Ground, JERVIS BAY AIRPORT DEFENCE RESERVE, JERVIS BAY TERRITORY, BOODEREE NATIONAL PARK, BEACHES, Newhaven Gap, Mount Bushwalker, DEFENCE RESERVE, Conjola, Swanhaven, Berrara, Cudmirrah, Fishermans Paradise, Beach, Cave Beach, Wreck Bay, Steamers Beach, St Georges Head, Cape St George

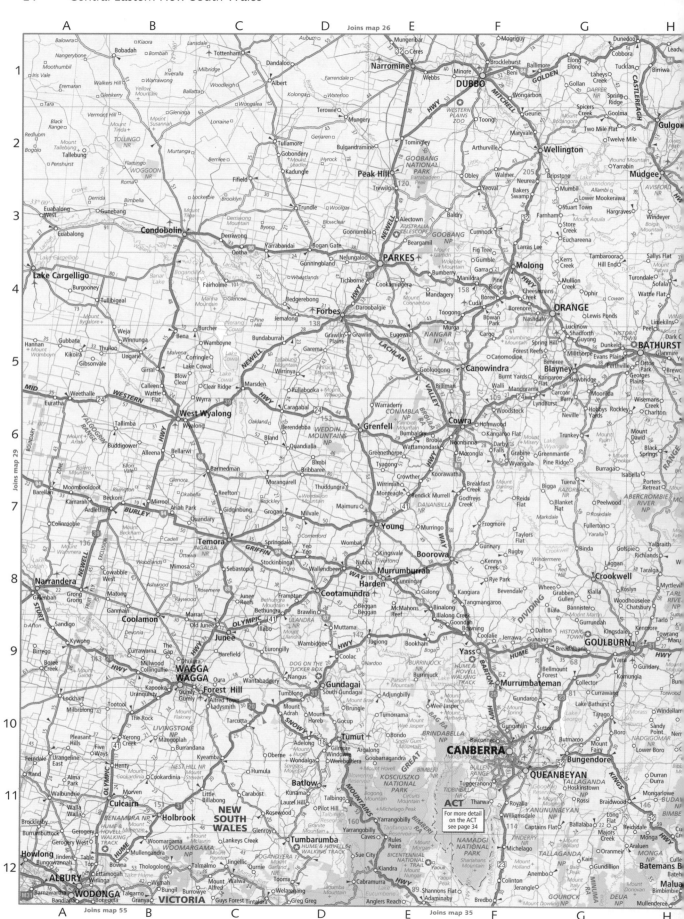

Joins map 26
Joins map 29
Joins map 55
Joins map 35

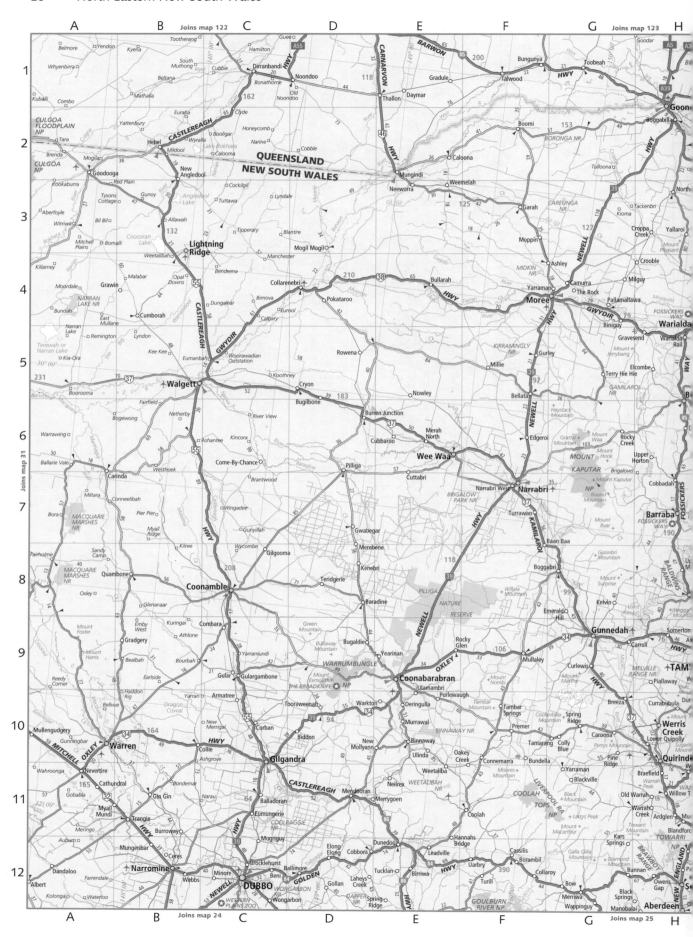

0 20 40 60 80 100 km

I J K L M N O P

WARNER BROS.
MOVIE WORLD,
WET 'N' WILD
DREAMWORLD,
SEA WORLD,
SURFING

GOLD COAST

NERANG

Paradise Point
Helensvale
Labrador
Main Beach
Surfers Paradise
Broadbeach
Burleigh Heads
Palm Beach
Coolangatta
Tweed Heads

Boonah
Beaudesert
Mudgeeraba
Numinbah Valley
Springbrook
Terranora
Banora Point
Chinderah
Kingscliff
Bogangar

1

Mount Bodumba
Karara
Greymare
Thanes Creek
Pratten
Berat
Goomburra
MAIN RANGE
Mount Alford
Josephville
Laravale
Kerry
Hillview
Lamington
Natural Bridge
Tumbulgum
Condong

Inglewood
CUNNINGHAM HWY
42
Lake Coolmunda
Braeside
Cunningham
Willowvale
Freestone
Yangan
WARWICK
Killarney
Moogerah
Mount Alford
Kooralbyn
Tamrookum
Rathdowney
143
LAMINGTON NP
Murwillumbah
Stokers Siding
Burringbar
Hastings Point
Pottsville

CORAL

2

QUEENSLAND
TOOLOOM NP
NEW ENGLAND HWY
Pozieres
Dalveen
Lower Acacia Creek
Woodenbong
Mulli Mulli
Urbenville
BORDER RANGES
Cougal
Grevillea
The Risk
Lynchs Creek
Wiangaree
Tyalgum
Kunghur
Uki
Crabbes Creek
Billinudgel
Ocean Shores
Brunswick Heads

Smithfield
Beebo
Limevale
Amiens
Thulimbah
The Summit
Applethorpe
Cottonvale
Stanthorpe
Liston
Amosfield
Tooloom
TOONUMBAR NP
Toonumbar
Old Bonalbo
Mount William
Bonalbo
RICHMOND RANGE NP
Ettrick
Cawongla
Georgica
Nimbin
The Channon
Tyagarah
Mullumbimby
NIGHTCAP NP

3

Texas
Mount Guyan
Pikedale
Cannon Creek
GRANITE BELT WINERIES
Glen Aplin
Eukey
Severnlea
Ballandean
BOONOO BOONOO NP
Wallangarra
Boonoo Boonoo
YABBRA NP
Haystack Mountain
Tabulam
Mummulgum
Fairy Hill
Bentley
Modanville
Goolmangar
Bexhill
Clunes
Bangalow
Byron Bay
Cape Byron
Suffolk Park
CAPE BYRON LIGHTHOUSE, WATEGO BEACH, WHALES

NEW SOUTH WALES
Bonshaw
Mingoola
44
Clifton
Mole River
Bungulla
NEW ENGLAND HWY
GIRRAWEEN NP
BALD ROCK NP
Drake
193
Mallanganee
Leeville
Casino
LISMORE
44
Wollongbar
Alstonville
Lennox Head

Round Mountain
Red Rock
Ashford
The Gulf
TORRINGTON SCA
Sugarloaf Mountain
Mount Misery
Bluff Rock
13
Black Mountain
DEMON NR
TIMBARRA
Sandy Hill
Tenterfield
Alice
MOUNT PIKAPENE
Coombell
Tatham
Coraki
Wardell
Empire Vale
BALLINA
Sand Point
Meerschaum Vale

4

Wallangra
Bukkulla
Emmaville
Deepwater
Dundee
CAPOOMPETA NP
WASHPOOL NATIONAL PARK
160
Cangai
Baryulgil
Camira Creek
Whiporie
Woodburn
1
Evans Head
Goanna Headland
BROADWATER NP
BROADWATER
29° 00'

Inverell
Gilgai
Brodies Plains
Elsmore
Stannifer
Tingha
Woodville
Wellingrove
KINGS PLAINS NP
BUTTERLEAF NP
38
GIBRALTAR RANGE NP
Jackadgery
Apple Tree Flat
Copmanhurst
FORTIS CREEK NP
Lawrence
Chatsworth
Harwood
Palmers Island
Maclean
Iluka
Yamba
Angourie
BUNDJALUNG NP
Shark Bay
Woody Head
131

5

Stanborough
Sapphire
Matheson
Stonehenge
Glencoe
Red Range
Glen Innes
Newton Boyd
161
Dalmorton
MANN RIVER NR
NYMBOIDA NP
GUY FAWKES RIVER NP
Mount Gundahl
RAMORNIE NP
Eatonsville
Waterview Heights
Seelands
Brushgrove
Junction Hill
GRAFTON
Coutts Crossing
Tyndale
Pillar Valley
YURAYGIR NP
Sandon Bluffs
Brooms Head

Bundarra
THE BASIN NR
Wandsworth
Ben Lomond
Guyra
Llangothlin Lake
Llangothlin
Clouds Creek
Towallum
Marengo
Dundurrabin
Billys Creek
Tyringham
Lowanna
Nana Glen
Corindi
Glenreagh
SHERWOOD NR
Safety Beach
Corindi Beach
Red Rock
SOLITARY ISLANDS MP
North Solitary Island
86
Kungala
Halfway Creek
Wooli
Minnie Water
Bare Point
Rocky Point
YURAYGIR

6

Kingstown
Yarrowyck
Black Mountain
Mount Lookout
Hernani
Bostobrick
Megan
Ulong
Lower Bucca
Coramba
Moonee Beach
Korora
Arrawarra
Mullaway
Woolgoolga
Sandy Beach
Emerald Beach
30° 00'

7

Brushgrove
Rocky River
Uralla
Dangarsleigh
Hillgrove
CUNNAWARRA NP
NEW ENGLAND NP
Mount Comara
HISTORIC TOWN
Wollomombi
Ebor
190
BICENTENNIAL NATIONAL TRAIL
Darkwood
Thora
Dorrigo
DORRIGO NP
Boambee
Bonville
COFFS HARBOUR
SAWTELL
BONGIL BONGIL NP
Bellingen
Raleigh
Mylestom

8

Kentucky
Wollun
Walcha Road
16
CATHEDRAL ROCK NP
Round Mountain
GANAY NR
Urunga
Wenonah Head
Valla Beach
WATERFALL WAY
Missabotti
Hyland Park
Nambucca Heads

9

Woolbrook
OXLEY
Walcha
ABERBALDIE NR
Moona Plains
OXLEY WILD RIVERS NP
Comara
Taylors Arm
Warrell Creek
Bellbrook
229
CARRAI NP
Willawarrin
Eungai Creek
167
Scotts Head
Macksville
Stuarts Point
Grassy Head
YARRAHAPINNI NP
South West Rocks
Smoky Cape

Kootingal
Brackendale
Niangala
Tia
Yarrowitch
259
WERRIKIMBE NP
Mount Werrikimbe
WILLI WILLI NP
Green Hill
Collombatti
Clybucca
Rail
Smithtown
Kinchela
Jerseyville
Frederickton
Korogoro Point
Kempsey
KUMBATINE NP
1
MARIA NP
Crescent Head
Kundabung
Racecourse Head

10

Dungowan
Bowling Alley Point
FOSSICKERS WAY
NEW ENGLAND
DIVIDING RANGE
Nowendoc
NOWENDOC NP
MUMMEL GULF NP
COTTAN-BIMBANG NP
Mount Seaview
Birdwood
Rollands Plains
Point Plomer
Telegraph Point
LIMEBURNERS CREEK NR

31° 00'

11

Barry
Gulf Road
MONKEYCOT NR
Mount Myra
BARAKEE NP
Cooplacurripa
BUGAN NP
TAPIN TOPS NP
Comboyne
Elands
Byabarra
Ellenborough
Beechwood
Bagnoo
Wauchope
PORT MACQUARIE
Nobby Head
Tacking Point
LAKE INNES NR
Lake Cathie
Bonny Hills
North Haven

TASMAN SEA

Illerston
nan Flat
BICENTENNIAL NATIONAL TRAIL
BRETTI NR
WOKO NP
KILLABAKH NR
Mount Gibralta
Herons Creek
Kendall
Lorne
Kew
Laurieton
CROWDY BAY NP
Diamond Head

Upper Bowman
Rawdon Vale
BARRINGTON TOPS NP
Mount Barrington
Rookhurst
Barrington
Copeland
Gloucester
Belbora
Wyoming
Bobin
Killabakh
Bretti
Marlee
Dingo Peak
Wingham
Lansdowne
Johns River
Bundook
Mount George
Tinonee
TAREE
24
Moorland
Coopernook
Crowdy Head
CAMELS HUMP NP

12

Gloucester
Burrell Creek
Purfleet
Harrington
Manning Point
Old Bar

I J K L M N O P

For more detail on the North Coast see page 21

For more detail on the Mid North Coast see page 20

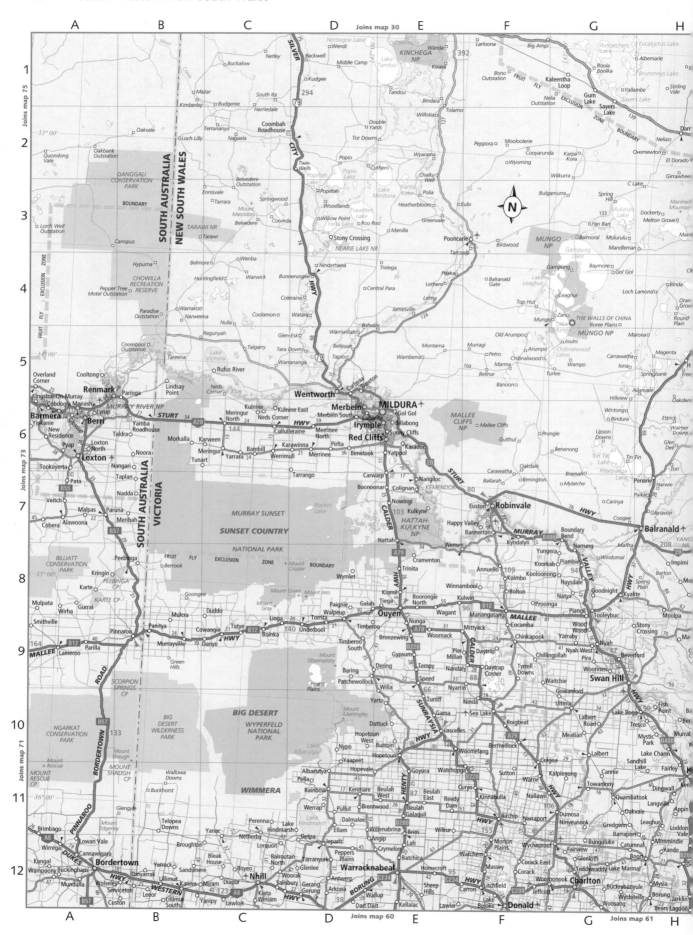

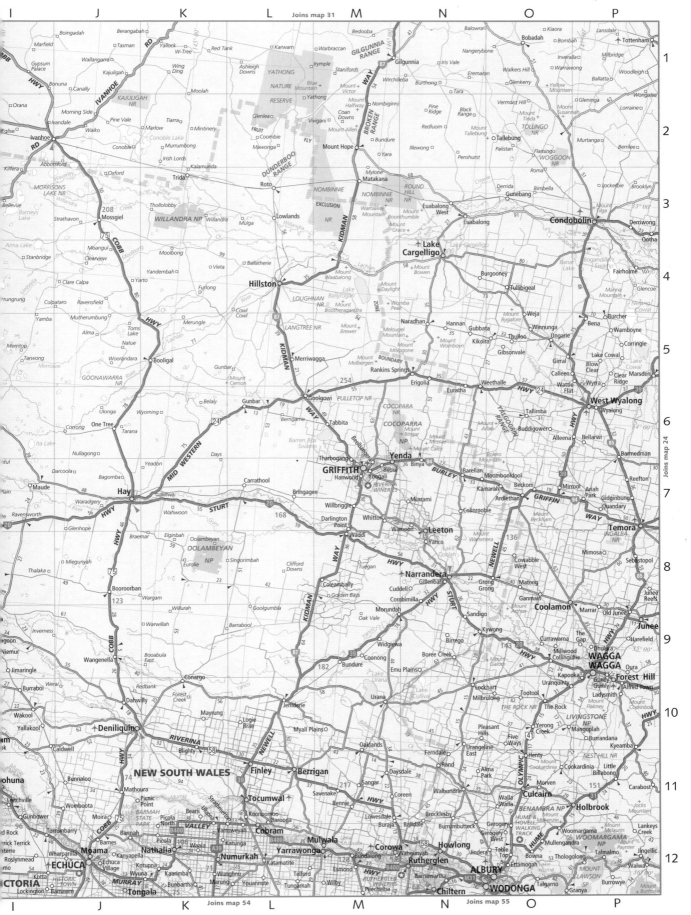

Joins map 31

0 20 40 60 80 100 km

I J K L M N O P

1

Boingadah
Berangabah
Marfield
Tasman
Yallock
W-Tree
Red Tank
Karwarn
Warbraccan
Bedooba
Balowra
Bobadah
Kiaora
Bombah
Lansdale
Milbridge
Tottenham
Gypsum Palace
Wallangarra
Wing Ding
Ashleigh Downs
Irymple
Staniforths
GILGUNNIA RANGE
Gilgunnia
Nangerybone
Iris Vale
Walkers Hill
Inveralla
Warrawong
Woodleigh
Bonuna
Canally
Kajuligah
Moolah
Glenlea
YATHONG NATURE RESERVE
Yathong
Blue Mountain
Vivigani
Mount Victor
Wirchilleba
Burthong
Tara
Eremaran
Glenkerry
Yellow Mountain
Mount Susannah
Gleninga
Lorraine
Wongalea

2

Orana
Morning Side
Pine Vale
Tiarra
Mintinery
Coombie
Mawonga
FRUIT FLY ZONE
Mount Allen
Mount Halfway
Coan Downs
Nombiginni
Pine Ridge
Black Range
Redluom
Vermont Hill
Mount Tinda
TOLLINGO NR
Mount Tallebung
Tallebung
Palistan
Murtanga
Berrilee
Ivanhoe
Waiko
Marlow
Conoble Lake
Murrumbong
Irish Lords
Kalamunda
Mount Hope
Yara
Bundure
Illewong
Penshurst
Roma
Flamingo
WOGGOON NR
Kilfera
Abbotsford
Oxford
Trida
Roto
Matakana
Mylone
Derrida
Gunebang
Bimbella
Lockerbie
Brooklyn

3

Bellevue
Barneys Lake
MORRISONS LAKE NR
Waverley
Strathavon
Thollolobby
Willandra
Lowlands
Mulga
NOMBINNIE EXCLUSION NR
NOMBINNIE NR
Warraway Mountain
Boonthumble
Mount Grace
Euabalong West
Euabalong
Condobolin
Derriwong
Ootha
Alma Lake
208
Mossgiel
WILLANDRA NP
Ballatherie
Lake Cargelligo
Banar Lake
Bogandillon Swamp
Mount Tilga
Fairholme
101
Stanbridge
Moangul
Clearview
Moolbong
Vieta
Mount Waabalong
Lake Ballyrogan
Mount Bowen
Euabalong
Burgooney
80
Manna Mountain
Glencoe
Nejanojo Cowal

4

Clare Calpa
Ravensfield
Mutherumbung
Yarto
Furlong
Hillston
LOUGHNAN NR
Mount Daylight
Womba Peak
Fullibigeal
Weja
Winnunga
Burcher
Bena
Wamboyne
Merritop
Yamba
Alma
Toms Lake
Natue
Merungle
Cowl Cowl
LANGTREE NR
Mount Brewer
Naradhan
Mount Bygalore
Gubbata
Thulloo
Ungarie
Corringle
Tarwong
Woorandara
Booligal
Merriwagga
Melougel Mountain
Mount Molgona
Mount Wombyn
Kikoira
Gibsonvale
Girral
Calleen
Lake Cowal
Blow Clear
Clear Ridge
Marsden

5

GOONAWARRA NR
Gunbar
Mount Melberger
BOUNDARY ZONE
Rankins Springs
Erigolia
Euratha
Weethalle
Wattle Flat
Wyrra
West Wyalong
Ulonga
Wyoming
Goolgowi
PULLETOP NR
COCOPARA NR
Tallimba
HWY 24
Wyalong

6

One Tree
Tarana
Belaly
Gunbar
Berngarne
Tabbita
COCOPARA NP
Mount Bingar
Mount Caley
Mount Mcrae
Bolero Mountain
Buddigower
Alleena
Bellarwi
Barmedman
Corrong
Nullagong
Yeadon
Days
Beelbangera
Tharbogang
Yenda
Binya
BURLEY GRIFFIN
254
Barellan
Moombooldool
Beckom
Mirrool
Ariah Park
Gidginbung
Quandary
Reefton

7

Maude
Darcoola
Bagomba
Carrathool
GRIFFITH
Hanwood
Bilbul
Yoogali
RIVERINA WINERIES
Murami
Kamarah
Ardlethan
Colinroobie
GRIFFIN WAY
Temora
INGALBA NR
Ita Lake
Hay
Jililiwa
Bringagee
Willbriggle
Whitton
Wamoon
Leeton
Mount Wammera
Mimosa
Sebastopol
Ravensworth
Glenhope
Braemar
Wahwoon
168
STURT HWY
Darlington Point
Waddi
Yanco
136
Junee Reefs

8

Thalaka
Miegunyah
Elginbah
Eurolie
Singorimbah
OOLAMBEYAN NP
Clifford Downs
Tuegan
Narrandera
Gillenbah
Grong Grong
Cowabbie West
Matong
Old Junee
NEWELL HWY
STURT HWY
49
123
Booroorban
Wargam
Willurah
Goolgumbla
Barrabool
Coleambally
Golden Bays
Corobimilla
Morundah
Sandigo
Ganmain
Coolamon
Marrar
Junee

9

Inverness
Warwillah
Oak Vale
Widgiewa
Birrego
Kywong
Currawarna
Millwood
Collingullie
The Gap
Harefield
Burraboi
Wangenella
Booabula East
Redbank
Conargo
Coonong
Bundure
Emu Plains
Boree Creek
Mount Galore
WAGGA WAGGA
143
Kapooka
Uranquinty
Forest Hill
Oura

10

Jimaringle
Dahwilly
Forest Creek
Jerilderie
Logie Brae
Myall Plains
Lake Urana
Urana
Lake Cullival
Lockhart
Milbrulong
Tootool
THE ROCK NR
The Rock
Gumly Gumly
Ladysmith
Mount Flakney
Mount Corinbobia
Wakool
Yallakool
182
LIVINGSTONE NP
Mangoplah
Burrandana
Kyeamba

11

Deniliquin
RIVERINA HWY
Blighty
58
Finley
Berrigan
Oaklands
Sangar
Coreen
Daysdale
Ferndale
Rand
Alma Park
Urangeline East
Pleasant Hills
Five Ways
Yerong Creek
41
Henty
Morven
Cookardinia
151
Carabost
Caldwell
NEW SOUTH WALES
Bunnaloo
Mathoura
94
74
Tocumwal
Rennie
Savernake
217
Walbundrie
Walla Walla
Culcairn
NEST HILL NR
Little Billabong
Leitchville
Wombota
Moira
Picola Point
Koonoomoo
Baroga
Lowesdale
Buraja
Brocklesby
Burrumbuttock
Gerogery
Gerogery West
BENAMBRA NP
Holbrook
HUME & HOVELL WALKING TRACK
Jocks Mountain
Lankeys Creek

12

Gunbower
Torrumbarry
Wharparilla
Moama
ECHUCA
Echuca Village
Barnes
BARMAH STATE PARK
Picola North
Strathmerton
Bearii
Ulupna
Katunga
Cobram
MURRAY VALLEY
Yarroweyah
Waaia
Numurkah
Katamatite
Mulwala
Yarrawonga
Bundalong
Corowa
Wahgunyah
Rutherglen
RUTHERGLEN WINERIES
Howlong
Jindera
Table Top
Bowna
Lake Hume
Thologolong
Talgarno
MOUNT LAWSON
Burrowye
Walwa
d Rock
Wakool
Kanyapella
Nathalia
Kotupna
Wunghnu
Youanmite
Wilby
Esmond
Telford
Tungamah
Marungan
Peechelba
ALBURY
Chiltern
WODONGA
Barnawartha
Ettamogah
Mount Mcleay
WOOMARGAMA NP
Woomargama
Mullengandra
Granya
Jingellic

Joins map 54   Joins map 55

Joins map 24

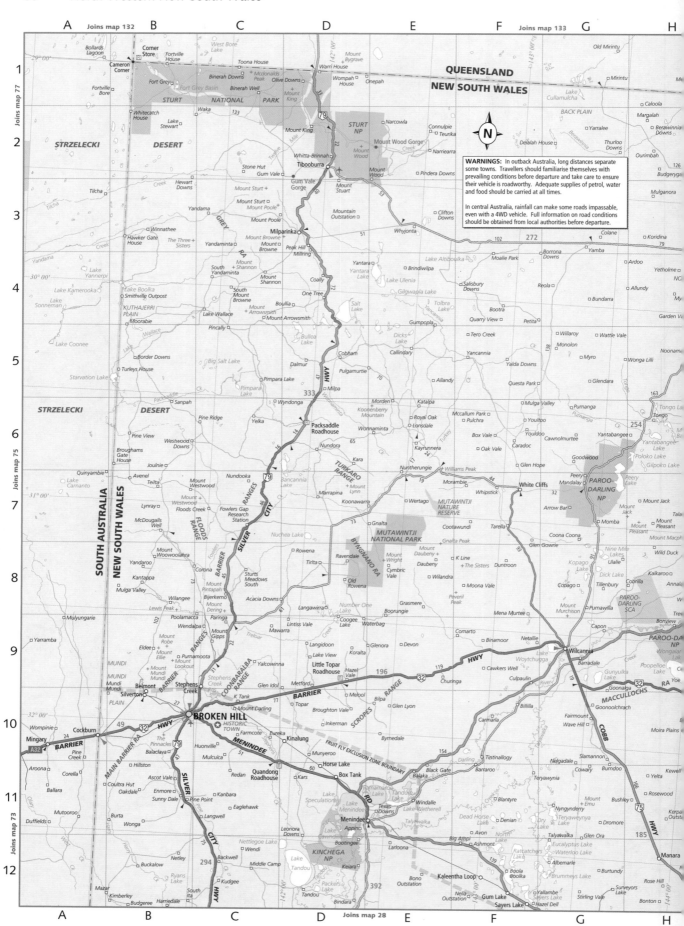

WARNINGS: In outback Australia, long distances separate some towns. Travellers should familiarise themselves with prevailing conditions before departure and take care to ensure their vehicle is roadworthy. Adequate supplies of petrol, water and food should be carried at all times.

In central Australia, rainfall can make some roads impassable, even with a 4WD vehicle. Full information on road conditions should be obtained from local authorities before departure.

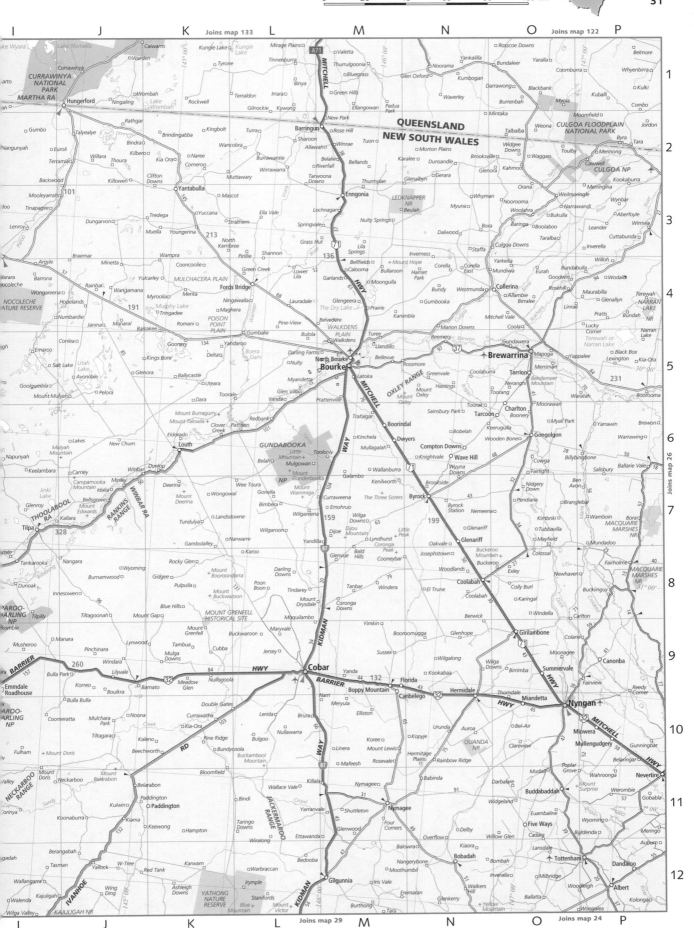

0   20   40   60   80   100 km

Joins map 133
Joins map 122
Joins map 26
Joins map 29
Joins map 24

QUEENSLAND
NEW SOUTH WALES

CURRAWINYA
NATIONAL
PARK
MARTHA RA

Hungerford

CULGOA FLOODPLAIN
NATIONAL PARK

CULGOA NP

Yantabulla

NOCOLECHE
NATURE RESERVE

MULCHACERA PLAIN

Fords Bridge

POISON
POINT
PLAIN

Enngonia

LEDKNAPPER
NR

WALKDENS
PLAIN
Walkdens

North Bourke
Bourke

Brewarrina

OXLEY RANGE

THOOLABOOL
RA

Tilpa

RANKINS RANGE

WINBAR RA

Louth

GUNDABOOKA
NP

Byrock

MACQUARIE
MARSHES
NR

Glenariff

MACQUARIE
MARSHES
NR

PAROO-
DARLING
NP

Emmdale
Roadhouse

PAROO-
DARLING
NP

MOUNT GRENFELL
HISTORICAL SITE

Coolabah

Girilambone

Cobar

BARRIER   HWY

Summervale

Canonba

Nyngan

Hermidale

Nevertire

NECKARBOO
RANGE

Paddington

JACKERMAROO
RANGE

Nymagee

Buddabaddah

Five Ways

IVANHOE

YATHONG
NATURE
RESERVE

KAJULIGAH NR

Gilgunnia

KIDMAN

Tottenham

Dandaloo

Albert

0   0.25   0.50   0.75   1 km

Legend

Accommodation ■
Best Western Motel Monaro 1 F12
Brassey of Canberra 2 E11
Crowne Plaza Canberra 3 D4
The Griffin Hotel 4 E11
Hyatt Hotel Canberra 5 C8
Hotel Kurrajong 6 D10
Medina Executive James Court 7 D2
Olims Canberra Hotel 8 F3
Rydges Capital Hill 9 D11
Rydges Lakeside 10 C4
Note: Only a sample range of accommodation is listed; inclusion is not necessarily a recommendation.

General Information ■
Bus Interchange 11 D3
Canberra Railway Station 12 G12
General Post Office 13 C3
Jolimont Centre 14 C3
Motoring Organisation (NRMA) 15 D2
Police Station 16 C4
Qantas Travel Centre 17 C3

Places of Interest ■
Australian National University 18 B4

Australian War Memorial 19 G4
Blundell's Cottage 20 F6
Canberra Glassworks 21 F11
Canberra Museum and Gallery 22 D3
Canberra Theatre Centre 23 D4
Captain Cook Memorial Water Jet 24 C6
High Court of Australia 25 E8
Legislative Assembly of the ACT 26 D4
The Lodge 27 A10
Manuka Oval 28 D12
National Capital Exhibition 29 D6
National Carillon 30 F8
National Film & Sound Archive 31 B4
National Gallery of Australia 32 E8
National Library of Australia 33 D7
National Museum of Australia 34 B6
Old Parliment House & National Portrait Gallery 35 C8
Parliament House 36 B10
Questacon – The National Science & Technology Centre 37 D8
St John the Baptist Church 38 E5

Map labels:

TO GOULBURN
Joins map 33
Mt Ainslie Lookout

Braddon
Corroboree Park
Ainslie Public School
Northbourne Oval
Ainslie Hostel
Canberra Nature Park

CSIRO Head Office
Campbell High School TRELOAR
Gorman House Arts Centre & Gorman House Markets (Sat)
Garema Place
Bus Interchange (Closed to traffic)

CANBERRA
Fellows Oval
South Oval
Australian National University
City Hill
CIRCLE
VERNON
Canberra Centre
Glebe Park
Casino Canberra

Reid
Reid Park
St John's Schoolhouse Museum
Australian War Memorial
Remembrance Nature Park
FAIRBAIRN AV
TO AIRPORT

Swimming Pool
Constitution
St John the Baptist Church
ANZAC Parade
Memorials
Campbell
Campbell Public School
St Thomas More Convent

Acton Ferry Terminal & Boat Hire
Footbridge
Commonwealth
West Basin
Nerang Pool
Footbridge

National Capital Exhibition
Regatta Point
Captain Cook Memorial Water Jet
LAKE
National Museum of Australia
Acton Peninsula

BURLEY
Central Basin
Gallipoli Reach
Kings Park
Griffin
Burley
WENDOUREE WAY
RUSSELL

National Carillon
Aspen Island
Footbridge
Russell
Australian–American Memorial
Canberra Nature Park
NORTHCOTT DR

Attunga Point
Flynn Place
National Library of Australia
ENID LYONS
Southern Cross Yacht Club
Lennox Gardens
Lotus Bay
Stirling
Questacon – The National Science & Technology Centre
Rose Gardens
High Court of Australia
National Gallery of Australia
Grevillea Park
MORSHEAD DR
TO AIRPORT

Parkes
Rose Gardens
George
Kings Avenue Bridge
Bowen Place

Yarralumla
National Archives of Australia
Victoria
GRIFFIN
East Basin
Molonglo River
Canberra Nature Park

CAPITAL CIRCLE
Parliament House
Capital Hill
Barton
KINGS
Bowen Park
Bowen Park

TO WODEN
ADELAIDE AV
The Lodge
York Park
Jerrabomberra Wetlands

Forrest
Forrest Public School
National Jewish Memorial Centre
Serbian Orthodox Church
Telopea Park High School
Canberra Glassworks
Old Bus Depot Markets (Sun)
Kingston
Boat Harbour

Deakin
Manuka Oval
Canberra Railway Museum
Canberra Railway Station
TO QUEANBEYAN
Joins map 33

North (N) compass indicator
Joins map 33 (left and right margins)

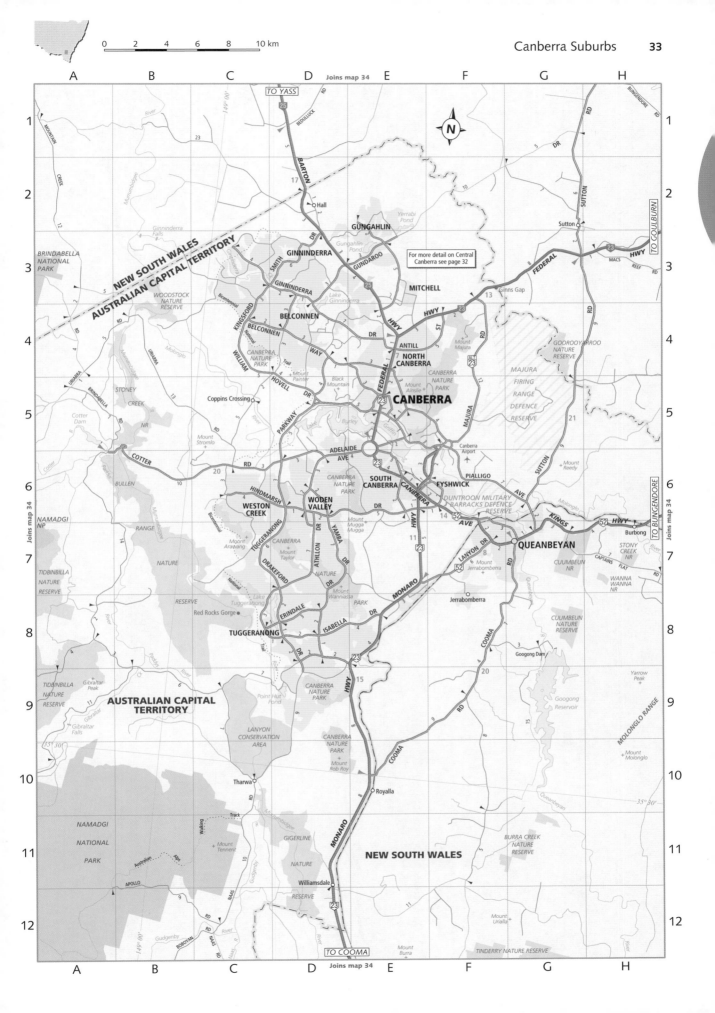

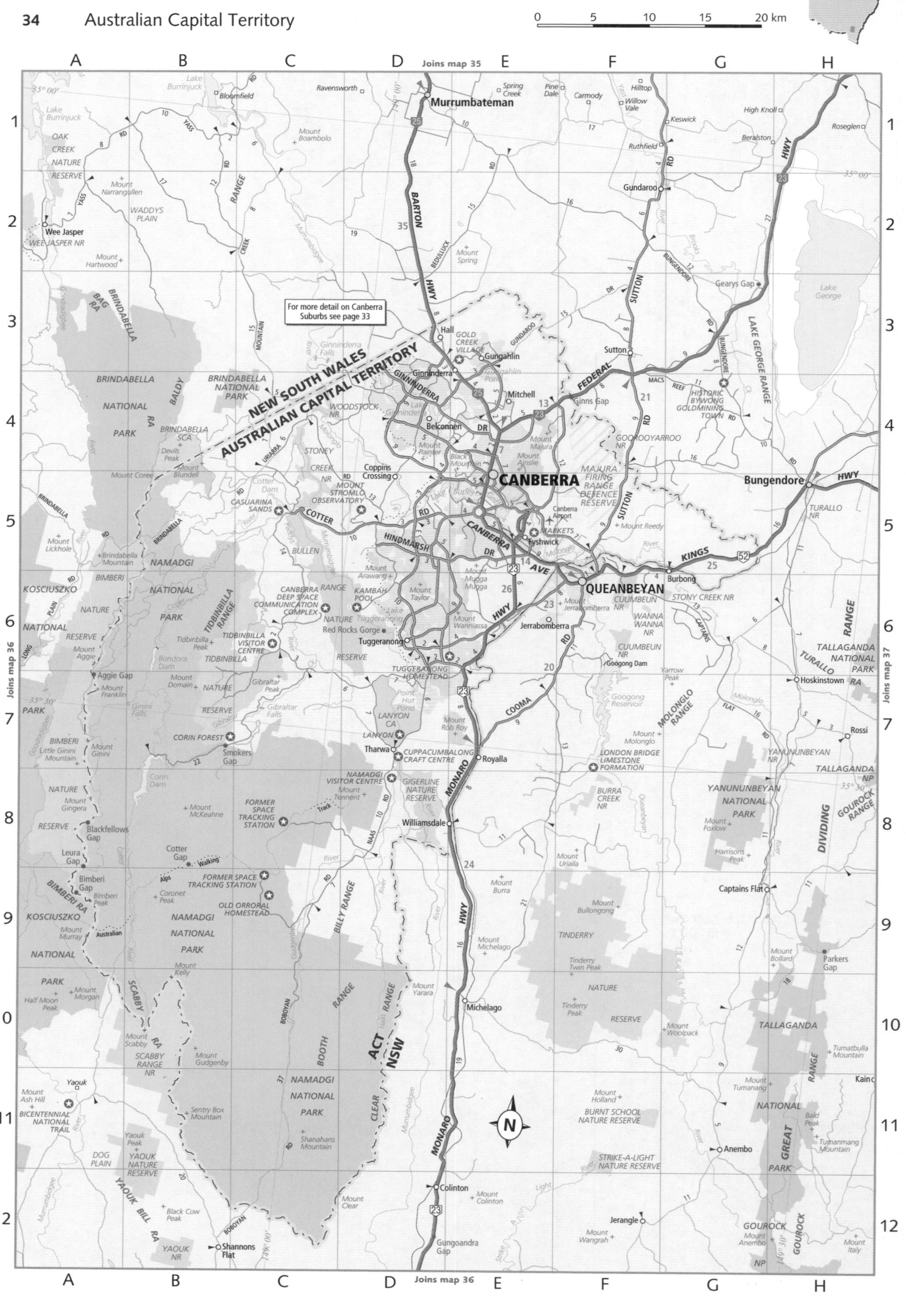

0 5 10 15 20 km

Joins map 35

For more detail on Canberra Suburbs see page 33

NEW SOUTH WALES
AUSTRALIAN CAPITAL TERRITORY

CANBERRA
QUEANBEYAN
Murrumbateman
Bungendore

OAK CREEK NATURE RESERVE
Lake Burrinjuck
Bloomfield
Ravensworth
Spring Creek
Pine Dale
Carmody
Hilltop
Willow Vale
Keswick
High Knoll
Roseglen
Mount Narrangullen
Waddys Plain
Mount Boambolo
Ruthfield
Beralston
Wee Jasper
WEE JASPER NR
Mount Hartwood
Gundaroo
Gearys Gap
Lake George
BRINDABELLA RA
BALDY RANGE MOUNTAIN
BRINDABELLA NATIONAL PARK
Ginninderra Falls
Hall
GOLD CREEK VILLAGE
Ginninderra
Gungahlin
Sutton
LAKE GEORGE RANGE
FEDERAL
Ginns Gap
MACS REEF
HISTORIC BYWONG GOLDMINING TOWN
Devils Peak
Mount Blundell
Mount Coree
WOODSTOCK NR
Belconnen
Mount Painter
Black Mountain
Mount Majura
Mount Ainslie
GOOROOYARROO
SUTTON
Bungendore
HWY
Coppins Crossing
CASUARINA SANDS
MOUNT STROMLO OBSERVATORY
COTTER
Mount Reedy
TURALLO NR
BRINDABELLA
Mount Lickhole
Brindabella Mountain
NAMADGI
STONEY CREEK NR
BULLEN
HINDMARSH
CANBERRA
Canberra Airport
MARKETS
Kingston
KINGS AVE
Burbong
STONY CREEK NR
KOSCIUSZKO NATIONAL NATURE RESERVE
BIMBERI
NATIONAL PARK
TIDBINBILLA RANGE
CANBERRA DEEP SPACE COMMUNICATION COMPLEX
KAMBAH POOL
Mount Arawang
Mount Taylor
Mount Mugga Mugga
Jerrabomberra
CUUMBEEN NR
WANNA WANNA NR
RANGE
TALLAGANDA NATIONAL PARK
TURALLO
Mount Aggie
Tidbinbilla Peak
TIDBINBILLA VISITOR CENTRE
TIDBINBILLA NATURE RESERVE
Red Rocks Gorge
Tuggeranong
Mount Wanniassa
CUUMBEEN NR
Googong Dam
MOLONGLO RANGE
Hoskinstown
Mount Domain
Gibraltar Peak
Gibraltar Falls
TUGGERANONG HOMESTEAD
Point Hut Pond
Mount Rob Roy
Mount Molonglo
Googong Reservoir
YANUNUNBEYAN NR
Rossi
CORIN FOREST
Smokers Gap
LANYON CA
LANYON
Tharwa
CUPPACUMBALONG CRAFT CENTRE
Royalla
LONDON BRIDGE LIMESTONE FORMATION
YANUNUNBEYAN NATIONAL PARK
TALLAGANDA NP
GOUROCK RANGE
Mount Ginini
NAMADGI VISITOR CENTRE
Mount Tennent
GIGERLINE NATURE RESERVE
BURRA CREEK NR
Mount Foxlow
DIVIDING RANGE
Blackfellows Gap
FORMER SPACE TRACKING STATION
Mount McKeahne
Williamsdale
Mount Uriaila
Harrisons Peak
Leura Gap
Bimberi Gap
Cotter Gap
Walking
FORMER SPACE TRACKING STATION
OLD ORRORAL HOMESTEAD
Mount Burra
Captains Flat
BIMBERI RA
KOSCIUSZKO
Bimberi Peak
Coronet Peak
NAMADGI NATIONAL PARK
Mount Bullongong
Mount Bollard
Parkers Gap
Mount Murray
Australian Alps
Mount Kelly
Mount Michelago
TINDERRY
Mount Tumanang
NATIONAL PARK
Half Moon Peak
Mount Morgan
SCABBY RA
Mount Gudgenby
BOOTH RANGE
BILLY RANGE
Mount Yarara
Tinderry Twin Peak
Tinderry Peak
Mount Woolpack
TALLAGANDA
Mount Scabby
SCABBY RANGE NR
NAMADGI NATIONAL PARK
Michelago
NATURE RESERVE
Mount Holland
Yaouk
Mount Ash Hill
BICENTENNIAL NATIONAL TRAIL
Sentry Box Mountain
Shanahans Mountain
BURNT SCHOOL NATURE RESERVE
Bald Peak
Kain
Tumanang Mountain
DOG PLAIN
Yaouk Peak
YAOUK NATURE RESERVE
STRIKE-A-LIGHT NATURE RESERVE
Anembo
GREAT
Tumatbulla Mountain
YAOUK BILL RA
BOBOYAN RD
CLEAR RANGE
ACT NSW
Colinton
Mount Colinton
Jerangle
GOUROCK
Mount Anembo
NATIONAL PARK
Black Cow Peak
Shannons Flat
YAOUK NR
Gungoandra Gap
Mount Clear
Mount Wangrah
Mount Italy
MONARO HWY
COOMA
BARTON HWY

Joins map 36
Joins map 37

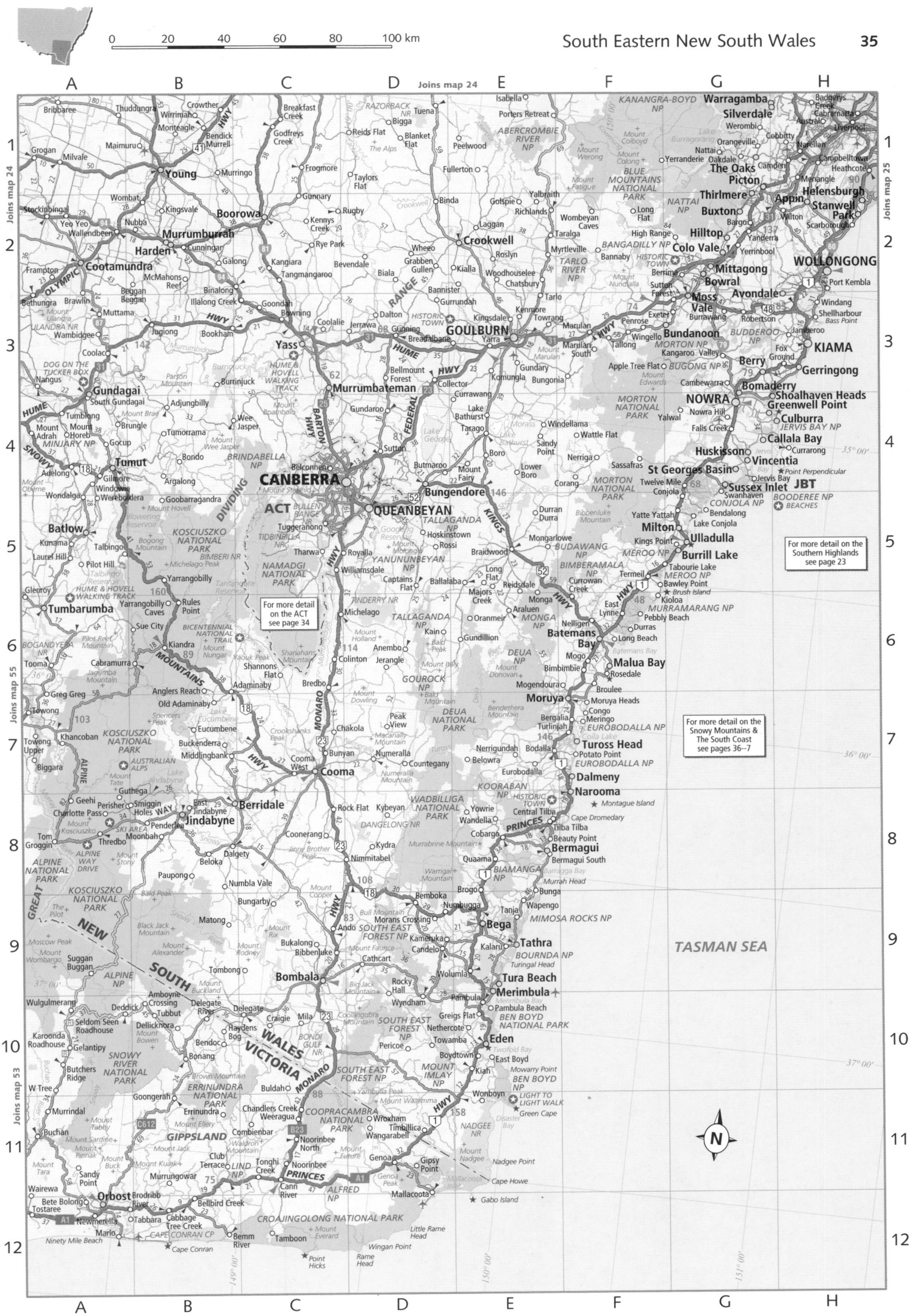

0 20 40 60 80 100 km

Joins map 24

Joins map 25

Joins map 24

Joins map 25

Joins map 55

Joins map 53

For more detail on the ACT see page 34

For more detail on the Southern Highlands see page 23

For more detail on the Snowy Mountains & The South Coast see pages 36--7

CANBERRA
QUEANBEYAN
GOULBURN
WOLLONGONG
NOWRA
KIAMA
Cooma
Bombala
Eden
Bega
Merimbula
Batemans Bay
Moruya
Narooma
Bermagui
Jindabyne
Berridale
Tumut
Gundagai
Cootamundra
Young
Boorowa
Crookwell
Yass
Murrumbateman
Bungendore
Tumbarumba
Batlow
Orbost

TASMAN SEA

KOSCIUSZKO NATIONAL PARK
ALPINE NATIONAL PARK
NAMADGI NATIONAL PARK
MORTON NATIONAL PARK
DEUA NATIONAL PARK
WADBILLIGA NATIONAL PARK
SOUTH EAST FOREST NP
COOPRACAMBRA NATIONAL PARK
CROAJINGOLONG NATIONAL PARK
ERRINUNDRA NATIONAL PARK
SNOWY RIVER NATIONAL PARK
BEN BOYD NATIONAL PARK

VICTORIA
NEW SOUTH WALES
GIPPSLAND

N

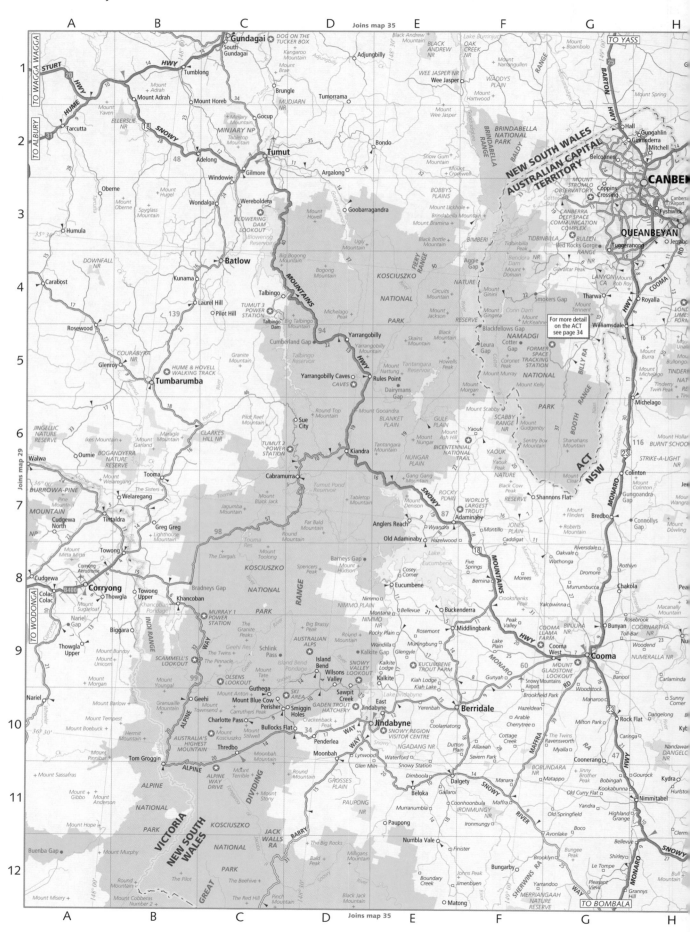

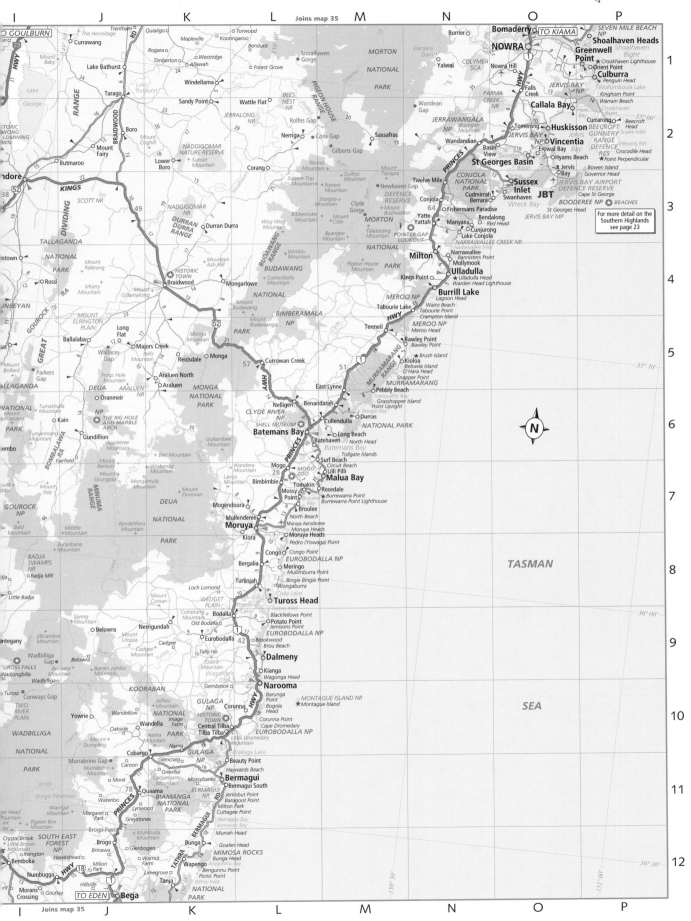

Joins map 35

0 10 20 30 40 km

For more detail on the
Southern Highlands
see page 23

MAPS

VICTORIA

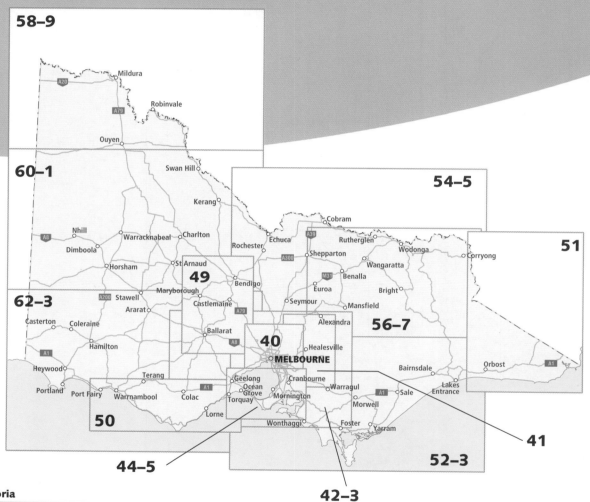

58–9
- Mildura
- Robinvale
- Ouyen

60–1
- Swan Hill
- Kerang
- Nhill
- Warracknabeal
- Charlton
- Rochester
- Echuca
- Dimboola
- St Arnaud
- Horsham
- Maryborough
- Bendigo

54–5
- Cobram
- Rutherglen
- Wodonga
- Shepparton
- Wangaratta
- Benalla
- Euroa
- Bright

51
- Corryong
- Orbost

49
- Castlemaine

62–3
- Casterton
- Coleraine
- Stawell
- Ararat
- Hamilton
- Ballarat

56–7
- Seymour
- Mansfield
- Alexandra

40
- MELBOURNE
- Healesville

50
- Heywood
- Portland
- Port Fairy
- Warrnambool
- Terang
- Colac
- Lorne
- Geelong
- Ocean Grove
- Torquay
- Mornington
- Wonthaggi

44–5

42–3

- Cranbourne
- Warragul
- Morwell
- Sale
- Foster
- Yarram

41

- Bairnsdale
- Lakes Entrance

52–3

Victoria

Central Melbourne	39
Melbourne Suburbs	40
Dandenong & Yarra Ranges	41
Melbourne & Surrounds	42–3
Mornington & Bellarine Peninsulas	44–5
Geelong	46
Ballarat	47
Bendigo	48
Goldfields	49
Great Ocean Road	50
Eastern Victoria	51
Southern Central Victoria	52–3
North Central Victoria	54–5
High Country	56–7
North Western Victoria	58–9
Central Western Victoria	60–1
South Western Victoria	62–3

INTER-CITY ROUTES		DISTANCE
Melbourne–Sydney via Hume Hwy/Fwy	M31 31	881 km
Melbourne–Sydney via Princes Hwy/Fwy	M1 A1 1	1037 km
Melbourne–Adelaide via Western & Dukes hwys	M8 A8 M1	733 km
Melbourne–Adelaide via Princes Hwy	M1 A1 B1 M1	906 km
Melbourne–Brisbane via Newell Hwy	M31 A39 39 A39 A2	1676 km

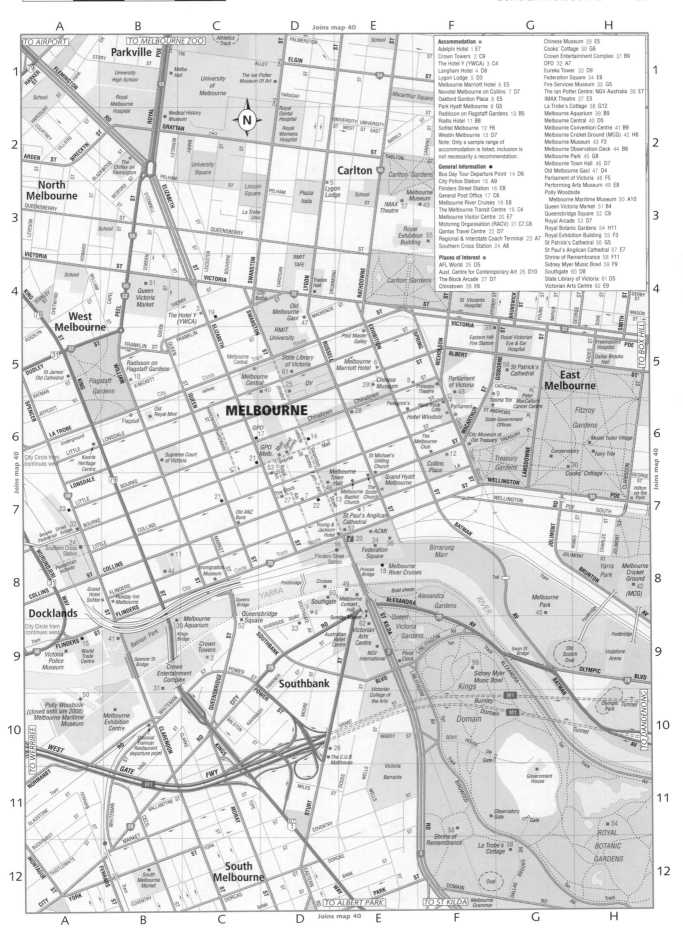

Accommodation ■
Adelphi Hotel 1 E7
Crown Towers 2 C9
The Hotel Y (YWCA) 3 C4
Langham Hotel 4 D8
Lygon Lodge 5 D3
Melbourne Marriott Hotel 6 E5
Novotel Melbourne on Collins 7 D7
Oakford Gordon Place 8 E5
Park Hyatt Melbourne 9 G5
Radisson on Flagstaff Gardens 10 B5
Rialto Hotel 11 B8
Sofitel Melbourne 12 F6
Westin Melbourne 13 D7
Note: Only a sample range of
accommodation is listed; inclusion is
not necessarily a recommendation.

General Information ■
Bus Day Tour Departure Point 14 D6
City Police Station 15 A9
Flinders Street Station 16 E8
General Post Office 17 C6
Melbourne River Cruises 18 E8
The Melbourne Transit Centre 19 C4
Melbourne Visitor Centre 20 E7
Motoring Organisation (RACV) 21 C7,C6
Qantas Travel Centre 22 D7
Regional & Interstate Coach Terminal 23 A7
Southern Cross Station 24 A8

Places of Interest ■
AFL World 25 D5
Aust. Centre for Contemporary Art 26 D10
The Block Arcade 27 D7
Chinatown 28 E6

Chinese Museum 29 E5
Cooks' Cottage 30 G6
Crown Entertainment Complex 31 B9
DFO 32 A7
Eureka Tower 33 D9
Federation Square 34 E8
Fire Services Museum 35 G5
The Ian Potter Centre: NGV Australia 36 E7
IMAX Theatre 37 E3
La Trobe's Cottage 38 G12
Melbourne Aquarium 39 B9
Melbourne Central 40 D5
Melbourne Convention Centre 41 B9
Melbourne Cricket Ground (MCG) 42 H8
Melbourne Museum 43 F3
Melbourne Observation Deck 44 B8
Melbourne Park 45 G8
Melbourne Town Hall 46 D7
Old Melbourne Gaol 47 D4
Parliament of Victoria 48 F5
Performing Arts Museum 49 E8
Polly Woodside
   Melbourne Maritime Museum 50 A10
Queen Victoria Market 51 B4
Queensbridge Square 52 C9
Royal Arcade 53 D7
Royal Botanic Gardens 54 H11
Royal Exhibition Building 55 F3
St Patrick's Cathedral 56 G5
St Paul's Anglican Cathedral 57 E7
Shrine of Remembrance 58 F11
Sidney Myer Music Bowl 59 F9
Southgate 60 D8
State Library of Victoria 61 D5
Victorian Arts Centre 62 E9

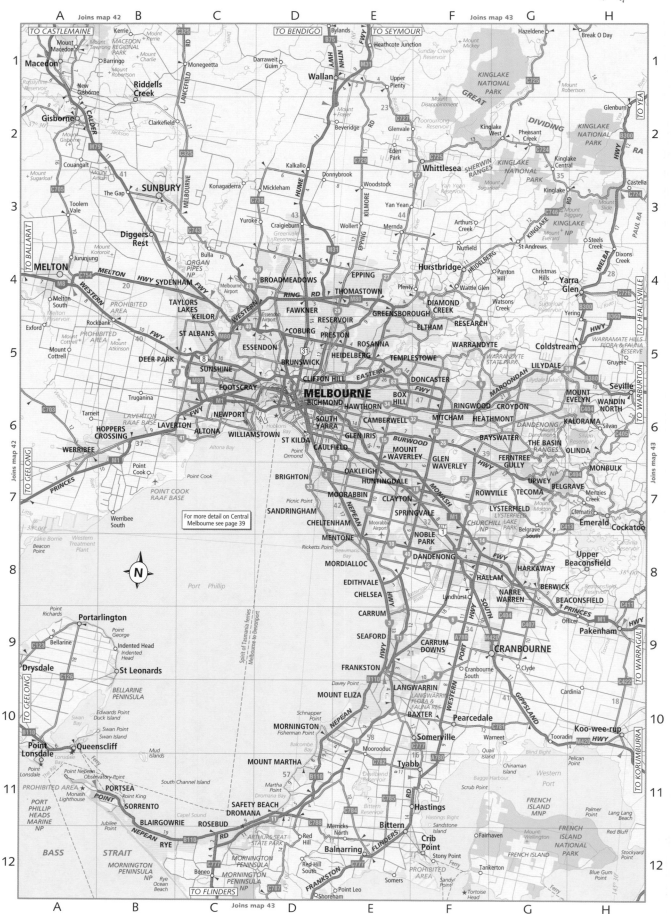

For more detail on Central Melbourne see page 39

0 5 10 15 20 km

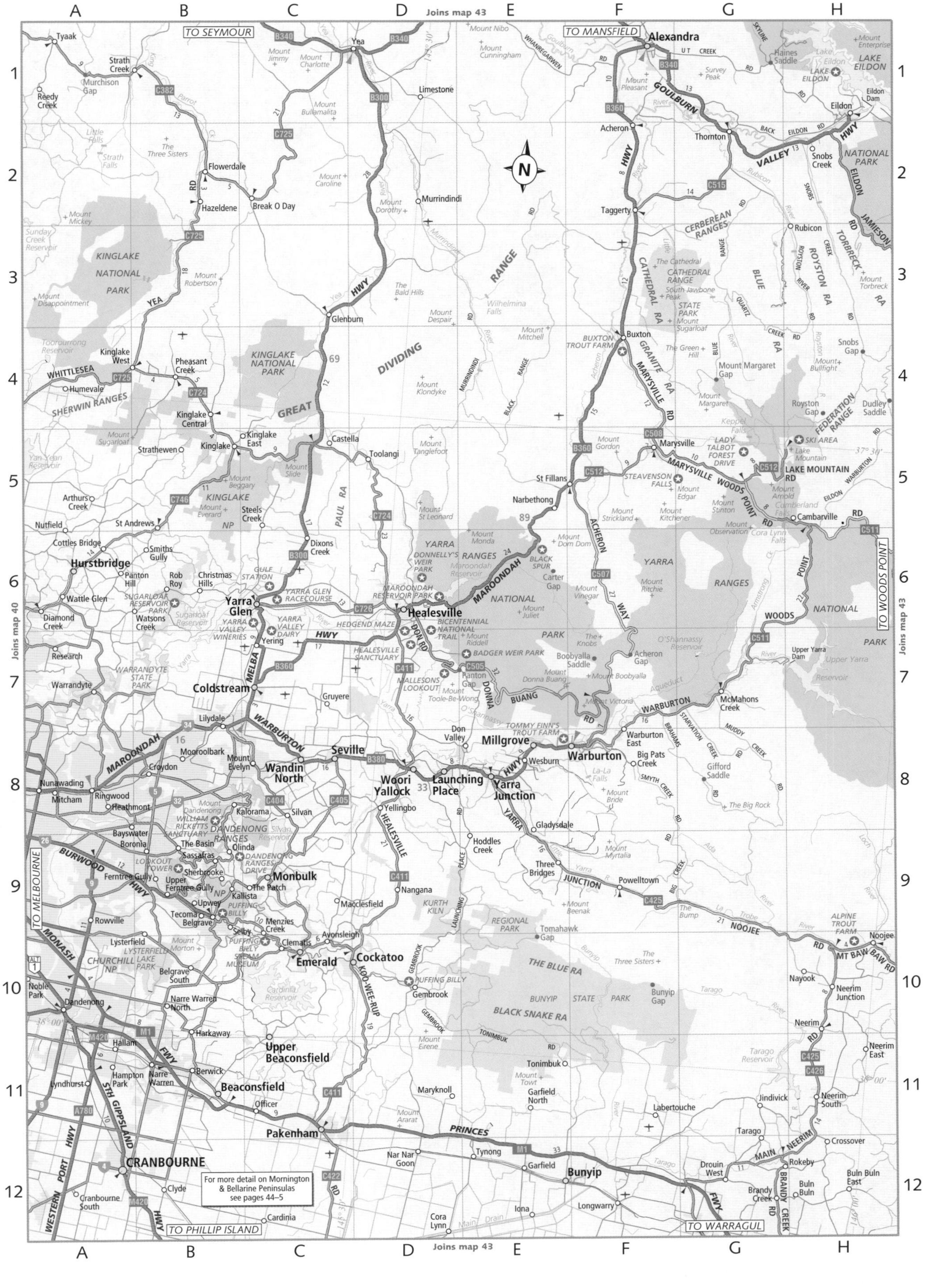

A
B
C
D
E
F
G
H
1
2
3
4
5
6
7
8
9
10
11
12
Joins map 43
Joins map 40
TO SEYMOUR
TO MANSFIELD
TO WOODS POINT
TO MELBOURNE
TO PHILLIP ISLAND
TO WARRAGUL
For more detail on Mornington & Bellarine Peninsulas see pages 44–5
Tyaak
Strath Creek
Reedy Creek
Murchison Gap
Yea
Mount Jimmy
Mount Charlotte
Mount Nibo
Mount Cunningham
Alexandra
Mount Pleasant
Survey Peak
Haines Saddle
LAKE EILDON
Mount Enterprise
Eildon Dam
Eildon
Limestone
Mount Bullamalita
Acheron
Thornton
Snobs Creek
EILDON NATIONAL PARK
Little Falls
Strath Falls
The Three Sisters
Flowerdale
Hazeldene
Break O Day
Mount Caroline
Mount Dorothy
Murrindindi
Taggerty
CERBEREAN RANGES
Rubicon
Mount Mickey
Sunday Creek Reservoir
KINGLAKE NATIONAL PARK
Mount Robertson
Mount Disappointment
The Bald Hills
DIVIDING RANGE
Wilhelmina Falls
The Cathedral
CATHEDRAL RANGE
South Jawbone Peak
CATHEDRAL RANGE STATE PARK
Mount Sugarloaf
Mount Torbreck
Glenburn
Mount Despair
Mount Mitchell
Buxton
BUXTON TROUT FARM
The Green Hill
Toorourrong Reservoir
Kinglake West
Pheasant Creek
WHITTLESEA
Humevale
SHERWIN RANGES
Mount Klondyke
GREAT
GRANITE RA
MARYSVILLE RD
Mount Margaret Gap
Mount Margaret
Snobs Gap
Mount Bullfight
Royston Gap
FEDERATION RANGE
Dudley Saddle
Kinglake Central
Kinglake
Kinglake East
Strathewen
Mount Sugarloaf
Yan Yean Reservoir
Castella
Toolangi
Mount Tanglefoot
Mount Gordon
Marysville
LADY TALBOT FOREST DRIVE
Keppel Falls
SKI AREA
Lake Mountain
LAKE MOUNTAIN RD
Mount Slide
Mount Beggary
KINGLAKE NP
Mount Everard
Steels Creek
PAUL RA
St Fillans
Narbethong
STEAVENSON FALLS
Mount Edgar
Mount Strickland
Mount Kitchener
Mount Stinton
Mount Arnold
Cumberland Falls
Cambarville
Arthurs Creek
Nutfield
St Andrews
Mount St Leonard
Mount Monda
YARRA RANGES
Mount Dom Dom
Mount Observation
Cora Lynn Falls
Cottles Bridge
Smiths Gully
Dixons Creek
DONNELLY'S WEIR PARK
Maroondah Reservoir
BLACK SPUR
Carter Gap
ACHERON WAY
YARRA RANGES NATIONAL PARK
Mount Ritchie
Hurstbridge
Panton Hill
Rob Roy
Christmas Hills
GULF STATION
YARRA GLEN RACECOURSE
MAROONDAH RESERVOIR PARK
Mount Vinegar
Mount Juliet
Wattle Glen
SUGARLOAF RESERVOIR PARK
Sugarloaf Reservoir
Yarra Glen
Healesville
BICENTENNIAL NATIONAL TRAIL
Mount Riddell
The Knobs
O'Shannassy Reservoir
WOODS POINT RD
Diamond Creek
Watsons Creek
YARRA VALLEY WINERIES
YARRA VALLEY DAIRY
HEDGEND MAZE
Yering
HEALESVILLE SANCTUARY
BADGER WEIR PARK
Boobyalla Saddle
Acheron Gap
Upper Yarra Dam
Upper Yarra Reservoir
Research
WARRANDYTE STATE PARK
MALLESONS LOOKOUT
Panton Gap
Mount Toole-Be-Wong
Mount Donna Buang
Mount Boobyalla
DONNA BUANG RD
Mount Victoria
Aqueduct
McMahons Creek
Warrandyte
Coldstream
Gruyere
TOMMY FINN'S TROUT FARM
Lilydale
MAROONDAH
WARBURTON
Don Valley
Millgrove
Warburton
Warburton East
Big Pats Creek
STARVATION CREEK
MUDDY CREEK
Mooroolbark
Croydon
Mount Evelyn
Wandin North
Seville
Woori Yallock
Launching Place
Yarra Junction
Wesburn
La-La Falls
Mount Bride
Gifford Saddle
The Big Rock
Nunawading
Mitcham
Ringwood
Heathmont
Mount Dandenong
Kalorama
Silvan
Yellingbo
WILLIAM RICKETTS SANCTUARY
DANDENONG RANGES
Silvan Reservoir
Gladysdale
Bayswater
Boronia
The Basin
Sassafras
Olinda
DANDENONG RANGES DRIVE
Hoddles Creek
Mount Myrtalia
BURWOOD HWY
LOOKOUT TOWER
Sherbrooke
Monbulk
Ferntree Gully
Upper Ferntree Gully
The Patch
Kallista
Three Bridges
Powelltown
Mount Beenak
The Bump
NOOJEE
ALPINE TROUT FARM
Noojee
Upwey
PUFFING BILLY
Tecoma
Belgrave
Rowville
Macclesfield
Nangana
KURTH KILN
Menzies Creek
Selby
Avonsleigh
Tomahawk Gap
REGIONAL PARK
The Three Sisters
MT BAW BAW RD
Lysterfield
LYSTERFIELD LAKE PARK
Mount Morton
CHURCHILL NP
Clematis
PUFFING BILLY STEAM MUSEUM
Emerald
Cockatoo
THE BLUE RA
Nayook
Belgrave South
Noble Park
Dandenong
Cardinia Reservoir
Gembrook
BUNYIP STATE PARK
Bunyip Gap
Tarago
Neerim Junction
Narre Warren North
BLACK SNAKE RA
MONASH
KOO-WEE-RUP
Harkaway
Hallam
Upper Beaconsfield
Mount Eirene
TONIMBUK RD
Tonimbuk
Neerim
Tarago Reservoir
Neerim East
Hampton Park
Narre Warren
Berwick
Lyndhurst
Beaconsfield
Mount Towt
Garfield North
Maryknoll
Jindivick
Neerim South
Officer
Labertouche
Mount Ararat
Pakenham
PRINCES
Tarago
Crossover
Nar Nar Goon
Tynong
MAIN NEERIM
Rokeby
CRANBOURNE
Garfield
Bunyip
Drouin West
Buln Buln East
Clyde
Brandy Creek
Buln Buln
Cranbourne South
Iona
Longwarry
WESTERN PORT HWY
STH GIPPSLAND HWY
Cardinia
Cora Lynn
FWY
BRANDY CREEK RD

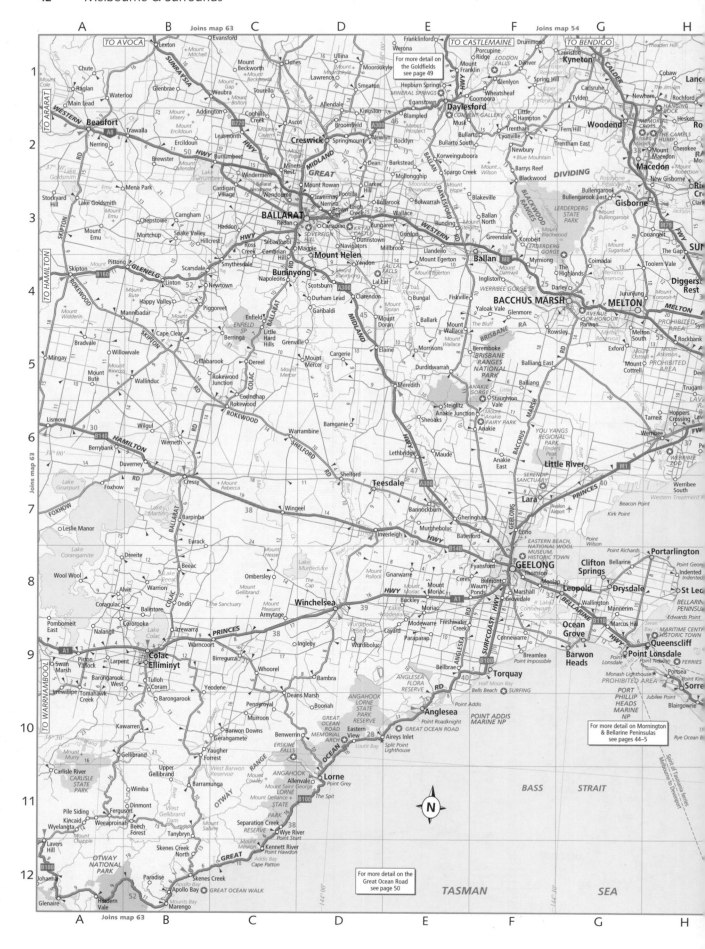

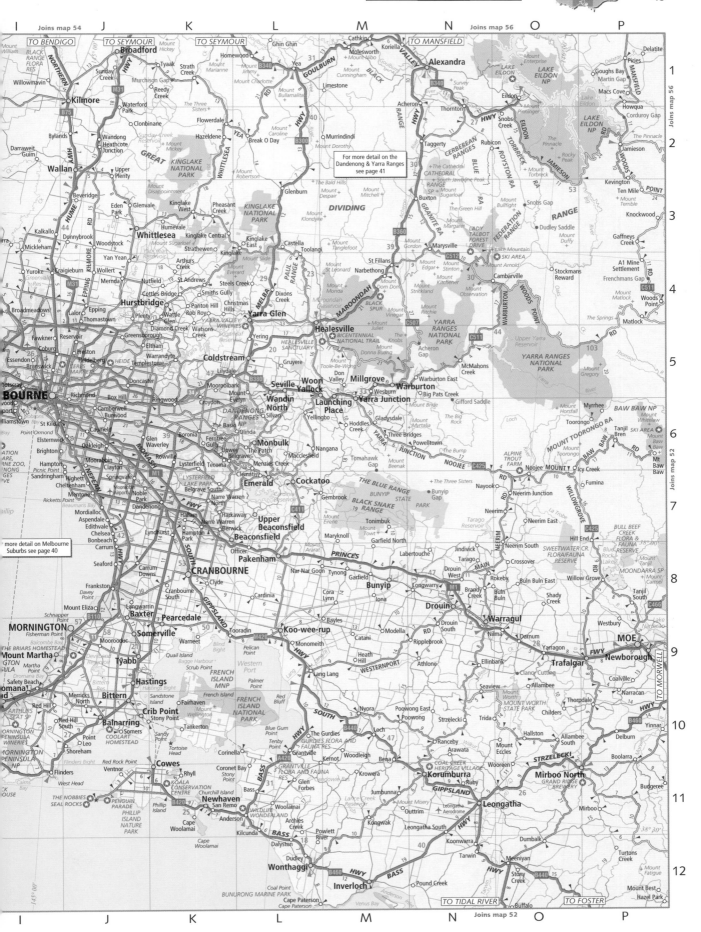

0   10   20   30 km

TO WERRIBEE

TO BALLARAT
TO HAMILTON
TO COLAC
TO LORNE

Joins map 42

Rothwell
Werribee South

SERENDIP
SANCTUARY
AVALON
RACEWAY

Lara
Lara Lake

PRINCES

FWY

Lake
Borrie

Western Treatment Plant

Beacon Point

Hovell
Park
Rosewall

LIMEBURNERS
LAGOON
NATURE
RESERVE

Kirk
Point

Lovely
Banks
Moorabool
Batesford
Norlane
Corio

Avalon
Airport

WILDLIFE
RESERVE

Port Phillip

Bell Park
North Shore

Avalon

Point Lillias

Point Wilson

Hamlyn Heights
Geelong North
Rippleside
Drumcondra

Corio Bay

Outer

Harbour

For more detail on
Geelong see page 46

POINT RICHARDS CHANNEL

Point Richards
Port Bellarine
Bellarine

Portarlington

Point
George

GEELONG
Geelong East

Fyansford

Eastern Beach,
National Wool Museum,
Historic Town

Point Henry

WILSON

SPIT

CHANNEL

CLIFTON
SPRINGS
GOLF
COURSE

PORTARLINGTON
GOLF COURSE

Indented Head
Indented Head

Clifton Springs

C123

Geelong South
Thomson
Moolap

Barwon Valley
Golf Course

Highton
Wandana
Heights
Belmont

GEELONG

PORTARLINGTON

St Albans
Park
Breakwater

Drysdale

DRYSDALE
REC RES

BELLARINE
PENINSULA
RAILWAY

Murradoc

St Leonards

C125

Leopold

Marshall
Grovedale

Curlewis
COUNTRY
CONNECTION
ADVENTURE
PARK

BELLARINE
PENINSULA

OCEAN GROVE RD

Mannerim

LOWER BLUFF
WILDLIFE
RESERVE

Mount
Dunned

Connewarre

Wallington

A MAZE 'N
GAMES

Fenwick

WILDLIFE
RESERVE

Lake
Connewarre

Marcus

Marcus Hill

Edwards
Point
Duck Island

PORT PHILLIP HEADS
MARINE NP
Swan Island
Swan Point
Swan Bay

JIRRAHLINGA
KOALA & WILDLIFE
RESERVE

DRYSDALE

Collendina

Lake
Victoria

MARITIME CENTRE,
BELLARINE PENINSULA
RAILWAY,
HISTORIC TOWN

PORT PHILLP HEADS
MARINE NP

SYMONDS CHANNEL

Mud
Islands

PINNACE CHANNEL

Barwon
Heads

BARWON HEADS
GOLF CLUB

Ocean
Grove

Barwon
Head

Queenscliff

Breamlea

Point
Impossible

SURFCOAST

SURFWORLD
AUSTRALIA

Torquay

Point Lonsdale
PORT PHILLIP HEADS
MARINE NP

Point
Lonsdale

Lonsdale Bay

BLACK LIGHTHOUSE,
FORT QUEENSCLIFF,
WHITE LIGHTHOUSE

FERRIES

South Channel Island

Spirit of Tasmania ferries

Jan Juc
Half Moon Bay

SURFING

POINT DANGER
MARINE SANCTUARY

The Rip

Point Nepean

PORT PHILLIP HEADS
MARINE NP
PROHIBITED
AREA

FORT
NEPEAN

Observatory
Point

Portsea

Point
Nepean

SOUTH

CHANNEL

LONDON
BRIDGE

Monash
Lighthouse

MORNINGTON

PENINSULA

NATIONAL

PARK

Point King

Sorrento

COLLINS
SETTLEMENT
HISTORIC SITE

Capel Sound

Rosebud

Blairgowrie
Jubilee Point

Rye

Tootgarook

Rosebud
West

MORNIN
PENINS

N

BASS

Rye Ocean Beach
Saint Andrews Beach

MORNINGTON

PENINSULA

NATIONAL

PARK

38° 30'

144° 30'

Boneo

Fingal

ROSEBUD
COUNTRY
CLUB

ROSEBUD FLINDERS RD

Gunnamatta
Beach

Cape Sch

MORNI
PENI
NAT
PA

CAPE SCHANCK
LIGHTHOUSE

Cape
Schanck

STRAIT

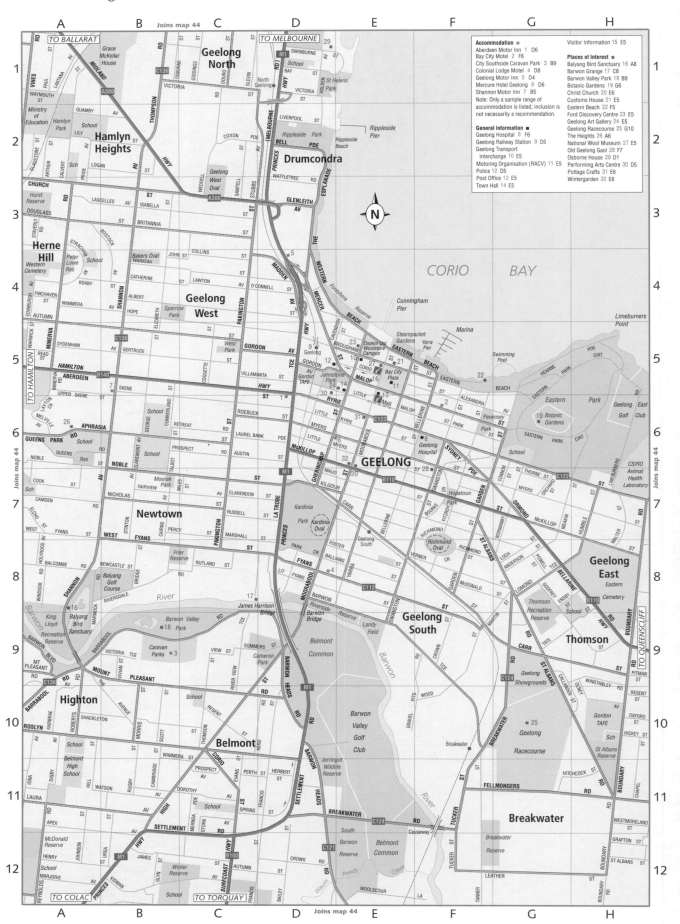

Joins map 44

Joins map 44

Joins map 44

Joins map 44

Accommodation
Aberdeen Motor Inn 1 D6
Bay City Motel 2 F6
City Southside Caravan Park 3 B9
Colonial Lodge Motel 4 D8
Geelong Motor Inn 5 D4
Mercure Hotel Geelong 6 D6
Shannon Motor Inn 7 B5
Note: Only a sample range of
accommodation is listed; inclusion is
not necessarily a recommendation.

General Information
Geelong Hospital 8 F6
Geelong Railway Station 9 D5
Geelong Transport
   Interchange 10 E5
Motoring Organisation (RACV) 11 E5
Police 12 D5
Post Office 13 E5
Town Hall 14 E5

Visitor Information 15 E5

Places of Interest
Balyang Bird Sanctuary 16 A8
Barwon Grange 17 C8
Barwon Valley Park 18 B9
Botanic Gardens 19 G6
Christ Church 20 E6
Customs House 21 E5
Eastern Beach 22 F5
Ford Discovery Centre 23 E5
Geelong Art Gallery 24 E5
Geelong Racecourse 25 G10
The Heights 26 A6
National Wool Museum 27 E5
Old Geelong Gaol 28 F7
Osborne House 29 D1
Performing Arts Centre 30 D5
Pottage Crafts 31 E5
Wintergarden 32 E6

TO BALLARAT

TO MELBOURNE

TO HAMILTON

TO COLAC

TO TORQUAY

TO QUEENSCLIFF

Geelong North

Geelong West

Hamlyn Heights

Herne Hill

Newtown

Highton

Belmont

GEELONG

Drumcondra

Geelong South

Geelong East

Thomson

Breakwater

CORIO BAY

0   0.5   1   1.5   2 km

Joins map 49

Accommodation

Bakery Hill Motel 1 F6
Ballarat Village Motor Inn & Conference Centre 2 F8
Central City Motor Inn 3 F6
Comfort Inn Main Lead 4 F7
Craig's Royal Hotel 5 E6
Eureka Lodge Motel 6 H6
George Hotel 7 E6
Lake Terrace Apartments 8 C5
Lake View Hotel/Motel 9 C5
Ballarat Mid City Accommodation & Conference Centre 10 D6
Miners Retreat Motel 11 H6
Peppinella Motel 12 A10
Ravenswood Cottage 13 E5
Red Lion Bar & Bistro 14 F7
Sovereign Hill Lodge 15 F8
Sovereign Park Motor Inn 16 F7
Tawana Lodge 17 E6
Victoriana Motor Inn 18 H5
Note: Only a sample range of accommodation is listed; inclusion is not necessarily a recommendation.

General Information

Ballarat Base Hospital 19 D6
Ballarat Railway Station 20 E6
Motoring Organisation (RACV) 21 E6
Police Station 22 E6
Post Office 23 E6
Visitor Information 24 E6, E7

Places of Interest

Adam Lindsay Gordon's Cottage 25 A5
Aquatic & Hockey Centre 26 A5
Ballarat Fine Art Gallery 27 E6
Ballarat Tramway Museum 28 A6
Ballarat Wildlife & Reptile Park 29 H7
The Conservatory 30 A5
Eureka Stockade Centre 31 H6
Gold Museum 32 F8
Her Majesty's Theatre 33 E6
The Mining Exchange 34 E6
Montrose Cottage and Museum 35 F7
The Robert Clark Conservatory 36 A5
Sovereign Hill Historical Park 37 F8
Town Hall 38 E6

Wendouree · Invermay · Nerrina · Black Hill · Brown Hill · Ballarat North · Lake Wendouree · Victoria Park · Ballarat South · BALLARAT · Canadian · Delacombe · Redan · Mount Pleasant · Sebastopol

TO ARARAT · TO MELBOURNE · TO HAMILTON · TO GEELONG

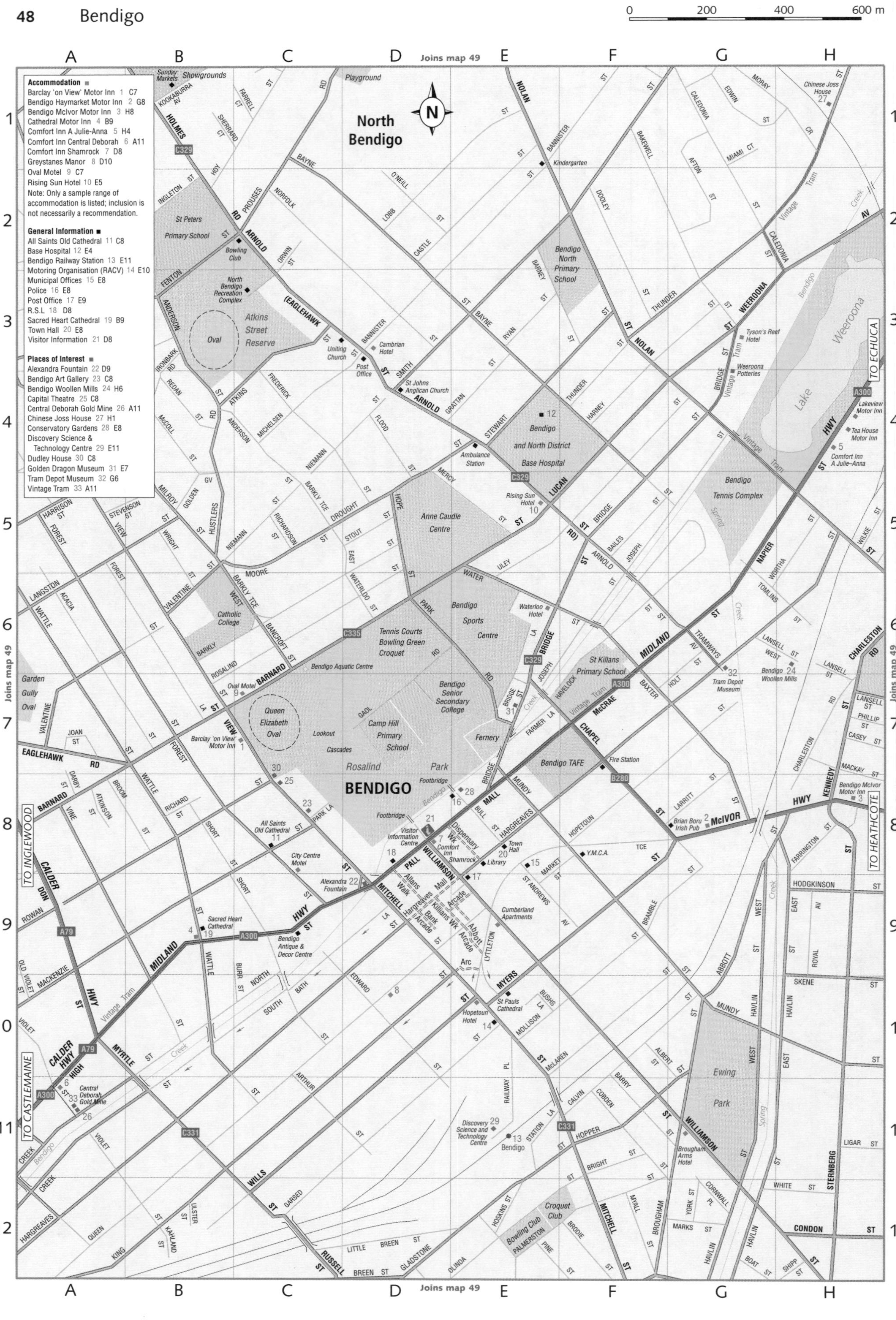

0 200 400 600 m

North Bendigo

N

Accommodation ■
Barclay 'on View' Motor Inn 1 C7
Bendigo Haymarket Motor Inn 2 G8
Bendigo McIvor Motor Inn 3 H8
Cathedral Motor Inn 4 B9
Comfort Inn A Julie-Anna 5 H4
Comfort Inn Central Deborah 6 A11
Comfort Inn Shamrock 7 D8
Greystanes Manor 8 D10
Oval Motel 9 C7
Rising Sun Hotel 10 E5
Note: Only a sample range of
accommodation is listed; inclusion is
not necessarily a recommendation.

General Information ■
All Saints Old Cathedral 11 C8
Base Hospital 12 E4
Bendigo Railway Station 13 E11
Motoring Organisation (RACV) 14 E10
Municipal Offices 15 E8
Police 16 E8
Post Office 17 E9
R.S.L 18 D8
Sacred Heart Cathedral 19 B9
Town Hall 20 E8
Visitor Information 21 D8

Places of Interest ■
Alexandra Fountain 22 D9
Bendigo Art Gallery 23 C8
Bendigo Woollen Mills 24 H6
Capital Theatre 25 C8
Central Deborah Gold Mine 26 A11
Chinese Joss House 27 H1
Conservatory Gardens 28 E8
Discovery Science &
  Technology Centre 29 E11
Dudley House 30 C8
Golden Dragon Museum 31 E7
Tram Depot Museum 32 G6
Vintage Tram 33 A11

Joins map 49

Joins map 49

Joins map 49

Joins map 49

TO ECHUCA

TO HEATHCOTE

TO INGLEWOOD

TO CASTLEMAINE

BENDIGO

Rosalind Park

Lake Weeroona

Ewing Park

Chinese Joss House 27

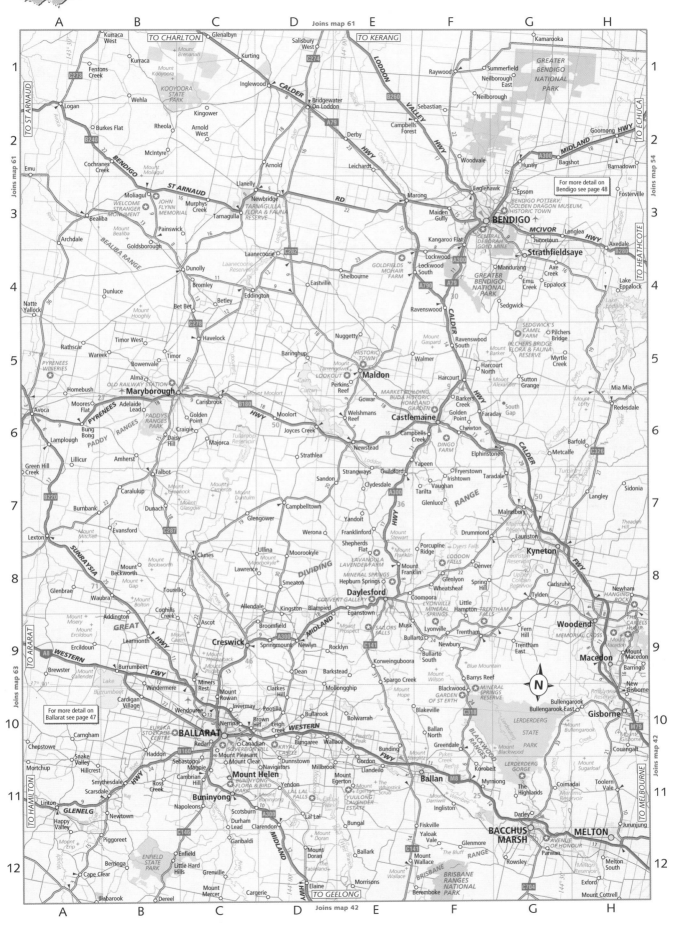

Joins map 61
Joins map 42

0 5 10 15 20 km

TO CHARLTON
TO KERANG
TO ST ARNAUD
TO ECHUCA
TO HEATHCOTE
TO ARARAT
TO HAMILTON
TO MELBOURNE
TO GEELOGN

Joins map 61
Joins map 54
Joins map 63
Joins map 42

For more detail on Bendigo see page 48

For more detail on Ballarat see page 47

GREATER BENDIGO NATIONAL PARK

BENDIGO
BALLARAT
Castlemaine
Maryborough
Maldon
Daylesford
Kyneton
Woodend
Macedon
Gisborne
MELTON
BACCHUS MARSH
Ballan
Strathfieldsaye
Buninyong
Creswick

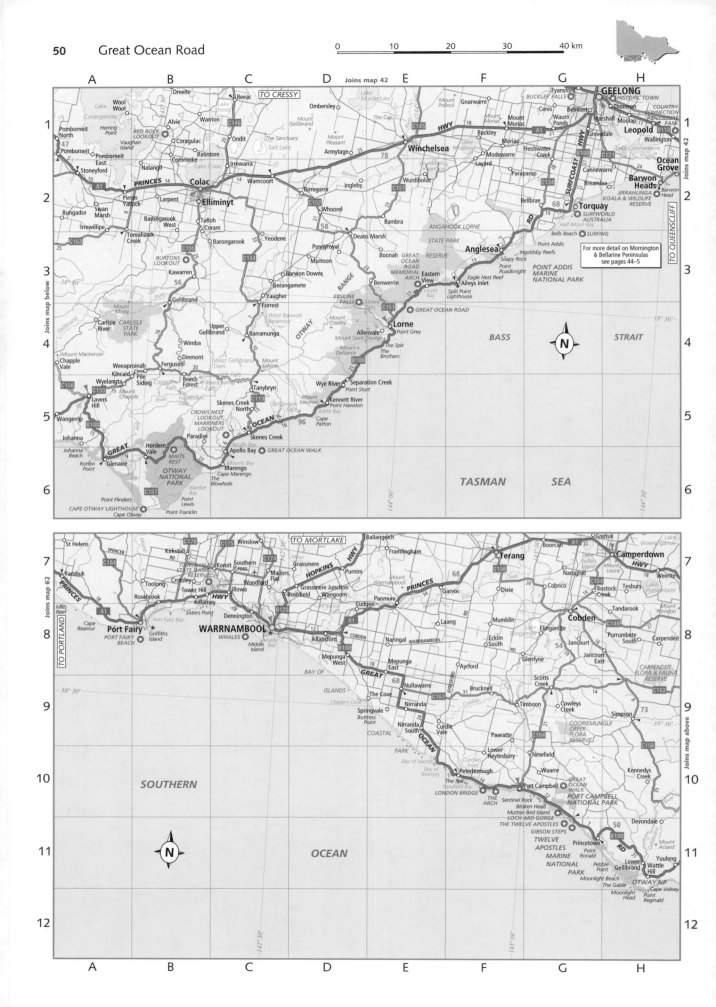

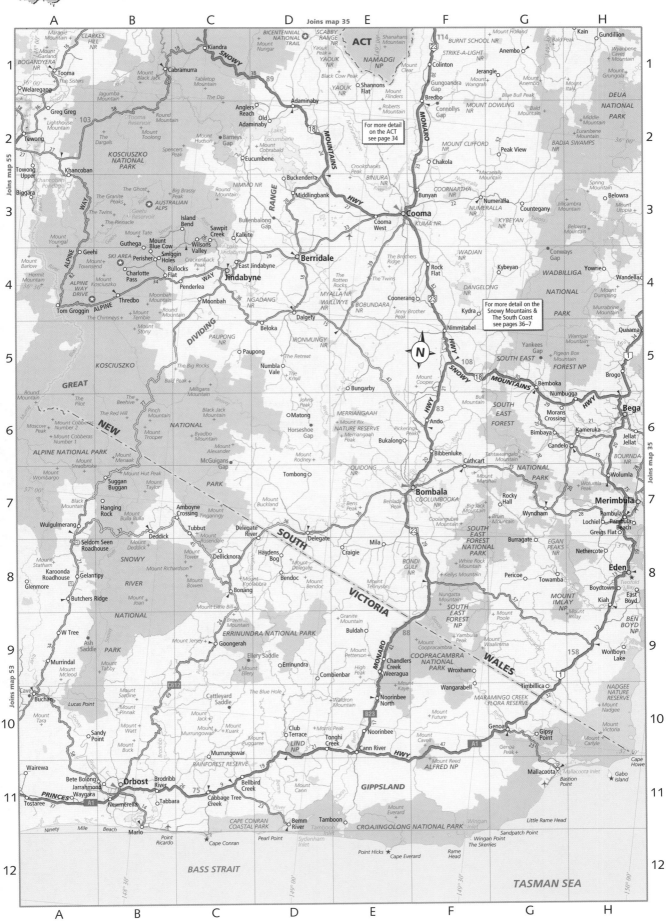

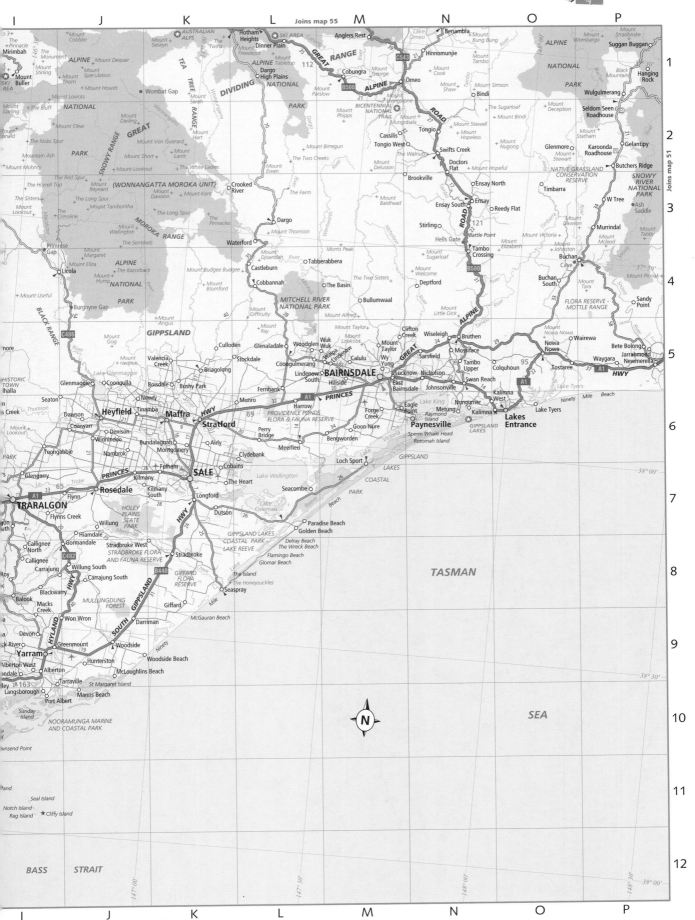

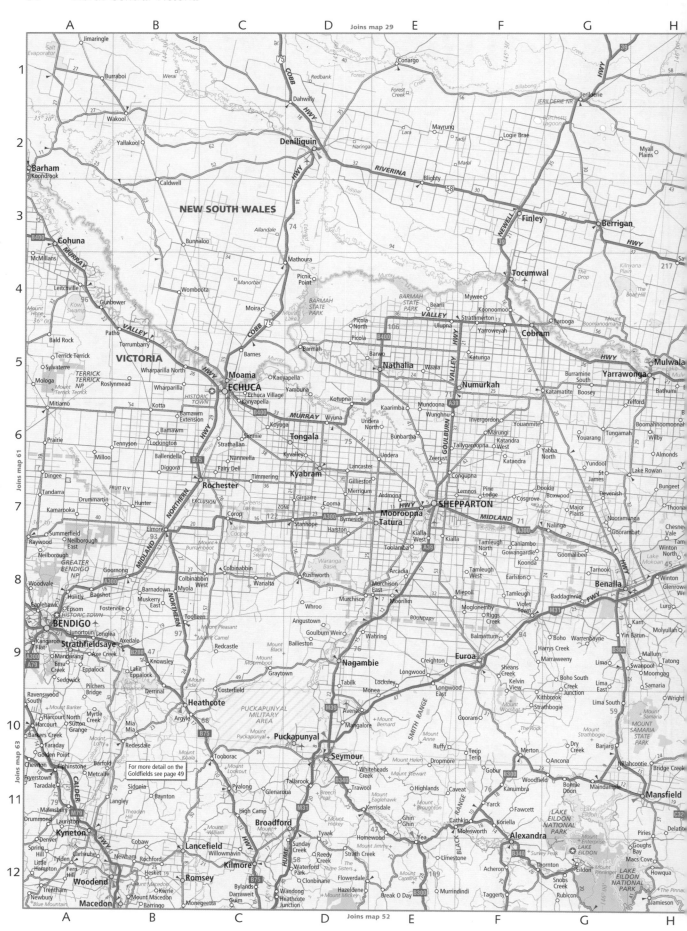

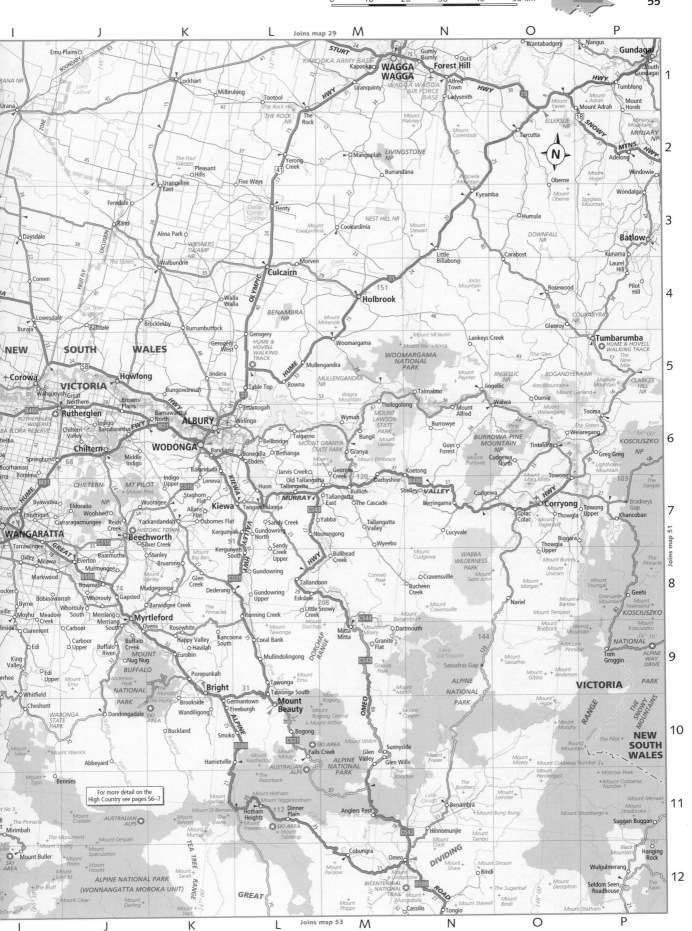

0   10   20   30   40   50 km

Joins map 29

Joins map 51

Joins map 53

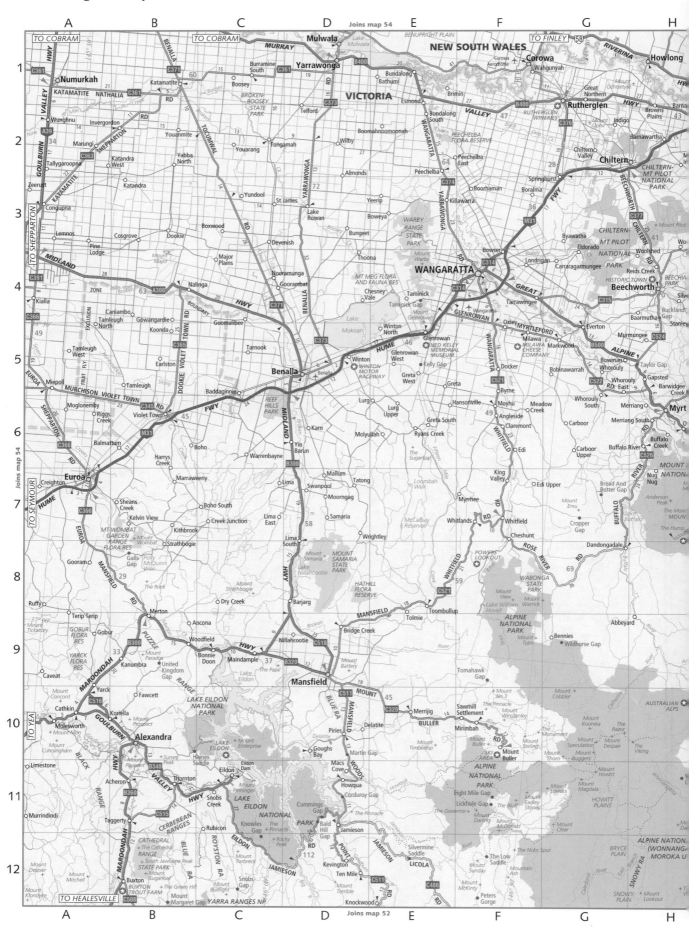

0   10   20   30 km

Joins map 55
Joins map 53
Joins map 51

NEW SOUTH WALES

VICTORIA

I   J   K   L   M   N   O   P

1   2   3   4   5   6   7   8   9   10   11   12

TO WAGGA WAGGA
TO HOLBROOK
TO THREDBO
TO BAIRNSDALE

Mullengandra
WOOMARGAMA NATIONAL PARK
MULLENGANDRA NR
The Glen
The Nine Mile
Paddys Ck
Jindera
Table Top
ETTAMOGAH PUB
Bowna
Lake Hume
Talmalmo
Mount Paynter
Jingellic
JINGELLIC NATURE RESERVE
Ournie
Marajie Mountain
Mount Garland
CLARKES HILL NR
Jindera Gap
HUME & HOVELL WALKING TRACK
Ettamogah
Thologolong
Mount Porcupine
MURRAY RIVER
Walwa
Mount Welaregang
BOGANDYERA NATURE RESERVE
Ikes Mountain
Mount Elliot
ALBURY
Wirlinga
Albury
MULLENGANDRA NR
Wagra Mountain
Wymah
Talmalmo
Burrowye
Mount Alfred
Tooma
The Sisters
WONGA
Bandiana
Hume Dam
Bonegilla
Ebden
TALGARNO
Talgarno
C542
Bungil
MOUNT LAWSON STATE PARK
Mount Lawson
Guys Forest
BURROWA-PINE MOUNTAIN NATIONAL PARK
Mount Burrowa
Cudgewa North
Tintaldra
Welaregang
Greg Greg
Leneva
Barranduda
Mount Granya
Bellbridge
Bethanga
Lake Hume
Jarvis Creek
Georges Creek
Granya
C546
Koetong
C547
Shelley
CUDGEWA
Cudgewa
Corryong Aerodrome
Mt Mitta Mitta Flora Reserve
Towong
KOSCIUSZKO NATIONAL PARK
Bradneys Gap
Staghorn Flat
Allans Flat
Osbornes Flat
KIEWA
Huon
Tangambalanga
Kiewa
Tallangatta
Old Tallangatta
MURRAY
Tallangatta East
Bullioh
Mount Bullioh
The Cascade
Darbyshire
VALLEY
Berringama
Colac Colac
Corryong
Mount Mitta Mitta
Towong Upper
Thowgla
Khancoban
Khancoban Pondage
DEDERANG
B400
Glen Creek
C531
Sandy Creek
Gundowring North
Sandy Creek Upper
Lockhart Gap
Yabba
C543
Tallangatta Valley
Wyeebo
Lucyvale
WABBA WILDERNESS PARK
Mount Cudgewa
Nariel Gap
Thowgla Upper
Biggara
KOSCIUSZKO NATIONAL PARK
C528
Kergunyah
Gundowring
Gundowring Upper
Noorongong
OMEO
Bullhead Creek
Tallandoon
Cravensville
Bucheen Creek
Mount Saint John
Mount Unicorn
Mount Morgan
SCAMMELL'S SPUR LOOKOUT
YOUNGAL NATIONAL PARK
Mount Youngal
Glen Creek
VALLEY
Dederang
Eskdale
Little Snowy Creek
Mount Tawonga
Mount Dorchap
Mitta Mitta
Connels Peak
Mount Cravensville
Nariel
Mount Barlow
Mount Tempest
Granuaille Mountain
Geehi
ALPINE WAY DRIVE
The Pinnacles
Running Creek
C534
Kancoona South
Coral Bank
Mullindolingong
DORCHAP RANGE
C544
Lake Banimboola
Dartmouth
Mount Benambra
Mount Misery
CORRYONG
Mount Sassafras
WILD BOAR RANGE
Hermit Mountain
Mount Pinnibar
ALPINE NATIONAL PARK
Tom Groggin
HAPPY VALLEY
Porepunkah
Bright
C536
Germantown
Freeburgh
Mount Yorke
Granite Flat
Granite Peak
C543
148
ALPINE NATIONAL PARK
SASSAFRAS GAP
Eustace Gap
Mount Gibbo
Mount Anderson
Mount Boebuck
ALPINE NATIONAL PARK
B500
GREAT
TROUT FARM
Smoko
Mount Beauty
TAWONGA GAP
Tawonga
Tawonga South
Bogong
C531
OMEO
Mount Bogong Central
Mount Bogong
Mount Cooper
Mount Emu
ALPINE NATIONAL PARK (COBBERAS - TINGARINGY)
Buenba Gap
Mount Murphy
THE PILOT
RAMS HEAD RANGE
Harrietville
Mount Fainter North
Mount Fainter South
Mount Feathertop
Mount Mckay
FALLS CREEK
SKI AREA
Mount Nelse North
Mount Nelse
Mount Wills
Sunnyside
Glen Wills
Glen Valley
The Knocker
Mount Fraser
C545
The Brothers
Beloka Gap
Mount Leinster
Mount Pendergast
Moscow Peak
Mount Cobberas Number 2
Mount Cobberas Number 1
RANGE
The Razorback
BOGONG HIGH PLAINS
Mount Niggerhead
Mount Jim
Mount Loch
Mount Hotham
Mount Cope
BUCKETY PLAIN
92
Trapyard Gap
HINNOMUNJIE BRIDGE
Lake Omeo
Benambra
Mount Pleasant
Mount Bung Bung
ALPINE NATIONAL PARK
Mount Stradbroke
Mount Wombargo
Mount Sugarloaf
AUSTRALIAN ALPS
DINNER PLAIN
Mount Higginbotham
Hotham Heights
The Twins
Mount Freezeout
Dinner Plain
SKI AREA
Mount Tabletop
BULL PLAIN
110
Anglers Rest
BENAMBRA RD
Hinnomunjie
Mount Tambo
FORLORN HOPE PLAIN
Black Mountain
DARGO
Mount Murray
DARGO HIGH PLAINS
ALPINE NATIONAL PARK
Cobungra
Mount Parslow
Omeo
C543
Mount George
Mount Cook
GREAT
DIVIDING
Mount Shaw
Mount Simson
BLUE SHIRT PLAINS
NUNNIONG PLAINS
MUNDY PLAIN
Wulgulmerang
GOW PLAIN
HIGH PLAINS
TREASURE PLAIN
B500
Mount Livingstone
Mount Phipps
Bindi
Mount Hopeless
The Sugarloaf
Mount Deception
Seldom Seen Roadhouse
TEA TREE RANGE
The Tablelands
Mount Birregun
GREAT
ALPINE
BICENTENNIAL NATIONAL TRAIL
Mount Mungobala
Mount Tongio
Mount Stawell
Tongio
Mount Bindi
Mount Nugong
LOW PLAINS
Mount Statham
C608
Gelantipy
Mount Sarah
Cassilis
Tongio West
Swifts Creek
Glenmore
Karoonda Roadhouse
Mount Von Guerard
The Two Creeks
The Walnuts
Brookville
Doctors Flat
Mount Delusion
Mount Hopeful
Camp Oven Gap
Mount Stewart
Butchers Ridge
NATIVE GRASSLAND CONSERVATION RES

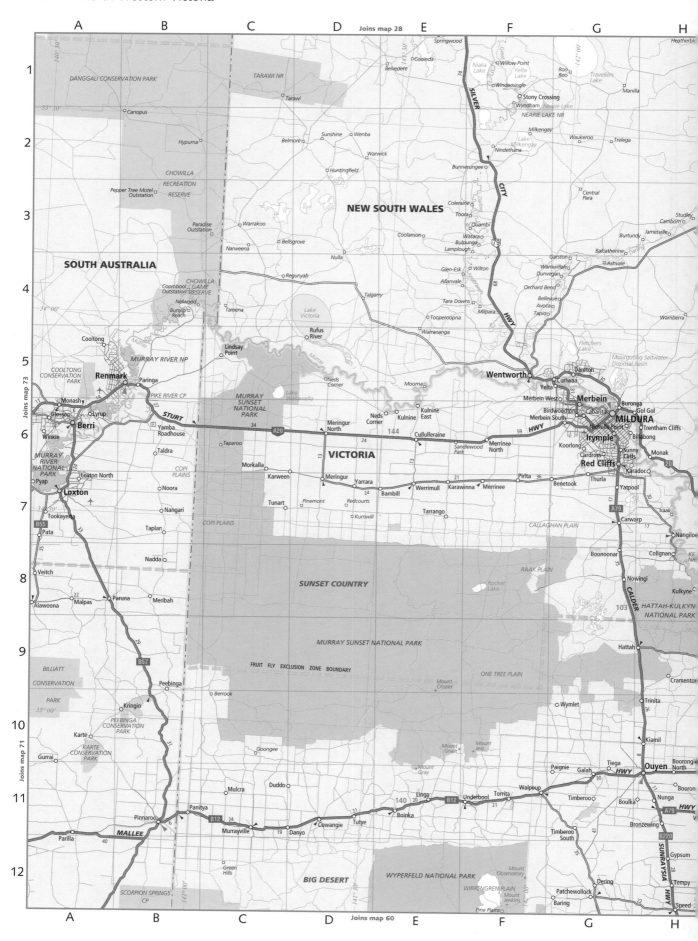

Joins map 28
Joins map 60
Joins map 73
Joins map 71

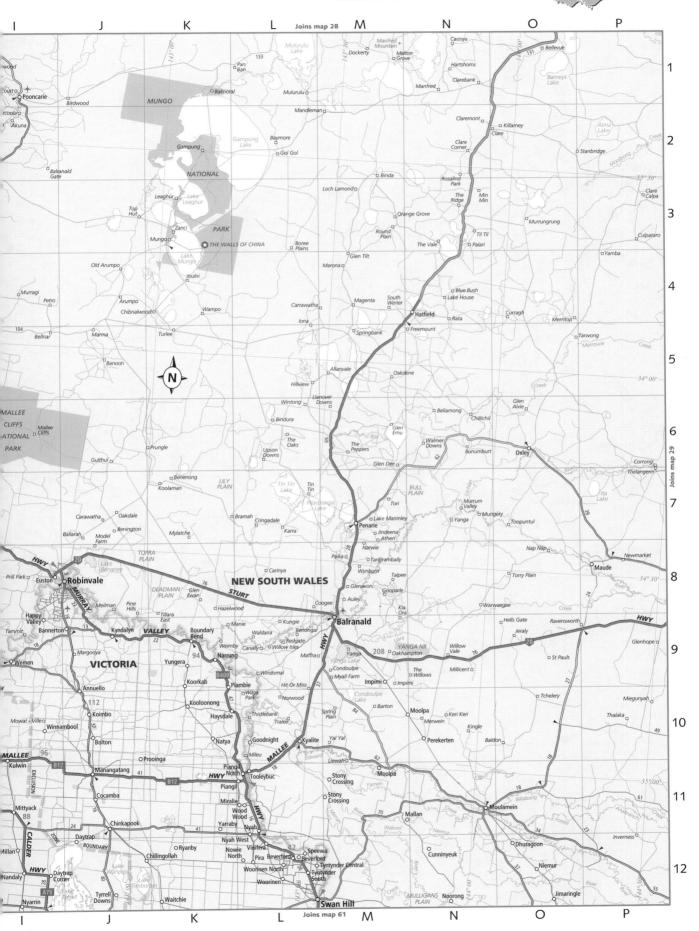

0 10 20 30 40 50 km

I J K L M N O P

1

Pooncarie
Birdwood
Balmoral
Pan Ban
133
Mururulu Lake
Dockerty
Manfred Mountain
Melton Grove
Carinya
Bellevue
131

rcoola
Akuna
MUNGO
Mandleman
Manfred
Hartshorns
Clarebank
Barneys Lake

2

Balranald Gate
NATIONAL
Gampung
Baymore
Gol Gol
Mururulu
Binda
Claremont
Clare Corner
Killarney
Clare
Stanbridge

Alma Lake

3

Leaghur
Lake Leaghur
PARK
Zanci
Mungo
THE WALLS OF CHINA
Boree Plains
Loch Lamond
Orange Grove
Round Plain
The Vale
Glen Tilt
Rosalind Park
The Ridge
Min Min
Til Til
Palari
Murrungrung
Clare Calpa
Culpataro
Yamba

4

Old Arumpo
Joulni
Marona
Magenta
South Winter
Hatfield
Rata
Blue Bush
Lake House
Curragh
Merritop
Tarwong

Murragi
Petro
Arumpo
Chibnalwood
Wampo
Carrawatha
Iona
Springbank
Freemount
Merrowie Creek

5

104
Bellnar
Marma
Turlee
Banoon
Hillview
Allanvale
Oakdene
Glen Alvie

6

MALLEE CLIFFS ATIONAL PARK
Mallee Cliffs
Prungle
Wintong
Llanover Downs
Bindura
The Oaks
The Peppers
Glen Emu
Glen Dee
Beliamong
Chillichil
Walmer Downs
Bunumburt
Oxley
Corrong
Thelangerin

Gulthul

7

Benenong
Koolaman
LILY PLAIN
Tin Tin Lake
Tin Tin
Pranbunga Lake
Bramah
Tori
Lake Marimley
Murrum Valley
Mungery
Toopuntul
Itta Lake

8

Carawatha
Oakdale
Benington
Mylatche
Cringadale
Karra
Penarie
Jindeena
Athen
Yanga
Nap Nap
Newmarket

Ballarah
Model Farm
HWY
20
TOPRA PLAIN
Narwie
Paika
Tangrambally
Torry Plain
Maude

Prill Park
Euston
Robinvale
Lake Benanee
DEADMAN PLAIN
Glen Ewan
Hazelwood
Coogee
Auley
NEW SOUTH WALES
STURT
Wynburn
Taipee
Glenavon
Gooparle
Kia Ora
Warwagae
Hells Gate
Ravensworth
HWY

9

Happy Valley
Bannerton
Meilman
Pine Hills
Tillara East
MURRAY VALLEY
Kyndalyn
Boundary Bend
Manie
Waldaira
Kungie
Benongal
Balranald
Jeraly
20
Glenhope

Tammit
Margooya
Weimby
Canally
Willow Isles
Maffra
Yanga
Oakhampton
YANGA NR
Willow Vale
St Pauls

10

Wemen
Yungera
Narrung
Windomal
Hit Or Miss
Myall Farm
Yanga Lake
Condoulpe
The Willows
Millicent
Tchelery
Miegunyah

Annuello
94
Koorkab
Piambie
Wulga Park
Norwood
Impimi
Impimi
Barton
Moolpa
Merwein
Keri Keri
Kingle
Baldon
Thalaka

Mowat-Ville
Koimbo
112
Kooloonong
Haysdale
Thistlebank
Tralee
Spring Plain
84
Perekerten
49

11

Winnambool
Bolton
Natya
Goodnight
Mileu
Kyalite
Yal Yal
Liewah
62
Moolpa
Moulamein

MALLEE
Kulwin
96
B12
Prooinga
Piangil North
Tooleybuc
Stony Crossing
Edward
18
61

Manangatang
41
B12
Piangil
Miralie
Stony Crossing
Yarrein
Mallan
Niemur Forest
Inverness

Mittyack
88
Cocamba
Wood Wood
HWY
Yarraby
70
34
23

CALDER ZONE
24
Daytrap
Chinkapook
41
Nyah
Nyah West
Vinifera
Nowie North
Pira
Beverford
Speewa
Cunninyeuk
Dhuragoon
Niemur

Millan
Nandaly
Daytrap Corner
BOUNDARY
Ryanby
Chillingollah
Woorinen North
Beverford
Tyntynder Central
Niemur
Jimaringle

HWY
Nyarrin
A79
Lake Tyrrell
Tyrrell Downs
Waitchie
Woorinen
Tyntynder South
MULLIGANS PLAIN
Noorong
Jimaringle

12

Swan Hill

I J K L M N O P

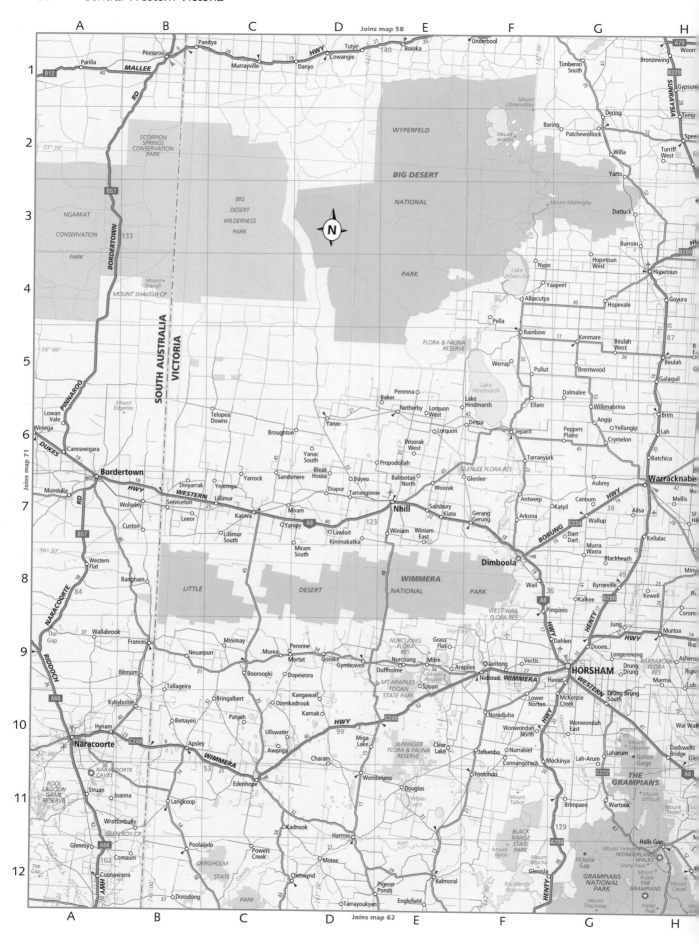

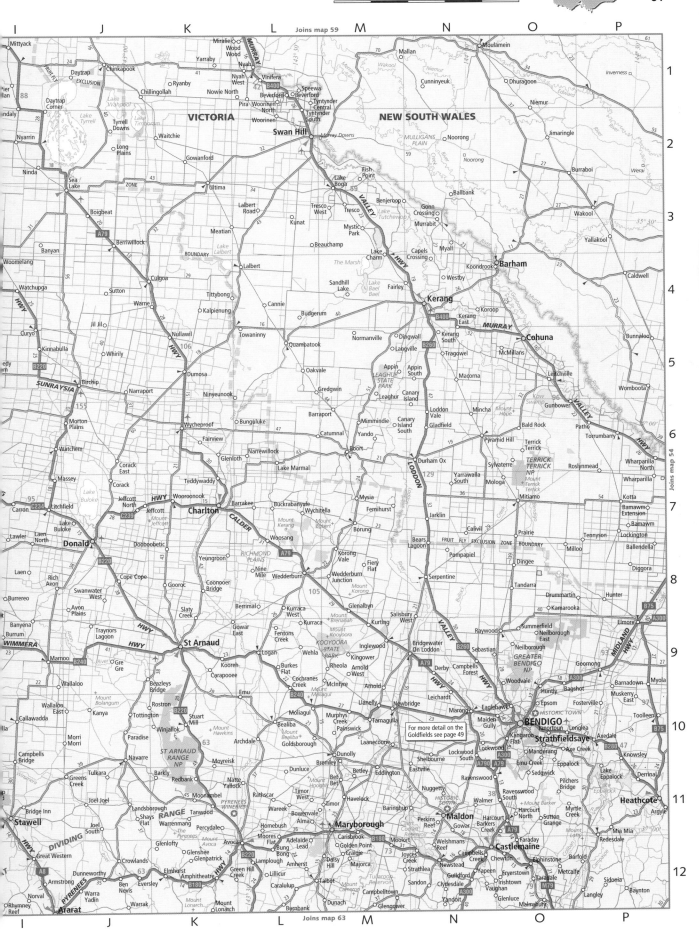

0 10 20 30 40 50 km

Joins map 59

VICTORIA

NEW SOUTH WALES

MULLIGANS PLAIN

MURRAY VALLEY HWY

Mittyack
Daytrap
Chinkapook
Miralie
Wood Wood
Yarraby
Nyah
Nyah West
Vinifera
B400
Speewa
Beverford
Tyntynder Central
Tyntynder South
Moulamein
Inverness
Dhuragoon
Niemur
Jimaringle

Daytrap Corner
EXCLUSION
Chillingollah
Ryanby
Nowie North
Pira
Woorinen North
Woorinen
Cunninyeuk
Noorong
Werai

Nyarrin
Lake Wahpool
Lake Tyrrell
Tyrrell Downs
Waitchie
Swan Hill
Murray Downs
Noorong
Burraboi

Ninda
Long Plains
Gowanford
Ultima
Fish Point
Lake Boga
Benjeroop
Ballbank
Niemur
Wakool

Sea Lake
Boigbeat
ZONE
Lalbert Road
Tresco West
Tresco
Gonn Crossing
Murrabit
Koondrook
Caldwell

Banyan
Berriwillock
Meatian
Kunat
Mystic Park
Lake Charm
Capels Crossing
Myall
Barham

Woomelang
Watchupga
Sutton
Warne
Tittybong
Cannie
Beauchamp
Sandhill Lake
The Marsh
Lake Bael Bael
Fairley
Kerang
Westby
Koondrook
Koroop
Cohuna

Curyo
Jil Jil
Nullawil
Kalpienung
Towaninny
Quambatook
Normanville
Dingwall
Langville
Kerang East
Kerang South
Tragowel
McMillans
Leitchville
Bunnaloo

Kinnabulla
Birchip
Narraport
Dumosa
Ninyeunook
Oakvale
Gredgwin
Appin
Appin South
Leaghur
Canary Island
Madorna
Bald Rock
Gunbower
Womboota

Watchem
Corack East
Corack
Teddywaddy
Wooroonook
Barrakee
Buckrabanyule
Wychitella
Mimmindie
Yando
Loddon Vale
Gladfield
Mincha
Mount Hope
Torrumbarry
Wharparilla North

Massey
Jeffcott North
Jeffcott
Charlton
Barraport
Catumnal
Boort
Mysia
Fernihurst
Durham Ox
Sylvaterre
Pyramid Hill
Terrick Terrick
Roslynmead
Wharparilla

Carron
Litchfield
Lake Buloke
Mount Jeffcott
Glenloth
Lake Marmal
Korong Vale
Borung
Jarklin
Calivil
Prairie
Mitiamo
Kotta
Bamawm Extension
Bamawm

Lawler
Laen North
Donald
Dooboobetic
Woosang
Wedderburn
Fiery Flat
Bears Lagoon
Pompapiel
Dingee
Tandarra
Milloo
Tennyson
Lockington
Ballendella
Diggora

Rich Avon
Swanwater West
Cope Cope
Yeungroon
Nine Mile
Wedderburn Junction
Glenalbyn
Salisbury West
Serpentine
Drummartin
Kamarooka
Hunter
Elmore

Banyena
Burrereo
Traynors Lagoon
Slaty Creek
Berrimal
Kurraca West
Kurraca
Kurting
Raywood
Summerfield
Neilborough East
Myola

Marnoo
Gre Gre
Gower East
Fentons Creek
Wehla
Inglewood
Bridgewater On Loddon
Sebastian
Neilborough
Goornong
Barnadown
Muskerry East

Wallaloo
Beazleys Bridge
St Arnaud
Logan
Burkes Flat
Rheola
Arnold West
Derby
Campbells Forest
Woodvale
Huntly
Epsom
Fosterville
Toolleen

Wallaloo East
Rostron
Stuart Mill
Kooreh
Carapooee
Cochranes Creek
McIntyre
Arnold
Llanelly
Newbridge
Leichardt
Marong
Eaglehawk
Bagshot

Callawadda
Kanya
Winjallok
Emu
Moliagul
Murphys Creek
Painswick
Tarnagulla
BENDIGO
Maiden Gully
Maldon
Strathfieldsaye
Axedale

Morri Morri
Paradise
Navarre
Barkly
Redbank
Bealiba
Goldsborough
Dunolly
Laanecoorie
Shelbourne
Lockwood South
Kangaroo Flat
Lockwood
Mandurang
Axe Creek
Knowsley

Campbells Bridge
Tulkara
Landsborough
Shays Flat
Moonambel
Natte Yallock
Rathscar
Timor West
Betley
Eddington
Eastville
Nuggetty
Ravenswood
Sedgwick
Pilchers Bridge
Lake Eppalock
Derrinal

Greens Creek
Joel Joel
Warrenmang
Percydale
Moyreisk
Archdale
Bromley
Bet Bet
Havelock
Baringhup
Walmer
Ravenswood South
Eppalock
Myrtle Creek
Heathcote

Bridge Inn
Joel South
Glenlofty
Avoca
Moores Flat
Timor
Carisbrook
Moolort
Joyces Creek
Maldon
Harcourt
Harcourt North
Sutton Grange
Mia Mia

Stawell
Great Western
Crowlands
Glenshee
Glenpatrick
Homebush
Bowenvale
Alma
Maryborough
Golden Point
Craigie
Welshmans Reef
Campbells Creek
Faraday
Redesdale
Argyle

Dunneworthy
Elmhurst
Amphitheatre
Lamplough
Bung Bong
Amherst
Daisy Hill
Majorca
Strathlea
Newstead
Guildford
Chewton
Castlemaine
Elphinstone
Barfold

Armstrong
Warra Yadin
Ben Nevis
Eversley
Green Hill Creek
Lillicur
Caralulup
Talbot
Sandon
Yapeen
Fryerstown
Vaughan
Irishtown
Metcalfe
Sidonia

Rhymney Reef
Norval
Warrak
Mount Lonarch
Burnbank
Dunach
Campbelltown
Glengower
Clydesdale
Glenluce
Guildford
Taradale
Malmsbury
Langley
Baynton

Ararat

Joins map 63

Joins map 54

For more detail on the Goldfields see page 49

HISTORIC TOWN

PYRENEES WINERIES

ST ARNAUD RANGE NP

KOOYOORA STATE PARK

LEAGHUR STATE PARK

TERRICK TERRICK NP

GREATER BENDIGO NP

GREAT DIVIDING RANGE

FRUIT FLY EXCLUSION ZONE

SUNRAYSIA HWY

WIMMERA HWY

CALDER HWY

LODDON VALLEY HWY

MIDLAND HWY

PYRENEES RANGE

I J K L M N O P

1 2 3 4 5 6 7 8 9 10 11 12

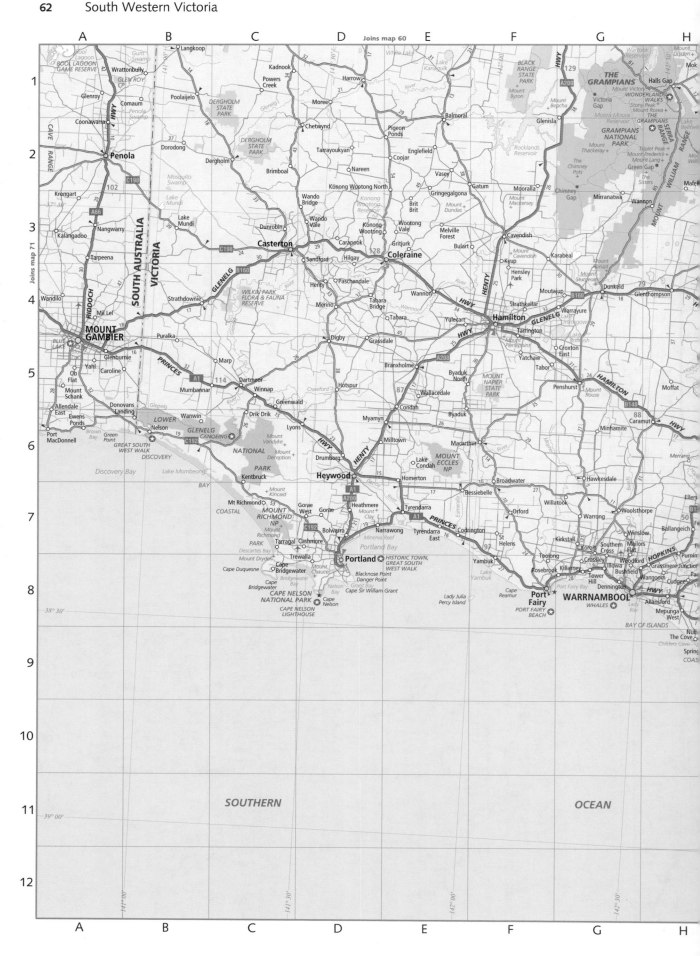

Joins map 61

For more detail on the Goldfields see page 49

For more detail on Melbourne & Surrounds see pages 42–3

For more detail on the Great Ocean Road see page 50

MAPS

SOUTH AUSTRALIA

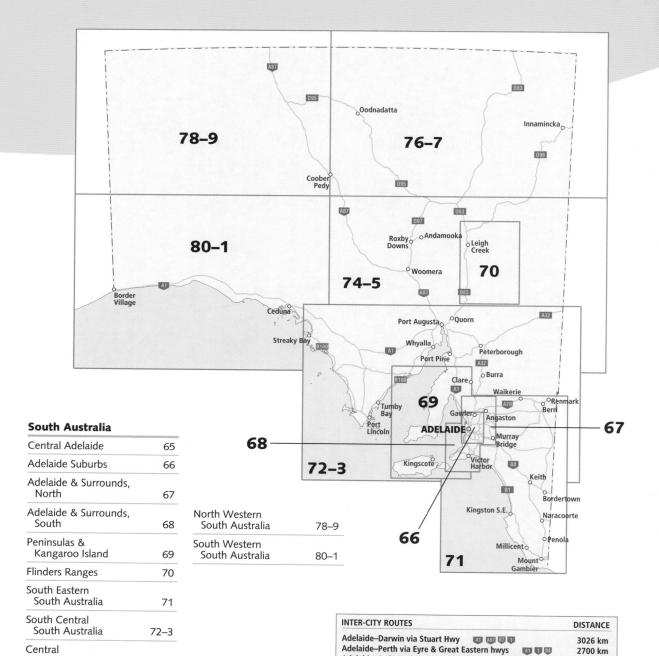

South Australia

Central Adelaide	65
Adelaide Suburbs	66
Adelaide & Surrounds, North	67
Adelaide & Surrounds, South	68
Peninsulas & Kangaroo Island	69
Flinders Ranges	70
South Eastern South Australia	71
South Central South Australia	72–3
Central South Australia	74–5
North Eastern South Australia	76–7

North Western South Australia	78–9
South Western South Australia	80–1

INTER-CITY ROUTES	DISTANCE
Adelaide–Darwin via Stuart Hwy	3026 km
Adelaide–Perth via Eyre & Great Eastern hwys	2700 km
Adelaide–Sydney via Sturt & Hume hwys	1417 km
Adelaide–Melbourne via Dukes & Western hwys	733 km
Adelaide–Melbourne via Princes Hwy	906 km

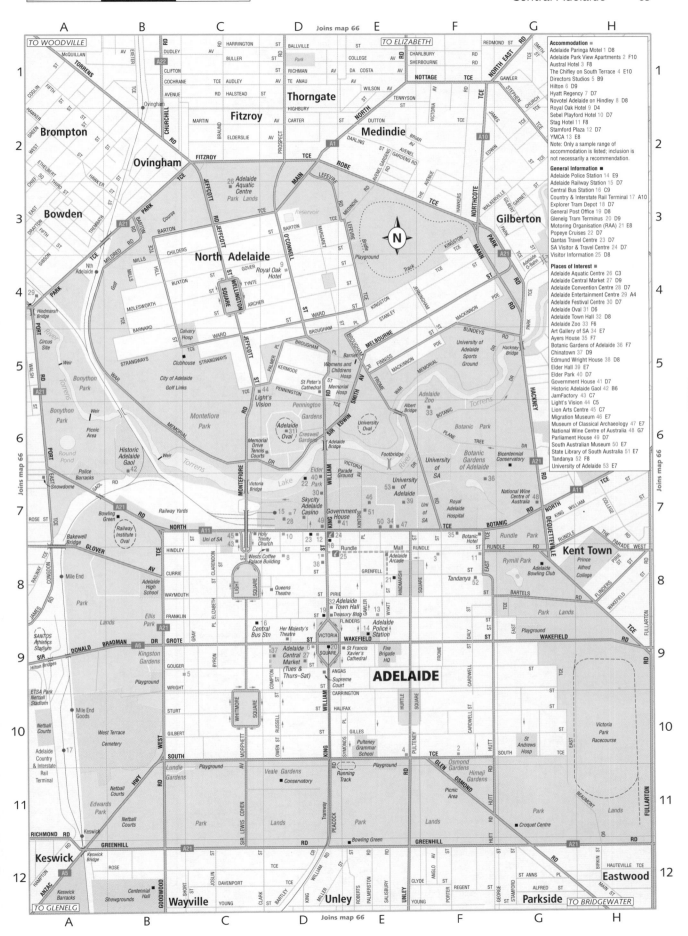

0   5   10   15 km

A   B   C   D   Joins map 67   E   F   G   H

TO PORT WAKEFIELD

A1

TO BURRA   A32   STURT   HWY   TO NURIOOTPA   TO NURIOOTPA

Kangaroo Flat   GAWLER   Rosedale

VALLEY WAY

Two Wells   BAROSSA   Rowland Flat

Lewiston   GAWLER   Sandy Creek   Lyndoch   B19

Middle Beach   Angle Vale   Williamstown

PORT   ANGLE   VALE   Virginia   SMITHFIELD   PARA WIRRA RECREATION PARK   South Para Dam   HALE CP   WARREN CP   B34

Port Gawler   Bolivar   NORTH   Barossa Reservoir

PORT GAWLER CONSERVATION PARK   Direk   Edinburgh Aerodrome   ELIZABETH   South Para Reservoir   WARREN CP   CRICKS MILL RD

St Kilda   WATERLOO CORNER   BLACK TOP RD   38   MOUNT GOULD   CROMER RANGE

Point Grey   SALISBURY   Little Para Reservoir   Mount Gawler   Kersbrook   LITTLE   B34

Pelican Point   TORRENS ISLAND CP   MAIN   Little Para Dam   Mount Gould   Forreston   PARA   WARREN RD

OUTER HARBOR   SALISBURY HWY   41   COBBLER CREEK RP   B31   Trail   RANGE

NORTH HAVEN   OSBORNE   PARAFIELD   Parafield Airport   GREEN FIELDS   TEA TREE GULLY   B10   Gumeracha   Birdwood

TAPEROO   A13   A20   BRIDGE   A18   ANSTEY HILL RP   Houghton   Torrens River   Mount Torrens

LARGS NORTH   LEFEVRE PENINSULA   DRY CREEK   PARA HILLS   30   Kangaroo Creek Reservoir   B31   B34

SEMAPHORE   Torrens Island   NORTHFIELD   Hope Valley Reservoir   Kangaroo Creek Dam   CUDLEE CREEK CP

Point Malcolm   PORT ADELAIDE   JUNCTION   RD   GORGE   BLACK HILL CP   MONTACUTE   RANGE   Lobethal

GRAND   A17   A10   A11   FOREST

GULF   ALBERTON   KILBURN   EAST   MORIALTA CP   KENNETH STIRLING CP   Charleston   CHARLESTON CP

PORT   ADELAIDE   ROSTREVOR   Heysen   TORRENS

ALBERT PARK   DUDLEY PARK   A11   MAGILL   RANGE

GRANGE   A7   NORTH   PORTRUSH   GREENHILL RD   MOUNT

BOWDEN   NORTH ADELAIDE   A17   HORSNELL GULLY RP   Woodside

ST VINCENT   A15   ADELAIDE   Summertown   Uraidla   B34   Oakbank   Brukunga

TAPLEYS   A6   Adelaide Airport   KESWICK   CLELAND CP   KENNETH STIRLING CP   Balhannah

Holdfast Bay   ANZAC HWY   GOODWOOD   A1   Stirling   Bridgewater

CROSS   UNLEY PARK   RD   Mount Lofty   Aldgate

GLENELG   A13   MITCHAM   12   BROWNHILL CREEK RP   SOUTH   MOUNT GEORGE   Hahndorf   Nairne

ASCOT PARK   BELAIR   31   Heathfield   PRINCES

HOVE   MARION   SOUTH   BELAIR NP   Upper Sturt   MARK OLIPHANT CP   Littlehampton   EASTERN   M1

BRIGHTON   EDEN HILLS   GLENALTA   Mylor   OLD   HWY

SEACLIFF   A15   BLACKWOOD   STURT GORGE RP   TOTNESS RP   Mount Barker   FWY

MARINO CP   EXP   Happy Valley Reservoir   Mount Barker

Marino Rocks Lighthouse   RD   SCOTT CREEK CONSERVATION PARK   Echunga   TO MURRAY BRIDGE

HALLETT COVE CONSERVATION PARK   21   REYNELLA   Clarendon   33   Mount Bold   Wistow

LONSDALE   SOUTHERN   A13   22   Mount Bold Reservoir   RD

CHRISTIES BEACH   A15   M2   MORPHETT VALE   Mount Bold Dam   B33   Macclesfield

PORT NOARLUNGA   NOARLUNGA CENTRE   MAIN   ONKAPARINGA RIVER NATIONAL PARK   Kangarilla   BATTUNGA   RD   B37

ONKAPARINGA RIVER RECREATION PARK   Blewitt Springs   DASHWOOD GULLY   RD   Meadows   B33

SEAFORD   OLD NOARLUNGA   SOUTH   McLaren Flat   34   Mount Wilson   VALLEY   Woodchester   Hartley

MOANA SANDS CP   B23   KANGARILLA   BROOKMAN   LONG   RD

Ochre Point   TATACHILLA   McLaren Vale   B34

Moana   A13   Maslin Beach   Bletchley

TO VICTOR HARBOR   Joins map 68

A   B   C   D   E   F   G   H

N

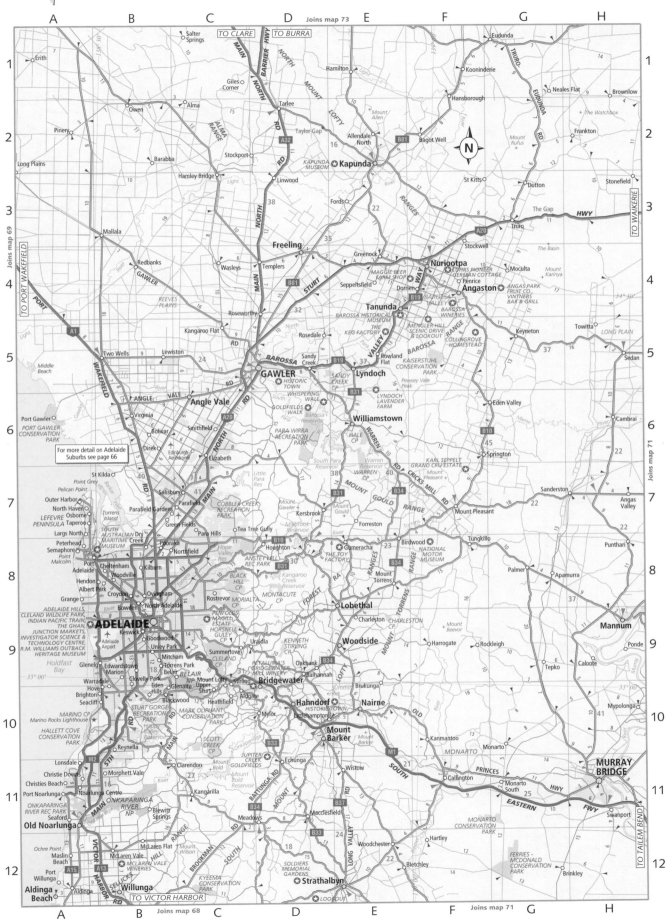

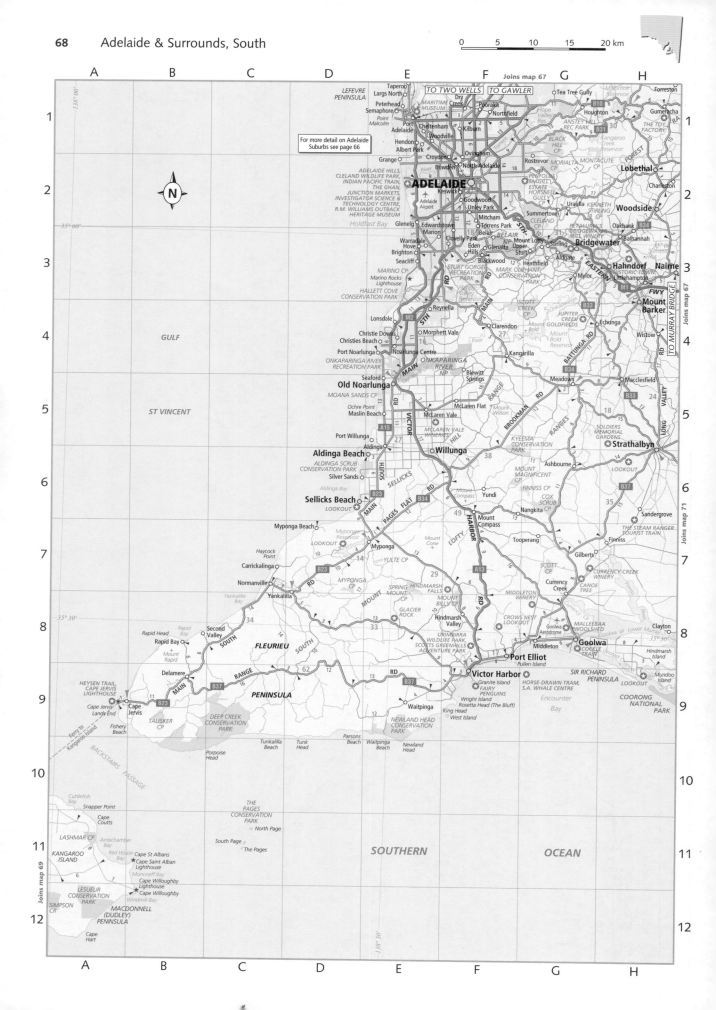

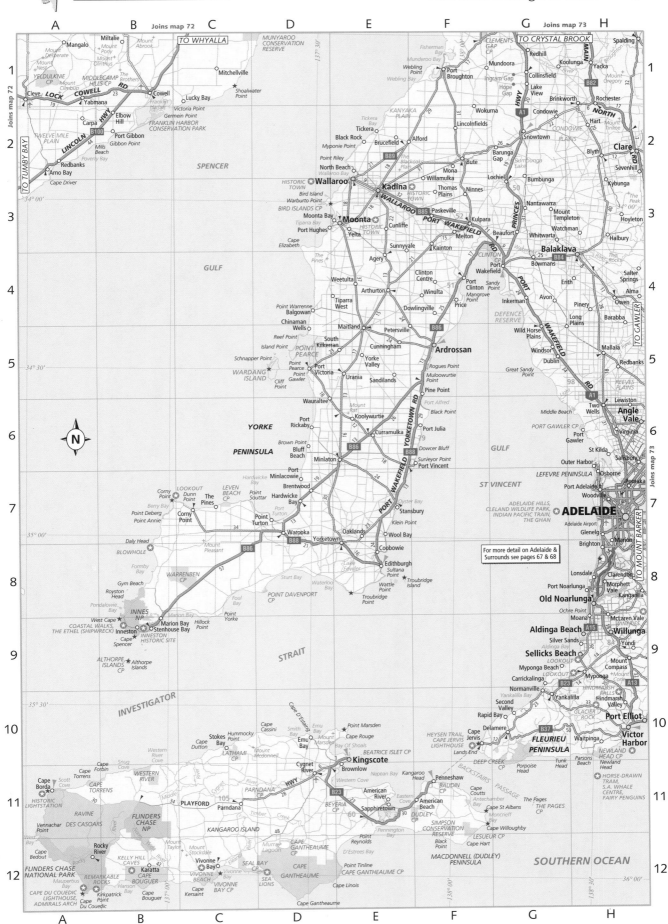

Joins map 72
Joins map 72
Joins map 73
Joins map 73
TO WHYALLA
TO CRYSTAL BROOK
TO TUMBY BAY
TO GAWLER

0   10   20   30   40   50 km

For more detail on Adelaide &
Surrounds see pages 67 & 68

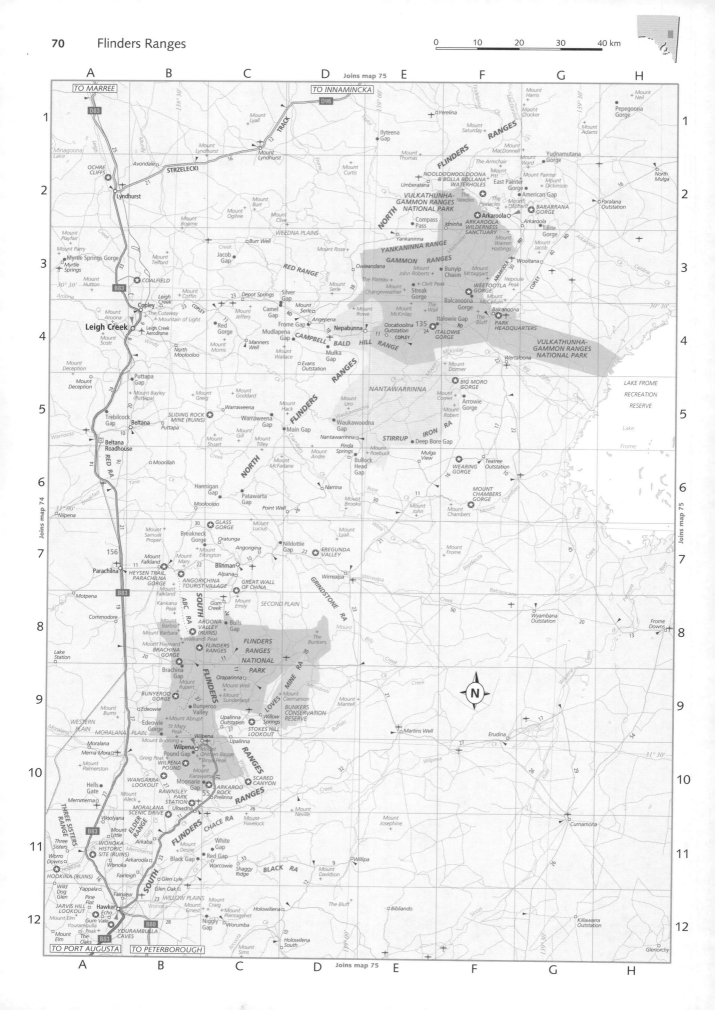

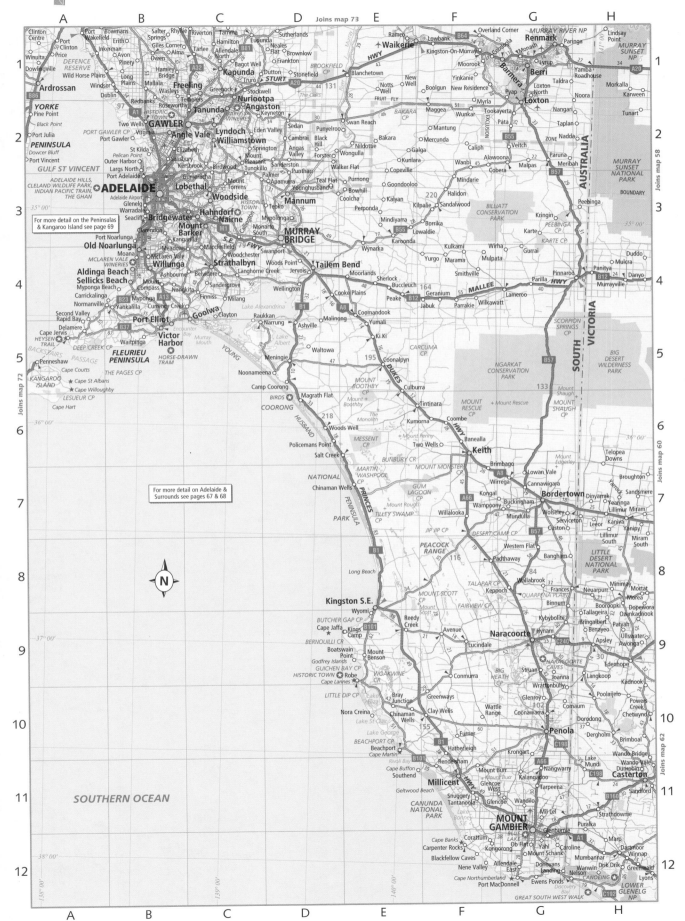

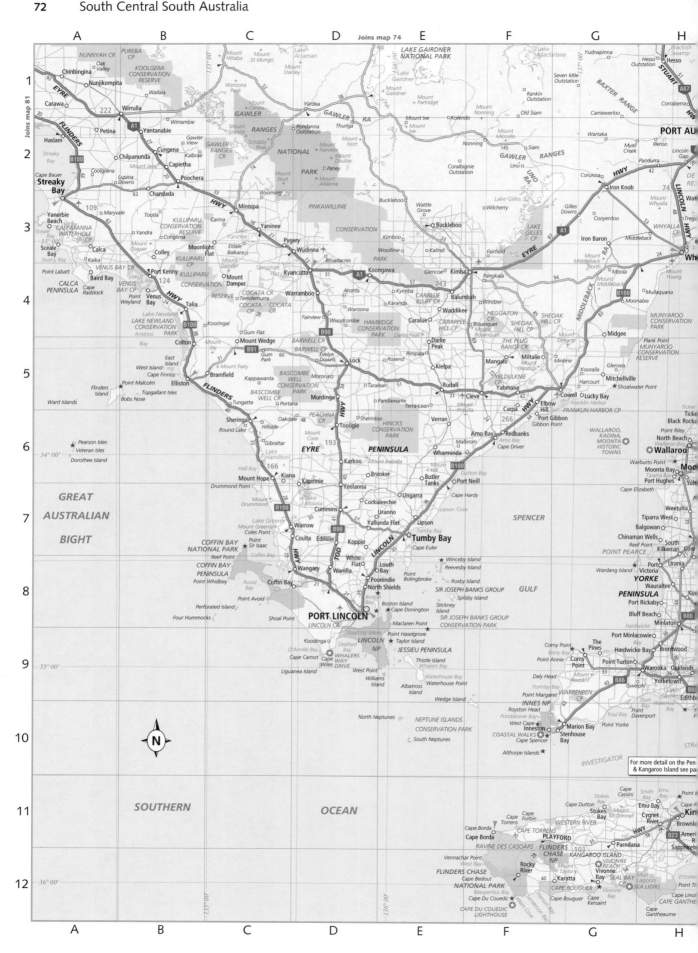

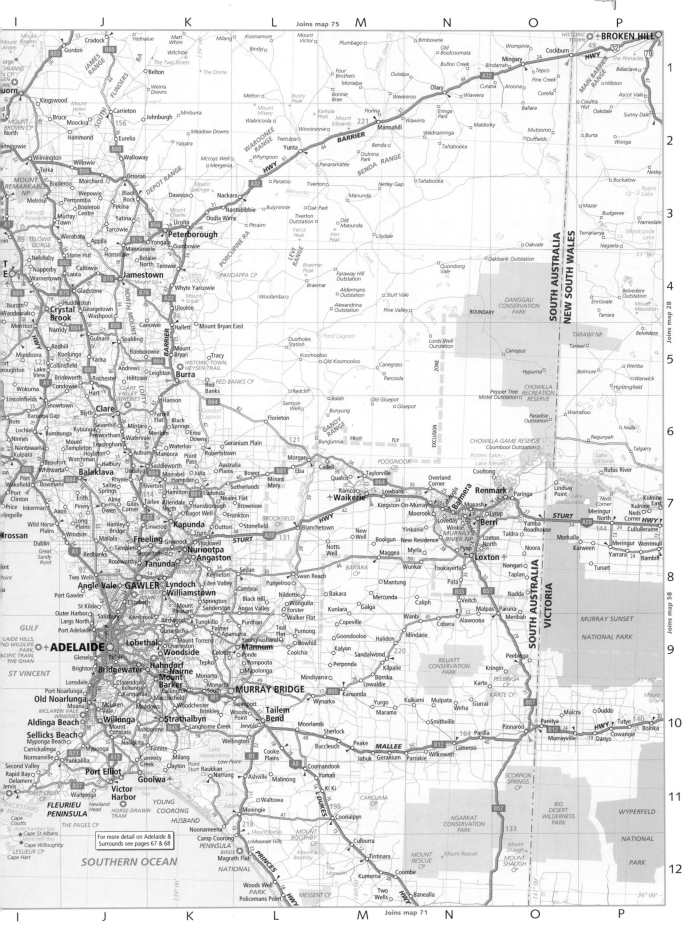

0   20   40   60   80   100 km

Joins map 75

BROKEN HILL

For more detail on Adelaide & Surrounds see pages 67 & 68

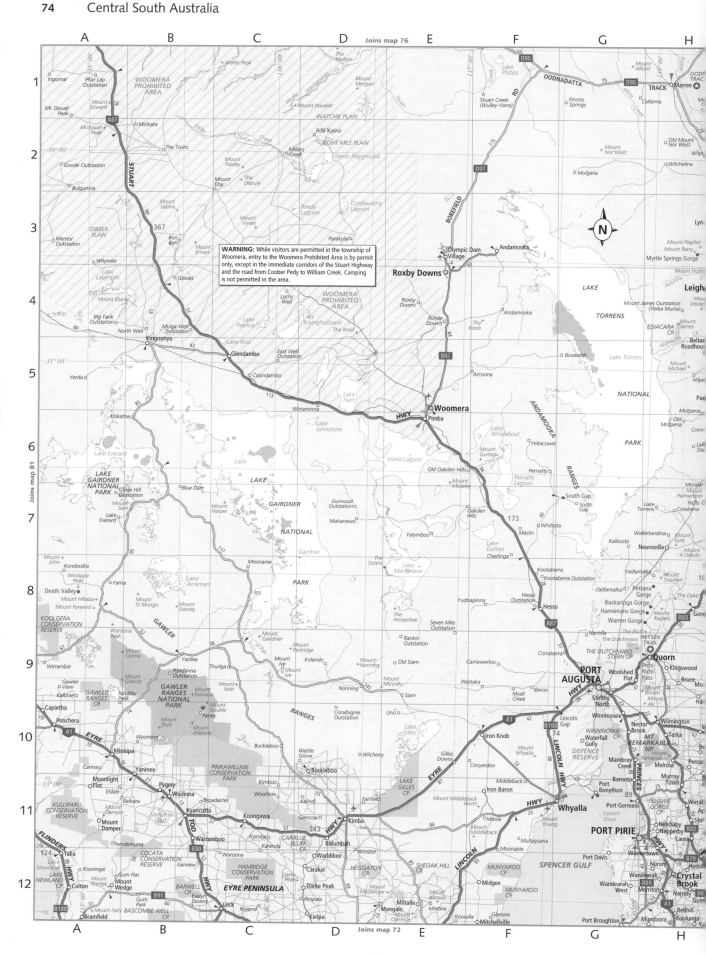

Joins map 76
Joins map 72
Joins map 81

WARNING: While visitors are permitted in the township of Woomera, entry to the Woomera Prohibited Area is by permit only, except in the immediate corridors of the Stuart Highway and the road from Coober Pedy to William Creek. Camping is not permitted in the area.

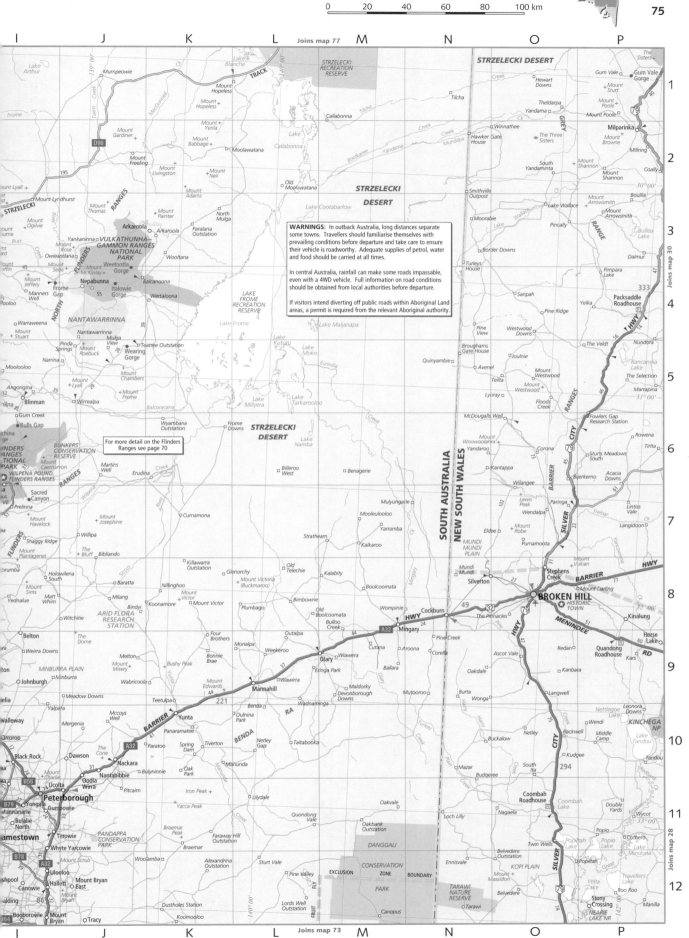

A   B   C   D   E   F   G   H

Joins map 109

1

PMER ULPERRE INGWEMIRNE

ARLETHERRE ABORIGINAL

LAND TRUST

SIMPSON

NORTHERN TERRITORY

QUEENSLAND

New Crown

Mount Peebles

APATULA ABORIGINAL LAND TRUST

Mount Daer

Mount Etingimbra

Mirranponga Ponguna Lake

Lake Poeppel

Poeppel Corner

Mount Willyunpa

2

NORTHERN TERRITORY

SOUTH AUSTRALIA

Lake Thomas

Mount Hearne   Mount Frank

Mount Dare

River   Mount Apperda

Mount Alinerta

WITJIRA

SIMPSON

Mount Weeahlakiminne

Mount Bagot

Mount Ludgate

DESERT

DESERT

Mount Barr

Mount Hammersley

NATIONAL

CONSERVATION

3

Stevenson

Mount Crispe

Mount Attachemikanna

Mount Emery

Mount Doorundina

PARK

Poolowanna Lake

Mount Ross

WARNING: Visitors planning to enter the Desert Parks are required to contact National Parks and Wildlife SA. A Desert Parks Pass is necessary.

Mount Hornet

Mount Dillon

Mount Goodiar

Mount Adnalgowara

SIMPSON

Peera Peera Poolanna Lake

Mount Algoochinna

Hamilton

Ck

DESERT

4

Hamilton

PEDIRKA

Mount Rebecca

MABEL RANGE

Mount Yangalee

Mount Onqueedinna

RECREATION

Lake Griselda

DESERT

Mount Sarah

Mount Sarah

RESERVE

27° 00'

Mount Alexander

Lake Umaroona

5

Todmorden

Alberga

River

Mount John

Macumba

SIMPSON

Lake Willawilaninna

DE

OODNADATTA

Mount Alice

Mount Narlee

Macumba

Mount Aggie

D95

Mount Midlargunna

Mount Tidnabakina

Tallacooppa

6

Mount Beviss

Mount Malua

Mount O'Halloran

Mount Arthur

Mount Edarteenya

Lake Pantoowarinna

Lake Warrandirinn

Mount Lucy

Mount Carulinia

Oodnadatta

Mount Guy

Ck

River

Mount Albany

Mount Areebunna

Woodmurra

Lake Noolyeana

Millyeewilpa Lake

Lake Peera Mudla Yeppa

Kalame

Allandale

Mount Carlootanna

Mount Toodla

7

Joins map 79

TRACK

Mount Perrypollkot

Pompapillinna

Warburton

140

Mount Andrews

Neales

Mount Dutton

Mount Harvey

Mount Robinson

Mount Toodley

TIR DES

28° 00'

Mount Minyalcooroo

Mount Toondina

Lewis Bay

Twin Lakes

Lake Koolkootinne

Kalam Lake

8

Mount Bray

Arckaringa

Ck

Mount Kingston North

DENISON RANGE

Mount Kingston

(Nappamurra)

River

LAKE EYRE

Lake Eyre (North)

LAKE EYRE NATIONAL

Lora

Mount Barry

Peake

Mount Denison

Mount Charles

NATIONAL

PARK

Ck

DAVENPORT RANGE

203

Lake Warrangarrana

Nilpinna

Mount Margaret

PARK

LAKE EYRE

Lake Mulapula

Lake Puntawolona

9

WARNING: While visitors are permitted in the township of Woomera, entry to the Woomera Prohibited Area is by permit only, except in the immediate corridors of the Stuart Highway and the road from Coober Pedy to William Creek. Camping is not permitted in the area.

405

Mount Anna

Ck

Halligan Bay

ELLIOT PRICE CONSERVATION PARK

10

151

DUGOUTS

Coober Pedy

Lake Cadibarrawirracanna

D95

Douglas

Anna Creek

William Creek

29° 00'

166

Mooloogoorana Swamp

Belt Bay

La Flc

STUART

WOOMERA

PROHIBITED

Lake William

OODNADATTA

Lake Callara

Lake Eyre (North)

11

STUART

82

Mount Woods

AREA

Warrena

THE ILLUSION PLAINS

Muloorina

Engenina

Mount Allafone

121

Lake Eyre (South)

LAKE EYRE NATIONAL PARK

Lake Ellen

A87

Mount Penrhyn

Wartawangoonga

Warrena

Ck

HERMIT RA

Lake Marion

D8

12

Ingomar

Phar Lap Outstation

RANGE

Wares Peak

Mount Purvis

Mount Riddoch

North

Margaret

WABMA KADARBU MOUND SPRINGS CONSERVATION PARK

Lake Phibbs

Stuart Creek (Wulley-Yarra)

BOREFIELD RD

TRACK

75

Mount Alford

OODNADATTA TRACK

Marree

BIRDSVILLE

SERRATED RANGE

Mount Morgan

TURRET RA

Stuart

Ck

Callanna

D95

Pit

STUART HWY

135° 00'

136° 00'

137° 00'

138° 00'

A   B   C   D   E   F   G   H

Joins map 74

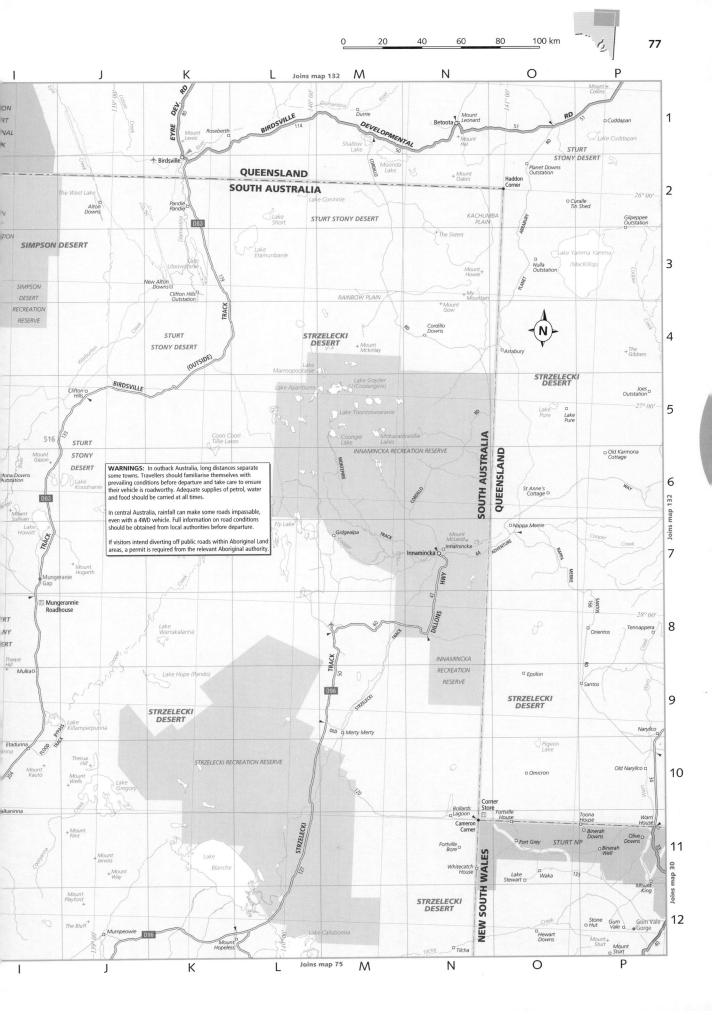

0 20 40 60 80 100 km

Joins map 132

I J K L M N O P

Mount Collins 1

EYRE DEV. RD
80
BIRDSVILLE 114 DEVELOPMENTAL RD 51 Cuddapan

Diamantina Durrie River

Mount Lewis Roseberth Betoota Mount Leonard 51

Mount Hal

Lake Cuddapan

Birdsville Shallow Lake 50 CORDILLO Mount Oakes STURT STONY DESERT

QUEENSLAND

SOUTH AUSTRALIA Haddon Corner 2

26° 00′

The West Lake Lake Coninnie Planet Downs Outstation Curalle Tin Shed

Alton Downs Pandie Pandie D83 Lake Short STURT STONY DESERT KACHUMBA PLAIN Gilpeppee Outstation

Diamantina The Sisters ARRABURY Nulla Outstation Lake Yamma Yamma (MacKillop) 3

SIMPSON DESERT Lake Uloowaranie Lake Etamunbanie Mount Howie PLANET

New Alton Downs Clifton Hills Outstation 179 RAINBOW PLAIN Mount Gow RD Cordillo Downs Mount Mountain Arrabury The Gibbers 4

SIMPSON DESERT RECREATION RESERVE TRACK STRZELECKI DESERT Mount Mckinlay

STURT STONY DESERT Warburton (OUTSIDE) Lake Marroopootanie Lake Goyder (Coolangirie) **STRZELECKI DESERT** 27° 00′ 5

Creek BIRDSVILLE Clifton Hills Lake Apanburra Lake Toontoowaranie RD Lake Pure Lake Pure Joes Outstation

Coori Coori Tillie Lakes MONTEPINE Coongie Lake Mitkacaldratillie Lakes CORDILLO St Anne's Cottage Old Karmona Cottage WAY 6

516 133 STURT STONY DESERT Lake Koodnanie INNAMINCKA RECREATION RESERVE

Mount Gason D83

ona Downs utstation Mount Sullivan Lake Howitt

WARNINGS: In outback Australia, long distances separate some towns. Travellers should familiarise themselves with prevailing conditions before departure and take care to ensure their vehicle is roadworthy. Adequate supplies of petrol, water and food should be carried at all times.

In central Australia, rainfall can make some roads impassable, even with a 4WD vehicle. Full information on road conditions should be obtained from local authorities before departure.

If visitors intend diverting off public roads within Aboriginal Land areas, a permit is required from the relevant Aboriginal authority.

Fly Lake Gidgealpa TRACK Mount McLeod Innamincka Nappa Merrie NAPPA Cooper Creek 7

TRACK Cooper Innamincka 44 ADVENTURE MERRIE 28° 00′

Mungeranie Gap Mount Hogarth HWY SANTOS 166 8

Mungerannie Roadhouse Lake Warrakalanna TRACK 60 DILLONS 47 Orientos Tennappera

INNAMINCKA RECREATION RESERVE Epsilon RD Santos

Theare Hill Lake Hope (Pando) TRACK 50 STRZELECKI **STRZELECKI DESERT** 9

Mulka D96

Etadunna FLOOD Lake Killamperpunna OLD Merty Merty Naryilco

TRACK **STRZELECKI DESERT** Pigeon Lake Old Naryilco 34 10

Mount Kauto Therua Hill Mount Wells Lake Gregory STRZELECKI RECREATION RESERVE 120 Omicron

alkaninna Mount Flint STRZELECKI Corner Store Toona House Warri House

Bollards Lagoon Fortville House 11

Coongarna Mount Jervois Cameron Corner Binerah Downs Olive Downs

Mount Way Lake Blanche 127 Fortville Bore Fort Grey **STURT NP** Binerah Well 33

NEW SOUTH WALES Whitecatch House Mount King

Mount Playford Lake Stewart Waka 133

The Bluff Murnpeowie D96 Mount Hopeless 141° 00′ Lake Callabonna **STRZELECKI DESERT** Creek Stone Hut Gum Vale Gum Vale Gorge

Hewart Downs Mount Sturt 40 12

Tilcha Tilcha Mount Sturt

I J K L M N O P

Joins map 75

Joins map 132
Joins map 30

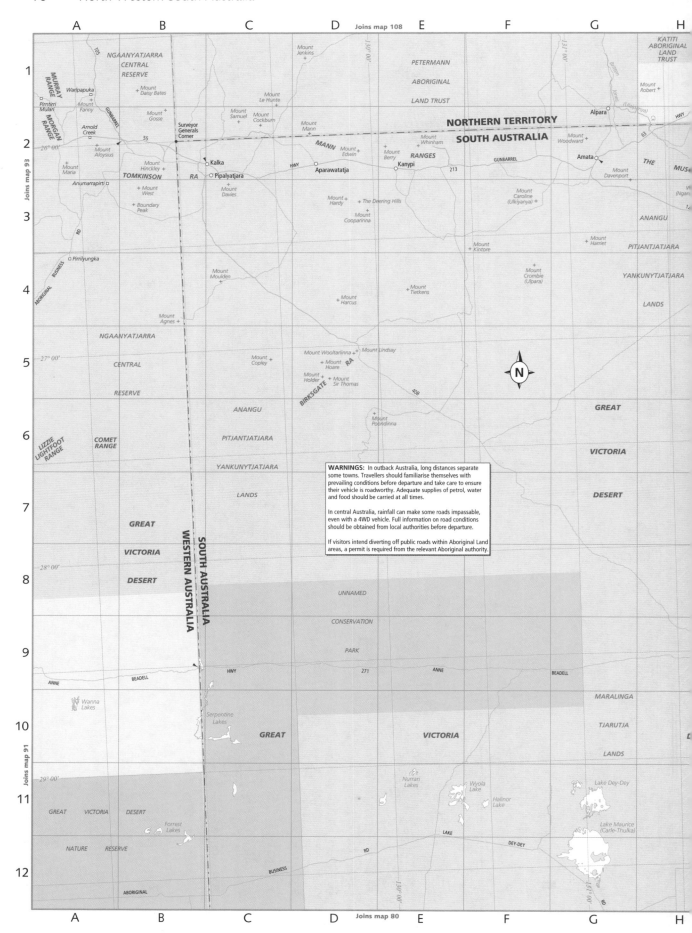

Joins map 108

Joins map 93

Joins map 91

Joins map 80

WARNINGS: In outback Australia, long distances separate some towns. Travellers should familiarise themselves with prevailing conditions before departure and take care to ensure their vehicle is roadworthy. Adequate supplies of petrol, water and food should be carried at all times.

In central Australia, rainfall can make some roads impassable, even with a 4WD vehicle. Full information on road conditions should be obtained from local authorities before departure.

If visitors intend diverting off public roads within Aboriginal Land areas, a permit is required from the relevant Aboriginal authority.

0 20 40 60 80 100 km

74

Mount Peebles

Mount Magarey
Umbeara
NEWLAND
Mount Falconer
Mount Hopetoun
Mount Gordon
Mount Peterswald
Mount Daniel
Mount Mcgowan
New Crown
APATULA ABORIGINAL LAND TRUST

Kulgera
Kulgera
Mount Reynolds
Mount Cavenagh
RANGES
Mount Beddome
BEDDOME RANGE
Mount Grundy
Mount Wilyunpa

Victory Downs
NORTHERN TERRITORY
SOUTH AUSTRALIA
AYERS RANGE
Goyder
Mount Cecil
Mount Darling
Mount Parlue
Mount Mead
Mount Anderson
Mount Hearne
Mount Frank
Mount Dare

New Well
Mount Cuthbert
Mount Everard
RANGES
Mount Warrabillinna
Sundown Outstation
180
Mount Howe
Tieyon
Mount Anthony
Mount Tieyon
Mount Treloar
Abminga
WITJIRA
Mount Hammersley
NATIONAL

Mount Mair
STUART
CENTRAL
AUSTRALIA
Agnes Creek
Mount Irwin
Mount Walter
Mount Britton
Mount Hornet
Akoolalunna
BAGOT RA
Mount Deane
Mount Algoochinna
Mount Ross
PARK

Fregon
ANANGU PITJANTJATJARA YANKUNYTJATJARA LANDS
Tarcoonyinna
River
Lambina
Mount Alberga
Mount Isabel
Hamilton
PEDIRKA DESERT
Mount Rebecca
Mount Sarah

Wallatalleena Peak
Mount Illbillee
Mount Carmeena
Mimili
THE EVERARD RA
Taddy Peak
Mount Barnet
Mount Etitinna
143
Iwantja (Indulkana)
Chandler
INDULKANA RANGE
Granite Downs
Mount Mystery
Christmas Well
Mount Randolph
Todmorden
Mount Alice
Mount Narlee

Mount John
Mount Weir
Mount Byilcaoora
Marla
OODNADATTA TRACK
Mount Gordon
D95
Mount Herbert North
Mount Jane North
212
TRACK

Mintabie
Wallatinna
Welbourn Hill
Mount Brougham South
Mount Todmorden
Mount Aggie
Mount Malua
Neales River

COMALCO
SURVEY TRACK
GREAT VICTORIA DESERT
COMALCO
Mount Beviss
Mount Lucy
Mount Carulinia
Mount Albany

COMALCO SURVEY TRACK
Kyber Pass
Mount Willoughby
Mount Andrews
Joins map 76

Wintinna
Mount Marron
Mount Waddikee
Mount Arckaringa
Mount Minyalcooroo

Cadney Homestead
Copper Hill
32
Mount Willoughby
Arckaringa
140

WOOMERA PROHIBITED AREA
235
Mount Furner
Mount Evelyn
Mount Bray

MARALINGA TJARUTJA LANDS
TALLARINGA CONSERVATION PARK
Mount Gillen
Evelyn Downs
Mcdonald Peak
Mount Barry

Lake Meramangye
48
BEADELL
284
HWY
BEADELL HWY
ANNE
Pootnoura
STUART
179
Mount Barry
Mount Euee

CENTRAL AUSTRALIA
Algebullcullia
Cadibarrawirracanna
Lake

WARNING: While visitors are permitted in the township of Woomera, entry to the Woomera Prohibited Area is by permit only, except in the immediate corridors of the Stuart Highway and the road from Coober Pedy to William Creek. Camping is not permitted in the area. Note the overlap with Aboriginal Land where you need additional seperate permits.

Mount Clarence
Mabel Creek
Manguri
STUART
23
DUGOUTS
Coober Pedy

WOOMERA PROHIBITED AREA
GREAT VICTORIA DESERT
Mabel
Mount Penrhyn
A87
RANGE HWY

WOOMERA PROHIBITED AREA
Lake Woorong
Lake Phillipson
Wirrida
Lake Wirrida
RAILWAY

Mount Igy
Garford
Sandstone
Ingomar
Phar Lap Outstation

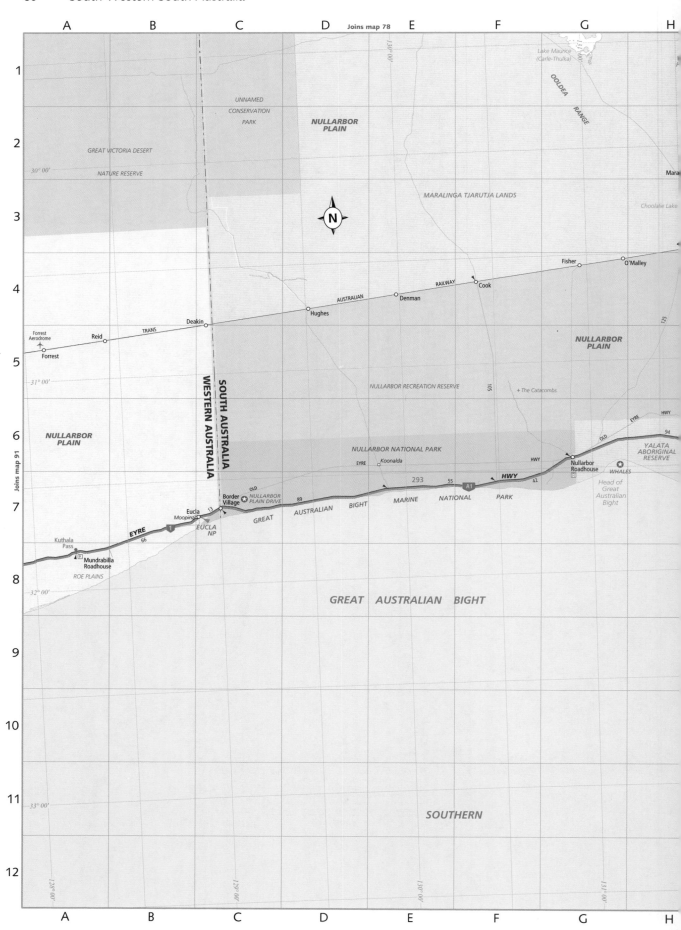

Joins map 78

Joins map 91

0   20   40   60   80   100 km

I   J   K   L   Joins map 79   M   N   O   P

WARNING: While visitors are permitted in the township of Woomera, entry to the Woomera Prohibited Area is by permit only, except in the immediate corridors of the Stuart Highway and the road from Coober Pedy to William Creek. Camping is not permitted in the area. Note the overlap with Aboriginal Land where you need additional seperate permits.

Wirrida

Lake Wirrida

Ingomar

Phar Lap Outstation

Mount Sandy

1

STUART

Mc Douall Peak

Mount Soward

Mirikata

WILKINSON LAKES

MARALINGA TJARUTJA LANDS

Indooroopilly Outstation

Jumbuck

Comet

Commonwealth Hill

A87

HWY

367

2

Lake Anthony

WOOMERA PROHIBITED AREA

Half Moon Lake

Irria Outstation

Muckanippie Outstation

Bradman Outstation

Gina Outstation

Goode Outstation

Bulgunnia

Lake Bring

Mulgathing

Mount Christie

Durkin Outstation

Gibraltar Outstation

Carne Outstation

Ooramina Outstation

Johns Outstation

3

oldea

Bates

Warrior Outstation

Ambrosia Outstation

Ealbara Outstation

Mentor Outstation

Whymlet

TRANS

AUSTRALIAN

Wynbring

Carnding Road Outstation

CENTRAL

Lake Labyrinth

Lyons Camp

Malbooma Outstation

RAILWAY

Tarcoola

Lake Moolkra

Mount Eba

Big Tank Outstation

4

Lake Ifould

Wilgena

North Well

Kingoonya

Mount Finke

Lake Harris

Lake Tallacootra

143

Yerda

Kokatha

5

YELLABINNA RECREATION RESERVE

LAKE GAIRDNER NATIONAL PARK

Lake Everard

6

YALATA ABORIGINAL RESERVE

Yalata

Glyde Hill Outstation

Joins map 74

Lake Everard

GUNYAH CONSERVATION PARK

IAN NP

55

EYRE

Nundroo

Nundroo Roadhouse

202

YUMBARRA CR

Northedge

YUMBARRA CONSERVATION PARK

Mount John

Lake Acraman

7

Pintumba

Coorabie

39

35

Cundilippy

YUMBARRA CR

Kondoolka

Mount Wallaby

Mount Pollard

Yarna

95

Wookata

FOWLERS BAY CR

31

Bookabie

CHADINGA CR

Penong

Koonibba

PUREBA CR

PUREBA CONSERVATION PARK

Winnilippe Peak

Mount Hiltaba

Mount St Mungo

Cape Adieu

Cheetima Beach

Fowlers Bay

Point Fowler

Fowlers Bay

CHADINGA CR

A1

73

Marbra

Corrong

NULLARBOR PLAIN DRIVE

Watchbrae

NUNNYAH CR

Mount Pyramid

Waroona Peak

8

Cape Nuyts

SURFING Cactus Beach Point Sinclair

Black Peak

Lake MacDonnell

HWY

Ceduna

EYRE

Mudamuckla

Oak Valley

KOOLGERA CR

NUYTS REEF CP

POINT BELL CR

Thevenard

Denial Bay

Chinbingina

92

Mount Centre

GAWLER RANGES NP

Point Bell

Point Peter

FLINDERS

Nunjikompita

Point Dillon

Purdie Islands

St Peter Island

Cape D'Estrees

Smoky Bay

Kara-Pine

Carawa

222

Wirrulla

61

Wirrambie

Wallala

Mount Granite

9

Goat Island

Lacy Island

Evans Island

Eyre Island

Smoky Bay

30

A1

Yantanabie

Gawler View

GAWLER RANGES CR

Scrubby Peak

NUYTS ARCHIPELAGO CP

Franklin Islands

ACRAMAN CREEK CP

Flagstaff

109

Petina

Cungena

27

Kalbrae

Scrubby Peak

ISLES OF ST. FRANCIS CP

St Francis Island

Point Brown

St Mary Bay

Gascoigne Bay

Haslam

B100

Chilpalunda

Capietha

74

Point Collinson

Streaky Bay

Mount Jane

20

Poochera

HWY

Coolgrana

The Bald Hills

Chandada

Wyoming

10

Cape Bauer

Eba Island

62

Parla Peak

Tootla

33

Minnipa

16

Corvisart Bay

Streaky Bay

Point Westall

Maryvale

Yandra

Carina

Yaninee

Yanerbie Beach

SCEALE BAY CR

CALPATANNA WATERHOLE CP

Mount Cooper

Conglima

Moonlight Flat

21

Sceale Bay

Calca

Colley

FLINDERS

Lake Yaninee

11

Slade Point

Searcy Bay

Mount Hall

Mount Misery

KULLIPARU CP

Mount Damper

Point Labatt

Baird Bay

Port Kenny

VENUS BAY CP

124

Mount Damper

OCEAN

Cape Radstock

Venus Bay

24

COCATA CP

Anxious Bay

Talia

12

Talia Beach

Lake Newland

B100

Kooringal

Mount Wedge

Mount Wedge

WALDEGRAVE ISLANDS CP

LAKE NEWLAND CP

HWY

Colton

Mount Fairy

B91

Bramfield

I   J   K   L   M   N   O   Joins map 72   P

MAPS

WESTERN AUSTRALIA

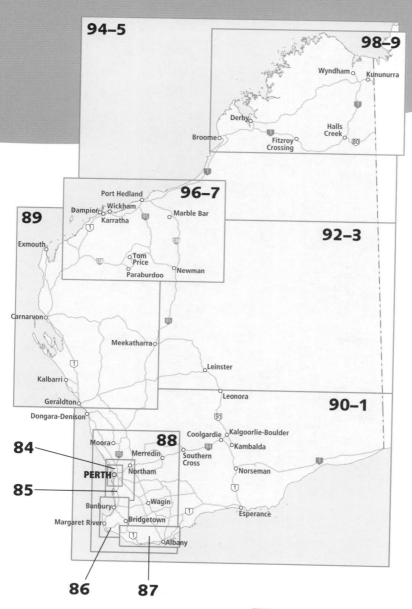

Western Australia

Central Perth	83
Perth Suburbs	84
Perth & Surrounds	85
South-West Coast	86
South Coast	87
South Western Western Australia	88
Central Western Western Australia	89
Southern Western Australia	90–1
Central Western Australia	92–3
Northern Western Australia	94–5
Pilbara	96–7
Kimberley	98–9

INTER-CITY ROUTES		DISTANCE
Perth–Adelaide via Great Eastern & Eyre hwys		2700 km
Perth–Darwin via Great Northern Hwy		4032 km

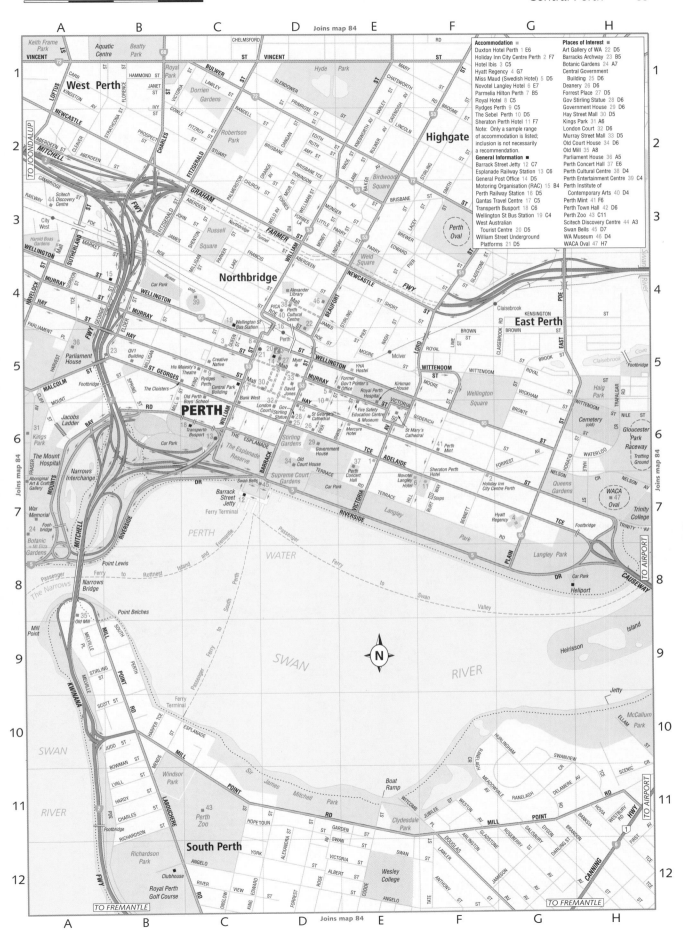

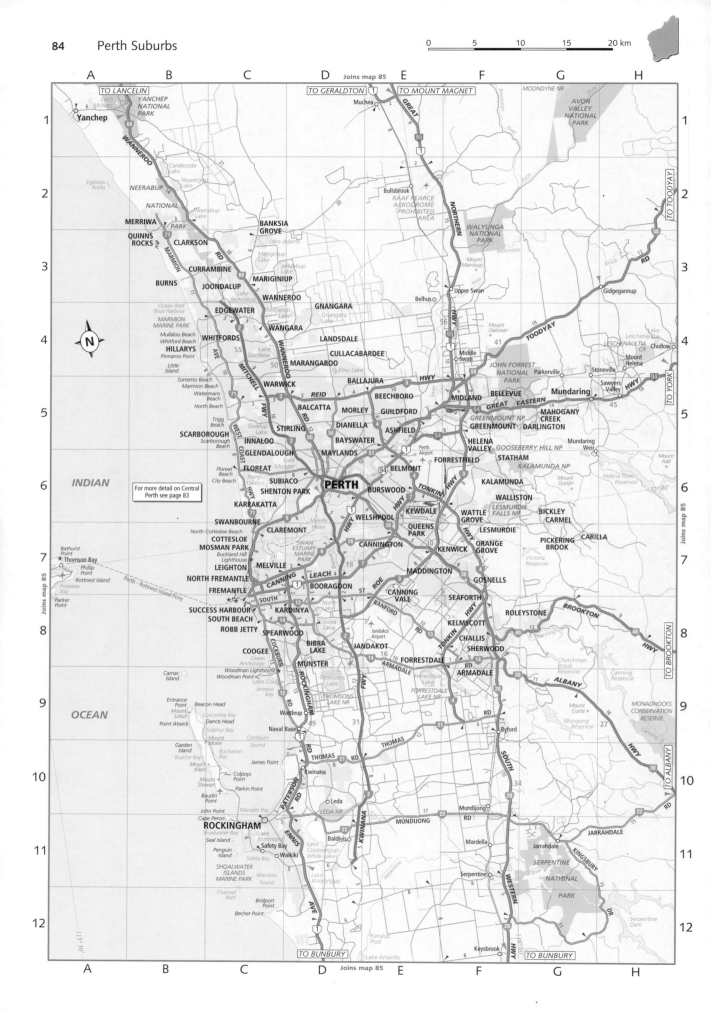

0   5   10   15   20 km

A   B   C   D   Joins map 85   E   F   G   H

TO LANCELIN
Loch McNess
6
Yanchep
YANCHEP NATIONAL PARK
60
WANNEROO

TO GERALDTON   1
TO MOUNT MAGNET
Muchea
GREAT
95
MOONDYNE NR
AVON VALLEY NATIONAL PARK
River
Brockman

Eglinton Rocks
Carabooda Lake
Nowergup Lake
21
NEERABUP
74
Bullsbrook
RAAF PEARCE AERODROME PROHIBITED AREA
NORTHERN
15
Avon
TO TOODYAY
50

NATIONAL
Neerabup Lake
Lake Adams
Lake Joondalup
MERRIWA
PARK
3
BANKSIA GROVE
WALYUNGA NATIONAL PARK
Wooroloo
Brook
RD
12

QUINNS ROCKS
CLARKSON
71
MARMION
10
Mariginiup Lake
Jandabup Lake
6
Upper Swan
River
Gidgegannup

BURNS
CURRAMBINE
60
MARIGINIUP
WANNEROO
GNANGARA
Belhus
95
HWY
56
Mount Mambup
TOODYAY
19
Leschenaultia CR
Chidlow

JOONDALUP
Badgerup Lake
Gnangara Lake
Emu Lake
Middle Swan
41
LESCHENAULTIA CR
Mount Helena

Ocean Reef Boat Harbour
EDGEWATER
WANGARA
LANDSDALE
10
1
JOHN FORREST NATIONAL PARK
Parkerville
Stoneville

MARMION MARINE PARK
2
WHITFORDS
55
CULLACABARDEE
HWY
Mount Oakover
Sawyers Valley
94

Mullaloo Beach
Whitford Beach
HILLARYS
Pinnaroo Point
MITCHELL
Lake Goollelal
MARANGAROO
BALLAJURA
3
BELLEVUE
MIDLAND
GREAT
EASTERN
HWY
Mundaring
45
TO YORK

Little Island
AVE
50
WARWICK
REID
BEECHBORO
10
Swan
GREENMOUNT NP
14
MAHOGANY CREEK
Mundaring Weir
Mount Hall

Sorrento Beach
Marmion Beach
Watermans Beach
North Beach
FWY
SCARBOROUGH
71
BALCATTA
RD
MORLEY
GUILDFORD
ASHFIELD
Helena
GREENMOUNT
DARLINGTON
Gooseberry Hill NP
River
32° 00'

Trigg Beach
WEST COAST
STIRLING
60
DIANELLA
BAYSWATER
94
HELENA VALLEY
STATHAM
KALAMUNDA NP
Helena River Reservoir

SCARBOROUGH
Scarborough Beach
INNALOO
2
56
MAYLANDS
51
Perth Airport
FORRESTFIELD
KALAMUNDA
Mount Gunjin

GLENDALOUGH
Lake Monger
BELMONT
94
1
HWY
Mount Hall

Floreat Beach
City Beach
FLOREAT
For more detail on Central Perth see page 83
SUBIACO
PERTH
BURSWOOD
TONKIN
WALLISTON
LESMURDIE FALLS NP
BICKLEY
CARMEL

INDIAN
SHENTON PARK
Perry Lakes
Swan
River
4
WELSHPOOL
KEWDALE
HWY
WATTLE GROVE
LESMURDIE
PICKERING BROOK
CARILLA

KARRAKATTA
Melville Water
HWY
QUEENS PARK
30
ORANGE GROVE
Victoria Reservoir

SWANBOURNE
71
CLAREMONT
5
26
CANNINGTON
30
KENWICK
SEAFORTH
ROLEYSTONE
BROOKTON
9

North Cottesloe Beach
COTTESLOE
MOSMAN PARK
SWAN ESTUARY MARINE PARK
Canning
5
LEACH
18
ROE
MADDINGTON
GOSNELLS
12
HWY

Bathurst Point
Thomson Bay
Phillip Point
Rottnest Island
LEIGHTON
NORTH FREMANTLE
MELVILLE
2
BOORAGOON
ST
CANNING VALE
Ranford
TONKIN
KELMSCOTT
CHALLIS
ALBANY
40
TO BROOKTON

Porpoise Bay
Parker Point
FREMANTLE
SOUTH
CANNING
North Lake
RD
Jandakot Airport
SHERWOOD
Churchman Brook Reservoir
Canning

SUCCESS HARBOUR
SOUTH BEACH
ROBB JETTY
KARDINYA
13
Bibra Lake
JANDAKOT
16
FORRESTDALE
ARMADALE
RD
ARMADALE
11
Canning Reservoir

COOGEE
SPEARWOOD
14
BIBRA LAKE
MUNSTER
2
10
FORRESTDALE
Forrestdale Lake
30
MONADNOCKS CONSERVATION RESERVE

Carnac Island
Owen Anchorage
Woodman Lighthouse
Woodman Point
COCKBURN
Lake Coogee
ROCKINGHAM
Thomsons Lake
FORRESTDALE LAKE NR
Mount Curtis
Wungong Reservoir
27

OCEAN
Entrance Point
Mount Lotus
Point Atwick
Beacon Head
Luscombe Bay
Dance Head
Sulphur Bay
Jervoise Bay
12
Wattleup
THOMSONS LAKE NR
31
21
Byford
ALBANY
16
HWY
30
TO ALBANY

Garden Island
Mount Moke
Buchanan Sound
Naval Base
1
49
THOMAS
RD
4
SOUTH
RD

Garden Island
Buache Point
Mount Klein
James Point
THOMAS
RD
Kwinana
21
THOMAS
12
20

Mount Stewart
Colpoys Point
Parkin Point
PATERSON
RD
34

Baudin Point
John Point
Cape Peron
Mangles Bay
ROCKINGHAM
ENNIS
Leda
LEDA NR
KWINANA
17
Mundijong
22
RD
MUNDIJONG
Mardella
22
JARRAHDALE
KINGSBURY

Shoalwater Bay
Seal Island
Penguin Island
Lake Richmond
Baldivis
5
Serpentine
Jarrahdale
15

Safety Bay
Waikiki
Lake Coolongup
White Lake
SERPENTINE
NATIONAL
DR

SHOALWATER ISLANDS MARINE PARK
Warnbro Sound
Lake Walyungup
Serpentine
River
PARK
15

Channel Reef
Bridport Point
Becher Point
1
WESTERN
HWY
20
Kerulup Pool
Lake Amarillo
Keysbrook
TO BUNBURY
Serpentine Dam

115° 30'

TO BUNBURY
Joins map 85

A   B   C   D   Joins map 85   E   F   G   H

1   2   3   4   5   6   7   8   9   10   11   12

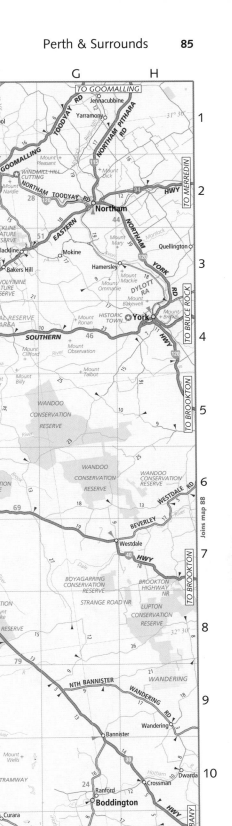

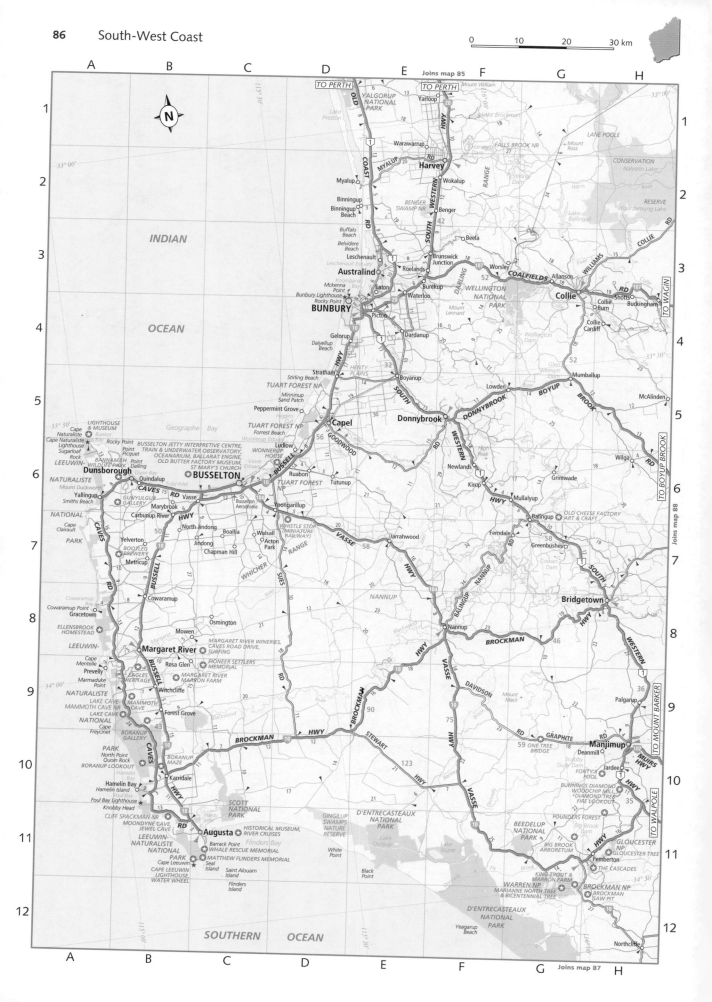

0   10   20   30 km

A   B   C   D   E   F   G   H

1

INDIAN

OCEAN

2

3

4

5

6

7

8

9

10

11

12

TO PERTH
TO PERTH
YALGORUP NATIONAL PARK
Yarloop
Mount William

Warawarrup
Lake Preston
Harvey
Wokalup
Myalup
Binningup
Binningup Beach
Benger
Buffalo Beach
Belvidere Beach
Leschenault
Brunswick Junction
Worsley
Allanson
Collie
Australind
Roelands
Eaton
Burekup
Shotts
Buckingham
Mckenna Point
Bunbury Lighthouse
Rocky Point
Waterloo
Collie Burn
BUNBURY
Picton
Dardanup
Collie Cardiff
Gelorup
Dalyellup Beach
Stratham
Boyanup
Mumballup
Stirling Beach
HENTY PLAINS
TUART FOREST NA
Minninup Sand Patch
Lowden
McAlinden
Peppermint Grove
Higgins
Forrest Beach
Capel
Donnybrook
Wilga
Ludlow
WONNERUP HOUSE
Newlands
Grimwade
BUSSELTON JETTY INTERPRETIVE CENTRE, TRAIN & UNDERWATER OBSERVATORY, OCEANARIUM, BALLARAT ENGINE, OLD BUTTER FACTORY MUSEUM, ST MARY'S CHURCH
Ruabon
Kirup
Mullalyup
Dunsborough
Quindalup
BUSSELTON
Tutunup
Balingup
OLD CHEESE FACTORY ART & CRAFT
Yallingup
Vasse
Marybrook
Busselton Aerodrome
Yoongarillup
WHISTLE STOP (MINIATURE RAILWAY)
Ferndale
Smiths Beach
GUNYULGUP GALLERY
Carbunup River
North Jindong
Boallia
Walsall
Acton Park
Jarrahwood
Greenbushes
Cape Clairault
Yelverton
Jindong
Chapman Hill
BOOTLEG BREWERY
Metricup
Cowaramup
Bridgetown
Cowaramup Point
Gracetown
Osmington
NANNUP
ELLENSBROOK HOMESTEAD
Mowen
MARGARET RIVER WINERIES, CAVES ROAD DRIVE, SURFING
Nannup
Cape Mentelle
Margaret River
Rosa Glen
PIONEER SETTLERS MEMORIAL
Prevelly
EAGLES HERITAGE
MARGARET RIVER MARRON FARM
Marmaduke Point
Witchcliffe
Mount Mack
Palgarup
LAKE CAVE
MAMMOTH CAVE
Forest Grove
GRAPHITE
Manjimup
Cape Freycinet
BORANUP GALLERY
BROCKMAN
ONE TREE BRIDGE
Deanmill
North Point
Quoin Rock
BORANUP LOOKOUT
BORANUP MAZE
Jardee
Hamelin Bay
Karridale
FONTY'S POOL
Hamelin Island
Foul Bay
Foul Bay Lighthouse
Knobby Head
BUNNINGS DIAMOND WOODCHIP MILL, DIAMOND TREE FIRE LOOKOUT
SCOTT NATIONAL PARK
FOUNDERS FOREST
CLIFF SPACKMAN NR
MOONDYNE CAVE, JEWEL CAVE
HISTORICAL MUSEUM, RIVER CRUISES
GINGILUP SWAMPS NATURE RESERVE
BEEDELUP NATIONAL PARK
BIG BROOK ARBORETUM
Pemberton
GLOUCESTER NP
GLOUCESTER TREE
Augusta
Barrack Point
WHALE RESCUE MEMORIAL
White Point
THE CASCADES
LEEUWIN-NATURALISTE NATIONAL PARK
MATTHEW FLINDERS MEMORIAL
Cape Leeuwin
CAPE LEEUWIN LIGHTHOUSE, WATER WHEEL
Seal Island
Saint Alouarn Island
Flinders Island
Black Point
KING TROUT & MARRON FARM
WARREN NP
MARIANNE NORTH TREE & BICENTENNIAL TREE
BROCKMAN NP
BROCKMAN SAW PIT
D'ENTRECASTEAUX NATIONAL PARK
Yeagarup Beach
Northcliffe

SOUTHERN   OCEAN

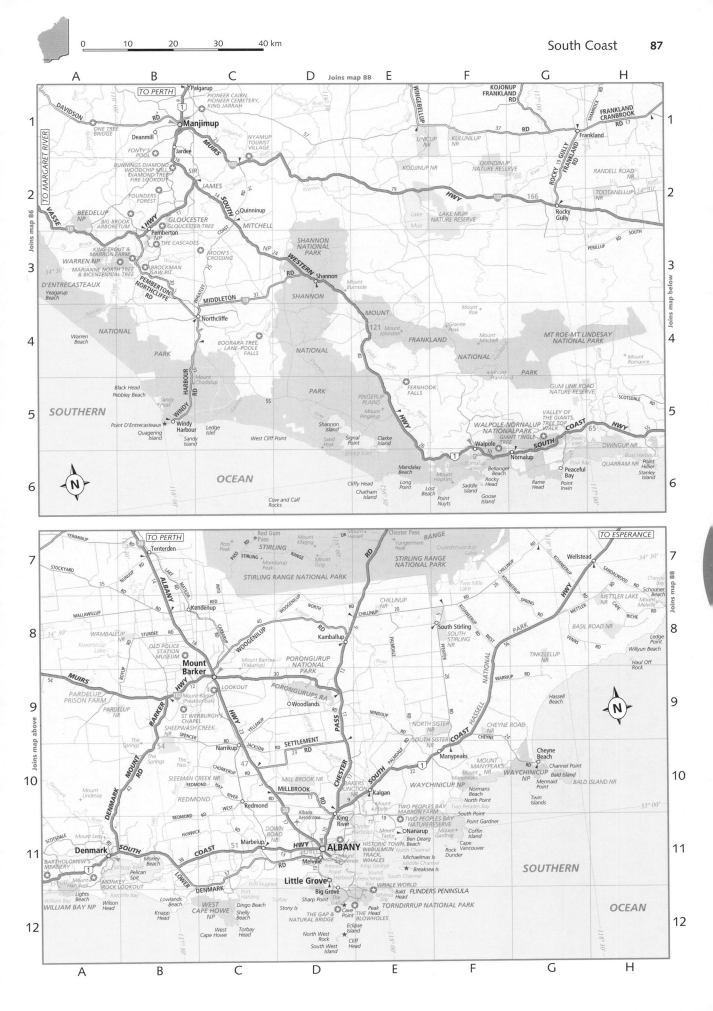

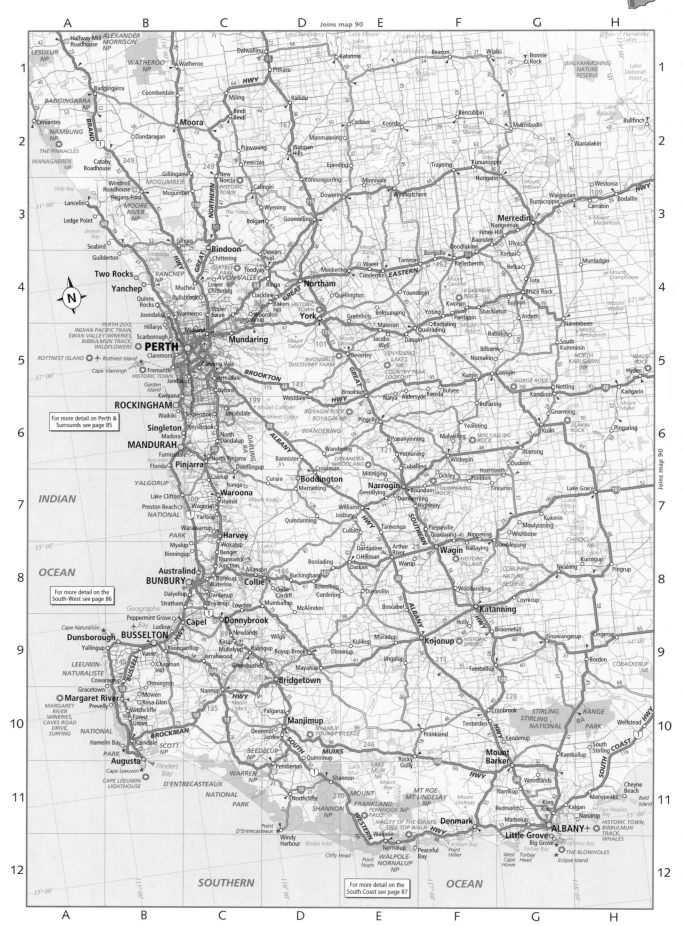

0   20   40   60   80 km

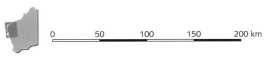

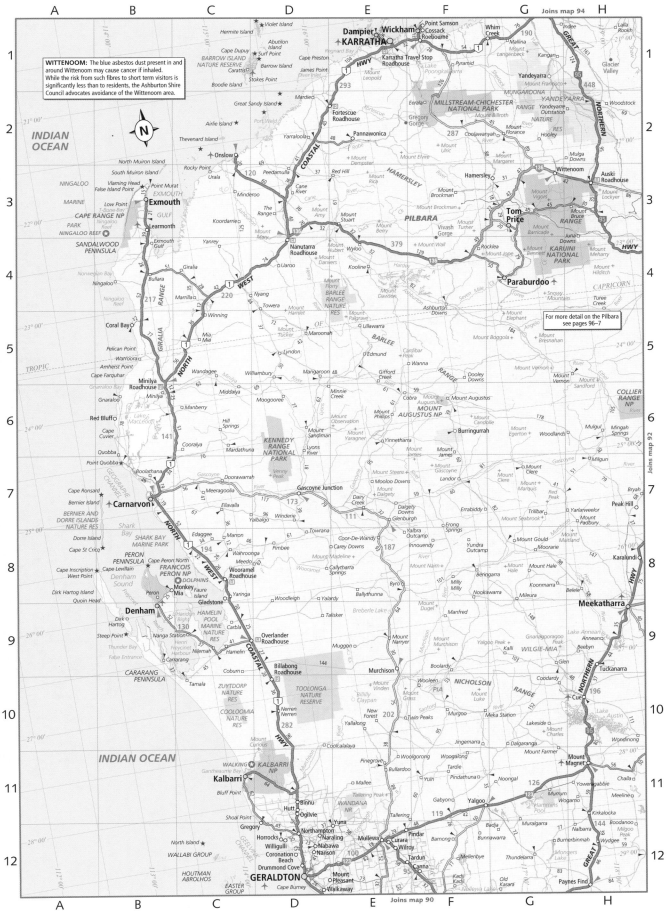

0   50   100   150   200 km

WITTENOOM: The blue asbestos dust present in and around Wittenoom may cause cancer if inhaled. While the risk from such fibres to short term visitors is significantly less than to residents, the Ashburton Shire Council advocates avoidance of the Wittenoom area.

INDIAN OCEAN

For more detail on the Pilbara see pages 96–7

INDIAN OCEAN

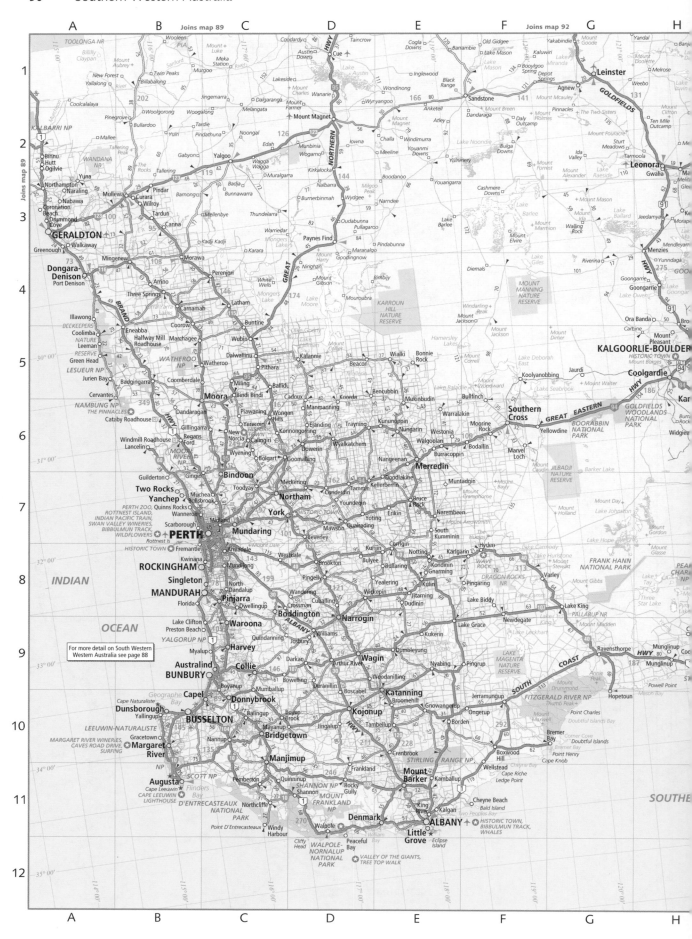

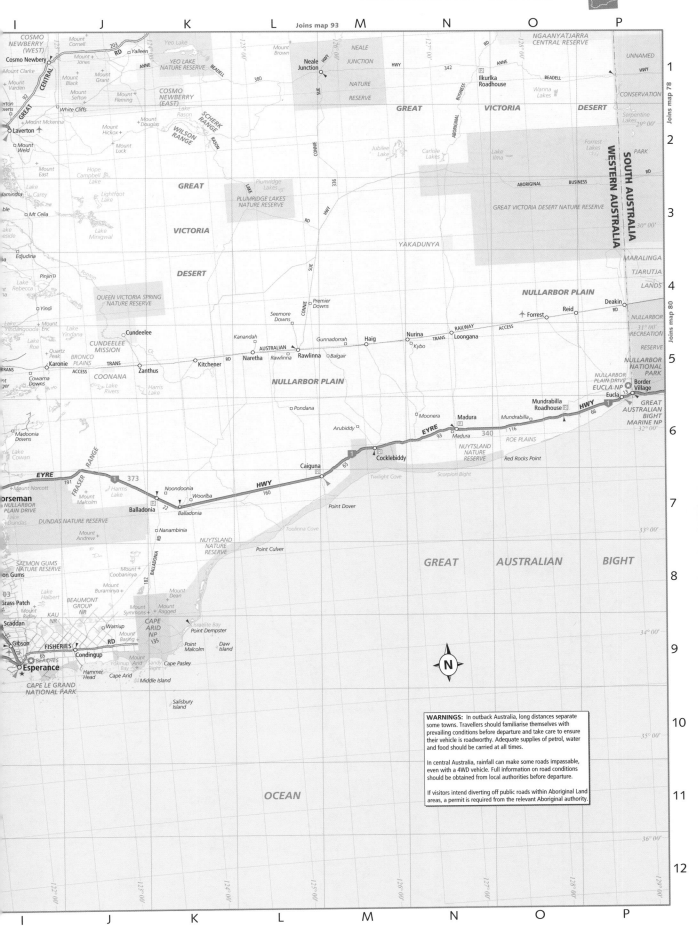

0   50   100   150   200 km

Joins map 93

Joins map 78

Joins map 80

COSMO NEWBERRY (WEST)
Cosmo Newberry
Mount Cornell
203 RD Yalleen
Yeo Lake
YEO LAKE NATURE RESERVE
Mount + Jones
Mount Grant
Mount Brown
Neale Junction
NEALE JUNCTION
NGAANYATJARRA CENTRAL RESERVE
RD
UNNAMED
HWY

Mount Clarke
Mount Black
Mount Varden
Mount Sefton
Mount + Fleming
COSMO NEWBERRY (EAST)
Lake Rason
SCHERK RANGE
CONNIE
SUE HWY
NATURE RESERVE
ANNE
BEADELL
ANNE
342
BUSINESS
Ilkurlka Roadhouse
ABORIGINAL
BEADELL
Wanna Lakes
CONSERVATION

White Cliffs
Mount Mckenna
Mount Hickox +
Mount + Douglas
WILSON RANGE
Lake Rason
GREAT
VICTORIA
DESERT
Jubilee Lake
Carlisle Lakes
Lake Ilma
VICTORIA
WESTERN AUSTRALIA
SOUTH AUSTRALIA
Serpentine Lakes
Forrest Lakes
PARK
29° 00'

Laverton
Mount Weld
Mount Luck +
GREAT
336
Lake Minigwal
ABORIGINAL
BUSINESS
GREAT VICTORIA DESERT NATURE RESERVE
MARALINGA
RD
30° 00'

Mount East
Hope Campbell Lake
Lightfoot Lake
VICTORIA
LAKE
Plumridge Lakes
PLUMRIDGE LAKES NATURE RESERVE
SUE
RD
YAKADUNYA
TJARUTJA LANDS

Lake Carey
Mt Celia
DESERT
CONNIE
NULLARBOR PLAIN
4
31° 00'

Edjudina
Lake Rebecca
QUEEN VICTORIA SPRING NATURE RESERVE
Seemore Downs
Premier Downs
Deakin
Forrest
Reid
RD
NULLARBOR RECREATION
RESERVE

Pinjin
Yindi
Cundeelee
Kanandah
Gunnadorrah
Haig
Nurina
Kybo
Loongana
RAILWAY
TRANS
ACCESS
NULLARBOR NATIONAL PARK

Karonie
Quartz Peak
Lake Yindana
Mount Enc
CUNDEELEE MISSION
BRONCO PLAINS
Zanthus
Kitchener
Naretha
Rawlinna
Rawlinna
AUSTRALIAN
Balgair
NULLARBOR PLAIN
NULLARBOR PLAIN DRIVE
EUCLA NP
Eucla
Border Village

Cowarna Downs
COONANA
TRANS
ACCESS
Lake Rivers
Harris Lake
Pondana
Moonera
Mundrabilla Roadhouse
Mundrabilla
HWY
GREAT AUSTRALIAN BIGHT MARINE NP
32° 00'

Madoonia Downs
Lake Cowan
Arubiddy
EYRE
93
Madura
340
116
ROE PLAINS
66

Mount Norcott
EYRE
191
FRASER RANGE
373
Harms Lake
Caiguna
65
Cocklebiddy
NUYTSLAND NATURE RESERVE
Red Rocks Point

orseman
NULLARBOR PLAIN DRIVE
Lake Dundas
DUNDAS NATURE RESERVE
Mount Malcolm
Noondoonia
Woorlba
HWY
160
Twilight Cove
Scorpion Bight
Point Dover
7
33° 00'

Balladonia
22
Balladonia
Nanambinia
Mount Andrew
NUYTSLAND NATURE RESERVE
Toolinna Cove

SALMON GUMS NATURE RESERVE
on Gums
Mount Coobaninya
BALLADONIA
182
Mount Buraminya +
Point Culver
GREAT
AUSTRALIAN
BIGHT
8

03
Grass Patch
Mount Ridley
KAU NR
Mount Symmons +
Mount Dean
Mount Ragged

Scaddan
BEAUMONT GROUP NR
CAPE ARID NP
135
Israelite Bay
Point Dempster
34° 00'

Gibson
Warriup
Mount Baring +
RD
Point Malcolm
Daw Island
9

FISHERIES
Condingup
BEACHES
65
Mount Baring
Mount
Duke of Orleans Bay
Cape Pasley

Esperance
Hammer Head
Cape Arid
Sandy Bight
Middle Island

CAPE LE GRAND NATIONAL PARK
Salisbury Island
10
35° 00'

WARNINGS: In outback Australia, long distances separate some towns. Travellers should familiarise themselves with prevailing conditions before departure and take care to ensure their vehicle is roadworthy. Adequate supplies of petrol, water and food should be carried at all times.

In central Australia, rainfall can make some roads impassable, even with a 4WD vehicle. Full information on road conditions should be obtained from local authorities before departure.

If visitors intend diverting off public roads within Aboriginal Land areas, a permit is required from the relevant Aboriginal authority.

OCEAN
11
36° 00'

12

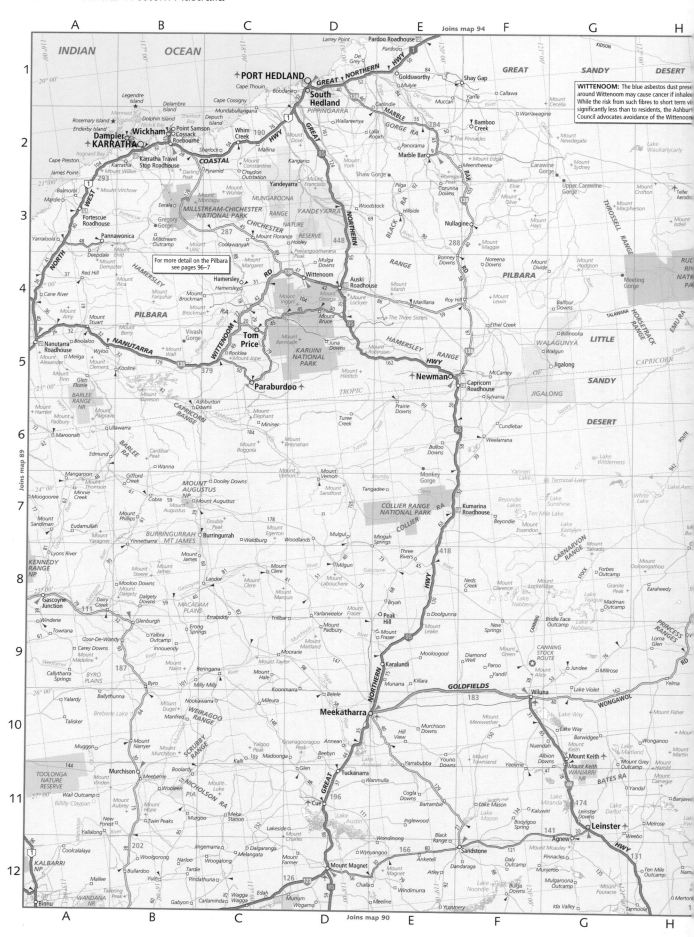

WITTENOOM: The blue asbestos dust prese around Wittenoom may cause cancer if inhalee While the risk from such fibres to short term vi significantly less than to residents, the Ashbur Council advocates avoidance of the Wittenoom

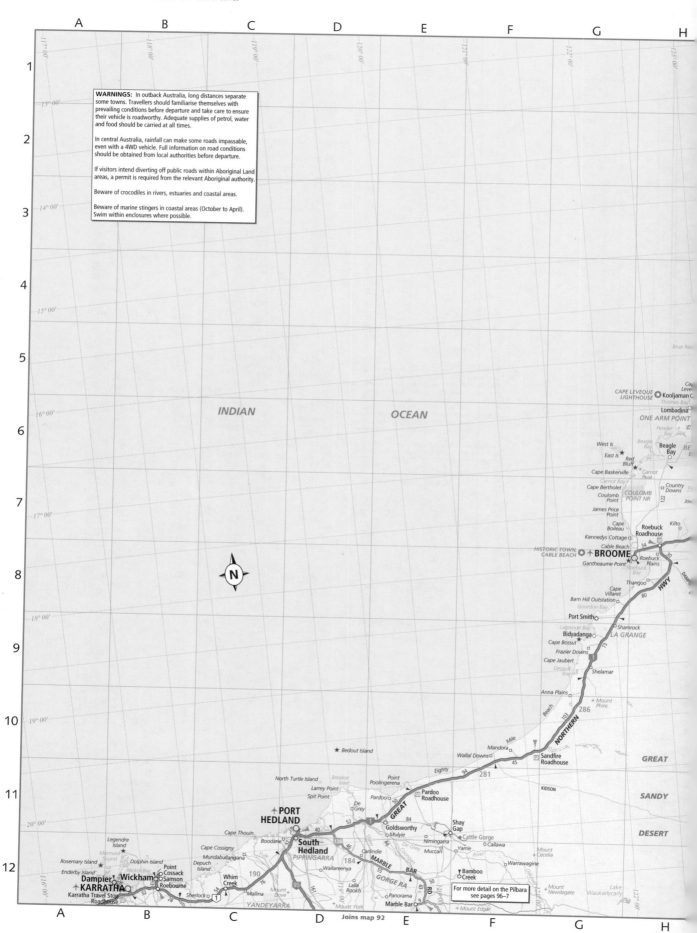

WARNINGS: In outback Australia, long distances separate some towns. Travellers should familiarise themselves with prevailing conditions before departure and take care to ensure their vehicle is roadworthy. Adequate supplies of petrol, water and food should be carried at all times.

In central Australia, rainfall can make some roads impassable, even with a 4WD vehicle. Full information on road conditions should be obtained from local authorities before departure.

If visitors intend diverting off public roads within Aboriginal Land areas, a permit is required from the relevant Aboriginal authority.

Beware of crocodiles in rivers, estuaries and coastal areas.

Beware of marine stingers in coastal areas (October to April). Swim within enclosures where possible.

INDIAN   OCEAN

N

For more detail on the Pilbara see pages 96–7

Joins map 92

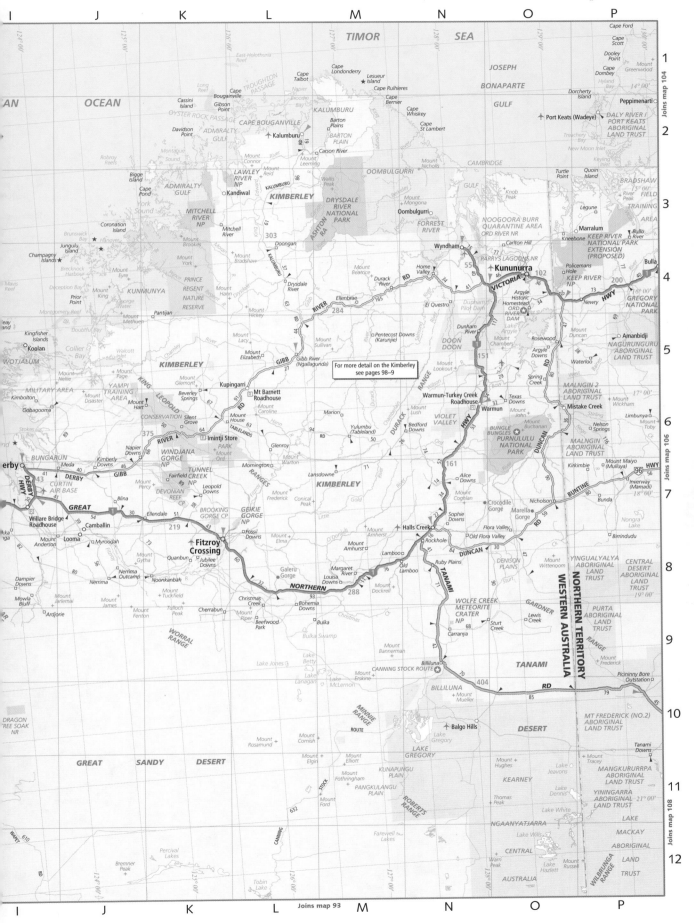

0   50   100   150   200 km

For more detail on the Kimberley
see pages 98–9

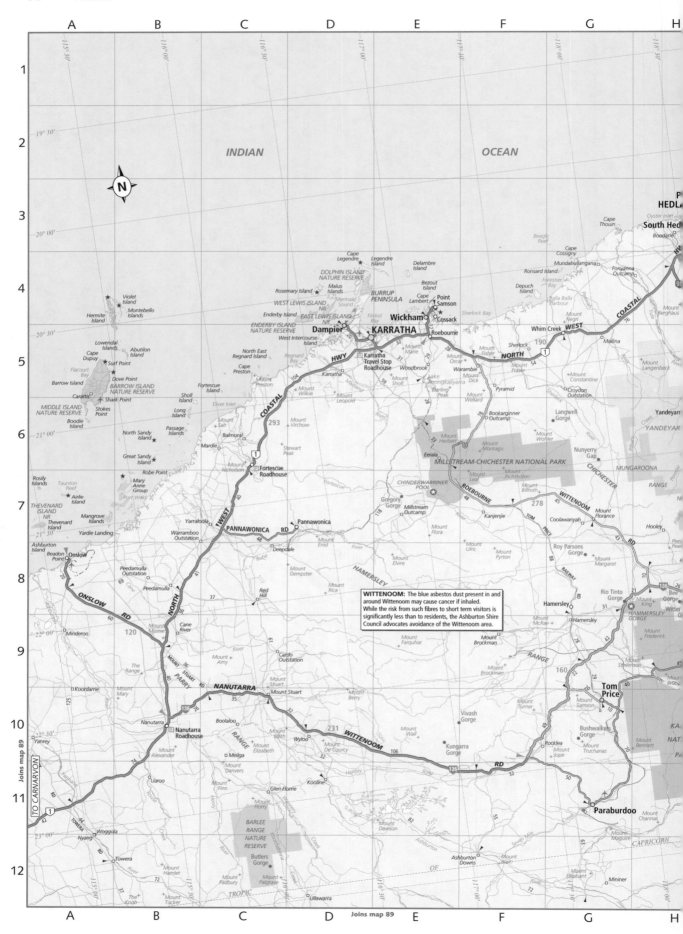

0 20 40 60 80 100 km

I J K L M N O P

Joins map 94

TO BROOME

Sandfire Roadhouse

Wallal Downs
Mile Beach
Mandora
45

Eighty
NORTHERN HWY 94
241
KIDSON

GREAT

Cape Keraudren
Pardoo Outcamp
Mount Blaze
Pardoo Roadhouse

SANDY

Point Poolingerena
Poissonnier Point
Cartaminia Point
Red Point
Pardoo

CAPE KERAUDREN RD
70
80

BORELINE
RD

DESERT

Breaker Inlet
Larrey Point
TRACK

GREAT
Ripon Island
De Grey

Goldsworthy
Mount Goldsworthy
84

Shay Gap
Cattle Gorge
Kennedy Gap

MARBLE
Mount Grant
Mulyie
Nimingarra

52
46
138

RD
RD

Callawa

Cundaline
Kimberley Gap
Muccan
Yarrie

Warrawagine

Carlindie
84
DeGrey
WARRAWAGINE RD

WOODIE WOODIE

GORGE
RANGE
RD
144
55

Wallareenya

Kittys Gap
Coppin Gap
Talga Peak
50

RIPON

GREGORY

Lalla Rookh

Doolena Peak
Doolena Gap
Bamboo Creek
The Pinnacles

Mount Newdegate

Panorama
The Sisters

RANGE

HILLS

Mount York
Strelley Gorge
9
Marble Bar
Limestone
Warrawoona Peak
Meentheena
Mount Edgar

RD
RD
Mount Sydney

TELFER

Lake Waukarlycarly

Glacier Valley
The Island Hill
92

Horrigan Peak

Carawine Gorge

MINE
RD

Mount Crofton

Shaw Gorge
Old Corunna Downs
Corunna Downs

MARBLE

Upper Carawine Gorge

THROSSELL

Pilga
Warrery Gap

RANGE
Emu

Mount Elsie

RD

103

Mount Olive
Mount Macpherson

Woodstock
Mount Webber
Hillside

138
BAR

SKULL
SPRINGS
Hallcomes Peak
Mount Hays

RANGE

NORTHERN
69

Beaton Gorge
201
Nullagine

Mount Cooke

PILBARA
BLACK

90

40

Mount Maggie

Mount Rudall

HWY
95

RANGE

Bonney Downs
Noreena Downs
Mount Hodgson

Meeting Gorge

RUDALL RIVER

Warrie
58

RD

Mount Divide

NATIONAL

Mount McKay

PARK

Auski Roadhouse
MUNJINA
Mount Lockyer
86
145
ROY HILL RD
Marillana
59

Lynn Peak
Roy Hill

Mount Marsh
Mount Lewin

Balfour Downs

HORSTRACK RANGE

TRACK

Munjina Gorge
DALES GORGE
95
35

HAMERSLEY

The Three Sisters

Ethel Creek

Talawana
Talawana
LITTLE

Mount Windell

RANGE
Marillana Creek

87

WALAGUNYA

Mount Meharry
34

WEELI WOLLI SPRING
HANCOCK RANGE
RANGE
89
PUNDA POOL

Billinooka

SANDY

Mount Robinson
WANNA MUNNA ROCK ART SITE
EAGLE ROCK FALLS
KALGANS POOL

Walgun

GREAT
The Governor
90
194 NORTHERN HWY
35
Cathedral Gorge

BAR
138

CAPRICORN

Mount Ella
Mount Newman
Jigalong

Spearhole

Newman
Ophthalmia Dam
McCamey

OF

DESERT

TROPIC
Capricorn Roadhouse
Sylvania

JIGALONG

Turee Creek
50
Prairie Downs
69

Cundlebar

95
TO MEEKATHARRA
Weelarrana

I J K L M N O P

Joins map 92

WARNINGS: In outback Australia, long distances separate some towns. Travellers should familiarise themselves with prevailing conditions before departure and take care to ensure their vehicle is roadworthy. Adequate supplies of petrol, water and food should be carried at all times.

In central Australia, rainfall can make some roads impassable, even with a 4WD vehicle. Full information on road conditions should be obtained from local authorities before departure.

If visitors intend diverting off public roads within Aboriginal Land areas, a permit is required from the relevant Aboriginal authority.

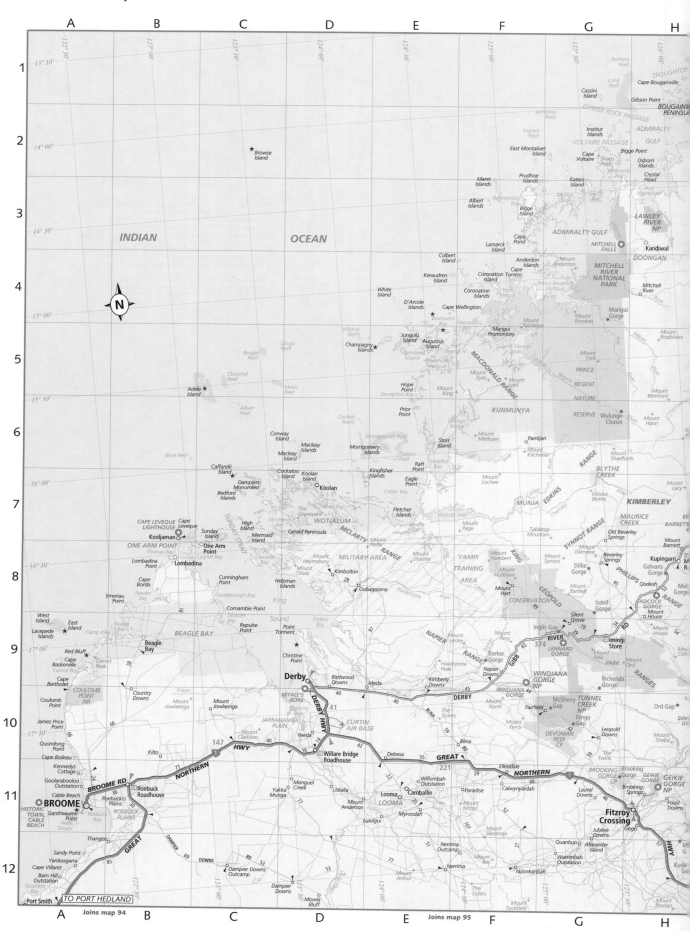

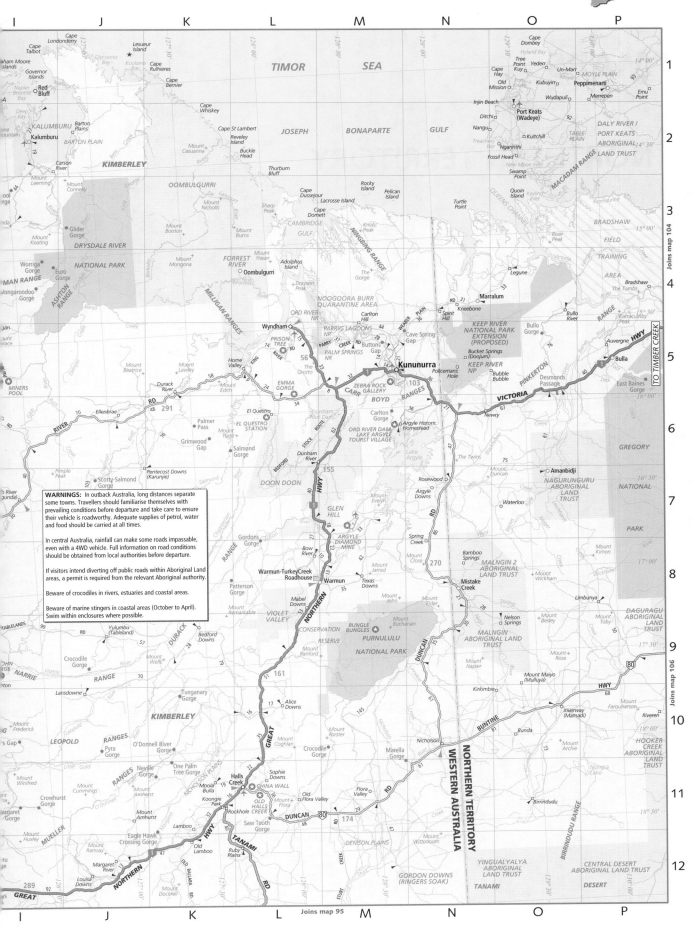

MAPS

NORTHERN TERRITORY

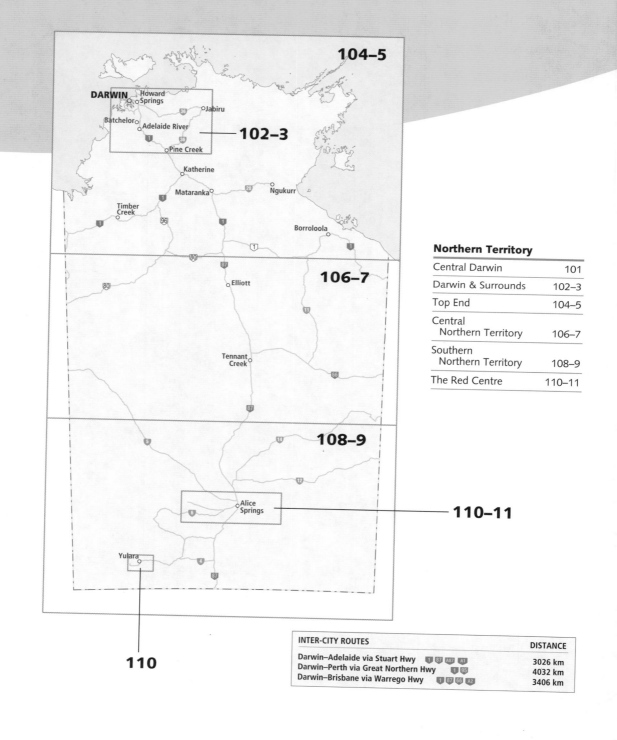

104–5

102–3

106–7

108–9

110–11

110

Northern Territory

Central Darwin	101
Darwin & Surrounds	102–3
Top End	104–5
Central Northern Territory	106–7
Southern Northern Territory	108–9
The Red Centre	110–11

INTER-CITY ROUTES		DISTANCE
Darwin–Adelaide via Stuart Hwy		3026 km
Darwin–Perth via Great Northern Hwy		4032 km
Darwin–Brisbane via Warrego Hwy		3406 km

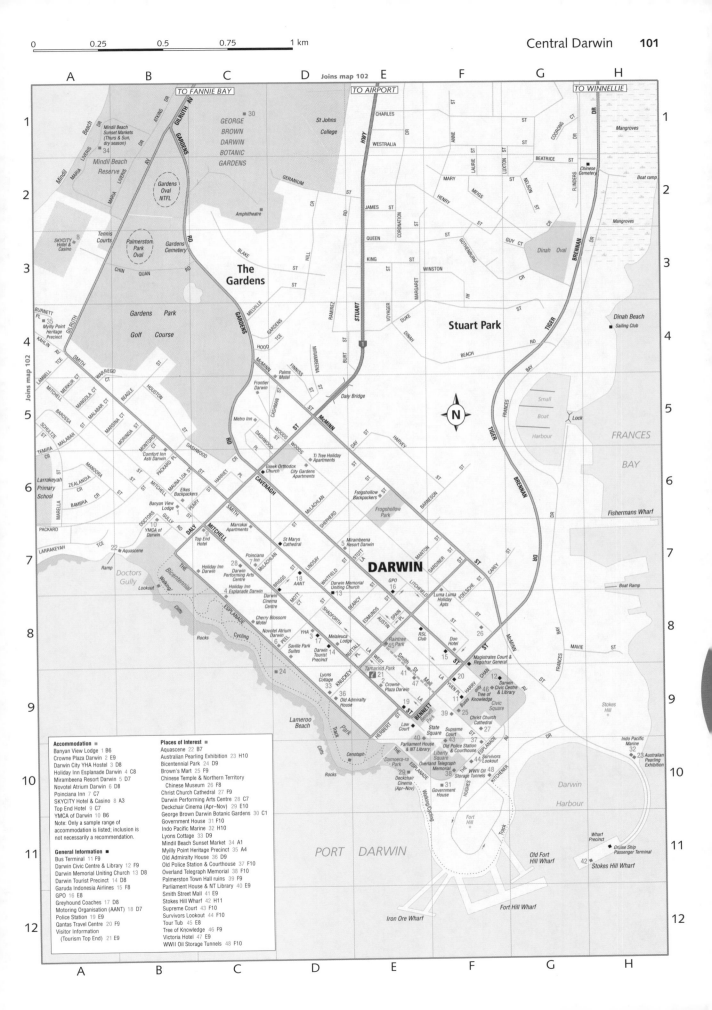

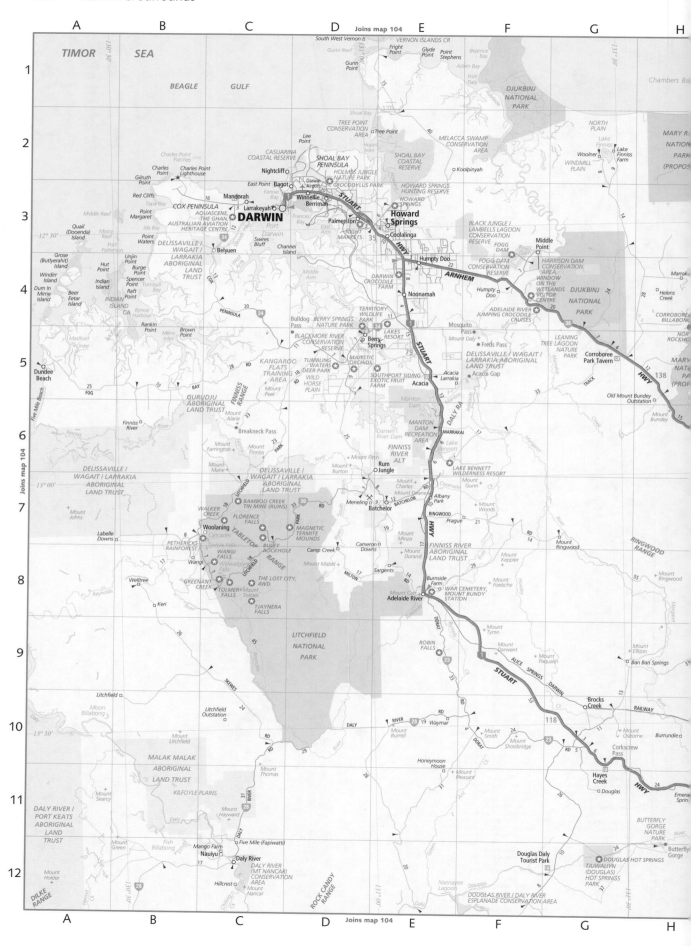

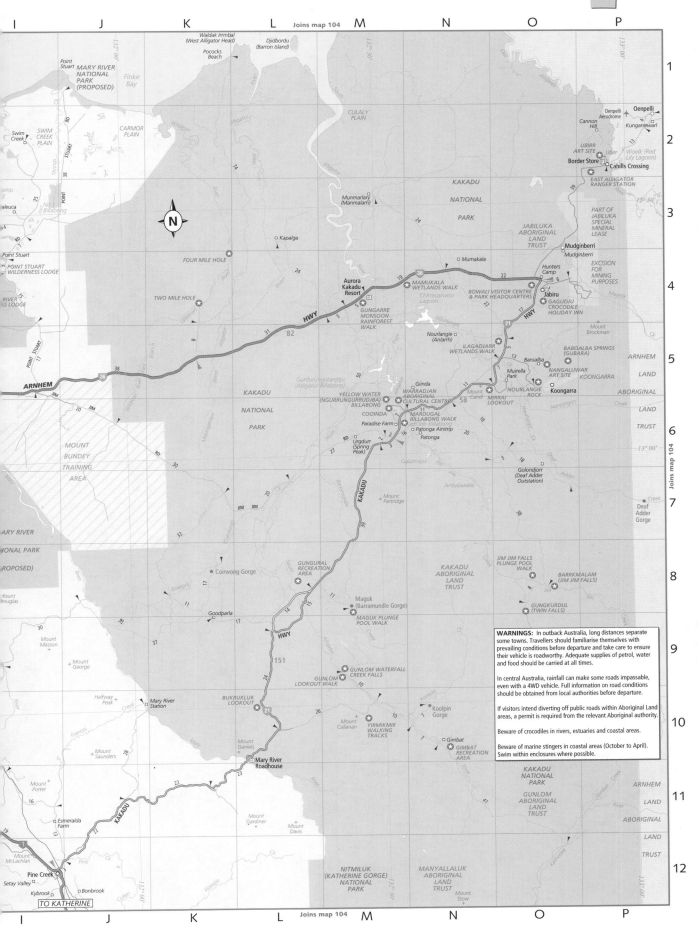

0   10   20   30   40 km

I   J   K   L   M   N   O   P

WARNINGS: In outback Australia, long distances separate some towns. Travellers should familiarise themselves with prevailing conditions before departure and take care to ensure their vehicle is roadworthy. Adequate supplies of petrol, water and food should be carried at all times.

In central Australia, rainfall can make some roads impassable, even with a 4WD vehicle. Full information on road conditions should be obtained from local authorities before departure.

If visitors intend diverting off public roads within Aboriginal Land areas, a permit is required from the relevant Aboriginal authority.

Beware of crocodiles in rivers, estuaries and coastal areas.

Beware of marine stingers in coastal areas (October to April). Swim within enclosures where possible.

I   J   K   L   M   N   O   P

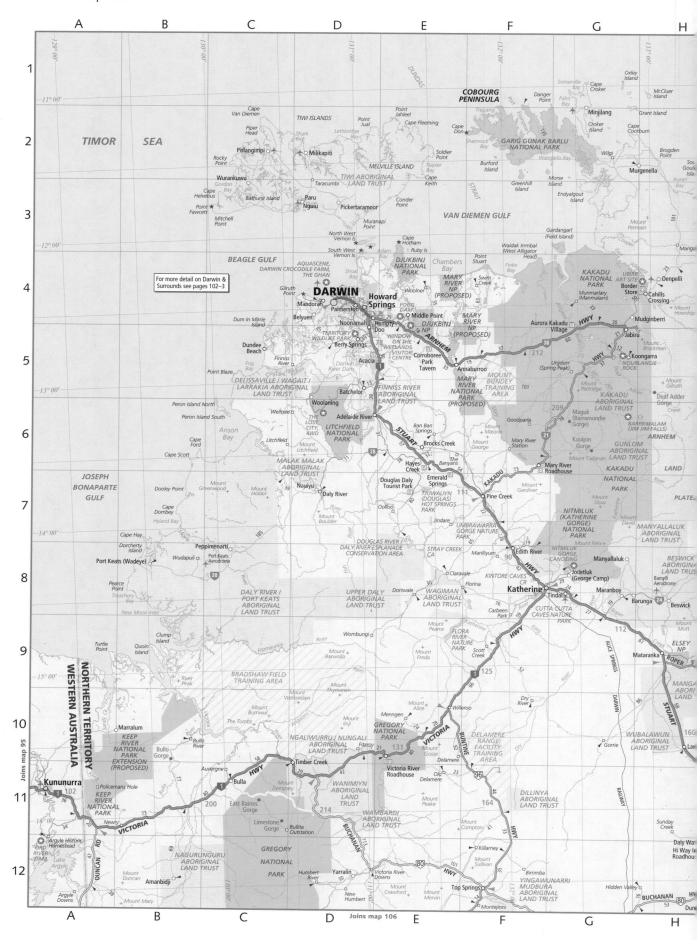

For more detail on Darwin & Surrounds see pages 102–3

Joins map 95

Joins map 106

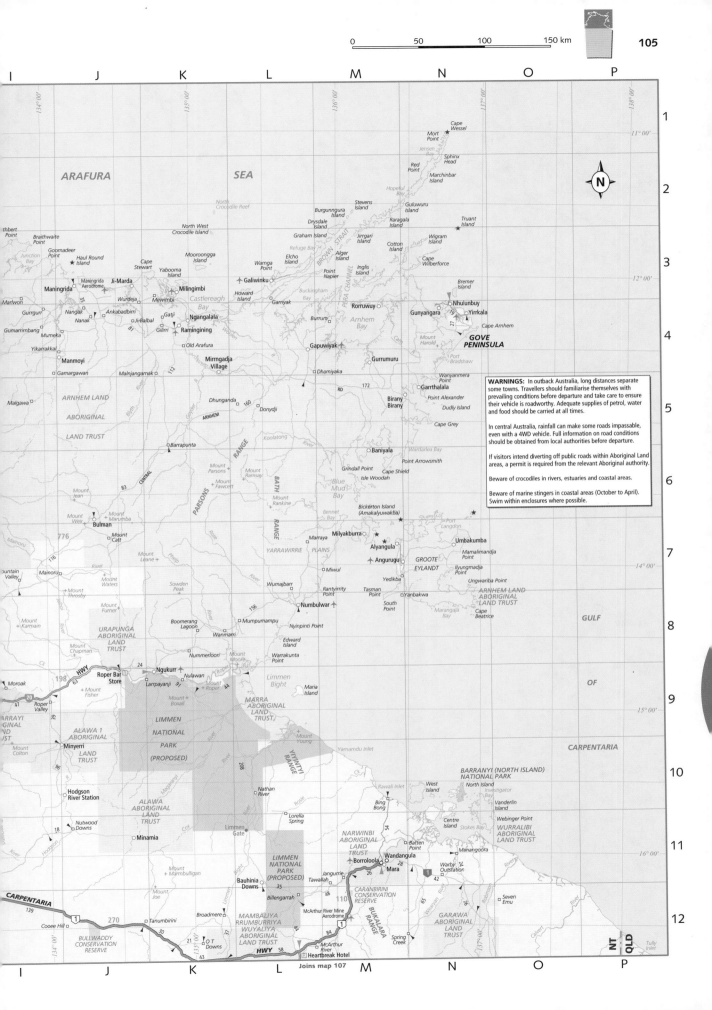

0 50 100 150 km

105

WARNINGS: In outback Australia, long distances separate some towns. Travellers should familiarise themselves with prevailing conditions before departure and take care to ensure their vehicle is roadworthy. Adequate supplies of petrol, water and food should be carried at all times.

In central Australia, rainfall can make some roads impassable, even with a 4WD vehicle. Full information on road conditions should be obtained from local authorities before departure.

If visitors intend diverting off public roads within Aboriginal Land areas, a permit is required from the relevant Aboriginal authority.

Beware of crocodiles in rivers, estuaries and coastal areas.

Beware of marine stingers in coastal areas (October to April). Swim within enclosures where possible.

Joins map 107

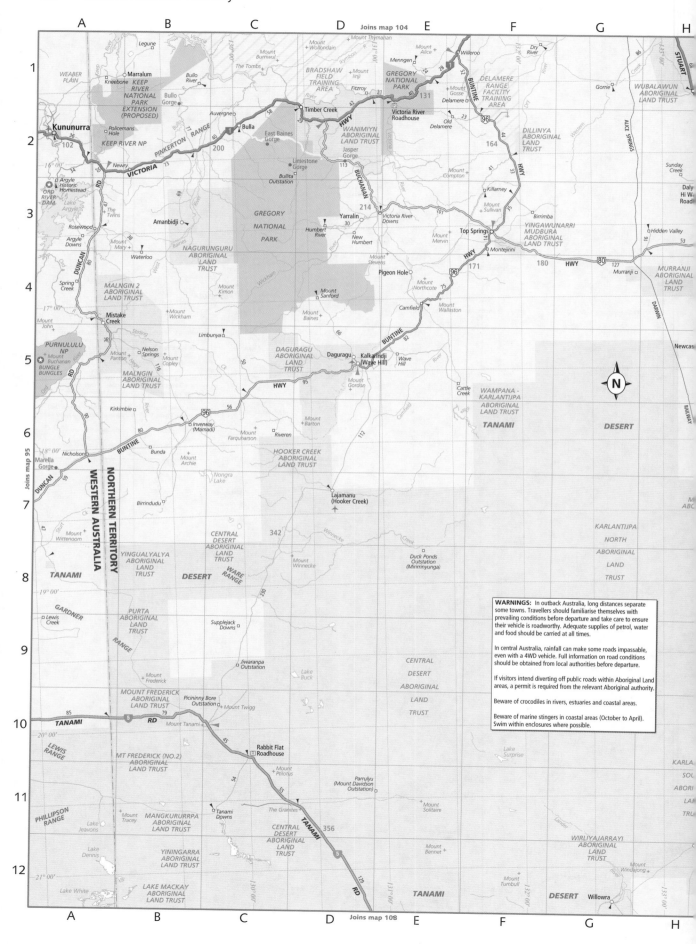

WARNINGS: In outback Australia, long distances separate some towns. Travellers should familiarise themselves with prevailing conditions before departure and take care to ensure their vehicle is roadworthy. Adequate supplies of petrol, water and food should be carried at all times.

In central Australia, rainfall can make some roads impassable, even with a 4WD vehicle. Full information on road conditions should be obtained from local authorities before departure.

If visitors intend diverting off public roads within Aboriginal Land areas, a permit is required from the relevant Aboriginal authority.

Beware of crocodiles in rivers, estuaries and coastal areas.

Beware of marine stingers in coastal areas (October to April). Swim within enclosures where possible.

0 50 100 150 km

Joins map 105

I J K L M N O P

ARAFURA SEA

Minyerri
ALAWA 1 ABORIGINAL LAND TRUST
Hodgson River Station
LIMMEN NATIONAL PARK (PROPOSED)
VIYINTYI RANGE
Yarnamdu Inlet
BARRANYI (NORTH ISLAND) NATIONAL PARK
GULF OF CARPENTARIA

Nutwood Downs
ALAWA ABORIGINAL LAND TRUST
Minamia
Nathan River
Lorella Spring
Rawali Inlet
West Island
North Island
Centre Island
Vanderlin Island
WURRALIBI ABORIGINAL LAND TRUST

Mount Marmbulligan
Limmen Gate
LIMMEN NATIONAL PARK (PROPOSED)
Billengarrah
Bing Bong
Batten Point
Stokes Bay

Mount Joe
Bauhinia Downs
NARWINBI ABORIGINAL LAND TRUST
Borroloola
Wandangula
Mara
Manangoora
Seven Emu

CARPENTARIA
Cooee Hill
Tanumbirini
Broadmere
Jangurrie
Tawallah
CARANBIRINI CONSERVATION RESERVE
BUKALARA RANGE
Warby Outstation

BULLWADDY CONSERVATION RESERVE
O T Downs
McArthur River Mine Aerodrome
McArthur River
Heartbreak Hotel
Spring Creek
GARAWA ABORIGINAL LAND TRUST
Robinson River

Beetaloo
MAMBALIYA RRUMBURRIYA WUYALIYA ABORIGINAL LAND TRUST
Mallapunyah
Kiana
Calvert Hills
Echo Gorge
Wollogorang Roadhouse
Westmoreland

BARKLY TABLELAND
Ucharonidge
Mungabroom
Walhallow
Bamadjina Claypan

Renner Springs
STOCK Eva Downs
ROUTE Anthony Lagoon
Cresswell Downs
CALVERT
Benmara
WAANYI / GARAWA ABORIGINAL LAND TRUST
BOODJAMULLA (LAWN HILL) NATIONAL PARK

Helen Springs
BARKLY JUNCTION RESERVE
Tarrabool Lake
Creswell
Caulfield Clay Flats
Murun Murula

Muckaty
Banka Banka Outstation
Corella Lake
Lake Sylvester
Ngunarra
RANKEN
CONNELLS LAGOON CONSERVATION RESERVE
Mount Morgan
Mittiebah
New Herbert Vale
Old Herbert Vale

Kalumpurlpa
Brunchilly
Rockhampton Downs
Lake De Burgh
WARUMUNGU ABORIGINAL LAND TRUST
TABLELANDS
Playford
MITTIEBAH RANGE
Alexandria
BARKLY TABLELAND
Gallipoli

Phillip Creek
Wogyala
KURNTURLPARA ABORIGINAL LAND TRUST
Alroy Downs
Norfolk
No 3 Outstation
Morstone

Three Ways Roadhouse
Likkaparta
BARKLY
Mount Lamb
Kerringnew Swamp
BURUDU ABORIGINAL LAND TRUST
Warrego
Tennant Creek
Barkly Homestead
Dalmore Downs
Oolgoolgarri Swamp
GULANGULU ABORIGINAL LAND TRUST
Camooweal

WARUMUNGU ABORIGINAL LAND TRUST
WAKAYA ABORIGINAL LAND TRUST
UDOONGUL ABORIGINAL LAND TRUST
Soudan
Avon Downs
CAMOOWEAL CAVES NP
Don

MUNGKARTA ABORIGINAL LAND TRUST
Mungkarta
Kalinjarri
Kurundi
Mount Cairns
Kurinelli Outstation
Wutunugurra
Canteen Creek
Old Wooroona
Wooroona

DEVIL'S MARBLES CR
DEVILS MARBLES
Wauchope
Singleton
DAVENPORT RANGE NATIONAL PARK (PROPOSED)
ANURRETE ABORIGINAL LAND TRUST
Austral Downs
Mount Michael
Arcadia
Bullecourt

Wycliffe Well Roadhouse
Ali-Curung
Imangara
Hatches Creek
RANGE
Elkedra
Lake Nash
Alpurrurulam
Georgina

WARRABRI ABORIGINAL LAND TRUST
OSBORNE RA
Mount Strzelecki
Mount Morphett
Elkedra
Mount Alone
Annitowa
SANDOVER
HWY

NORTHERN TERRITORY
QUEENSLAND

Joins map 129
Joins map 130
Joins map 109

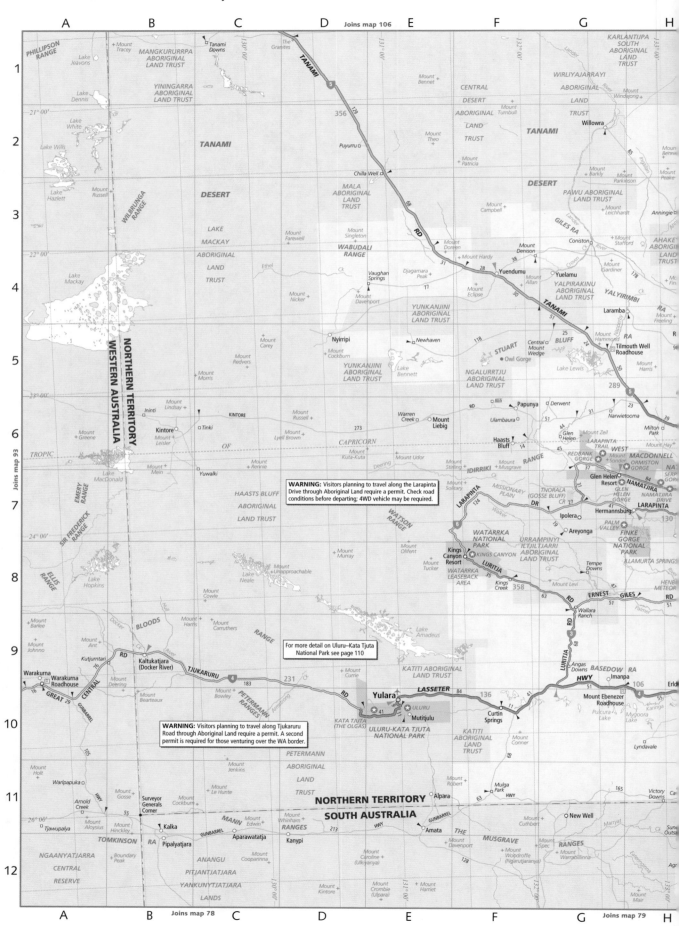

Joins map 106

Joins map 93

WARNING: Visitors planning to travel along the Larapinta Drive through Aboriginal Land require a permit. Check road conditions before departing; 4WD vehicle may be required.

For more detail on Uluru–Kata Tjuta National Park see page 110

WARNING: Visitors planning to travel along Tjukaruru Road through Aboriginal Land require a permit. A second permit is required for those venturing over the WA border.

NORTHERN TERRITORY
SOUTH AUSTRALIA

Joins map 78

Joins map 79

0   50   100   150 km

Joins map 107

WARNINGS: In outback Australia, long distances separate some towns. Travellers should familiarise themselves with prevailing conditions before departure and take care to ensure their vehicle is roadworthy. Adequate supplies of petrol, water and food should be carried at all times.

In central Australia, rainfall can make some roads impassable, even with a 4WD vehicle. Full information on road conditions should be obtained from local authorities before departure.

If visitors intend diverting off public roads within Aboriginal Land areas, a permit is required from the relevant Aboriginal authority.

For more detail on Alice Springs & the MacDonnell Ranges see page 110–11

Joins map 76

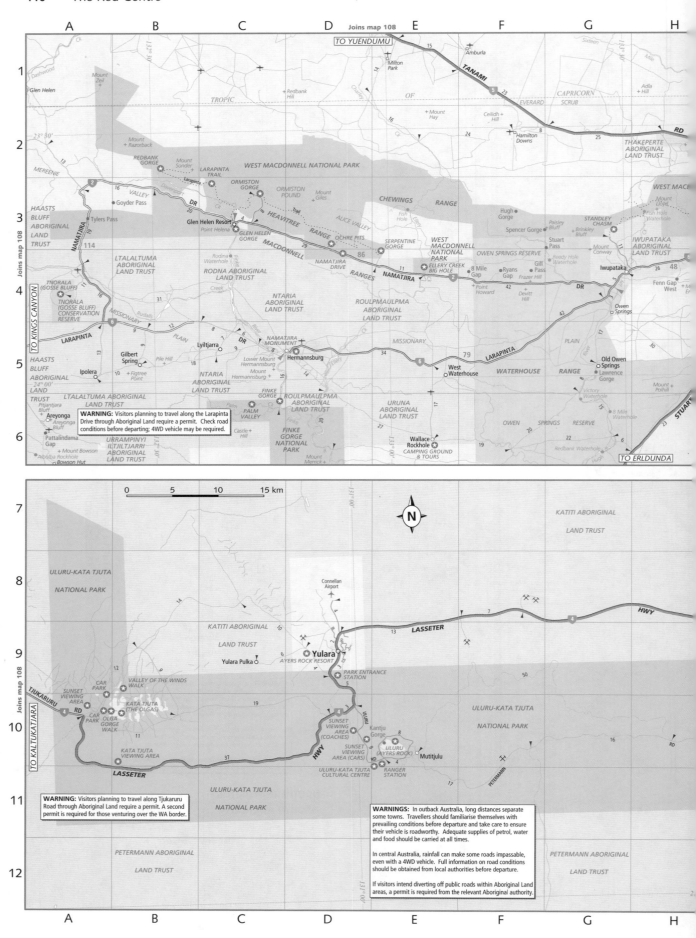

Joins map 108

Joins map 108

WARNING: Visitors planning to travel along the Larapinta Drive through Aboriginal Land require a permit. Check road conditions before departing; 4WD vehicle may be required.

WARNING: Visitors planning to travel along Tjukaruru Road through Aboriginal Land require a permit. A second permit is required for those venturing over the WA border.

WARNINGS: In outback Australia, long distances separate some towns. Travellers should familiarise themselves with prevailing conditions before departure and take care to ensure their vehicle is roadworthy. Adequate supplies of petrol, water and food should be carried at all times.

In central Australia, rainfall can make some roads impassable, even with a 4WD vehicle. Full information on road conditions should be obtained from local authorities before departure.

If visitors intend diverting off public roads within Aboriginal Land areas, a permit is required from the relevant Aboriginal authority.

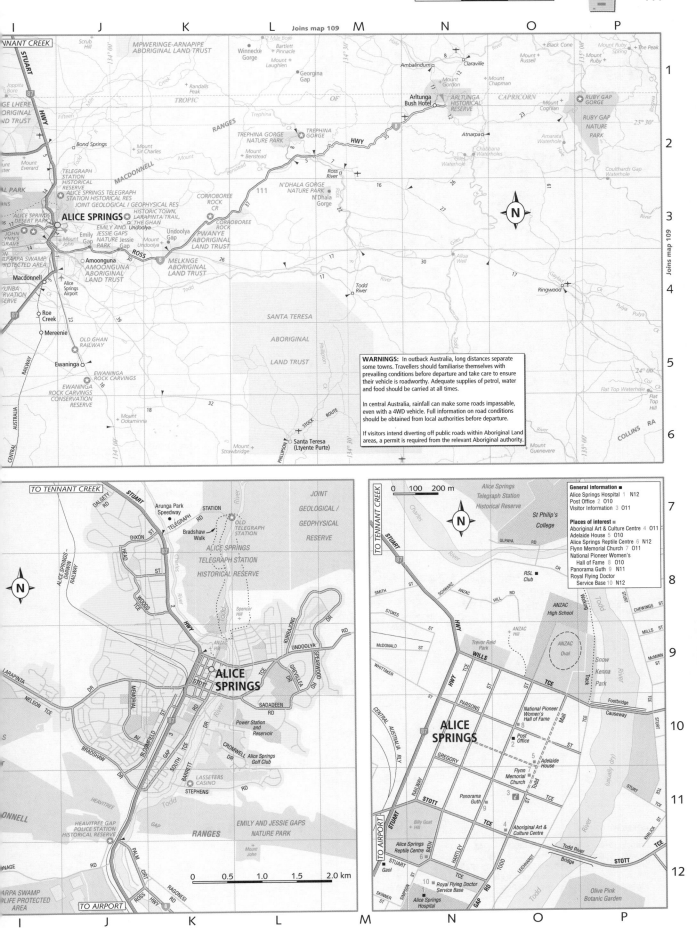

MAPS

QUEENSLAND

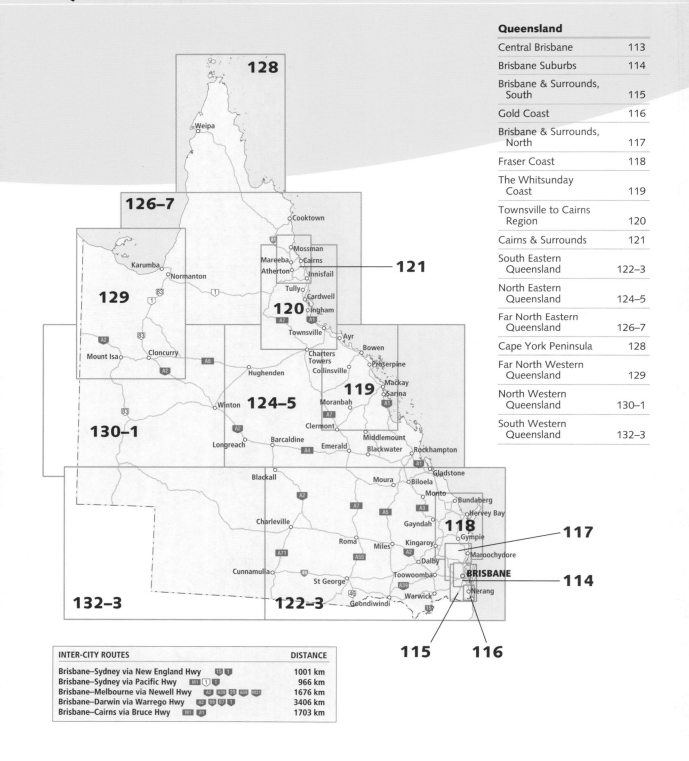

Queensland

Central Brisbane	113
Brisbane Suburbs	114
Brisbane & Surrounds, South	115
Gold Coast	116
Brisbane & Surrounds, North	117
Fraser Coast	118
The Whitsunday Coast	119
Townsville to Cairns Region	120
Cairns & Surrounds	121
South Eastern Queensland	122–3
North Eastern Queensland	124–5
Far North Eastern Queensland	126–7
Cape York Peninsula	128
Far North Western Queensland	129
North Western Queensland	130–1
South Western Queensland	132–3

INTER-CITY ROUTES	DISTANCE
Brisbane–Sydney via New England Hwy	1001 km
Brisbane–Sydney via Pacific Hwy	966 km
Brisbane–Melbourne via Newell Hwy	1676 km
Brisbane–Darwin via Warrego Hwy	3406 km
Brisbane–Cairns via Bruce Hwy	1703 km

0   0.25   0.5   0.75   1 km

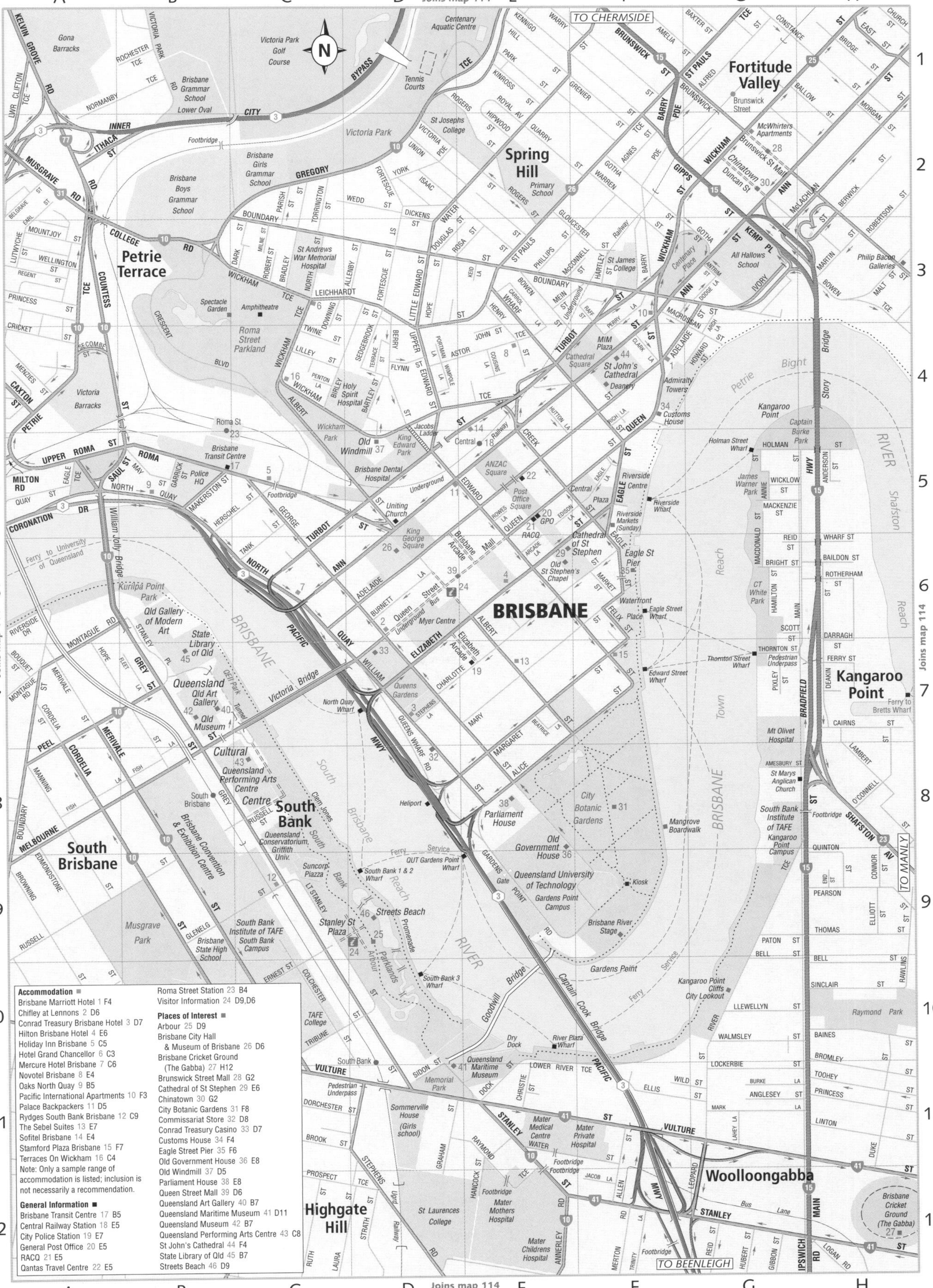

Joins map 114

Fortitude Valley

Spring Hill

Petrie Terrace

BRISBANE

Kangaroo Point

South Bank

South Brisbane

Highgate Hill

Woolloongabba

TO CHERMSIDE
TO MANLY
TO BEENLEIGH

Joins map 114

Brisbane Cricket Ground (The Gabba) 27

Accommodation
Brisbane Marriott Hotel 1 F4
Chifley at Lennons 2 D6
Conrad Treasury Brisbane Hotel 3 D7
Hilton Brisbane Hotel 4 E6
Holiday Inn Brisbane 5 C5
Hotel Grand Chancellor 6 C3
Mercure Hotel Brisbane 7 C6
Novotel Brisbane 8 E4
Oaks North Quay 9 B5
Pacific International Apartments 10 F3
Palace Backpackers 11 D5
Rydges South Bank Brisbane 12 C9
The Sebel Suites 13 E7
Sofitel Brisbane 14 E4
Stamford Plaza Brisbane 15 F7
Terraces On Wickham 16 C4
Note: Only a sample range of accommodation is listed; inclusion is not necessarily a recommendation.

General Information
Brisbane Transit Centre 17 B5
Central Railway Station 18 E5
City Police Station 19 E7
General Post Office 20 E5
RACQ 21 E5
Qantas Travel Centre 22 E5
Roma Street Station 23 B4
Visitor Information 24 D9,D6

Places of Interest
Arbour 25 D9
Brisbane City Hall & Museum of Brisbane 26 D6
Brisbane Cricket Ground (The Gabba) 27 H12
Brunswick Street Mall 28 G2
Cathedral of St Stephen 29 E6
Chinatown 30 G2
City Botanic Gardens 31 F8
Commissariat Store 32 D8
Conrad Treasury Casino 33 D7
Customs House 34 F4
Eagle Street Pier 35 F6
Old Government House 36 E8
Old Windmill 37 D5
Parliament House 38 E8
Queen Street Mall 39 D6
Queensland Art Gallery 40 B7
Queensland Maritime Museum 41 D11
Queensland Museum 42 B7
Queensland Performing Arts Centre 43 C8
St John's Cathedral 44 F4
State Library of Qld 45 B7
Streets Beach 46 D9

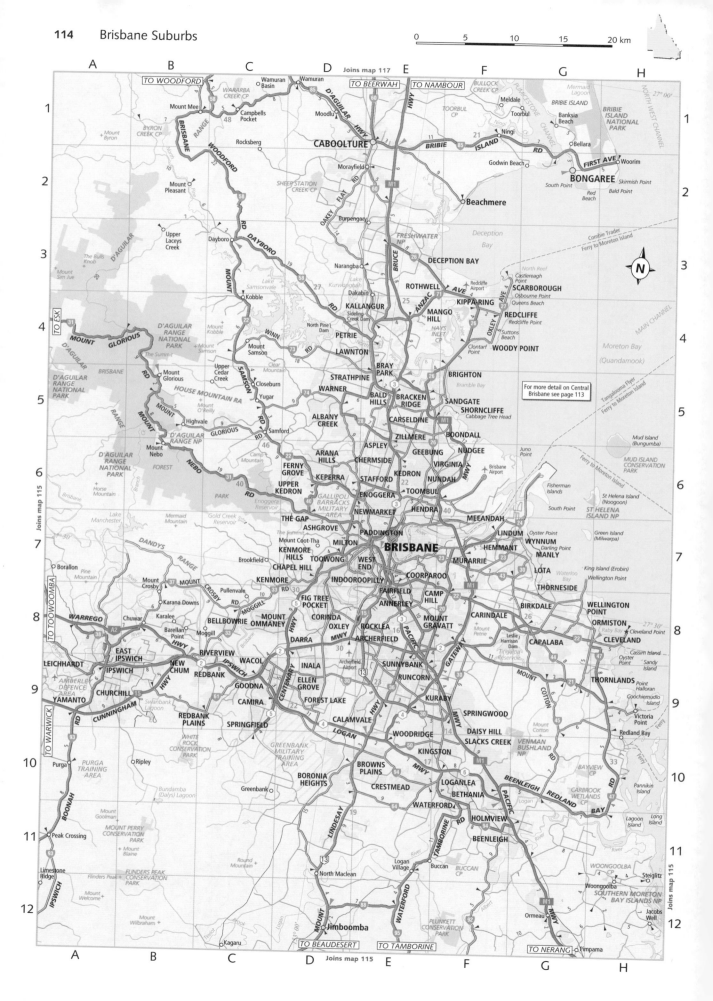

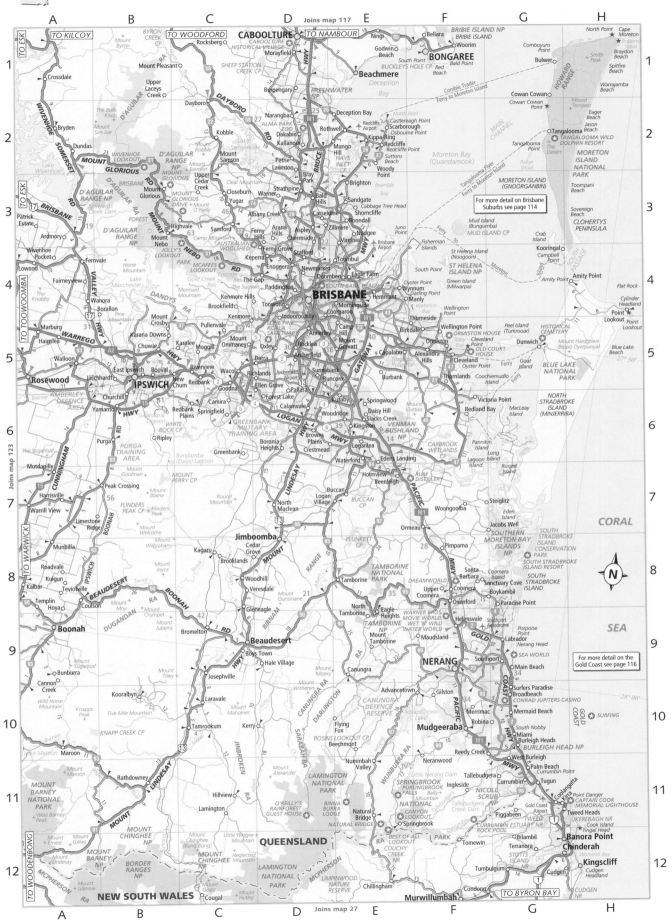

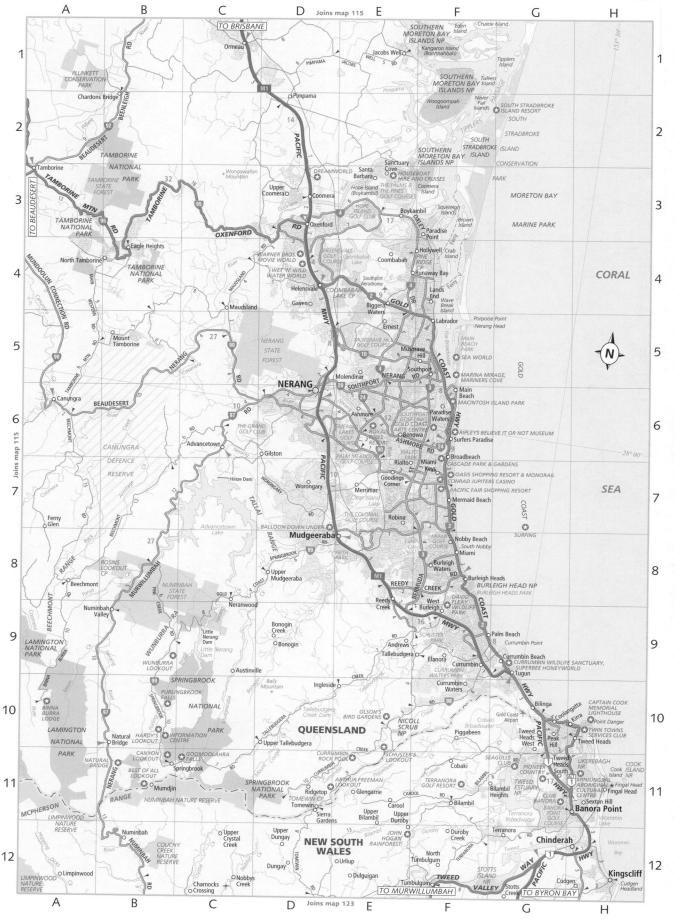

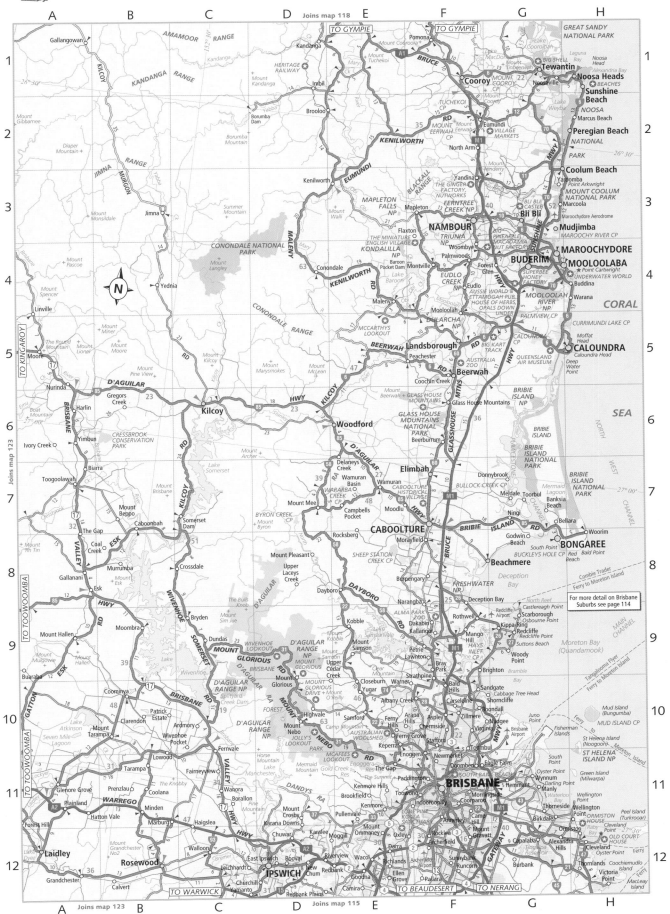

Joins map 118
Joins map 123
Joins map 115

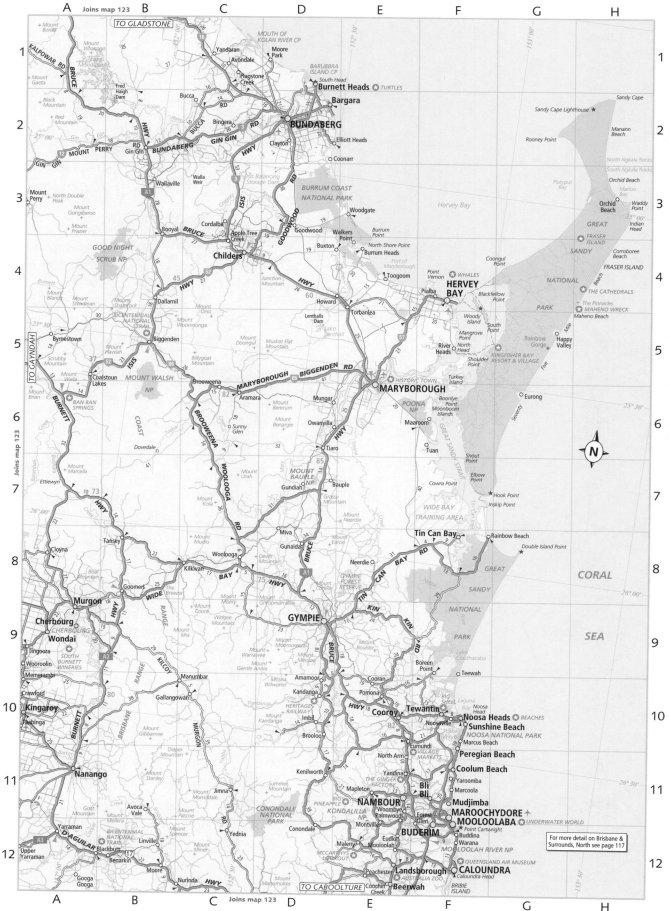

0   10   20   30   40   50 km

TO GLADSTONE

TO GAYNDAH

Joins map 123

TO CABOOLTURE

For more detail on Brisbane & Surrounds, North see page 117

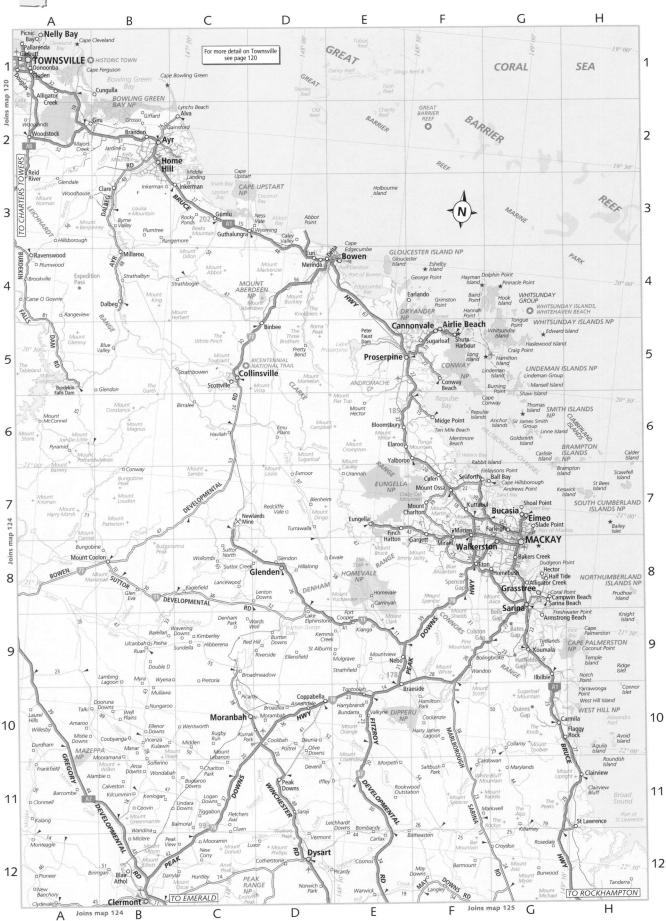

For more detail on Townsville see page 120

0   20   40   60   80   100 km

Joins map 120

Joins map 124

Joins map 124

Joins map 125

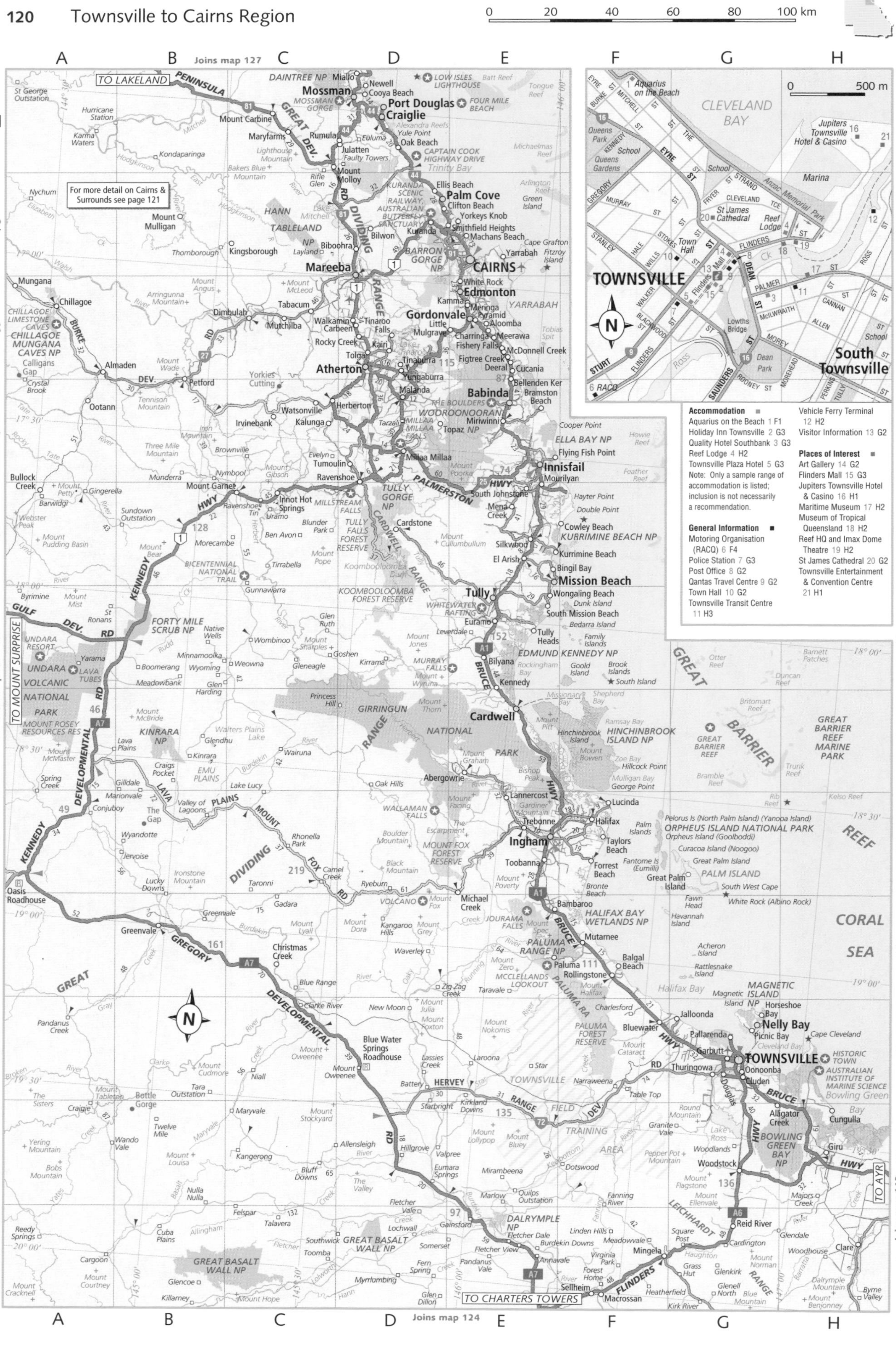

0 20 40 60 80 100 km

TOWNSVILLE (inset map)

0 500 m

N

CLEVELAND BAY

South Townsville

Accommodation
Aquarius on the Beach 1 F1
Holiday Inn Townsville 2 G3
Quality Hotel Southbank 3 G3
Reef Lodge 4 H2
Townsville Plaza Hotel 5 G3
Note: Only a sample range of accommodation is listed; inclusion is not necessarily a recommendation.

General Information
Motoring Organisation (RACQ) 6 F4
Police Station 7 G3
Post Office 8 G2
Qantas Travel Centre 9 G2
Town Hall 10 G2
Townsville Transit Centre 11 H3

Vehicle Ferry Terminal 12 H2
Visitor Information 13 G2

Places of Interest
Art Gallery 14 G2
Flinders Mall 15 G3
Jupiters Townsville Hotel & Casino 16 H1
Maritime Museum 17 H2
Museum of Tropical Queensland 18 H2
Reef HQ and Imax Dome Theatre 19 H2
St James Cathedral 20 G2
Townsville Entertainment & Convention Centre 21 H1

TO LAKELAND
Joins map 127
PENINSULA DEV RD
GREAT DIVIDING RANGE
DAINTREE NP
Mossman
Port Douglas
Craiglie
Palm Cove
CAIRNS
Mareeba
Atherton
Gordonvale
Edmonton
Babinda
Innisfail
Mission Beach
Tully
Cardwell
Ingham
Halifax
Lucinda
Paluma
Rollingstone
Nelly Bay
TOWNSVILLE
Thuringowa
Greenvale
Oasis Roadhouse
GULF DEV RD
KENNEDY DEV RD
GREGORY DEVELOPMENTAL RD
GREAT DIVIDING RANGE
BRUCE HWY
FLINDERS HWY
TO CHARTERS TOWERS
Joins map 124
Joins map 119
TO AYR

CORAL SEA
GREAT BARRIER REEF MARINE PARK
MAGNETIC ISLAND
ORPHEUS ISLAND NATIONAL PARK
HINCHINBROOK ISLAND NP
BOWLING GREEN BAY NP

N

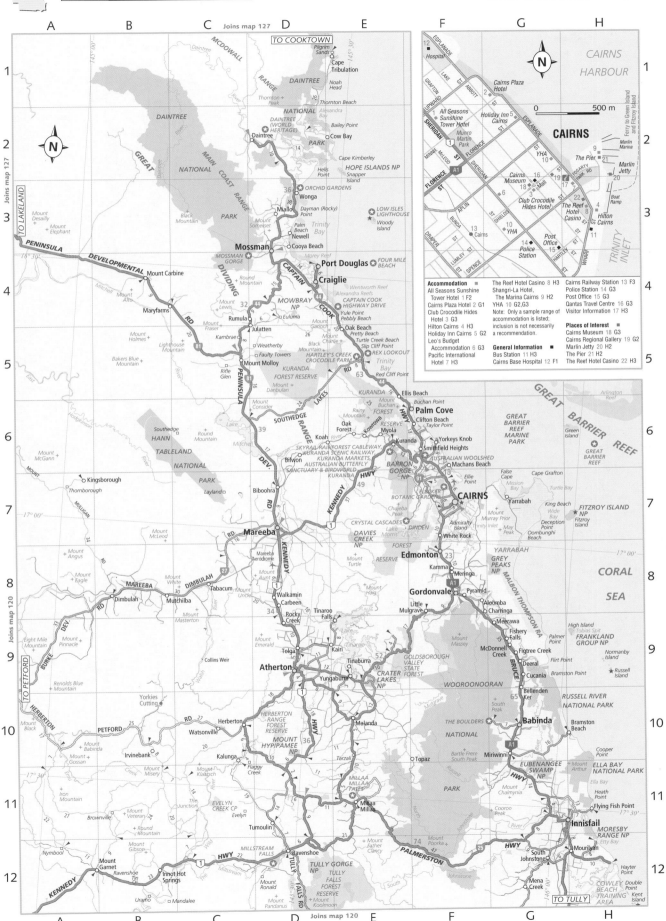

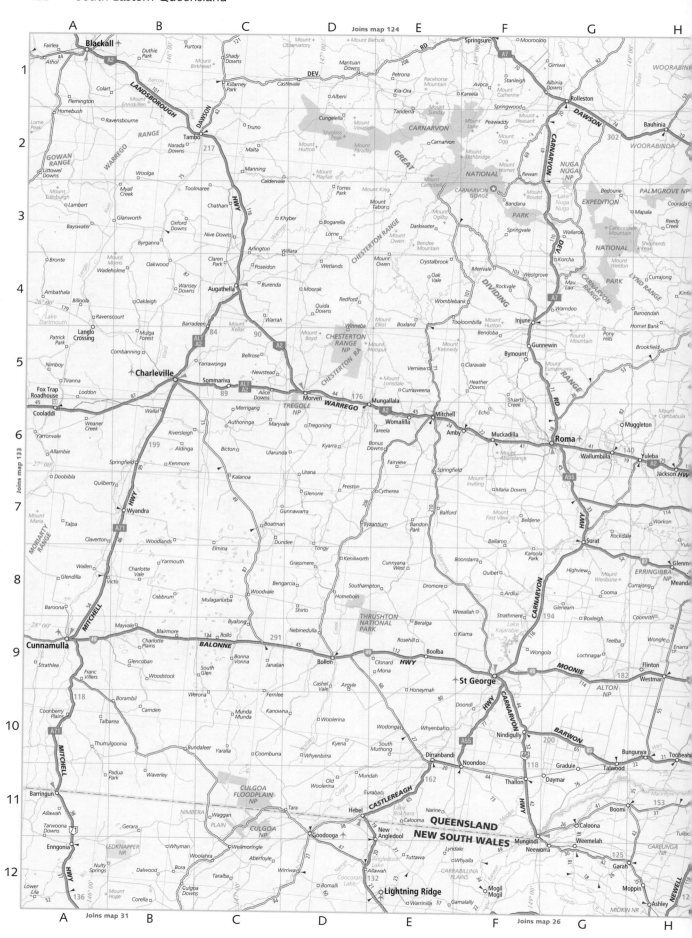

Joins map 124
Joins map 31
Joins map 26
Joins map 133

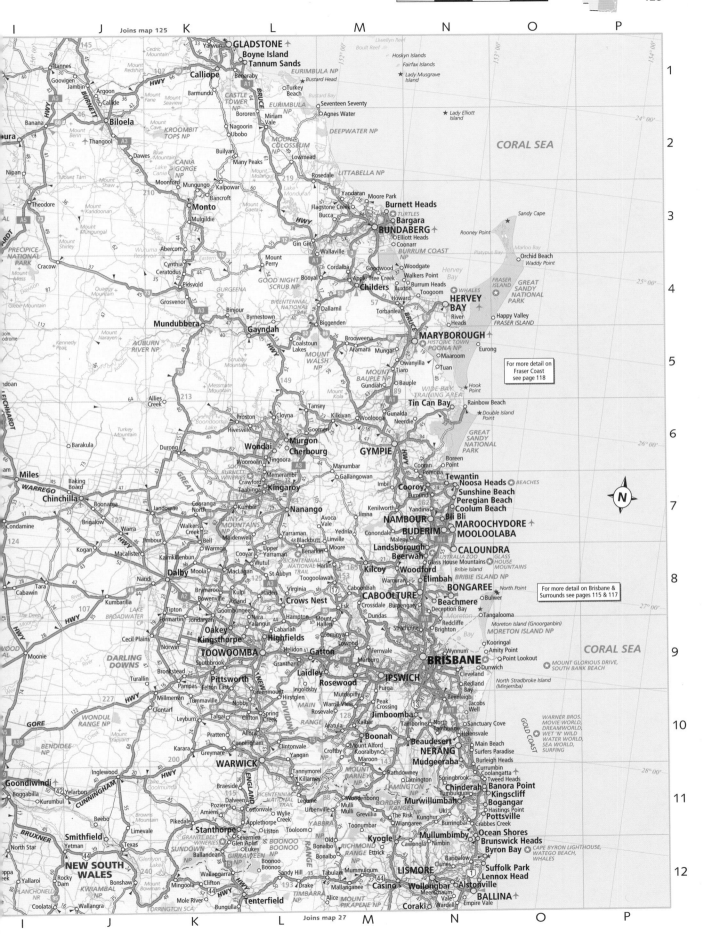

0 25 50 75 100 km

I   **J**   **K**   **L**   **M**   **N**   **O**   **P**

Joins map 125

1

2

3

4

5

6

7

8

9

10

11

12

CORAL SEA

GLADSTONE
Boyne Island
Tannum Sands
Calliope
Benaraby
Yarwun

Argoon
Calide
Biloela
Banana

Theodore

Nipan

Cracow

PRECIPICE
NATIONAL
PARK

Miles

Chinchilla
WARREGO

Condamine

Tara
Cabawin

Moonie

GORE

BENDIDEE
NP

Goondiwindi
Boggabilla
Kurumbul

Smithfield
Yetman
North Star

NEW SOUTH
WALES

Yallaroi
Coolatai
Wallangra

Monto
Mulgildie

Mundubbera

Gayndah

Wondai
Murgon
Cherbourg

Kingaroy

Nanango

Dalby

Oakey
Kingsthorpe
TOOWOOMBA

Pittsworth

WARWICK

Stanthorpe

Tenterfield

BUNDABERG
Bargara
Burnett Heads
Childers
HERVEY BAY
MARYBOROUGH

GYMPIE

Tin Can Bay

Rainbow Beach

GREAT
SANDY
NATIONAL
PARK

FRASER
ISLAND

Orchid Beach

Cooroy
NAMBOUR
Noosa Heads
Sunshine Beach
Peregian Beach
Coolum Beach
MAROOCHYDORE
MOOLOOLABA
BUDERIM
CALOUNDRA
Landsborough
Beerwah
Woodford
Kilcoy
Elimbah
CABOOLTURE
BONGAREE
Beachmere
Deception Bay
Redcliffe
Brighton

BRISBANE
IPSWICH

Jimboomba
Boonah
Beaudesert
NERANG
Mudgeeraba

GOLD COAST
Surfers Paradise
Southport

Murwillumbah
Chinderah
Banora Point
Kingscliff
Bogangar
Pottsville

Mullumbimby
Brunswick Heads
Byron Bay
Ocean Shores

LISMORE
Ballina
Lennox Head
Alstonville

Casino
Kyogle

CORAL SEA

For more detail on Fraser Coast
see page 118

For more detail on Brisbane &
Surrounds see pages 115 & 117

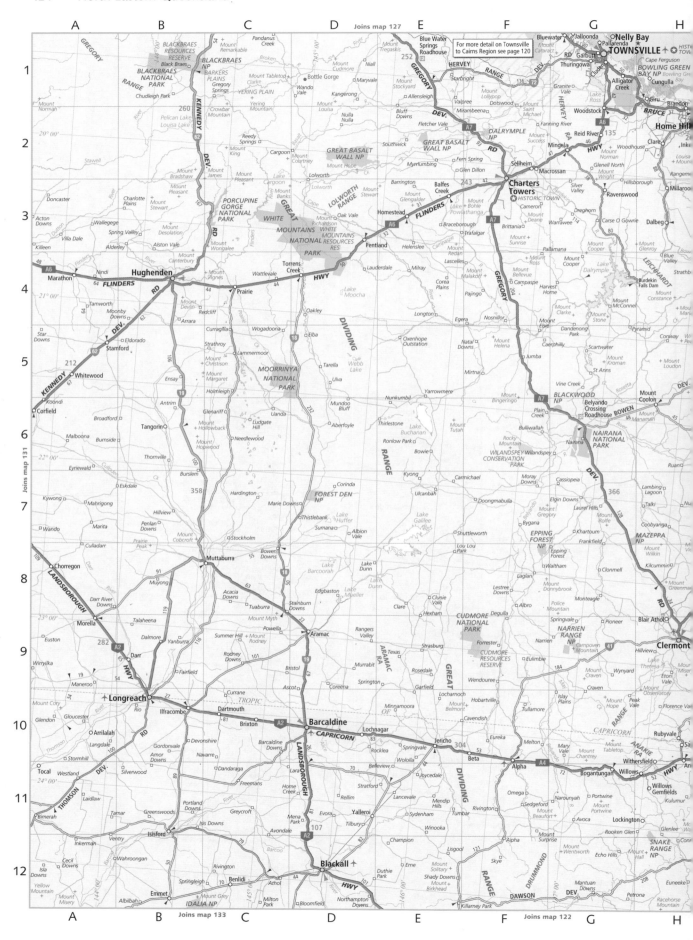

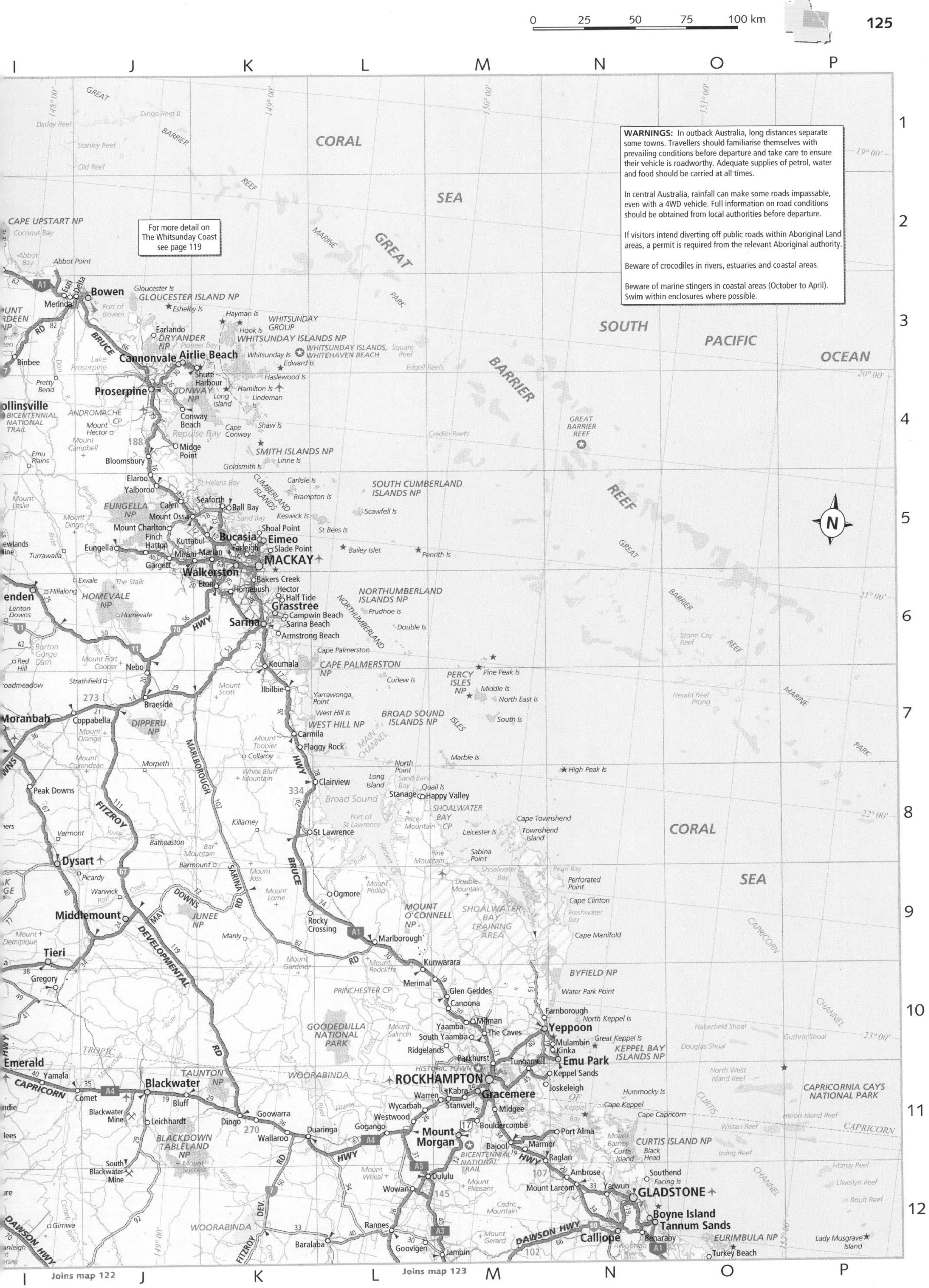

0 25 50 75 100 km

For more detail on The Whitsunday Coast see page 119

CORAL SEA

GREAT BARRIER REEF

SOUTH PACIFIC OCEAN

MARINE PARK

19° 00'
20° 00'
21° 00'
22° 00'
23° 00'

GREAT BARRIER REEF

Darley Reef
Dingo Reef B
Stanley Reef
Old Reef

CAPE UPSTART NP
Coconut Bay
Abbot Bay
Abbot Point
Bowen
Merinda
Euri Delta
BRUCE RD
Binbee
Pretty Bend
Gloucester Is
GLOUCESTER ISLAND NP
Eshelby Is
Hayman Is
Hook Is
WHITSUNDAY GROUP
WHITSUNDAY ISLANDS NP
Whitsunday Is
WHITSUNDAY ISLANDS, WHITEHAVEN BEACH
Square Reef
Edgell Reefs
Earlando
DRYANDER NP
Pioneer Bay
Cannonvale Airlie Beach
Shute Harbour
CONWAY NP
Hamilton Is
Haslewood Is
Lindeman Is
Proserpine
Lake Proserpine
ANDROMACHE CP
Mount Hector
Conway Beach
Long Island
Cape Conway
Shaw Is
Credlin Reefs
GREAT BARRIER REEF
Mount Campbell
Repulse Bay
Midge Point
SMITH ISLANDS NP
Linne Is
Bloomsbury
Goldsmith Is
Collinsville
BICENTENNIAL NATIONAL TRAIL
Emu Plains
Elaroo
Yalboroo
EUNGELLA NP
Calen
Mount Ossa
Seaforth
Ball Bay
CUMBERLAND ISLANDS
Carlisle Is
Brampton Is
SOUTH CUMBERLAND ISLANDS NP
Mount Leslie
Mount Dingo
Mount Charlton
Finch Hatton
Kuttabul
Keswick Is
Shoal Point
St Bees Is
Scawfell Is
GREAT BARRIER REEF
Turrawalla
Eungella
Gargett
Mirani Marian
Bucasia
Eimeo
Slade Point
Fashleigh
MACKAY
Bailey Islet
Penrith Is
Exvale
The Stalk
HOMEVALE NP
Walkerston
Eton
Bakers Creek
Homebush
Hector
NORTHUMBERLAND ISLANDS NP
enden
Hillalong
Lenton Downs
Homevale
Grasstree
Half Tide
Campwin Beach
Prudhoe Is
Double Is
Barton Gorge Dam
HWY
Sarina
Sarina Beach
Armstrong Beach
Cape Palmerston
Red Hill
Mount Fort Cooper
Nebo
Koumala
CAPE PALMERSTON NP
Curlew Is
roadmeadow
Strathfield
Mount Scott
Ilbilbie
Yarrawonga Point
West Hill Is
PERCY ISLES NP
Pine Peak Is
Middle Is
North East Is
Herald Reef Prong
Moranbah
Coppabella
Mount Orange
Braeside
DIPPERU NP
Carmila
WEST HILL NP
BROAD SOUND ISLANDS NP
South Is
Peak Downs
Mount Coxendean
Morpeth
Flaggy Rock
Mount Toobier
Collaroy
Marble Is
High Peak Is
Vermont
Killarney
Mount Joss
Clairview
White Bluff Mountain
Long Island
North Point
Sand Bank Bay
Quail Is
Happy Valley
Stanage
MARINE PARK
Dysart
Picardy
Barmount
Bar Mountain
Batheaston
St Lawrence
Broad Sound
SHOALWATER BAY
Port of St Lawrence
Price Mountain
Leicester Is
Cape Townshend
Townshend Island
CORAL SEA
Warwick Roll
Middlemount
DOWNS
JUNEE NP
Mount Gardiner
Manly
Ogmore
Mount Lorne
Mount Phillip
Pine Mountain
Sabina Point
Shoalwater Bay
Pearl Bay
Perforated Point
Cape Clinton
Freshwater Bay
Tieri
Gregory
Rocky Crossing
Marlborough
MOUNT O'CONNELL NP
Double Mountain
Cape Manifold
DEVELOPMENTAL RD
Mount Redcliffe
Kunwarara
Merimal
SHOALWATER BAY TRAINING AREA
Emerald
Yamala
TROPIC OF CAPRICORN
TAUNTON NP
PRINCHESTER CP
Glen Geddes
Canoona
Farnborough
North Keppel Is
Water Park Point
BYFIELD NP
CAPRICORN
Comet
Blackwater
Bluff
Leichhardt
Dingo
Goowarra
Duaringa
WOORABINDA
GOODEDULLA NATIONAL PARK
Mount Salmon
Yaamba
South Yaamba
Ridgelands
Milman
The Caves
Parkhurst
Yeppoon
Mulambin
Kinka
Tungamull
Great Keppel Is
KEPPEL BAY ISLANDS NP
Emu Park
Keppel Sands
Haberfield Shoal
Douglas Shoal
North West Island Reef
Blackwater Mine
Wycarbah
Warren
Kabra
HISTORIC TOWN
ROCKHAMPTON
Stanwell
Gracemere
Midgee
Bouldercombe
Joskeleigh
Cape Keppel
Cape Capricorn
CAPRICORNIA CAYS NATIONAL PARK
Heron Island Reef
Wistari Reef
BLACKDOWN TABLELAND NP
Mount Success
Wallaroo
Westwood
Gogango
Mount Morgan
Bajool
Marmor
Raglan
CURTIS ISLAND NP
Mount Barney
Curtis Island
Black Head
Irving Reef
South Blackwater Mine
Mount Wheal
Dululu
Mount Pleasant
BICENTENNIAL NATIONAL TRAIL
Ambrose
Mount Larcom
Southend
Facing Is
Fitzroy Reef
Wowan
Cedric Mountain
Yarwun
GLADSTONE
Llewellyn Reef
Boult Reef
WOORABINDA
Rannes
Mount Gerard
Goovigen
Jambin
DAWSON HWY
Calliope
Boyne Island
Tannum Sands
Benaraby
EURIMBULA NP
Lady Musgrave Island
DAWSON HWY
Baralaba
Turkey Beach

Joins map 122
Joins map 123

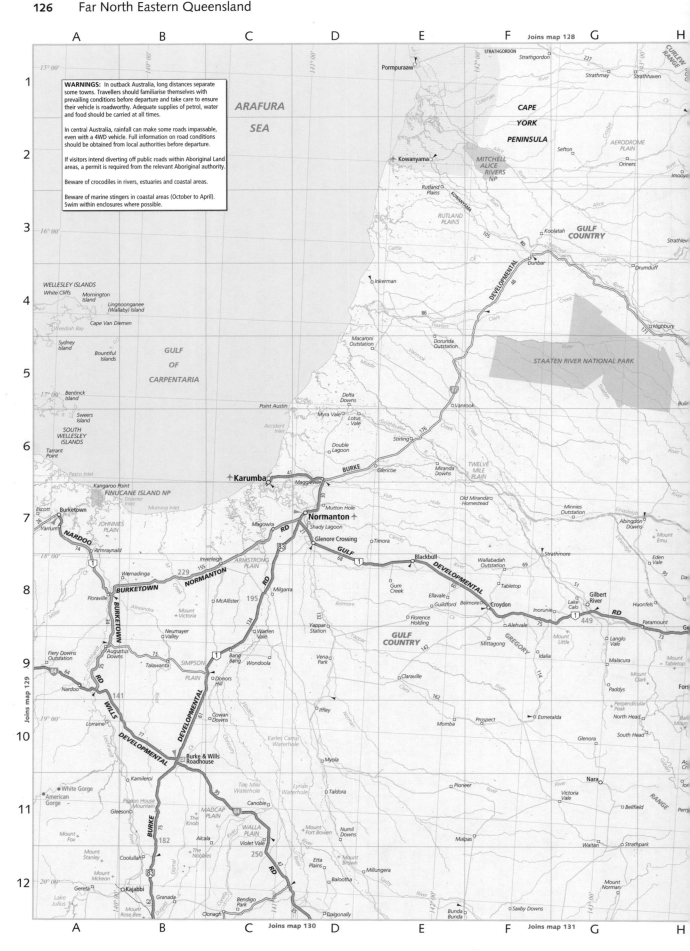

WARNINGS: In outback Australia, long distances separate some towns. Travellers should familiarise themselves with prevailing conditions before departure and take care to ensure their vehicle is roadworthy. Adequate supplies of petrol, water and food should be carried at all times.

In central Australia, rainfall can make some roads impassable, even with a 4WD vehicle. Full information on road conditions should be obtained from local authorities before departure.

If visitors intend diverting off public roads within Aboriginal Land areas, a permit is required from the relevant Aboriginal authority.

Beware of crocodiles in rivers, estuaries and coastal areas.

Beware of marine stingers in coastal areas (October to April). Swim within enclosures where possible.

ARAFURA SEA

CAPE YORK PENINSULA

AERODROME PLAIN

MITCHELL ALICE RIVERS NP

GULF COUNTRY

RUTLAND PLAINS

STAATEN RIVER NATIONAL PARK

WELLESLEY ISLANDS

GULF OF CARPENTARIA

SOUTH WELLESLEY ISLANDS

FINUCANE ISLAND NP

BURKE

Karumba

Normanton

Glenore Crossing

GULF

Blackbull

DEVELOPMENTAL

Burketown

NARDOO

JOHNNIES PLAIN

BURKETOWN

NORMANTON

ARMSTRONG PLAIN

RD

Croydon

Gilbert River

GREGORY

GULF COUNTRY

SIMPSON PLAIN

BURKETOWN

WILLS

DEVELOPMENTAL

Burke & Wills Roadhouse

BURKE

MADCAP PLAIN

WALLA PLAIN

RANGE

RD

Kajabbi

0 25 50 75 100 km

I J K L M N O P

WAKOOKA

CAPE
MELVILLE
NP

TURTLE
GROUP
NP

LIZARD ISLAND NP

Eyrie Reef

Turtle Group

★ Lizard Is
★ Palfrey Is
Martin Reef

1

LAKEFIELD

Bizant
Breeza Plains
Outstation

LAKEFIELD

MUNBURRA
RESOURCES
RES

Lookout Point

Flattery
Harbour

CORAL

NATIONAL

Koolburra
Mountain

Koolburra

Hann River
Roadhouse

Mount
Stuckey (Numbargulmi)

STARCKE
NP

Mount
Beardmore

BRIDGE
CREEK
NP

MOUNT WEBB NP

THREE ISLANDS NP

Mount
Baird

Cape
Bedford

South Cape
Bedford

Forrester Reef

Cape Flattery

SEA

2

GREAT

PARK

PENINSULA

DEVELOPMENTAL

Mount
Emma

Mount
Daintree

Maiden
Peak

Fairlight

BURKE

Bellevue

Welcome

Laura

Mount
Sampson

QUINKAN

McCormack

HOPE
VALE

Hope
Vale

ENDEAVOUR RIVER NP

Marton

Cooktown ✈

BICENTENNIAL
NATIONAL
TRAIL

★ Archer Point

BLACK MOUNTAIN NP

Helenvale

15° 00'

3

GREAT

WEST
QUINKAN

DIVIDING

Mount
Lukin

Rossville

Cedar Bay

Lakeland

COOKTOWN DEV. RD

Mount
Eykin

Rattlesnake Point
(North Head)

CEDAR BAY
NP

Ayton

Wujal Wujal

REEF

MARINE

Palmer River
Roadhouse

PALMER GOLDFIELD
RESOURCES RES

Mount
Hurford

RANGE

DAINTREE
(WORLD
HERITAGE)

DAINTREE
NP

Cape Tribulation

DAINTREE
NATIONAL PARK

St Crispin Reef

16° 00'

4

PALMERVILLE

Mount
Bennett

Racecourse
Mountain

Daintree

Thornton
Peak

Alexandra
Bay

Cow Bay

Cape Kimberley

HOPE ISLANDS NP

Wonga

Miallo

Trinity Bay

LOW ISLES
★ LIGHTHOUSE

Tongue Reef

PARK

PENINSULA DEV. RD

Mount Carbine

Mossman

Cooya Beach

Port Douglas
Craiglie

Oak Beach

FOUR MILE
BEACH

Michaelmas Reef

GREAT

5

Nychum

Maryfarms

Julatten

CAPTAIN COOK
HIGHWAY DRIVE

Trinity Bay

Arlington Reef

BARRIER

Mount Molloy

Ellis Beach

Mount
Mulligan

Kingsborough

HANN
TABLELAND
NP

Koah

Biboohra

Kuranda

Palm Cove

Clifton Beach

Smithfield Heights

Green Is ★

KURANDA SCENIC
RAILWAY,
AUSTRALIAN
BUTTERFLY
SANCTUARY

Elford Reef

GREAT
BARRIER
REEF

6

Chillagoe

Mungana

CHILLAGOE
MUNGANA
CAVES NP

Mount
Mulgrave

Dimbulah

Tabacum

Mareeba

BARRON
GORGE
NP

CAIRNS

Edmonton

Gordonvale

Aloomba

Fitzroy Is ★

Sudbury Reef

17° 00'

7

Almaden

Petford

Mutchilba

Walkamin

Tinaroo Falls

Tolga

Kairi

Atherton

Tinaburra

Yungaburra

Fishery Falls

Deeral

Russell Is ★

RUSSELL RIVER NP

Gibson Reef

Howie Reef

For more detail on
Townsville to Cairns Region
see page 120

Herberton

Irvinebank

Kalunga

Malanda

Millaa Millaa

Babinda

Miriwinni

Bramston Beach

ELLA BAY NP

8

Ootann

Mount
Beauty

Three Mile
Mountain

Tumoulin

Ravenshoe

WOOROONOORAN
NP

Innisfail

Mourilyan

South Johnstone

Flying Fish Point

COWLEY BEACH
TRAINING AREA

Cowley Beach

KURRIMINE BEACH NP

Potter Reef

Mount
Garnet

Innot Hot
Springs

TULLY
GORGE NP

Mena Creek

Cardstone

Silkwood

El Arish

Kurrimine Beach

Bingil Bay

Mission Beach

Wongaling Beach

Dunk Is

Yamacutta Reef

REEF

Springfield

BICENTENNIAL
NATIONAL
TRAIL

FORTY MILE
SCRUB NP

TULLY FALLS
FOREST RESERVE

KOOMBOOLOOMBA
FOREST RESERVE

Glen
Ruth

WHITEWATER
RAFTING

Tully

Euramo

Tully Heads

South Mission Beach

Bedarra Is ★

18° 00'

9

Mount
Surprise

UNDARA
VOLCANIC
NATIONAL
PARK

MOUNT-ROSEY
RESOURCES RESERVE

Kinrara

KINRARA
NP

Native
Wells
Swamp

GIRRINGUN

Bilyana

Kennedy

Cardwell

EDMUND KENNEDY NP

Rockingham Bay

South Is ★

Cape Sandwich

HINCHINBROOK ISLAND
NP

Hinchinbrook
Island

Hillcock
Point

Britomart
Reef

Trunk
Reef

MARINE

PARK

Oasis
Roadhouse

GREGORY

Greenvale

Christmas
Creek

Abergowrie

Lannercost

Trebonne

Ingham

Toobanna

Lucinda

Halifax

Taylors
Beach

PALM
ISLANDS

Pelorus Is (North Palm Island) (Yanooa)

ORPHEUS ISLAND NP

Orpheus Is (Goolboddi)

Curacoa Is (Noogoo)

10

Kidston

FOX

Michael
Creek

Forrest
Beach

Great Palm Is

★ White Rock (Albino Rock)

Great Palm Island

HALIFAX BAY WETLANDS NP

Havannah Is

11

GREAT

DIVIDING

Greenvale

Mount
Dora

Bambaroo

PALUMA
RANGE NP

Mutarnee

Paluma

Balgal Beach

Rollingstone

Taravale

Jalloonda

Pallarenda

Nelly Bay

Horseshoe Bay

MAGNETIC ISLAND NP

Halifax Bay

Rattlesnake Is ★

Picnic Bay

19° 00'

RANGE

Blue Water
Springs
Roadhouse

HERVEY

Mount
Cataract

Bluewater

Thuringowa

TOWNSVILLE ✈

Cape Cleveland

HISTORIC
TOWN

For more detail on
The Whitsunday Coast
see page 119

TOWNSVILLE
FIELD
TRAINING AREA

Granite
Vale

Alligator Creek

Cungulla

Bowling Green

Cape Bowling
Green

BOWLING
GREEN
BAY NP

12

KENNEDY

Valpree

Woodstock

Reid River

DALRYMPLE
NP

Mount
Success

Giru

BOWLING
GREEN
BAY NP

Brandon

Alva

Ayr

Home Hill

Cape
Upstart

I J K L M N O P

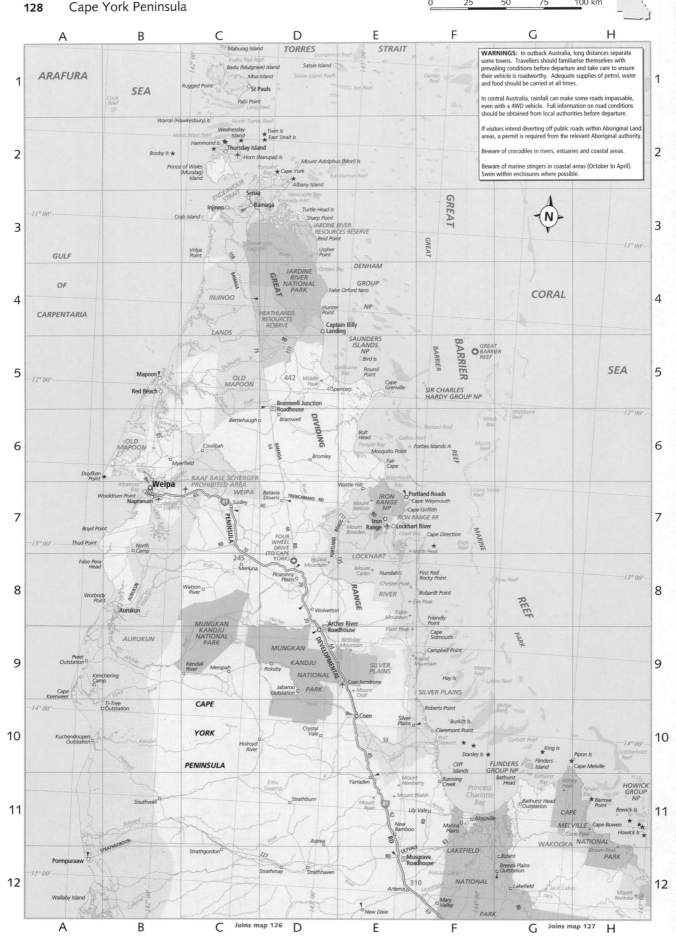

0   25   50   75   100 km

WARNINGS: In outback Australia, long distances separate some towns. Travellers should familiarise themselves with prevailing conditions before departure and take care to ensure their vehicle is roadworthy. Adequate supplies of petrol, water and food should be carried at all times.

In central Australia, rainfall can make some roads impassable, even with a 4WD vehicle. Full information on road conditions should be obtained from local authorities before departure.

If visitors intend diverting off public roads within Aboriginal Land areas, a permit is required from the relevant Aboriginal authority.

Beware of crocodiles in rivers, estuaries and coastal areas.

Beware of marine stingers in coastal areas (October to April). Swim within enclosures where possible.

ARAFURA SEA

TORRES STRAIT

GULF OF CARPENTARIA

GREAT BARRIER REEF

CORAL SEA

MARINE REEF PARK

Weipa

CAPE YORK PENINSULA

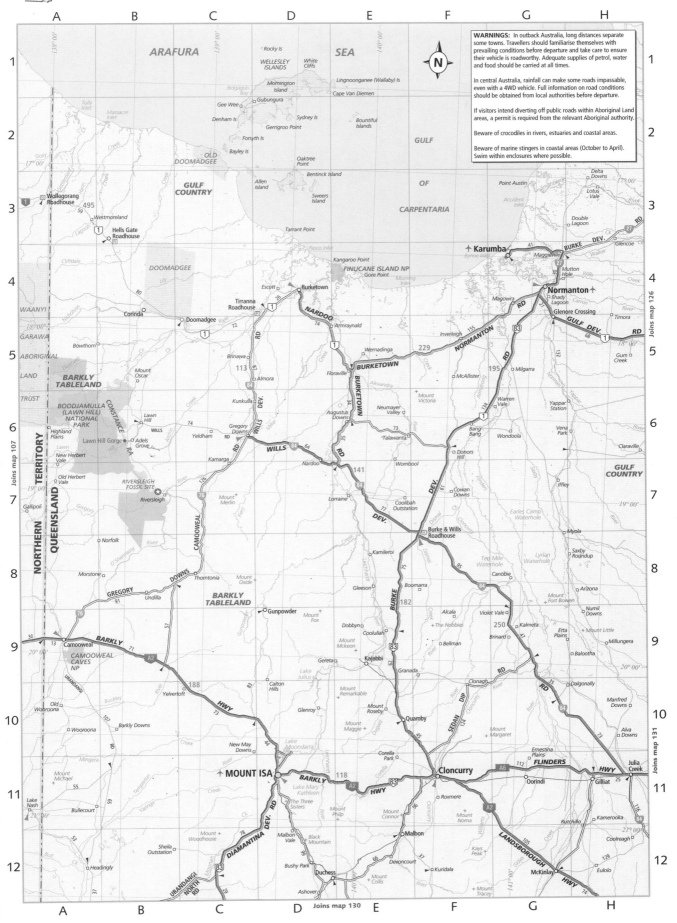

0   25   50   75   100 km

WARNINGS: In outback Australia, long distances separate some towns. Travellers should familiarise themselves with prevailing conditions before departure and take care to ensure their vehicle is roadworthy. Adequate supplies of petrol, water and food should be carried at all times.

In central Australia, rainfall can make some roads impassable, even with a 4WD vehicle. Full information on road conditions should be obtained from local authorities before departure.

If visitors intend diverting off public roads within Aboriginal Land areas, a permit is required from the relevant Aboriginal authority.

Beware of crocodiles in rivers, estuaries and coastal areas.

Beware of marine stingers in coastal areas (October to April). Swim within enclosures where possible.

ARAFURA   SEA

WELLESLEY ISLANDS
Rocky Is
White Cliffs
Lingnoonganee (Wallaby) Is
Mornington Island
Cape Van Diemen
Gee Wee
Gubungura
Denham Is
Sydney Is
Forsyth Is
Bountiful Islands
Gerrigroo Point
Bayley Is
Oaktree Point

GULF

OF

CARPENTARIA

Bentinck Island
Allen Island
Sweers Island
Point Austin
Accident Inlet
Delta Downs
Lotus Vale

GULF COUNTRY

OLD DOOMADGEE

Wollogorang Roadhouse
495
59
Westmoreland
Hells Gate Roadhouse

DOOMADGEE

Kangaroo Point
Pasco Inlet
Tarrant Point
FINUCANE ISLAND NP
Gore Point
Morning Inlet

Karumba
Maggieville
Byno-e Inlet
41
BURKE DEV.
Walker
Glencoe
27
RD

Mutton Hole
Normanton
Magowra
Shady Lagoon
Carron
Timora
River

WAANYI

GARAWA

ABORIGINAL

LAND

TRUST

Bowthorn
Mount Oscar
Corinda
Escott
Burketown
Tirranna Roadhouse
Doomadgee
26
NARDOO
Armraynald
74
1
Wernadinga
229
Floraville
BURKETOWN
McAllister
Mount Victoria
Neumayer Valley
Glenore Crossing
68
1
Gum Creek

BARKLY TABLELAND

Brinawa
113
Almora
84
DEV.
Kunkulla
WILLS
Augustus Downs
34
BURKETOWN
Warren Vale
195
Milgarra
132
Yappar Station
Vena Park
Claraville

Inverleigh
155
NORMANTON
RD
83
Amprong
134
1

BOODJAMULLA (LAWN HILL) NATIONAL PARK
Highland Plains
Lawn Hill
WILLS
74
Gregory Downs
RD
WILLS
84
64
Nardoo
141
84
Yeldham
Kamarga
Lorraine
77
DEV.
Coolibah Outstation

Bang Bang
73
Talawanta
Wondoola
Donors Hill
DEV.
61
Cowan Downs
Iffley

GULF COUNTRY

Lawn Hill Gorge
Adels Grove
RIVERSLEIGH FOSSIL SITE
Riversleigh
76
Mount Merlin
126

New Herbert Vale
Old Herbert Vale
Gallipoli
Norfolk
Morstone

CAMOOWEAL

GREGORY
DOWNS
91
Undilla
Thorntonia
57

BARKLY TABLELAND

Gunpowder
Mount Fox
Mount Oxide

Wombool
Womboo
Burke & Wills Roadhouse
Demal

Ten Mile Waterhole
Earles Camp Waterhole
Lyrian Waterhole
Myola
Saxby Roundup

Kamileroi
Gleeson
BURKE
182
Boomarra
75
Canobie
84
Arizona
Mount Fort Bowen
Numil Downs
Mount Little
Millungera
Baalootha

CAMOOWEAL
30
Camooweal
13
71
A2
BARKLY
CAMOOWEAL CAVES NP
URANDANGI

BARKLY
HWY
188
Yelvertoft
83
73
Calton Hills
Glenroy

Dobbyn
Coolullah
Gereta
Kajabbi
83
Granada
Bellman
Alcala
The Nobbies
Violet Vale
250
Brinard
Kalmeta
47
Etta Plains

Mount Mckeon
Lake Julius
Mount Remarkable
Mount Roseby
Mount Maggie
Quamby
45
SEDAN
DIP
124
Mount Margaret
Clonagh
RD
35
Dalgonally
Manfred Downs
84

New May Downs
44
Lake Moondarra
MOUNT ISA
BARKLY
118
A2
HWY
Corella Park
Cloncurry
Oorindi
A6
Gilliat
FLINDERS
Julia Creek
HWY
25
116

Lake Mary Kathleen
The Three Sisters
Mount Philp
83
Roxmere
Mount Connor
Mount Norna
A2
Oorindi

Mount Michael
55
59
Lake Nash
Bullecourt
53
Mount Woodhouse
78
Sheila Outstation
DIAMANTINA
DEV.
RD
83
URANDANGI
NORTH
RD
Malbon Vale
Black Mountain
Bushy Park
99
Duchess
Mount Collis
66
Devoncourt
37
Kuridala
Malbon
58
Kays Peak
McKinlay
105
LANDSBOROUGH
141
HWY
74
Eulolo
Coolreagh
129
Kamerooka
Rutchillo
84
27°00'
Ashover
Mount Tracey

NORTHERN TERRITORY
QUEENSLAND

Joins map 107
Joins map 126
Joins map 131
Joins map 130

1   2   3   4   5   6   7   8   9   10   11   12

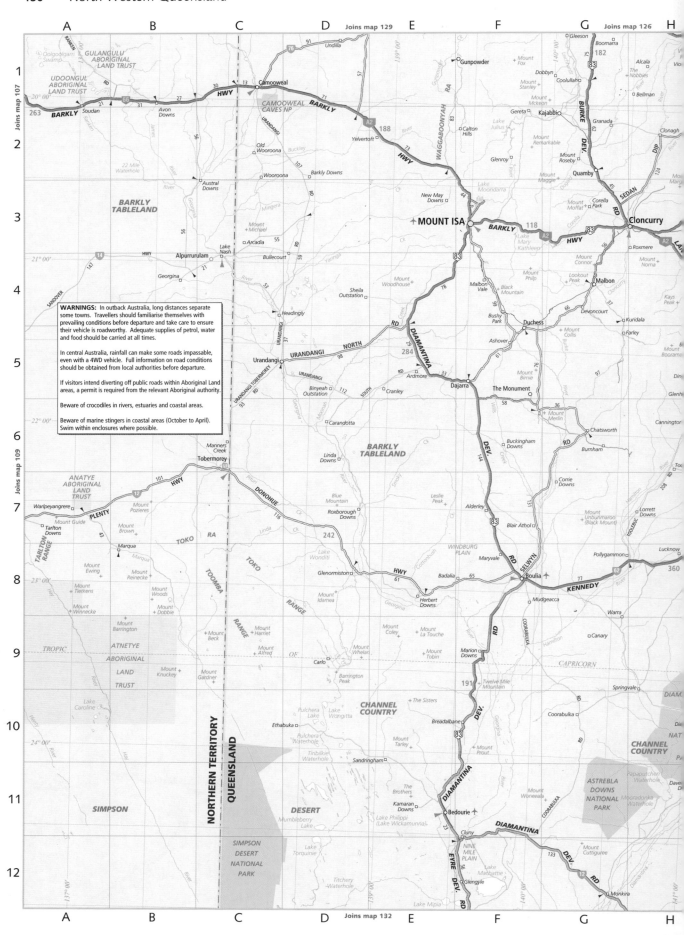

Joins map 107
Joins map 129
Joins map 126
Joins map 109
Joins map 132

WARNINGS: In outback Australia, long distances separate some towns. Travellers should familiarise themselves with prevailing conditions before departure and take care to ensure their vehicle is roadworthy. Adequate supplies of petrol, water and food should be carried at all times.

In central Australia, rainfall can make some roads impassable, even with a 4WD vehicle. Full information on road conditions should be obtained from local authorities before departure.

If visitors intend diverting off public roads within Aboriginal Land areas, a permit is required from the relevant Aboriginal authority.

Beware of crocodiles in rivers, estuaries and coastal areas.

Beware of marine stingers in coastal areas (October to April). Swim within enclosures where possible.

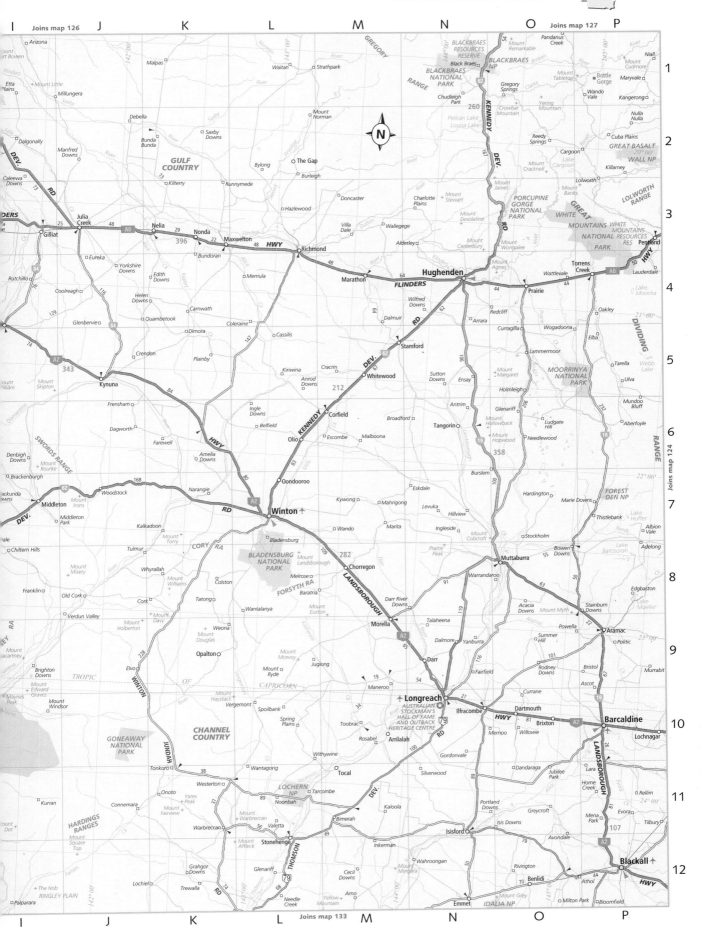

0   25   50   75   100 km

Arizona
rt Bowen
Flinders
Etta
Plains
+ Mount Little

Malpas
Waitan
Strathpark

GREGORY

Mount
Remarkable

BLACKBRAES
RESOURCES
RESERVE
Black Braes
BLACKBRAES
NP

Pandanus
Creek

Niall

Mount
Cudmore

Maryvale

Millungera
Debella
Bunda
Bunda
Saxby
Downs

RANGE

BLACKBRAES
NATIONAL
PARK

Chudleigh
Park
260

Gregory
Springs
Crowbar
Mountain

Mount
Tabletop

Bottle
Gorge

Wando
Vale

Kangerong

Dalgonally
Manfred
Downs

GULF
COUNTRY
Bylong
The Gap

River

62

Pelican Lake
Louisa Lake

Yering
Mountain
Cargoon
Lake
Cargoon

Nulla
Nulla
Cuba Plains

GREAT BASALT
WALL NP

Caleewa
Downs

Kilterry
Runnymede
Burleigh
Mount
Cracknell

Killarney

DERS
Gilliat
25
Julia
Creek
48
A6
Nelia
29
Nonda
22
Maxwelton
48
HWY
Richmond
64
Hughenden

Eureka
Yorkshire
Downs
Bundoran

Marathon
FLINDERS

Wilfred
Downs
62
Redcliff

Curragilla
Lammermoor

Elba

DIVIDING

Coolreagh
Helen
Downs
Edith
Downs
Merriula
Dalmuir
Arrara
Wogadoona
Oakley
Tarella
Webb
Lake

Glenbervie
Quambetook
Coleraine
Cassilis
Stamford
Sutton
Downs
Ensay
Mount
Margaret
Lammermoor
Ludgate
Hill

MOORRINYA
NATIONAL
PARK

Ulva

Mundoo
Bluff

RANGE

Kynuna
Crendon
Dimora
Plainby
Kiriwina
Cracrin
Whitewood
212
Antrim
Holmleigh
Needlewood
Aberfoyle

Frensham
Ingle
Downs
Corfield
Broadford
Tangorin
Mount
Hollowback
Mount
Hopwood
358

FOREST
DEN NP

Dagworth
Belfield
Olio
Escombe
Malboona
Burslem

Farewell
Amelia
Downs
Oondooroo
Kywong
Eskdale
Hardington
Marie Downs
Thistlebank

Middleton
Woodstock
Narangie
Winton
Mahrigong
Levuka
Hillview
Stockholm
Albion
Vale
Adelong

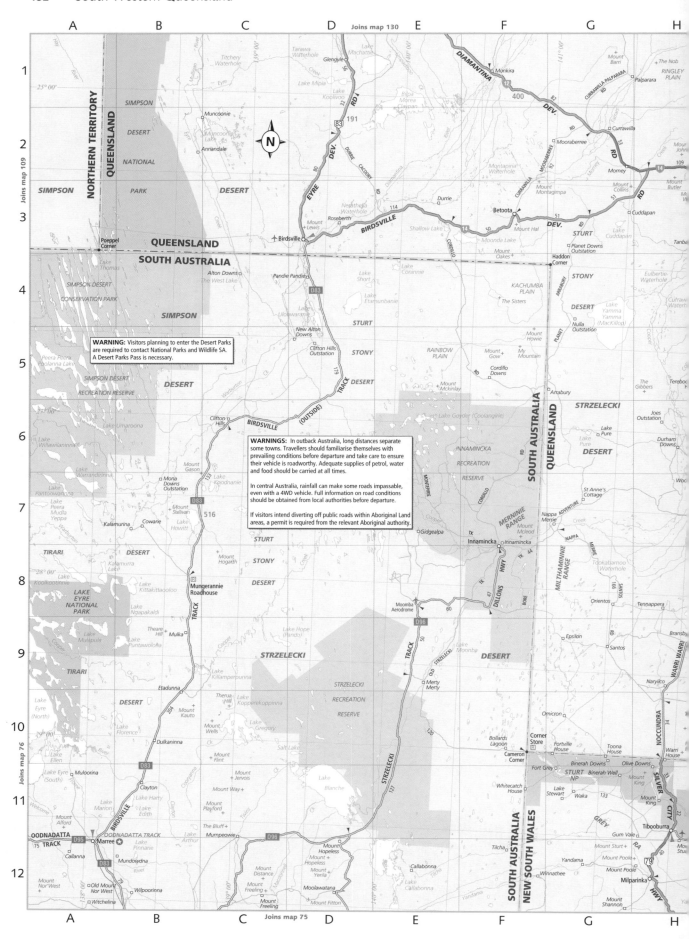

Joins map 130

Joins map 109

Joins map 76

WARNING: Visitors planning to enter the Desert Parks are required to contact National Parks and Wildlife SA. A Desert Parks Pass is necessary.

WARNINGS: In outback Australia, long distances separate some towns. Travellers should familiarise themselves with prevailing conditions before departure and take care to ensure their vehicle is roadworthy. Adequate supplies of petrol, water and food should be carried at all times.

In central Australia, rainfall can make some roads impassable, even with a 4WD vehicle. Full information on road conditions should be obtained from local authorities before departure.

If visitors intend diverting off public roads within Aboriginal Land areas, a permit is required from the relevant Aboriginal authority.

Joins map 75

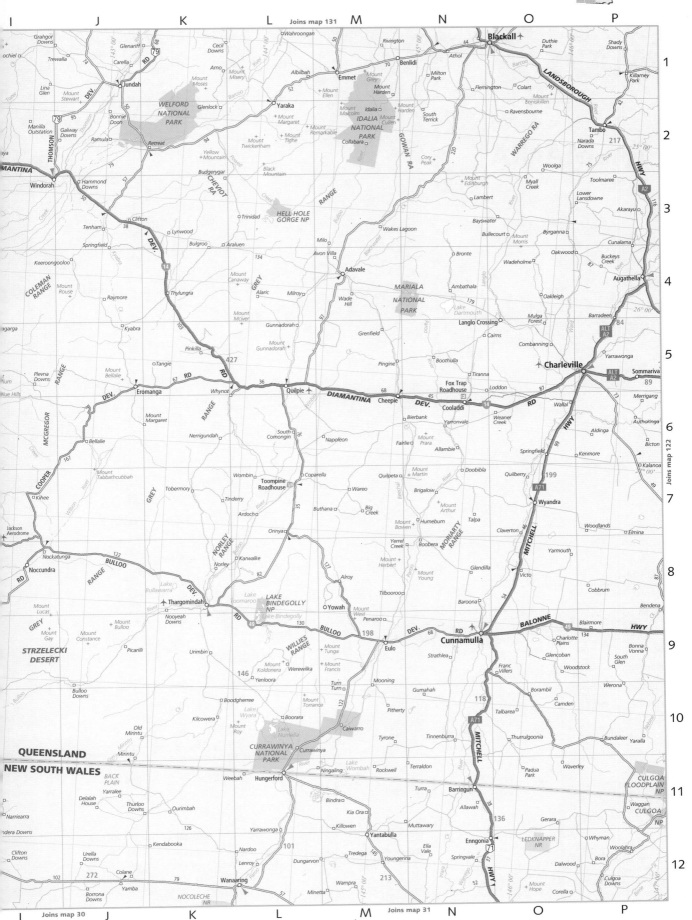

0 25 50 75 100 km

I J K L M N O P

Grahgor Downs
Trewalla
Glenariff
Glenariff
Cecil Downs
Arno
Mount Misery
Wahroongan
Rivington
Blackall
Duthie Park
Shady Downs
Killarney Park

ochiel
Lina Glen
Jundah
Carella
RD 79
Mount Moses
Albilbah
Emmet
Benlidi
Athol
Milton Park
Flemington
Colart
LANDSBOROUGH
101

1

Mount Stewart
THOMSON
Barcoo
Yaraka
Mount Ellen
Mount Grey
Mount Harden
Idalia
Mount Cullen
South Terrick
Ravensbourne
Mount Enniskillen
Tambo
Narada Downs
217

2

iya
Manilla Outstation
79 95
Galway Downs
Bonnie Doon
WELFORD NATIONAL PARK
Glenlock
Mount Margaret
Mount Remarkable
IDALIA NATIONAL PARK
Collabara
Mount Harden
Mount Edinburgh
Woolga
GOWAN RA
Myall Creek
WARREGO RA
Toolmaree
HWY
A2

MANTINA
Manilla
Ramula
Hammond Downs
Retreat
Budgerygar
Yellow Mountain
Mount Twickenham
Black Mountain
Mount Malcolm
Mount Tighe
Cheepie
Lambert
Bayswater
Lower Lansdowne
Akarayu
116

3

Windorah
MANTINA
DEV
57
CHEVIOT RA
Trinidad
HELL HOLE GORGE NP
Milo
Wakes Lagoon
Bullecourt
Mount Morris
Byrganna
Oakwood
Cunalama
Buckeys Creek
87

4

Keeroongooloo
COLEMAN RANGE
Mount Rouse
Springfield
Tenham
38
Lynwood
Bulgroo
Araluen
GREY
134
Avon Villa
Adavale
Bronte
Wade Hill
MARIALA NATIONAL PARK
Ambathala
Wadeholme
Oakleigh
Barradeen
Augathella
84

DEV
14
Raymore
Thylunga
Mount Canaway
Alaric
Milroy
179
Lake Dartmouth
Cairns
Mulga Forest
ALT A2

5

Mount Bellalie
Kyabra
Mount Mclver
Gunnadorah
Grenfield
Langlo Crossing
Combanning
Charleville
Yarrawonga
Sommariva
89

Plevna Downs
RANGE
Pinkilla
Tangie
Mount Gunnadorah
Pingine
Boothulla
Tiranna
Loddon
Wallal
Merrigang
A2

6

um
blue Hills
MCGREGOR
67 RD
427
36
Whynot
Quilpie
DIAMANTINA
68
Cheepie
45
Fox Trap Roadhouse
Cooladdi
Weaner Creek
87
Authoringa
73
Bicton

Eromanga
DEV
Mount Margaret
Nerrigundah
South Comongin
Napoleon
Fairlie
Bierbank
Yarronvale
Allambie
Mount Prara
Springfield
99
199
Aldinga
Kenmore
Kalanoa
49

7

COOPER
Bellalie
RANGE
Tobermory
76
Wombin
Coparella
Wareo
Quilpeta
Mount Martin
Doobibla
Quilberry
Wyandra
A71
Elmina
Woodlands

Kihee
Mount Tabbathcubbah
Tindery
Ardoch
35
Buthana
Big Creek
Brigalow
Mount Arthur
Talpa
Claverton
MITCHELL
Yarmouth

8

Jackson Aerodrome
Nockatunga
Noccundra
BULLOO
122
RANGE
GREY
Norley
Karwalke
82
Orinya
Yerrel Creek
Boobera
MONIARTY RANGE
Mount Herbert
Glendilla
Victo
Baroona
Cobbrum
Bendena

Mount Lucas
Mount Gay
Mount Constance
Thargomindah
Nooyeah Downs
NORLEY RANGE
Alroy
Mount Young
Tilbooroo
BALONNE
49
Blairmore
134

9

STRZELECKI DESERT
Picarilli
Urimbin
LAKE BINDEGOLLY NP
Lake Bindegolly
130
Yowah
BULLOO
198
Eulo
DEV
68
Cunnamulla
Franc Villers
Charlotte Plains
Glencoban
Woodstock
South Glen
Bonna Vonna
Werona

Bulloo Downs
Mount Bulloo
146
Yenloora
WILLIES RANGE
Mount Koldonera
Werewilka
Mount Francis
Strathlea
Mooning
Gumahah
118
Borambil
Talbarea
Camden
Yaralla
Bundaleer

10

Kilcowera
Boodgherree
Lake Wyara
Mount Torrance
Boorara
Caiwarro
122
Tyrone
Pitherty
Tinnenburra
MITCHELL
A71
Thurrulgoonia
Padua Park
Waverley

QUEENSLAND
Old Mirintu
CURRAWINYA NATIONAL PARK
Currawinya
Lake Wombah
Rockwell
Terraldon
CULGOA FLOODPLAIN NP

11

NEW SOUTH WALES
BACK PLAIN
Minintu
Weebah
Hungerford
Ningaling
Turra
Barringun
Waggan
CULGOA NP

Narrearra
Delalah House
Yarralee
Thurloo Downs
Ourimbah
126
Bindra
Kia Ora
Killowen
Muttaway
Allawah
136
Gerara
Whyman
LEDKNAPPER NR

12

Clifton Downs
ndera Downs
Urella Downs
Colane
79
272
Yarrawonga
101
Nardoo
Lenroy
Dungarvon
145
Tredega
Yantabulla
Youngerina
Ella Vale
Springvale
Enngonia
71
HWY
Dalwood
Bora
Woolahra
Culgoa Downs

Yamba
Borrona Downs
Kendabooka
Wanaaring
NOCOLECHE NR
Minetta
57
Wampra
213
52
Mount Hope
Corella
Mount

I J K L M N O P

MAPS

TASMANIA

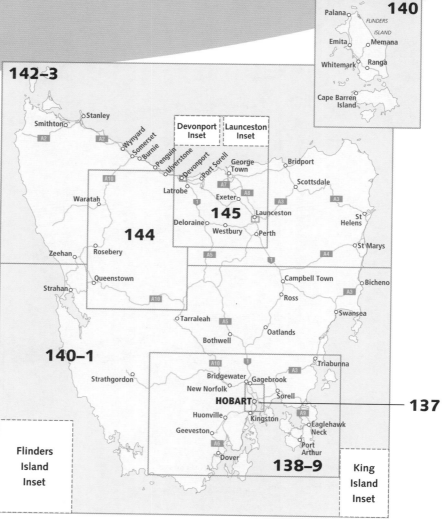

Tasmania

Central Hobart	136
Hobart Suburbs	137
Hobart & Surrounds	138–9
Southern Tasmania	140–1
Northern Tasmania	142–3
Tasmanian Highlands	144
Launceston Region	145

INTER-CITY ROUTES	DISTANCE
Hobart–Launceston via Midland Hwy	200 km
Hobart–Devonport via Midland & Bass hwys	286 km

Approximate Distances TASMANIA	Burnie	Campbell Town	Deloraine	Devonport	Geeveston	George Town	Hobart	Launceston	New Norfolk	Oatlands	Port Arthur	Queenstown	Richmond	Rosebery	St Helens	St Marys	Scottsdale	Smithton	Sorell	Strahan	Swansea	Ulverstone
Burnie		200	101	50	391	204	333	152	328	247	432	163	304	110	300	263	222	88	318	185	267	28
Campbell Town	200		99	150	191	119	133	67	128	47	232	304	104	357	122	85	137	288	118	344	67	172
Deloraine	101	99		51	290	103	232	51	227	146	331	207	203	211	199	162	121	189	217	247	166	73
Devonport	50	150	51		341	154	283	102	278	197	382	213	254	160	250	213	172	138	268	235	217	22
Geeveston	391	191	290	341		310	58	258	95	144	157	308	85	361	313	276	328	479	84	348	197	363
George Town	204	119	103	154	310		252	52	247	166	351	310	223	314	182	182	83	292	237	350	186	176
Hobart	333	133	232	283	58	252		200	37	86	99	250	27	303	265	228	270	421	26	290	139	305
Launceston	152	67	51	102	258	52	200		195	114	299	258	171	262	167	130	70	240	185	298	134	124
New Norfolk	328	128	227	278	95	247	37	195		81	136	213	64	266	250	213	265	416	63	253	176	300
Oatlands	247	47	146	197	144	166	86	114	81		175	257	57	310	169	132	184	335	71	297	125	219
Port Arthur	432	232	331	382	157	351	99	299	136	175		349	87	402	312	275	369	520	73	389	186	404
Queenstown	163	304	207	213	308	310	250	258	213	257	349		277	53	426	389	328	253	276	40	389	191
Richmond	304	104	203	254	85	223	27	171	64	57	87	277		330	226	189	241	392	14	317	123	276
Rosebery	110	357	211	160	361	314	303	262	266	310	402	53	330		410	373	332	222	329	75	442	138
St Helens	300	122	199	250	313	182	265	167	250	169	312	426	226	410		37	99	388	240	466	126	272
St Marys	263	85	162	213	276	182	228	130	213	132	275	389	189	373	37		136	351	203	429	89	235
Scottsdale	222	137	121	172	328	83	270	70	265	184	369	328	241	332	99	136		310	255	368	204	194
Smithton	88	288	189	138	479	292	421	240	416	335	520	253	392	222	388	351	310		406	275	355	116
Sorell	318	118	217	268	84	237	26	185	63	71	73	276	14	329	240	203	255	406		316	113	290
Strahan	185	344	247	235	348	350	290	298	253	297	389	40	317	75	466	429	368	275	316		429	213
Swansea	267	67	166	217	197	186	139	134	176	125	186	389	123	442	126	89	204	355	113	429		239
Ulverstone	28	172	73	22	363	176	305	124	300	219	404	191	276	138	272	235	194	116	290	213	239	

Distances on this chart have been calculated over main roads and do not necessarily reflect the shortest route between towns.

0   0.25   0.5   0.75   1 km

A   B   C   D   E   F   G   H

Joins map 137

TO GLENORCHY

TO GLENORCHY

TO AIRPORT

Joins map 137

RIVER

DERWENT

Pavilion Point

TASMAN HWY

Tasman Bridge

Ross Bay

QUEENS

DOMAIN

Royal Tasmanian Botanical Gardens

Government House 27

Crossroads Sports Grounds

Domain Athletic Centre

35

DOMAIN

TCA Ground

Domain Tennis Centre

TASMAN HWY

Cenotaph 21

Macquarie Point

Sacred Heart College

Clare Street Oval

Calvary Hospital

New Town

North Hobart

New Town

North Hobart Football Oval

Friends Junior School

Clemes College

Friends High School

North Hobart

Glebe

School

Hobart TAFE

TAFE

Tattersall's Hobart Aquatic Centre

ABC Radio, TV

AUSSAT Earth Station

West Hobart

John Doggett Park

Elizabeth College

Hobart Fire Brigade

Ambulance HQ

Police Headquarters 15

Theatre Royal 41

Royal Hobart Hospital

Wapping

Evans

Railway Goods Yard

Centre for the Arts

18

RACT 14

Car Park

City Hall

28

26

43

Macquarie

Wharf

St Marys College

Caldew Park

St Virgils College

Criterion

39

20

Mall

13

23

29

11

42

40

3

25

St David's Cathedral

22

Wharf

Hunter

HOBART

Franklin Square

17

Sullivans Cove

Government Offices

Brooke Street Pier 10

Parliament House

33

SALAMANCA

Royal Tennis Club

St David's Park

5

Salamanca Market

Salamanca Sq

36

30

6

Kelly's Steps

38

CSIRO

Princes Park

Bellerive

Ferry

Anglesea Barracks (Department of Defence)

Battery Point

19

32

31

School

St George's Anglican Church

Secheron Point

Short Beach

Hobart

School

Fitzroy Gardens

Parliament St Reserve

Sth Hobart Sports Ground

Sandy Bay

School

Royal Yacht Club of Tasmania

University of Tasmania

Derwent Sailing Squadron

RIVER

DERWENT

TO CASCADES

Dynnyrne

TO TAROONA

Wrest Point

Wrest Point Casino 44

N

Accommodation
Barton Cottage 1 F9
Colville Cottage 2 G9
Hadley's Hotel 3 E7
The Henry Jones Art Hotel 4 G6
Hobart Macquarie 5 E8
Lenna of Hobart 6 G8
The Old Woolstore 7 G6
Salamanca Inn 8 F8
Somerset on the Pier 9 G7
Note: Only a sample range of accommodation is listed; inclusion is not necessarily a recommendation.

General Information
Brooke Street Pier 10 F7
General Post Office 11 F7
Hobart Transit Centre 12 D8
Metro Tasmania Bus Terminal 13 F7
Motoring Organisation (RACT) 14 D6
Police Headquarters 15 F6
Qantas Travel Centre 16 E7
Tasmanian Travel & Information Centre 17 F7
Tigerline Coach Terminal 18 E6

Places of Interest
Arthur's Circus 19 G9
Cat and Fiddle Arcade 20 E7
Cenotaph 21 G5
Constitution Dock 22 F7
Elizabeth Street Mall 23 E7
Federation Concert Hall 24 G6
Franklin Square 25 F7
Gasworks Shopping Village 26 G6
Government House 27 G3
Hope and Anchor Tavern 28 F6
Ingle Hall 29 F7
Kelly's Steps 30 G8
Maritime Museum of Tasmania 31 F7
Narryna Heritage Museum 32 F9
Parliament House 33 F8
Penitentiary Chapel & Criminal Court (National Trust HQ) 34 E5
Queens Domain 35 E3
Salamanca Arts Centre 36 G8
Salamanca Place 37 F8
Signal Station 38 G8
State Library/Allport Library & Museum of Fine Arts 39 E7
Tasmanian Museum & Art Gallery 40 F7
Theatre Royal 41 F6
Town Hall 42 F7
Victoria Dock 43 G7
Wrest Point Casino 44 G12

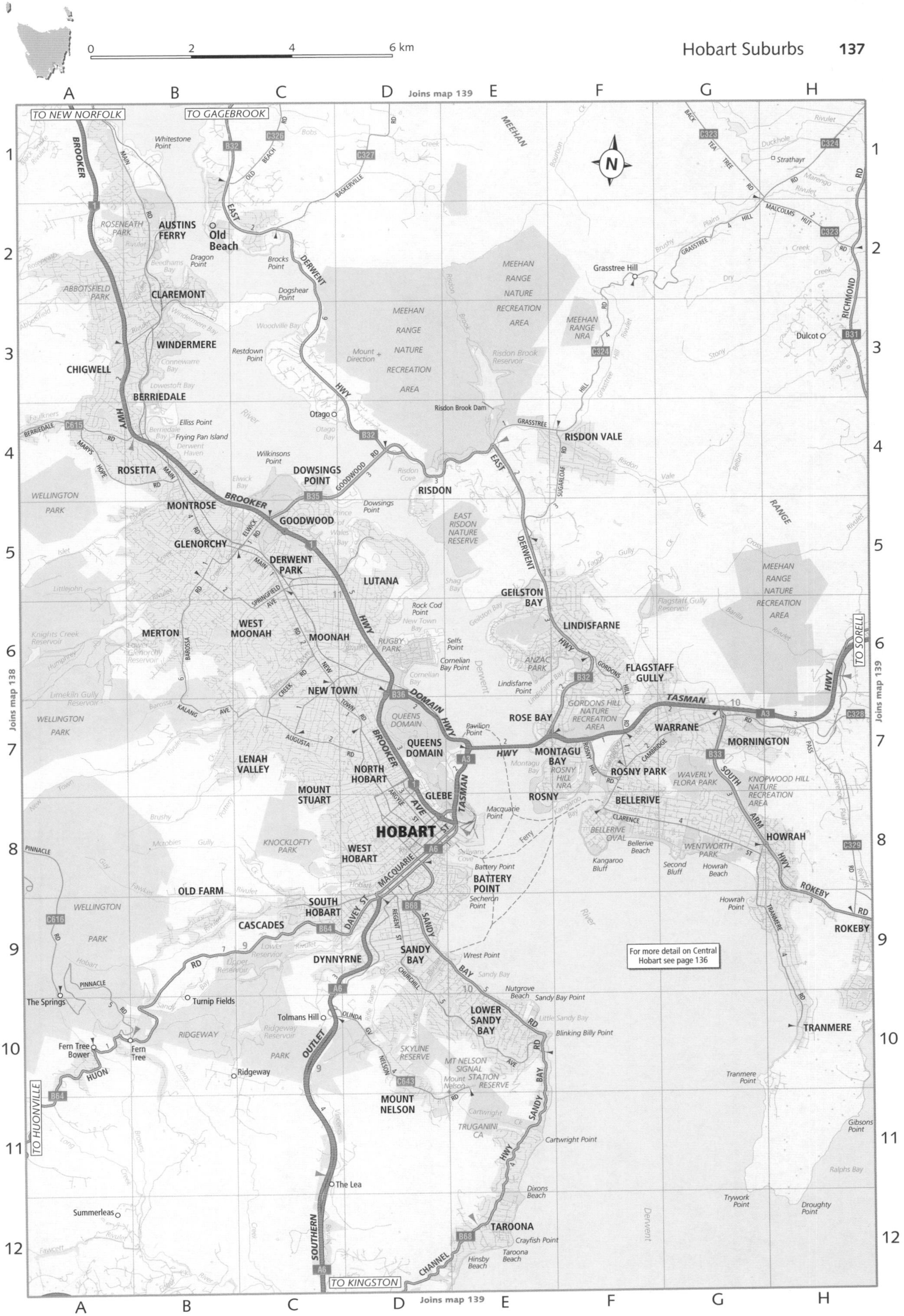

0 2 4 6 km

Joins map 139

TO NEW NORFOLK
TO GAGEBROOK

BROOKER

MEEHAN

N

Whitestone Point

AUSTINS FERRY
Old Beach
Dragon Point
Brocks Point

DERWENT

Dogshear Point

Woodville Bay

MEEHAN RANGE NATURE RECREATION AREA

MEEHAN RANGE NRA

Grasstree Hill

CLAREMONT
ABBOTSHIELD PARK

WINDERMERE
Connewarre Bay
Restdown Point

Mount Direction

Risdon Brook Reservoir

Dulcot

CHIGWELL

Lowestoft Bay

BERRIEDALE
Elliss Point
Frying Pan Island
Derwent Haven

River

Otago

Risdon Brook Dam

Grasstree
RISDON VALE

BERRIEDALE

ROSETTA
Wilkinsons Point

DOWSINGS POINT
Dowsings Point

RISDON

EAST RISDON NATURE RESERVE

MONTROSE
GOODWOOD

GLENORCHY

DERWENT PARK

Lake of Wales

DERWENT

GEILSTON BAY

MEEHAN RANGE NATURE RECREATION AREA

LUTANA

Rock Cod Point
New Town Bay

Shag Bay

LINDISFARNE

Flagstaff Gully Reservoir

MERTON
WEST MOONAH

Lower Glenorchy Reservoir

MOONAH

Selfs Point

Cornelian Bay Point

ANZAC PARK

Lindisfarne Point

FLAGSTAFF GULLY

WELLINGTON PARK

Knights Creek Reservoir

Limekiln Gully Reservoir

NEW TOWN

RUGBY PARK

Cornelian Bay

ROSE BAY

GORDONS HILL NATURE RECREATION AREA

TASMAN

WARRANE

MORNINGTON

LENAH VALLEY

Queens Domain

Pavilion Point

QUEENS DOMAIN

MONTAGU BAY

ROSNY HILL NRA

ROSNY PARK

Cambridge

KNOPWOOD HILL NATURE RECREATION AREA

MOUNT STUART
NORTH HOBART

GLEBE

Montagu Bay

ROSNY

WAVERLY FLORA PARK

BELLERIVE

HOWRAH

HOBART

WEST HOBART
MACQUARIE

Macquarie Point

Ferry

BELLERIVE OVAL
Kangaroo Bluff
Bellerive Beach

WENTWORTH PARK

Second Bluff
Howrah Beach

OLD FARM

Knocklofty Park

Battery Point

BATTERY POINT
Secheron Point

Howrah Point

ROKEBY

ROKEBY

SOUTH HOBART
CASCADES

DAVEY ST

SANDY BAY

Wrest Point

Nutgrove Beach
Sandy Bay Beach

DYNNYRNE

CHURCHILL

Sandy Bay Point

For more detail on Central Hobart see page 136

The Springs

Turnip Fields

Little Sandy Bay
Blinking Billy Point

TRANMERE

Fern Tree Bower
Fern Tree

RIDGEWAY

Tolmans Hill
OLINDA

Ridgeway Reservoir

LOWER SANDY BAY

SANDY BAY RD

Tranmere Point

HUON

TO HUONVILLE

Ridgeway

OUTLET

SKYLINE RESERVE

MT NELSON SIGNAL STATION RESERVE

Mount Nelson

Cartwright Point

Gibsons Point

Summerleas

The Lea

MOUNT NELSON

TRUGANINI CA

Cartwright Point

Trywork Point

Droughty Point

Ralphs Bay

SOUTHERN

CHANNEL

TAROONA
Crayfish Point

Dixons Beach

Hinsby Beach
Taroona Beach

Dixons Point

TO KINGSTON

Joins map 139
Joins map 138
Joins map 139

TO SORELL

WELLINGTON PARK

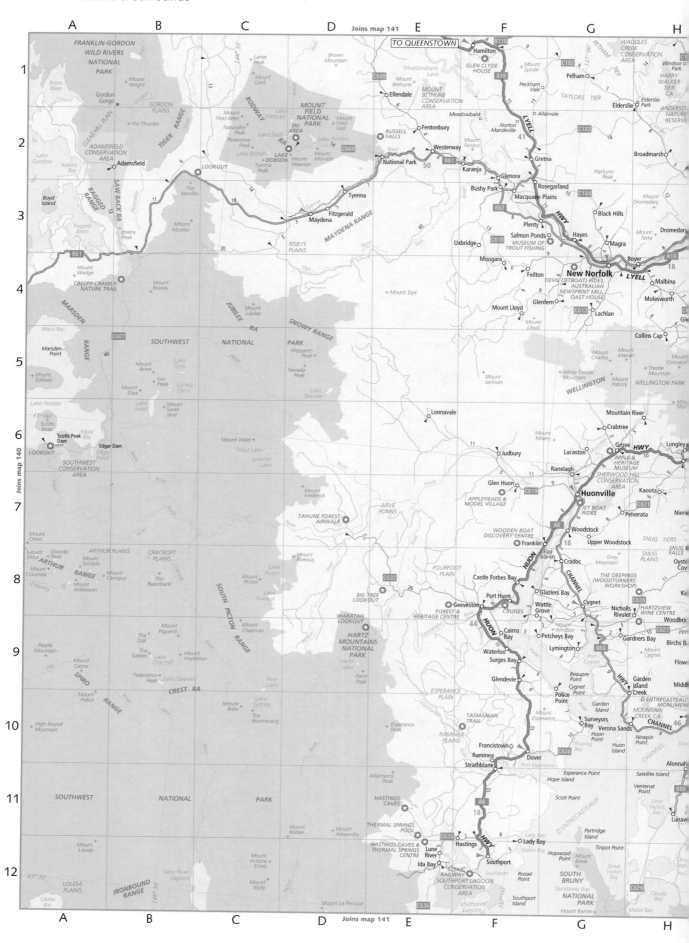

0 5 10 15 20 km

TO LAUNCESTON
Joins map 141
TO SWANSEA

42°30'
43°00'

N

Places and labels:

Eldon, Colebrook, Levendale, Mount Hobbs, Mount Douglas, BUCKLAND MILITARY PROHIBITED AREA, Triabunna, Rostrevor Reservoir, Woodstock, Cape Bougainville, Okehampton, Lords Bluff

Quoin Mountain, Fair View, Craigbourne Dam, GRAVELLY RIDGE CONSERVATION AREA, Mount Bairns, Stonehurst, The Cobs, Prosser River, Louisville, Point Home Lookout Lighthouse, Point Home Lookout

Chauncy Vale, Lowdina, Brown Mountain, C312, Buckland, Court Farm, Orford, Shelly Beach, Quarry Point, Ile Du Nord, Cape Boullanger, Fossil Bay

angalore, PONTVILLE RIFLE RANGE PROHIBITED AREA, Campania, Runnymede, Whitemarsh, Mount Calvary, Sally Peak, HISTORIC CHURCH, THREE THUMBS STATE RESERVE, FLASH TIER, Spring Beach, Johnsons Point, Painted Cliffs, Darlington, HISTORIC PENAL SETTLEMENT

TASMAN, Pontville, Tea Tree, Rekuna, Campania House, Mount Phipps, Mount Morrison, C335, Rheban, Lachlan, Lachlan Island, Mount Maria, MARIA ISLAND NATIONAL PARK

water, Gagebrook, BONORONG WILDLIFE PARK, COAL RIVER TIER, Strathay, Richmond, Park View, Orielton, Pawleena, NELSONS TIER, Nugent, Middle Peak, CAPE BERNIER NATURE RESERVE, Sandspit Point, Booming Bay, Point Lesueur, Perpendicular Mountain, Mistaken Cape

CADBURY SCHWEPPES CHOCOLATE FACTORY, Old Beach, Grasstree Hill, HISTORIC TOWN, C351, Penna, Sorell, Wattle Hill, Hillcrest, ILES TIER, Point Des Galets, Point Mauge, Green Bluff, MARIA ISLAND, Cape Bald, Cape Maurouard

Mount Direction, Risdon Brook, Mount Lord, WOODVINE NATURE RESERVE, Kellevie, Point Du Ressac, Cape Peron, Barren Head

Risdon Vale, Pittwater Bluff, PITT WATER NR, Mount Elizabeth, Forcett, RAGGED TIER, Marion Bay, Cape Bernier

Lindisfarne, Cambridge Aerodrome, Barilla, Midway Point, Woody Is, ARTHUR HWY, Bream Creek, Marion Bay, LONG SPIT PRIVATE NR, Long Spit, Cape Paul Lamanon, Visscher Island

New Town, HOBART, Rosny Park, BELLERIVE OVAL, LOOKOUT, Mount Rumney, CHINA TIER, Copping MUSEUM, Cape Frederick Hendrick

Howrah, Rokeby, Seven Mile Beach, Hobart Airport, Sandy Point, Park Beach, Dodges Ferry, Carlton, Connellys Marsh, Denison Canal, Bangor Point, BLACKMAN PLAINS, Kelly Islands, Humper Bluff, TASMAN

BATTERY POINT, WREST POINT CASINO, Lauderdale, Mays Point, Carlton Bluff, Primrose Sands, Dunalley, Mount Forestier, PENINSULA TRAIL DRIVE, FORESTIER PENINSULA, High Yellow Bluff, NATIONAL

Sandy Bay, MT NELSON SIGNAL STATION, Droughty Point, Mount Mather, Sandford, Cremorne, Pipe Clay Head, Fulham Point, Fulham Island, Mount Reynolds

Taroona, SHOT TOWER, Gellibrand Point, Ralphs Bay, Pipe Clay Lagoon, Green Head, Whitehouse Point, Smooth Island, Dunbabin Point, Murdunna, Cape Surville, Deep Glen Bluff

Kingston, Opossum Bay, Cape Deslacs, Clifton Beach, Sloping Island, Sloping Lagoon, LIME BAY STATE RES, Lobster Point, Monk Bay, Chronicle Point, FAZACKERLEYS WA, View Peak, Macgregor Peak, PARK

Blackmans Bay, Halfmoon Bay, SOUTH ARM CA, South Arm, North West Head, Mount Wilmot, COAL MINES HISTORIC SITE, Deer Point, Norfolk Bay, Flinders Bay, EAGLEHAWK BAY-FLINDERS BAY CONSERVATION AREA, PIRATES BAY LOOKOUT, TESSELLATED PAVEMENT

Mount Louis, Piersons Point, Tinderbox, Cape Deliverance, Cape Contrariety, Saltwater River, Heather Point, Eaglehawk Bay, Dart Island, Eaglehawk Neck, Pirates Bay, TASMAN BLOWHOLE

Killora, Dennes Point, Cape De La Sortie, Bull Bay, Little Betsey Island, Betsey Island, Outer North Head, Prices Bay, Halfway Bluff, TASMANIAN DEVIL PARK, Cascades Bay, Taranna, Penzance, Doo Town, TASMANS ARCH, DEVIL'S KITCHEN, Waterfall Bay

Barnes Bay, Yellow Bluff, Mount Communication, Premaydena, Koonya, B37, Mount Koonya, Clemes Peak, TASMAN, O'Hara Bluff, Thumbs Point

Roaring Beach Bay, Wedge Bay, Nubeena, Mount Clark, Oakwood, ARTHUR, PENINSULA, NATIONAL

White Beach, Wedge Island, TASMAN, Mount Tonga, BUSH MILL STEAM RAILWAY, Dolomieu Point, The Lanterns, Cape Hauy, Hippolyte Rocks

Mount Spaulding, Highcroft, HISTORIC TOWN, Port Arthur, PALMERS LOOKOUT, Point Puer, TUNAH PLAINS, TASMAN, Mount Fortescue

Storm Bay, Two Island Bay, Stormlea, Mount Arthur, Black Mountain, Safety Cove, NATIONAL

Curio Bay, Salters Point, REMARKABLE CAVE, Mount Raoul, Mount Brown, West Arthur Head, Budget Head, Haines Bluff, Black Head, Cape Pillar

Cape Queen Elizabeth, Neck Beach, LOOKOUT, Adventure Bay, Maingon Bay, Raoul Bay, Black Head, TASMAN PASSAGE

MORELLA ISLAND RETREAT, Coal Point, Cape Raoul, Tasman Island, Tasman Island Lighthouse

Grass Point, Penguin Island, CAPTAIN COOK'S LANDING PLACE, SOUTH BRUNY, Fluted Cape, Cookville

Mount Cook, Cape Connella, Bay of Islands, NATIONAL, Mangana Bluff, Arched Island, PARK

TASMAN SEA

For more detail on Hobart Suburbs see page 137

Road numbers: B31, C318, B31, C321, C350, C322, A3, C324, B31, B32, B33, B68, B66, C625, A3, C331, C349, C334, C337, C341, C344, A9, B37, C320, C321, C310

A B C D E F G H

Joins map 142

1
2
3
4
5
6
7
8
9
10
11
12

42° 00'
42° 30'
43° 00'
40° 00'
40° 30'

145° 00'
148° 30'
146° 00'
145° 30'

TYNDALL RR
Mount Geikie
Lake Dora
LAKE BEATRICE
Lake Margaret
Castle Mountain
Mount Nereus
Mount Hyperion
Mount Gould
WALLS OF JERUSALEM NATIONAL PARK
CENTRAL PLATEAU CA
Lake Meston
GREAT PINE TIER

ZEEHAN HWY
MOUNT DUNDAS REGIONAL RESERVE
Lake Margaret
Queenstown
Linda
Gormanston
PRINCESS RIVER CA
CRADLE MOUNTAIN- LAKE ST CLAIR NATIONAL PARK
Mount Ida
SKULLBONE PLAINS

For more detail on the Tasmanian Highlands see page 144

OCEAN BEACH
B27
GORDON RIVER CRUISE
Strahan
LYELL HWY
Lynchford
Mount Olympus
Lake Saint Clair
CHEYNE RANGE
Pine Tier Lagoon

Surging Point
Cape Sorell
Regatta Point
B24
King
Crotty Dam
Mount Huxley
Mount Gell
Mount Rufus
LYELL HWY
Derwent Bridge
A10
Pine Tier Dam
Bronte Park
B

Round Head
Betsys Bay
ABT WILDERNESS RAILWAY
WESTCOAST RANGE RR
Darwin Dam
Mount Jukes
CROTTY CA
Mount Maud
Mount Arrowsmith
Laughing Jack Dam
Bronte Lagoon
A10

Sloop Point
Macquarie
Mount Sorell
Mount Mullens
KING WILLIAM RA
Mount King William I
Clark Dam
Tungatinah Dam
Brady
Binney Dam

Gorge Point
Harbour
Rum Point
Frenchmans Cap
Mount Emma
Mount King William II
Mount King William III
Butlers Gorge
Tarraleah
LYELL

Birthday Bay
Varna Bay
WESTERN PLAINS
WHITE HILL PLAIN
Mount Propsting
Mount Seal
Mount Llewellyn
Mount Norway
Observation Peak
FRANKLIN-GORDON WILD RIVERS NATIONAL PARK
Mount Shakespeare
Wayatinah
Wayatinah Dam

Pennerowne Point
Hibbs Bay
SOUTHWEST
Mount Discovery
TASMANIAN WILDERNESS AREA (WORLD HERITAGE)
Mount Diamond Peak
Convict Peak
Conical Mountain
GORDON RANGE
Mount Dawson

Point Hibbs
Spero Bay
Conder Point
Endeavour Bay
WAROUNRIM PLAINS
Mount Lee
Innes Peak
Mount Humboldt
PRINCE OF WALES RA
Reeds Peak
Mount Wright
GORDON PLAINS
Mount Lord
Mount Field West
SKI AREA

SOUTHERN
CONSERVATION
High Rocky Point
Mount Lewis
Gordon Dam
Strathgordon
Serpentine Dam
Adamsfield
ADAMSFIELD CA
Lake Gordon
Mount Mawson
Mount Mueller
Fit

AREA
Mount Osmond
Mount Eleanor
Mount Jean
Mount Sprent
Koruna Peak
Mount Wedge
B61
Mount Helder
Mount Bowes
Mount Jubilee

Veridian Point
Black Is
Hudson
LAWSON RANGE
TOP PLAIN
Coronation Peak
FRANKLAND RA
Lake Pedder
Mount Anne
Lake Judd
Mount Weld

OCEAN
Low Rocky Point
Elliott Bay
SOUTHWEST
ROOKERY PLAIN
Frankland Peak
Pedder
Scotts Peak Dam
SOUTHWEST CA
Mount Frederic

Nye Bay
Bottom Rocks
Elliott Point
NATIONAL
Mount Gaffney
Piners Peak
Mount Giblin
CROSSING PLAINS
Edgar Dam
SOUTHWEST CA

Mulcahy Bay
Brier Holme Head
Svenor Point
Wreck Bay
DE WITT RANGE
Mount Hean
Mount Robinson
Mount Braddon
Mount Hesperus
ARTHUR RANGE
GRACROFT PLAINS
Mount Rivaeux
Mount Picton

TASMAN SEA
0 10 20 km
Althild Bight
Sandblow Bay
PARK
Mount Legge
TASMANIAN WILDERNESS AREA (WORLD HERITAGE)
Mount Aldebaran
Mount Piguenit
Mount Chapman

Craggy Island
SISTER ISLANDS CONSERVATION AREA
Outer Sister Island
Inner Sister Island
Stanley Point
Holloway Point
South East Bight
North Head
Mount King
ROWITTA PLAINS
Mount Norold
Federation Peak

Blyth Point
Palana
Quoin Hill
Foochow Beach
N
South East Bight
Point Saint Vincent
Mount Berry
Port Davey
Mount Rugby
Mount Pollux
High Round Mountain
Mount Bobs

Mount Killiecrankie
Killiecrankie Bay
Killiecrankie
Mount Blyth
WINGAROO NR
Mount Boyes
FLINDERS ISLAND
Bathurst Harbour

Cape Frankland
Mount Tanner
Leeka
PASCO GROUP
Pine Scrub
Foochow Inlet
Hilliard Head
Stephens Bay
Mount Rallinga
Mount Fulton
SOUTHWEST
Mount Louisa
Mount Bisdee

Marshall Bay
Lughrata
Memana
Babel Island
Cat Island
Mutton Bird Is
SOUTH COAST TRACK
Melaleuca
Mount Counsel
NATIONAL
Mount Wylly

Emita
Wybalenna
HISTORIC TOWN
South Patriarch
Sellars Point
Planter Beach
Sellars Lagoon
Flying Cloud Point
Island Bay
SOUTHWEST CA
Mount Melaleuca
LOUISA PLAINS

Prime Seal Island
Blue Rocks
Chalky Island
Parrys Bay
Flinders Island Airport
Survey Hill
Cameron Inlet
Window Pane Bay
Mount Karamu
Mount Wylly
New River Lagoon

Low Islets
Whitemark
Mount Hauland
LOGAN LAGOON CA
Mount Karamu
LOUISA PLAINS
Prion Bay
Pindars Peak

East Kangaroo Island
B85
Ranga
Logan Lagoon
South West Cape
Telopea Point
Red Point
Ile Du Golfe
Point Vivian

FURNEAUX
Big Green Island
Loccota
STRZELECKI NP
Cooma
Vinegat Hill
Lady Barron
Great Dog Island
Karamu Bay
Flat Witch Is
De Witt Is
MAATSUYKER GROUP
Surprise Bay
Shoemaker Point

CHAPPELL ISLANDS
Mount Chappell Island
Goose Island
Badger Island
Anderson Island
Tin Kettle Island
Vansittart Island
Puncheon Point
Needle Rocks
Maatsuyker Island
South Cape

CHAPPELL ISLANDS NR
GROUP
Long Island
Cape Barren Island
Mount Munro
Deep Bay
Big Stony Hill
Harleys Point

Sir John Cape
River Point
Preservation Island
Double Peak
Cape Barren Island
Phils Hill
Hogans Hill
Jamiesons Bay

BASS STRAIT
Dyas Bay
Foam Point
Home Hill
Spike Bay
Green Hill
CLARKE ISLAND NR
Kent Bay
Mount Kerford
Cone Point
Passage Island
Mewstone

Clarke Island
Forsyth Island
Moriarty Point

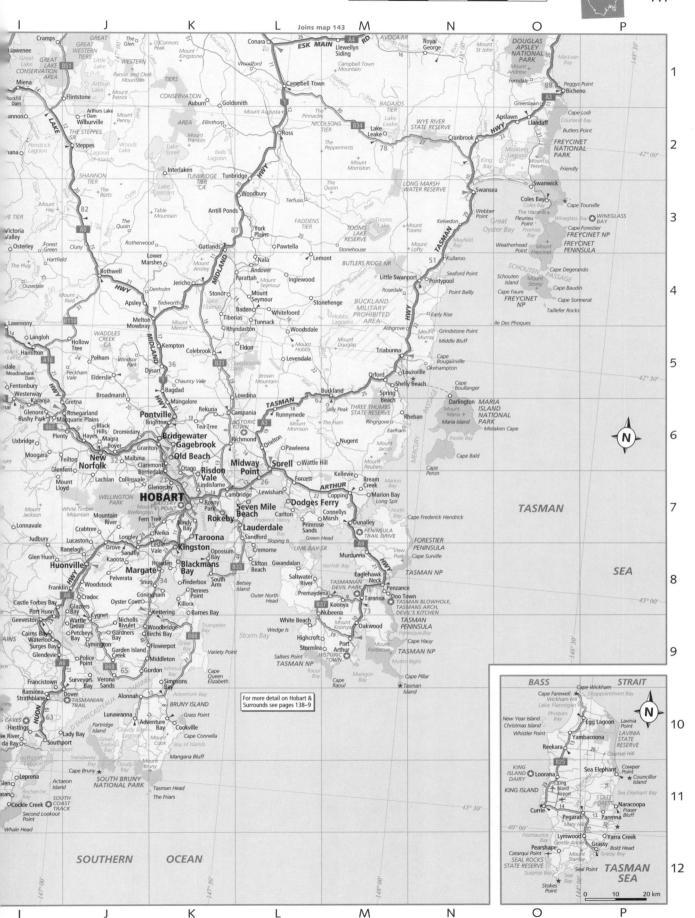

Joins map 143

0   10   20   30   40   50 km

Main map labels (I–P columns, rows 1–12):

Cramps · Liawenee · GREAT WESTERN TIERS · The Glen · O'Connors Peak · Mount Kingstone · Conara · Llewellyn Siding · ESK MAIN RD · A4 · AVOCA RR · St Pauls · Royal George · Mount St John · DOUGLAS APSLEY NATIONAL PARK · MacLean Bay

GREAT LAKE CONSERVATION AREA · Great Lake · B51 · Little Lake · WESTERN TIERS · Parson and Clerk Mountain · Woodford · Campbell Town Mountain · BADAJOS TIER · Mount Andrew · Ferndale

Miena · Flintstone · Arthurs Lake · Arthurs Lake Dam · Mount Penny · Campbell Town · Greenlawn · Apslawn · Peggys Point · Bicheno · 89

Rockfill Dam · Cannon · Wilburville · Mount Patrick · CONSERVATION AREA · Auburn · Goldsmith · The Pinnacles · Campbell Town · Lake Leake · WYE RIVER STATE RESERVE · Cranbrook · A3 · Cape Lodi · Llandaff · Courland Bay · FREYCINET NATIONAL PARK

THE STEPPES SR · Mount Penny · Ellinthorp · Ross · NICOLSONS TIER · B34 · Lake Leake · 78 · Swan · Coles Bay · Cape Tourville · Swanwick · 42°00'

Steppes · Interlaken · Lake Sorell · Tunbridge · HWY · The Peppermints · Mount Morriston · Swansea · Coles Bay · The Hazards · Fleurieu Point · WINEGLASS BAY · Cape Forestier · FREYCINET NP

SHANNON TIER · Lagoon of Islands · TUNBRIDGE TIER CA · Tunbridge · Woodbury · Terfusis · FADDENS TIER · TOOMS LAKE RESERVE · Tooms Lake · Mount Tooms · Kelvedon · Webber Point · Great Oyster Bay · Promise Bay · Cape Baudin · Promise Bay · FREYCINET PENINSULA

82 · The Butts · Table Mountain · Antill Ponds · Pawtella · Stonehouse · Mount Lofty · Little Swanport · Seaford Point · Pontypool · Weatherhead Point · Mount Freycinet · SCHOUTEN PASSAGE · Cape Degerando

87 · York Plains · Nala · Lemont · BUTLERS RIDGE NR · 51 · Kullaroo · Schouten Island · Mount Storey · Cape Faure

Osterley · Cluny · Rotherwood · Oatlands · Andover · Inglewood · Stonehenge · BUCKLAND MILITARY PROHIBITED AREA · Rosedale · Point Bailly · FREYCINET NP · Cape Sonnerat · Taillefer Rocks

Hartfield · Bothwell · Lower Marshes · Jericho · Parattah · Mount Seymour · Early Rise · Ashgrove · Ile Des Phoques

The Plug · Denham · Apsley · Tedworth · Stonor · Baden · Tunnack · Woodsdale · Mount Murray · Grindstone Point · Middle Bluff

Victoria Valley · Melton Mowbray · Mount Mercer · Tiberias · Whiteford · Hobbs Lagoons · Mount Douglas · Triabunna · Cape Bougainville · Okehampton

Lawrenny · Langloh · Hollow Tree · Kempton · Rhyndaston · Eldon · Levendale · Mount Hobbs · Orford · Louisville · MARIA ISLAND NATIONAL PARK

Hamilton · Pelham · Colebrook · Lowdina · TASMAN · Buckland · Shelly Beach · Darlington · Maria Island · Mistaken Cape · 42°30'

Meadowbank Dam · Fentonbury · Westerway · Karanja · Gretna · Eldersie · Dysart · B31 · Campania · Richmond · Runnymede · HISTORIC TOWN · Spring Beach · Rheban · Mount Maria · Riedle Bay

Glenora · Rosegarland · Macquarie Plains · Bushy Park · Broadmarsh · Bagdad · Mangalore · Rekuna · A3 · Onelton · Mount Morrison · The Ham · Ringrove · Earlham · Cape Bald

Uxbridge · Plenty · Hayes · Magra · Boyer · Pontville · Brighton · Tea Tree · Richmond · Pawleena · Nugent · Mount Jacob · Cape Peron

Moogara · Feilton · Malbina · Bridgewater · Gagebrook · Granton · Otago · Midway Point · Forcett · Kellevie · Mount Reuben · N

New Norfolk · Claremont · Old Beach · Risdon Vale · Sorell · Bream Creek · Marion Bay · Cape Frederick Hendrick · TASMAN

Glenfern · Lachlan · Berriedale · Lindisfarne · Cambridge · Lewisham · Copping · ARTHUR · Long Spit

Mount Lloyd · Collinsvale · Glenorchy · HOBART · Rosny · BATTERY POINT · Dodges Ferry · Connellys Marsh · Dunalley · North Head · FORESTIER PENINSULA · SEA

WELLINGTON PARK · White Timber Mountain · Mount Wellington · Fern Tree · Rokeby · Seven Mile Beach · Carlton · Primrose Sands · Green Head · PENINSULA TRAIL DRIVE · Cape Surville · TASMAN NP

Lonnavale · Crabtree · Mountain River · Neika · Taroona · Lauderdale · Sandford · Sloping Is · LIME BAY SR · Murdunna · View Peak · 43°00'

Judbury · Lucaston · Longley · Grove · Kingston · Cremorne · Gwandalan · TASMANIAN DEVIL PARK · Eaglehawk Neck · A9 · HWY

Glen Huon · Ranelagh · Sandfly · Blackmans Bay · Clifton Beach · Saltwater River · Penzance · TASMAN NP

Huonville · Woodstock · Pelverata · Howden · Snug · Tinderbox · South Arm · White Beach · Premaydena · Koonya · Taranna · Doo Town · TASMAN BLOWHOLE, TASMANS ARCH, DEVIL'S KITCHEN · 73

Franklin · Cradoc · Coningham · Dennes Point · Betsey Island · Outer North Head · B37 · Nubeena · Oakwood · TASMAN PENINSULA

Castle Forbes Bay · Glaziers Bay · Cygnet · Oyster Cove · Killora · Barnes Bay · Wedge Is · Mount Koonya · Port Arthur · Fortescue Bay

Port Huon · Wattle Grove · Nicholls Rivulet · Woodbridge · Birchs Bay · Trumpeter Bay · Highcroft · HISTORIC TOWN · Cape Hauy

Geeveston · Cairns Bay · Petcheys Bay · Gardners Bay · Flowerpot · Middleton · Stormlea · Port Arthur · TASMAN NP · Musra Bight

Waterloo · Surges Bay · Lymington · Garden Island Creek · Variety Point · Salters Point · TASMAN NP · Maingon Bay

Glendevie · A6 · Police Point · Gordon · Cape Queen Elizabeth · Raoul Bay · Cape Pillar

Francistown · Surveyors Bay · Verona Sands · Simpsons Bay · 65 · Isthmus Bay · Cape Raoul · Tasman Island

Raminea · Dover · Alonnah · Adventure Bay · For more detail on Hobart & Surrounds see pages 138–9

Strathblane · TASMANIAN TRAIL · 63 · Lunawanna · BRUNY ISLAND · Grass Point

HUON · D'ENTRECASTEAUX · Partridge Island · Adventure Bay · Cookville · Cape Connella

Hastings · Lady Bay · Cloudy Bay Lagoon · Mount Cook · Bay of Islands

Leprena · CAVES · Actaeon Island · Mangana Bluff

Cockle Cook · SOUTH COAST TRACK · Cape Bruny · SOUTH BRUNY NATIONAL PARK · Tasman Head · The Friars

Whale Head · Second Lookout Point · Recherche Bay

SOUTHERN OCEAN · 43°30'

King Island inset (BASS STRAIT):

Cape Wickham · Wickham Hill · Disappointment Bay

Cape Farewell · New Year Island · Christmas Island · Whistler Point · Phoques Bay · Egg Lagoon · Lavinia Point · LAVINIA STATE RESERVE

Reekara · Yambacoona · 26 · Sea Elephant · Cowper Point · Councillor Island

KING ISLAND DAIRY · Loorana · B25 · King Island Airport · Sea Elephant Bay

Currie · 14 · KING ISLAND · Naracoopa · Fraser Bluff · STATE FOREST · Parenna

Pegarah · Mary Hill · 12 · Bold Head

Lymwood · Gentle Annie · Grassy · Grassy Bay

Pearshape · Catarqui Point · SEAL ROCKS STATE RESERVE · Mount Stanley · Yarra Creek · Seal Point

Surprise Bay · Seal Bay · Stokes Point · 40°00' · TASMAN SEA

0   10   20 km

148°30' · 148°00' · 147°30' · 147°00'

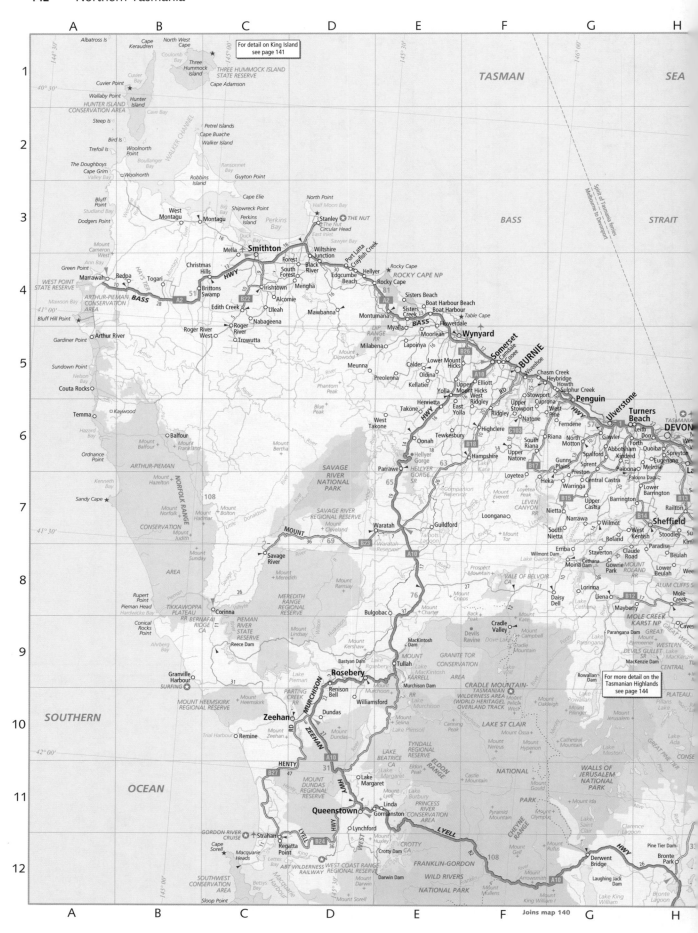

0 10 20 30 40 50 km

I J K L M N O P

1

TASMAN SEA

For more detail on Flinders Island
see page 140

FURNEAUX
GROUP

CHAPPELL ISLANDS

CHAPPELL ISLANDS NR

Goose
Is

East Kangaroo Is

Big
Green
Is

Barclay Hill
Mount Boobstead
Trousers Point
Loccota
Mount Razorback

Ranga
FLINDERS
ISLAND
STRZELECKI
NP
B85
Lady Barron

Mount Chappell Is

Anderson Is

Pigs Head Point
Tin Kettle
Is

Great Dog Is

Long Is
Neds Point

Boxen Is

Badger
Island

Cape Barren
Island
Barretts Hill
Double
Peak
Mount
Munro
Lascars Hill

Cape Barren Island

Big Stony Hill

Phils Hill

Deep
Bay

Mount
Kerferd

2

Sir John Cape

Preservation Is

Rum Is

Foam Point

Dyas
Bay
Battery
Point
Home Hill
Clarke Island
Green
Hill
Lookout Head

CLARKE
ISLAND NR
Seal Point
Forsyth
Is
Black Point
Passage
Is

Kent
Bay
Crystal
Lagoon

40° 30'

3

South
Head

Moriarty Point

BANKS   STRAIT

TASMAN SEA

Foster
Islands

Cape
Portland

Petal Point

Cape
Portland

Lyme
Regis
Swan
Island

Rushy
Lagoon

Great Musselroe

Icena

MUSSELROE BAY
CONSERVATION AREA
Musselroe Point
Musselroe Bay
Cape Naturaliste
Stumpys
Bay
Boulder Point

Mount
William

Cod Bay

4

Ninth
Island

Waterhouse
Island

Waterhouse
Point

Croppies Point

West Sandy Point
St Albans
Bay
East Sandy Point
Anderson Bay

Waterhouse

Tomahawk

Boobyalla

Waterhouse

WATERHOUSE
CONSERVATION
AREA

Ringarooma
Bay

Gladstone

Eddystone Point

MOUNT WILLIAM
NATIONAL PARK

Purdon Bay

41° 00'

5

Stony Head

STONY HEAD ARTILLERY
RANGE PROHIBITED AREA
Lulworth
Noland Bay
Weymouth
Bellingham
Back
Creek
Leura

DOUBLE SANDY
POINT CA

Bridport

CAMERON
REGIONAL
RESERVE
Mount
Cameron

South
Mount Cameron

B82

Ansons Bay
Ansons Bay

more detail on
ceston Region
see page 145

West Head

Low
Head
Greens
Beach
Low Head
PENGUINS
George
Town
Kelso
Beechford

NARAWNTAPU
NP
Clarence Point
Beauty Point
Bell Bay
Kayena
Rowella
Sidmouth

NORTHERN
TASMANIA
WINERIES
Beaconsfield

Badger
Head

ell

Lefroy
Pipers
River
The
Glen
Glen
Lebrina

Pipers Brook

B82

B84

Jetsonville
North
Scottsdale

Forester

Warrentinna

Mount
Horror

Winnaleah
Herrick
Moorina
Pioneer

Derby

Policemans
Point

BAY OF FIRES

6

West
Frankford
Frankford

Flowery Gully
Holwell

Exeter
Deviot
Hillwood
Robigana
Gravelly
Beach
Windermere
Mount
Direction

Lower Turners
Marsh
Bangor
North
Lilydale
Karoola
Lilydale
Turners
Marsh

Golconda

B81

Lisle

Wyena

Nabowla

West
Scottsdale

Scottsdale

Tonganah

Springfield
Cuckoo

Telita

Kamona

Tulendeena
Branxholm

Legerwood

Weldborough

Lottah
Goulds Country

The Shades
Big
Lagoon

The Gardens

CONSERVATION
AREA

Binalong Bay
Grants Point

7

B71

Winkleigh

Glengarry
Lanena
Rosevears
Dilston
Underwood
Myrtle
Bank
Targa

Patersonia

Ringarooma
Alberton

Talawa

Goshen
Priory
Pyengana

St Helens Point

RATTLER RANGE

Legana
Rocherlea

St Patricks River

Diddleum
Plains

Mount
Maurice

Trenah

Mount
Victoria

8

Reedy
Marsh
Birralee
Rosevale
Selbourne

Notley
Hills
Bridgenorth

B72

Riverside
Trevallyn
Waverley
Mowbray

LAUNCESTON

HISTORIC TOWN,
CATARACT GORGE

Numamara

Mount
Barrow

Tayene

Mount
Saddleback

Mount
Blackboy

Mount
Young

Mount
Albert

George

Pyengana

St Helens

Akaroa
Stieglitz
Parnella

St Helens Island

Dianas Basin

ST HELENS CA

Weetah

Deloraine

Westwood
Hadspen
Carrick
St Leonards
Kings Meadows
Relbia
Corra Linn
White Hills

Burns Creek

Musselboro

Upper
Esk

Roses Tier

Mathinna

Beaumaris
Shelly Point

SIDA TIER

9

Exton
Westbury
Osmaston
Glenore
Hagley
Whitemore
Oaks
Toiberry
Perth
Pateena
Breadalbane
Western Junction

Blessington

Upper
Blessington
Carr Villa

Legges Tor
BEN
LOMOND
NATIONAL
PARK
SKI AREA
The
Knuckle

Tower Hill

Upper
Scamander

Cornwall

Scamander

Henderson Lagoon

Falmouth

41° 30'

Quamby Brook
Cluan

Bracknell
Bishopsbourne
Longford

Deddington

Clarendon
Nile
Hampden

English
Town

FISHERS TIER

Mangana

St Marys

B43

Four Mile Creek

A3

Golden
Valley

Evandale

10

A5

Liffey

Jackeys
Marsh

Blackwood
Creek

Cressy
Kilrae

Poatina

Talentyre
Pisa

Parknook

B51

WESTERN

Epping Forest

B53

MIDLAND

Esk Vale

Kelvin
Grove
Ellerslie

Cleveland

Brambletey

Bona-Vista Estate
South

Avoca

Llewellyn
Siding

Conara

Rossarden
Rostrevor
Ormley

CASTLE
CARY
RR

B42

Fingal

Royal
George

Gray

Mount
Malcolm

AVOCA RR
St Pauls

Mount
St John

MAIN

Mount
Foster

RD

Seymour

DOUGLAS
APSLEY
NATIONAL
PARK

Wardlaws Point

Chain of Lagoons

Piccaninny Point

Long Point

TASMAN

SEA

10

Breona

Liawenee

Cramps

GREAT
WESTERN

TIERS

Mount
Kingstone

The
Retreat

Mount
Blackwood

Connors
Peak

Rokeby

Woodford

Campbell Town

ESK

Avoca

AVOCA RR

BADAJOS TIER

Mount
Henry

FINGAL

MacLean Bay

11

Miena

GREAT
LAKE
CA

Flintstone

Little
Lake
Parson and Clerk
Mountain

Arthurs
Lake

CONSERVATION

TIERS
AREA

Auburn
Goldsmith

Auburn

The
Pinnacles

Campbell
Town
Mountain

Campbell Town

Elizabeth

Ferndale

Apslawn

B89

Peggys Point

APSLEY
CA

Bicheno

Cape Lodi

42° 00'

St Patricks
Plains

Penstock
Lagoon

Arthurs Lake
Dam

Mount
Penny

Wilburville

Mount
Patrick

Ellinthorp

Mount
Franklin

Bells
Lagoon

The
Peppermints

WYE RIVER
STATE RESERVE

Mount
Morrison

TASMAN

Greenlawn

Llandaff

Courland Bay

Butlers
Point

FREYCINET
NATIONAL
PARK

COLES
BAY

12

THE STEPPES
SR
Steppes

Shannon

Interlaken

Lake
Crescent

TUNBRIDGE TIER
CONSERVATION
AREA

Tunbridge

Ross

Lake Leake

WINGS TIER

LONG MARSH
WATER RESERVE

Cranbrook

PARAMORES TIER

A3

Swansea

Swanwick

Kings
Bay
Mount Peter

Friendly Point

Mount Stacey

A5

Lake
Sorell

Mount
Franklin

DOGS HEAD

Lagoon
of Islands

Woods
Lake

Lake
Crescent

Mount
Morrison
The Quoin

Joins map 141

I J K L M N O P

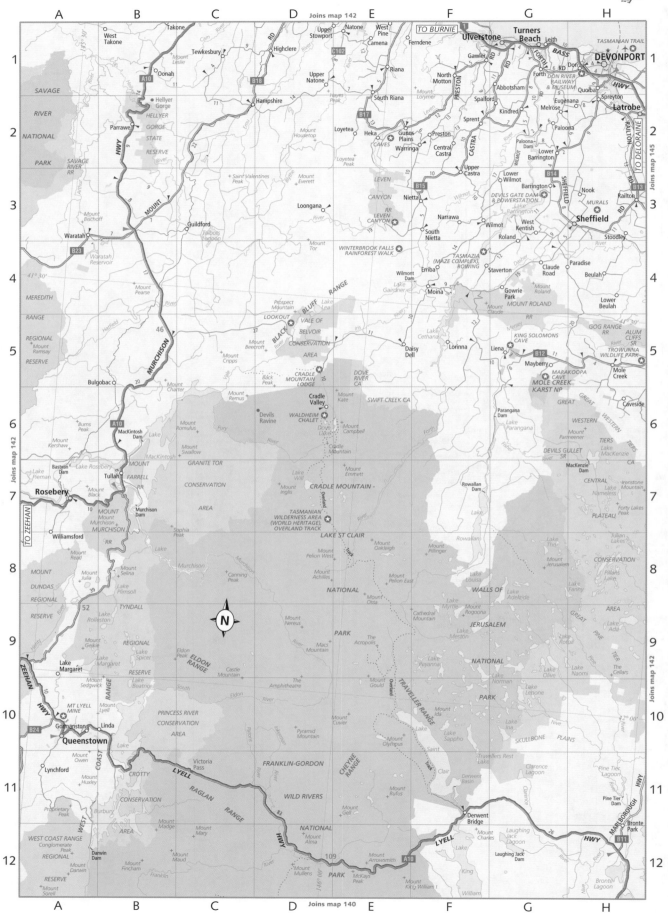

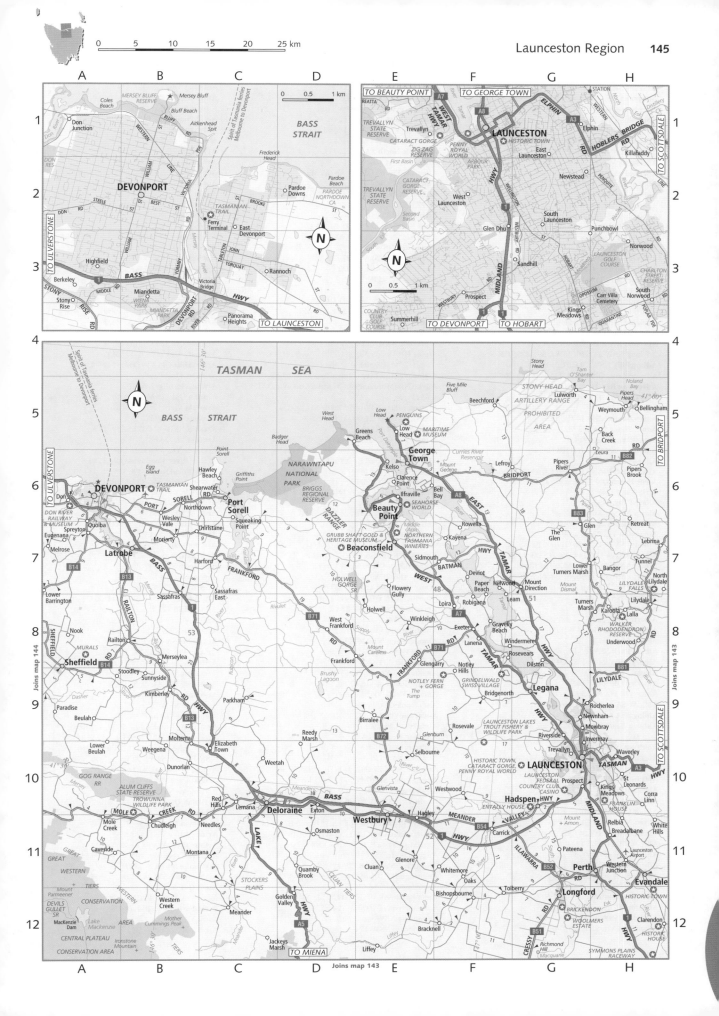

Index of Place Names

A1 Mine Settlement Vic. 43 P4, 52 H3
Abbeyard Vic. 55 J10, 56 H9
Abbotsford Vic. xv N9, xvii O1
Abbotsham Tas. 142 G6, 144 G1
Abercorn Qld 123 K3
Abercrombie River NP NSW 24 H7, 35 E1
Aberdeen NSW 25 K1, 26 H12
Aberfeldie Vic. xiv D2
Aberfeldy Vic. 52 H4
Abergowrie Qld 120 E7, 127 L9
Abermain NSW 13 E2, 19 A8, 25 L4
Acacia NT 102 E5, 104 D5
Acheron Vic. 41 F2, 43 N1, 52 F1, 54 F12, 56 B11
Acland Qld 123 K8
Acton ACT 32 A3
Acton Park WA 86 C7
Adaminaby NSW 24 E12, 35 B6, 36 E7, 51 D2
Adamsfield Tas. 138 A2, 140 G6
Adavale Qld 133 M4
Addington Vic. 42 C2, 49 B8, 63 L3
Adelaide SA xxi J6, 65, 66 C7, 67 B9, 68 F2, 69 H7,
    71 B3, 73 J9
Adelaide Airport SA xx D8
Adelaide Lead Vic. 49 B6, 61 L12
Adelaide River NT 102 E8, 104 D6
Adelong NSW 24 D10, 35 A4, 36 B2, 55 P2
Adjungbilly NSW 24 E10, 35 B4, 36 D1
Advancetown Qld 21 G1, 115 F10, 116 C6
Adventure Bay Tas. 139 I11, 141 K10
Agery SA 69 E4, 72 H7
Agnes Vic. 52 H10
Agnes Banks NSW 14 H4, 17 N7
Agnes Water Qld 123 M2
Agnew WA 90 G1, 92 G11
Aileron Roadhouse NT 108 H5
Ailsa Vic. 60 G7
Aireys Inlet Vic. 42 D10, 50 F3, 63 N9
Airlie Beach Qld 119 F5, 125 J3
Airly Vic. 53 K6
Akaroa Tas. 143 P8
Alawa NT xxvii D4
Alawoona SA 28 A7, 58 A8, 71 G2, 73 N9
Albacutya Vic. 28 D11, 60 F4
Albany WA 87 D11, 88 G11, 90 E11
Albany Creek Qld 114 D5, 115 D3, 117 F10
Albert NSW 24 C1, 26 A12, 31 P12
Albert Park SA 66 B6, 67 B8, 68 E1
Albert Park Vic. xvii I7
Alberton SA 66 B6
Alberton Tas. 143 N7
Alberton Vic. 53 I9
Alberton West Vic. 53 I9
Albion Qld xxxi I4
Albion Park NSW 23 E6
Albury NSW 24 A12, 29 O12, 55 K6, 57 I2
Alcomie Tas. 142 C4
Alderley Qld xxx E3
Aldersyde WA 88 E5
Aldgate SA 66 E8, 67 C10, 68 G3
Aldinga SA 67 A12, 68 E5
Aldinga Beach SA 67 A12, 68 E6, 69 H9, 71 B4,
    73 J10
Alectown NSW 24 E3
Alexander Morrison NP WA 88 A1, 90 B5
Alexandra Vic. 41 F1, 43 N1, 52 F1, 54 F12, 56 B10
Alexandra Hills Qld 115 F5, 117 G12
Alexandria NSW viii D9
Alford SA 69 F2, 73 I6
Alfred Cove WA xxiv E10
Alfred NP Vic. 35 C11, 51 F11
Alfred Town NSW 24 C10, 29 P10, 55 N1
Alice NSW 21 C5, 27 M4, 123 M12
Alice Springs NT 109 I7, 111 J3, 111 K9
Ali-Curung NT 107 J12, 109 J1
Alison NSW 19 E4, 20 B10
Allambee Vic. 43 O9, 52 G7
Allambee South Vic. 43 O10, 52 G8
Allambie Heights NSW xi L1
Allandale NSW 13 E1, 19 A7
Allans Flat Vic. 55 K7, 57 I4

Allansford Vic. 50 D8, 62 H8
Allanson WA 86 G3, 88 C8
Alleena NSW 24 B6, 29 P6
Allenby Gardens SA xx F2
Allendale Vic. 42 D2, 49 D8, 63 M3
Allendale East SA 62 A6, 71 G12
Allendale North SA 67 E2, 71 C1, 73 K7
Allens Rivulet Tas. 138 H7
Allenvale Vic. 42 D11, 50 E4, 63 M9
Allies Creek Qld 123 K6
Alligator Creek Qld 119 G8, 120 G11, 124 G1,
    127 N12
Allora Qld 123 L10
Alma SA 67 C2, 69 H4, 71 B1, 73 J7
Alma Vic. 49 B5, 61 L11, 63 L1
Alma Park NSW 24 A11, 29 N11, 55 K3
Almaden Qld 120 A3, 127 J7
Almonds Vic. 54 H6, 56 D2
Almurta Vic. 45 P10
Almurta East Vic. 45 P10
Alonnah Tas. 138 H10, 141 J10
Alpara NT 78 G2, 108 E11
Alpha Qld 124 F10
Alphadale NSW 21 G5, 27 O3
Alpine NP Vic. 35 A9, 36 B11, 51 A6, 52 H1, 53 J1,
    54 H12, 55 N9, 56 F9, 57 K8
Alpine NP (Cobberas–Tingaringy) Vic. 55 N9, 57 N8
Alpine NP (Wonnangatta Moroka Unit) Vic. 53 K3,
    55 J12, 56 H12
Alpurrurulam NT 107 P12, 109 P1, 130 C4
Alstonville NSW 21 G5, 27 O3, 123 N12
Alton NP Qld 122 G9
Altona Vic. 40 C6, 43 I6, 52 B5
Alva Qld 119 C2, 124 H1, 127 O12
Alvie Vic. 42 A8, 50 B1, 63 K7
Alyangula NT 105 M7
Amamoor Qld 118 D10
Amanbidji NT 95 P5, 99 O7, 104 B12, 106 B3
Amata SA 78 G2, 108 E11
Amboyne Crossing Vic. 35 B10, 51 C7
Ambrose Qld 125 N12
Amby Qld 122 F6
American Beach SA 69 F11, 73 I11
American River SA 69 E11, 72 H11
Amherst Vic. 49 B6, 61 L12, 63 L1
Amiens Qld 21 A3, 27 K2, 123 K11
Amity Point Qld 115 H4, 123 N9
Amoonguna NT 109 I7, 111 J4
Amosfield NSW 21 B3, 27 L2
Amphion WA 85 F10
Amphitheatre Vic. 61 K12, 63 K2
Ampilatwatja NT 109 K3
Anakie Qld 124 H10
Anakie Vic. 42 F6, 63 N6
Anakie East Vic. 42 F6, 63 O6
Anakie Junction Vic. 42 F6, 63 N6
Ancona Vic. 54 G10, 56 B9
Andamooka SA 74 F3
Anderson Vic. 43 L11, 45 N11, 52 E8
Ando NSW 35 C9, 51 F6
Andover Tas. 141 L4
Andrews Qld 116 E9
Andrews SA 73 J5
Anembo NSW 24 G12, 34 G11, 35 D6, 37 I6, 51 G1
Angas Valley SA 67 H7, 71 D2, 73 L8
Angaston SA 67 F4, 71 C2, 73 K8
Angip Vic. 28 D12, 60 G6
Angle Vale SA 66 D2, 67 C6, 69 H6, 71 B2, 73 J8
Anglers Reach NSW 24 E12, 35 B6, 36 E7, 51 D2
Anglers Rest Vic. 53 M1, 55 M11, 57 L10
Anglesea Vic. 42 E10, 50 F3, 63 N9
Angleside Vic. 55 I8, 56 F6
Angourie NSW 21 F8, 27 O5
Angurugu NT 105 M7
Angustown Vic. 54 D9
Anna Bay NSW 19 G8, 20 C12, 25 M4
Annaburroo NT 102 H6, 104 E5
Annandale NSW viii C5, x C12
Annangrove NSW 12 C3, 15 J6

Annerley Qld xxx G12, 114 E8, 115 D5, 117 F11
Annuello Vic. 28 F8, 59 J9
Ansons Bay Tas. 143 P6
Antill Ponds Tas. 141 L3
Antwerp Vic. 28 D12, 60 F7
Anula NT xxvii E5
Apamurra SA 67 G8, 71 D3, 73 K9
Aparawatatja SA 78 D2, 108 C11
Apollo Bay Vic. 42 B12, 50 C6, 63 L10
Appila SA 73 J3, 74 H11
Appin NSW 23 F2, 25 J8, 35 H2
Appin Vic. 28 H11, 61 M5
Appin South Vic. 61 N5
Apple Tree Creek Qld 118 C4, 123 M4
Apple Tree Flat NSW 14 C7, 16 F12, 21 C8, 23 A8,
    25 I9, 27 M5, 35 F3
Applecross WA xxiv E9
Applethorpe Qld 21 A3, 27 L2, 123 L11
Apslawn Tas. 141 O2, 143 O11
Apsley Tas. 141 J4
Apsley Vic. 60 B10, 71 H9
Arakwal NP NSW 21 H4, 27 O3, 123 N12
Araluen NSW 24 H12, 35 E6, 37 K5
Araluen North NSW 37 K5
Aramac Qld 124 D9, 131 P9
Aramara Qld 118 C6, 123 M5
Arana Hills Qld 114 D6, 115 D3, 117 E10
Arapiles Vic. 60 E9
Ararat Vic. 61 I12, 63 I2
Aratula Qld 123 M10
Arawata Vic. 43 N10, 52 F8
Arawerr NT 109 K3
Arcadia NSW 12 D3, 13 A10, 15 K5
Arcadia Vic. 54 E8
Archdale Vic. 49 A3, 61 L10
Archer River Roadhouse Qld 128 D9
Archerfield Qld 114 E8, 115 D5, 117 F12
Archies Creek Vic. 43 L11, 45 P12, 52 E9
Ardath WA 88 G4
Ardeer Vic. 43 I5, 63 P5
Ardglen NSW 26 H11
Ardlethan NSW 24 B7, 29 O7
Ardmona Vic. 54 E7
Ardmory Qld 115 A3, 117 C10
Ardross WA xxiv F10
Ardrossan SA 69 F5, 71 A1, 73 I7
Areegra Vic. 61 I7
Areyonga NT 108 G7, 110 A6
Argalong NSW 24 E10, 35 B4, 36 D2
Argoon Qld 123 J1
Argyle Vic. 54 B10, 61 P11, 63 P1
Ariah Park NSW 24 B7, 29 P7
Arkaroola SA 70 F2, 75 K3
Arkona Vic. 28 D12, 60 F7
Arltunga Bush Hotel NT 109 K6, 111 N1
Armadale Vic. xvii O9
Armadale WA 84 F9, 85 D6, 88 C5, 90 C8
Armatree NSW 26 C10
Armidale NSW 20 B1, 27 J8
Armstrong Vic. 61 I12, 63 I2
Armstrong Beach Qld 119 G9, 125 K6
Armytage Vic. 42 C8, 50 D1, 63 M8
Arncliffe NSW viii A12, 12 E9, 15 L10
Arno Bay SA 69 A2, 72 F6
Arnold Vic. 49 D2, 61 M9
Arnold West Vic. 49 C2, 61 M9
Arrawarra NSW 21 E10, 27 N7
Arrilalah Qld 124 A10, 131 M10
Arrino WA 90 B4
Artarmon NSW x E5
Arthur River Tas. 142 A5
Arthur River WA 88 E8, 90 D9
Arthurs Creek Vic. 40 F3, 41 A5, 43 K4, 52 D3
Arthurton SA 69 E4, 72 H7
Arthurville NSW 24 F2
Ascot Qld xxxi K4
Ascot Vic. 42 C2, 49 C9, 63 M3
Ascot Park SA xx F12, 66 C8
Ascot Vale Vic. xiv F5
Ascot WA xxv C5

Ashbourne SA 68 G6, 71 C4, 73 J10
Ashens Vic. 60 H9
Ashfield WA xxv C4, 84 E5, 85 C5
Ashford NSW 27 I4
Ashford SA xx G7
Ashgrove Qld xxx D4, 114 D7
Ashley NSW 26 F4, 122 H12
Ashmore Qld 116 E6
Ashville SA 71 D5, 73 L11
Aspendale Vic. 43 J7, 45 K2, 52 C5
Aspendale Gardens Vic. 45 K2
Aspley Qld 114 E5, 115 D3, 117 F10
Asquith NSW 12 E4, 13 B10, 15 L6
Astrebla Downs NP Qld 130 G11
Atherton Qld 120 D3, 121 D9, 127 L7
Athlone Vic. 43 N9, 52 F7
Atitjere NT 109 K5
Atneltyey NT 109 J3
Attadale WA xxiv D10
Attunga NSW 26 H9
Aubrey Vic. 60 G7
Auburn NSW 12 D7, 13 A12, 15 K8
Auburn SA 73 J6
Auburn Tas. 141 K1, 143 K11
Auburn River NP Qld 123 K5
Auchenflower Qld xxx D7
Augathella Qld 122 C4, 133 P4
Augusta WA 86 C11, 88 B10, 90 B11
Auldana SA xxi P5
Aurora Kakadu Resort NT 103 M4, 104 G4
Aurukun Qld 128 B8
Auski Roadhouse WA 89 H3, 92 D4, 97 I9
Austinmer NSW 23 G4
Austins Ferry Tas. 137 B2
Austinville Qld 116 C9
Austral NSW 14 H9, 25 J7, 35 H1
Australia Plains SA 73 K7
Australind WA 86 E3, 88 C8, 90 C9
Avalon NSW 12 H3, 13 C10, 15 N6
Avalon Vic. 44 B2
Avenel Vic. 54 D10
Avenue SA 71 F9
Avoca Tas. 143 M10
Avoca Vic. 49 A6, 61 L12, 63 L1
Avoca Beach NSW 13 E8, 15 O3
Avoca Vale Qld 118 B11, 123 L7
Avon SA 69 G4, 71 B1, 73 J7
Avon Plains Vic. 61 J8
Avon Valley NP WA 84 G1, 85 E2, 88 C4, 90 C7
Avondale NSW 13 E4, 19 A10, 23 E5, 25 J8, 35 H3
Avondale Qld 118 C1
Avondale Heights Vic. xiv A1
Avonsleigh Vic. 41 C10, 45 O1
Awaba NSW 13 F4, 19 B10
Awonga Vic. 60 C10, 71 H9
Axe Creek Vic. 49 G4, 54 A9, 61 O10
Axedale Vic. 49 H3, 54 B9, 61 P10
Ayr Qld 119 B2, 124 H2, 127 O12
Ayrford Vic. 50 F8, 63 I8
Ayton Qld 127 L4

Baan Baa NSW 26 F7
Baandee WA 88 F3
Baarmutha Vic. 55 J8, 56 H4
Babakin WA 88 G5
Babinda Qld 120 E4, 121 G10, 127 M7
Bacchus Marsh Vic. 42 G4, 49 G11, 52 A3, 63 O5
Back Creek Tas. 143 K5, 145 H5
Baddaginnie Vic. 54 G8, 56 C5
Baden Tas. 141 L4
Badgerys Creek NSW 14 H8, 25 J7, 35 H1
Badgingarra WA 88 A1, 90 B5
Badgingarra NP WA 88 A1, 90 B5
Badjaling WA 88 F5
Baerami NSW 25 J2
Bagdad Tas. 139 I2, 141 K5
Bagnoo NSW 20 E6, 27 L11
Bago Bluff NP NSW 20 E6, 27 L11
Bagot NT 102 D3
Bagot Well SA 67 F2, 71 C1, 73 K7
Bagshot Vic. 49 G2, 54 A8, 61 O9
Bailieston Vic. 54 D9
Baird Bay SA 72 A4, 81 N11
Bairnsdale Vic. 53 M5

Bajool Qld 125 M11
Bakara SA 71 E2, 73 M8
Baker Vic. 60 E6
Bakers Creek Qld 119 G8, 125 K6
Bakers Hill WA 85 F3, 88 D4
Bakers Swamp NSW 24 F3
Baking Board Qld 123 J7
Balaclava Vic. xvii M11
Balaklava SA 69 H4, 73 J7
Balcatta WA xxiv D1, 84 D5
Balcombe Vic. 45 J6
Bald Hills Qld 114 E5, 115 D3, 117 F10
Bald Rock Vic. 29 I12, 54 A5, 61 O6
Bald Rock NP NSW 21 A4, 27 L3, 123 L12
Baldivis WA 84 D11, 85 C7
Baldry NSW 24 E3
Balfes Creek Qld 124 E3
Balfour Tas. 142 B6
Balga WA xxiv E1
Balgal Beach Qld 120 F9, 127 M11
Balgo Hills WA 95 N10
Balgowan SA 69 D4, 72 H7
Balgowlah NSW xi L4, 12 G6, 13 C12, 15 M8
Balgowlah Heights NSW xi L5
Balgownie NSW 22 C3, 23 F4
Balhannah SA 66 F8, 67 D9, 68 H3
Balingup WA 86 G6, 88 C9, 90 C10
Balintore Vic. 42 B8, 50 B1, 63 L8
Ball Bay Qld 119 G7, 125 K5
Balladonia WA 91 K7
Balladoran NSW 26 C11
Ballajura WA xxv A1, 84 D5, 85 C4
Ballalaba NSW 24 G11, 35 E5, 37 J5
Ballan Vic. 42 F3, 49 F11, 63 N4
Ballan North Vic. 42 F3, 49 F10, 63 N4
Ballandean Qld 21 A4, 27 K3, 123 K12
Ballangeich Vic. 50 D7, 62 H7
Ballarat Vic. 42 D3, 47, 49 C10, 63 M4
Ballarat North Vic. 47 E4
Ballarat South Vic. 47 C7
Ballark Vic. 42 E4, 49 E12, 63 N5
Ballaying WA 88 F8
Ballbank NSW 28 H10, 61 N3
Balldale NSW 29 N11, 55 J4
Ballendella Vic. 54 B6, 61 P8
Balliang Vic. 42 F5, 52 A4, 63 O5
Balliang East Vic. 42 F5, 52 A4, 63 O5
Ballidu WA 88 D1, 90 C5
Ballimore NSW 24 F1, 26 D12
Ballina NSW 21 G5, 27 O3, 123 N12
Ballyrogan Vic. 63 J3
Balmain NSW viii D3, x D10
Balmain East NSW viii E3, x E11
Balmattum Vic. 54 F9, 56 B6
Balmoral NSW xi K6, 13 F4, 19 B10
Balmoral Qld xxxi J6
Balmoral Vic. 60 E12, 62 E2
Balnarring Vic. 40 E12, 43 J10, 45 K8, 52 C7
Balnarring Beach Vic. 45 K9
Balook Vic. 53 I8
Balranald NSW 28 H7, 59 M9
Balrootan North Vic. 28 C12, 60 E7
Balumbah SA 72 E4, 74 D11
Bamaga Qld 128 C3
Bamawm Vic. 29 I12, 54 B6, 61 P7
Bamawm Extension Vic. 54 B6, 61 P7
Bambaroo Qld 120 E9, 127 M10
Bambill Vic. 28 C6, 58 E7, 73 P8
Bamboo Creek WA 92 F2, 94 F12, 97 L4
Bambra Vic. 42 D9, 50 E2, 63 M8
Bamganie Vic. 42 D6, 63 M6
Banana Qld 123 I2
Bancroft Qld 123 K3
Bandiana Vic. 24 A12, 55 K6, 57 I2
Bandon Grove NSW 19 D3, 20 B9, 25 M2
Banealla SA 71 F6, 73 N12
Bangadilly NP NSW 23 A4, 25 I8, 35 F2
Bangalow NSW 21 G4, 27 O3, 123 N12
Bangerang Vic. 60 H6
Bangham SA 60 B8, 71 G8
Bangor Tas. 143 K7, 145 H7
Baniyala NT 105 M6
Banksia NSW 15 L10
Banksia Beach Qld 114 G1, 117 G7

Banksia Grove WA 84 C3
Bankstown NSW 12 C8, 15 K9
Bannaby NSW 24 H8, 35 F2
Bannerton Vic. 28 F7, 59 J9
Bannister NSW 24 G8, 35 E2
Bannister WA 85 G9, 88 D6
Bannockburn Vic. 42 E7, 63 N7
Banora Point NSW 21 H2, 27 O2, 115 G12, 116 H11, 123 N11
Banyan Vic. 61 I3
Banyena Vic. 61 I9
Bar Beach NSW 18 C9
Barabba SA 67 B2, 69 H4
Baradine NSW 26 D8
Barakee NP NSW 20 B6, 27 J11
Barakula Qld 123 J6
Baralaba Qld 123 I1, 125 L12
Baranduda Vic. 55 K6, 57 I3
Barcaldine Qld 124 D10, 131 P10
Bardon Qld xxx C6
Barellan NSW 24 A7, 29 N7
Barellan Point Qld 114 B8
Barfold Vic. 49 H6, 54 A11, 61 P12, 63 P1
Bargara Qld 118 D2, 123 M3
Bargo NSW 23 D3, 25 J8, 35 G2
Barham NSW 29 I10, 54 A2, 61 O4
Baring Vic. 28 D9, 58 G12, 60 G2
Baringhup Vic. 49 D5, 61 N11, 63 N1
Barjarg Vic. 54 G10, 56 D8
Bark Hut Inn NT 102 H6
Barkers Creek Vic. 49 F6, 54 A10, 61 O11, 63 O1
Barkly Vic. 61 L12
Barkly Homestead NT 107 L9
Barkstead Vic. 42 E2, 49 E9, 63 N3
Barmah Vic. 29 J12, 54 D5
Barmedman NSW 24 C6, 29 P6
Barmera SA 28 A6, 71 G1, 73 N7
Barmundu Qld 123 K1
Barnadown Vic. 49 H2, 54 B8, 61 P9
Barnard Island Group NP Qld 120 F5, 121 H12, 127 M8
Barnawartha Vic. 24 A12, 29 N12, 55 J6, 56 H2
Barnawartha North Vic. 55 K6, 56 H2
Barnes NSW 29 J12, 54 C5
Barnes Bay Tas. 139 I8, 141 K8
Barongarook Vic. 42 B10, 50 B3, 63 L9
Barongarook West Vic. 42 B9, 50 B2, 63 K8
Barooga NSW 29 L11, 54 G4
Barool NP NSW 21 B8, 27 L5
Baroota SA 73 I3, 74 G11
Barpinba Vic. 42 B7, 63 L7
Barraba NSW 26 H7
Barrakee Vic. 61 L7
Barramunga Vic. 42 B11, 50 C4, 63 L9
Barranyi (North Island) NP NT 105 N10, 107 N1
Barraport Vic. 28 H11, 61 M6
Barringo Vic. 40 B1, 49 H9, 52 B2, 54 B12
Barrington NSW 20 C8, 25 M1, 27 J12
Barrington Tas. 142 H7, 144 G3
Barrington Tops NP NSW 19 C1, 20 A8, 25 L1, 27 I12
Barringun NSW 31 M2, 122 A11, 133 N11
Barron Gorge NP Qld 120 D2, 121 E6, 127 L6
Barrow Creek NT 109 I2
Barry NSW 24 G5, 27 I11
Barrys Reef Vic. 42 F2, 49 F9, 52 A2, 63 O3
Barton ACT 32 D10
Barton Vic. 63 I2
Barunga NT 104 G8
Barunga Gap SA 69 G2, 73 I6
Barwidgee Creek Vic. 55 K8, 56 H5
Barwo Vic. 54 D5
Barwon Downs Vic. 42 C10, 50 C3, 63 L9
Barwon Heads Vic. 42 G9, 44 C6, 50 H2, 52 A7, 63 O8
Baryulgil NSW 21 C6, 27 M4
Basin View NSW 23 C11, 37 O2
Basket Swamp NP NSW 21 B5, 27 L3, 123 L12
Bass Vic. 43 L11, 45 O11', 52 E8
Bass Landing Vic. 45 N11
Bassendean WA xxv C4
Batchelor NT 102 E7, 104 D5
Batchica Vic. 28 E12, 60 H6
Bateau Bay NSW 13 E8, 15 P2

Batehaven NSW 24 H12, 37 L6
Bateman WA xxiv F11
Batemans Bay NSW 24 H12, 35 F6, 37 L6
Bates SA 81 J3
Batesford Vic. 42 F7, 44 A2, 63 N7
Bathumi Vic. 54 H5, 56 E1
Bathurst NSW 24 H5
Batlow NSW 24 D11, 35 A5, 36 C4, 55 P3
Battery Point Tas. xxxiv F12, 1 B8, 136 F8, 137 E8
Bauhinia Qld 122 H2
Bauhinia Downs NT 105 L11, 107 L2
Baulkham Hills NSW 12 C5, 15 J7
Bauple Qld 118 D7, 123 M5
Baw Baw NP Vic. 43 P6, 52 H5, 53 I5
Bawley Point NSW 25 I11, 35 F5, 37 N5
Baxter Vic. 40 E10, 43 J9, 45 K5, 52 D6
Bayles Vic. 43 M9, 52 E6
Baynton Vic. 54 B11, 61 P12, 63 P2
Bayswater Vic. 40 G6, 41 A8
Bayswater WA xxiv H3, xxv B4, 84 E5
Bayview NSW 12 H4, 13 C10, 15 N6
Bayview NT xxvii C9
Beachmere Qld 114 F2, 115 E1, 117 F8, 123 N8
Beachport SA 71 E10
Beacon WA 88 F1, 90 D5
Beaconsfield NSW viii E10
Beaconsfield Tas. 143 J6, 145 E7
Beaconsfield Vic. 40 G8, 41 B11, 43 K7, 45 N3, 52 E6
Beaconsfield WA xxiv C12
Beagle Bay WA 94 H6, 98 B9
Bealiba Vic. 49 A3, 61 L10
Beardmore Vic. 53 I5
Beargamil NSW 24 E3
Bearii Vic. 29 K11, 54 E4
Bears Lagoon Vic. 28 H12, 61 N7
Beauchamp Vic. 61 L3
Beaudesert Qld 21 F1, 27 N1, 115 C9, 123 M10
Beaufort SA 69 G3, 73 I6
Beaufort Vic. 42 A2, 63 K3
Beaumaris Tas. 143 O8
Beaumaris Vic. 45 J1
Beaumont SA xxi N8
Beauty Point NSW xi J5, 13 E5, 19 A11, 35 E8, 37 K11
Beauty Point Tas. 143 J6, 145 E6
Beazleys Bridge Vic. 61 J9
Beckenham WA xxv E10
Beckom NSW 24 B7, 29 O7
Bedford WA xxiv G3, xxv A4
Bedgerebong NSW 24 D4
Bedourie Qld 130 E11
Beeac Vic. 42 B8, 50 C1, 63 L7
Beebo Qld 27 I2, 123 J11
Beech Forest Vic. 42 B11, 50 B4, 63 K10
Beechboro WA xxv B2, 84 E5
Beechford Tas. 143 J5, 145 F5
Beechmont Qld 21 F1, 115 E10, 116 A8
Beechwood NSW 20 F6, 27 L11
Beechworth Vic. 55 J7, 56 H4
Beechworth Park Vic. 55 J7
Beedelup NP WA 86 G11, 87 A2, 88 C10, 90 C11
Beela WA 86 F3
Beelbangera NSW 29 M7
Beenleigh Qld 114 G11, 115 E7, 123 N10
Beerburrum Qld 117 F6
Beerwah Qld 117 F5, 118 E12, 123 N8
Bega NSW 35 E9, 37 J12, 51 H6
Beggan Beggan NSW 24 D8, 35 B2
Beilpajah NSW 28 H2
Belair SA xxi L12, 66 C8, 67 C9, 68 F3, 73 J9
Belair NP SA 66 D8, 67 C9, 68 F3, 69 H8, 71 B3, 73 J9
Belalie North SA 73 J4, 75 I11
Belbora NSW 20 C8, 25 N1, 27 K12
Belconnen ACT 24 F10, 33 D4, 34 D4, 35 C4, 36 G2
Belford NSW 25 L3
Belford NP NSW 19 A6, 25 L3
Belgrave Vic. 40 G7, 41 B9, 43 K6, 52 E5
Belgrave South Vic. 40 G7, 41 B10, 43 K7, 45 N1
Belhus WA 84 E3, 85 D4
Belka WA 88 G4
Bell NSW 14 D2, 16 F3, 25 I5
Bell Qld 123 K7

Bell Bay Tas. 143 J6, 145 E6
Bell Park Vic. 44 A3
Bellambi NSW 23 G4
Bellara Qld 114 G1, 115 F1, 117 G7
Bellarine Vic. 40 A9, 42 G8, 44 E3, 52 B6, 63 P7
Bellarwi NSW 24 B6, 29 P6
Bellata NSW 26 F5
Bellbird NSW 13 D2, 25 L4
Bellbird Creek Vic. 35 B12, 51 C11
Bellbowrie Qld 114 C8
Bellbrae Vic. 42 E9, 50 G2, 63 N8
Bellbridge Vic. 55 L6, 57 J2
Bellbrook NSW 20 F3, 27 L9
Bellellen Vic. 61 I12, 63 I1
Bellenden Ker Qld 120 E3, 121 G9
Bellerive Tas. 1 E7, 137 F8
Bellevue WA xxv G3, 84 F5
Bellevue Hill NSW ix K6
Bellingen NSW 20 G1, 21 D12, 27 M8
Bellinger River NP NSW 20 F1, 21 C12, 27 M8
Bellingham Tas. 143 K5, 145 H5
Bellmount Forest NSW 24 F9, 35 D3
Belltrees NSW 13 C8, 15 N2, 25 K1, 27 I12
Belmont NSW 13 G4, 19 C10, 30 B10
Belmont Qld xxxi O12
Belmont Vic. 42 F8, 44 A4, 46 C10, 50 G1, 52 A6, 63 O7
Belmont WA xxv C6, 84 E6, 85 C5
Belmore NSW 15 K9
Belmunging WA 88 E4
Beloka NSW 35 B8, 36 E11, 51 D5
Belowra NSW 35 E7, 37 J9, 51 H3
Belrose NSW 12 F5, 13 B11, 15 M7
Beltana SA 70 B5, 74 H4
Beltana Roadhouse SA 70 A5, 74 H4
Belton SA 73 K1, 75 I9
Belvidere SA 71 C4
Belyando Crossing Roadhouse Qld 124 G6
Belyuen NT 102 C3, 104 D4
Bemboka NSW 35 D9, 37 I12, 51 G5
Bemm River Vic. 35 B12, 51 D11
Ben Boyd NP NSW 35 E10, 51 H9
Ben Bullen NSW 25 I4
Ben Halls Gap NP NSW 27 I11
Ben Lomond NSW 27 J6
Ben Lomond NP Tas. 143 M9
Ben Nevis Vic. 61 J12, 63 J2
Bena NSW 24 B5, 29 P5
Bena Vic. 43 M10, 52 F8
Benalla Vic. 54 G8, 56 D5
Benambra Vic. 53 N1, 55 N11, 57 M9
Benambra NP NSW 24 B11, 29 O11, 55 L4
Benandarah NSW 37 M6
Benaraby Qld 123 L1, 125 N12
Benarkin Qld 118 B12, 123 L8
Benayeo Vic. 60 B10, 71 H9
Bencubbin WA 88 F2, 90 D5
Bendalong NSW 25 I11, 35 G5, 37 N3
Bendemeer NSW 27 I9
Bendick Murrell NSW 24 E7, 35 B1
Bendidee NP Qld 26 H1, 123 I10
Bendigo Vic. 48, 49 F3, 54 A9, 61 O10
Bendoc Vic. 35 B10, 51 D8
Bendolba NSW 19 D3, 20 B10, 25 M2
Beneree NSW 24 G5
Benetook Vic. 28 D6, 58 G7
Benger WA 86 E2, 88 C8
Bengworden Vic. 53 M6
Beni NSW 24 F1, 26 C12
Benjeroop Vic. 28 H10, 61 M3
Benlidi Qld 124 C12, 131 O12, 133 M1
Bennies Vic. 55 I11, 56 G9
Benowa Qld 116 E6
Bentley NSW 21 F4, 27 N3
Bentley WA xxiv H8, xxv B9
Benwerrin Vic. 42 D10, 50 E3, 63 M9
Berambing NSW 14 E3, 17 I4
Berat Qld 27 L1
Beremboke Vic. 42 E5, 49 F12, 63 N5
Berendebba NSW 24 D6
Beresfield NSW 13 G2, 19 C8, 20 A12, 25 L4
Bergalia NSW 35 F7, 37 L8
Berkeley Tas. 145 A3

Berkeley Vale NSW 13 E7, 15 P2
Bermagui NSW 35 E8, 37 K11
Bermagui South NSW 35 E8, 37 K11
Berowra NSW 12 F3, 13 B10, 15 L5
Berowra Heights NSW 12 E3, 13 B10, 15 L5
Berowra Waters NSW 12 E2, 13 B9, 15 L5
Berrara NSW 23 C12, 37 O3
Berri SA 28 A6, 58 A6, 71 G1, 73 N7
Berridale NSW 35 B8, 36 E10, 51 D4
Berriedale Tas. xxxiv B3, 137 B3, 139 I4, 141 K6
Berrigan NSW 29 L11, 54 G3
Berrima NSW 23 B5, 25 I8, 35 G2
Berrimah NT xxvii G7, 102 D3
Berrimal Vic. 61 L8
Berringa Vic. 42 C5, 49 B12, 63 L5
Berringama Vic. 55 N7, 57 M3
Berriwillock Vic. 28 F10, 61 J3
Berry NSW 23 D8, 25 J9, 35 G3
Berry Springs NT 102 D5, 104 D5
Berrybank Vic. 42 A6, 63 K6
Berwick Vic. 40 G8, 41 B11, 43 K7, 45 N2, 52 D6
Bessiebelle Vic. 62 E7
Beswick NT 104 H8
Bet Bet Vic. 49 C4, 61 M11
Beta Qld 124 F10
Bete Bolong Vic. 35 A12, 51 B11, 53 P5
Bethanga Vic. 55 L6, 57 J2
Bethania Qld 114 F10
Bethungra NSW 24 D8, 35 A3
Betley Vic. 49 C4, 61 M11
Betoota Qld 77 N1, 132 F3
Beulah Tas. 142 H8, 144 H4, 145 A9
Beulah Vic. 28 E11, 60 H5
Beulah East Vic. 28 E11, 60 H5
Beulah Park SA xxi M4
Beulah West Vic. 28 E11, 60 G5
Bevendale NSW 24 F8, 35 D2
Beverford Vic. 28 G9, 59 L12, 61 L1
Beveridge Vic. 40 E2, 43 J3, 52 C2
Beverley SA xx E2
Beverley WA 88 E5, 90 D7
Beverly Hills NSW 12 D9, 15 K10
Bexhill NSW 21 G4, 27 O3
Biala NSW 24 G8, 35 D2
Biamanga NP NSW 35 E8, 37 K11, 51 H5
Biarra Qld 117 A7
Bibbenluke NSW 35 C9, 51 F6
Biboohra Qld 120 D2, 121 D7, 127 L6
Bibra Lake WA 84 D8, 85 C6
Bicheno Tas. 141 O1, 143 O11
Bickley WA 84 G6, 85 D5
Bicton WA xxiv D10
Biddon NSW 26 D10
Bidyadanga WA 94 G9
Big Grove WA 87 D11, 88 G12
Big Pats Creek Vic. 41 F8, 43 N5
Bigga NSW 24 G7, 35 D1
Biggara Vic. 35 A7, 36 B9, 51 A3, 55 P7, 57 P4
Biggenden Qld 118 B5, 123 L4
Biggera Waters Qld 116 E4
Bilambil NSW 21 G2, 115 G12, 116 F11
Bilambil Heights NSW 116 G11
Bilbarin WA 88 G5
Bilbul NSW 29 M7
Bilinga Qld 116 G10
Billabong Vic. 28 E6, 58 G6
Billabong Roadhouse WA 89 D10
Billimari NSW 24 E5
Billinudgel NSW 21 G3, 27 O2
Billys Creek NSW 21 C11, 27 M7
Biloela Qld 123 J2
Bilpin NSW 14 F3, 17 K4, 25 J5
Bilwon Qld 120 D2, 121 D6
Bilyana Qld 120 E6, 127 M9
Bimbaya NSW 51 G6
Bimberamala NP NSW 24 H11, 35 F5, 37 L4
Bimbi NSW 24 D6
Bimbimbie NSW 24 H12, 35 F6, 37 L7
Binalong NSW 24 E8, 35 C2
Binalong Bay Tas. 143 P7
Binbee Qld 119 D5, 125 I3
Binda NSW 24 G8, 35 D2
Bindarri NP NSW 20 G1, 21 D11, 27 M7

Bindi Vic. 53 N1, 55 N12, 57 N11
Bindi Bindi WA 88 C2, 90 C5
Bindoon WA 85 D1, 88 C3, 90 C7
Bingara NSW 26 H6
Bingera Qld 118 C2
Bingil Bay Qld 120 E5, 127 M8
Binginwarri Vic. 52 H9
Biniguy NSW 26 G4
Binjour Qld 123 K4
Binnaway NSW 26 E10
Binningup WA 86 D2, 88 C8
Binningup Beach WA 86 D2
Binnu WA 89 D11, 90 A2, 92 A12
Binnum SA 60 B9, 71 G8
Binya NSW 29 N7
Birany Birany NT 105 N5
Birchgrove NSW viii D2, x D10
Birchip Vic. 28 F11, 61 J5
Birchs Bay Tas. 138 H9, 141 J9
Birdsville Qld 77 K2, 132 D3
Birdwood NSW 20 E5, 27 L10
Birdwood SA 66 H5, 67 E8, 71 C2, 73 K9
Birdwoodton Vic. 58 G6
Biriwal Bulga NP NSW 20 D6, 27 K11
Birkdale Qld 114 G8, 115 F5, 117 G11
Birralee Tas. 143 J8, 145 E9
Birrego NSW 24 A9, 29 N9
Birregurra Vic. 42 C9, 50 D2, 63 L8
Birriwa NSW 24 H1, 26 E12
Birrong NSW 12 C8, 15 K9
Bishopsbourne Tas. 143 J9, 145 F12
Bittern Vic. 40 E12, 43 J10, 45 K8, 52 D7
Black Bobs Tas. 140 H4
Black Forest SA xx H9
Black Hill SA 71 C2, 73 L8
Black Hill Vic. 47 F4
Black Hills Tas. 138 G3, 141 J6
Black Mountain NSW 27 J7
Black Mountain NP Qld 127 L3
Black River Tas. 142 D4
Black Rock SA 69 E2, 72 H6, 73 J3, 75 I10
Black Springs NSW 24 H6, 26 H12, 27 I5
Black Springs SA 73 K6
Blackall Qld 122 A1, 124 D12, 131 P12, 133 O1
Blackberry Corner Vic. 45 I10
Blackbraes NP Qld 124 B1, 127 I11, 131 N1
Blackbull Qld 126 E8
Blackbutt Qld 118 A12, 123 L8
Blackdown Tableland NP Qld 125 J11
Blackfellow Caves SA 71 F12
Blackheath NSW 14 C4, 16 F6, 25 I6
Blackheath Vic. 60 G8
Blackmans Bay Tas. 139 I7, 141 K8
Blacksmiths NSW 13 G5, 19 C11
Blacktown NSW 12 B5, 15 J7, 25 J6
Blackville NSW 26 G11
Blackwarry Vic. 53 I8
Blackwater Qld 125 J11
Blackwood SA 66 C9, 67 B10, 68 F3
Blackwood Vic. 42 F2, 49 F10, 52 A2, 63 O3
Blackwood Creek Tas. 143 J10
Blackwood NP Qld 124 G6
Bladensburg NP Qld 131 L8
Blair Athol Qld 119 B12, 124 H9
Blairgowrie Vic. 40 B12, 42 H10, 44 F8, 52 B7, 63 P9
Blakeville Vic. 42 E3, 49 E10, 63 N4
Blampied Vic. 42 E2, 49 D9
Blanchetown SA 71 E1, 73 L7
Bland NSW 24 C6
Blandford NSW 26 H11
Blanket Flat NSW 24 G7, 35 D1
Blaxland NSW 14 G6, 17 K10, 25 J6
Blaxlands Ridge NSW 14 H3, 17 O4
Blayney NSW 24 G5
Bleak House Vic. 28 C12, 60 D7
Blessington Tas. 143 L9
Bletchley SA 66 H12, 67 E12
Blewitt Springs SA 66 C11, 67 B11, 68 F4
Bli Bli Qld 117 G3, 118 F11, 123 N7
Blighty NSW 29 K10, 54 E3
Blind Bight Vic. 45 N6
Blinman SA 70 C7, 75 I5
Bloomsbury Qld 119 E6, 125 J4

Blow Clear NSW 24 B5, 29 P5
Blue Lake NP Qld 115 H5, 123 N9
Blue Mountains NP NSW 14 E7, 16 G7, 17 J6, 23 A1, 24 H7, 25 I7, 35 F1
Blue Rocks Tas. 140 B10
Blue Water Springs Roadhouse Qld 120 D10, 124 E1, 127 L11
Bluewater Qld 120 F10, 124 G1, 127 N11
Blueys Beach NSW 20 E10, 25 O3
Bluff Qld 125 J11
Bluff Beach SA 69 D6, 72 H8
Bluff Rock NSW 21 A6, 27 L4
Blyth SA 69 H2, 73 J6
Boallia WA 86 C7
Boambee NSW 20 H1, 21 E12, 27 N8
Boat Harbour NSW 19 G8, 20 C12
Boat Harbour Tas. 142 E4
Boat Harbour Beach Tas. 142 E4
Boatswain Point SA 71 E9
Bobadah NSW 24 B1, 29 O1, 31 N12
Bobbin Head NSW 12 F4, 13 B10, 15 L6
Bobin NSW 20 D7, 25 N1, 27 K12
Bobinawarrah Vic. 55 I8, 56 G5
Bodalla NSW 35 E7, 37 L9
Bodallin WA 88 H3, 90 F6
Boddington WA 85 G10, 88 D7, 90 C8
Bogan Gate NSW 24 D3
Bogangar NSW 21 H3, 27 O2, 123 N11
Bogantungan Qld 124 G11
Boggabilla NSW 26 H2, 123 I11
Boggabri NSW 26 G8
Bogong Vic. 55 L10, 57 K8
Boho Vic. 54 G9, 56 B6
Boho South Vic. 54 G9, 56 C7
Boigbeat Vic. 28 F10, 61 J3
Boinka Vic. 28 C9, 58 E11, 60 E1, 73 P10
Boisdale Vic. 53 K5
Bolgart WA 88 D3, 90 C6
Bolinda Vic. 42 H2, 52 B2
Bolivar SA 66 C3, 67 B6
Bolivia NSW 21 A6, 27 K4
Bollon Qld 122 D9
Bolton Vic. 28 F8, 59 J10
Bolwarra NSW 13 G1, 19 C7, 20 A11
Bolwarrah Vic. 42 E3, 49 E10, 63 N4
Bomaderry NSW 23 D9, 25 I9, 35 G4, 37 O1
Bombala NSW 35 C9, 51 F7
Bombo NSW 23 F7
Bonalbo NSW 21 D4, 27 M3, 123 M12
Bonang Vic. 35 B10, 51 C8
Bonbeach Vic. 43 J7, 45 K3
Bondi NSW ix K8
Bondi Beach NSW ix L8
Bondi Junction NSW ix J8, 12 F8, 15 M9
Bondo NSW 24 E10, 35 B4, 36 E2
Bonegilla Vic. 24 A12, 55 L6, 57 J2
Boneo Vic. 40 C12, 43 I10, 44 H9, 52 C8
Bongaree Qld 114 G2, 115 F1, 117 G8, 123 N8
Bongil Bongil NP NSW 20 H1, 21 E12, 27 M8
Bonnells Bay NSW 13 F5, 19 B11
Bonnie Doon Vic. 54 G11, 56 C9
Bonnie Rock WA 88 G1, 90 E5
Bonny Hills NSW 20 F7, 27 M11
Bonogin Qld 116 D9
Bonogin Creek Qld 116 D9
Bonshaw NSW 27 J3, 123 J12
Bonville NSW 20 H1, 21 D12, 27 M8
Booborowie SA 73 K5, 75 I12
Boobyalla Tas. 143 N5
Booderee NP JBT 23 D12, 25 J10, 35 G4, 37 O3
Bookabie SA 81 K7
Bookar Vic. 63 J7
Bookham NSW 24 E9, 35 B3
Boolading WA 88 D8
Boolaroo NSW 13 G3, 19 C9
Boolarra Vic. 43 P10, 52 H8
Boolba Qld 122 E9
Booleroo SA 73 J3, 74 H10
Booleroo Centre SA 73 J3, 74 H10
Boolgun SA 71 F1, 73 M8
Booligal NSW 29 K5
Boomahnoomoonah Vic. 54 H6, 56 E2

Boomi NSW 26 F2, 122 H11
Boonah Qld 21 D1, 27 M1, 115 A9, 123 M10
Boonah Vic. 42 D10, 50 E3, 63 M9
Boonarga Qld 123 J7
Boondall Qld 114 F5, 115 E3, 117 F10
Boonoo Boonoo NSW 21 B4, 27 L3, 123 L12
Boonoo Boonoo NP NSW 21 B4, 27 L3, 123 L12
Boonoonar Vic. 28 E7, 58 G8
Boorabbin NP WA 90 G6
Booragoon WA xxiv F10, 84 D7, 85 C6
Booral NSW 19 F5, 20 B10, 25 M3
Boorcan Vic. 50 G7, 63 I7
Boorhaman Vic. 55 I6, 56 F3
Boorindal NSW 31 M6
Boorongie Vic. 58 H11
Boorongie North Vic. 28 E8, 58 H11
Booroopki Vic. 60 C9, 71 H8
Booroorban NSW 29 J8
Boorowa NSW 24 E8, 35 C2
Boort Vic. 28 H12, 61 M6
Boosey Vic. 54 G5, 56 C1
Booti Booti NP NSW 20 E10, 25 N2
Booval Qld 115 B5, 117 D12
Booyal Qld 118 B3, 123 M4
Boppy Mountain NSW 31 M9
Borallon Qld 114 A7, 115 B4, 117 C11
Boralma Vic. 55 I6, 56 F3
Borambil NSW 25 I1, 26 F12
Borden WA 88 H9, 90 E10
Border Ranges NP NSW 21 E2, 27 N2, 115 B12, 123 M10
Border Store NT 103 P2, 104 H4
Border Village SA 80 C7, 91 P5
Bordertown SA 28 A12, 60 A7, 71 G7
Boree NSW 13 B4, 24 F4, 25 K4
Boree Creek NSW 24 A9, 29 N9
Boreen Point Qld 118 F9, 123 N6
Borenore NSW 24 F4
Boro NSW 24 G10, 35 E4, 37 J2
Boronia Vic. 41 B9, 43 K6, 52 D5
Boronia Heights Qld 114 D10, 115 D6
Bororen Qld 123 L2
Borrika SA 71 F3, 73 M9
Borroloola NT 105 M11, 107 M2
Borung Vic. 28 H12, 61 M7
Boscabel WA 88 E8, 90 D10
Bostobrick NSW 21 C11, 27 M7
Bostock Creek Vic. 50 G7, 63 J8
Botany NSW 12 F9, 15 L10, 25 K7
Botany Bay NP NSW 12 F10, 15 L11, 25 K7
Bothwell Tas. 141 J4
Bouddi NP NSW 13 D9, 15 O4, 25 L6
Bouldercombe Qld 125 M11
Boulia Qld 130 F8
Boulka Vic. 58 H11
Boundain WA 88 F7
Boundary Bend Vic. 28 G7, 59 K9
Bourke NSW 31 M5
Bournda NP NSW 35 E9, 51 H7
Bow NSW 25 J1, 26 G12
Bowan Park NSW 24 F4
Bowden SA xx H3, 65 A3, 66 C7, 67 B8, 68 F2
Bowelling WA 88 D8, 90 C9
Bowen Qld 119 E4, 125 J3
Bowen Hills Qld xxx H5
Bowen Mountain NSW 14 G4, 17 L6
Bowenfels NSW 14 B2, 16 D2
Bowenvale Vic. 49 B5, 61 L11, 63 L1
Bowenville Qld 123 K8
Bower SA 73 L7
Boweya Vic. 54 H7, 56 E3
Bowhill SA 71 E3, 73 L9
Bowling Alley Point NSW 27 I10
Bowling Green Bay NP Qld 119 B2, 120 G11, 124 H1, 127 O12
Bowman Vic. 55 J8, 56 G5
Bowmans SA 69 G4, 71 A1, 73 I7
Bowna NSW 24 B12, 29 O12, 55 L5, 57 K1
Bowning NSW 24 F9, 35 C3
Bowral NSW 23 C5, 25 I8, 35 G2
Bowraville NSW 20 G2, 27 M9
Bowser Vic. 55 I7, 56 F4
Box Hill Vic. 40 E6, 43 J6, 52 D4

149

Box Tank NSW 30 D11
Boxwood Vic. 54 G7, 56 C3
Boxwood Hill WA 90 F10
Boya WA xxv H3
Boyanup WA 86 E5, 88 C8, 90 C10
Boydtown NSW 35 E10, 51 H8
Boyeo Vic. 28 C12, 60 D7
Boyer Tas. 138 H4, 141 J6
Boykambil Qld 115 F8, 116 E3
Boyne Island Qld 123 L1, 125 N12
Boys Town Qld 115 C9
Boyup Brook WA 88 D9, 90 C10
Bracken Ridge Qld 114 E5
Brackendale NSW 20 B4, 27 J10
Bracknell Tas. 143 J9, 145 F12
Braddon ACT 32 D2
Bradvale Vic. 42 A5, 63 K5
Braefield NSW 26 H11
Braemar NSW 23 C4
Braeside Qld 21 A2, 27 L2, 119 E10, 123 L11, 125 J7
Braeside Vic. 45 K2
Braidwood NSW 24 H11, 35 E5, 37 K4
Bramfield SA 72 C5, 74 A12, 81 P12
Brampton Islands NP Qld 119 G6, 125 K5
Bramston Beach Qld 120 E4, 121 H10, 127 M7
Bramwell Junction Roadhouse Qld 128 D6
Brandon Qld 119 B2, 124 H2, 127 O12
Brandy Creek Vic. 41 G12, 43 N8, 52 G6
Branxholm Tas. 143 M7
Branxholme Vic. 62 E5
Branxton NSW 19 A6, 25 L3
Brawlin NSW 24 D8, 35 A2
Bray Junction SA 71 E10
Bray Park Qld 114 E5, 115 D3, 117 F9
Breadalbane NSW 24 G9, 35 E3
Breadalbane Tas. 143 K8, 145 H11
Break O Day Vic. 40 H1, 41 C2, 43 L2, 52 E2, 54 E12
Breakfast Creek NSW 24 F7, 35 C1
Breakfast Creek NSW 25 I3
Breakwater Vic. 44 B4, 46 G11
Bream Creek Tas. 139 M5, 141 M7
Breamlea Vic. 42 F9, 44 B6, 50 H2, 52 A7, 63 O8
Bredbo NSW 24 F12, 35 C6, 36 G7, 51 F2
Breeza NSW 26 G10
Bremer Bay WA 90 G10
Brentwood SA 69 D7, 72 H9
Brentwood Vic. 28 D11, 60 G5
Brentwood WA xxiv G10
Breona Tas. 143 I10
Bretti NSW 20 C7, 25 M1, 27 K12
Brewarrina NSW 31 O5
Brewongle NSW 24 H5
Brewster Vic. 42 B2, 49 A9, 63 L3
Briagolong Vic. 53 K5
Bribbaree NSW 24 D7, 35 A1
Bribie Island NP Qld 114 G1, 115 F1, 117 G6, 118 F12, 123 N8
Bridge Creek Vic. 54 H10, 56 D9
Bridge Creek NP Qld 127 K2
Bridge Inn Vic. 61 I11, 63 I1
Bridgenorth Tas. 143 J7, 145 F9
Bridgetown WA 86 H8, 88 D9, 90 C10
Bridgewater SA 66 E8, 67 D10, 68 G3, 71 C3, 73 J9
Bridgewater Tas. 139 I3, 141 K6
Bridgewater On Loddon Vic. 49 D2, 61 N9
Bridport Tas. 143 L5
Brigalow Qld 123 J7
Bright Vic. 55 K9, 57 I7
Brighton Qld 114 F5, 115 E3, 117 F9, 123 N9
Brighton SA 66 B9, 67 B10, 68 E3, 69 H8, 73 J9
Brighton Tas. 139 I3, 141 K6
Brighton Vic. 40 D7, 43 J6, 52 C5
Brightwaters NSW 13 F5, 19 B11
Brim Vic. 28 E11, 60 H6
Brimbago SA 28 A11, 71 F7
Brimboal Vic. 62 C2, 71 H10
Brimin Vic. 55 I5, 56 E1
Brimpaen Vic. 60 G11
Brindabella NP NSW 24 E10, 33 A3, 34 A4, 35 C4, 36 F2
Bringagee NSW 29 L7
Bringalbert Vic. 60 C10, 71 H9
Bringelly NSW 14 H9

Brinkin NT xxvii D4
Brinkley SA 67 G12, 73 K10
Brinkworth SA 69 H1, 73 J5
Brisbane Qld xxx G7, 113, 114 E7, 115 D4, 117 F11, 123 N9
Brisbane Airport Qld xxxi M2
Brisbane Ranges NP Vic. 42 F5, 49 F12, 52 A4, 63 N5
Brisbane Water NP NSW 12 G1, 13 C8, 15 M3, 25 K5
Brit Brit Vic. 62 E3
Brittons Swamp Tas. 142 B4
Brixton Qld 124 C10, 131 O10
Broad Arrow WA 90 H4
Broad Sound Islands NP Qld 119 H10, 125 L7
Broadbeach Qld 21 G1, 27 O1, 115 G10, 116 F6
Broadford Vic. 43 J1, 52 D1, 54 D11
Broadmarsh Tas. 138 H2, 141 J6
Broadmeadows Vic. 40 D4, 43 I4, 52 C3
Broadview SA xxi K1
Broadwater NSW 21 G6, 27 O4
Broadwater Vic. 62 F6
Broadwater NP NSW 21 G6, 27 O4
Broadway NSW 10 A12
Brocklehurst NSW 24 F1, 26 C12
Brocklesby NSW 24 A11, 29 N11, 55 J4
Brockman NP WA 86 H11, 87 B3, 88 D11, 90 C11
Brocks Creek NT 102 G10, 104 E6
Brodies Plains NSW 27 J5
Brodribb River Vic. 35 A12, 51 B11
Brogo NSW 35 E8, 37 J12, 51 H5
Broke NSW 13 C1, 25 K3
Broken Hill NSW 30 B10, 73 P1, 75 Q8
Bromelton Qld 21 E1, 115 C9
Bromley Vic. 49 C4, 61 M10
Brompton SA xx H2, 65 A2
Bronte NSW ix K9
Bronte Park Tas. 140 H2, 142 H12, 144 H11
Bronzewing Vic. 28 E9, 58 H11, 60 H1
Brook Islands NP Qld 120 F6, 127 M9
Brooker SA 72 D6
Brookfield NSW 19 E5, 20 B10, 25 M3
Brookfield Qld 114 C7, 115 C4, 117 E11
Brooklands Qld 115 C8
Brooklyn NSW 12 G2, 13 C9, 15 M4
Brooklyn Park SA xx E5
Brookside Vic. 55 K10, 57 I7
Brookstead Qld 123 K9
Brookton WA 88 E5, 90 D8
Brookvale NSW 12 G6, 13 C11, 15 M7
Brookville Vic. 53 N3, 57 M12
Brooloo Qld 117 E2, 118 D10
Broome WA 94 H8, 98 A11
Broomehill WA 88 F9, 90 E10
Broomfield Vic. 42 D2, 49 D9, 63 M3
Brooms Head NSW 21 F8, 27 N6
Brooweena Qld 118 C6, 123 M5
Broughton Vic. 28 C12, 60 D6, 71 H7
Broula NSW 24 E6
Broulee NSW 24 H12, 35 F6, 37 L7
Brown Hill Vic. 42 D3, 47 H4, 49 C10
Brown Hill Creek SA xxi M11
Brownlow SA 67 H1, 69 E11, 71 D1, 72 H11, 73 L7
Browns Plains Qld 114 E10, 115 D6
Browns Plains Vic. 55 J6, 56 H2
Bruarong Vic. 55 K8, 57 I5
Bruce SA 73 I2, 81 P10
Bruce Rock WA 88 G4, 90 E7
Brucefield SA 69 E2, 72 H6
Brucknell Vic. 50 F9, 63 I9
Brukunga SA 66 H8, 67 E9
Brungle NSW 24 D10, 35 A4, 36 C1
Brunkerville NSW 13 F3, 19 B9
Brunswick Vic. xv K3, 40 D5, 43 I5, 52 C4
Brunswick East Vic. xv L4
Brunswick Heads NSW 21 H4, 27 O3, 123 N12
Brunswick Junction WA 86 E3, 88 C8
Brunswick West Vic. xv I3
Brushgrove NSW 20 A1, 21 E8, 27 I8
Bruthen Vic. 53 N5
Bryden Qld 115 A2, 117 C9
Brymaroo Qld 123 K8
Buangor Vic. 63 J3

Buaraba Qld 117 A9
Bucasia Qld 119 G7, 125 K5
Bucca Qld 118 C2, 123 M3
Buccan Qld 114 E11, 115 E7
Buccleuch SA 71 E4, 73 M10
Buchan Vic. 35 A11, 51 A10, 53 P4
Buchan South Vic. 53 O4
Bucheen Creek Vic. 55 N8, 57 M5
Buckenderra NSW 35 B7, 36 E8, 51 D3
Bucketty NSW 13 C4, 25 K4
Buckingham SA 28 A12, 71 G7
Buckingham WA 86 H3, 88 D8
Buckland Tas. 139 M2, 141 M5
Buckland Vic. 55 K10, 56 H8
Buckleboo SA 72 E3, 74 D10
Buckley Vic. 42 E8, 50 F1, 63 N8
Buckrabanyule Vic. 28 G12, 61 L7
Budawang NP NSW 24 H11, 35 F5, 37 L4
Buddabaddah NSW 31 O11
Budderoo NP NSW 23 D7, 25 J9, 35 G3
Buddigower NSW 24 B6, 29 O6
Buddina Qld 117 H4, 118 F12
Buderim Qld 117 G4, 118 F12, 123 N7
Budgeree Vic. 43 P11, 52 H8
Budgeree East Vic. 52 H8
Budgerum Vic. 61 L4
Budgewoi NSW 13 F6, 19 B12
Buffalo Vic. 43 O12, 52 G9
Buffalo Creek Vic. 55 J9, 56 H6
Buffalo River Vic. 55 J9, 56 H6
Bugaldie NSW 26 D9
Bugilbone NSW 26 D5
Bugong NP NSW 23 C8, 25 I9, 35 G3
Builyan Qld 123 L2
Bukalong NSW 35 C9, 51 E6
Bukkulla NSW 27 I5
Bulahdelah NSW 19 H4, 20 C10, 25 N3
Bulart Vic. 62 F3
Buldah Vic. 35 C10, 51 E9
Bulga NSW 25 K3
Bulgandramine NSW 24 E2
Bulgobac Tas. 142 E8, 144 B5
Bulimba Qld xxxi J6
Bull Creek WA xxiv G11, xxv A12
Bulla NT 95 P4, 99 P5, 104 C11, 106 C2
Bulla Vic. 40 C4, 43 I4, 52 B3
Bullaburra NSW 14 E6, 16 H9
Bullarah NSW 26 E4
Bullaring WA 88 F6, 90 E8
Bullarook Vic. 42 D3, 49 D10, 63 M4
Bullarto Vic. 42 F2, 49 F9, 63 N3
Bullarto South Vic. 42 F2, 49 F9
Bullengarook Vic. 42 G3, 49 H10, 52 A2, 63 O4
Bullengarook East Vic. 42 G3, 49 H10, 52 A2
Bulleringa NP Qld 127 I7
Bullfinch WA 88 H2, 90 F6
Bullhead Creek Vic. 55 M8, 57 K4
Bullioh Vic. 55 M7, 57 L3
Bullock Creek Qld 120 A5, 127 J7
Bullocks Flat NSW 36 D10, 51 B4
Bullsbrook WA 84 E2, 85 C3, 88 C4, 90 C7
Bullumwaal Vic. 53 M4
Bulman NT 105 J6
Buln Buln Vic. 41 H12, 43 N8, 52 G6
Buln Buln East Vic. 41 H12, 43 O8, 52 G6
Bulwer Qld 115 G1, 123 N8
Bulyee WA 88 F5, 90 D8
Bumbaldry NSW 24 E6
Bumberry NSW 24 E4
Bumbunga SA 69 G2, 73 I6
Bunbartha Vic. 29 K12, 54 E6
Bunburra Qld 21 D1, 115 A9
Bunbury WA 86 D4, 88 C8, 90 C9
Bundaberg Qld 118 D2, 123 M3
Bundaburrah NSW 24 D5
Bundalaguah Vic. 53 K6
Bundalong Vic. 29 M12, 54 H5, 56 E1
Bundalong South Vic. 54 H6, 56 E2
Bundanoon NSW 23 A7, 25 I9, 35 G3
Bundarra NSW 27 I7
Bundeena NSW 12 E11, 15 L12, 25 K7
Bundella NSW 26 F10

Bunding Vic. 42 E3, 49 E10, 63 N4
Bundjalung NP NSW 21 F7, 27 O5
Bundook NSW 20 C8, 25 N1, 27 K12
Bundure NSW 29 M9
Bung Bong Vic. 49 A6, 61 L12, 63 L1
Bungador Vic. 50 A2, 63 K8
Bungal Vic. 42 E4, 49 E11, 63 N5
Bungarby NSW 35 C9, 36 F12, 51 E5
Bungaree Vic. 42 D3, 49 D10, 63 M4
Bungaree Vic. 42 D3, 49 D10, 63 M4
Bungawalbin NP NSW 21 F6, 27 N4
Bungeet Vic. 54 H7, 56 D3
Bungendore NSW 24 G10, 34 H5, 35 D4, 37 I3
Bungil Vic. 24 B12, 55 M6, 57 L2
Bungonia NSW 24 H9, 35 F3
Bungowannah NSW 24 A12, 55 K5, 57 I1
Bungulla NSW 21 A5, 27 L4, 123 L12
Bungulla WA 88 F4
Bunguluke Vic. 28 G12, 61 L6
Bungunya Qld 26 F1, 122 H10
Bungwahl NSW 20 D10, 25 N3
Buninyong Vic. 42 D4, 49 C11, 63 M4
Bunnaloo NSW 29 J11, 54 B3, 61 P5
Bunnan NSW 25 J1, 26 G12
Buntine WA 90 C5
Bunya Mountains NP Qld 123 K7
Bunyah NSW 20 D9, 25 N2
Bunyan NSW 35 C7, 36 G9, 51 F3
Bunyip Vic. 41 E12, 43 M8, 52 F6
Buraja NSW 29 M11, 55 I4
Burbank Qld 115 E5, 117 G12
Burbong NSW 33 H7, 34 G5, 36 H3
Burcher NSW 24 C5, 29 P5
Burekup WA 86 E3, 88 C8
Burgooney NSW 24 A4, 29 N4
Burke & Wills Roadhouse Qld 126 B10, 129 F8
Burkes Flat Vic. 49 A2, 61 L9
Burketown Qld 126 A7, 129 D4
Burleigh Head NP Qld 21 G1, 27 O1, 115 G10, 116 F8, †23 N11
Burleigh Heads Qld 21 G1, 27 O1, 115 G10, 116 F8, 123 N11
Burleigh Waters Qld 116 F8
Burnbank Vic. 49 A7, 61 L12, 63 L2
Burnett Heads Qld 118 D1, 123 M3
Burnie Tas. 142 F5
Burnley Vic. xv O12, xvii O4
Burns WA 84 B3, 85 B4
Burns Creek Tas. 143 L8
Burnside SA xxi O7
Burnt Yards NSW 24 F5
Buronga NSW 58 G6
Burpengary Qld 114 E2, 115 D1, 117 F8, 123 N8
Burra SA 73 K5
Burraboi NSW 29 I10, 54 A1, 61 O2
Burracoppin WA 88 G3, 90 E6
Burradoo NSW 23 B5
Burraga NSW 24 G6
Burragate NSW 51 G8
Burramine South Vic. 54 G5, 56 C1
Burrandana NSW 24 B10, 29 P10, 55 M2
Burrawang NSW 23 C6, 25 I9, 35 G3
Burrell Creek NSW 20 D8, 25 N1, 27 K12
Burren Junction NSW 26 D6
Burrereo Vic. 61 I8
Burrier NSW 23 B9, 37 N1
Burrill Lake NSW 25 I11, 35 G5, 37 N4
Burringbar NSW 21 G3, 27 O2, 123 N11
Burringurrah WA 89 F6, 92 C7
Burrinjuck NSW 24 E9, 35 B3
Burroin Vic. 28 E10, 60 H3
Burrowa–Pine Mountain NP Vic. 24 C12, 29 P12, 36 A7, 55 N6, 57 N2
Burroway NSW 26 B11
Burrowye Vic. 24 C12, 29 P12, 55 N6, 57 M2
Burrum Coast NP Qld 118 D3, 123 M4
Burrum Vic. 61 I9
Burrum Heads Qld 118 E4, 123 N4
Burrumbeet Vic. 42 C2, 49 B9, 63 L3
Burrumbuttock NSW 24 A11, 29 N11, 55 K4
Burswood WA xxiv H5, xxv A6, 84 E6, 85 C5
Burwood NSW 12 D7
Burwood Vic. 43 J6

Bushfield Vic. 50 C7, 62 G8
Bushy Park Tas. 138 F3, 141 I6
Bushy Park Vic. 53 K5
Busselton WA 86 C6, 88 B9, 90 B10
Butchers Ridge Vic. 35 A10, 51 A8, 53 P2, 57 P12
Bute SA 69 F2, 73 I6
Butler Tanks SA 72 E6
Butlers Gorge Tas. 140 G3
Butmaroo NSW 24 G10, 35 D4, 37 I2
Butterleaf NP NSW 21 A7, 27 K5
Buxton NSW 23 D3, 25 I8, 35 G2
Buxton Qld 118 D4, 123 M4
Buxton Vic. 41 F4, 43 N3, 52 F2, 56 B12
Byabarra NSW 20 E6, 27 L11
Byaduk Vic. 62 E5
Byaduk North Vic. 62 E5
Byawatha Vic. 55 J7, 56 G3
Byfield NP Qld 125 N10
Bylands Vic. 40 D1, 43 J2, 52 C2, 54 C12
Bylong NSW 25 I2
Bymount Qld 122 F5
Byrne Vic. 55 I8, 56 F5
Byrneside Vic. 54 D7
Byrnestown Qld 118 A5, 123 L4
Byrneville Vic. 60 G8
Byrock NSW 31 N7
Byron Bay NSW 21 H4, 27 O3, 123 N12

Cabarita Vic. 28 D6, 58 G6
Cabarlah Qld 123 L9
Cabawin Qld 123 I8
Cabbage Tree Creek Vic. 35 B12, 51 C11
Caboolture Qld 114 E1, 115 D1, 117 F7, 123 N8
Caboonbah Qld 117 B7, 123 M8
Cabramatta NSW 12 B7, 15 J9, 25 J7, 35 H1
Cabramurra NSW 24 D12, 35 B6, 36 D7, 51 B1
Cadell SA 73 M6
Cadney Homestead SA 79 N7
Cadoux WA 88 E2, 90 D6
Cahills Crossing NT 103 P2, 104 H4
Caiguna WA 91 M7
Caiguna Roadhouse WA 91 M7
Cairns Qld 120 E2, 121 F7, 121 G2, 127 L6
Cairns Bay Tas. 138 F9, 141 I9
Calala NSW 27 I9
Calamvale Qld 114 E9, 115 D6
Calca SA 72 A3, 81 N11
Calder Tas. 142 E5
Caldermeade Vic. 45 P6
Caldwell NSW 29 I10, 54 B2, 61 P4
Calen Qld 119 F7, 125 J5
Calga NSW 13 C8, 15 M3
Calingiri WA 88 C3, 90 C6
Caliph SA 71 F2, 73 N8
Calivil Vic. 61 N7
Callala Bay NSW 23 D10, 25 J10, 35 G4, 37 O2
Callawadda Vic. 61 I10
Calleen NSW 24 B5, 29 O5
Callide Qld 123 J1
Callignee Vic. 53 I8
Callignee North Vic. 53 I8
Callington SA 67 F11, 71 C3, 73 K10
Calliope Qld 123 K1, 125 N12
Caloona NSW 26 E2, 122 G11
Caloote SA 67 H9, 73 K9
Caloundra Qld 117 H5, 118 F12, 123 N8
Caltowie SA 73 J4, 74 H11
Calulu Vic. 53 M5
Calvert Qld 117 B12
Calvert Vic. 63 I3
Camballin WA 95 J7, 98 E11
Cambarville Vic. 41 H5, 43 O4, 52 G3
Camberwell NSW 25 K2
Camberwell Vic. 40 E6, 43 J6
Cambewarra NSW 23 C8, 25 I9, 35 G3
Cambrai SA 67 H6, 71 D2, 73 L8
Cambrian Hill Vic. 42 C4, 49 C11
Cambridge Tas. 1 G2, 139 J5, 141 K7
Camdale Tas. 142 F5
Camden NSW 14 G11, 23 E1, 25 J7, 35 H1
Camden Park SA xx E9
Camena Tas. 144 E1

Camira Qld 114 C9, 115 C6, 117 E12
Camira Creek NSW 21 E7, 27 N4
Cammeray NSW x G6, 11 E1
Camooweal Qld 107 P10, 129 A9, 130 C1
Camooweal Caves NP Qld 107 P10, 129 A9, 130 C1
Camp Coorong SA 71 D5, 73 L12
Camp Hill Qld xxxi J10, 114 E8, 115 E5, 117 F11
Campania Tas. 139 J2, 141 K6
Campbell ACT 32 G6
Campbell Town Tas. 141 L1, 143 L11
Campbells Bridge Vic. 61 I10
Campbells Creek Vic. 49 F6, 61 N12, 63 N1
Campbells Forest Vic. 49 F2, 61 N9
Campbells Pocket Qld 114 C1, 117 E7
Campbelltown NSW 14 H11, 23 F1, 25 J7, 35 H1
Campbelltown SA xxi O1
Campbelltown Vic. 49 D7, 61 M12, 63 M2
Camperdown NSW viii D6
Camperdown Vic. 50 H7, 63 J7
Campwin Beach Qld 119 G8, 125 K6
Camurra NSW 26 G4
Canadian Vic. 42 D3, 47 H9, 49 C10
Canary Island Vic. 61 N6
Canary Island South Vic. 61 M6
Canbelego NSW 31 M9
Canberra ACT 24 F10, 32, 33 E5, 34 E5, 35 D4, 36 H3
Candelo NSW 35 D9, 51 H6
Cangai NSW 21 C7, 27 L5
Cania Gorge NP Qld 123 K2
Caniambo Vic. 54 F8, 56 B4
Cann River Vic. 35 C11, 51 E10
Canna WA 89 F12, 90 B3
Cannawigara SA 28 A12, 60 A6, 71 G7
Cannie Vic. 28 G11, 61 L4
Canning Vale WA xxv C12, 84 E8, 85 C6, 88 C5
Cannington WA xxv D9, 84 E7, 85 C5
Cannon Creek Qld 21 A3, 27 K2, 115 A9
Cannon Hill Qld xxxi L8
Cannons Creek Vic. 45 M6
Cannonvale Qld 119 F5, 125 J3
Cannum Vic. 60 G7
Canomodine NSW 24 F5
Canonba NSW 31 P9
Canoona Qld 125 M10
Canowie SA 73 K4, 75 I12
Canowindra NSW 24 F5
Canteen Creek NT 107 L11, 109 L1
Canterbury NSW 12 E8, 15 L9
Canunda NP SA 71 F11
Canungra Qld 21 F1, 115 E9, 116 A6
Capalaba Qld 114 G8, 115 E5, 117 G12
Cape Arid NP WA 91 J9
Cape Barren Island Tas. 140 B11, 143 O2
Cape Borda SA 69 A11, 72 F11
Cape Bridgewater Vic. 62 C8
Cape Clear Vic. 42 B5, 49 A12, 63 L5
Cape Hillsborough NP Qld 119 G7, 125 K5
Cape Jaffa SA 71 E9
Cape Jervis SA 68 A9, 69 F10, 71 A5, 73 I11
Cape Le Grand NP WA 91 I9
Cape Melville NP Qld 127 K1, 128 G11
Cape Nelson NP Vic. 62 D8
Cape Palmerston NP Qld 119 H9, 125 K6
Cape Paterson Vic. 43 L12, 52 E9
Cape Range NP WA 89 B3
Cape Schanck Vic. 44 H10
Cape Tribulation Qld 121 E1, 127 L4
Cape Upstart NP Qld 119 C3, 125 I2, 127 P12
Cape Woolamai Vic. 43 K11, 45 M11, 52 D8
Capel WA 86 D5, 88 B9, 90 C10
Capella Qld 125 I9
Capels Crossing Vic. 61 N4
Capertee NSW 25 I4
Capietha SA 72 B2, 74 A10, 81 O10
Capital Hill ACT 32 B10
Capoompeta NP NSW 21 A7, 27 K4
Capricorn Coast NP Qld 125 N10
Capricorn Roadhouse WA 92 E5, 97 L11
Capricornia Cays NP Qld 123 M1, 125 P11
Captain Billy Landing Qld 128 D4
Captains Flat NSW 24 G11, 34 G9, 35 D5, 37 I5
Carabost NSW 24 C11, 29 P11, 36 A4, 55 O4

Caragabal NSW 24 D6
Caralue SA 72 E4, 74 D12
Caralulup Vic. 49 B7, 61 L12, 63 L2
Caramut Vic. 62 H6
Carapooee Vic. 61 K9
Carapook Vic. 62 D3
Carawa SA 72 A1, 81 N9
Carbeen Qld 120 D3, 121 D8
Carboor Vic. 55 J9, 56 G6
Carboor Upper Vic. 55 J9, 56 G6
Carbunup River WA 86 B7
Carcoar NSW 24 G5
Cardiff NSW 13 G3, 19 C9
Cardigan Village Vic. 42 C3, 49 B10, 63 L3
Cardinia Vic. 40 H10, 41 C12, 43 L8, 45 O5, 52 E6
Cardross Vic. 58 G6
Cardstone Qld 120 D5, 127 L8
Cardwell Qld 120 E7, 127 M9
Cargerie Vic. 42 D5, 49 D12, 63 M5
Cargo NSW 24 F5
Carilla WA 84 G7
Carina Qld xxxi M10
Carina Heights Qld xxxi L11
Carinda NSW 26 A6
Carindale Qld xxxi N12, 114 F8
Carine WA xxiv B1
Caringbah NSW 12 D10, 15 K11
Carisbrook Vic. 49 C6, 61 M11, 63 M1
Carlingford NSW 12 D6, 15 K7
Carlisle WA xxv C7
Carlisle River Vic. 42 A11, 50 A4, 63 K9
Carlsruhe Vic. 42 G1, 49 H8, 52 A1, 54 A12, 63 O3
Carlton Tas. 139 L5, 141 L7
Carlton Vic. xv K9, xvii J1, 39 E2
Carlton North Vic. xv K7
Carlwood NSW 24 H5
Carmel WA 84 G6
Carmila Qld 119 G10, 125 K7
Carnamah WA 90 B4
Carnarvon WA 89 B7
Carnarvon NP Qld 122 E2
Carnegie Homestead WA 93 I8
Carngham Vic. 42 B3, 49 A10, 63 L4
Caroline SA 62 A5, 71 G12
Carool NSW 116 E11
Caroona NSW 26 G10
Carpa SA 69 A2, 72 F5
Carpendeit Vic. 50 H8, 63 J8
Carpenter Rocks SA 71 F12
Carrabin WA 88 H3
Carrai NP NSW 20 D3, 27 L9
Carrajung Vic. 53 I8
Carrajung South Vic. 53 J8
Carranballac Vic. 63 J4
Carraragarmungee Vic. 55 I7, 56 G4
Carrathool NSW 29 L7
Carrick Tas. 143 J8, 145 F11
Carrickalinga SA 68 C7, 69 G9, 71 B4, 73 I10
Carrieton SA 73 J2, 75 I9
Carrington NSW 18 B2, 19 F7, 20 C11
Carroll NSW 26 G9
Carron Vic. 28 F12, 61 I7
Carrum Vic. 40 E9, 43 J8, 45 K3, 52 D6
Carrum Downs Vic. 40 F9, 43 J8, 45 L3, 52 D6
Carseldine Qld 114 E5, 115 D3, 117 F10
Carwarp Vic. 28 E7, 58 G7
Cascade WA 90 H9
Cascade NP NSW 21 C11, 27 M7
Cascades Tas. 137 C9
Cashmore Vic. 62 D7
Casino NSW 21 E5, 27 N3, 123 M12
Cassilis NSW 25 I1, 26 F12
Cassilis Vic. 53 M2, 55 M12, 57 M12
Castella Vic. 40 H3, 41 C5, 43 L3, 52 E3
Casterton Vic. 62 C3, 71 H11
Castle Cove NSW x H2
Castle Forbes Bay Tas. 138 F8, 141 I8
Castle Hill NSW 12 D5, 13 A11, 15 K7
Castle Rock NSW 25 K2
Castle Tower NP Qld 123 L1, 125 N12
Castleburn Vic. 53 L4
Castlecrag NSW x H4
Castlemaine Vic. 49 F6, 61 N12, 63 N1

Castlereagh NSW 14 G5, 17 M8
Casuarina NT xxvii E4
Casula NSW 12 B8, 15 I9
Cataby Roadhouse WA 88 B2, 90 B6
Catamaran Tas. 141 I11
Catani Vic. 43 M9
Cathcart NSW 35 D9, 51 F7
Cathcart Vic. 63 I2
Cathedral Rock NP NSW 20 E1, 21 A12, 27 L8
Catherine Hill Bay NSW 13 F5, 19 C11, 25 L5
Cathkin Vic. 43 M1, 52 F1, 54 F11, 56 A10
Cathundral NSW 26 A11
Cattai Vic. 12 B1, 15 J4
Cattai NP NSW 12 B1, 15 J4, 25 K6
Catumnal Vic. 28 G12, 61 L6
Caulfield Vic. 40 E6, 43 J6, 52 C5
Caulfield North Vic. xvii O11
Caveat Vic. 54 E11, 56 A9
Cavendish Vic. 62 F3
Caversham WA xxv D1
Caveside Tas. 142 H9, 144 H6, 145 A11
Cawdor NSW 14 G11, 23 E1
Cawongla NSW 21 F4, 27 N3, 123 N12
Cecil Park NSW 12 A7, 15 I8
Cecil Plains Qld 123 K9
Cedar Bay NP Qld 127 L3
Cedar Brush Creek NSW 13 D5
Cedar Grove Qld 115 D8
Ceduna SA 81 M8
Centennial Park NSW ix I8
Central Castra Tas. 142 G7, 144 F2
Central Colo NSW 15 I2, 17 P2, 25 J5
Central Mangrove NSW 13 C6, 15 N1, 25 K5
Central Tilba NSW 35 E8, 37 K10
Centreville Vic. 45 L4
Ceratodus Qld 123 K4
Ceres NSW 24 E1, 26 B12
Ceres Vic. 42 F8, 50 G1, 63 N7
Cervantes WA 88 A2, 90 A5
Cessnock NSW 13 E2, 19 A8, 25 L4
Chaelundi NP NSW 21 C9, 27 M6
Chain Valley Bay NSW 13 F6, 19 B11
Chakola NSW 35 C7, 36 G8, 51 F2
Challis WA 84 F8
Chandada SA 72 B2, 81 O10
Chandler SA 79 L4
Chandlers Creek Vic. 35 C11, 51 E9
Chapel Hill Qld xxx A9, 114 D7
Chapman Hill WA 86 C7, 88 B9
Chapple Vale Vic. 50 A4, 63 K10
Charam Vic. 60 D10
Chardons Bridge Qld 116 B2
Charles Darwin NT xxvij D9
Charles Darwin NP NT xxvii E8, 102 D3, 104 D4
Charleston SA 66 G7, 67 E9, 68 H2, 73 K9
Charlestown NSW 13 G4, 19 C10
Charleville Qld 122 B5, 133 P5
Charlotte Pass NSW 35 A8, 36 C10, 51 B4
Charlton NSW 24 H6, 31 O6
Charlton Vic. 28 G12, 61 K7
Charnocks Crossing NSW 116 C12
Charringa Qld 120 E3, 121 F8
Charters Towers Qld 124 F2
Chasm Creek Tas. 142 F5
Chatsbury NSW 24 H8, 35 E2
Chatswood NSW x F3, 12 F6, 13 B11, 15 L8
Chatswood West NSW x D3
Chatsworth NSW 21 F7, 27 N5
Chatsworth Vic. 62 H5
Cheepie Qld 133 M6
Cheesemans Creek NSW 24 F4
Chelmer Qld xxx C11
Chelsea Vic. 40 E8, 43 J7, 45 K2, 52 D6
Chelsea Heights Vic. 45 K2
Cheltenham NSW 12 D5, 13 A11
Cheltenham SA 67 B8, 68 E1
Cheltenham Vic. 40 E7, 43 J7, 45 J1, 52 C5
Chepstowe Vic. 42 B3, 49 A10, 63 L4
Cherbourg Qld 118 A9, 123 L6
Chermside Qld 114 E6, 115 D3, 117 F10
Cherokee Vic. 42 H2, 52 B2
Cheshunt Vic. 55 I10, 56 F7
Chesney Vale Vic. 54 H7, 56 D4

Chesterton Range NP Qld 122 D5
Chetwynd Vic. 60 D12, 62 D2, 71 H10
Chewton Vic. 49 F6, 54 A10, 61 O12, 63 O1
Cheyne Beach WA 87 G10, 88 H11, 90 F11
Chidlow WA 84 H4, 85 E4
Chigwell Tas. 137 A3
Childers Qld 118 C4, 123 M4
Childers Vic. 43 O10, 52 G7
Chillagoe Qld 120 A3, 127 J6
Chillagoe–Mungana Caves NP Qld 120 A3, 127 J6
Chillingham NSW 21 G2, 115 E12
Chillingollah Vic. 28 F9, 59 J12, 61 J1
Chilpanunda SA 72 A2, 81 O10
Chiltern Vic. 29 N12, 55 J6, 56 H2
Chiltern–Mt Pilot NP Vic. 24 A12, 29 N12, 55 J7, 56 G3
Chiltern Valley Vic. 55 J6, 56 G2
Chinaman Wells SA 69 D5, 71 E7, 72 H7
Chinbingina SA 72 A1, 81 N8
Chinchilla Qld 123 J7
Chinderah NSW 21 H2, 27 O2, 115 G12, 116 H12, 123 N11
Chinkapook Vic. 28 F9, 59 J11, 61 J1
Chippendale NSW viii E6
Chiswick NSW viii A1, x A9
Chittering WA 85 D1, 88 C4
Chorregon Qld 124 A8, 131 M8
Christie Downs SA 67 A11, 68 E4
Christies Beach SA 66 A10, 67 A11, 68 E4
Christmas Creek Qld 120 C9, 127 K11
Christmas Hills Tas. 142 C4
Christmas Hills Vic. 40 G4, 41 B6, 43 K4
Chudleigh Tas. 142 H8, 145 B11
Church Point NSW 12 H4, 13 C10, 15 N6
Churchill Qld 114 A9, 115 B6, 117 D12
Churchill Vic. 52 H8
Churchill NP Vic. 40 F7, 41 A10, 43 K7, 45 M1, 52 D5
Churchlands WA xxiv C4
Chute Vic. 42 A1, 63 K2
Chuwar Qld 114 B8, 115 B5, 117 D12
City Beach WA xxiv B5
Clackline WA 85 F3, 88 D4
Clairview Qld 119 H11, 125 L8
Clandulla NSW 25 I3
Clapham SA xxi J12
Clare Qld 119 B3, 120 H12, 124 H2
Clare SA 69 H2, 73 J6
Claremont Tas. xxxiv A1, 137 B2, 139 I4, 141 K6
Claremont Vic. 55 I9, 56 F6
Claremont WA xxiv C7, 84 C6, 85 B5, 88 B5
Claremont Isles NP Qld 128 F10
Clarence NSW 14 C2, 16 E2, 25 I5
Clarence Gardens SA xx H10
Clarence Park SA xx H9
Clarence Point Tas. 143 J6, 145 E6
Clarence Town NSW 19 E6, 20 B11, 25 M3
Clarendon NSW 15 I5, 17 O7
Clarendon Qld 117 B10
Clarendon SA 66 C10, 67 B11, 68 F4, 69 H8, 71 B3, 73 J9
Clarendon Tas. 143 K9, 145 H12
Clarendon Vic. 42 D4, 49 D11, 63 M5
Clarkefield Vic. 40 B2, 42 H3, 52 B2, 63 P4
Clarkes Hill Vic. 42 D3, 49 D10, 63 M3
Clarkson WA 84 B3
Claude Road Tas. 142 G8, 144 G4
Clay Wells SA 71 F10
Clayfield Qld xxxi J3
Clayton Qld 118 D2
Clayton SA 68 H8, 71 C4, 73 K11
Clayton Vic. 40 E7, 43 J6
Clear Lake Vic. 60 E10
Clear Ridge NSW 24 C5, 29 P5
Cleland SA xxi P10
Clematis Vic. 40 H7, 41 C10, 43 L7, 45 O1
Clermont Qld 119 B12, 124 H9
Cleve SA 69 A1, 72 F5
Cleveland Qld 114 H8, 115 F5, 117 H12, 123 N9
Cleveland Tas. 143 L10
Cliff Island NP Qld 128 F10
Clifton NSW 23 G3, 27 K3, 123 K12
Clifton Qld 123 L10

Clifton Beach Qld 120 D2, 121 F6, 127 L6
Clifton Beach Tas. 139 K7, 141 L8
Clifton Creek Vic. 53 M5
Clifton Gardens NSW ix J1, xi J9
Clifton Hill Vic. xv N7, 40 D5
Clifton Springs Vic. 42 G8, 44 D4, 52 A6, 63 O7
Clinton Centre SA 69 F4, 71 A1, 73 I7
Clintonvale Qld 21 B1, 27 L1, 123 L10
Clonbinane Vic. 43 J2, 52 D2, 54 D12
Cloncurry Qld 129 F11, 130 H3
Clontarf NSW xi K5
Clontarf Qld 123 K10
Closeburn Qld 114 C5, 115 C3, 117 E10
Clouds Creek NSW 21 C10, 27 M7
Clovelly NSW ix K10
Clovelly Park SA 67 B9, 68 F3
Cloven Hills Vic. 63 J6
Cloverdale WA xxv D6
Cloyna Qld 118 A8, 123 L6
Cluan Tas. 143 J9, 145 E11
Club Terrace Vic. 35 B11, 51 D10
Cluden Qld 119 A1, 120 G10, 124 G1
Clump Mountain NP Qld 120 E5, 127 M8
Clunes NSW 21 G4, 27 O3, 123 N12
Clunes Vic. 42 C1, 49 C8, 63 M2
Clybucca NSW 20 G4, 27 M9
Clyde Vic. 40 G9, 41 B12, 43 K8, 45 M4, 52 D6
Clyde North Vic. 45 N4
Clyde River NP NSW 24 H12, 35 F6, 37 L6
Clydebank Vic. 53 L6
Clydesdale Vic. 49 E7, 61 N12
Coal Creek Qld 117 B8
Coalcliff NSW 23 G3
Coaldale NSW 21 D7, 27 M5
Coalstoun Lakes Qld 118 A5, 123 L5
Coalstoun Lakes NP Qld 118 A5, 123 L5
Coalville Vic. 43 P9, 52 H7
Cobains Vic. 53 K7
Cobaki NSW 116 F11
Cobar NSW 31 L9
Cobargo NSW 35 E8, 37 K10
Cobaw Vic. 42 H1, 52 B1, 54 B12
Cobbadah NSW 26 H7
Cobbannah Vic. 53 L4
Cobbitty NSW 14 G10, 25 J7, 35 H1
Cobbora NSW 24 G1, 26 D12
Cobden Vic. 50 G8, 63 J8
Cobdogla SA 28 A6, 71 F1, 73 N7
Cobera SA 28 A7, 71 F2, 73 N9
Cobram Vic. 29 L12, 54 F4
Cobrico Vic. 50 G7, 63 I8
Cobungra Vic. 53 M1, 55 M12, 57 L10
Coburg Vic. xv J1, 40 D5, 43 I5
Cocamba Vic. 28 F9, 59 J11
Cochranes Creek Vic. 49 B2, 61 L9
Cockaleechie SA 72 D7
Cockatoo Vic. 40 H7, 41 D10, 43 L7, 45 P1, 52 E5
Cockburn SA 30 A10, 73 O1, 75 N8
Cockle Creek Tas. 141 I11
Cocklebiddy WA 91 M6
Coconut Grove NT xxvii B5
Cocoparra NP NSW 29 M6
Codrington Vic. 62 E7
Coen Qld 128 E10
Coffin Bay SA 72 D8
Coffin Bay NP SA 72 C8
Coffs Harbour NSW 20 H1, 21 E12, 27 N8
Coghills Creek Vic. 42 C2, 49 B9, 63 M3
Cohuna Vic. 29 I11, 54 A3, 61 O5
Coimadai Vic. 42 G4, 49 G11, 52 A3, 63 O4
Colac Vic. 42 B9, 50 B2, 63 L8
Colac Colac Vic. 36 A8, 55 O7, 57 N4
Colbinabbin Vic. 54 C8
Colbinabbin West Vic. 54 C8
Coldstream Vic. 40 H5, 41 C7, 43 L5, 52 E4
Coleambally NSW 29 M8
Colebrook Tas. 139 J1, 141 K5
Coledale NSW 23 G3
Coleraine Vic. 62 E3
Coles Bay Tas. 141 O3
Colignan Vic. 28 E7, 58 H8
Colinroobie NSW 24 A7, 29 N7
Colinton NSW 24 F12, 34 D12, 35 C6, 36 G7, 51 F1

Collarenebri NSW 26 D4
Collaroy NSW 25 I1, 26 F12
Collaroy Plateau NSW 12 H5, 13 C11, 15 N7
Collector NSW 24 G9, 35 D3
College Park SA xxi K4
Collendina Vic. 44 D6
Collerina NSW 31 O4
Colley SA 72 B3, 81 O11
Collie NSW 26 B10
Collie WA 86 G3, 88 D8, 90 C9
Collie Burn WA 86 G4
Collie Cardiff WA 86 H4, 88 D8
Collier Range NP WA 89 H6, 92 E7
Collingullie NSW 24 B9, 29 O9
Collingwood Vic. xv M9, xvii M1
Collins Cap Tas. 138 H5
Collinsfield SA 69 G1, 73 I5
Collinsvale Tas. 138 H4, 141 J7
Collinsville Qld 119 C5, 125 I4
Collinswood SA xxi J1
Collombatti Rail NSW 20 G4, 27 M10
Colly Blue NSW 26 G10
Colo NSW 15 I2, 17 P3, 25 J5
Colo Heights NSW 15 I1, 17 O1, 25 J5
Colo Vale NSW 23 C4, 25 I8, 35 G2
Colonel Light Gardens SA xxi I11
Colquhoun Vic. 53 O5
Colton SA 72 B5, 74 A12, 81 P12
Comara NSW 20 E3, 27 L9
Comaum SA 60 B12, 62 B1, 71 G10
Combara NSW 26 C9
Combienbar Vic. 35 C11, 51 D9
Comboyne NSW 20 E6, 27 L11
Come-By-Chance NSW 26 C6
Comet Qld 125 I11
Como NSW 12 D10, 15 K10, 23 H1
Como WA xxiv G8, xxv A9
Compton Downs NSW 31 N6
Conara Tas. 141 L1, 143 L10
Conargo NSW 29 K10, 54 E1
Concord NSW 12 D7, 15 K8
Condah Vic. 62 E5
Condamine Qld 123 I7
Condingup WA 91 J9
Condobolin NSW 24 B3, 29 P3
Condong NSW 21 G2, 27 O2, 115 F12
Condowie SA 69 G2, 73 I5
Congo NSW 35 F7, 37 L8
Congupna Vic. 54 E7, 56 A3
Conimbla NP NSW 24 E6
Coningham Tas. 139 I8, 141 K8
Coniston NSW 22 C11, 23 F5
Conjola NSW 23 B12, 25 I11, 35 G5, 37 N3
Conjola NP NSW 23 B12, 25 I10, 35 G5, 37 N3
Conmurra SA 71 F9
Connangorach Vic. 60 F10
Connellys Marsh Tas. 139 L5, 141 L7
Connemarra NSW 26 F10
Conneware Vic. 42 F9, 44 B6, 50 H2, 52 A7, 63 O8
Conondale Qld 117 D4, 118 D12, 123 M7
Conondale NP Qld 117 C4, 118 D11, 123 M7
Conway Beach Qld 119 F5, 125 J4
Conway NP Qld 119 F5, 125 J4
Coober Pedy SA 76 A10, 79 O10
Coobowie SA 69 E8, 72 H9
Coochin Creek Qld 117 F5, 118 E12
Cooee Tas. 142 F5
Coogee NSW ix J12
Coogee WA 84 C8
Coojar Vic. 62 E2
Cook SA 80 F4
Cookamidgera NSW 24 E4
Cookardinia NSW 24 B11, 29 O11, 55 M3
Cooke Plains SA 71 D4, 73 L10
Cooks Gap NSW 24 H2
Cooks Hill NSW 18 D7, 19 D9
Cooktown Qld 127 L3
Cookville Tas. 139 I11, 141 K10
Coolabah NSW 31 N8
Coolac NSW 24 D9, 35 A3
Cooladdi Qld 122 A6, 133 N6
Coolah NSW 26 F11
Coolah Tops NP NSW 26 F11

Coolalie NSW 24 F9, 35 C3
Coolalinga NT 102 E3
Coolamon NSW 24 B8, 29 O8
Coolana Qld 117 B11
Coolangatta Qld 21 H2, 27 O1, 115 G11, 116 G10, 123 N11
Coolatai NSW 27 I4, 123 I12
Coolbellup WA xxiv E12
Coolbinia WA xxiv F3
Coolcha SA 71 D3, 73 L9
Coolgardie WA 90 H5
Coolimba WA 90 A5
Coolongolook NSW 20 D9, 25 N2
Cooltong SA 28 A5, 58 A5, 73 O7
Coolum Beach Qld 117 G3, 118 F11, 123 N7
Coolup WA 85 D10, 88 C7
Cooma NSW 35 C7, 36 G9, 51 E3
Cooma Tas. 140 B11
Cooma Vic. 54 D7
Cooma West NSW 35 C7, 36 G9, 51 E3
Coomalbidgup WA 90 H9
Coomandook SA 71 E4, 73 L11
Coomba NSW 20 E10, 25 N2
Coombabah Qld 116 E4
Coombah Roadhouse NSW 28 C2, 75 O11
Coombe SA 71 F6, 73 M12
Coombell NSW 21 E5, 27 N4
Coomberdale WA 88 B1, 90 C5
Coomera Qld 115 F8, 116 D3
Coominya Qld 117 B10, 123 M9
Coomoora Vic. 42 E1, 49 E8, 63 N3
Coonabarabran NSW 26 E9
Coonalpyn SA 71 E5, 73 M11
Coonamble NSW 26 C8
Coonarr Qld 118 D2, 123 M3
Coonawarra NT xxvii F8
Coonawarra SA 60 A12, 62 A2, 71 G10
Coonerang NSW 35 C8, 36 G10, 51 F4
Coongulla Vic. 53 J5
Coongulmerang Vic. 53 L5
Coonong NSW 29 M9
Coonooer Bridge Vic. 61 K8
Coopernook NSW 20 E8, 25 O1, 27 L12
Cooplacurripa NSW 20 C6, 27 K11
Coopracambra NP Vic. 35 C11, 51 F9
Coorabakh NP NSW 20 E7, 25 O1, 27 L12
Coorabie SA 81 J8
Cooran Qld 118 E10, 123 N6
Cooranbong NSW 13 E4, 19 A10, 25 L4
Cooranga North Qld 123 K7
Coorong NP SA 68 H9, 71 D6, 73 K11
Coorow WA 90 B4
Cooroy Qld 117 F1, 118 E10, 123 N7
Coorparoo Qld xxxi I11, 114 F7, 115 D4, 117 F11
Cootamundra NSW 24 D8, 35 A2
Cooya Beach Qld 120 D1, 121 D3, 127 L5
Cooyal NSW 24 H2
Cooyar Qld 123 L8
Copacabana NSW 13 D9, 15 O4
Cope Cope Vic. 61 J8
Copeland NSW 20 B8, 25 M1, 27 J12
Copeville SA 71 E2, 73 M9
Copley SA 70 B4, 75 I4
Copmanhurst NSW 21 D8, 27 M5
Coppabella Qld 119 D10, 125 I7
Copping Tas. 139 M5, 141 M7
Coppins Crossing ACT 33 C5, 34 D5, 36 G3
Cora Lynn Vic. 41 D12, 43 M8, 52 E6
Corack Vic. 28 F12, 61 J7
Corack East Vic. 28 F12, 61 J6
Coragulac Vic. 42 A8, 50 B1, 63 K8
Coraki NSW 21 F6, 27 O4, 123 N12
Coral Bank Vic. 55 L9, 57 J6
Coral Bay WA 89 B5
Coram Vic. 42 B9, 50 B2, 63 L8
Coramba NSW 21 D11, 27 M7
Corang NSW 24 H10, 35 F4, 37 L2
Corattum SA 71 F12
Cordalba Qld 118 C3, 123 M4
Cordering WA 88 E8
Coreen NSW 29 M11, 55 I4
Corfield Qld 124 A6, 131 M6

153

Corinda Qld 114 D8, 129 B4
Corindhap Vic. 42 C5, 63 L6
Corindi NSW 21 E10, 27 N7
Corindi Beach NSW 21 E10, 27 N7
Corinella Vic. 43 L10, 45 N9, 52 E8
Corinna Tas. 142 C8
Corio Vic. 42 F7, 44 B2, 52 A6, 63 O7
Corlette NSW 19 G7
Corner Store Qld 30 B1, 77 N11, 132 F10
Cornwall Tas. 143 O9
Corny Point SA 69 C7, 72 G9
Corobimilla NSW 29 N8
Coromby Vic. 60 H8
Coronation Beach WA 89 D12, 90 A3
Coronet Bay Vic. 43 L11, 45 O10, 52 E8
Corop Vic. 54 C7
Cororooke Vic. 42 A9, 50 B1, 63 K8
Corowa NSW 29 M12, 55 I5, 56 F1
Corra Linn Tas. 143 K8, 145 H10
Corrigin WA 88 F5, 90 E8
Corrimal NSW 22 F1, 23 G4
Corringle NSW 24 C5, 29 P5
Corroboree Park Tavern NT 102 G5, 104 E5
Corryong Vic. 36 A8, 55 O7, 57 O3
Corunna NSW 37 L10
Cosgrove Vic. 54 F7, 56 B3
Cosmo Newbery WA 91 I1, 93 I11
Cossack WA 89 F1, 92 B2, 94 B12, 96 E4
Costerfield Vic. 54 C9
Cottan–Bimbang NP NSW 20 C5, 27 K10
Cottesloe WA xxiv B9, 84 C7, 85 B5
Cottles Bridge Vic. 41 A6, 43 K4
Cottonvale Qld 21 A3, 27 L2, 123 L11
Couangalt Vic. 40 A2, 42 H3, 49 H10, 52 B3, 63 P4
Cougal NSW 21 E2, 27 N2, 115 C12
Coulson Qld 115 A8
Coulta SA 72 D7
Countegany NSW 35 D7, 37 I9, 51 G3
Couridjah NSW 23 D2
Couta Rocks Tas. 142 A5
Coutts Crossing NSW 21 D9, 27 M6
Cow Bay Qld 121 E2, 127 L4
Cowabbie West NSW 24 A8, 29 O8
Cowan NSW 12 F2, 13 B9, 15 M5, 25 K6
Cowan Cowan Qld 115 G1
Cowandilla SA xx F6
Cowangie Vic. 28 C9, 58 D11, 60 D1, 73 P10
Cowaramup WA 86 B8, 88 B9
Cowell SA 69 B1, 72 G5
Cowes Vic. 43 K11, 45 L10, 52 D8
Cowley Beach Qld 120 F5, 127 M8
Cowleys Creek Vic. 50 G9, 63 J9
Cowper NSW 21 E8, 27 N5
Cowra NSW 24 F6
Cowwarr Vic. 53 J6
Coyrecup WA 88 G8
Crabbes Creek NSW 21 G3, 27 O2, 123 N11
Crabtree Tas. 138 G6, 141 J7
Cracow Qld 123 I4
Cradle Mountain–Lake St Clair NP Tas. 140 F1, 142 F10, 144 D7
Cradle Valley Tas. 142 F9, 144 D6
Cradoc Tas. 138 G8, 141 J8
Cradock SA 73 J1, 75 I8
Crafers West SA xxi O12
Craigie NSW 35 C10, 51 E8
Craigie Vic. 49 C6, 61 M12, 63 M1
Craigieburn Vic. 40 D3, 43 I4, 52 C3
Craiglie Qld 120 D1, 121 D4, 127 L5
Cramenton Vic. 28 E8, 58 H9
Cramps Tas. 141 I1, 143 I10
Cranbourne Vic. 40 G9, 41 A12, 43 K8, 45 M4, 52 D6
Cranbourne North Vic. 45 M3
Cranbourne South Vic. 40 F9, 41 A12, 43 K8, 45 L4, 52 D6
Cranbourne West Vic. 45 M4
Cranbrook Tas. 141 N2, 143 N12
Cranbrook WA 88 F10, 90 E10
Crater Lakes NP Qld 120 D3, 121 E9, 127 L7
Craven NSW 19 G2, 20 C9, 25 M2
Cravensville Vic. 55 N8, 57 M5
Crawford Qld 118 A10, 123 L7

Crawley WA xxiv E7
Crayfish Creek Tas. 142 D4
Creek Junction Vic. 54 G9, 56 C7
Creighton Vic. 54 E9, 56 A7
Cremorne NSW x H7
Cremorne Tas. 139 K6, 141 L8
Cremorne Vic. xvii M5
Cremorne Point NSW ix I1, xi I9
Crescent Head NSW 20 G5, 27 M10
Cressy Tas. 143 K9
Cressy Vic. 42 B7, 63 L6
Crestmead Qld 114 E10, 115 D6
Creswick Vic. 42 D2, 49 C9, 63 M3
Crib Point Vic. 40 F12, 43 J10, 45 L8, 52 D7
Croajingolong NP Vic. 35 C12, 51 E11
Croftby Qld 21 D1, 27 M1, 123 M10
Cronulla NSW 12 E11, 15 L11, 25 K7
Crooble NSW 26 H4, 123 I12
Crooked River Vic. 53 K3
Crookwell NSW 24 G8, 35 E2
Croppa Creek NSW 26 H3, 123 I12
Crossdale Qld 115 A1, 117 C8, 123 M8
Crossley Vic. 50 B7, 62 G8
Crossman WA 85 H10, 88 D7, 90 C8
Crossover Vic. 41 H12, 43 O8, 52 G6
Crowdy Bay NP NSW 20 F7, 25 O1, 27 L12
Crowlands Vic. 61 J12, 63 J1
Crows Nest NSW x G7, 11 B1
Crows Nest Qld 123 L8
Crows Nest NP Qld 123 L8
Crowther NSW 24 E7, 35 B1
Croxton East Vic. 62 F5
Croydon NSW 15 L9
Croydon Qld 126 F8
Croydon SA xx G2, 67 B8, 68 F2
Croydon Vic. 40 G6, 41 B8, 43 K5
Croydon Park SA xx G1
Crymelon Vic. 28 E12, 60 G6
Cryon NSW 26 D5
Crystal Brook SA 73 I4, 74 H12
Cuballing WA 88 E6, 90 D8
Cubbaroo NSW 26 E6
Cucania Qld 120 E3, 121 G9
Cuckoo Tas. 143 M7
Cudal NSW 24 F4
Cuddell NSW 29 N8
Cudgee Vic. 50 D8, 62 H8
Cudgen NSW 115 G12, 116 H12
Cudgera Creek NSW 21 H3
Cudgewa Vic. 36 A8, 55 O7, 57 N3
Cudgewa North Vic. 36 A7, 55 O6, 57 N3
Cudmirrah NSW 23 C12, 37 O3
Cudmore NP Qld 124 F9
Cue WA 89 H10, 90 D1, 92 D11
Culbin WA 88 E7
Culburra NSW 23 E10, 25 J10, 35 H4, 37 P1
Culburra SA 71 E5, 73 M12
Culcairn NSW 24 B11, 29 O11, 55 L4
Culgoa Vic. 28 F10, 61 K4
Culgoa NP NSW 26 A2, 31 P2, 122 C11, 133 P11
Culgoa Floodplain NP Qld 26 A2, 31 P2, 122 C11, 133 P11
Cullacabardee WA 84 D4
Cullen Bullen NSW 25 I5
Cullendulla NSW 24 H12, 37 M6
Culloden Vic. 53 K5
Cullulleraine Vic. 28 C6, 58 E6, 73 P7
Cumberland Park SA xx H10
Cumborah NSW 26 B4
Cummins SA 72 D7
Cumnock NSW 24 F3
Cundeelee WA 91 J5
Cunderdin WA 88 E4, 90 D7
Cundletown NSW 20 E8
Cungena SA 72 B2, 81 O9
Cungulla Qld 119 B1, 120 H11, 124 H1, 127 O12
Cunliffe SA 69 E3, 72 H6
Cunnamulla Qld 122 A9, 133 N9
Cunnawarra NP NSW 20 D2, 21 A12, 27 K8
Cunningar NSW 24 E8, 35 B2
Cunningham Qld 21 A1, 27 K1, 123 K10
Cunningham SA 69 E5, 72 H7

Cunninyeuk NSW 28 H9, 59 N12, 61 N1
Cuprona Tas. 142 F6
Curara WA 85 F11, 88 D7, 89 E12, 90 B3
Curban NSW 26 C10
Curdie Vale Vic. 50 E9, 63 I9
Curl Curl NSW xi G1
Curlewis NSW 26 G9
Curlewis Vic. 44 C4
Curlwaa NSW 28 D5, 58 G5
Currababula NSW 26 H10
Currambine WA 84 B3
Curramulka SA 69 E6, 72 H8
Currarong NSW 23 E11, 25 J10, 35 H4, 37 P2
Currawang NSW 24 G10, 35 E4, 37 J1
Currawarna NSW 24 B9, 29 O9
Currawinya NP Qld 31 I1, 133 L10
Currency Creek SA 68 G7, 71 C4, 73 J10
Currie Tas. 141 O11
Currowan Creek NSW 24 H12, 35 F6, 37 L5
Currumbin Qld 21 H2, 27 O1, 115 G11, 116 F9, 123 N11
Currumbin Beach Qld 116 G9
Currumbin Waters Qld 116 F10
Curtin Springs NT 108 F10
Curtis Island NP Qld 125 N11
Curyo Vic. 28 F11, 61 I5
Custon SA 28 B12, 60 B7, 71 G7
Cuttabri NSW 26 E6
Cygnet Tas. 138 G8, 141 J9
Cygnet River SA 69 D11, 72 H11
Cynthia Qld 123 K4

Daceyville NSW viii G12
Dadswells Bridge Vic. 60 H10
Daglish WA xxiv D6
D'Aguilar Range NP Qld 114 B4, 115 C3, 117 D9, 123 M9
Daguragu NT 106 D5
Dahlen Vic. 60 G9
Dahwilly NSW 29 J10, 54 D1
Daintree Qld 121 D2, 127 L4
Daintree NP Qld 120 C1, 121 B2, 127 K4
Daisy Dell Tas. 142 G8, 144 E5
Daisy Hill Qld 114 F9, 115 E6
Daisy Hill Vic. 49 B6, 61 M12, 63 M1
Dajarra Qld 130 F5
Dakabin Qld 114 E3, 115 D2, 117 F9
Dalbeg Qld 119 B4, 124 H3
Dalby Qld 123 K8
Dalgety NSW 35 B8, 36 E11, 51 D4
Dalkeith WA xxiv D8
Dallarnil Qld 118 B4, 123 M4
Dalmalee Vic. 28 D11, 60 G5
Dalmeny NSW 35 F7, 37 L9
Dalmore Vic. 45 O5
Dalmorton NSW 21 B9, 27 L6
Dalrymple NP Qld 120 E12, 124 F2, 127 M12
Dalton NSW 24 F9, 35 D3
Dalveen Qld 21 A2, 27 L2, 123 L11
Dalwallinu WA 88 D3, 90 C5
Daly River NT 102 C12, 104 D7
Daly Waters NT 104 H12, 106 H3
Dalyellup WA 88 C8
Dalyston Vic. 43 L12, 45 P12, 52 E9
Dalyup WA 91 I9
Dampier WA 89 E1, 92 B2, 94 B12, 96 D5
Dandaloo NSW 24 D1, 26 A12, 31 P12
Dandaragan WA 88 B2, 90 B6
Dandenong Vic. 40 F8, 41 A10, 43 K7, 45 L1, 52 D5
Dandenong North Vic. 45 L1
Dandenong Ranges NP Vic. 40 G6, 41 B8, 43 K6, 45 N1, 52 D5
Dandenong South Vic. 45 L2
Dandongadale Vic. 55 J10, 56 G8
Dangarfield NSW 25 K1, 26 H12
Dangarsleigh NSW 20 B1, 27 J8
Dangin WA 88 E5
Danyo Vic. 28 C9, 58 D11, 60 D1, 71 H4, 73 P10
Dapto NSW 23 F5
Darby Falls NSW 24 F6
Darbyshire Vic. 55 M6, 57 L3
Dardadine WA 88 E8
Dardanup WA 86 E4, 88 C8

Dareton NSW 28 D5, 58 G5
Dargo Vic. 53 L3
Dargo High Plains Vic. 53 L1
Dark Corner NSW 24 H5
Darkan WA 88 E8, 90 D9
Darke Peak SA 72 E5, 74 D12
Darkwood NSW 20 F1, 21 C12, 27 M8
Darley Vic. 42 G4, 49 G11, 52 A3, 63 O4
Darling Harbour NSW 10 B9
Darlinghurst NSW viii G6, 10 G10
Darlington NSW viii E7
Darlington Tas. 139 P2, 141 N5
Darlington Vic. 63 J6
Darlington WA 84 G5, 85 D4
Darlington Point NSW ix I5, xi I12, 29 M7
Darnick NSW 28 H2
Darnum Vic. 43 O9, 52 G7
Daroobalgie NSW 24 D4
Darr Qld 124 B9, 131 N9
Darra Qld 114 D8, 115 D5, 117 E12
Darraweit Guim Vic. 40 D1, 43 I2, 52 C2, 54 C12
Darriman Vic. 53 J9
Dart Dart Vic. 28 D12, 60 G7
Dartmoor Vic. 62 C5, 71 H12
Dartmouth Qld 124 C10, 131 O10
Dartmouth Vic. 55 M9, 57 L6
Darwin NT xxvii C10, 101, 102 C3, 104 D4
Dattuck Vic. 28 E10, 60 G3
Davenport Range NP (Proposed) NT 107 K11, 109 K1
Davidson NSW 12 F5, 15 M7
Davis Creek NSW 25 L2
Davies Creek NP Qld 120 D3, 121 E7, 127 L6
Davistown NSW 13 D8, 15 O4
Daw Park SA xx H12
Dawes Qld 123 J2
Dawes Point NSW viii F3, x F10, 10 C2, 11 D11
Dawson SA 73 K3, 75 J10
Dawson Vic. 53 J6
Dawsons Hill NSW 25 L2
Dayboro Qld 114 C3, 115 C2, 117 E8
Daylesford Vic. 42 E1, 49 E8, 63 N3
Daymar Qld 26 E1, 122 G11
Daysdale NSW 29 M11, 55 I3
Daytrap Vic. 28 F9, 59 J12, 61 J1
Daytrap Corner Vic. 28 F9, 59 I12, 61 I2
Deakin ACT 32 A12
Deakin WA 80 C4, 91 P4
Dean Vic. 42 D2, 49 D9, 63 M3
Deanmill WA 86 H10, 87 B1, 88 D10
Deans Marsh Vic. 42 C10, 50 D3, 63 M8
Deception Bay Qld 114 E3, 115 E2, 117 F8, 123 N8
Deddick Vic. 35 A10, 51 B7
Deddington Tas. 143 L9
Dederang Vic. 55 L8, 57 J5
Dee Lagoon Tas. 140 H3
Deep Lead Vic. 61 I11
Deepwater NSW 27 K5
Deepwater NP Qld 123 M2
Deer Park Vic. 40 B5, 42 H5, 52 B4, 63 P5
Deeral Qld 120 E3, 121 G9, 127 M7
Delacombe Vic. 47 A10
Delamere SA 68 B9, 69 G10, 71 A5, 73 I11
Delaneys Creek Qld 117 E6
Delatite Vic. 43 P1, 52 H1, 54 H11, 56 D10
Delburn Vic. 43 P10, 52 H8
Delegate NSW 35 C10, 51 D7
Delegate River Vic. 35 B10, 51 D8
Dellicknora Vic. 35 B10, 51 C8
Deloraine Tas. 143 I8, 145 C10
Delta Qld 119 D4, 125 J3
Delungra NSW 27 I5
Denham WA 89 B9
Denham Group NP Qld 128 E4
Denicull Creek Vic. 63 I2
Deniliquin NSW 29 J10, 54 D2
Denison Vic. 53 J6
Denman NSW 25 J2
Denman SA 80 E4
Denmark WA 87 A11, 88 F11, 90 E11
Dennes Point Tas. 139 I7, 141 K8
Dennington Vic. 50 C8, 62 G8

D'Entrecasteaux NP WA 86 E11, 87 A3, 88 C11, 90 C11
Denver Vic. 42 F1, 49 F8, 52 A1, 54 A12, 63 O2
Deptford Vic. 53 N4
Derby Tas. 143 N6
Derby Vic. 49 E2, 61 N9
Derby WA 95 I7, 98 D9
Dereel Vic. 42 C5, 49 B12, 63 L5
Dergholm Vic. 62 C2, 71 H10
Dering Vic. 28 D9, 58 G12, 60 G2
Deringulla NSW 26 E10
Derrinal Vic. 54 B9, 61 P11
Derrinallum Vic. 63 J6
Derriwong NSW 24 C3, 29 P3
Derwent Bridge Tas. 140 G2, 142 G12, 144 F11
Derwent Park Tas. xxxiv D6, 1 A1, 137 C5
Detpa Vic. 28 D12, 60 F6
Deua NP NSW 24 G12, 35 D7, 37 K7, 51 H1
Devenish Vic. 54 G7, 56 C3
Deviot Tas. 143 J7, 145 F7
Devon Vic. 53 I9
Devon Meadows Vic. 45 M5
Devon Park SA xx H1
Devondale Vic. 50 H11, 63 J10
Devonport Tas. 142 H6, 144 H1, 145 B2
Dewars Pool WA 85 F1, 88 C4
Dharug NP NSW 13 B7, 15 L2, 25 K5
Dhulura NSW 24 B9, 29 P9
Dhuragoon NSW 29 I9, 59 O12, 61 O1
Diamantina NP Qld 130 H10, 131 I10
Diamond Beach NSW 20 E9, 25 O2
Diamond Creek Vic. 40 F4, 41 A6, 43 K4
Dianella WA xxiv G2, xxv A3, 84 D5, 85 C5
Diapur Vic. 28 C12, 60 D7
Diddleum Plains Tas. 143 L7
Digby Vic. 62 D5
Diggers Rest Vic. 40 B3, 42 H4, 52 B3, 63 P4
Diggora Vic. 54 B7, 61 P8
Dilston Tas. 143 K7, 145 G8
Dimboola Vic. 60 F8
Dimbulah Qld 120 C3, 121 B8, 127 K6
Dingee Vic. 54 A7, 61 O8
Dingley Village Vic. 45 K1
Dingo Qld 125 K11
Dingwall Vic. 28 H11, 61 M5
Dinmont Vic. 42 B11, 50 B4, 63 K10
Dinner Plain Vic. 53 L1, 55 L11, 57 K10
Dinninup WA 88 D9
Dinoga NSW 26 H6
Dinyarrak Vic. 28 B12, 60 B7, 71 H7
Dipperu NP Qld 119 E10, 125 J7
Direk SA 66 C3, 67 B6
Dirranbandi Qld 26 C1, 122 E10
Dixie Vic. 50 F7, 63 I8
Dixons Creek Vic. 40 H4, 41 C6, 43 L4, 52 E3
Djukbinj NP NT 102 G4, 104 E4
Dobie Vic. 63 J2
Docker Vic. 55 I8, 56 F5
Docklands Vic. xiv G11, xvi G2, 39 A8
Doctors Flat Vic. 53 N2, 57 M12
Dodges Ferry Tas. 139 L5, 141 L7
Don Tas. 142 H6, 144 H1, 145 A6
Don Junction Tas. 145 A1
Don Valley Vic. 41 E8, 43 M5
Donald Vic. 28 F12, 61 J7
Doncaster Vic. 40 E5, 43 J5, 52 D4
Dongara–Denison WA 90 A4
Donnybrook Qld 117 G7
Donnybrook Vic. 40 D3, 43 J3, 52 C3
Donnybrook WA 86 F5, 88 C9, 90 C10
Donovans Landing SA 62 B6, 71 G12
Doo Town Tas. 139 N8, 141 M8
Dooboobetic Vic. 61 K8
Doodlakine WA 88 F4, 90 E7
Dooen Vic. 60 G9
Dookie Vic. 54 F7, 56 B3
Doomadgee Qld 129 C5
Doomben Qld 115 E4, 117 F11
Doonside NSW 12 A5, 15 I7, 17 P11
Dooragan NP NSW 20 F7, 25 O1, 27 L12
Dooralong NSW 13 D5
Dopewora Vic. 60 C9, 71 H8
Dora Creek NSW 13 E5, 19 B10

Dorodong Vic. 60 B12, 62 B2, 71 H10
Dorrien SA 67 F4
Dorrigo NSW 20 G1, 21 C12, 27 M8
Dorrigo NP NSW 20 G1, 21 D12, 27 M8
Double Bay NSW ix I6
Doubleview WA xxiv B3
Douglas Qld 119 A1, 120 G10
Douglas Vic. 60 E11
Douglas Apsley NP Tas. 141 O1, 143 O10
Douglas Daly Tourist Park NT 102 G12, 104 E7
Douglas Park NSW 23 E2
Dover Tas. 138 F10, 141 J10
Dover Heights NSW ix M6
Doveton Vic. 45 M1
Dowerin WA 88 E3, 90 D6
Dowlingville SA 69 F4, 71 A1, 73 I7
Dowsings Point Tas. xxxiv D4, 137 C4
Doyalson NSW 13 F6, 19 B12, 25 L5
Drake NSW 21 C5, 27 L3, 123 L12
Dreeite Vic. 42 A8, 63 K7
Drik Drik Vic. 62 C6, 71 H12
Drillham Qld 123 I6
Dripstone NSW 24 G2
Dromana Vic. 40 D11, 43 I10, 45 I7, 52 C7
Dromedary Tas. 138 H3, 141 J6
Dropmore Vic. 54 E11
Drouin Vic. 43 N8, 52 F6
Drouin South Vic. 43 N9, 52 F7
Drouin West Vic. 41 G12, 43 N8, 52 F6
Drovers Cave NP WA 88 A1, 90 A5
Drumborg Vic. 62 D6
Drumcondra Vic. 44 B3, 46 D2
Drummartin Vic. 54 A7, 61 O8
Drummond Vic. 42 F1, 49 F7, 52 A1, 54 A11, 63 O2
Drummond Cove WA 89 D12, 90 A3
Drummoyne NSW viii B1, x A9, 12 E7, 13 B12, 15 L8
Drung Drung Vic. 60 G9
Drung Drung South Vic. 60 G10
Dry Creek SA 66 C5, 67 B8, 68 F1
Dry Creek Vic. 54 G10, 56 C8
Dryander NP Qld 119 E4, 125 J3
Drysdale Vic. 40 A9, 42 G8, 44 D4, 52 A6, 63 O7
Drysdale River NP WA 95 M3, 99 J3
Duaringa Qld 125 K11
Dubbo NSW 24 F1, 26 C12
Dublin SA 69 G5, 71 B1, 73 J8
Duchess Qld 129 D12, 130 F5
Duckenfield NSW 13 G1, 19 D7
Duddo Vic. 28 C9, 58 D11, 71 H4, 73 P10
Dudinin WA 88 G6, 90 E8
Dudley Vic. 43 L12, 52 E9
Dudley Park SA xx H1, 66 C6
Duffholme Vic. 60 E9
Duffys Forest NSW 12 F4, 13 B10, 15 M6
Dulacca Qld 122 H6
Dularcha NP Qld 117 F5, 118 E12, 123 N7
Dulcie Range NP NT 109 L4
Dulcot Tas. 137 H3
Dulguigan NSW 116 E12
Dululu Qld 125 L12
Dulwich SA xxi L6
Dumbalk Vic. 43 O12, 52 G9
Dumberning WA 88 E7, 90 E9
Dumosa Vic. 28 G11, 61 K5
Dunach Vic. 49 B7, 61 M12, 63 M2
Dunalley Tas. 139 M6, 141 M7
Dunbogan NSW 20 F7
Dundas Qld 115 A2, 117 C9, 123 M9
Dundas Tas. 142 D10
Dundee NSW 27 K5
Dundee Beach NT 102 A5, 104 C5
Dundonnell Vic. 63 I5
Dundurrabin NSW 21 C11, 27 L7
Dunedoo NSW 24 H1, 26 E12
Dungay NSW 116 D12
Dungog NSW 19 E4, 20 B10, 25 M2
Dungowan NSW 27 I10
Dunkeld NSW 24 G5
Dunkeld Vic. 62 G4
Dunluce Vic. 49 B4, 61 L11
Dunmarra NT 104 H12, 106 H3
Dunneworthy Vic. 61 J12, 63 J2
Dunnstown Vic. 42 D3, 49 D10, 63 M4

Dunolly Vic. 49 C4, 61 M10
Dunoon NSW 21 G4, 27 O3
Dunorlan Tas. 142 H8, 145 B10
Dunrobin Vic. 62 C3, 71 H11
Dunsborough WA 86 B6, 88 B9, 90 B10
Dunwich Qld 115 G5, 123 N9
Dural NSW 12 D4, 13 A10, 15 K6
Duranillin WA 88 E8, 90 D9
Durdidwarrah Vic. 42 E5, 63 N5
Durham Lead Vic. 42 D4, 49 C11, 63 M5
Durham Ox Vic. 28 H12, 61 N6
Duri NSW 26 H10
Duroby Creek NSW 116 F12
Durong Qld 123 K6
Durran Durra NSW 24 H11, 35 E5, 37 K3
Durras NSW 25 I12, 35 F6, 37 M6
Dutson Vic. 53 K7
Dutton SA 67 G3, 71 D1, 73 K7
Dutton Park Qld xxx G9
Duverney Vic. 42 B6, 63 L6
Dwarda WA 85 H10
Dwellingup WA 85 E10, 88 C7, 90 C8
Dwyers NSW 31 M6
Dynnyrne Tas. 1 A10, 136 C12, 137 D9
Dysart Qld 119 D12, 125 I8
Dysart Tas. 139 I1, 141 K5

Eagle Farm Qld xxxi L5, 115 E4, 117 F11
Eagle Heights Qld 115 E9, 116 B4
Eagle Point Vic. 53 M6
Eaglehawk Vic. 49 F3, 54 A8, 61 O10
Eaglehawk Neck Tas. 139 N7, 141 M8
Earlando Qld 119 F4, 125 J3
Earlston Vic. 54 F8, 56 B5
East Arm NT xxvii H10
East Bairnsdale Vic. 53 M5
East Boyd NSW 35 E10, 51 H8
East Brisbane Qld xxxi I9
East Cannington WA xxv E9
East Devonport Tas. 145 C2
East Fremantle WA xxiv C10
East Gresford NSW 19 C4, 20 A10, 25 L2
East Hills NSW 12 C9, 15 J10
East Ipswich Qld 114 A9, 115 B5, 117 D12
East Jindabyne NSW 35 B8, 36 E10, 51 C4
East Kurrajong NSW 15 I3, 17 O5
East Launceston Tas. 145 G1
East Lynne NSW 35 F6, 37 M5
East Melbourne Vic. xv M11, xvii M2, 39 G5
East Perth WA xxiv G6, xxv A7, 83 G4
East Point NT xxvii A6
East Ryde NSW x A4
East Victoria Park WA xxiv H7, xxv B8
East Yolla Tas. 142 E6
Eastern Creek NSW 12 A5, 15 I7, 17 P12
Eastern View Vic. 42 D10, 50 E3, 63 M9
Eastlakes NSW viii F12
Eastville Vic. 49 D4, 61 N10
Eastwood NSW 12 D6, 15 K7
Eastwood SA xxi K7, 65 H12
Eaton WA 86 E3
Eatonsville NSW 21 D8, 27 M6
Eba SA 73 L6
Ebden Vic. 55 L6, 57 J3
Ebenezer NSW 12 B1, 15 J4
Ebor NSW 20 E1, 21 B12, 27 L8
Eccleston NSW 19 C2, 20 A9, 25 L2
Echuca Vic. 29 J12, 54 C5
Echuca Village Vic. 29 J12, 54 C5
Echunga SA 66 F10, 67 D11, 68 G4, 73 J9
Ecklin South Vic. 50 F8, 63 I8
Eddington Vic. 49 C4, 61 M11
Eddystone Point Tas. 143 P6
Eden NSW 35 E10, 51 H8
Eden Hill WA xxv C3
Eden Hills SA 66 C9, 67 B10, 68 F3
Eden Park Vic. 40 E2, 43 J3, 52 D3
Eden Valley SA 67 G6, 71 C2, 73 K8
Edenhope Vic. 60 C11, 71 H9
Edens Landing Qld 115 E6
Edgcumbe Beach Tas. 142 D4
Edgecliff NSW ix I6, 12 F8, 15 M9
Edgeroi NSW 26 F6

Edgewater WA 84 C4, 85 B4
Edi Vic. 55 I9, 56 F6
Edi Upper Vic. 55 I9, 56 F7
Edillilie SA 72 D7
Edith NSW 24 H6
Edith Creek Tas. 142 C4
Edith River NT 104 F8
Edithburgh SA 69 E8, 72 H9
Edithvale Vic. 40 E8, 43 J7, 45 K2, 52 D6
Edmonton Qld 120 E3, 121 F8, 127 L6
Edmund Kennedy NP Qld 120 E6, 127 M9
Edwardstown SA xx G11, 67 B9, 68 F3
Eganstown Vic. 42 E2, 49 E8, 63 N3
Egg Lagoon Tas. 141 P10
Eidsvold Qld 123 K4
Eildon Vic. 41 H1, 43 O1, 52 G1, 54 G12, 56 C11
Eimeo Qld 119 G7, 125 K5
Einasleigh Qld 127 I9
Ejanding WA 88 E2, 90 D6
El Arish Qld 120 E5, 127 M8
Elaine Vic. 42 D5, 49 D12, 63 M5
Elands NSW 20 D7, 27 K11
Elanora Qld 116 F9
Elanora Heights NSW 12 G4, 13 C11, 15 N6
Elaroo Qld 119 E6, 125 J5
Elbow Hill SA 69 B2, 72 F5
Elcombe NSW 26 H5
Elderslie Tas. 138 H1, 141 J5
Eldon Tas. 139 J1, 141 L5
Eldorado Vic. 55 J7, 56 G4
Electrona Tas. 139 I7
Elermore Vale NSW 13 G3, 19 C9
Elimbah Qld 117 F7, 123 N8
Elingamite Vic. 50 G8, 63 I8
Elizabeth SA 66 D3, 67 C6, 71 B2, 73 J8
Elizabeth Bay NSW viii H5
Elizabeth Beach NSW 20 E10, 25 N2
Elizabeth Town Tas. 143 I8, 145 C10
Ella Bay NP Qld 120 E4, 121 H11, 127 M7
Ellalong NSW 13 D3, 25 L4
Ellam Vic. 28 D11, 60 F5
Ellen Grove Qld 114 D9, 115 D5, 117 E12
Ellenborough NSW 20 E6, 27 L11
Ellendale Tas. 138 E1, 141 I5
Ellerslie Vic. 62 H7
Ellerston NSW 25 L1, 27 I12
Elliminyt Vic. 42 B9, 50 B2, 63 L8
Ellinbank Vic. 43 N9, 52 G7
Elliott NT 107 I5
Elliott Tas. 142 F5
Elliott Heads Qld 118 D2, 123 M3
Ellis Beach Qld 120 D2, 121 E5, 127 L5
Elliston SA 72 B5
Elmhurst Vic. 61 K12, 63 K1
Elmore Vic. 54 B7, 61 P9
Elong Elong NSW 24 G1, 26 D12
Elphin Tas. 145 G1
Elphinstone Vic. 49 G6, 54 A11, 61 O12, 63 O1
Elsey NP NT 104 H9
Elsmore NSW 27 J6
Elsternwick Vic. 43 J6, 52 C5
Eltham NSW 21 G4
Eltham Vic. 40 F5, 43 J5, 52 D4
Elwood Vic. xvii L12
Embleton WA xxiv H2, xxv B3
Emerald Qld 125 I10
Emerald Vic. 40 H7, 41 C10, 43 L7, 45 O1, 52 E5
Emerald Beach NSW 21 E11, 27 N7
Emerald Hill NSW 26 G8
Emerald Springs NT 102 H11, 104 E7
Emita Tas. 140 B10
Emmaville NSW 27 K5
Emmdale Roadhouse NSW 31 I9
Emmet Qld 124 B12, 131 N12, 133 M1
Empire Bay NSW 13 D9, 15 O4
Empire Vale NSW 21 G5, 27 O4, 123 N12
Emu Vic. 49 A2, 61 L10
Emu Bay SA 69 D10, 72 H11
Emu Creek Vic. 49 G4, 54 A9, 61 O10
Emu Downs SA 73 K6
Emu Park Qld 125 N10
Emu Plains NSW 14 G6, 17 M10, 29 N9, 55 J1
Endeavour Hills Vic. 45 M1

Endeavour River NP Qld 127 L2
Eneabba WA 90 B5
Enfield Vic. 42 C4, 49 B12, 63 M5
Engadine NSW 12 C11, 15 J11, 23 H1
Engawala NT 109 J5
Englefield Vic. 60 E12, 62 E2
English Town Tas. 143 L9
Enmore NSW viii B8
Enngonia NSW 31 M3, 122 A12, 133 N12
Enoggera Qld xxx D3, 114 D6, 115 D4, 117 F11
Ensay Vic. 53 N3
Ensay North Vic. 53 N3
Ensay South Vic. 53 N3
Eppalock Vic. 49 G4, 54 A9, 61 O10
Epping NSW 12 D5, 13 A11, 15 K7
Epping Vic. 40 E4, 43 J4, 52 C3
Epping Forest Tas. 143 L10
Epping Forest NP Qld 124 F8
Epsom Vic. 49 G3, 54 A8, 61 O10
Eraring NSW 13 F4, 19 B10
Ercildoun Vic. 42 B2, 49 A9, 63 L3
Erica Vic. 52 H6
Erigolia NSW 29 N5
Erikin WA 90 E7
Erina NSW 13 D8, 15 O3
Erindale SA xxi N6
Erith SA 67 A1, 69 H4, 71 B1, 73 J7
Erldunda NT 108 H9
Ernest Qld 116 E5
Eromanga Qld 133 J5
Erowal Bay NSW 23 D11, 37 O2
Erriba Tas. 142 G8, 144 F4
Erringibba NP Qld 122 H8
Errinundra Vic. 35 B11, 51 D9
Errinundra NP Vic. 35 B10, 51 D9
Erskine Park NSW 14 H7, 17 O12
Erskineville NSW viii D8
Esk Qld 117 A8, 123 M8
Eskdale Vic. 55 L8, 57 K5
Esmond Vic. 29 M12, 54 H6, 56 E1
Esperance WA 91 I9
Essendon Vic. xiv E1, 40 D5, 43 I5, 52 C4
Essendon West Vic. xiv B1
Etmilyn WA 85 E10
Eton Qld 119 F8, 125 K6
Ettalong Beach NSW 12 H1, 13 D9, 15 N4
Ettamogah NSW 24 A12, 29 O12, 55 L6, 57 J1
Ettrick NSW 21 E4, 27 N3, 123 M12
Euabalong NSW 24 A3, 29 N3
Euabalong West NSW 24 A3, 29 N3
Eubenangee Swamp NP Qld 120 E4, 121 G11, 127 M7
Euchareena NSW 24 G3
Eucla WA 80 C7, 91 P6
Eucla NP WA 80 C7, 91 P5
Eucumbene NSW 35 B7, 36 E8, 51 C2
Eudlo Qld 117 F4, 118 E12
Eudlo Creek NP Qld 117 F4, 118 E12, 123 N7
Eudunda SA 67 G1, 71 C1, 73 K7
Eugenana Tas. 142 H6, 144 H2, 145 A7
Eugowra NSW 24 E5
Eujinyn WA 88 G4
Eukey Qld 21 A4, 27 L3, 123 L12
Eulo Qld 133 M9
Eumemmerring Vic. 45 M2
Eumundi Qld 117 F2, 118 E10, 123 N7
Eumungerie NSW 26 C11
Eungai Creek NSW 20 G3, 27 M9
Eungella Qld 119 E7, 125 J5
Eungella NP Qld 119 E7, 125 J5
Eurack Vic. 42 B8, 63 L7
Euramo Qld 120 E6, 127 M8
Euratha NSW 24 A6, 29 N6
Eurelia SA 73 J2, 75 I9
Euri Qld 119 D4, 125 I3
Eurimbula NP Qld 123 L1, 125 O12
Euroa Vic. 54 F9, 56 A7
Eurobin Vic. 55 K9, 57 I6
Eurobodalla NSW 35 E7, 37 K9
Eurobodalla NP NSW 35 F7, 37 L9
Euroka NSW 14 C6, 16 D9, 20 F4
Eurong Qld 118 G6, 123 N5
Eurongilly NSW 24 C9

156

Euston NSW 28 F7, 59 I8
Evandale SA xxi L3
Evandale Tas. 143 K9, 145 H11
Evans Head NSW 21 G6, 27 O4
Evans Plains NSW 24 G5
Evansford Vic. 42 B1, 49 B7, 63 L2
Eveleigh NSW viii E8
Everard Junction WA 93 K7
Everard Park SA xx H8
Eversley Vic. 61 J12, 63 J2
Everton Vic. 55 J8, 56 G5
Everton Park Qld xxx E1
Ewaninga NT 111 J5
Ewens Ponds SA 62 A6, 71 G12
Exeter NSW 23 B6, 25 I9, 35 G3
Exeter Tas. 143 J7, 145 F8
Exford Vic. 40 A5, 42 G5, 49 H12, 52 B4, 63 P5
Exmouth WA 89 B3
Expedition NP Qld 122 G3
Exton Tas. 143 I8, 145 D10

Fairfield NSW 12 B7
Fairfield Qld xxx F11, 114 E8
Fairfield Vic. xv P7
Fairhaven Vic. 40 F12, 43 K10, 45 M8, 52 D7
Fairholme NSW 24 C4, 29 P4
Fairley Vic. 28 H10, 61 N4
Fairlies Knob NP Qld 118 C5, 123 M5
Fairlight NSW xi M4
Fairneyview Qld 115 A4, 117 C11
Fairview Vic. 28 G12, 61 K6
Fairy Dell Vic. 54 C7
Fairy Hill NSW 21 E4, 27 N3
Fairy Meadow NSW 22 F4, 23 F4
Falls Creek NSW 23 C10, 25 I10, 35 G4, 37 O1
Falls Creek Vic. 55 L10, 57 K8
Falmouth Tas. 143 O9
Family Islands NP Qld 120 F6, 127 M8
Fannie Bay NT xxvii B8
Faraday Vic. 49 F6, 54 A10, 61 O12, 63 O1
Farleigh Qld 119 G7, 125 K5
Farnborough Qld 125 M10
Farnham NSW 24 G3
Farrell Flat SA 73 K6
Faulconbridge NSW 14 F5, 17 K9
Fawcett Vic. 52 F1, 54 F11, 56 B10
Fawkner Vic. 40 D5, 43 I5, 52 C4
Feilton Tas. 138 F4, 141 I6
Felixstow SA xxi M1
Felton East Qld 123 K9
Fentonbury Tas. 138 E2, 141 I5
Fentons Creek Vic. 49 A1, 61 L9
Fenwick Vic. 44 C5
Ferguson Vic. 42 A11, 50 B4, 63 K10
Fern Hill Vic. 42 G2, 49 G9, 52 A2, 54 A12
Fern Tree Tas. 137 A10, 139 I6, 141 K7
Fern Tree Bower Tas. 137 A10
Fernbank Vic. 53 L5
Ferndale NSW 24 A11, 29 N11, 55 J3
Ferndale WA xxv C10, 86 G7
Ferndene Tas. 142 G6, 144 E1
Fernhill NSW 22 D2
Fernihurst Vic. 61 M7
Fernlees Qld 125 I11
Ferntree Creek NP Qld 117 F3, 118 E11, 123 N7
Ferntree Gully Vic. 40 G7, 41 B9, 43 K6, 52 D5
Fernvale Qld 115 A4, 117 C10, 123 M9
Ferny Glen Qld 116 A7
Ferny Grove Qld 114 D6, 115 D4, 117 E10
Ferny Hills Qld 115 D3, 117 E10
Fiery Flat Vic. 61 M8
Fifield NSW 24 C2
Fig Tree NSW 24 F4
Fig Tree Pocket Qld xxx A12, 114 D8
Figtree NSW 22 A10, 23 F5
Figtree Creek Qld 120 E3, 121 G9
Finch Hatton Qld 119 E7, 125 J5
Findon SA xx D2
Fingal Tas. 143 N9
Fingal Vic. 44 H9
Fingal Bay NSW 19 H8, 20 C12
Fingal Head NSW 116 H11
Finke NT 109 J10

Finke Gorge NP NT 108 H7, 110 C6
Finley NSW 29 L11, 54 F3
Finniss SA 68 H7, 71 C4, 73 K10
Finucane Island NP Qld 126 A7, 129 E4
Firle SA xxi N3
Fish Creek Vic. 52 G10
Fish Point Vic. 28 H10, 61 M2
Fisher SA 80 G4
Fishermans Paradise NSW 23 B12, 37 N3
Fishery Falls Qld 120 E3, 121 G9, 127 M6
Fiskville Vic. 42 F4, 49 F11, 63 N5
Fitzgerald Tas. 138 D3, 140 H6
Fitzgerald River NP WA 90 F10
Fitzroy SA xxi I2, 65 C2
Fitzroy Vic. xv L9, xvii L1
Fitzroy Crossing WA 95 K8, 98 H11
Fitzroy Island NP Qld 120 E2, 121 H7, 127 M6
Fitzroy North Vic. xv M6
Five Ways NSW 24 A10, 29 O10, 31 O11, 55 L2
Five Ways Vic. 45 L10
Fiveways Vic. 45 M5
Flaggy Rock Qld 119 G10, 125 K7
Flagstaff Gully Tas. 137 F6
Flagstone Creek Qld 118 C1, 123 M3
Flat Tops NSW 19 E5, 20 B10
Flaxton Qld 117 F3
Flemington Vic. xiv F6
Fletcher Qld 21 A4, 27 K3
Flinders Vic. 43 I11, 45 I10, 52 C8
Flinders Chase NP SA 69 A12, 72 F12
Flinders Group NP Qld 128 G10
Flinders Park SA xx E3
Flinders Ranges NP SA 70 C8, 75 I6
Flinton Qld 122 H9
Flintstone Tas. 141 J1, 143 J11
Floreat WA xxiv C5, 84 C6, 85 B5
Florida NSW 31 M9
Florida WA 85 B10, 88 B6, 90 B8
Florieton SA 73 L6
Flowerdale Tas. 142 E4
Flowerdale Vic. 41 B2, 43 K2, 52 D2, 54 D12
Flowerpot Tas. 138 H9, 141 K9
Flowery Gully Tas. 143 J7, 145 E7
Flying Fish Point Qld 120 E4, 121 H11, 127 M7
Flying Fox Qld 21 F1, 115 E10
Flynn Vic. 53 J7
Flynns Creek Vic. 53 I7
Footscray Vic. xiv C8, xvi D1, 40 D5, 43 I5, 52 C4
Forbes NSW 24 D4
Forbes Islands NP Qld 128 E6
Forcett Tas. 139 L4, 141 L7
Fords SA 67 E3
Fords Bridge NSW 31 L4
Fordwich NSW 25 K3
Forest Tas. 142 D4
Forest Den NP Qld 124 D7, 131 P7
Forest Glen NSW 12 D1, 13 A9, 15 K4
Forest Glen Qld 117 G4, 118 F12
Forest Grove WA 86 B9, 88 B10
Forest Hill NSW 24 C10, 29 P10, 55 N1
Forest Hill Qld 117 A11
Forest Lake Qld 114 D9, 115 D6
Forest Lodge NSW viii D6
Forest Reefs NSW 24 G5
Forester Tas. 143 M6
Forestville SA xx H8
Forge Creek Vic. 53 M6
Formartin Qld 123 K8
Forrest ACT 32 B11
Forrest Vic. 42 B10, 50 C3, 63 L9
Forrest WA 80 A5, 91 O4
Forrest Beach Qld 120 F8, 127 M10
Forrestdale WA 84 E8
Forrestfield WA xxv F7, 84 F6
Forreston SA 66 G5, 67 E7, 68 H1
Forsayth Qld 126 H9
Forster SA 71 D2, 73 L8
Forster–Tuncurry NSW 20 E9, 25 O2
Fort Lytton NP Qld 114 F6, 115 E4, 117 G11, 123 N9
Fortescue Roadhouse WA 89 E2, 92 A3, 96 C6
Forth Tas. 142 G6, 144 G1
Fortis Creek NP NSW 21 D7, 27 M5
Fortitude Valley Qld xxx H6, 113 G1

Forty Mile Scrub NP Qld 120 B6, 127 K8
Foster Vic. 52 G9
Fosterville Vic. 49 H3, 54 B8, 61 P10
Fountain Gate Vic. 45 M2
Fountaindale NSW 13 D7, 15 O2
Four Mile Creek Tas. 143 O9
Fowlers Bay SA 81 J8
Fox Ground NSW 23 E8, 25 J9, 35 H3
Fox Trap Roadhouse Qld 122 A6, 133 N6
Foxeys Hangout Vic. 45 J7
Foxhow Vic. 42 A7, 63 K6
Framlingham Vic. 50 E7, 62 H7
Framlingham East Vic. 62 H7
Frampton NSW 24 D8, 35 A2
Frances SA 60 B9, 71 G8
Francistown Tas. 138 F10, 141 I9
Francois Peron NP WA 89 B8
Frank Hann NP WA 90 G8
Frankford Tas. 143 I7, 145 E8
Frankland WA 87 G1, 88 F10, 90 D11
Frankland Group NP Qld 120 F3, 121 H9, 127 M7
Franklin Tas. 138 G7, 141 J8
Franklinford Vic. 42 E1, 49 E7, 63 N2
Franklin–Gordon Wild Rivers NP Tas. 138 A1, 140 G4, 142 E12, 144 D11
Frankston Vic. 40 E9, 43 J8, 45 K4, 52 D6
Frankton SA 67 H2, 71 D1, 73 K7
Fredericton NSW 20 G4, 27 M10
Freeburgh Vic. 55 K10, 57 J7
Freeling SA 67 D4, 71 C1, 73 K8
Freemans Reach NSW 12 A1, 15 I4, 17 O6, 25 J6
Freestone Qld 21 B1, 27 L1
Fregon SA 79 I4
Fremantle WA xxiv C11, 84 C8, 85 B6, 88 B5, 90 B8
French Island NP Vic. 40 G12, 43 K10, 45 N8, 52 E7
Frenchs Forest NSW 12 F5, 13 B11, 15 M7, 25 K6
Freshwater NP Qld 114 E3, 115 D1, 117 F8, 123 N8
Freshwater Creek Vic. 42 E9, 50 G2, 63 N8
Frewville SA xxi L8
Freycinet NP Tas. 141 O3, 143 O12
Frogmore NSW 24 F7, 35 C1
Fryerstown Vic. 49 F7, 54 A11, 61 O12, 63 O2
Fulham SA xx C5
Fulham Vic. 53 K7
Fulham Gardens SA xx C4
Fullarton SA xxi L8
Fullerton NSW 24 G7, 35 E1
Fumina Vic. 43 P7, 52 G5
Furner SA 71 F10
Furnissdale WA 85 C9, 88 C6
Fyansford Vic. 42 F8, 44 A3, 50 G1, 63 N7
Fyshwick ACT 33 F6, 34 E5, 36 H3

Gaffneys Creek Vic. 43 P3, 52 H3
Gagebrook Tas. 139 I3, 141 K6
Galah Vic. 28 D8, 58 G11
Galaquil Vic. 28 E11, 60 H5
Galaquil East Vic. 60 H5
Galga SA 71 E2, 73 M8
Galiwinku NT 105 L3
Gallanani Qld 117 A8
Gallangowan Qld 117 A1, 118 C10, 123 M7
Galong NSW 24 E8, 35 B2
Galston NSW 12 D3, 13 A10, 15 K5, 25 K6
Gama Vic. 28 E10, 60 H3
Ganmain NSW 24 B8, 29 O8
Gapsted Vic. 55 J8, 56 H5
Gapuwiyak NT 105 L4
Garah NSW 26 F3, 122 H12
Garbutt Qld 119 A1, 120 G10, 124 G1
Garden Island Creek Tas. 138 H9, 141 J9
Gardens of Stone NP NSW 25 I4
Gardners Bay Tas. 138 G9, 141 J9
Garema NSW 24 D5
Garfield Vic. 41 E12, 43 M8, 52 F6
Garfield North Vic. 41 E11, 43 M8, 52 F6
Gargett Qld 119 F7, 125 J5
Garibaldi Vic. 42 D4, 49 C12, 63 M5
Garig Gunak Barlu NP NT 104 F2
Garigal NP NSW x H1, xi I1, 12 F5, 13 B11, 15 M7, 25 K6
Garra NSW 24 F4
Garrthalala NT 105 N5

Garvoc Vic. 50 E7, 63 I8
Gary Junction WA 93 K3
Gascoyne Junction WA 89 D7, 92 A8
Gatton Qld 123 L9
Gatum Vic. 62 E2
Gaven Qld 116 D4
Gawler SA 66 E2, 67 D5, 71 C2, 73 J8
Gawler Tas. 142 G6, 144 F1
Gawler Ranges NP SA 72 C1, 74 B9, 81 P9
Gayndah Qld 123 L5
Gaythorne Qld xxx E2
Geebung Qld 114 E6
Geehi NSW 35 A8, 36 B10, 51 A4, 55 P8, 57 P5
Geelong Vic. 42 F8, 44 B4, 46, 50 G1, 52 A6, 63 O7
Geelong East Vic. 44 B4, 46 H8
Geelong North Vic. 44 B3, 46 C1
Geelong South Vic. 44 A4, 46 E9
Geelong West Vic. 46 C4
Geeralying WA 88 E7
Geeveston Tas. 138 F8, 141 I9
Geikie Gorge NP WA 95 L7, 98 H11
Geilston Bay Tas. xxxiv H6, 1 D2, 137 F6
Gelantipy Vic. 35 A10, 51 A8, 53 P2, 57 P12
Gellibrand Vic. 42 A10, 50 B3, 63 K9
Gelliondale Vic. 53 I9
Gelorup WA 86 D4
Gembrook Vic. 41 D10, 43 M7, 52 E5
Gemtree NT 109 J5
Genoa Vic. 35 D11, 51 G10
George Town Tas. 143 J6, 145 E6
Georges Creek Vic. 55 M6, 57 K3
Georges Heights NSW xi K8
Georges Plains NSW 24 H5
Georges River NP NSW 12 C9, 15 J10, 23 H1, 25 K7, 35 H1
Georgetown Qld 126 H9
Georgetown SA 73 J4, 74 H12
Georgica NSW 21 F4, 27 N3
Geraldton WA 89 D12, 90 A3
Gerang Gerung Vic. 28 D12, 60 F7
Gerangamete Vic. 42 C10, 50 C3, 63 L9
Geranium SA 71 F4, 73 M10
Geranium Plain SA 73 K6
Germantown Vic. 55 K10, 57 I7
Gerogery NSW 24 A12, 29 O12, 55 L5
Gerogery West NSW 24 A12, 29 O12, 55 L5
Gerringong NSW 23 F8, 25 J9, 35 H3
Gerroa NSW 23 E8
Geurie NSW 24 F2
Gheringhap Vic. 42 E7, 63 N7
Ghin Ghin Vic. 43 L1, 52 E1, 54 E11
Ghin-Doo-Ee NP NSW 19 H3, 20 C9, 25 M2
Gibraltar Range NP NSW 21 B7, 27 L5
Gibson WA 91 I9
Gibsonvale NSW 24 A5, 29 O5
Gidgegannup WA 84 H3, 85 E4, 88 C4
Gidginbung NSW 24 C7, 29 P7
Giffard Vic. 53 K8
Gilbert River Qld 126 G8
Gilbert Spring NT 110 B5
Gilberton SA xxi K2, 65 G3
Gilberts SA 68 G7
Giles Corner SA 67 C1, 71 C1, 73 J7
Gilgai NSW 27 I6
Gilgandra NSW 26 C10
Gilgooma NSW 26 C8
Gilgunnia NSW 29 M1, 31 M12
Gillenbah NSW 24 A8, 29 N8
Gilliat Qld 129 H11, 131 I3
Gillieston Vic. 54 E7
Gillingarra WA 88 C2, 90 C6
Gilmore NSW 24 D10, 35 A4, 36 C2
Gilston Qld 21 G1, 115 F10, 116 D6
Gin Gin NSW 26 B11
Gin Gin Qld 118 B2, 123 L3
Gindie Qld 125 I11
Gingin WA 85 C1, 88 B3, 90 C7
Ginninderra ACT 33 D3, 34 E3, 36 G2
Gipsy Point Vic. 35 D11, 51 G10
Girgarre Vic. 54 D7
Girilambone NSW 31 O9
Girral NSW 24 B5, 29 O5
Girraween NP Qld 21 A4, 27 K3, 123 K12

Girringun NP Qld 120 D7, 127 L9
Giru Qld 119 A2, 120 H11, 124 H1, 127 O12
Gisborne Vic. 40 A2, 42 H3, 49 H10, 52 B2, 63 P4
Gladfield Qld 21 B1
Gladfield Vic. 28 H12, 61 N6
Gladstone NSW 20 G4, 27 M10
Gladstone Qld 123 K1, 125 N12
Gladstone SA 73 J4, 74 H12
Gladstone Tas. 143 O5
Gladstone WA 89 C8
Gladysdale Vic. 41 E8, 43 M6, 52 F5
Glandore SA xx G9
Glanmire Vic. 24 H5
Glass House Mountains Qld 117 F6, 123 N8
Glass House Mountains NP Qld 117 F6, 118 E12, 123 N8
Glaziers Bay Tas. 138 F8, 141 J8
Glebe NSW viii D5, x D12
Glebe Tas. xxxiv F10, 1 A6, 136 E3, 137 D8
Glen Tas. 143 K6, 145 G7
Glen Alice NSW 25 I4
Glen Aplin Qld 21 A4, 27 K3, 123 K12
Glen Creek Vic. 55 K8, 57 I5
Glen Davis NSW 25 I4
Glen Dhu Tas. 145 F2
Glen Forbes Vic. 43 L11, 45 P10, 52 E8
Glen Geddes Qld 125 M10
Glen Helen Resort NT 108 G7, 110 C3
Glen Huon Tas. 138 F7, 141 I8
Glen Innes NSW 27 K5
Glen Iris Vic. 40 E6
Glen Martin NSW 19 E5, 20 B11
Glen Oak NSW 19 D6, 20 A11, 25 M3
Glen Osmond SA xxi M9
Glen Valley Vic. 55 M10, 57 L9
Glen Waverley Vic. 40 F6, 43 J6, 52 D5
Glen William NSW 19 E5, 20 B10
Glen Wills Vic. 55 M10, 57 L9
Glenaire Vic. 42 A12, 50 A6, 63 K10
Glenaladale Vic. 53 L5
Glenalbyn Vic. 49 C1, 61 M8
Glenalta SA 66 C8, 67 B10, 68 F3
Glenariff NSW 31 N7
Glenaroua Vic. 54 C11
Glenbrae Vic. 42 B1, 49 A8, 63 L3
Glenbrook NSW 14 G6, 17 L10, 25 J6
Glenburn Vic. 40 H2, 41 C3, 43 L3, 52 E2
Glenburnie SA 62 A5, 71 G12
Glencoe NSW 27 K6
Glencoe SA 71 G11
Glencoe West SA 71 F11
Glendalough WA xxiv D4, 84 D6, 85 C5
Glendambo SA 74 C5
Glenden Qld 119 D8, 125 I6
Glendevie Tas. 138 F9, 141 I9
Glendon Brook NSW 19 A5, 25 L3
Gleneagle Qld 115 C8
Glenelg SA xx C11, 66 B8, 67 B9, 68 E2, 69 H7, 71 B3, 73 J9
Glenelg East SA xx D11
Glenelg North SA xx C10
Glenelg South SA xx B12
Glenfern Tas. 138 G4, 141 J6
Glenfyne Vic. 50 F8, 63 I8
Glengarrie NSW 116 E11
Glengarry Tas. 143 J7, 145 E8
Glengarry Vic. 53 I7
Glengower Vic. 49 C7, 61 M12, 63 M2
Glengowrie SA xx D12
Glenhaven NSW 12 C4, 13 A10, 15 K6
Glenisla Vic. 60 G12, 62 G1
Glenlee Vic. 28 D12, 60 E7
Glenlofty Vic. 61 K12, 63 K1
Glenloth Vic. 28 G12, 61 K6
Glenluce Vic. 49 F7, 61 N12, 63 N2
Glenlusk Tas. 138 H4
Glenlyon Vic. 42 F1, 49 F8, 63 N2
Glenmaggie Vic. 53 J5
Glenmore NSW 14 F11, 23 D1
Glenmore Vic. 42 F4, 49 F12, 51 A8, 52 A3, 53 O2, 57 O12, 63 O5
Glenmorgan Qld 122 H8
Glenora Tas. 138 F2, 141 I6

Glenorchy Tas. xxxiv A6, 137 B5, 139 I4, 141 K7
Glenorchy Vic. 60 H10
Glenore Tas. 143 J9, 145 E11
Glenore Crossing Qld 126 D7, 129 G5
Glenore Grove Qld 117 A11
Glenorie NSW 12 D2, 13 A9, 15 K4
Glenormiston Vic. 63 I7
Glenormiston North Vic. 63 I7
Glenpatrick Vic. 61 K12, 63 K1
Glenreagh NSW 21 D10, 27 M7
Glenrowan Vic. 54 H8, 56 E5
Glenrowan West Vic. 54 H8, 56 E5
Glenroy NSW 14 B3, 16 D4, 24 C11, 25 I5, 35 A6, 36 B5, 55 O4
Glenroy SA 60 A12, 62 A1, 71 G10
Glenshee Vic. 61 K12, 63 K1
Glenside SA xxi L7
Glenthompson Vic. 62 H4
Glenunga SA xxi L8
Glenvale Vic. 40 F2, 43 J3, 52 D2
Glossodia NSW 15 I3, 17 O5
Glossop SA 28 A6, 58 A6, 73 N7
Gloucester NSW 20 C8, 25 M1, 27 K12
Gloucester Island NP Qld 119 E4, 125 J3
Gloucester NP WA 86 H11, 87 B2, 88 D10, 90 C11
Glynde SA xxi N2
Gnangara WA 84 D4, 85 C4
Gnarming WA 88 G6, 90 E8
Gnarwarre Vic. 42 E8, 50 F1, 63 N7
Gnotuk Vic. 50 G7, 63 J7
Gnowangerup WA 88 G9, 90 E10
Gobondery NSW 24 C2
Gobur Vic. 54 F11, 56 A9
Gocup NSW 24 D10, 35 A4, 36 C2
Godfreys Creek NSW 24 F7, 35 C1
Godwin Beach Qld 114 G2, 115 E1, 117 G8
Gogango Qld 125 L11
Gol Gol NSW 28 E6, 58 G6
Golconda Tas. 143 L6
Golden Beach Vic. 53 L7
Golden Point Vic. 49 F6, 54 A10, 61 M12
Golden Valley Tas. 143 I9, 145 D12
Goldfields Woodlands NP WA 90 G5
Goldsborough Vic. 49 B3, 61 L10
Goldsmith Tas. 141 K1, 143 K11
Goldsworthy WA 92 E1, 94 E11, 97 J3
Gollan NSW 24 G1, 26 D12
Golspie NSW 24 H8, 35 E2
Goneaway NP Qld 131 J10
Gongolgon NSW 31 O6
Gonn Crossing Vic. 61 N3
Goobang NP NSW 24 E3
Goobarragandra NSW 24 E11, 35 B5, 36 D3
Good Night Scrub NP Qld 118 A4, 123 L4
Goodedulla NP Qld 125 L10
Goodings Corner Qld 116 E7
Goodna Qld 114 C9, 115 C5, 117 E12
Goodnight NSW 28 G8, 59 L10
Goodooga NSW 26 A2, 122 D11
Goodwood Qld 118 D3, 123 M4
Goodwood SA xxi I8, 66 C7, 67 B9, 68 F2
Goodwood Tas. xxxiv D5, 137 C5
Googa Googa Qld 118 A12
Goold Island NP Qld 120 F6, 127 M9
Goolgowi NSW 29 L6
Goolma NSW 24 G2
Goolmangar NSW 21 F4, 27 N3
Gooloogong NSW 24 E5
Goolwa SA 68 G8, 71 C4, 73 J11
Goomalibee Vic. 54 G8, 56 C4
Goomalling WA 88 D3, 90 C6
Goombungee Qld 123 L8
Goomburra Qld 27 L1
Goomeri Qld 118 B8, 123 L6
Goon Nure Vic. 53 M6
Goondah NSW 24 E9, 35 C3
Goondiwindi Qld 26 H1, 123 I11
Goondooloo SA 71 E3, 73 M9
Goonengerry NP NSW 21 G4, 27 O3, 123 N12
Goongarrie WA 90 H4
Goongarrie NP WA 90 H4
Goongerah Vic. 35 B11, 51 C9
Goonumbla NSW 24 E3

Gooram Vic. 54 F10, 56 A8
Goorambat Vic. 54 G7, 56 C4
Goornong Vic. 49 H2, 54 B8, 61 P9
Gooroc Vic. 61 K8
Gooseberry Hill WA xxv H5
Gooseberry Hill NP WA xxv H4, 84 F5, 85 D5, 88 C5, 90 C7
Goovigen Qld 123 J1, 125 L12
Goowarra Qld 125 K11
Gorae Vic. 62 D7
Gorae West Vic. 62 D7
Gordon SA 73 J1, 74 H8
Gordon Tas. 138 H10, 141 J9
Gordon Vic. 42 E3, 49 E10, 63 N4
Gordon Park Qld xxx H2
Gordonvale Qld 120 E3, 121 F8, 127 L6
Gormandale Vic. 53 J8
Gormanston Tas. 140 E1, 142 E11, 144 A10
Gorokan NSW 13 E6, 15 P1, 19 B12
Goroke Vic. 60 D9
Gosford NSW 13 D8, 15 O3, 25 L5
Goshen Tas. 143 O7
Gosnells WA xxv F12, 84 F7, 85 D6
Goughs Bay Vic. 43 P1, 52 H1, 54 H12, 56 D10
Goulburn NSW 24 H9, 35 E3
Goulburn River NP NSW 24 H1, 25 I1, 26 F12
Goulburn Weir Vic. 54 D9
Goulds Country Tas. 143 O7
Gourock NP NSW 24 G12, 34 G12, 35 D6, 37 I7, 51 G1
Gowanford Vic. 28 G10, 61 K2
Gowangardie Vic. 54 F8, 56 B4
Gowar Vic. 49 E5, 61 N11, 63 N1
Gowar East Vic. 61 K9
Gowrie Park Tas. 142 G8, 144 G4
Goyura Vic. 28 E11, 60 H4
Grabben Gullen NSW 24 G8, 35 D2
Grabine NSW 24 F6
Grace Vic. 45 L4
Gracemere Qld 125 M11
Gracetown WA 86 A8, 88 B9, 90 B10
Graceville Qld xxx C12
Gradgery NSW 26 B9
Gradule Qld 26 E1, 122 G10
Grafton NSW 21 D9, 27 M6
Graman NSW 27 I4
Grampians NP Vic. 60 G12, 62 G2
Grandchester Qld 117 A12
Grange Qld xxx G3
Grange SA xx A3, 66 B7, 67 A8, 68 E2
Granite Flat Vic. 55 M9, 57 L6
Grantham Qld 123 L9
Granton Tas. 139 I3, 141 K6
Grantville Vic. 43 L10, 45 P9, 52 E8
Granville NSW 12 C6, 13 A12, 15 K8
Granville Harbour Tas. 142 B9
Granya Vic. 24 B12, 29 O12, 55 M6, 57 L2
Grasmere NSW 14 G11, 23 E1
Grass Flat Vic. 60 E9
Grass Patch WA 91 I8
Grassdale Vic. 62 D5
Grassmere Vic. 50 D7
Grassmere Junction Vic. 50 D7, 62 H8
Grasstree Qld 119 G8, 125 K6
Grasstree Hill Tas. xxxiv H1, 137 F2, 139 J4
Grassy Tas. 141 P12
Gravelly Beach Tas. 143 J7, 145 F8
Gravesend NSW 26 H5
Grawin NSW 26 B4
Grawlin NSW 24 D5
Grawlin Plains NSW 24 D5
Gray Tas. 143 O9
Graytown Vic. 54 C9
Gre Gre Vic. 61 J9
Great Australian Bight Marine NP SA 80 C7, 81 I7, 91 P6
Great Barrier Reef Marine Park Qld 119 F2, 120 H7, 121 G6, 125 K2, 127 M3, 128 F6
Great Basalt Wall NP Qld 120 B12, 124 D2, 127 L12, 131 P2
Great Northern Vic. 55 J6, 56 G1
Great Palm Island Qld 120 G8, 127 N10
Great Sandy NP Qld 117 G1, 118 G4, 123 O4

Great Western Vic. 61 I12, 63 I1
Greater Bendigo NP Vic. 49 G1, 54 A8, 61 O9
Gredgwin Vic. 28 G11, 61 L5
Green Fields SA 66 C5, 67 B7
Green Head WA 90 A5
Green Hill NSW 20 G4, 27 M10
Green Hill Creek Vic. 49 A7, 61 K12, 63 K2
Green Island NP Qld 120 E2, 121 H6, 127 M6
Green Island Marine Park Qld 120 E2, 121 H6
Green Point NSW 13 D8, 15 O3, 20 E10, 25 O2
Greenbank Qld 114 C10, 115 C6
Greenbushes WA 86 G7, 88 C9
Greendale Vic. 42 F3, 49 F10, 52 A3, 63 O4
Greenethorpe NSW 24 E6
Greenhill SA xxi P8
Greenhills WA 88 E4
Greenmantle NSW 24 F6
Greenmount Qld 123 L9
Greenmount Vic. 53 I9
Greenmount WA xxv G2, 84 F5, 85 D4
Greenmount NP WA xxv H3, 84 F5, 85 D5, 88 C5, 90 C7
Greenock SA 67 E4, 71 C1, 73 K8
Greenough WA 90 A3
Greens Beach Tas. 143 I6, 145 D5
Greens Creek Vic. 61 J11
Greensborough Vic. 40 E4, 43 J5, 52 D4
Greenslopes Qld xxx H11
Greenvale Qld 120 B9, 127 K10
Greenwald Vic. 62 C5, 71 H12
Greenways SA 71 F10
Greenwell Point NSW 23 E9, 25 J10, 35 G4, 37 P1
Greenwich NSW viii D1, x E7
Greg Greg NSW 24 D12, 35 A6, 36 B7, 51 A2, 55 P6, 57 P2
Gregors Creek Qld 117 B6
Gregory Qld 125 I10
Gregory WA 89 D12
Gregory NP NT 95 P4, 99 P6, 104 C12, 106 C3
Greigs Flat NSW 35 E10, 51 H7
Grenfell NSW 24 D6
Grenville Vic. 42 D5, 49 C12, 63 M5
Gresford NSW 19 C4, 20 A10, 25 L2
Greta Vic. 55 I8, 56 E5
Greta South Vic. 54 H9, 56 E6
Greta West Vic. 54 H8, 56 E5
Gretna Tas. 138 F2, 141 J6
Grevillia NSW 21 E3, 27 N2, 123 M11
Grey Peaks NP Qld 120 E2, 121 G8, 127 M6
Greymare Qld 21 A1, 27 K1, 123 K10
Griffith NSW 29 M7
Grimwade WA 86 G6
Gringegalgona Vic. 62 E2
Gritjurk Vic. 62 E3
Grogan NSW 24 D7, 35 A1
Grong Grong NSW 24 A8, 29 O8
Grose Vale NSW 14 G4, 17 M6
Grosvenor Qld 123 K4
Grove Tas. 138 G6, 141 J7
Grovedale Vic. 42 F8, 44 A4, 50 G1, 63 O8
Gruyere Vic. 40 H5, 41 C7, 43 L5
Gubbata NSW 24 A5, 29 N5
Guilderton WA 88 B4, 90 B7
Guildford NSW 12 C7, 15 J8
Guildford Tas. 142 E7, 144 C3
Guildford Vic. 49 E7, 61 N12, 63 N2
Guildford WA xxv D3, 84 E5, 85 C4
Gulaga NP NSW 35 E8, 37 K10
Gular NSW 26 C9
Gulargambone NSW 26 C9
Gulf Creek NSW 26 H7
Gulgong NSW 24 H2
Gulnare SA 73 J5, 74 H12
Guluguba Qld 123 I6
Gum Lake NSW 28 G1, 30 F12
Gumble NSW 24 F4
Gumbowie SA 73 K3, 75 I11
Gumdale Qld xxxi P11
Gumeracha SA 66 G5, 67 E8, 68 H1, 71 C3, 73 K9
Gumlu Qld 119 C3, 125 I2
Gumly Gumly NSW 24 C9, 29 P9, 55 N1
Gunalda Qld 118 D8, 123 M6
Gunbar NSW 29 L6

Gunbower Vic. 29 I11, 54 A4, 61 O6
Gundabooka NP NSW 31 L6
Gundagai NSW 24 D9, 35 A3, 36 C1, 55 P1
Gundaring WA 88 F7
Gundaroo NSW 24 G10, 34 F2, 35 D4, 36 H1
Gundary NSW 24 H9, 35 E3
Gunderman NSW 13 B8, 15 L3
Gundiah Qld 118 D7, 123 M5
Gundillion NSW 24 G12, 35 E6, 37 J6, 51 H1
Gundowring Vic. 55 L8, 57 J5
Gundowring North Vic. 55 L7, 57 J4
Gundowring Upper Vic. 55 L8, 57 J5
Gundy NSW 25 K1, 26 H12
Gunebang NSW 24 A3, 29 O3
Gungahlin ACT 24 F10, 33 E3, 34 E3, 36 H2
Gungal NSW 25 J2
Gunnary NSW 24 F7, 35 C2
Gunnedah NSW 26 G9
Gunnewin Qld 122 F5
Gunning NSW 24 G9, 35 D3
Gunningbland NSW 24 D4
Gunns Plains Tas. 142 G6, 144 E2
Gunpowder Qld 129 D9, 130 F1
Gunyangara NT 105 N4
Gurley NSW 26 F5
Gurrai SA 28 A8, 58 A10, 71 G4, 73 N10
Gurrumuru NT 105 M4
Gurrundah NSW 24 G9, 35 D3
Guthalungra Qld 119 D3, 125 I2
Guthega NSW 35 A8, 36 C10, 51 B4
Guy Fawkes River NP NSW 21 A9, 27 L6
Guyong NSW 24 G5
Guyra NSW 27 J7
Guys Forest Vic. 24 C12, 55 N6, 57 M2
Gwabegar NSW 26 D7
Gwalia WA 90 H2
Gwandalan NSW 13 F5, 19 B11
Gwandalan Tas. 139 L7, 141 L8
Gwelup WA xxiv C2
Gwynneville NSW 22 C7
Gymbowen Vic. 60 D9
Gympie Qld 118 D9, 123 M6
Gypsum Vic. 28 E9, 58 H12, 60 H1

Haasts Bluff NT 108 F6
Haberfield NSW viii A4, x A12
Hackney SA xxi K4
Haddon Vic. 42 C3, 49 B10, 63 L4
Haden Qld 123 L8
Hadspen Tas. 143 K8, 145 G10
Hagley Tas. 143 J8, 145 E11
Hahndorf SA 66 F9, 67 D10, 68 H3, 71 C3, 73 K9
Haig WA 91 M5
Haigslea Qld 115 A5, 117 C11
Halbury SA 69 H3, 73 J6
Hale Village Qld 21 F1, 115 D9
Half Tide Qld 119 G8, 125 K6
Halfway Creek NSW 21 E10, 27 N6
Halfway Mill Roadhouse WA 88 A1, 90 B5
Halidon SA 71 F3, 73 M9
Halifax Qld 120 F8, 127 M10
Halifax Bay Wetlands NP Qld 120 F9, 127 M10
Hall ACT 33 D2, 34 D3, 36 G2
Hallam Vic. 40 F8, 41 A11, 43 K7, 45 M2
Hallett SA 73 K5, 75 I12
Hallidays Point NSW 20 E9, 25 O2
Halls Creek WA 95 N7, 99 L11
Halls Gap Vic. 60 H12, 62 H1
Halls Head WA 85 B9
Hallston Vic. 43 O10, 52 G8
Halton NSW 19 C3, 20 A9, 25 L2
Hamel WA 85 D11, 88 C7
Hamelin Bay WA 86 B10, 88 B10
Hamersley WA xxiv C1, 85 H3, 89 G3, 92 C4, 96 G8
Hamilton NSW 19 D9
Hamilton Qld xxxi J4
Hamilton SA 67 E1, 71 C1, 73 K7
Hamilton Tas. 138 F1, 141 I5
Hamilton Vic. 62 F4
Hamilton East NSW 18 A6
Hamley Bridge SA 67 C3, 71 B1, 73 J7
Hamlyn Heights Vic. 44 A3, 46 A2
Hammond SA 73 J2, 74 H9

159

Hampden SA 73 K7
Hampshire Tas. 142 F6, 144 C2
Hampton NSW 14 A4, 16 B6, 25 I6
Hampton Qld 123 L9
Hampton Vic. 43 J6
Hampton Park Vic. 41 A11, 43 K7, 45 M2
Hanging Rock Vic. 51 B7, 53 P1, 55 P12
Hann River Roadhouse Qld 127 I2
Hann Tableland NP Qld 120 C2, 121 B6, 127 K6
Hannahs Bridge NSW 26 E11
Hannan NSW 24 A5, 29 N5
Hansborough SA 67 F1, 73 K7
Hanson SA 73 K6
Hansonville Vic. 55 I8, 56 E6
Hanwood NSW 29 M7
Happy Valley Qld 118 G5, 123 O4, 125 L8
Happy Valley Vic. 28 F7, 42 B4, 49 A12, 55 K9, 57 I6, 59 I9, 63 L5
Harbord NSW xi N2
Harcourt Vic. 49 F5, 54 A10, 61 O11, 63 O1
Harcourt North Vic. 49 F5, 54 A10, 61 O11, 63 O1
Harden NSW 24 E8, 35 B2
Hardwicke Bay SA 69 D7, 72 H9
Harefield NSW 24 C9, 29 P9
Harford Tas. 143 I6, 145 C7
Hargraves NSW 24 H3
Harkaway Vic. 40 G8, 41 B10, 43 K7, 45 N2
Harlin Qld 117 A6, 123 M8
Harrietville Vic. 55 L10, 57 J9
Harrington NSW 20 F8, 25 O1, 27 L12
Harrismith WA 88 G7
Harrisville Qld 115 A7
Harrogate SA 67 F9
Harrow Vic. 53 L6, 60 D11, 62 D1
Harrys Creek Vic. 54 F9, 56 B6
Harston Vic. 54 D7
Hart SA 69 H2, 73 J6
Hartley NSW 14 B3, 16 D4, 25 I5
Hartley SA 66 H12, 67 F12
Hartley Vale NSW 14 C3, 16 F4
Hartz Mountains NP Tas. 138 D9, 141 I9
Harvey WA 86 F2, 88 C7, 90 C9
Harwood NSW 21 F8, 27 N5
Haslam SA 72 A2, 81 N9
Hassell NP WA 87 F8, 88 H10, 90 F11
Hasties Swamp NP Qld 120 D3, 121 D9, 127 L7
Hastings Tas. 138 F11, 141 I10
Hastings Vic. 40 F11, 43 J9, 45 K7, 52 D7
Hastings Point NSW 21 H3, 27 O2, 123 N11
Hat Head NSW 20 G4, 27 M10
Hat Head NP NSW 20 G4, 27 M10
Hatches Creek NT 107 K12, 109 K1
Hatfield NSW 28 H5, 59 N4
Hatherleigh SA 71 F10
Hattah Vic. 28 E7, 58 H9
Hattah–Kulkyne NP Vic. 28 E7, 58 H8, 59 I9
Hatton Vale Qld 117 A11
Havelock Vic. 49 C5, 61 M11
Haven Vic. 60 G9
Havilah Vic. 55 K9, 57 I6
Hawker SA 70 A12, 74 H8
Hawkesbury Heights NSW 14 G5, 17 L8
Hawkesdale Vic. 62 G6
Hawks Nest NSW 19 H7, 20 C11, 25 N3
Hawley Beach Tas. 143 I6, 145 C6
Hawthorn SA xxi J10
Hawthorn Vic. xv P12, xvii P3, 40 E6
Hawthorne Qld xxxi I7
Hay NSW 29 J7
Haydens Bog Vic. 35 B10, 51 D8
Hayes Creek NT 102 G10, 104 E6
Hayes Tas. 138 G3, 141 J6
Haymarket NSW viii F6, 10 C11
Haysdale Vic. 28 G8, 59 K10
Hazel Park Vic. 43 P12, 52 H9
Hazelbrook NSW 14 E6, 17 I9
Hazeldene Vic. 40 G1, 41 B2, 43 K2, 52 D2, 54 D12
Hazelmere WA xxv G4, 85 D4
Hazelwood Vic. 52 H7
Hazelwood Park SA xxi N7
Healesville Vic. 41 D6, 43 L4, 52 E4
Heartbreak Hotel NT 105 L12, 107 L3
Heath Hill Vic. 43 M9, 52 F7
Heathcote NSW 12 C11, 15 J11, 23 H1, 25 K7, 35 H1

Heathcote Vic. 54 B10, 61 P11
Heathcote Junction Vic. 40 E1, 43 J2, 52 C2, 54 C12
Heathcote NP NSW 12 B11, 15 J12, 23 G2, 25 J7, 35 H1
Heatherton Vic. 45 K1
Heathfield SA 66 E9, 67 C10, 68 G3
Heathmere Vic. 62 D7
Heathmont Vic. 40 F6, 41 A8
Heathpool SA xxi M6
Hebden NSW 25 K2
Hebel Qld 26 B2, 122 D11
Hector Qld 119 G8, 125 K6
Hectorville SA xxi O2
Heddon Greta NSW 13 F2, 19 B8, 20 A12
Hedley Vic. 53 I9
Heidelberg Vic. 40 E5, 43 J5
Heka Tas. 142 F7, 144 E2
Helena Valley WA xxv H4, 84 F5
Helensburgh NSW 23 H2, 25 K8, 35 H2
Helensvale Qld 21 G1, 27 O1, 115 F9, 116 D4, 123 N10
Helenvale Qld 127 L3
Helidon Qld 123 L9
Hell Hole Gorge NP Qld 133 L3
Hells Gate Roadhouse Qld 129 B3
Hellyer Tas. 142 D4
Hemmant Qld xxxi O7, 114 F7, 115 E4, 117 G11
Hendon SA 67 B8, 68 E1
Hendra Qld xxxi K3, 114 E6
Henley Beach SA xx A4
Henley Beach South SA xx B5
Henley Brook WA 85 D4
Henrietta Tas. 142 E6
Hensley Park Vic. 62 F4
Henty NSW 24 B11, 29 O11, 55 L3
Henty Vic. 62 D4
Hepburn Springs Vic. 42 E1, 49 E8, 63 N2
Herberton Qld 120 C4, 121 C10, 127 L7
Herdsman WA xxiv E7
Hermannsburg NT 108 H7, 110 D5
Hermidale NSW 31 N10
Hernani NSW 21 B11, 27 L7
Herne Hill Vic. 46 A3
Herons Creek NSW 20 F7, 27 L11
Herrick Tas. 143 N6
Herston Qld xxx G5
Hervey Bay Qld 118 F4, 123 N4
Hesket Vic. 42 H2, 52 B2, 54 B12, 63 P3
Hesso SA 72 H1, 74 F8
Hexham NSW 13 G2, 19 D8, 20 A12, 25 L4
Hexham Vic. 62 H6
Heybridge Tas. 142 F5
Heyfield Vic. 53 J6
Heywood Vic. 62 D6
Hi Way Inn Roadhouse NT 104 H12, 106 H3
Hiamdale Vic. 53 J7
Hiawatha Vic. 53 I9
Hidden Valley NT xxvii G9
Hidden Valley NP WA 95 O4, 99 M5, 104 A11, 106 A2
High Camp Vic. 52 C1, 54 C11
High Range NSW 23 B4, 25 I8, 35 G2
High Wycombe WA xxv F5
Highbury WA 88 F7
Highclere Tas. 142 F6, 144 D1
Highcroft Tas. 139 L9, 141 M9
Highett Vic. 43 J7
Highfield Tas. 145 A3
Highfields Qld 123 L9
Highgate SA xxi K9
Highgate WA xxiv G5, 83 F2
Highgate Hill Qld xxx F9, 113 C12
Highlands Vic. 54 E11
Highton Vic. 44 A4, 46 A10
Highvale Qld 114 B5, 115 C3, 117 D10
Hilgay Vic. 62 D4
Hill End NSW 24 G4
Hill End Vic. 43 P7, 52 H6
Hillarys WA 84 B4, 85 B4, 88 B5
Hillcrest Vic. 42 B3, 49 A11
Hilldale NSW 19 D5, 20 A10
Hillgrove NSW 20 C1, 27 K8
Hillman WA 88 E8
Hillside Vic. 53 M5

Hillston NSW 29 L4
Hilltop NSW 23 C4, 25 I8, 35 G2
Hilltown SA 73 J5
Hillview Qld 21 F2, 27 N1, 115 C11
Hillwood Tas. 143 J7, 145 F7
Hilton SA xx G6
Hilton WA xxiv D12
Hinchinbrook Island NP Qld 120 F7, 127 M9
Hindmarsh SA xx G3
Hindmarsh Valley SA 68 F8, 69 H10
Hines Hill WA 88 G3
Hinnomunjie Vic. 53 N1, 55 N11, 57 M10
Hinton NSW 13 G1, 19 C7
Hirstglen Qld 123 L10
Hivesville Qld 123 L6
HMAS Cerberus Vic. 45 K8
Hobart Tas. xxxiv F11, 1 A7, 136, 137 D8, 139 I5, 141 K7
Hobbys Yards NSW 24 G6
Hoddle Vic. 52 G10
Hoddles Creek Vic. 41 E9, 43 M6, 52 E5
Hodgson River Station NT 105 J10, 107 J1
Holbourne Island NP Qld 119 E3, 125 J2
Holbrook NSW 24 B11, 29 O11, 55 M4
Holgate NSW 13 D8, 15 O2
Holland Park Qld xxxi I12
Hollow Tree Tas. 141 J5
Holly WA 88 F9
Hollydeen NSW 25 J2
Hollywell Qld 116 F4
Holmview Qld 114 F11, 115 E7
Holmwood NSW 24 F6
Holwell Tas. 143 J7, 145 E8
Home Hill Qld 119 B2, 124 H2, 127 O12
Homebush NSW 12 D7
Homebush Qld 119 G8, 125 K6
Homebush Vic. 49 A5, 61 L11, 63 L1
Homecroft Vic. 28 E12, 60 H7
Homerton Vic. 62 E6
Homestead Qld 124 E3
Homevale NP Qld 119 E8, 125 J6
Homewood Vic. 43 L1, 52 E1, 54 E11
Hope Islands NP Qld 121 E2, 127 L4
Hope Vale Qld 127 K2
Hopetoun Vic. 28 E10, 60 H4
Hopetoun WA 90 G10
Hopetoun West Vic. 28 D10, 60 G3
Hopevale Vic. 28 E11, 60 G4
Hoppers Crossing Vic. 40 B6, 42 H6, 52 B5, 63 P6
Hordern Vale Vic. 42 A12, 50 B6, 63 K10
Hornsby NSW 12 E4, 13 B10, 15 L6, 25 K6
Hornsby Heights NSW 12 E4, 13 B10, 15 L6
Hornsdale SA 73 J4, 75 I11
Horrocks WA 89 D12
Horse Lake NSW 30 D11, 75 P9
Horseshoe Bay Qld 120 G10, 127 N11
Horseshoe Bend Vic. 45 P2
Horsham Vic. 60 G9
Horsley Park NSW 12 A6, 15 I8
Horsnell Gully SA xxi P7
Hoskinstown NSW 24 G11, 34 H7, 35 D5, 37 I4
Hotham Heights Vic. 53 L1, 55 L11, 57 J9
Hotspur Vic. 62 D5
Houghton SA 66 E5, 67 D8, 68 G1
Hove SA 66 B8, 67 B10, 68 E3
Hovell Park Vic. 44 B2
Howard Qld 118 D4, 123 M4
Howard Springs NT 102 E3, 104 D4
Howden Tas. 139 I7, 141 K8
Howes Valley NSW 25 K3
Howick Group NP Qld 128 H11
Howlong NSW 24 A12, 29 N12, 55 J5, 56 H1
Howqua Vic. 43 P1, 52 H1, 54 H12, 56 D11
Howrah Tas. 1 H9, 137 G8, 139 J5
Howth Tas. 142 G5
Hoya Qld 115 A8
Hoyleton SA 69 H3, 73 J6
Huddleston SA 73 J4, 74 H12
Hughenden Qld 124 B4, 131 N4
Hughes SA 80 D4
Hull River NP Qld 120 E6, 127 M8
Humevale Vic. 41 A4, 43 K3, 52 D3
Humpty Doo NT 102 E4, 104 D4
Humula NSW 24 C11, 36 A3, 55 O3

Hungerford Qld 31 J1, 133 L11
Hunter Vic. 54 B7, 61 P8
Hunters Hill NSW x B7
Hunterston Vic. 53 J9
Huntingdale Vic. 40 E7
Huntingdale WA xxv F12
Huntleys Cove NSW x A7
Huntleys Point NSW x A8
Huntly Vic. 49 G2, 54 A8, 61 O9
Huon Vic. 55 L7, 57 J3
Huonville Tas. 138 G7, 141 J8
Hurstbridge Vic. 40 F4, 41 A6, 43 K4, 52 D3
Hurstville NSW 12 D9, 15 K10
Huskisson NSW 23 D11, 25 J10, 35 G4, 37 O2
Hutt WA 89 D11, 90 A2
Hyams Beach NSW 23 D11, 37 O2
Hyde Park SA xxi J8
Hyden WA 88 H5, 90 F8
Hyland Park NSW 20 H2, 27 M9
Hynam SA 60 A10, 71 G9

Icy Creek Vic. 43 O6, 52 G5
Ida Bay Tas. 138 E12, 141 I10
Idalia NP Qld 124 B12, 131 N12, 133 M2
Ilbilbie Qld 119 G9, 125 K7
Ilford NSW 24 H4
Ilfracombe Qld 124 B10, 131 N10
Ilfraville Tas. 145 E6
Ilkurlka Roadhouse WA 91 N1, 93 N11
Illabarook Vic. 42 B5, 49 A12, 63 L5
Illabo NSW 24 C9
Illalong Creek NSW 24 E9, 35 C3
Illawarra Vic. 61 I11, 63 I1
Illawong NSW 12 C9, 15 J10
Illawong WA 90 A4
Illowa Vic. 50 C7, 62 G8
Iluka NSW 21 F7, 27 O5
Imangara NT 107 K12, 109 K1
Imanpa NT 108 G9
Imbil Qld 117 D1, 118 D10, 123 M7
Imintji Store WA 95 K6, 98 G9
Impimi NSW 28 H8, 59 M9
Inala Qld 114 D9
Indaringinya NT 109 K3
Indented Head Vic. 40 B9, 42 H8, 44 F4, 52 B6, 63 P7
Indigo Vic. 55 J6, 56 G2
Indigo Upper Vic. 55 K7, 57 I3
Indooroopilly Qld xxx C10, 114 D7, 115 D4, 117 E11
Indwarra NP NSW 27 J6
Ingham Qld 120 E8, 127 M10
Ingleby Vic. 42 C9, 50 D2, 63 M8
Ingleside NSW 12 G4, 13 C10, 15 N6
Ingleside Qld 21 G2, 115 F11, 116 E10
Inglewood Qld 27 J1, 123 J11
Inglewood Tas. 141 L4
Inglewood Vic. 49 D1, 61 M9
Inglewood WA xxiv G4, xxv A5
Ingliston Vic. 42 F4, 49 F11, 63 O4
Ingoldsby Qld 123 L9
Injinoo Qld 128 C3
Injune Qld 122 F4
Inkerman Qld 119 C3, 124 H2
Inkerman SA 69 G4, 71 A1, 73 I7
Innaloo WA 84 C5, xxiv C3
Innamincka SA 77 N7, 132 F8
Innes NP SA 69 B8, 72 F10
Inneston SA 69 B9, 72 F10
Innisfail Qld 120 E4, 121 G11, 127 M7
Innot Hot Springs Qld 120 C5, 121 B12, 127 K7
Interlaken Tas. 141 K2, 143 K12
Inverell NSW 27 I5
Invergordon Vic. 54 F6, 56 B2
Inverleigh Vic. 42 D7, 63 M7
Inverloch Vic. 43 M12, 52 F9
Invermay Tas. 145 G10
Invermay Vic. 42 D3, 47 D2, 49 C10
Iona Vic. 41 E12, 43 M8
Ipolera NT 108 G7, 110 A5
Ipswich Qld 114 A9, 115 B5, 117 D12, 123 M9
Irishtown Tas. 142 C4
Irishtown Vic. 49 F7, 61 N12, 63 N2
Iron Baron SA 72 G3, 74 F11
Iron Knob SA 72 G2, 74 F10
Iron Range Qld 128 E7

Iron Range NP Qld 128 E7
Irrewarra Vic. 42 B9, 50 C2, 63 L8
Irrewillipe Vic. 42 A9, 50 A2, 63 K8
Irrwelty NT 109 K3
Irvinebank Qld 120 C4, 121 B10, 127 K7
Irymple Vic. 28 E6, 58 G6
Isabella NSW 24 H7, 35 E1
Isisford Qld 124 B11, 131 N11
Isla Gorge NP Qld 123 I3
Island Bend NSW 36 D9, 51 C3
Islington NSW 13 H3, 19 D9
Ivanhoe NSW 29 I2
Ivory Creek Qld 117 A6
Iwantja (Indulkana) SA 79 L4
Iwupataka NT 109 I7, 110 G4

Jabiru NT 103 O4, 104 G5
Jabuk SA 71 F4, 73 M10
Jack River Vic. 53 I9
Jackadgery NSW 21 C8, 27 M5
Jackeys Marsh Tas. 143 I9, 145 C12
Jackie Junction WA 93 M8
Jackson Qld 122 H6
Jacobs Well Qld 114 H12, 115 F7, 116 E1, 123 N10
Jacobs Well WA 88 E5
Jalloonda Qld 120 G10, 124 G1, 127 N11
Jallumba Vic. 60 F10
Jam Jerrup Vic. 45 P8
Jamberoo NSW 23 E7, 25 J9, 35 H3
Jambin Qld 123 J1, 125 M12
Jamestown SA 73 J4, 75 I11
Jamieson Vic. 43 P2, 52 H2, 54 H12, 56 D11
Jan Juc Vic. 44 A7
Jancourt Vic. 50 G8, 63 J8
Jancourt East Vic. 50 H8, 63 J8
Jandakot WA xxiv H12, 84 D8, 85 C6, 88 C5
Jandowae Qld 123 K7
Jane Brook WA xxv H1
Jannali NSW 12 D10
Japoon NP Qld 120 E5, 127 M8
Jardee WA 86 H10, 87 B1, 88 D10
Jardine River NP Qld 128 D4
Jarklin Vic. 28 H12, 61 N7
Jarra Jarra NT 106 H12, 108 H1
Jarrahdale WA 84 G11, 85 D7, 88 C6
Jarrahmond Vic. 51 B11, 53 P5
Jarrahwood WA 86 E7, 88 B9
Jarvis Creek Vic. 55 L6, 57 K3
Jaurdi WA 90 G5
Jeffcott Vic. 28 F12, 61 J7
Jeffcott North Vic. 61 J7
Jellat Jellat NSW 51 H6
Jemalong NSW 24 D4
Jennacubbine WA 85 G1
Jenolan Caves NSW 16 A11, 25 I6
Jeogla NSW 20 D1, 21 A12, 27 K8
Jeparit Vic. 28 D12, 60 F6
Jerangle NSW 24 F12, 34 F12, 35 D6, 36 H7, 51 G1
Jericho Qld 124 E10
Jericho Tas. 141 K4
Jericho Vic. 52 H4
Jerilderie NSW 29 L10, 54 G1
Jerrabomberra NSW 33 F8, 34 E6, 36 H3
Jerramungup WA 90 F10
Jerrawa NSW 24 F9, 35 D3
Jerrawangala NP NSW 23 B11, 25 I10, 35 G4, 37 N2
Jerrys Plains NSW 25 K2
Jerseyville NSW 20 G4, 27 M9
Jervis Bay JBT 23 D12, 25 J10, 35 G4, 37 O3
Jervis Bay NP NSW 23 D10, 25 J10, 35 G4, 37 O2
Jervois SA 71 D4, 73 L10
Jetsonville Tas. 143 L6
Jigalong WA 92 G5, 97 N11
Jilliby NSW 13 D6, 19 A12
Ji-Marda NT 105 J3
Jimaringle NSW 29 I9, 54 A1, 59 O12, 61 O2
Jimboomba Qld 114 D12, 115 D8, 123 N10
Jimbour Qld 123 K7
Jimna Qld 117 B3, 118 C11, 123 M7
Jindabyne NSW 35 B8, 36 E10, 51 C4
Jindera NSW 24 A12, 29 O12, 55 K5, 57 I1
Jindivick Vic. 41 G11, 43 N8, 52 G6
Jindong WA 86 B7

Jingalup WA 88 E9, 90 D10
Jingellic NSW 24 C12, 29 P12, 55 N5, 57 N1
Jingili NT xxvii D5
Jitarning WA 88 G6, 90 E8
Joanna SA 60 A11, 71 G9
Jodetluk (George Camp) NT 104 G8
Joel Joel Vic. 61 J11, 63 J1
Joel South Vic. 61 J11, 63 J1
Johanna Vic. 42 A12, 50 A5, 63 K10
John Forrest NP WA xxv H1, 84 F4, 85 D4, 88 C5, 90 C7
Johnburgh SA 73 J2, 75 I9
Johns River NSW 20 F7, 25 O1, 27 L12
Johnsonville Vic. 53 N5
Jolimont WA xxiv D5
Jondaryan Qld 123 K8
Joondalup WA 84 C3, 85 B4, 88 B4
Joondanna WA xxiv E3
Josbury WA 88 E7, 90 D9
Josephville Qld 21 E1, 27 N1, 115 C9
Joskeleigh Qld 125 M11
Joslin SA xxi L2
Joyces Creek Vic. 49 D6, 61 N12, 63 N1
Judbury Tas. 138 F6, 141 I8
Jugiong NSW 24 E9, 35 B3
Julatten Qld 120 D1, 121 D5, 127 L5
Julia SA 73 K7
Julia Creek Qld 129 H11, 131 J3
Jumbuk Vic. 53 I8
Jumbunna Vic. 43 M11, 52 F8
Junction Hill NSW 21 D8, 27 M6
Junction Village Vic. 45 M4
Jundah Qld 133 J1
Junee NSW 24 C9, 29 P9
Junee NP Qld 119 F12, 125 J9
Junee Reefs NSW 24 C8, 29 P8
Jung Vic. 60 G9
Junortoun Vic. 49 G3, 54 A9, 61 O10
Junuy Juluum NP NSW 20 G1, 21 C11, 27 M7
Jura WA 88 G4
Jurien Bay WA 90 A5
Jurunjung Vic. 40 A4, 42 H4, 49 H11, 52 B3, 63 P5

Kaarimba Vic. 29 K12, 54 E6
Kabra Qld 125 M11
Kadina SA 69 E3, 72 H6
Kadnook Vic. 60 C11, 62 C1, 71 H10
Kadungle NSW 24 D2
Kagaru Qld 114 C12, 115 C8
Kaimkillenbun Qld 123 K8
Kain NSW 24 G12, 34 H11, 35 D6, 37 I6, 51 H1
Kainton SA 69 F3, 73 I7
Kairi Qld 120 D3, 121 E9, 127 L7
Kajabbi Qld 126 B12, 129 E9, 130 G2
Kakadu NP NT 103 L5, 104 G4
Kalamunda WA xxv H7, 84 F6, 85 D5
Kalamunda NP WA 84 F6, 85 D5, 88 C5, 90 C7
Kalangadoo SA 62 A3, 71 G11
Kalannie WA 88 D1, 90 D5
Kalaru NSW 35 E9
Kalbar Qld 115 A8, 123 M10
Kalbarri WA 89 C11
Kalbarri NP WA 89 D11, 90 A2, 92 A12
Kaleentha Loop NSW 28 G1, 30 F12
Kalgan WA 87 E10, 88 G11, 90 E11
Kalgoorlie–Boulder WA 90 H5
Kalimna Vic. 53 O6
Kalimna West Vic. 53 N6
Kalinjarri NT 107 J11
Kalka SA 78 C2, 93 P8, 108 B11
Kalkallo Vic. 40 D2, 43 I3, 52 C3
Kalkarindji (Wave Hill) NT 106 D5
Kalkee Vic. 60 G8
Kalkite NSW 36 E9, 51 C3
Kallangur Qld 114 E4, 115 D2, 117 F9
Kallista Vic. 41 B9
Kalorama Vic. 40 G6, 41 B8
Kalpienung Vic. 28 G11, 61 K4
Kalpowar Qld 123 K2
Kaltukatjara (Docker River) NT 93 P6, 108 B9
Kalumburu WA 95 L2, 99 I2
Kalumpurlpa NT 107 I8
Kalunga Qld 120 C4, 121 C10, 127 L7
Kalyan SA 71 E3, 73 M9

Kamarah NSW 24 A7, 29 O7
Kamarooka Vic. 49 G1, 54 A7, 61 O8
Kamballda WA 90 H5
Kamballup WA 87 D8, 88 G10, 90 E11
Kameruka NSW 35 D9, 51 H6
Kamma Qld 120 E3, 121 F8
Kamona Tas. 143 M6
Kanangra–Boyd NP NSW 14 A7, 16 B11, 23 A1, 24 H7, 25 I7, 35 F1
Kancoona South Vic. 55 K9, 57 I6
Kandanga Qld 117 D1, 118 D10
Kandiwal WA 95 K3, 98 H3
Kandos NSW 25 I3
Kangaloon NSW 23 C6
Kangarilla SA 66 D11, 67 C11, 68 F4, 69 H8, 71 B3, 73 J10
Kangaroo Flat NSW 24 F6
Kangaroo Flat SA 66 D1, 67 C5
Kangaroo Flat Vic. 49 F3, 54 A9, 61 O10
Kangaroo Point Qld xxx H7, 113 H7
Kangaroo Valley NSW 23 C8, 25 I9, 35 G3
Kangawall Vic. 60 D10
Kangiara NSW 24 F8, 35 C2
Kaniva Vic. 28 B12, 60 C7, 71 H7
Kanmantoo SA 67 F10
Kanumbra Vic. 54 F11, 56 B9
Kanya Vic. 61 J10
Kanyapella Vic. 29 J12, 54 C6
Kanypi SA 78 E2, 108 D11
Kaoota Tas. 138 H7, 141 J8
Kapinnie SA 72 D7
Kapooka NSW 24 B10, 29 P10, 55 M1
Kapunda SA 67 E2, 71 C1, 73 K7
Karabeal Vic. 62 F3
Karadoc Vic. 28 E6, 58 H6
Karalee Qld 114 B8, 115 C5, 117 D12
Karalundi WA 89 H8, 92 E9
Karama NT xxvii G5
Karana Downs Qld 114 B8, 115 B5, 117 D11
Karanja Tas. 138 F2, 141 I6
Karara Qld 27 K1, 123 K10
Karatta SA 69 B12, 72 G12
Karawara WA xxiv G8, xxv A9
Karawinna Vic. 28 D6, 58 E7
Kardinya WA xxiv E12, 84 D8, 85 C6
Kariah Vic. 63 J7
Karijini NP WA 89 G3, 92 D5, 96 H10, 97 I9
Karingal Vic. 45 K4
Kariong NSW 13 C8, 15 N3
Karkoo SA 72 D6
Karlgarin WA 88 H5, 90 F8
Karn Vic. 54 H9, 56 D6
Karnak Vic. 60 D10
Karonie WA 91 I5
Karoola Tas. 143 K7, 145 H8
Karoonda SA 71 E3, 73 M10
Karoonda Roadhouse Vic. 35 A10, 51 A8, 53 P2, 57 P12
Karrakatta WA xxiv D7, 84 C6, 85 B5
Karratha WA 89 E1, 92 B2, 94 B12, 96 D5
Karratha Travel Stop Roadhouse WA 89 E1, 92 B2, 94 B12, 96 D5
Karridale WA 86 B10, 88 B10
Karrinyup WA xxiv B2
Kars Springs NSW 25 J1, 26 G12
Karte SA 28 A8, 58 A10, 71 G3, 73 N9
Karuah NSW 19 F7, 20 B11, 25 M3
Karumba Qld 126 C7, 129 G4
Karween Vic. 28 C6, 58 C6, 71 H1, 73 P8
Katamatite Vic. 29 L12, 54 F5, 56 B1
Katandra Vic. 54 F6, 56 B3
Katandra West Vic. 54 F6, 56 A2
Katanning WA 88 F8, 90 E9
Katherine NT 104 F8
Katoomba NSW 14 D5, 16 F9, 25 I6
Katunga Vic. 29 K12, 54 F5
Katyil Vic. 60 G7
Kawarren Vic. 42 B10, 50 B3, 63 L9
Kayena Tas. 143 J6, 145 H7
Kedron Qld xxx H1, 114 E6
Keep River NP NT 95 O4, 99 N5, 104 A11, 106 A2
Keep River NP Extension (Proposed) NT 95 P3, 99 N4, 104 B10, 106 B1

Keilor Vic. 40 C5, 43 I5, 52 B4
Keiraville NSW 22 A7, 23 F5
Keith SA 71 F6
Kellalac Vic. 28 E12, 60 H7
Kellatier Tas. 142 E5
Kellerberrin WA 88 F4, 90 D7
Kellevie Tas. 139 M4, 141 M7
Kelmscott WA 84 F8, 85 D6
Kelso Tas. 143 J6, 145 E6
Kelvin NSW 26 G8
Kelvin Grove Qld xxx F5
Kelvin View Vic. 54 F9, 56 B7
Kempsey NSW 20 G4, 27 M10
Kempton Tas. 139 I1, 141 K5
Kendall NSW 20 F7, 27 L11
Kendenup WA 87 B8, 88 G10
Kenebri NSW 26 D8
Kenilworth Qld 117 E3, 118 D11, 123 M7
Kenmare Vic. 28 D11, 60 G5
Kenmore NSW 24 H9, 35 E3
Kenmore Qld xxx A11, 114 D7, 115 D5, 117 E11
Kenmore Hills Qld 114 D7, 115 D4, 117 E11
Kennedy Qld 120 E6, 127 M9
Kennedy Range NP WA 89 D6, 92 A8
Kennedys Creek Vic. 50 H10, 63 J9
Kennett River Vic. 42 C12, 50 D5, 63 M10
Kennys Creek NSW 24 F8, 35 C2
Kensington NSW viii G10
Kensington SA xxi M5
Kensington Vic. xiv F7
Kensington WA xxiv G7, xxv A8
Kensington Gardens SA xxi N4
Kensington Park SA xxi N4
Kent Town SA xxi K5, 65 G8
Kentbruck Vic. 62 C6
Kenthurst NSW 12 D3, 13 A10, 15 K5
Kentlyn NSW 12 A10, 15 I11, 23 G1
Kentucky NSW 20 A2, 27 J8
Kenwick WA xxv F9, 84 E7, 85 D5
Keperra Qld xxx B1, 114 D6, 115 D4, 117 E10
Keppel Bay Islands NP Qld 125 N10
Keppel Sands Qld 125 N11
Keppoch SA 71 G8
Kerang Vic. 28 H11, 61 N4
Kerang East Vic. 28 H11, 61 N4
Kerang South Vic. 28 H11, 61 N5
Kergunyah Vic. 55 L7, 57 J4
Kergunyah South Vic. 55 L8, 57 J4
Kernot Vic. 43 L10, 45 P10, 52 E8
Kerrabee NSW 25 J2
Kerrie Vic. 40 B1, 52 B2, 54 B12
Kerrisdale Vic. 52 D1, 54 D11
Kerrs Creek NSW 24 G4
Kerry Qld 21 F1, 27 N1, 115 D10
Kersbrook SA 66 F5, 67 D7, 71 C2, 73 K9
Keswick SA xx H7, 65 A12, 66 C7, 67 B9, 68 F2
Keswick Terminal SA xx H6
Kettering Tas. 138 H8, 141 K8
Kevington Vic. 43 P2, 52 H2, 56 D12
Kew NSW 20 F7, 27 L11
Kew Vic. xv P10, xvii P2
Kewdale WA xxv D7, 84 E6
Kewell Vic. 60 H8
Keyneton SA 67 G5, 71 C2, 73 K8
Keysborough Vic. 45 L1
Keysbrook WA 84 F12, 85 D8, 88 C6
Khancoban NSW 35 A7, 36 B8, 51 A3, 55 P7, 57 P4
Ki Ki SA 71 E5, 73 M11
Kiah NSW 35 E10, 51 H8
Kialla NSW 24 G8, 35 E2
Kialla Vic. 54 E7, 56 A4
Kialla West Vic. 54 E7
Kiama NSW 23 F7, 25 J9, 35 H3
Kiamil Vic. 28 E8, 58 H10
Kiana SA 72 C6
Kiandra NSW 24 E12, 35 B6, 36 D6, 51 C1
Kianga NSW 37 L9
Kiara WA xxv C2
Kiata Vic. 28 C12, 60 E7
Kidman Park SA xx D4
Kidston Qld 127 I10
Kielpa SA 72 E5, 74 D12
Kiewa Vic. 55 L7, 57 J3

Kikoira NSW 24 A5, 29 O5
Kilburn SA 66 C6, 67 B8, 68 F1
Kilcoy Qld 117 C6, 123 M8
Kilcunda Vic. 43 L11, 45 O12, 52 E9
Kilkenny SA xx F1
Kilkivan Qld 118 C8, 123 M6
Killabakh NSW 20 E7, 25 N1, 27 L12
Killafaddy Tas. 145 H1
Killara NSW x B1, 12 F5, 15 L7
Killarney Qld 21 C2, 27 L1, 123 L11
Killarney Vic. 50 B7, 62 G8
Killarney Heights NSW xi I1
Killawarra Vic. 55 I6, 56 E3
Killiecrankie Tas. 140 A9
Killingworth NSW 13 F3, 19 B9
Killora Tas. 139 I8, 141 K8
Kilmany Vic. 53 J7
Kilmany South Vic. 53 J7
Kilmore Vic. 43 J1, 52 C1, 54 C12
Kilpalie SA 71 F3, 73 M9
Kimba SA 72 F4, 74 D11
Kimberley Tas. 142 H7, 145 B9
Kinalung NSW 30 D10, 75 P8
Kincaid Vic. 42 A11, 50 B5, 63 K10
Kinchega NP NSW 28 E1, 30 D12, 75 P10
Kinchela NSW 20 G4, 27 M10
Kincumber NSW 13 D8, 15 O3, 25 L6
Kindred Tas. 142 G6, 144 G2
King River WA 87 D10, 88 G11, 90 E11
King Valley Vic. 55 I9, 56 F7
Kingaroy Qld 118 A10, 123 L7
Kinglake Vic. 40 G3, 41 B5, 43 L3, 52 E3
Kinglake Central Vic. 40 G2, 41 B4, 43 K3, 52 E3
Kinglake East Vic. 41 C5, 43 L3
Kinglake NP Vic. 40 F1, 41 A3, 43 K2, 52 D2, 54 D12
Kinglake West Vic. 40 G2, 41 B4, 43 K3, 52 D2
Kingoonya SA 74 B5, 81 P5
Kingower Vic. 49 C2, 61 M9
Kings Camp SA 71 E9
Kings Canyon Resort NT 108 F8
Kings Cross NSW 10 H8, 12 F8, 13 B12, 15 M9
Kings Meadows Tas. 143 K8, 145 H10
Kings Park SA xxi I9
Kings Park WA xxiv E6
Kings Plains NP NSW 27 J5
Kings Point NSW 25 I11, 35 G5, 37 N4
Kingsborough Qld 120 C2, 121 A7, 127 K6
Kingscliff NSW 21 H2, 27 O2, 115 H12, 116 H12, 123 N11
Kingscote SA 69 E10, 72 H11
Kingsdale NSW 24 H9, 35 E3
Kingsford NSW viii H12, 12 F8, 15 M10
Kingsthorpe Qld 123 L9
Kingston ACT 32 F12
Kingston Qld 114 F10, 115 E6
Kingston Tas. 139 I6, 141 K8
Kingston Vic. 42 D2, 49 D9, 63 M3
Kingston-On-Murray SA 28 A6, 71 F1, 73 N7
Kingston S.E. SA 71 E8
Kingstown NSW 27 I8
Kingsvale NSW 24 E8, 35 B2
Kingsville Vic. xiv A9, xvi A1
Kingswood NSW 14 H6, 17 N11
Kingswood SA xxi J10, 73 I2, 74 H9
Kinimakatka Vic. 60 D7
Kinka Qld 125 N10
Kinnabulla Vic. 28 F11, 61 I5
Kinrara NP Qld 120 B7, 127 K9
Kintore NT 93 P4, 108 B6
Kioloa NSW 25 I12, 35 F6, 37 M5
Kiora NSW 37 L7
Kippa-Ring Qld 114 F4, 115 E2, 117 G9
Kirkstall Vic. 50 B7, 62 G7
Kirra Qld 115 G11, 116 H10
Kirrawee NSW 12 D10, 15 K11
Kirribilli NSW viii G2, x G10, 11 G9
Kirup WA 86 F6, 88 C9
Kitchener NSW 13 E2, 19 A8
Kitchener WA 91 K5
Kithbrook Vic. 54 F10, 56 B7
Kiwirrkurra WA 93 N4
Klemzig SA xxi M1

Knockrow NSW 21 G5, 27 O3
Knockwood Vic. 43 P3, 52 H3, 56 E12
Knowsley Vic. 54 B9, 61 P10
Knuckey Lagoon NT xxvii H7
Koah Qld 121 D6, 127 L6
Kobble Qld 114 C4, 115 C2, 117 E9
Koetong Vic. 55 N6, 57 M3
Kogan Qld 123 J8
Kogarah NSW 12 E9, 15 L10
Koimbo Vic. 28 F8, 59 J10
Kojonup WA 88 F9, 90 D10
Koloona NSW 26 H5
Kolora Vic. 63 I7
Komungla NSW 24 G9, 35 E3
Konagaderra Vic. 40 C3, 43 I3
Kondalilla NP Qld 117 E4, 118 E11, 123 N7
Kondinin WA 88 G5, 90 E8
Kongal SA 28 A12, 71 G7
Kongorong SA 71 F12
Kongwak Vic. 43 M11, 52 F8
Konnongorring WA 88 D3, 90 C6
Konong Wootong Vic. 62 E3
Konong Wootong North Vic. 62 E2
Kookynie WA 90 H3
Koolan WA 95 I5, 98 D7
Koolewong NSW 13 D8, 15 N3
Kooljaman WA 94 H5, 98 B7
Kooloonong Vic. 28 G8, 59 K10
Koolunga SA 69 G1, 73 J5, 74 H12
Koolyanobbing WA 90 F5
Koolywurtie SA 69 E1, 69, 72 H8
Koonda Vic. 54 F8, 56 B5
Koondrook Vic. 29 I10, 54 A2, 61 O4
Koongamia WA xxv G3
Koongarra NT 103 O5, 104 G5
Koongawa SA 72 D4, 74 C11
Koonibba SA 81 L7
Kooninderie SA 67 F1
Koonoomoo Vic. 29 L11, 54 F4
Koonwarra Vic. 43 N12, 52 G9
Koonya Tas. 139 M8, 141 M8
Kooraban NP NSW 35 E7, 37 K10, 51 H3
Kooralbyn Qld 21 E1, 27 N1, 115 B10, 123 M10
Koorawatha NSW 24 E6
Koorda WA 88 E2, 90 D6
Kooreh Vic. 61 K9
Kooringal Qld 115 G4, 123 N9
Koorkab Vic. 28 G8, 59 K9
Koorlong Vic. 58 G6
Kootingal NSW 27 I9
Koo-Wee-Rup Vic. 40 H10, 43 L9, 45 O6, 52 E7
Koo-Wee-Rup North Vic. 45 P5
Koppio SA 72 D7
Korbel WA 88 G4
Koreelah NP NSW 21 C2, 27 M1, 123 L11
Koriella Vic. 43 M1, 52 F1, 54 F11, 56 B10
Korobeit Vic. 42 F3, 49 F11, 52 A3, 63 O4
Koroit Vic. 50 C7, 62 G7
Korong Vale Vic. 61 M8
Koroop Vic. 61 N4
Korora NSW 20 H1, 21 E11, 27 N7
Korumburra Vic. 43 N11, 52 F8
Korweinguboora Vic. 42 E2, 49 E9, 63 N3
Kosciuszko NP NSW 24 E11, 34 A6, 35 A7, 36 E4,
  51 B2, 55 P6, 57 P3
Kotta Vic. 29 I12, 54 B6, 61 P7
Kotupna Vic. 29 K12, 54 D6
Koumala Qld 119 G9, 125 K6
Kowanyama Qld 126 E2
Kowrowa Qld 121 E6
Koyuga Vic. 54 C6
Krambach NSW 20 D8, 25 N2
Kringin SA 28 A8, 58 B10, 71 G3, 73 O9
Krongart SA 62 A3, 71 G10
Kroombit Tops NP Qld 123 K2
Krowera Vic. 43 M11, 52 F8
Kukerin WA 88 G7, 90 E9
Kulgera NT 79 L1, 109 I11
Kulgun Qld 115 A8
Kulikup WA 88 E9
Kulin WA 88 G6, 90 E8
Kulkami SA 71 F4, 73 N10
Kulkyne Vic. 28 E7, 58 H8

Kulnine Vic. 28 C6, 58 E6, 73 P7
Kulnine East Vic. 28 C6, 58 E6, 73 P7
Kulnura NSW 13 C6, 25 K5
Kulpara SA 69 F3, 73 I6
Kulpi Qld 123 K8
Kulwin Vic. 28 E8, 59 I10
Kumarina Roadhouse WA 92 E7
Kumarl WA 91 I8
Kumbarilla Qld 123 J8
Kumbatine NP NSW 20 F4, 27 L10
Kumbia Qld 123 L7
Kumorna SA 71 F6, 73 M12
Kunama NSW 24 D11, 35 A5, 36 B4, 55 P3
Kunat Vic. 61 L3
Kundabung NSW 20 G5, 27 M10
Kungala NSW 21 E10, 27 N7
Kunghur NSW 21 F3, 27 O2, 123 N11
Kunjin WA 88 F5, 90 E8
Kunlara SA 71 E2, 73 M8
Kununoppin WA 88 F2, 90 E6
Kununurra WA 95 O4, 99 M5, 104 A11, 106 A2
Kunwarara Qld 125 L10
Kupingarri WA 95 L6, 98 H8
Kuraby Qld 114 E9, 115 E6
Kuranda Qld 120 D2, 121 E6, 127 L6
Ku-Ring-Gai Chase NP NSW 12 G3, 13 C10, 15 M5,
  25 K6
Kuringup WA 88 H8
Kurmond NSW 14 H4, 17 N5
Kurnell NSW 12 F10, 15 L11, 25 K7
Kurraca Vic. 49 B1, 61 L9
Kurraca West Vic. 49 B1, 61 L8
Kurrajong NSW 14 G4, 17 M5
Kurrajong Heights NSW 14 G3, 17 L5, 25 J5
Kurralta Park SA xx G8
Kurri Kurri NSW 13 F2, 19 B8, 25 L4
Kurrimine Beach Qld 120 E5, 127 M8
Kurrimine Beach NP Qld 120 E5, 127 M8
Kurting Vic. 49 C1, 61 M9
Kurumbul Qld 26 H2, 123 I11
Kuttabul Qld 119 F7, 125 K5
Kweda WA 88 F5
Kwiambal NP NSW 27 I3, 123 J12
Kwinana WA 84 D10, 85 C7, 88 B5, 90 C8
Kwolyin WA 88 F4
Kyabram Vic. 54 D6
Kyalite NSW 28 G8, 59 L10
Kyancutta SA 72 D4, 74 B11
Kybeyan NSW 35 D8, 36 H10, 51 G4
Kybunga SA 69 H3, 73 J6
Kybybolite SA 60 B10, 71 G9
Kydra NSW 35 D8, 36 H11, 51 F4
Kyeamba NSW 24 C10, 29 P10, 55 N3
Kyndalyn Vic. 28 F7, 59 J9
Kyneton Vic. 42 G1, 49 G8, 52 A1, 54 A11, 63 O2
Kynuna Qld 131 I3
Kyogle NSW 21 E4, 27 N3, 123 M12
Kyup Vic. 62 F3
Kyvalley Vic. 54 D6
Kywong NSW 24 A9, 29 N9

Laanecoorie Vic. 49 D4, 61 M10
Laang Vic. 50 E8, 63 I8
Labertouche Vic. 41 F11, 43 N8, 52 F6
Labrador Qld 21 G1, 27 O1, 115 G9, 116 F5
Lachlan Tas. 138 G4, 141 J7
Lackrana Tas. 140 B10
Lady Barron Tas. 140 B11, 143 P1
Lady Bay Tas. 138 F11, 141 I10
Ladysmith NSW 24 C10, 29 P10, 55 N1
Laen Vic. 61 I8
Laen North Vic. 61 I7
Laggan NSW 24 G8, 35 E2
Lah Vic. 28 E12, 60 H6
Lah-Arum Vic. 60 G10
Laheys Creek NSW 24 G1, 26 D12
Laidley Qld 117 A12, 123 M9
Lajamanu (Hooker Creek) NT 106 D7
Lake Bathurst NSW 24 G10, 35 E4, 37 J1
Lake Biddy WA 90 F8
Lake Bindegolly NP Qld 133 L8
Lake Boga Vic. 28 H10, 61 M3
Lake Bolac Vic. 63 I4

Lake Buloke Vic. 28 F12, 61 J7
Lake Cargelligo NSW 24 A4, 29 N4
Lake Cathie NSW 20 F6, 27 M11
Lake Charm Vic. 28 H10, 61 M4
Lake Clifton WA 85 C11, 88 B7, 90 C9
Lake Condah Vic. 62 E6
Lake Conjola NSW 25 I11, 35 G5, 37 N3
Lake Cowal NSW 24 C5, 29 P5
Lake Eildon NP Vic. 41 H1, 43 O1, 52 G1, 54 G12,
  56 C11
Lake Eppalock Vic. 49 H4, 54 B9, 61 P11
Lake Eyre NP SA 74 F1, 76 F9, 132 A8
Lake Gairdner NP SA 72 E1, 74 A6, 81 P6
Lake Goldsmith Vic. 42 A3, 63 K4
Lake Grace WA 88 H7, 90 E9
Lake Hindmarsh Vic. 28 D11, 60 E6
Lake King WA 90 G8
Lake Leake Tas. 141 M2, 143 M12
Lake Margaret Tas. 140 D1, 142 D11, 144 A9
Lake Marmal Vic. 28 G12, 61 L6
Lake Mundi Vic. 62 B3, 71 H11
Lake Munmorah NSW 13 F6, 19 B12, 25 L5
Lake Rowan Vic. 54 G7, 56 D3
Lake Torrens NP SA 74 G4
Lake Tyers Vic. 53 O6
Lake View SA 69 G1, 73 I5
Lakefield NP Qld 127 I1, 128 F12
Lakeland Qld 127 K3
Lakes Entrance Vic. 53 O6
Lakeside Vic. 45 O1
Lakesland NSW 14 E12, 23 D2
Lal Lal Vic. 42 D4, 49 D11, 63 M4
Lalbert Vic. 28 G10, 61 L4
Lalbert Road Vic. 28 G10, 61 L3
Lalla Tas. 143 K7, 145 H8
Lallat Vic. 61 I8
Lalor Vic. 43 J4
Lameroo SA 28 A9, 71 G4, 73 N10
Lamington Qld 21 F2, 27 N1, 115 C11, 123 M11
Lamington NP Qld 21 F2, 27 N2, 115 D11, 116 A10,
  123 N11
Lamplough Vic. 49 A6, 61 L12, 63 L1
Lancaster Vic. 54 D6
Lancefield Vic. 42 H1, 52 B1, 54 B12, 63 P2
Lancelin WA 88 A3, 90 B6
Lands End Qld 116 F4
Landsborough Qld 117 F5, 118 E12, 123 N8
Landsborough Vic. 61 J11, 63 J1
Landsdale WA 84 D4, 85 C4
Lane Cove NSW x C5, 12 E6, 13 B12, 15 L8
Lane Cove NP NSW x B1, 12 E5, 13 B11, 15 L7,
  25 K6
Lane Cove North NSW x C3
Lane Cove West NSW x B4
Lanena Tas. 143 J7, 145 F8
Lang Lang Vic. 43 L9, 45 P7, 52 E7
Langford WA xxv D10
Langhorne Creek SA 71 C4, 73 K10
Langi Logan Vic. 63 I2
Langkoop Vic. 60 B11, 62 B1, 71 H9
Langley Vic. 49 H7, 54 A11, 61 P12, 63 P2
Langlo Crossing Qld 122 A5, 133 O5
Langloh Tas. 141 I5
Langsborough Vic. 53 I10
Langville Vic. 28 H11, 61 M5
Langwarrin Vic. 40 E10, 43 J8, 45 K5
Lankeys Creek NSW 24 C12, 29 P12, 55 N5
Lannercost Qld 120 E8, 127 M10
Lansdowne NSW 20 E7, 25 O1, 27 L12
Lapoinya Tas. 142 E5
Lapstone NSW 14 G7, 17 L11
Lara Vic. 42 F7, 44 B1, 52 A5, 63 O7
Lara Lake Vic. 44 B1
Laramba NT 108 H4
Laravale Qld 21 E1, 27 N1, 115 C10
Largs North SA 66 B5, 67 A7, 68 E1, 71 B2, 73 J9
Larpent Vic. 42 A9, 50 B2, 63 K8
Larrakeyah NT xxvii A10, 102 C3
Larras Lee NSW 24 F3
Larrimah NT 104 H10, 106 H1
Lascelles Vic. 28 E10, 60 H3
Latham WA 90 C4
Lathlain WA xxiv H6, xxv B7

Latrobe Tas. 142 H6, 144 H2, 145 B7
Lauderdale Tas. 139 K6, 141 L7
Laughtondale NSW 13 A7, 15 K2
Launceston Tas. 143 K8, 145 F1
Launching Place Vic. 41 D8, 43 M5, 52 E4
Laura Qld 127 J3
Laura SA 73 J4, 74 H11
Laurel Hill NSW 24 D11, 35 A5, 36 B4, 55 P4
Laurieton NSW 20 F7, 25 O1, 27 L12
Lauriston Vic. 42 F1, 49 G8, 52 A1, 54 A11, 63 O2
Lavender Bay NSW viii G1, x G9
Lavers Hill Vic. 42 A12, 50 A5, 63 K10
Laverton Vic. 40 B6, 42 H6, 52 B4, 63 P6
Laverton WA 91 I2, 93 I12
Lawler Vic. 28 E12, 61 I7
Lawley River NP WA 95 L3, 98 H3
Lawloit Vic. 28 C12, 60 D7
Lawnton Qld 114 E4, 115 D2, 117 F9
Lawrence NSW 21 E8, 27 N5
Lawrence Vic. 42 D1, 49 D8, 63 M2
Lawrence Road NSW 21 E7, 27 N5
Lawrenny Tas. 141 I5
Lawson NSW 14 E6, 16 H9, 25 I6
Layard Vic. 42 E9, 50 F1, 63 N8
Le Roy Vic. 53 I8
Leabrook SA xxi N6
Leadville NSW 24 F11, 26 E12
Leaghur Vic. 28 H11, 61 M5
Leam Tas. 145 F8
Leanyer NT xxvii F4
Learmonth Vic. 42 C2, 49 B9, 63 L3
Learmonth WA 89 B3
Leasingham SA 73 J6
Leawarra Vic. 45 K4
Leawood Gardens SA xxi O10
Lebrina Tas. 143 K6, 145 H7
Leda WA 84 D10, 85 C7
Ledge Point WA 88 A3
Lee Point NT xxvii F2
Leederville WA xxiv E5
Leeka Tas. 140 A9
Leeman WA 90 A5
Leeming WA xxiv H12, xxv A12
Leeor Vic. 28 B12, 60 B7, 71 H7
Leeton NSW 29 N8
Leets Vale NSW 13 A7, 15 J2
Leeville NSW 21 E5, 27 N4
Lefroy Tas. 143 J6, 145 G6
Legana Tas. 143 K7, 145 G9
Legerwood Tas. 143 M7
Legume NSW 21 C2, 27 L2, 123 L11
Leichardt Vic. 49 E2, 61 N10
Leichhardt NSW viii A5, x A12, 12 E8
Leichhardt Qld 114 A9, 115 B5, 117 C12, 125 J11
Leigh Creek SA 70 B4, 74 H4
Leigh Creek Vic. 42 D3, 49 D10, 63 M4
Leighton SA 73 K5
Leighton WA 84 C7
Leinster WA 90 G1, 92 G11
Leitchville Vic. 29 I11, 54 A4, 61 O5
Leith Tas. 142 H6, 144 G1
Lemana Tas. 145 C10
Lemnos Vic. 54 E7, 56 A3
Lemon Tree Passage NSW 19 G8, 20 C12, 25 M4
Lemont Tas. 141 L4
Lenah Valley Tas. xxxiv B10, 137 C7
Leneva Vic. 55 K6, 57 I3
Lennox Head NSW 21 H5, 27 O3, 123 N12
Leongatha Vic. 29 N11, 52 G8
Leongatha South Vic. 43 N11, 52 F9
Leonora WA 90 H2
Leopold Vic. 42 G8, 44 C4, 50 H1, 52 A6, 63 O7
Leppington NSW 14 H9
Leprena Tas. 141 I11
Leschenault WA 86 E3
Leslie Manor Vic. 42 A7, 63 K7
Leslie Vale Tas. 138 H6, 141 K7
Lesmurdie WA xxv H8, 84 F7
Lesmurdie Falls NP WA xxv H7, 84 F6, 85 D5,
    88 C5, 90 C7
Lesueur NP WA 88 A1, 90 A5
Lethbridge Vic. 42 E6, 63 N6
Leumeah NSW 14 H11, 23 F1

Leura NSW 14 D5, 16 G9, 25 I6
Levendale Tas. 139 L1, 141 L5
Lewis Ponds NSW 24 G4
Lewisham NSW viii A7, 12 E8
Lewisham Tas. 139 L5, 141 L7
Lewiston SA 66 C1, 67 B5, 69 H6
Lexton Vic. 42 B1, 49 A7, 63 L2
Leyburn Qld 123 K10
Liawenee Tas. 141 I1, 143 I11
Licola Vic. 53 J4
Lidcombe NSW 15 K8
Liena Tas. 142 G8, 144 G5
Lietinna Tas. 143 L6
Liffey Tas. 143 J9, 145 E12
Lightning Ridge NSW 26 B3, 122 E12
Likkaparta NT 107 J9
Lileah Tas. 142 C4
Lilli Pilli NSW 37 M7
Lillicur Vic. 49 A6, 61 L12, 63 L1
Lillimur Vic. 28 B12, 60 C7, 71 H7
Lillimur South Vic. 28 B12, 60 C7, 71 H7
Lilydale Tas. 143 K7, 145 H8
Lilydale Vic. 40 G5, 41 B7, 43 L5, 52 E4
Lilyfield NSW viii C4, x B11
Lima Vic. 54 G9, 56 C7
Lima East Vic. 54 G9, 56 C7
Lima South Vic. 54 G10, 56 D7
Limeburners Creek NSW 19 F6, 20 B11, 25 M3
Limekilns NSW 24 H4
Limestone Vic. 41 D1, 43 M1, 52 E1, 54 E12, 56 A11
Limestone Ridge Qld 114 A12, 115 B7
Limevale Qld 27 J2, 123 J11
Limmen NP (Proposed) NT 105 K9, 107 L2
Limpinwood NSW 116 A12
Lincoln NP SA 72 D9
Lincolnfields SA 69 F2, 73 I6
Lind NP Vic. 35 B11, 51 D10
Linda Tas. 140 E1, 142 E11, 144 B10
Lindeman Islands NP Qld 119 G5, 125 K4
Linden NSW 14 F6, 17 J9
Linden Park SA xxi M7
Lindenow Vic. 53 M5
Lindenow South Vic. 53 M5
Lindfield NSW x C1
Lindisfarne Tas. xxxiv H7, 1 E3 , 137 F6, 139 J5,
    141 K7
Lindsay Point Vic. 28 B5, 58 C5, 71 H1, 73 O7
Lindum Qld 114 G7
Linga Vic. 28 C9, 58 E11
Linley Point NSW x B6
Linton Vic. 42 B4, 49 A11, 63 L4
Linville Qld 117 A4, 118 B12, 123 M7
Linwood SA 67 D3, 73 J7
Lipson SA 72 E7
Lisarow NSW 13 D7, 15 O2
Lisle Tas. 143 L7
Lismore NSW 21 F5, 27 O3, 123 N12
Lismore Vic. 42 A6, 63 K6
Liston NSW 21 B3, 27 L2, 123 L11
Litchfield Vic. 28 F12, 61 I7
Litchfield NP NT 102 D9, 104 D6
Lithgow NSW 14 B2, 16 D2, 25 I5
Littabella NP Qld 118 C1, 123 M2
Little Billabong NSW 24 C11, 29 P11, 55 N3
Little Desert NP Vic. 28 B12, 60 C8, 71 G8
Little Grove WA 87 D11, 88 G12, 90 E11
Little Hampton Vic. 42 F2, 49 F9, 52 A2, 54 A12,
    63 O3
Little Hard Hills Vic. 42 C4, 49 B12
Little Hartley NSW 14 C3, 16 E5
Little Jilliby NSW 13 D6
Little Mulgrave Qld 120 E3, 121 F8
Little River Vic. 42 G6, 52 A5, 63 O6
Little Snowy Creek Vic. 55 L8, 57 K6
Little Swanport Tas. 141 N4
Little Topar Roadhouse NSW 30 D9
Littlehampton SA 66 G9, 67 D10, 68 H3
Liverpool NSW 12 B8, 15 J9, 25 J7, 35 H1
Livingstone NP NSW 24 B10, 29 P10, 55 M2
Lizard Island NP Qld 127 L1
Llandaff Tas. 141 O2, 143 O11
Llandeilo Vic. 42 E3, 49 E11, 63 N4
Llanelly Vic. 49 D3, 61 M10

Llangothlin NSW 27 K7
Llewellyn Siding Tas. 141 M1, 143 M10
Lobethal SA 66 G7, 67 E8, 68 H2, 71 C3, 73 K9
Loccota Tas. 140 B11, 143 O1
Loch Vic. 43 M10, 52 F8
Loch Sport Vic. 53 M6
Lochern NP Qld 131 L11
Lochiel NSW 51 H7
Lochiel SA 69 G3, 73 I6
Lochinvar NSW 13 F1, 19 B7, 25 L3
Lochnagar Qld 124 D10, 131 P10
Lock SA 72 D5, 74 C12
Lockhart NSW 24 A10, 29 N10, 55 K1
Lockhart River Qld 128 E7
Lockington Qld 124 H11
Lockington Vic. 29 I12, 54 B6, 61 P7
Lockleys SA xx D5
Lockridge WA xxv C2
Locksley NSW 24 H5
Locksley Vic. 54 E9
Lockwood Vic. 49 F4, 61 N10
Lockwood South Vic. 49 F4, 61 N10
Loddon Vale Vic. 28 H11, 61 N6
Loftus NSW 12 C10, 15 K11, 23 H1
Logan Vic. 49 A2, 61 L9
Logan Village Qld 114 E11, 115 E7
Loganlea Qld 114 F10, 115 E6
Logie Brae NSW 29 L10, 54 F2
Loira Tas. 143 J7, 145 F8
Lombadina WA 94 H6, 98 B8
Londonderry NSW 14 H5, 17 N8
Londrigan Vic. 55 I7, 56 F4
Long Beach NSW 35 F6, 37 M6
Long Flat NSW 20 E6, 24 G11, 25 I8, 27 L11, 35 F2,
    37 J5
Long Jetty NSW 13 E7, 15 P2, 25 L5
Long Plains SA 67 A2, 69 H5, 71 B1, 73 J7
Long Plains Vic. 61 J2
Long Pocket Qld 127 L12
Longerenong Vic. 60 G9
Longford Tas. 143 K9, 145 G12
Longford Vic. 53 K7
Longlea Vic. 49 G3, 54 A9, 61 O10
Longley Tas. 138 H6, 141 J7
Longreach Qld 124 B10, 131 N10
Longueville NSW x C7
Longwarry Vic. 41 F12, 43 N8, 52 F6
Longwood Vic. 54 E9
Longwood East Vic. 54 E9
Lonnavale Tas. 138 E6, 141 I7
Lonsdale SA 66 B10, 67 A11, 68 E4, 69 H8, 73 J9
Looma WA 95 J7, 98 E11
Loongana Tas. 142 F7, 144 D3
Loongana WA 91 N5
Loorana Tas. 141 O11
Lorinna Tas. 142 G8, 144 F5
Lorne NSW 20 E7, 27 L11
Lorne Vic. 42 D11, 50 E4, 63 M9
Lorquon Vic. 28 C12, 60 E6
Lorquon West Vic. 60 E6
Lostock NSW 19 B3, 20 A9, 25 L2
Lota Qld 114 G7
Lottah Tas. 143 O7
Louisville Tas. 139 N1, 141 M5
Louth NSW 31 K6
Louth Bay SA 72 D8
Loveday SA 73 N7
Lovely Banks Vic. 44 A2
Low Head Tas. 143 J6, 145 E5
Lowaldie SA 71 E3, 73 M9
Lowan Vale SA 28 A12, 60 A6, 71 G7
Lowanna NSW 21 D11, 27 M7
Lowbank SA 71 F1, 73 M7
Lowden WA 86 F5, 88 C8
Lowdina Tas. 139 J2, 141 K5
Lower Acacia Creek NSW 21 B2, 27 L2
Lower Barrington Tas. 142 H7, 144 G2, 145 A7
Lower Beulah Tas. 142 H8, 144 H4, 145 A10
Lower Boro NSW 24 H10, 35 E4, 37 K2
Lower Bucca NSW 21 E11, 27 N7
Lower Chittering WA 85 D2, 88 C4
Lower Creek NSW 20 E2, 27 L9
Lower Gellibrand Vic. 50 H11, 63 J10

Lower Glenelg NP Vic. 62 B6, 71 H12
Lower Heytesbury Vic. 50 F10, 63 I9
Lower Mangrove NSW 13 B8, 15 M2
Lower Marshes Tas. 141 K4
Lower Mitcham SA xxi J11
Lower Mookerawa NSW 24 G3
Lower Mount Hicks Tas. 142 F5
Lower Norton Vic. 60 F10
Lower Quipolly NSW 26 H10
Lower Sandy Bay Tas. 137 E10
Lower Turners Marsh Tas. 143 K6, 145 G7
Lower Wilmot Tas. 144 G3
Lowesdale NSW 29 M11, 55 I4
Lowlands NSW 14 H4, 17 O6, 29 L3
Lowmead Qld 123 L2
Lowood Qld 115 A4, 117 B10, 123 M9
Lowther NSW 14 B4, 16 C6, 25 I6
Loxton SA 28 A6, 58 A7, 71 G2, 73 N8
Loxton North SA 28 A6, 58 A7, 71 G1, 73 N8
Loyetea Tas. 142 F7, 144 E2
Lubeck Vic. 60 H9
Lucas Heights NSW 12 B10, 15 J11, 23 H1
Lucaston Tas. 138 G6, 141 J7
Lucinda Qld 120 F8, 127 M10
Lucindale SA 71 F9
Lucknow NSW 24 G5
Lucknow Vic. 53 M5
Lucky Bay SA 69 C1, 72 G5
Lucyvale Vic. 55 N7, 57 M4
Luddenham NSW 14 G8
Ludlow WA 86 D6, 88 B9
Ludmilla NT xxvii B7
Lue NSW 24 H3
Lughrata Tas. 140 B10
Lulworth Tas. 143 K5, 145 G5
Lunawanna Tas. 138 H11, 141 J10
Lune River Tas. 138 E12, 141 I10
Lurg Vic. 54 H8, 56 E6
Lurg Upper Vic. 54 H8, 56 E6
Lutana Tas. xxxiv E6, 1 A2 , 137 D5
Lutwyche Qld xxx H3
Lyiltjarra NT 110 C5
Lyme Regis Tas. 143 O4
Lymington Tas. 138 G9, 141 J9
Lymwood Tas. 141 P12
Lynchford Tas. 140 D2, 142 D11, 144 A11
Lynchs Creek NSW 21 E3, 27 N2
Lyndhurst NSW 24 F5
Lyndhurst SA 70 A2, 74 H3
Lyndhurst Vic. 40 F8, 41 A11, 43 K7, 45 M3, 52 D6
Lyndoch SA 66 G2, 67 E5, 71 C2, 73 K8
Lynton SA xxi J12
Lynwood WA xxv C11
Lyons NT xxvii E3
Lyons Vic. 62 D6, 71 H12
Lyonville Vic. 42 F2, 49 F9, 63 O3
Lyrup SA 28 A6, 58 A6, 71 G1, 73 N7
Lysterfield Vic. 40 G7, 41 B9, 43 K6, 52 D5
Lysterfield Lake Park Vic. 40 G8, 43 K7, 45 M1
Lytton Qld xxxi P5

Maaroom Qld 118 F6, 123 N5
McAlinden WA 86 H5, 88 D8
Macalister Qld 123 J8
Macarthur Vic. 62 F6
Macclesfield SA 66 F11, 67 D11, 68 H5, 71 C4, 73 K10
Macclesfield Vic. 41 C9, 43 L6, 52 E5
McCrae Vic. 44 H8
McCullys Gap NSW 25 K2
Macdonnell NT 111 I4
McDonnell Creek Qld 120 E3, 121 G9
Macedon Vic. 40 A1, 42 G2, 49 H9, 52 B2, 54 B12, 63 P3
McGraths Hill NSW 12 A2, 15 I5, 17 P7
Machans Beach Qld 120 E2, 121 F6
McIntyre Vic. 49 B2, 61 M9
Mackay Qld 119 G8, 125 K5
McKees Hill NSW 21 F5
McKenzie Creek Vic. 60 G9
McKinlay Qld 129 G12, 131 I4
Macks Creek Vic. 53 I9
Macksville NSW 20 G2, 27 M9

Maclagan Qld 123 K8
McLaren Flat SA 66 C12, 67 B12, 68 F5
McLaren Vale SA 66 B12, 67 B12, 68 E5, 69 H9, 71 B4, 73 J10
Maclean NSW 21 F8, 27 N5
McLoughlins Beach Vic. 53 J9
McMahons Creek Vic. 41 G7, 43 N5, 52 F4
McMahons Point NSW viii F2, x F9, 11 B9
McMahons Reef NSW 24 E8, 35 B2
McMillans Vic. 29 I11, 54 A4, 61 O5
Macorna Vic. 28 H11, 61 N5
Macquarie Fields NSW 12 A9, 15 I10
Macquarie Park NSW x A2
Macquarie Pass NP NSW 23 D6, 25 J9, 35 G3
Macquarie Plains Tas. 138 F3, 141 I6
Macrossan Qld 120 F12, 124 F2
Macs Cove Vic. 43 P1, 52 H1, 54 H12, 56 D11
Madalya Vic. 53 I9
Maddington WA 84 F7, 85 D6
Maddington WA xxv F11
Madora WA 85 C9, 88 B6
Madura Roadhouse WA 91 N6
Madura WA 91 N6
Mafeking Vic. 62 H2
Maffra Vic. 53 K6
Maggea SA 71 F2, 73 M8
Magill SA xxi O3
Magnetic Island NP Qld 119 A1, 120 G10, 124 G1, 127 N11
Magpie Vic. 42 C3, 49 C11
Magra Tas. 138 G3, 141 J6
Magrath Flat SA 71 D6, 73 L12
Mahogany Creek WA 84 G5
Maianbar NSW 12 D11, 15 K12
Maida Vale WA xxv G6
Maiden Gully Vic. 49 F3, 61 O10
Maidenwell Qld 123 L7
Maidstone Vic. xiv A5
Mailors Flat Vic. 50 C7, 62 G7
Maimuru NSW 24 D7, 35 B1
Main Beach Qld 21 G1, 27 O1, 115 G9, 116 F6, 123 N10
Main Lead Vic. 42 A1, 63 K3
Main Range NP Qld 21 C1, 27 M1, 123 L10
Main Ridge Vic. 45 I9
Maindample Vic. 54 G11, 56 C9
Maitland NSW 13 F1, 19 C7, 20 A11, 25 L3
Maitland SA 69 E5, 72 H7
Major Plains Vic. 54 G7, 56 C4
Majorca Vic. 49 C6, 61 M12, 63 M1
Majors Creek NSW 24 G11, 35 E5, 37 J5
Malaga WA xxiv G1, xxv A1
Malak NT xxvii F5
Malanda Qld 120 D4, 121 E10, 127 L7
Malbina Tas. 138 H4, 141 J6
Malbon Qld 129 E12, 130 G4
Malcolm WA 90 H2
Maldon NSW 14 F12, 23 E2
Maldon Vic. 49 E5, 61 N11, 63 N1
Maleny Qld 117 E4, 118 E12, 123 N7
Malinong SA 71 D5, 73 L11
Mallacoota Vic. 35 D11, 51 G11
Mallala SA 67 B3, 69 H5, 71 B1, 73 J7
Mallan NSW 28 H9, 59 M11, 61 M1
Mallanganee NSW 21 D5, 27 M3, 123 M12
Mallanganee NP NSW 21 D5, 27 M3, 123 M12
Mallee Cliffs NP NSW 28 E5, 58 H5, 59 I6
Mallum Vic. 54 H9, 56 D7
Malmsbury Vic. 49 G7, 52 A1, 54 A11, 61 O12, 63 O2
Malpas SA 28 A7, 58 A8, 71 G2, 73 N9
Malua Bay NSW 24 H12, 35 F6, 37 M7
Malvern SA xxi J9
Malyalling WA 88 F6
Mambray Creek SA 73 I3, 74 G10
Manangatang Vic. 28 F8, 59 J11
Manara NSW 29 I1, 30 H12
Mandagery NSW 24 E4
Mandalong NSW 13 E5, 19 A11
Mandorah NT 102 C3, 104 D4
Mandurah WA 85 C9, 88 B6, 90 C8
Mandurama NSW 24 F5
Mandurang Vic. 49 G4, 54 A9, 61 O10

Mangalo SA 69 A1, 72 F5, 74 E12
Mangalore Tas. 139 I2, 141 K6
Mangalore Vic. 54 D10
Mangana Tas. 143 N9
Mangerton NSW 22 C10
Mango Hill Qld 114 E4, 115 E2, 117 F9
Mangoola NSW 25 J2
Mangoplah NSW 24 B10, 29 O10, 55 M2
Mangrove Creek NSW 13 B7, 15 M1, 25 K5
Mangrove Mountain NSW 13 C6, 15 M1, 25 K5
Manguri SA 79 N10
Manildra NSW 24 F4
Manilla NSW 26 H8
Maningrida NT 105 J3
Manjimup WA 86 H10, 87 B1, 88 D10, 90 C10
Manly NSW xi O5, 12 G6, 13 C12, 15 M8, 25 K6
Manly Qld 114 G7, 115 E4, 117 G11
Manly Vale NSW xi M2
Manmanning WA 88 E2, 90 D6
Manmoyi NT 105 J4
Mannahill SA 73 M2, 75 L9
Mannanarie SA 73 J3, 75 I11
Mannerim Vic. 42 G8, 44 D5, 52 A6
Mannering Park NSW 13 F5, 19 B11, 25 L5
Mannibadar Vic. 42 A4, 63 K5
Manning WA xxiv G9, xxv A10
Manning Point NSW 20 E8, 25 O1, 27 L12
Manns Beach Vic. 53 J10
Mannum SA 67 H9, 71 D3, 73 L9
Manobalai NSW 25 J1, 26 H12
Manoora SA 73 K6
Mansfield Vic. 54 H11, 56 D9
Mantung SA 71 F2, 73 M8
Manumbar Qld 118 C10, 123 M6
Many Peaks Qld 123 L2
Manyallaluk NT 104 G8
Manyana NSW 37 N3
Manypeaks WA 87 F10, 88 H11
Mapleton Qld 117 F3, 118 E11
Mapleton Falls NP Qld 117 E3, 118 E11, 123 N7
Mapoon Qld 128 B5
Mara NT 105 M11, 107 M2
Maralinga SA 80 H3
Marama SA 71 F4, 73 M10
Maranboy NT 104 G8
Marangaroo WA 84 C4, 85 C4
Marathon Qld 124 A4, 131 M4
Maraylya NSW 12 B2, 15 J4
Marbelup WA 87 C11, 88 G11
Marble Bar WA 92 E2, 94 E12, 97 K5
Marburg Qld 115 A5, 117 B11, 123 M9
Marchagee WA 90 B5
Marcoola Qld 117 G3, 118 F11
Marcus Vic. 44 D5
Marcus Beach Qld 117 H2, 118 F10
Marcus Hill Vic. 42 G9, 44 D5, 52 A7
Mardella WA 84 F11, 85 D7
Marden SA xxi L2
Mareeba Qld 120 D2, 121 D7, 127 L6
Marengo NSW 21 B11, 27 L7
Marengo Vic. 42 B12, 50 C6, 63 L11
Margaret River WA 86 B8, 88 B10, 90 B10
Margate Tas. 139 I7, 141 K8
Maria Creek NP Qld 120 E5, 127 M8
Maria Island NP Tas. 139 O3, 141 N6
Maria NP NSW 20 G5, 27 M10
Mariala NP Qld 133 N4
Marian Qld 119 F7, 125 K5
Maribyrnong Vic. xiv B4
Mariginiup WA 84 C3
Marion SA 66 B8, 67 B9, 68 E3, 69 H8
Marion Bay SA 69 B9, 72 G10
Marion Bay Tas. 139 N5, 141 M7
Markwell NSW 19 H4, 20 C10, 25 N2
Markwood Vic. 55 I8, 56 G5
Marla SA 79 M5
Marlborough Qld 125 L9
Marlee NSW 20 D7, 25 N1, 27 K12
Marleston SA xx F7
Marlo Vic. 35 A12, 51 B11
Marma Vic. 60 H9
Marmion WA xxiv A1
Marmor Qld 125 M11

Marnoo Vic. 61 I9
Marong Vic. 49 E3, 61 N10
Maroochydore Qld 117 G4, 118 F11, 123 N7
Maroon Qld 21 D1, 27 N1, 115 A10, 123 M10
Maroona Vic. 63 I3
Maroota NSW 13 A8, 15 K3, 25 K5
Marp Vic. 62 C5, 71 H12
Marrabel SA 71 C1, 73 K7
Marradong WA 85 G11, 88 D7
Marralum NT 95 P3, 99 N4, 104 B10, 106 B1
Marramarra NP NSW 12 E1, 13 B9, 15 K3, 25 K5
Marrangaroo NSW 14 B1, 16 C1, 25 I5
Marrar NSW 24 B9, 29 P9
Marrara NT xxvii E6
Marrawah Tas. 142 A4
Marraweeny Vic. 54 F9, 56 B7
Marree SA 74 H1, 76 H12, 132 A12
Marrickville NSW viii A9, 12 E8, 15 L9
Marrinup WA 85 E10
Marryatville SA xxi M6
Marsden NSW 24 C5, 29 P5
Marshall Vic. 42 F8, 44 A4, 50 G1, 52 A6, 63 O7
Marshdale NSW 19 E4, 20 B10, 25 M3
Martin WA xxv H12
Martindale NSW 25 J2
Martins Creek NSW 19 C5, 20 A11, 25 L3
Martinsville NSW 13 E4, 19 A10
Marton Qld 127 L3
Marulan NSW 24 H9, 35 F3
Marulan South NSW 24 H9, 35 F3
Marungi Vic. 29 L12, 54 F6, 56 A2
Marvel Loch WA 90 F6
Mary River NP (Proposed) NT 102 H1, 103 I4, 104 E4
Mary River Roadhouse NT 103 L10, 104 F6
Maryborough Qld 118 E6, 123 N5
Maryborough Vic. 49 C5, 61 M11, 63 M1
Marybrook WA 86 B6
Maryfarms Qld 120 C1, 121 B4, 127 K5
Maryknoll Vic. 41 D11, 43 M7, 52 E6
Maryland NP NSW 21 B3, 27 L2, 123 L11
Marysville Vic. 41 F5, 43 N3, 52 F3
Maryvale NSW 24 F2
Maryvale Qld 21 C1
Maryville NSW 18 A2
Mascot NSW viii E12, 12 F8, 15 L9
Maslin Beach SA 66 A12, 67 A12, 68 E5
Massey Vic. 28 F12, 61 I7
Matakana NSW 29 M3
Mataranka NT 104 H9
Matcham NSW 13 D8, 15 O3
Matheson NSW 27 J5
Mathinna Tas. 143 N8
Mathoura NSW 29 J11, 54 D4
Matlock Vic. 43 P4, 52 H4
Matong NSW 24 B8, 29 O8, 35 B9, 36 E12, 51 D6
Maude NSW 29 I7, 59 P8
Maude Vic. 42 E6, 63 N6
Maudsland Qld 115 F9, 116 C4
Mawbanna Tas. 142 D4
Mawson WA 88 E5, 90 D7
Maxwelton Qld 131 K3
Mayanup WA 88 D9, 90 D10
Mayberry Tas. 142 H8, 144 G5
Maydena Tas. 138 D3, 140 H6
Maylands SA xxi L4
Maylands WA xxiv H4, xxv A5, 84 D6, 85 C5
Mayrung NSW 29 K10, 54 E2
Mazeppa NP Qld 119 A10, 124 G7
Meadow Creek Vic. 55 I8, 56 F6
Meadowbank NSW 15 K8
Meadows SA 66 E11, 67 D11, 68 G5, 71 C4, 73 J10
Meandarra Qld 122 H8
Meander Tas. 143 I9, 145 C12
Meatian Vic. 28 G10, 61 K3
Mebbin NP NSW 21 F3, 27 N2, 123 N11
Meckering WA 88 E4, 90 D7
Medindie SA xxi J2, 65 E2
Medindie Gardens SA xxi J1
Medlow Bath NSW 14 C5, 16 F8, 25 I6
Medowie NSW 19 E7
Meeandah Qld 114 F7
Meekatharra WA 89 H9, 92 E10

Meelon WA 85 D10
Meeniyan Vic. 43 O12, 52 G9
Meerawa Qld 120 E3, 121 G9
Meerlieu Vic. 53 L6
Meerschaum Vale NSW 21 G5, 27 O4, 123 N12
Megalong NSW 14 C5, 16 E8
Megan NSW 21 C11, 27 M7
Melaleuca Tas. 140 F10
Melbourne Vic. xv J11, xvii J2, 39, 40 D6, 43 I5, 52 C4
Meldale Qld 114 F1, 117 G7
Mella Tas. 142 C4
Mellis Vic. 60 H7
Melros WA 85 B10
Melrose SA 73 I3, 74 H10
Melrose Tas. 142 H6, 144 G2, 145 A7
Melrose Park SA xx H11
Melton SA 69 F3, 73 I6
Melton Vic. 40 A4, 42 G4, 49 H12, 52 B3, 63 P5
Melton Mowbray Tas. 141 K4
Melton South Vic. 40 A4, 42 G4, 49 H12, 52 B4, 63 P5
Melville WA xxiv D10, 84 D7, 85 C6, 87 D11
Melville Forest Vic. 62 E3
Memana Tas. 140 B10
Memerambi Qld 118 A10, 123 L6
Mena Creek Qld 120 E5, 121 G12, 127 M8
Mena Park Vic. 42 A3, 63 K4
Menai NSW 12 C10, 15 J11, 23 H1
Menangle NSW 14 G12, 23 F2, 25 J7, 35 H1
Menangle Park NSW 14 H11, 23 F1
Mendooran NSW 26 D11
Mengha Tas. 142 D4
Menindee NSW 30 E11
Meningie SA 71 D5, 73 L11
Menora WA xxiv F4
Mentone Vic. 40 E8, 43 J7, 45 J1, 52 C5
Menzies WA 90 H3
Menzies Creek Vic. 40 H7, 41 C9, 43 L6
Mepunga East Vic. 50 E8, 62 H8
Mepunga West Vic. 50 D8, 62 H8
Merah North NSW 26 E6
Merbein Vic. 28 D6, 58 G6
Merbein South Vic. 28 D6, 58 G6
Merbein West Vic. 58 G5
Mercunda SA 71 F2, 73 M8
Merebene NSW 26 D7
Meredith Vic. 42 E5, 63 N5
Mereenie NT 111 I5
Merewether NSW 13 H3, 18 A10, 19 D9
Meribah SA 28 B7, 58 B8, 71 G2, 73 O8
Merildin SA 73 K6
Merimal Qld 125 M10
Merimbula NSW 35 E9, 51 H7
Merinda Qld 119 D4, 125 I3
Meringa Qld 120 E3, 121 F8
Meringo NSW 35 F7, 37 L8
Meringur Vic. 28 C6, 58 D7, 73 P8
Meringur North Vic. 28 C6, 58 D6, 73 P7
Merino Vic. 62 D4
Mermaid Beach Qld 21 G1, 115 G10, 116 F7
Mernda Vic. 40 E3, 43 J4, 52 D3
Meroo NP NSW 25 I11, 35 F5, 37 N4
Merredin WA 88 G3, 90 E6
Merriang Vic. 55 J8, 56 H6
Merriang South Vic. 55 J9, 56 H6
Merricks Vic. 45 J9
Merricks Beach Vic. 45 J9
Merricks North Vic. 40 E12, 43 J10, 45 J8, 52 C7
Merrigum Vic. 54 D7
Merrijig Vic. 52 H1, 54 H11, 56 E10
Merrimac Qld 115 F10, 116 E7
Merrinee Vic. 28 D6, 58 F7
Merrinee North Vic. 28 D6, 58 F6
Merriton SA 73 I5, 74 H12
Merriwa NSW 25 J1, 26 G12
Merriwa WA 84 B2
Merriwagga NSW 29 L5
Merrygoen NSW 26 D11
Merrylands NSW 15 J8
Merseylea Tas. 142 H7, 145 B8
Merton Tas. 137 B6
Merton Vic. 54 F10, 56 B9

Metcalfe Vic. 49 G6, 54 A11, 61 O12, 63 O1
Metricup WA 86 B7
Metung Vic. 53 N6
Meunna Tas. 142 D5
Mia Mia Vic. 49 H5, 54 B10, 61 P11, 63 P1
Miallo Qld 120 D1, 121 D3, 127 L5
Miami Qld 21 G1, 115 G10, 116 F8
Miami Keys Qld 116 F7
Miandetta NSW 31 O10
Miandetta Tas. 145 B3
Michael Creek Qld 120 E8, 127 L10
Michaelmas and Upolu Cays NP Qld 120 E1, 121 H5, 127 M5
Michelago NSW 24 F12, 34 E10, 35 C6, 36 H5
Mickleham Vic. 40 D3, 43 I3, 52 C3
Middle Cove NSW x H3
Middle Creek Vic. 63 K3
Middle Dural NSW 12 D3, 13 A10, 15 K5
Middle Indigo Vic. 55 J6, 56 H2
Middle Park Vic. xvii J8
Middle Point NT 102 F3, 104 E4
Middle Swan WA xxv F1, 84 F4, 85 D4
Middlemount Qld 125 J9
Middleton Qld 131 I7
Middleton SA 68 G8
Middleton Tas. 138 H9, 141 J9
Middlingbank NSW 35 B7, 36 E9, 51 D3
Midge Point Qld 119 F6, 125 J4
Midgee Qld 125 M11
Midgee SA 72 G4, 74 F12
Midland WA xxv F2, 84 F5, 85 D4, 88 C5, 90 C7
Midvale WA xxv G2
Midway Point Tas. 139 K4, 141 L7
Miena Tas. 141 I1, 143 I11
Miepoll Vic. 54 E8, 56 A5
Miga Lake Vic. 60 D10
Mil Lel SA 62 A4, 71 G11
Mila NSW 35 C10, 51 E8
Milabena Tas. 142 E5
Milang SA 71 C4, 73 K10
Milawa Vic. 55 I8, 56 F5
Milbrulong NSW 24 A10, 29 O10, 55 K1
Mildura Vic. 28 E6, 58 G6
Mile End SA xx G5
Mile End South SA xx G6
Miles Qld 123 I7
Milguy NSW 26 G4, 122 H12
Milikapiti NT 104 D2
Miling WA 88 C1, 90 C5
Milingimbi NT 105 K3
Millaa Millaa Qld 120 D4, 121 E11, 127 L7
Millaroo Qld 119 B4, 124 H3
Millbrook Vic. 42 E3, 49 D11
Millers Point NSW viii F3, x F11, 10 B4
Millfield NSW 13 D2, 25 L4
Millgrove Vic. 41 E8, 43 M5, 52 F4
Millicent SA 71 F11
Millie NSW 26 F5
Millmerran Qld 123 K9
Milloo Vic. 54 A6, 61 O8
Millstream–Chichester NP WA 89 F2, 92 B3, 96 E6
Millstream Falls NP Qld 120 D5, 121 D12, 127 L7
Millswood SA xxi I9
Millthorpe NSW 24 G5
Milltown Vic. 62 D6
Millwood NSW 24 B9, 29 O9
Milman Qld 125 M10
Milparinka NSW 30 D3, 75 P2, 132 H12
Milsons Point NSW viii G2, x G10
Miltalie SA 69 B1, 72 F5, 74 E12
Milton NSW 25 I11, 35 G5, 37 N4
Milton Qld xxx F7, 114 E7
Milvale NSW 24 D7, 35 A1
Milyakburra NT 105 M7
Mimili SA 79 K5
Mimmindie Vic. 28 H12, 61 M6
Mimosa NSW 24 B8, 29 P8
Mimosa Rocks NP NSW 35 E9, 37 K12, 51 H6
Minamia NT 105 J11, 107 J2
Mincha Vic. 28 H11, 61 N6
Mindarie SA 71 F3, 73 M9
Minden Qld 117 B11

Mindiyarra SA 71 E3, 73 M9
Miners Rest Vic. 42 C2, 49 C9, 63 M3
Minerva Hills NP Qld 124 H12, 125 I12
Mingary SA 30 A10, 73 O1, 75 M8
Mingay Vic. 42 A5, 63 K5
Mingela Qld 120 F12, 124 G2
Mingenew WA 90 B4
Mingoola NSW 27 K3, 123 K12
Minhamite Vic. 62 G6
Minilya Roadhouse WA 89 B6
Minimay Vic. 60 C9, 71 H8
Mininera Vic. 63 I4
Minjary NP NSW 24 D10, 35 A4, 36 C2, 55 P2
Minjilang NT 104 G1
Minlaton SA 69 E6, 72 H8
Minmi NSW 13 G3, 19 C9, 20 A12
Minnamurra NSW 23 F7
Minnie Water NSW 21 F9, 27 N6
Minniging WA 88 E7
Minnipa SA 72 C3, 74 A10, 81 P10
Minnivale WA 88 E3
Minore NSW 24 E1, 26 C12
Mintabie SA 79 L5
Mintaro SA 73 J6
Minto NSW 15 I10, 23 G1
Minyerri NT 105 J10, 107 J1
Minyip Vic. 60 H8
Miowera NSW 31 P10
Miralie Vic. 59 L11, 61 L1
Miram Vic. 28 C12, 60 C7, 71 H7
Miram South Vic. 60 D7, 71 H7
Miranda NSW 12 D10, 15 K11
Mirannie NSW 19 B3, 25 L2
Mirboo Vic. 43 P11, 52 H8
Mirboo North Vic. 43 P11, 52 G8
Miriam Vale Qld 123 L2
Mirimbah Vic. 53 I1, 55 I11, 56 F10
Miriwinni Qld 120 E4, 121 G10, 127 M7
Mirrabooka WA xxiv F1
Mirranatwa Vic. 62 G3
Mirrngadja Village NT 105 K4
Mirrool NSW 24 B7, 29 O7
Missabotti NSW 20 G2, 27 M8
Mission Beach Qld 120 E5, 127 M8
Mistake Creek NT 95 O6, 99 N8, 106 A4
Mitcham SA xxi K11, 66 C8, 67 B9, 68 F2
Mitcham Vic. 40 F6, 41 A8
Mitchell ACT 33 E3, 34 E4, 36 H2
Mitchell Qld 122 E6
Mitchell Alice Rivers NP Qld 126 F2
Mitchell River NP Vic. 53 L4
Mitchell River NP WA 95 K3, 98 G4
Mitchellville SA 69 C1, 72 G5, 74 F12
Mitchelton Qld xxx C1
Mitiamo Vic. 29 I12, 54 A6, 61 O7
Mitre Vic. 60 E9
Mitta Mitta Vic. 55 M9, 57 L6
Mittagong NSW 23 C5, 25 I8, 35 G2
Mittyack Vic. 28 F9, 59 I11, 61 I1
Miva Qld 118 D8
Moama NSW 29 J12, 54 C5
Moana SA 66 A12, 69 H9, 71 B4, 73 J10
Moats Corner Vic. 45 I7
Mockinya Vic. 60 F10
Moculta SA 67 G4
Modanville NSW 21 F4, 27 O3
Modella Vic. 43 M9, 52 F7
Modewarre Vic. 42 E9, 50 F1, 63 N8
Moe Vic. 43 P9, 52 H7
Moffat Vic. 62 H5
Mogendoura NSW 35 F6, 37 L7
Moggill Qld 114 C8, 115 C5, 117 D12
Mogil Mogil NSW 26 D3, 122 F12
Moglonemby Vic. 54 F8, 56 A6
Mogo NSW 35 F6, 37 L7
Mogriguy NSW 24 F1, 26 C12
Mogumber WA 88 C3
Moil NT xxvii E5
Moina Tas. 142 G8, 144 F4
Moira NSW 29 J11, 54 C4
Mokepilly Vic. 60 H11, 62 H1
Mokine WA 85 G3

Mole Creek Tas. 142 H8, 144 H5, 145 A11
Mole Creek Karst NP Tas. 142 G8, 144 G5, 145 A11
Mole River NSW 27 K4, 123 K12
Molendinar Qld 116 E5
Molesworth Tas. 138 H4
Molesworth Vic. 43 M1, 52 F1, 54 F11, 56 A10
Moliagul Vic. 49 B3, 61 L10
Molle Islands NP Qld 119 F5, 125 K3
Mollongghip Vic. 42 E2, 49 D9
Mollymook NSW 37 N4
Mologa Vic. 54 A5, 61 O7
Molong NSW 24 F4
Moltema Tas. 142 H8, 145 B10
Molyullah Vic. 54 H9, 56 E6
Mona SA 69 F2
Mona Vale NSW 12 H4, 13 C10, 15 N6, 25 K6
Monak NSW 58 H6
Monarto SA 67 G10, 73 K9
Monarto South SA 67 G11, 71 C3, 73 K10
Monash SA 28 A6, 58 A6, 71 G1, 73 N7
Monbulk Vic. 40 H7, 41 C9, 43 L6, 52 E5
Monea Vic. 54 E10
Monegeetta Vic. 40 C1, 42 H2, 52 B2, 54 B12, 63 P3
Monga NSW 24 H11, 35 E5, 37 K5
Monga NP NSW 24 H12, 35 E6, 37 K5
Mongarlowe NSW 24 H11, 35 E5, 37 K4
Monkey Mia WA 89 B8
Monomeith Vic. 43 L9, 45 P6, 52 E7
Montagu Tas. 142 B3
Montagu Bay Tas. xxxiv H10, 1 D5, 137 F7
Montana Tas. 143 I9, 145 C11
Monteagle NSW 24 E7, 35 B1
Montgomery Vic. 53 K6
Monto Qld 123 K3
Montrose Tas. xxxiv A5, 137 B5
Montumana Tas. 142 E4
Montville Qld 117 F4, 118 E11
Mooball NSW 21 G3
Mooball NP NSW 21 G3, 27 O2, 123 N11
Moockra SA 73 J2, 74 H9
Moodlu Qld 114 D1, 117 E7
Moogara Tas. 138 F4, 141 I6
Moogerah Qld 21 D1, 27 M1
Moogerah Peaks NP Qld 21 D1, 27 M1, 115 A8, 123 M10
Moola Qld 123 K8
Moolap Vic. 42 F8, 44 B4, 50 H1
Mooloolaba Qld 117 H4, 118 F12, 123 N7
Mooloolah Qld 117 F5, 118 E12
Mooloolah River NP Qld 117 G4, 118 F12, 123 N7
Moolort Vic. 49 D6, 61 M12, 63 M1
Moolpa NSW 28 H8, 59 M11
Moombooldool NSW 24 A7, 29 N7
Moombra Qld 117 B9
Moona Plains NSW 20 C3, 27 K9
Moonah Tas. xxxiv D7, 137 C6, 139 I5
Moonambel Vic. 61 K11
Moonan Flat NSW 25 L1, 27 I12
Moonbah NSW 35 B8, 36 D10, 51 C4
Moonbi NSW 27 I9
Moondarra Vic. 52 H6
Moonee Beach NSW 21 E11, 27 N7
Moonee Ponds Vic. xiv E3
Mooney Mooney NSW 12 G1, 13 C9, 15 M4
Moonford Qld 123 K3
Moonie Qld 123 I9
Moonlight Flat SA 72 C3, 74 A11, 81 P11
Moonta SA 69 E3, 72 H6
Moonta Bay SA 69 E3, 72 H6
Moora WA 88 B2, 90 B6
Moorabbin Vic. 40 E7, 43 J6, 52 C5
Moorabool Vic. 44 A2
Mooralla Vic. 62 F2
Moore Qld 117 A5, 118 B12, 123 M8
Moore Park NSW viii G8
Moore Park Qld 118 D1, 123 M3
Moore River NP WA 88 B3, 90 B6
Moores Flat Vic. 49 A6, 61 L11, 63 L1
Moorilda NSW 24 G5
Moorilim Vic. 54 E8
Moorina Tas. 143 N6
Moorine Rock WA 90 F6
Moorland NSW 20 E7, 25 O1, 27 L12

Moorlands SA 71 E4, 73 L10
Moorleah Tas. 142 E5
Moorngag Vic. 54 H9, 56 D7
Moorooduc Vic. 40 E10, 43 J9, 45 K6, 52 C7
Moorook SA 71 F1, 73 N7
Moorookyle Vic. 42 D1, 49 D8, 63 M2
Mooroolbark Vic. 41 B8, 43 K5
Mooroopna Vic. 54 E7
Moorrinya NP Qld 124 C5, 131 P5
Moppin NSW 26 F3, 122 H12
Moranbah Qld 119 C10, 125 I7
Morangarell NSW 24 C7
Morans Crossing NSW 35 D9, 37 I12, 51 G6
Morawa WA 90 B4
Morayfield Qld 114 E2, 115 D1, 117 F8
Morchard SA 73 J2, 75 I10
Mordialloc Vic. 40 E8, 43 J7, 45 K2, 52 C5
Morea Vic. 60 C9, 71 H8
Moree NSW 26 G4
Moree Vic. 60 D12, 62 D1
Morella Qld 124 A9, 131 M9
Moresby Range NP Qld 120 E4, 121 H11, 127 M7
Moreton Island NP Qld 115 H2, 123 N9
Morgan SA 73 L6
Moriac Vic. 42 E8, 50 F1, 63 N8
Moriarty Tas. 142 H6, 145 B7
Morisset NSW 13 E5, 19 B11, 25 L4
Morkalla Vic. 28 B6, 58 C6, 71 H1, 73 P8
Morley WA xxiv G2, xxv A3, 84 D5
Morningside Qld xxxi K7, 115 E4, 117 F11
Mornington Tas. 1 G5
Mornington Tas. 137 G7
Mornington Vic. 40 D10, 43 J9, 45 J5, 52 C7
Mornington Peninsula NP Vic. 40 B12, 42 H10, 43 I10, 44 H9, 45 I9, 52 C8, 63 P9
Morongla NSW 24 F6
Morpeth NSW 13 G1, 19 C7, 20 A11, 25 L3
Morphett Vale SA 66 B10, 67 B11, 68 E4, 69 H8
Morphettville SA xx E11
Morri Morri Vic. 61 J10
Morrisons Vic. 42 E5, 49 E12, 63 N5
Mortat Vic. 60 D9, 71 H8
Mortchup Vic. 42 B3, 49 A11, 63 L4
Mortdale NSW 12 D9
Mortlake Vic. 63 I6
Morton NP NSW 23 A8, 24 H11, 25 I10, 35 F4, 37 M1
Morton Plains Vic. 28 F12, 61 J6
Morundah NSW 29 M9
Moruya NSW 35 F7, 37 L7
Moruya Heads NSW 35 F7, 37 L7
Morven NSW 24 B11, 29 O11, 55 L4
Morven Qld 122 D5
Morwell Vic. 52 H7
Morwell NP Vic. 52 H8
Mosman NSW ix J1, xi J8, 12 G7, 13 C12, 15 M8
Mosman Park WA xxiv C9, 84 C7, 85 B5
Moss Glen Tas. 141 I11
Moss Vale NSW 23 B6, 25 I9, 35 G3
Mossgiel NSW 29 J3
Mossiface Vic. 53 N5
Mossman Qld 120 D1, 121 D3, 127 L5
Mossy Point NSW 37 L7
Moulamein NSW 29 I9, 59 N11, 61 N1
Moulyinning WA 88 G7
Mount Aberdeen NP Qld 119 D4, 125 I3
Mount Adrah NSW 24 D10, 35 A4, 36 B1, 55 P1
Mount Alford Qld 21 D1, 27 M1, 123 M10
Mount Alfred Vic. 24 C12, 55 N6, 57 M1
Mount Archer NP Qld 125 M11
Mount Augustus NP WA 89 F6, 92 B7
Mount Barker SA 66 F10, 67 D10, 68 H3, 71 C3, 73 K9
Mount Barker WA 87 C9, 88 G11, 90 E11
Mount Barnett Roadhouse WA 95 L6, 98 H8
Mount Barney NP Qld 21 D2, 27 M1, 115 A11, 123 M11
Mount Bauple NP Qld 118 D7, 123 M5
Mount Baw Baw Vic. 43 P6, 52 H5
Mount Beauty Vic. 55 L10, 57 J7
Mount Beckworth Vic. 42 C1, 49 B8, 63 L2
Mount Benson SA 71 E9
Mount Beppo Qld 117 B7

Mount Best Vic. 43 P12, 52 H9
Mount Blue Cow NSW 36 C10, 51 B4
Mount Bryan SA 73 K5, 75 I12
Mount Bryan East SA 73 K5, 75 J12
Mount Buffalo NP Vic. 55 J9, 56 H7, 57 I7
Mount Buller Vic. 53 I1, 55 I12, 56 F10
Mount Burnett Vic. 45 P2
Mount Burr SA 71 F11
Mount Bute Vic. 42 A5, 63 K5
Mount Carbine Qld 120 C1, 121 B4, 127 K5
Mount Charlton Qld 119 F7, 125 J5
Mount Chinghee NP Qld 21 E2, 27 N2, 115 B12, 123 M11
Mount Claremont WA xxiv C6
Mount Clear Vic. 49 C11
Mount Clunie NP Qld 21 C2, 27 M1, 123 M11
Mount Colah NSW 12 E4, 13 B10, 15 L6
Mount Colosseum NP Qld 123 L2
Mount Compass SA 68 F6, 69 H9, 71 B4, 73 J10
Mount Cook NP Qld 127 L3
Mount Coolon Qld 119 B8, 124 H6
Mount Coolum NP Qld 117 G3, 118 F11, 123 N7
Mount Coot-Tha Qld xxx B7, 114 D7
Mount Cottrell Vic. 40 A5, 42 H5, 49 H12, 52 B4, 63 P5
Mount Crosby Qld 114 B8, 115 B5, 117 D11
Mount Damper SA 72 C4, 74 A11, 81 P11
Mount David NSW 24 H6
Mount Direction Tas. 143 K7, 145 G7
Mount Doran Vic. 42 D4, 49 D12, 63 M5
Mount Druitt NSW 12 A5, 15 I7, 17 O11
Mount Dunned Vic. 44 A5
Mount Ebenezer Roadhouse NT 108 G10
Mount Eccles Vic. 43 O10, 52 G8
Mount Eccles NP Vic. 62 E6
Mount Egerton Vic. 42 E4, 49 E11, 63 N4
Mount Eliza Vic. 40 E10, 43 J8, 45 K5, 52 C6
Mount Emu Vic. 42 A3, 63 K4
Mount Etna Caves NP Qld 125 M10
Mount Evelyn Vic. 40 H6, 41 C8, 43 L5
Mount Fairy NSW 24 G10, 35 E4, 37 J2
Mount Field NP Tas. 138 D2, 140 H5, 141 I5
Mount Frankland NP WA 87 E4, 88 E11, 90 D11
Mount Franklin Vic. 42 E1, 49 E8, 63 N2
Mount Gambier SA 62 A5, 71 G12
Mount Garnet Qld 120 C5, 121 A12, 127 K7
Mount George NSW 20 D8, 25 N1, 27 K12
Mount Glorious Qld 114 B5, 115 B3, 117 D9
Mount Gravatt Qld 114 E8, 115 E5, 117 F12
Mount Hallen Qld 117 A9, 123 M9
Mount Hawthorn WA xxiv E4
Mount Helen Vic. 42 D4, 49 C11, 63 M4
Mount Helena WA 84 H4, 85 E4
Mount Hope NSW 29 M2
Mount Hope SA 72 C6
Mount Horeb NSW 24 D10, 35 A4, 36 B1, 55 P1
Mount Hunter NSW 14 F11, 23 E1
Mount Hypipamee NP Qld 120 D4, 121 D10, 127 L7
Mount Imlay NP NSW 35 D10, 51 G8
Mount Irvine NSW 14 E2, 17 J3
Mount Isa Qld 129 D11, 130 F3
Mount Jerusalem NP NSW 21 G3, 27 O2, 123 N12
Mount Jim Crow NP Qld 125 M10
Mount Kaputar NP NSW 26 G6
Mount Keira NSW 22 A8
Mount Keith WA 92 G10
Mount Kembla NSW 23 F5
Mount Kuring-Gai NSW 12 E3, 13 B10, 15 L6
Mount Lambie NSW 14 A1, 16 A1, 25 I5
Mount Larcom Qld 125 N12
Mount Lawley WA xxiv F4, xxv A5
Mount Liebig NT 108 E6
Mount Lloyd Tas. 138 F4, 141 I7
Mount Lofty SA 66 D8, 67 C10, 68 G3
Mount Lonarch Vic. 61 K12, 63 K2
Mount Macedon Vic. 40 A1, 42 H2, 49 H9, 52 B2, 54 B12, 63 P3
Mount Magnet WA 89 H11, 90 D2, 92 D12
Mount Martha Vic. 40 D11, 43 I9, 45 I6, 52 C7
Mount Martin NP Qld 119 F7, 125 K5
Mount Mary SA 73 L7
Mount Mee Qld 114 B1, 117 D7
Mount Mercer Vic. 42 D5, 49 C12, 63 M5

Mount Molloy Qld 120 C1, 121 C5, 127 L5
Mount Morgan Qld 125 M11
Mount Moriac Vic. 42 E8, 50 F1, 63 N8
Mount Mulligan Qld 120 B2, 127 K6
Mount Nebo Qld 114 B6, 115 B3, 117 D10
Mount Nelson Tas. 1 A12, 137 D10
Mount Nothofagus NP Qld 21 D2, 27 M1, 115 A12, 123 M11
Mount O'Connell NP Qld 125 L9
Mount Ommaney Qld 114 D8, 115 C5, 117 E12
Mount Osmond SA xxi N9
Mount Ossa Qld 119 F7, 125 J5
Mount Ossa NP Qld 119 F7, 125 J5
Mount Ousley NSW 22 D5, 23 F4
Mount Perry Qld 118 A3, 123 L4
Mount Pikapene NP NSW 21 D5, 27 M4, 123 M12
Mount Pinbarren NP Qld 118 E10, 123 N6
Mount Pleasant NSW 22 A5
Mount Pleasant Qld 114 B2, 115 C1, 117 D8
Mount Pleasant SA 67 F7, 71 C2, 73 K9
Mount Pleasant Vic. 47 E9, 49 C10
Mount Pleasant WA xxiv F10, 89 D12, 90 H5
Mount Remarkable NP SA 73 I3, 74 H10
Mount Richmond Vic. 62 C7
Mount Richmond NP Vic. 62 C7
Mount Roe–Mt Lindesay NP WA 87 G4, 88 F11, 90 D11
Mount Rowan Vic. 42 D3, 49 C10, 63 M3
Mount Royal NP NSW 19 A1, 25 L2
Mount St Thomas NSW 22 B12
Mount Samson Qld 114 C4, 115 C2, 117 E9
Mount Schank SA 62 A5, 71 G12
Mount Seaview NSW 20 D5, 27 K11
Mount Seymour Tas. 141 L4
Mount Stuart Tas. xxxiv D10, 137 C7
Mount Surprise Qld 127 J8
Mount Tamborine Qld 21 G1, 115 E9, 116 B5
Mount Tarampa Qld 117 B10
Mount Taylor Vic. 53 M5
Mount Templeton SA 69 G3, 73 J6
Mount Thorley NSW 25 K3
Mount Tomah NSW 14 E3, 17 I4
Mount Torrens SA 66 H6, 67 E8, 71 C3, 73 K9
Mount Victoria NSW 14 C4, 16 E5, 25 I6
Mount Wallace Vic. 42 E5, 49 E12, 63 N5
Mount Walsh NP Qld 118 B5, 123 L5
Mount Warning NP NSW 21 G3, 27 O2, 123 N11
Mount Waverley Vic. 40 E6
Mount Webb NP Qld 127 L2
Mount Wedge SA 72 C5, 74 A12, 81 P12
Mount White NSW 13 C8, 15 M3, 25 K5
Mount William NP Tas. 143 P5
Mount Wilson NSW 14 D3, 16 H4, 25 I5
Mountain River Tas. 138 H6, 141 J7
Moura Qld 123 I2
Mourilyan Qld 120 E5, 121 H12, 127 M7
Moutajup Vic. 62 G4
Mowbray Tas. 143 K8, 145 G9
Mowbray NP Qld 120 D1, 121 D4, 127 L5
Mowbray Park NSW 14 E12, 23 D2
Mowen WA 86 B8, 88 B10
Moyhu Vic. 55 I8, 56 F6
Moyreisk Vic. 61 K10
Moyston Vic. 63 I2
Muchea WA 84 E1, 85 C2, 88 C4, 90 C7
Muckadilla Qld 122 F6
Mudamuckla SA 81 N8
Mudgee NSW 24 H2
Mudgeeraba Qld 21 G1, 27 O1, 115 F10, 116 E8, 123 N10
Mudginberri NT 103 O3, 104 G4
Mudjimba Qld 117 G3, 118 F11
Muggleton Qld 122 G6
Muirhead NT xxvii F3
Mukinbudin WA 88 G2, 90 E6
Mulambin Qld 125 N10
Mulbring NSW 13 F3, 19 B9
Mulcra Vic. 28 B9, 58 C11, 71 H4, 73 O10
Mulgildie Qld 123 K3
Mulgoa NSW 14 G8, 25 J6
Mullaley NSW 26 F9
Mullalyup WA 86 F6, 88 C9

Mullaway NSW 21 E11, 27 N7
Mullenderee NSW 24 H12, 37 L7
Mullengandra NSW 24 B12, 29 O12, 55 L5, 57 K1
Mullengudgery NSW 26 A10, 31 P10
Mullewa WA 89 E12, 90 B3
Mulli Mulli NSW 21 D3, 27 M2, 123 M11
Mullindolingong Vic. 55 L9, 57 J7
Mullion Creek NSW 24 G4
Mullumbimby NSW 21 G4, 27 O3, 123 N12
Mulpata SA 28 A8, 71 F4, 73 N10
Mulwala NSW 29 M12, 54 H5, 56 D1
Mumballup WA 86 G5, 88 D8, 90 C10
Mumbannar Vic. 62 C5, 71 H12
Mumbil NSW 24 G3
Mumblin Vic. 50 F8, 63 I8
Mumdjin NSW 116 B11
Mummel Gulf NP NSW 20 C5, 27 J10
Mummulgum NSW 21 D5, 27 M3, 123 M12
Munbilla Qld 115 A8
Mundaring WA 84 G5, 85 E4, 88 C5, 90 C7
Mundaring Weir WA 84 G6, 85 E5
Mundijong WA 84 F10, 85 D7, 90 C8
Mundoona Vic. 54 E6
Mundoora SA 69 F1, 73 I5, 74 H12
Mundrabilla Roadhouse WA 80 A8, 91 O6
Mundubbera Qld 123 K4
Mundulla SA 28 A12, 60 A7, 71 G7
Mungalawurru NT 107 I9
Mungallala Qld 122 D6
Mungana Qld 120 A3, 127 J6
Mungar Qld 118 D6, 123 M5
Mungerannie Roadhouse SA 77 I8, 132 B8
Mungeribar NSW 24 E1, 26 B12
Mungery NSW 24 D2
Mungindi NSW 26 E2, 122 F11
Mungkan Kandju NP Qld 128 D9
Mungkarta NT 107 J11
Munglinup WA 90 H9
Mungo NP NSW 28 G4, 59 K1
Mungungo Qld 123 K3
Munro Vic. 53 L6
Munster WA 84 D9, 85 C6
Muntadgin WA 88 H4, 90 E7
Muradup WA 88 E9
Murarrie Qld xxxi M7, 114 F7
Murchison Vic. 54 D8
Murchison WA 89 E9, 92 B11
Murchison East Vic. 54 E8
Murdinga SA 72 D5
Murdoch WA xxiv F12
Murdunna Tas. 139 N6, 141 M8
Murga NSW 24 E4
Murgenella NT 104 G2
Murgheboluc Vic. 42 E7, 63 N7
Murgon Qld 118 A9, 123 L6
Murmungee Vic. 55 J8, 56 H5
Murphys Creek Vic. 49 C3, 61 M10
Murra Warra Vic. 60 G8
Murrabit Vic. 28 H10, 61 N3
Murradoc Vic. 44 E4
Murramarang NP NSW 24 H12, 25 I12, 35 F6, 37 M5
Murrami NSW 29 N7
Murrawal NSW 26 E10
Murray Bridge SA 67 H11, 71 D3, 73 K10
Murray River NP SA 28 A6, 58 A6, 71 G1, 73 N7
Murray Sunset NP Vic. 28 C7, 58 D9, 71 H2, 73 P9
Murray Town SA 73 I3, 74 H11
Murrays Run NSW 13 C4, 25 K4
Murrayville Vic. 28 B9, 58 C11, 60 C1, 71 H4, 73 O10
Murrindal Vic. 35 A11, 51 A9, 53 P3
Murrindindi Vic. 41 D2, 43 M2, 52 E2, 54 E12, 56 A11
Murringo NSW 24 E7, 35 B1
Murroon Vic. 42 C10, 50 D3, 63 L9
Murrumba Qld 117 B8
Murrumbateman NSW 24 F9, 34 D1, 35 C3
Murrumburrah NSW 24 E8, 35 B2
Murrungowar Vic. 35 B11, 51 C10
Murrurundi NSW 26 H11
Murtoa Vic. 60 H9
Murun Murula NT 107 O7

Murwillumbah NSW 21 G2, 27 O2, 115 F12, 123 N11
Musgrave Hill Qld 116 F5
Musgrave Roadhouse Qld 128 E12
Musk Vic. 42 E2, 49 E9, 63 N3
Muskerry East Vic. 54 B8, 61 P10
Musselboro Tas. 143 L8
Musselroe Bay Tas. 143 O5
Muswellbrook NSW 25 K2
Mutarnee Qld 120 F9, 127 M10
Mutawintji NP NSW 30 D7
Mutchilba Qld 120 C3, 121 B8, 127 K6
Mutdapilly Qld 115 A7, 123 M10
Mutitjulu NT 108 E10, 110 E10
Muttaburra Qld 124 C8, 131 O8
Muttama NSW 24 D9, 35 A3
Myall Vic. 28 H10, 61 N3
Myall Lakes NP NSW 19 H7, 20 D11, 25 N3
Myall Mundi NSW 26 B11
Myall Plains NSW 29 M10, 54 H2
Myalla Tas. 142 E5
Myalup WA 86 D2, 88 C8, 90 C9
Myamyn Vic. 62 E6
Myaree WA xxiv E11
Mylestom NSW 20 H1, 21 D12, 27 M8
Mylor SA 66 E9, 67 D10, 68 G3
Myola Qld 121 E6
Myola Vic. 54 B8, 61 P9
Mypolonga SA 67 H10, 71 D3, 73 L9
Myponga SA 68 E7, 69 H9, 71 B4, 73 J10
Myponga Beach SA 68 D7, 69 G9, 71 B4, 73 J10
Myrla SA 71 F2, 73 N8
Myrniong Vic. 42 F4, 49 F11, 52 A3, 63 O4
Myrrhee Vic. 43 P6, 52 H4, 55 I9, 56 F7
Myrtle Bank SA xxi L9
Myrtle Bank Tas. 143 L7
Myrtle Creek Vic. 49 G5, 54 A10, 61 O11, 63 O1
Myrtleford Vic. 55 J8, 56 H6
Myrtleville NSW 24 H8, 35 E2
Mysia Vic. 28 H12, 61 M7
Mystic Park Vic. 28 H10, 61 M3
Mywee Vic. 54 F4

Nabageena Tas. 142 C4
Nabawa WA 89 D12, 90 A3
Nabiac NSW 20 D9, 25 N2
Nabowla Tas. 143 L6
Nackara SA 73 L3, 75 J10
Nadda SA 28 B7, 58 B8, 71 H2, 73 O8
Nagambie Vic. 54 D9
Nagoorin Qld 123 K2
Nailsworth SA xxi J1
Nairana NP Qld 119 A8, 124 G6
Nairne SA 66 G9, 67 E10, 68 H3, 71 C3, 73 K9
Nakara NT xxvii E4
Nala Tas. 141 L4
Nalangil Vic. 42 A9, 50 B2, 63 K8
Nalinga Vic. 54 G7, 56 B4
Nalya WA 88 E5
Namadgi NP ACT 24 F12, 33 A11, 34 B5, 35 C5, 36 F5, 51 E1
Nambour Qld 117 F3, 118 E11, 123 N7
Nambrok Vic. 53 J6
Nambucca Heads NSW 20 H2, 27 M9
Nambung NP WA 88 A2, 90 A6
Nana Glen NSW 21 D11, 27 M7
Nanango Qld 118 A11, 123 L7
Nanarup WA 87 E11, 88 H11
Nandaly Vic. 28 F9, 59 I12, 61 I1
Nandi Qld 123 K8
Nanga WA 85 E11, 88 C7
Nangana Vic. 41 D9, 43 L6, 52 E5
Nangar NP NSW 24 E5
Nangari SA 28 B6, 58 B7, 71 H2, 73 O8
Nangeenan WA 88 G3, 90 E6
Nangiloc Vic. 28 E7, 58 H7
Nangkita SA 68 F6, 71 B4, 73 J10
Nangus NSW 24 D9, 35 A3, 55 P1
Nangwarry SA 62 A3, 71 G11
Nanneella Vic. 54 C6
Nannup WA 86 F8, 88 C10, 90 C10
Nanson WA 89 D12
Nantabibbie SA 73 K3, 75 J10

Nantawarra SA 69 G3, 73 I6
Nanutarra Roadhouse WA 89 D4, 92 A5, 96 B10
Napoleons Vic. 42 C4, 49 C11, 63 M4
Napperby SA 73 I4, 74 H11
Napranum Qld 128 B7
Nar Nar Goon Vic. 41 D12, 43 M8, 52 E6
Nar Nar Goon North Vic. 45 P2
Nara Qld 123 L8, 126 G11
Naracoopa Tas. 141 P11
Naracoorte SA 60 A10, 71 G9
Naracoorte Caves NP SA 60 A11, 71 G9
Naradhan NSW 29 N5
Naraling WA 89 D12, 90 A3
Narangba Qld 114 D3, 115 D2, 117 F9
Narara NSW 13 D8, 15 O2
Narawntapu NP Tas. 143 I6, 145 D6
Narbethong Vic. 41 E5, 43 M4, 52 F3
Nareen Vic. 62 D2
Narellan NSW 14 G10, 23 F1, 25 J7, 35 H1
Narembeen WA 88 G4, 90 E7
Naremburn NSW x F6
Naretha WA 91 L5
Nariel Vic. 36 A10, 55 O8, 57 N5
Naringal Vic. 50 E8, 62 H8
Naroghid Vic. 50 G7, 63 J7
Narooma NSW 35 F8, 37 L10
Narrabri NSW 26 F7
Narrabri West NSW 26 F7
Narracan Vic. 43 P10, 52 H7
Narrandera NSW 24 A8, 29 N8
Narraport Vic. 28 F11, 61 J5
Narrawa Tas. 142 G7, 144 F3
Narrawallee NSW 37 N4
Narraweena NSW 12 G5, 13 C11, 15 M7
Narrawong Vic. 62 D7
Narre Warren Vic. 40 G8, 41 B11, 43 K7, 45 M2, 52 D6
Narre Warren East Vic. 45 N1
Narre Warren North Vic. 41 B10, 43 K7, 45 N1
Narre Warren South Vic. 45 M3
Narrewillock Vic. 61 L6
Narridy SA 73 J5, 74 H12
Narrien Range NP Qld 124 G9
Narrikup WA 88 G11
Narrogin WA 88 E7, 90 D9
Narromine NSW 24 E1, 26 B12
Narrung SA 71 C5, 73 K11
Narrung Vic. 28 G8, 59 K9
Nashdale NSW 24 F4
Nathalia Vic. 29 K12, 54 E5
Natimuk Vic. 60 F9
National Park Tas. 138 E2, 141 I6
Natone Tas. 142 F6, 144 E1
Nattai NSW 14 D11, 23 C1, 25 I7, 35 G1
Nattai NP NSW 14 D12, 23 C2, 25 I8, 35 G2
Natte Yallock Vic. 49 A4, 61 L11
Natural Bridge Qld 21 G2, 27 O1, 115 E11, 116 B10
Natya Vic. 28 G8, 59 K10
Nauiyu NT 102 C12, 104 D7
Naval Base WA 84 D9, 85 C7
Navarre Vic. 61 J10
Navigators Vic. 42 D3, 49 D11, 63 M4
Nayook Vic. 41 H10, 43 O7, 52 G5
Neale Junction WA 91 M1, 93 M11
Neales Flat SA 67 G1, 71 D1, 73 K7
Neath NSW 13 E2, 19 A8
Nebo Qld 119 E9, 125 J7
Nectar Brook SA 73 I2, 74 G10
Nedlands WA xxiv D7
Neds Corner Vic. 28 C6, 58 E6, 73 P7
Needles Tas. 143 I8, 145 C11
Neerabup NP WA 84 B2, 85 B3, 88 B4, 90 B7
Neerdie Qld 118 E8, 123 N6
Neerim Vic. 41 H10, 43 O7, 52 G5
Neerim East Vic. 41 H11, 43 O7, 52 G6
Neerim Junction Vic. 41 H10, 43 O7, 52 G5
Neerim South Vic. 41 H11, 43 O7, 52 G6
Neeworra NSW 26 E3, 122 G12
Neika Tas. 138 H6, 141 K7
Neilborough Vic. 49 F1, 54 A8, 61 O9
Neilborough East Vic. 49 G1, 54 A7, 61 O9
Neilrex NSW 26 E11
Nelia Qld 131 K3

Nelligen NSW 24 H12, 35 F6, 37 L6
Nelly Bay Qld 119 A1, 120 G10, 124 G1, 127 N11
Nelshaby SA 73 I4, 74 H11
Nelson NSW 12 B3, 15 J5
Nelson Vic. 62 B6, 71 G12
Nelson Bay NSW 19 G8, 20 C12, 25 N4
Nelsons Plains NSW 13 H1, 19 D7, 20 A11
Nelungaloo NSW 24 D4
Nemingha NSW 27 I9
Nene Valley SA 71 F12
Nepabunna SA 70 E4, 75 J4
Nerang Qld 21 G1, 27 O1, 115 F9, 116 D6, 123 N10
Neranwood Qld 115 F11, 116 C8
Nerriga NSW 24 H10, 35 F4, 37 L2
Nerrigundah NSW 35 E7, 37 K9
Nerrin Nerrin Vic. 63 J5
Nerrina Vic. 42 D3, 47 H3, 49 C10, 63 M4
Nerring Vic. 42 A2, 63 K3
Netherby SA xxi K10
Netherby Vic. 28 C11, 60 E6
Nethercote NSW 35 E10, 51 H8
Netley SA xx E8
Neuarpurr Vic. 60 B9, 71 H8
Neurea NSW 24 F3
Neuroodla SA 74 H7
Neutral Bay NSW viii H1, x H8, 11 G5
Nevertire NSW 26 A11, 31 P11
Neville NSW 24 G6
New Angledool NSW 26 B2, 122 E11
New Brighton NSW 21 H3
New Chum Qld 114 B9, 115 C5, 117 D12
New England NP NSW 20 E1, 21 A12, 27 L8
New Farm Qld xxxi I7
New Gisborne Vic. 40 A2, 42 H3, 49 H10, 52 B2, 63 P3
New Italy NSW 21 F6, 27 N4
New Lambton NSW 13 G3, 19 D9
New Mollyann NSW 26 E10
New Norcia WA 88 C2, 90 C6
New Norfolk Tas. 138 G4, 141 J6
New Residence SA 28 A6, 71 F1, 73 N7
New Town Tas. xxxiv E8, 1 A4, 136 A2, 137 C7, 139 I5
New Well SA 71 E1, 73 M7, 79 I2, 108 G11
Newborough Vic. 43 P9, 52 H7
Newbridge NSW 24 G5
Newbridge Vic. 49 D3, 61 M10
Newbury Vic. 42 F2, 49 F9, 52 A2, 54 A12, 63 O3
Newcastle NSW 13 H3, 18, 19 D9, 20 A12, 25 M4
Newcastle Waters (Marlinja) NT 106 H5
Newcastle West NSW 18 B6
Newdegate WA 90 F8
Newell Qld 120 D1, 121 D3
Newfield Vic. 50 G10, 63 I9
Newham Vic. 42 H1, 49 H8, 52 B1, 54 B12, 63 P3
Newhaven Vic. 43 K11, 45 M11, 52 D8
Newlands WA 86 F6, 88 C9
Newlyn Vic. 42 D2, 49 D9, 63 M3
Newman WA 92 E5, 97 L11
Newmarket Qld xxx F4, 114 E6, 115 D4, 117 F11
Newmerella Vic. 35 A12, 51 B11, 53 P5
Newnes NSW 25 I4
Newnes Junction NSW 14 C2, 16 F2
Newnham Tas. 145 G9
Newport NSW 12 H4, 13 C10, 15 N6, 25 K6
Newport Vic. xvi B6, 40 C6, 43 I6
Newry Vic. 53 J6
Newry Islands NP Qld 119 F7, 125 K5
Newrybar NSW 21 G4, 27 O3
Newstead Qld xxxi I6
Newstead Tas. 145 G2
Newstead Vic. 49 E6, 61 N12, 63 N1
Newton SA xxi P1
Newton Boyd NSW 21 B9, 27 L6
Newtown NSW viii C7, 12 F8, 15 L9
Newtown Vic. 42 B4, 46 B7, 49 B11, 63 L4
Ngangalala NT 105 K4
Nguiu NT 104 D3
Ngukurr NT 105 K9
Ngunarra NT 107 M7
Nhill Vic. 28 C12, 60 E7
Nhulunbuy NT 105 N4
Niagara Park NSW 13 D7, 15 O2

Niangala NSW 20 A4, 27 J10
Nicholls Point Vic. 58 G6
Nicholls Rivulet Tas. 138 H8, 141 J9
Nicholson Vic. 53 N5
Nicoll Scrub NP Qld 21 G2, 27 O1, 115 G11, 116 E10, 123 N11
Niemur NSW 29 I9, 59 O12, 61 O1
Nierinna Tas. 138 H7
Nietta Tas. 142 G7, 144 F3
Nightcap NP NSW 21 F3, 27 O2, 123 N12
Nightcliff NT xxvii B5, 102 C2
Nildottie SA 71 E2, 73 L8
Nile Tas. 143 L9
Nillahcootie Vic. 54 G11, 56 D9
Nilma Vic. 43 O9, 52 G7
Nimbin NSW 21 F4, 27 O3, 123 N12
Nimmitabel NSW 35 D8, 36 H11, 51 F5
Ninda Vic. 28 F10, 61 I2
Nindigully Qld 122 F10
Nine Mile Vic. 61 L8
Ningaloo Marine Park WA 89 B4
Ningi Qld 114 F1, 115 E1, 117 G7
Ninnes SA 69 F3, 73 I6
Ninyeunook Vic. 28 G11, 61 L5
Nipan Qld 123 I2
Nippering WA 88 F7
Nirranda Vic. 50 E9, 62 H9
Nirranda South Vic. 50 E9, 63 I9
Nitmiluk (Katherine Gorge) NP NT 103 M12, 104 G7
Noarlunga Centre SA 66 B11, 67 A11, 68 E4
Nobby Qld 123 L10
Nobby Beach Qld 116 F8
Nobbys Creek NSW 116 C12
Nobelius Vic. 45 O1
Noble Park Vic. 40 F7, 41 A10, 43 J7, 45 L1
Noccundra Qld 133 I8
Nollamara WA xxiv E2
Nonda Qld 131 K3
Noojee Vic. 41 H10, 43 O7, 52 G5
Nook Tas. 144 H3, 145 A8
Noonamah NT 102 E4, 104 D5
Noonameena SA 71 D5, 73 K11
Noonbinna NSW 24 E6
Noondoo Qld 26 D1, 122 F10
Noora SA 28 B6, 58 B7, 71 H2, 73 O8
Nooramunga Vic. 54 G7, 56 C4
Noorat Vic. 63 I7
Noorinbee Vic. 35 C11, 51 E10
Noorinbee North Vic. 35 C11, 51 E10
Noorong NSW 28 H9, 59 N12, 61 N2
Noorongong Vic. 55 L7, 57 K4
Noosa Heads Qld 117 H1, 118 F10, 123 N7
Noosa NP Qld 117 H2, 118 F10, 123 N7
Noosaville Qld 117 G1, 118 F10
Nora Creina SA 71 E10
Noradjuha Vic. 60 F10
Norah Head NSW 13 F7, 19 B12, 25 L5
Norahville NSW 13 F7, 19 B12
Noranda WA xxiv N1, xxv A2
Nords Wharf NSW 13 F5, 19 C11
Norlane Vic. 44 B2
Norman Park Qld xxxi I9
Normanhurst NSW 12 E5, 15 L6
Normanton Qld 126 D7, 129 G4
Normanville SA 68 C7, 69 G10, 71 B4, 73 I10
Normanville Vic. 61 M5
Nornakin WA 88 F5
Nornalup WA 87 G6, 88 E12
Norseman WA 91 I7
North Adelaide SA xxi J3, 65 C4, 66 C7, 67 B8, 68 F2
North Arm Qld 117 F2, 118 E11
North Arm Cove NSW 19 G7, 20 C11
North Balgowlah NSW xi K2
North Beach SA 69 E2, 72 H6
North Beach WA xxiv A1
North Bendigo Vic. 48 D1
North Bondi NSW ix L7, 12 G8, 13 C12, 15 M9
North Bourke NSW 31 M5
North Cremorne NSW xi I7, 11 H1
North Dandalup WA 85 D9, 88 C6, 90 C8
North Fremantle WA xxiv B11, 84 C7, 85 B6

North Haven NSW 20 F7, 27 M12
North Haven SA 66 B5, 67 A7
North Hobart Tas. xxxiv E10, 1 A6, 136 A3, 137 D7
North Jindong WA 86 B7
North Lake WA xxiv F12
North Lilydale Tas. 143 K7, 145 H7
North Maclean Qld 114 D11, 115 D7
North Manly NSW xi M1
North Melbourne Vic. xiv H9, xvii I1, 39 A3
North Motton Tas. 142 G6, 144 F1
North Perth WA xxiv F4
North Pinjarra WA 85 D9, 88 C6
North Plympton SA xx E8
North Richmond NSW 14 H4, 17 N6
North Rothbury NSW 19 A6, 25 L3
North Ryde NSW x B3
North Scottsdale Tas. 143 M6
North Shields SA 72 D8
North Shore Vic. 44 B3
North Star NSW 26 H3, 123 I12
North Sydney NSW viii G1, x G8, 11 C6, 12 F7, 15 M8
North Tamborine Qld 115 E9, 116 B4, 123 N10
North Tumbulgum NSW 116 F12
North Willoughby NSW x G3
North Wollongong NSW 22 F7, 23 F5
Northam WA 85 G2, 88 D4, 90 C7
Northampton WA 89 D12, 90 A3
Northbridge NSW x H5
Northbridge WA xxiv F5, 83 C4
Northcliffe WA 86 H12, 87 C4, 88 D11, 90 C11
Northcote Vic. xv O4
Northdown Tas. 142 H6, 145 B6
Northfield SA 66 C5, 67 B8, 68 F1
Northgate Qld xxxi L1
Northmead NSW 12 C5, 13 A11, 15 J7
Northumberland Islands NP Qld 119 H8, 125 L6
Northwood NSW x D7
Norval Vic. 61 I12, 63 I2
Norwin Qld 123 K9
Norwood SA xxi L5
Norwood Tas. 145 H3
Notley Hills Tas. 143 J7, 145 F9
Notting WA 88 G5, 90 E8
Notts Well SA 71 E1, 73 M8
Novar Gardens SA xx D9
Nowa Nowa Vic. 53 O5
Nowendoc NSW 20 B6, 27 J11
Nowendoc NP NSW 20 A5, 27 J11
Nowie North Vic. 59 L12, 61 L1
Nowingi Vic. 28 E7, 58 G8
Nowley NSW 26 E5
Nowra NSW 23 D9, 25 I10, 35 G4, 37 O1
Nowra Hill NSW 23 C10, 25 I10, 35 G4, 37 O1
Nturiya NT 108 H4
Nubba NSW 24 D8, 35 B2
Nubeena Tas. 139 L8, 141 L8
Nudgee Qld 114 F6, 115 E3, 117 F10
Nug Nug Vic. 55 J9, 56 H7
Nuga Nuga NP Qld 122 G2
Nugent Tas. 139 M3, 141 M6
Nuggetty Vic. 49 E5, 61 N11
Nulkaba NSW 13 E2, 19 A8
Nullagine WA 92 F3, 97 L7
Nullan Vic. 60 H8
Nullarbor NP SA 80 E6, 91 P5
Nullarbor Roadhouse SA 80 G6
Nullawarre Vic. 50 E9, 62 H9
Nullawil Vic. 28 G11, 61 K5
Numbla Vale NSW 35 B8, 36 E12, 51 D5
Numbugga NSW 35 D9, 37 I12, 51 H6
Numbulwar NT 105 L8
Numeralla NSW 35 D7, 36 H9, 51 F3
Numinbah NSW 116 B12
Numinbah Valley Qld 21 G1, 27 O1, 115 E11, 116 B9
Numurkah Vic. 29 K12, 54 F5, 56 A1
Nunamara Tas. 143 L8
Nunawading Vic. 41 A8
Nundah Qld xxxi K1, 114 E6
Nundle NSW 27 I10
Nundroo Roadhouse SA 81 J7
Nunga Vic. 28 E9, 58 H11
Nungarin WA 88 G2, 90 E6

Nungurner Vic. 53 N6
Nunjikompita SA 72 A1, 81 N9
Nurcoung Vic. 60 E9
Nurina WA 91 N5
Nurinda Qld 117 A5, 118 C12
Nuriootpa SA 67 F4, 71 C1, 73 K8
Nurom SA 73 I4, 74 H12
Nurrabiel Vic. 60 F10
Nutfield Vic. 40 F3, 41 A5, 43 K4, 52 D3
Nyabing WA 88 G8, 90 E9
Nyah Vic. 28 G9, 59 L11, 61 L1
Nyah West Vic. 28 G9, 59 L11, 61 L1
Nyarrin Vic. 28 F9, 59 I12, 61 I2
Nyirripi NT 108 D5
Nymagee NSW 31 M11
Nymboi–Binderay NP NSW 21 C10, 27 M7
Nymboida NSW 21 C10, 27 M6
Nymboida NP NSW 21 B8, 27 L5
Nyngan NSW 31 O10
Nyora Vic. 43 M10, 52 F7
Nypo Vic. 28 D10, 60 F4

Oak Beach Qld 120 D1, 121 E5, 127 L5
Oak Flats NSW 23 F6
Oak Forest Qld 121 E6
Oakbank SA 66 F8, 67 D9, 68 H3
Oakdale NSW 14 E11, 23 D1, 25 J7, 35 G1
Oakey Qld 123 K9
Oakey Creek NSW 26 F11
Oaklands NSW 29 M10, 55 I3
Oaklands SA 69 E7, 72 H9
Oakleigh Vic. 40 E7, 43 J6, 52 C5
Oaks Tas. 143 J9, 145 F11
Oakvale Vic. 28 G11, 61 L5
Oakwood Tas. 139 M8, 141 M9
Oasis Roadhouse Qld 120 A8, 127 J10
Oatlands Tas. 141 K3
Oatley NSW 12 D9, 15 K10
Ob Flat SA 62 A5, 71 G12
Oberne NSW 24 C10, 36 A3, 55 O3
Oberon NSW 24 H6
Obley NSW 24 F2
Obx Creek NSW 21 D9, 27 M6
Ocean Grove Vic. 42 G9, 44 C6, 50 H2, 52 A7, 63 O8
Ocean Shores NSW 21 H3, 27 O2, 123 N11
Ockley WA 88 F7
O'Connor WA xxiv D11
Oenpelli NT 103 P2, 104 H4
Officer Vic. 40 H9, 41 C11, 43 L8, 45 O3, 52 E6
Ogilvie WA 89 D11, 90 A2
Ogmore Qld 125 L9
Olary SA 73 N1, 75 M9
Old Adaminaby NSW 35 B7, 36 E7, 51 D2
Old Bar NSW 20 E8, 25 O1, 27 L12
Old Beach Tas. xxxiv E1, 137 B2, 139 I4, 141 K6
Old Bonalbo NSW 21 D4, 27 M3, 123 M12
Old Bowenfels NSW 14 B2, 16 C3
Old Farm Tas. 137 B9
Old Junee NSW 24 C9, 29 P9
Old Noarlunga SA 66 B11, 67 A11, 68 E5, 69 H8, 71 B4, 73 J10
Old Owen Springs NT 110 G5
Old Tallangatta Vic. 55 M7, 57 K3
Old Tyabb Vic. 45 L7
Old Warrah NSW 26 H11
Oldina Tas. 142 E5
Olinda NSW 25 I3
Olinda Vic. 40 G6, 41 B9, 43 L6, 52 E5
Olio Qld 131 L6
Olympic Dam Village SA 74 E3
O'Malley SA 80 G4
Ombersley Vic. 42 C8, 50 D1, 63 M7
Omeo Vic. 53 M1, 55 M12, 57 M11
Ondit Vic. 42 B8, 50 C1, 63 L8
One Arm Point WA 94 H5, 98 C8
One Tree NSW 29 J6
Ongerup WA 88 H9, 90 F10
Onkaparinga River NP SA 66 B11, 67 B11, 68 E4, 69 H8, 71 B3, 73 J10
Onslow WA 89 C2, 96 A8
Oodla Wirra SA 73 K3, 75 J10
Oodnadatta SA 76 B6
Oolambeyan NP NSW 29 K8

Ooldea SA 81 I3
Oombulgurri WA 95 N3, 99 L4
Oonah Tas. 142 E6, 144 B1
Oondooroo Qld 131 L7
Oonoonba Qld 119 A1, 120 G10
Oorindi Qld 129 G11, 131 I3
Ootann Qld 120 A4, 127 J7
Ootha NSW 24 C3, 29 P3
Opalton Qld 131 K9
Ophir NSW 24 G4
Opossum Bay Tas. 139 J7, 141 K8
Ora Banda WA 90 H4
Orange NSW 24 G4
Orange Grove WA xxv H10, 84 F7, 85 D5
Orangeville NSW 14 F10, 25 J7, 35 G1
Oranmeir NSW 24 G12, 35 E6, 37 J6
Orbost Vic. 35 A12, 51 B11
Orchid Beach Qld 118 H3, 123 O4
Orford Tas. 139 N2, 141 M5
Orford Vic. 62 F7
Organ Pipes NP Vic. 40 C4, 42 H4, 52 B3, 63 P5
Orielton Tas. 139 K3, 141 L6
Orient Point NSW 23 E10, 37 P1
Ormeau Qld 114 G12, 115 F7, 116 C1
Ormiston Qld 114 H8, 115 F5, 117 H12
Orpheus Island NP Qld 120 F8, 127 N10
Orroroo SA 73 J3, 75 I10
Orrtipa–Thurra NT 109 M5
Orton Park NSW 24 H5
Osborne SA 66 B5, 67 A7, 69 H7
Osborne Park NSW x E6
Osborne Park WA xxiv D3
Osbornes Flat Vic. 55 K7, 57 I4
Osmaston Tas. 143 I8, 145 D11
Osmington WA 86 C8, 88 B10
Osterley Tas. 141 I3
Otago Tas. xxxiv E2, 137 C4, 139 I4, 141 K7
Otford NSW 23 H3
Otway NP Vic. 42 A12, 50 B6, 63 K11
Oura NSW 24 C9, 29 P9, 55 N1
Ourimbah NSW 13 D7, 15 O2, 25 L5
Ournie NSW 24 C12, 36 A6, 55 O5, 57 O1
Ouse Tas. 141 I4
Outer Harbor SA 66 B4, 67 A7, 69 H6, 71 B2, 73 J8
Outtrim Vic. 43 M11, 52 F8
Ovens Vic. 55 J9, 56 H6
Overland Corner SA 28 A5, 71 F1, 73 N7
Overlander Roadhouse WA 89 D9
Ovingham SA xx H2, 65 B2, 67 B8, 68 F2
Owanyilla Qld 118 D6, 123 M5
Owen SA 67 B2, 69 H4, 71 B1, 73 J7
Owens Gap NSW 25 K1, 26 H12
Oxenford Qld 115 F8, 116 D3
Oxley NSW 29 I6, 59 O6
Oxley Qld 114 D8, 115 D5, 117 E12
Oxley Vic. 55 I8, 56 F5
Oxley Wild Rivers NP NSW 20 C3, 21 A12, 27 K9
Oyster Cove Tas. 138 H8, 141 J8
Ozenkadnook Vic. 60 C10, 71 H9

Paaratte Vic. 50 F9, 63 I9
Pacific Palms NSW 20 E10, 25 N3
Packsaddle Roadhouse NSW 30 D6, 75 P4
Paddington NSW viii H7, 10 H11, 31 K11
Paddington Qld xxx M10, 114 E7, 115 D4, 117 F11
Padthaway SA 71 F8
Pagewood NSW viii G12
Paignie Vic. 28 D8, 58 G11
Painswick Vic. 49 C3, 61 M10
Pakenham Vic. 40 H9, 41 C11, 43 L8, 45 O3, 52 E6
Pakenham South Vic. 45 P4
Pakenham Upper Vic. 45 P2
Palana Tas. 140 A9
Palgarup WA 86 H9, 87 B1, 88 D10
Pallamallawa NSW 26 G4
Pallara Qld 115 D5, 117 F12
Pallarenda Qld 119 A1, 120 G10, 124 G1, 127 N11
Palm Beach NSW 12 H3, 13 C10, 15 N5, 25 K6
Palm Beach Qld 21 H2, 27 O1, 115 G11, 116 F9
Palm Cove Qld 120 D2, 121 F6, 127 L5
Palm Dale NSW 15 O1
Palm Grove NSW 13 D7, 15 N1

Palmdale NSW 13 D7
Palmer SA 67 G8, 71 D3, 73 K9
Palmer River Roadhouse Qld 127 K4
Palmers Island NSW 21 F8, 27 N5
Palmers Oakey NSW 24 H4
Palmerston NT 102 D3, 104 D4
Palmerston Rocks NP Qld 120 E4, 121 G12, 127 M7
Palmgrove NP Qld 122 H3
Palmwoods Qld 117 F4, 118 E11
Palmyra WA xxiv D11
Paloona Tas. 142 H6, 144 G2
Paluma Qld 120 E9, 127 M11
Paluma Range NP Qld 120 E9, 127 M10
Pambula NSW 35 E10, 51 H7
Pambula Beach NSW 35 E10, 51 H7
Pampas Qld 123 K9
Panitya Vic. 28 B9, 58 B11, 60 B1, 71 H4, 73 O10
Panmure Vic. 50 E7, 62 H8
Pannawonica WA 89 E2, 92 A3, 96 D7
Panorama SA xxi I12
Panorama Heights Tas. 145 C4
Pantapin WA 88 F4
Panton Hill Vic. 40 G4, 41 A6, 43 K4
Paper Beach Tas. 145 F8
Pappinbarra NSW 20 E5
Papunya NT 108 F6
Para Hills SA 66 D5, 67 C7
Paraburdoo WA 89 G4, 92 C5, 96 G11
Parachilna SA 70 A7, 74 H5
Paradise Tas. 142 H8, 144 G4, 145 A9
Paradise Vic. 42 B12, 50 B5, 61 J10, 63 L10
Paradise Beach Vic. 53 L7
Paradise Point Qld 27 O1, 115 G8, 116 F3
Paradise Waters Qld 116 F6
Parafield SA 66 D5, 67 C7
Parafield Gardens SA 67 B7
Parap NT xxvii B8
Paraparap Vic. 42 E9, 50 F2, 63 N8
Parattah Tas. 141 L4
Pardoe Downs Tas. 145 D2
Pardoo Roadhouse WA 92 E1, 94 E11, 97 K2
Parenna Tas. 141 P11
Parilla SA 28 A9, 58 A11, 60 A1, 71 G4, 73 N10
Paringa SA 28 B5, 58 B5, 71 G1, 73 O7
Park Beach Tas. 139 L5
Park Holme SA xx F12
Parkdale Vic. 45 K1
Parkers Corner Vic. 52 H6
Parkerville WA 84 G4, 85 D4
Parkes ACT 32 D8
Parkes NSW 24 E4
Parkham Tas. 143 I7, 145 C9
Parkhurst Qld 125 M10
Parkside SA xxi K7, 65 G12
Parkville NSW 25 K1, 26 H12
Parkville Vic. xv I7, 39 B1
Parkwood WA xxv C11
Parndana SA 69 C11, 72 G11
Parnella Tas. 143 P8
Paroo–Darling NP NSW 30 G7, 31 I8
Parrakie SA 71 F4, 73 N10
Parramatta NSW 12 C6, 13 A12, 15 J8, 25 K6
Parrawe Tas. 142 E6, 144 B2
Paru 104 D3
Paruna SA 28 A7, 58 A8, 71 G2, 73 O8
Parwan Vic. 42 G4, 49 G12, 52 A4, 63 O5
Paschendale Vic. 62 D4
Pascoe Vale South Vic. xv I1
Paskeville SA 69 F3, 73 I6
Pata SA 28 A7, 58 A7, 71 G2, 73 N8
Patchewollock Vic. 28 D9, 58 G12, 60 G2
Pateena Tas. 143 K9, 145 G11
Paterson NSW 19 C6, 20 A11, 25 L3
Patersonia Tas. 143 L7
Patho Vic. 54 B5, 61 P6
Patonga NSW 12 H2, 13 C9, 15 N4
Patrick Estate Qld 115 A3, 117 B10
Patterson Lakes Vic. 45 K3
Patyah Vic. 60 C10, 71 H9
Paupong NSW 35 B8, 36 E11, 51 C5
Pawleena Tas. 139 L3, 141 L6
Pawtella Tas. 141 L3
Paxton NSW 13 D3

Payneham SA xxi M2
Payneham South SA xxi M3
Paynes Crossing NSW 13 B2, 25 K4
Paynes Find WA 89 H12, 90 D3
Paynesville Vic. 53 N6
Peaceful Bay WA 87 G6, 88 E12, 90 D11
Peachester Qld 117 F5, 118 E12
Peak Charles NP WA 90 H8
Peak Crossing Qld 114 A11, 115 B7, 123 M10
Peak Downs Qld 119 D11, 125 I8
Peak Hill NSW 24 E2, 116 G10
Peak Hill WA 89 H7, 92 E8
Peak Range NP Qld 119 C12, 124 H8, 125 I9
Peak View NSW 35 D7, 36 H8, 51 G2
Peake SA 71 E4, 73 M10
Pearcedale Vic. 40 F10, 43 K9, 45 L5, 52 D7
Pearl Beach NSW 12 H2, 13 C9, 15 N4
Pearshape Tas. 141 O12
Peats Ridge NSW 13 C7, 15 N1, 25 K5
Pebbly Beach NSW 25 I12, 35 F6, 37 M6
Peebinga SA 28 B8, 58 B9, 71 H3, 73 O9
Peechelba Vic. 29 M12, 55 I6, 56 E2
Peechelba East Vic. 55 I6, 56 E2
Peel NSW 24 H5
Peelwood NSW 24 G7, 35 E1
Pegarah Tas. 141 P11
Pekina SA 73 J3, 75 I10
Pelaw Main NSW 13 F2, 19 B8
Pelham Tas. 138 G1, 141 J5
Pella Vic. 28 D11, 60 F4
Pelverata Tas. 138 G7, 141 J8
Pemberton WA 86 H11, 87 B3, 88 D11, 90 C11
Pembroke NSW 20 F6, 27 L11
Penarie NSW 28 H7, 59 M7
Penderlea NSW 35 B8, 36 D10, 51 C4
Pendle Hill NSW 12 B6, 15 J7
Penguin Tas. 142 G6
Pennant Hills NSW 12 D5, 13 A11, 15 K7
Penneshaw SA 69 F11, 71 A5, 73 I11
Pennyroyal Vic. 42 C10, 50 D3, 63 M9
Penola SA 62 A2, 71 G10
Penong SA 81 K8
Penrice SA 67 F4
Penrith NSW 14 H6, 17 M11, 25 J6
Penrose NSW 23 A7, 25 I9, 35 F3
Penshurst NSW 15 K10
Penshurst Vic. 62 G5
Pentland Qld 124 D3, 131 P3
Penwortham SA 73 J6
Penzance Tas. 139 N8, 141 M8
Peppermint Grove WA xxiv C9, 86 D5, 88 B9
Peppers Plains Vic. 28 D12, 60 G6
Peppimenarti NT 95 P2, 99 P1, 104 C8
Percy Isles NP Qld 125 M7
Percydale Vic. 61 K11, 63 K1
Peregian Beach Qld 117 H2, 118 F10, 123 N7
Perekerten NSW 28 H8, 59 N10
Perenjori WA 90 C4
Perenna Vic. 28 C11, 60 E5
Pericoe NSW 35 D10, 51 G8
Perisher NSW 35 A8, 36 C10, 51 B4
Perkins Reef Vic. 49 E5, 61 N11, 63 N1
Peronne Vic. 60 C9
Perponda SA 71 E3, 73 M9
Perroomba SA 73 J3, 74 H10
Perry Bridge Vic. 53 L6
Perth Tas. 143 K9, 145 H11
Perth WA xxiv F6, 83, 84 D6, 85 C5, 88 C5, 90 C7
Perth Airport WA xxv E6
Perthville NSW 24 H5
Petcheys Bay Tas. 138 F9, 141 J9
Peterborough SA 73 K3, 75 I11
Peterborough Vic. 50 F10, 63 I9
Peterhead SA 67 A8, 68 E1
Petersham NSW viii A7
Petersville SA 69 F5, 73 I7
Petford Qld 120 B3, 127 K7
Petina SA 72 A2, 81 N9
Petrie Qld 114 D4, 115 D2, 117 F9
Petrie Terrace Qld 113 B3
Pheasant Creek Vic. 40 G2, 41 B4, 43 K3, 52 D3
Pialba Qld 118 F4

Piallaway NSW 26 H9
Piambie Vic. 28 G8, 59 K9
Piangil Vic. 28 G8, 59 L11
Piangil North Vic. 59 L11
Piawaning WA 88 C2, 90 C6
Pickering Brook WA 84 G7
Pickertaramoor NT 104 D3
Picnic Bay Qld 119 A1, 120 G10, 127 N11
Picnic Point NSW 29 J11, 54 D4
Picola Vic. 29 K12, 54 D5
Picola North Vic. 29 K12, 54 D5
Picton NSW 14 F12, 23 D2, 25 J7, 35 G1
Picton WA 86 E4
Pier Millan Vic. 28 F9, 59 I12, 61 I1
Piesseville WA 88 F7
Pigeon Hole NT 106 E4
Pigeon Ponds Vic. 60 E12, 62 E2
Piggabeen NSW 21 G2, 115 G11, 116 F10
Piggoreet Vic. 42 B4, 49 A12, 63 L5
Pikedale Qld 27 K2, 123 K11
Pilchers Bridge Vic. 49 G5, 54 A10, 61 O11
Pile Siding Vic. 42 A11, 50 B4
Pillar Valley NSW 21 E9, 27 N6
Pilliga NSW 26 D6
Pilot Hill NSW 24 D11, 35 A5, 36 C4, 55 P4
Pimba SA 74 E6
Pimpama Qld 114 G12, 115 F8, 116 D2
Pimpinio Vic. 60 F8
Pindar WA 89 E12, 90 B3
Pine Creek NT 103 I12, 104 F7
Pine Gap NT 111 I4
Pine Lodge Vic. 54 F7, 56 A3
Pine Point SA 69 F5, 71 A2, 73 I8
Pine Ridge NSW 24 F4, 26 G10
Pine Scrub Tas. 140 A9
Pinery SA 67 A2, 69 H4, 71 B1, 73 J7
Pingaring WA 88 H6, 90 F8
Pingelly WA 88 E6, 90 D8
Pingrup WA 88 H8, 90 F9
Pinjarra WA 85 D10, 88 C6, 90 C8
Pinkenba Qld xxxi O4
Pinnaroo SA 28 B9, 58 B11, 60 B1, 71 H4, 73 O10
Pioneer Tas. 143 N6
Pioneer Peaks NP Qld 119 F7, 125 K5
Pipalyatjara SA 78 C2, 93 P8, 108 B12
Pipeclay NP Qld 118 F8, 123 N6
Piper Islands NP Qld 128 E6
Pipers Brook Tas. 143 K6, 145 H6
Pipers River Tas. 143 K6, 145 G6
Pira Vic. 28 G9, 59 L12, 61 L1
Piries Vic. 43 P1, 52 H1, 54 H11, 56 D10
Pirlangimpi NT 104 C2
Pirlta Vic. 28 D6, 58 F7
Pirron Yallock Vic. 42 A9, 50 A2, 63 K8
Pithara WA 88 D1, 90 C5
Pitt Town NSW 12 B2, 15 I4, 17 P7
Pittong Vic. 42 B4, 63 K4
Pittsworth Qld 123 K9
Plainland Qld 117 A11
Pleasant Hills NSW 24 A10, 29 N10, 55 K2
Plenty Tas. 138 F3, 141 J6
Plenty Vic. 40 F4, 43 J4
Plympton SA xx F9
Plympton Park SA xx F10
Pmara Jutunta NT 109 I4
Poatina Tas. 143 J10
Point Addis Marine NP Vic. 42 E10, 50 G3, 63 O9
Point Clare NSW 13 D3, 15 N3
Point Cook Vic. 40 B7, 42 H6, 52 B5, 63 P6
Point Leo Vic. 40 E12, 43 J10, 45 J9, 52 C8
Point Lonsdale Vic. 40 A11, 42 G9, 44 E6, 52 B7, 63 P8
Point Lookout Qld 115 H4, 123 O9
Point Pass SA 73 K6
Point Piper NSW ix J5, xi K12
Point Samson WA 89 F1, 92 B2, 94 B12, 96 E4
Point Turton SA 69 D7, 72 G9
Pokataroo NSW 26 D4
Pokolbin NSW 13 D2
Police Point Tas. 138 G9, 141 J9
Policemans Point SA 71 D6, 73 L12
Pomborneit Vic. 50 A1, 63 K8
Pomborneit East Vic. 42 A9, 50 A1

Pomborneit North Vic. 50 A1
Pomona Qld 117 F1, 118 E10, 123 N7
Pomonal Vic. 60 H12, 62 H1
Pompapiel Vic. 61 N8
Pompoota SA 73 L9
Ponde SA 67 H9, 73 L9
Pontville Tas. 139 I3, 141 K6
Pontypool Tas. 141 N4
Poochera SA 72 B2, 74 A10, 81 O10
Poolaijelo Vic. 60 B12, 62 B1, 71 H10
Poona NP Qld 118 E6, 123 N5
Pooncarie NSW 28 F3, 59 I1
Poonindie SA 72 D8
Pooraka SA 67 B8, 68 F1, 69 H7
Pootilla Vic. 42 D3, 49 D10
Pootnoura SA 79 N9
Poowong Vic. 43 M10, 52 F7
Poowong East Vic. 43 N10, 52 F7
Popanyinning WA 88 E6
Popran NP NSW 12 F1, 13 C7, 15 M2, 25 K5
Porcupine Gorge NP Qld 124 C3, 131 O3
Porcupine Ridge Vic. 42 F1, 49 F8, 63 N2
Porepunkah Vic. 55 K9, 57 I7
Pormpuraaw Qld 126 E1, 128 A12
Porongurup SA 66 B6, 67 A8, 68 E1, 69 H7, 71 B3, 73 J9
Port Adelaide SA 66 B6, 67 A8, 68 E1, 69 H7, 71 B3, 73 J9
Port Albert Vic. 53 I10
Port Alma Qld 125 N11
Port Arthur Tas. 139 M9, 141 M9
Port Augusta SA 72 H2, 74 G9
Port Bellarine Vic. 44 E3
Port Bonython SA 72 H3, 74 G11
Port Broughton SA 69 F1, 73 I5, 74 G12
Port Campbell Vic. 50 F10, 63 I9
Port Campbell NP Vic. 50 G10, 63 J10
Port Clinton SA 69 F4, 71 A1, 73 I7
Port Davis SA 73 I4, 74 G11
Port Denison WA 90 A4
Port Douglas Qld 120 D1, 121 D4, 127 L5
Port Elliot SA 68 F8, 69 H10, 71 B5, 73 J11
Port Fairy Vic. 50 B8, 62 F8
Port Franklin Vic. 52 H10
Port Gawler SA 66 A3, 67 A6, 69 H6, 71 B2, 73 J8
Port Germein SA 73 I3, 74 G11
Port Gibbon SA 69 B2, 72 F6
Port Hedland WA 92 D1, 94 D11, 96 H3
Port Hughes SA 69 D3, 72 H6
Port Huon Tas. 138 F8, 141 I9
Port Julia SA 69 F6, 71 A2, 73 I8
Port Keats (Wadeye) NT 95 P2, 99 O2, 104 B8
Port Kembla NSW 23 F5, 25 J8, 35 H2
Port Kenny SA 72 B4, 81 O11
Port Latta Tas. 142 D4
Port Lincoln SA 72 D8
Port Macdonnell SA 62 A6, 71 G12
Port Macquarie NSW 20 G6, 27 M11
Port Melbourne Vic. xiv E12, xvi E5
Port Minlacowie SA 69 D7, 72 H9
Port Neill SA 72 E6
Port Noarlunga SA 66 A11, 67 A11, 68 E4, 69 H8, 71 B3, 73 J10
Port Pirie SA 73 I4, 74 H11
Port Rickaby SA 69 D6, 72 H8
Port Smith WA 94 G8, 98 A12
Port Sorell Tas. 143 I6, 145 C6
Port Victoria SA 69 D5, 72 H8
Port Vincent SA 69 F6, 71 A2, 73 I8
Port Wakefield SA 69 G4, 71 A1, 73 I7
Port Welshpool Vic. 52 H10
Port Willunga SA 67 A12, 68 E5
Portarlington Vic. 40 A9, 42 H8, 44 E3, 52 B6, 63 P7
Porters Retreat NSW 24 H7, 35 E1
Portland NSW 25 I5
Portland Vic. 62 D8
Portland Roads Qld 128 E7
Portsea Vic. 40 B11, 42 H9, 44 F7, 52 B7, 63 P8
Possession Island NP Qld 128 C2
Potato Point NSW 35 F7, 37 L9
Potts Point NSW viii H4, x H12, xi I11, 10 H7
Pottsville NSW 21 H3, 27 O2, 123 N11
Pound Creek Vic. 43 N12, 52 F9
Powelltown Vic. 41 F9, 43 N6, 52 F5

Powers Creek Vic. 60 C12, 62 C1, 71 H10
Powlett River Vic. 43 L12, 45 P12, 52 E9
Powranna Tas. 143 K9
Pozieres Qld 21 A3, 27 K2, 123 K11
Prahran Vic. xvii N8
Prairie Qld 124 C4, 131 O4
Prairie Vic. 29 I12, 54 A6, 61 O7
Pratten Qld 27 K1, 123 K10
Precipice NP Qld 123 I4
Premaydena Tas. 139 M8, 141 M8
Premer NSW 26 F10
Prenzlau Qld 117 B11
Preolenna Tas. 142 E5
Preston Tas. 142 G7, 144 F2
Preston Vic. xv P1, 40 D5, 43 J5, 52 C4
Preston Beach WA 85 C12, 88 B7, 90 C9
Prevelly WA 86 A9, 88 B10
Price SA 69 F4, 71 A1, 73 I7
Primbee NSW 23 F6
Primrose Sands Tas. 139 L5, 141 L7
Princes Hill Vic. xv K6
Princetown Vic. 50 G11, 63 J10
Priory Tas. 143 O7
Prooinga Vic. 28 F8, 59 J10
Propodollah Vic. 60 D6
Proserpine Qld 119 E5, 125 J4
Prospect SA xxi I1
Prospect Tas. 145 G10
Proston Qld 123 L6
Puckapunyal Vic. 54 D10
Pullabooka NSW 24 D5
Pullenvale Qld 114 C8, 115 C5, 117 E11
Pullut Vic. 28 D11, 60 F5
Punchbowl NSW 12 D8
Punchbowl Tas. 145 G3
Punthari SA 67 H8, 71 D3, 73 L9
Punyelroo SA 71 E2, 73 L8
Pura Pura Vic. 63 J5
Puralka Vic. 62 B5, 71 H12
Purfleet NSW 20 E8, 25 N1, 27 L12
Purga Qld 114 A10, 115 B6, 123 M9
Purlewaugh NSW 26 E10
Purnim Vic. 50 D7, 62 H7
Purnong SA 71 E3, 73 L9
Purnululu NP WA 95 O6, 99 M9, 106 A5
Purrumbete South Vic. 50 H8
Putty NSW 25 J4
Pyalong Vic. 54 C11
Pyap SA 28 A6, 58 A7, 71 G1, 73 N8
Pyengana Tas. 143 N7
Pygery SA 72 C3, 74 B11
Pymble NSW 12 E5, 13 B11, 15 L7
Pyramid Qld 120 E3, 121 F8
Pyramid Hill Vic. 29 I12, 61 N6
Pyrmont NSW viii E4, x E12, 10 A7

Quaama NSW 35 E8, 37 J11, 51 H5
Quairading WA 88 E5, 90 D7
Quakers Hill NSW 12 B4, 15 I6
Qualco SA 73 M7
Quambatook Vic. 28 G11, 61 L5
Quambone NSW 26 B8
Quamby Qld 129 E10, 130 G2
Quamby Brook Tas. 143 I9, 145 D11
Quandary NSW 24 B7, 29 P7
Quandialla NSW 24 D6
Quandong Roadhouse NSW 30 C11, 75 P9
Quantong Vic. 60 F9
Queanbeyan NSW 24 F11, 33 G7, 34 F6, 35 D5, 36 H3
Queens Domain Tas. xxxiv F10, 1 A6, 137 D7
Queens Park NSW ix J8
Queens Park WA xxv D8, 84 E7
Queenscliff NSW xi N3
Queenscliff Vic. 40 A10, 42 H9, 44 E6, 52 B7, 63 P8
Queensferry Vic. 45 O9
Queenstown Tas. 140 D1, 142 D11, 144 A10
Quellington WA 85 H3, 88 D4
Quilpie Qld 133 L5
Quindalup WA 86 B6
Quindanning WA 85 H12, 88 D7, 90 C9
Quinninup WA 87 C2, 88 D10, 90 C11
Quinns Rocks WA 84 B3, 85 B3, 88 B4, 90 B7

Quirindi NSW 26 H10
Quoiba Tas. 142 H6, 144 H1, 145 A6
Quoin Island NP Qld 128 F6
Quorn SA 73 I1, 74 H9
Quorrobolong NSW 13 E3, 19 A9

Rabbit Flat Roadhouse NT 106 C10
Raglan Qld 125 M11
Raglan Vic. 42 A1, 63 K3
Railton Tas. 142 H7, 144 H3, 145 B8
Rainbow Vic. 28 D11, 60 F5
Rainbow Beach Qld 118 F8, 123 N6
Rainbow Flat NSW 20 E8, 25 N2
Raleigh NSW 20 H1, 21 D12, 27 M8
Ramco SA 71 E1, 73 M7
Raminea Tas. 138 F10, 141 I10
Ramingining NT 105 K4
Ramornie NP NSW 21 C9, 27 M6
Ranceby Vic. 43 N10, 52 F8
Rand NSW 24 A11, 29 N11, 55 J3
Randwick NSW ix I10, 12 F8, 15 M9, 25 K7
Ranelagh Tas. 138 G6, 141 J8
Ranford WA 85 G10
Ranga Tas. 140 B10, 143 O1
Rankins Springs NSW 29 N5
Rannoch Tas. 145 C3
Rapid Bay SA 68 B8, 69 G10, 71 A5, 73 I11
Rapid Creek NT xxvii C4
Rappville NSW 21 E6, 27 N4
Rathdowney Qld 21 E2, 27 N1, 115 B11, 123 M11
Rathmines NSW 13 F4, 19 B10, 25 L4
Rathscar Vic. 49 A5, 61 L11
Raukkan SA 71 C5, 73 K11
Ravensbourne NP Qld 123 L9
Ravensdale NSW 13 D5
Ravenshoe Qld 120 D4, 121 D12, 127 L7
Ravensthorpe WA 90 G9
Ravenswood Qld 119 A4, 124 G3
Ravenswood Vic. 49 F4, 61 N11
Ravenswood South Vic. 49 F5, 54 A10, 61 O11
Ravensworth NSW 25 K2
Rawdon Vale NSW 20 B8, 25 M1, 27 J12
Rawlinna WA 91 L5
Raymond Terrace NSW 13 H2, 19 D7, 20 A12, 25 M4
Raywood Vic. 49 F1, 54 A7, 61 O9
Red Banks SA 73 K5
Red Beach Qld 128 B5
Red Bluff WA 89 B6, 99 I2
Red Cliffs Vic. 28 E6, 58 G6
Red Hill Qld xxx E5
Red Hill Vic. 40 D12, 43 I10, 45 I8, 52 C7
Red Hill South Vic. 40 D12, 43 I10, 45 I8
Red Hills Tas. 143 I8, 145 C10
Red Jacket Vic. 52 H4
Red Range NSW 27 K6
Red Rock NSW 21 E10, 27 N7
Redan Vic. 42 C3, 47 C9, 49 C10
Redbank Qld 114 C9, 115 C5, 117 D12
Redbank Vic. 61 K11
Redbank Plains Qld 114 B9, 115 C6, 117 D12
Redbanks SA 67 B4, 69 H5, 71 B1, 72 F6, 73 J8
Redcastle Vic. 54 C9
Redcliffe Qld 114 F4, 115 E2, 117 G9, 123 N9
Redcliffe WA xxv C5
Redesdale Vic. 49 H6, 54 B10, 61 P11, 63 P1
Redfern NSW viii F7, 12 F8, 13 B12, 15 L9
Redhead NSW 13 G4, 19 D10
Redhill SA 69 G1, 73 I5, 74 H12
Redland Bay Qld 114 H9, 115 F6, 123 N9
Redmond WA 87 C10, 88 G11
Redpa Tas. 142 B4
Reedy Creek Qld 115 F10, 116 E8
Reedy Creek SA 71 E9
Reedy Creek Vic. 41 A1, 43 K1, 52 D1, 54 D12
Reedy Dam Vic. 28 E11, 61 I5
Reedy Flat Vic. 53 O3
Reedy Marsh Tas. 143 I8, 145 D10
Reef Hills Park Vic. 54 G8
Reefton NSW 24 C7, 29 P7
Reekara Tas. 141 O10
Regans Ford WA 88 B3, 90 B6

Regatta Point Tas. 140 C2, 142 C12
Regents Park NSW 12 C7, 13 A12, 15 K9
Reid ACT 32 F4
Reid WA 80 A5, 91 O4
Reid River Qld 119 A3, 120 G12, 124 G2, 127 N12
Reids Creek Vic. 55 J7, 56 H4
Reids Flat NSW 24 F7, 35 D1
Reidsdale NSW 24 H11, 35 E5, 37 K5
Rekuna Tas. 139 J3, 141 K6
Relbia Tas. 143 K8, 145 H11
Reliance Creek NP Qld 119 G7, 125 K5
Remine Tas. 142 C10
Rendelsham SA 71 F11
Renison Bell Tas. 142 D9
Renmark SA 28 A5, 58 B5, 71 G1, 73 O7
Renner Springs NT 107 I7
Rennie NSW 29 M11, 54 H4
Renown Park SA xx H2
Repulse Islands NP Qld 119 F6, 125 K4
Research Vic. 40 F5, 41 A7
Reservoir Vic. 40 E5, 43 J5
Restoration Island NP Qld 128 E7
Retreat Tas. 143 K6, 145 H6
Revesby NSW 12 C9, 15 J10
Reynella SA 66 B10, 67 B10, 68 E4
Rheban Tas. 139 N2, 141 M6
Rheola Vic. 49 B2, 61 M9
Rhodes NSW 12 D7, 13 A12, 15 K8
Rhyll Vic. 43 K11, 45 M10, 52 D8
Rhymney Reef Vic. 61 I12, 63 I2
Rhyndaston Tas. 141 K5
Rhynie SA 71 B1, 73 J7
Riachella Vic. 61 I10
Rialto Qld 116 E7
Riana Tas. 142 F6, 144 E1
Rich Avon Vic. 61 I8
Richlands NSW 24 H8, 35 E2
Richlands Qld 115 D5, 117 E12
Richmond NSW 14 H4, 17 N7, 25 J6
Richmond Qld 131 L3
Richmond SA xx F6
Richmond Tas. 139 J3, 141 K6
Richmond Vic. xv N12, xvii M4, 40 D6, 43 J5, 52 C4
Richmond Range NP NSW 21 D4, 27 M3, 123 M12
Riddells Creek Vic. 40 B2, 42 H3, 52 B2, 63 P3
Ridgelands Qld 125 M10
Ridgetop Qld 116 D11
Ridgeway Tas. 137 B10, 139 I6
Ridgley Tas. 142 F6
Ridleyton SA xx G2
Riggs Creek Vic. 54 F8, 56 A6
Ringa WA 85 F2, 88 D4
Ringarooma Tas. 143 M7
Ringwood Vic. 40 F6, 41 A8, 43 K6, 52 D4
Ripley Qld 114 B10, 115 B6
Ripplebrook Vic. 43 N9, 52 F7
Rippleside Vic. 44 B3
Ripponlea Vic. xvii M12
Risdon Tas. xxxiv G3, 1 B1, 137 D4, 139 I4
Risdon Vale Tas. xxxiv H4, 1 E1, 137 F4, 139 J4, 141 K7
River Heads Qld 118 F5, 123 N4
Riverside Tas. 143 K8, 145 G9
Riverstone NSW 12 A3, 15 I6, 17 P9
Riverton SA 71 C1, 73 J7
Riverton WA xxiv H10, xxv B10
Rivervale WA xxv C7
Riverview NSW x C6
Riverview Qld 114 B9, 115 C5, 117 D12
Riverwood NSW 15 K10
Roadvale Qld 115 A8
Rob Roy Vic. 41 B6, 43 K4
Robb Jetty WA 84 C8
Robe SA 71 E9
Robertson NSW 23 D6, 25 J9, 35 G3
Robertstown SA 73 K6
Robigana Tas. 143 J7, 145 F8
Robina Qld 115 G10, 116 E7
Robinson River NT 107 N4
Robinvale Vic. 28 F7, 59 J8
Rocherlea Tas. 143 K8, 145 G9
Rochester SA 69 H1, 73 J5
Rochester Vic. 54 C7

Rochford Vic. 42 H1, 52 B1, 54 B12, 63 P3
Rock Flat NSW 35 C8, 36 G10, 51 F4
Rockbank Vic. 40 B5, 42 H5, 52 B4, 63 P5
Rockdale NSW 12 E9
Rockhampton Qld 125 M11
Rockingham WA 84 C11, 85 B7, 88 B6, 90 B8
Rocklea Qld 114 E8, 115 D5, 117 F12
Rockleigh SA 67 F9
Rockley NSW 24 H6
Rocklyn Vic. 42 E2, 49 D9, 63 N3
Rocksberg Qld 114 C2, 115 C1, 117 E7
Rocky Cape Tas. 142 D4
Rocky Cape NP Tas. 142 E4
Rocky Creek NSW 26 G6
Rocky Creek Qld 120 D3, 121 D9
Rocky Crossing Qld 125 K9
Rocky Dam NSW 27 I3, 123 I12
Rocky Glen NSW 26 E9
Rocky Gully WA 87 G2, 88 E10, 90 D11
Rocky Hall NSW 35 D10, 51 G7
Rocky Islets NP Qld 127 L1
Rocky River NSW 20 B1, 27 J8
Rocky River SA 69 A12, 72 F12
Rodd Point NSW viii A3, x A11
Roe Creek NT 111 I4
Roebourne WA 89 F1, 92 B2, 94 B12, 96 E5
Roebuck Roadhouse WA 94 H7, 98 B11
Roelands WA 86 E3
Roger River Tas. 142 C4
Roger River West Tas. 142 C5
Rokeby Tas. 137 H9, 139 J5, 141 K7
Rokeby Vic. 41 G12, 43 N8, 52 G6
Rokewood Vic. 42 C6, 63 L6
Rokewood Junction Vic. 42 B5, 63 L5
Roland Tas. 142 G7, 144 G4
Rolands Plains NSW 20 F5, 27 L10
Rolleston Qld 122 G1
Rollingstone Qld 120 F9, 127 M11
Roma Qld 122 G6
Romsey Vic. 42 H2, 52 B2, 54 B12, 63 P3
Rookhurst NSW 20 B8, 25 M1, 27 J12
Rookwood NSW 12 D7
Rooty Hill NSW 12 A5, 15 I7, 17 P11
Roper Bar Store NT 105 J9
Rorruwuy NT 105 M4
Rosa Glen WA 86 B9, 88 B10
Rosanna Vic. 40 E5
Rose Bay NSW ix L6, xi L12
Rose Bay Tas. xxxiv H9, 1 D5 , 137 F7
Rose Park SA xxi L6
Rosebery NSW viii F11
Rosebery Tas. 142 D9, 144 A7
Rosebrook NSW 19 B6, 20 A11
Rosebrook Vic. 50 B7, 62 G8
Rosebud Vic. 40 C12, 43 I10, 44 H8, 52 C7
Rosebud West Vic. 44 H8
Rosedale NSW 35 F6, 37 L7
Rosedale Qld 123 L2
Rosedale SA 66 G1, 67 D5
Rosedale Vic. 53 J7
Rosegarland Tas. 138 F2, 141 J6
Rosehill NSW 12 C6
Rosenthal NSW 19 H4, 20 C10, 25 N2
Roses Tier Tas. 143 M8
Rosetta Tas. 137 B4
Rosetta Tas. xxxiv A4
Rosevale Qld 123 M10
Rosevale Tas. 143 J8, 145 F9
Rosevears Tas. 143 J7, 145 F8
Roseville NSW x E1, 12 F6, 13 B11
Roseville Chase NSW x G1
Rosewall Vic. 44 B2
Rosewhite Vic. 55 K9, 57 I6
Rosewood NSW 24 C11, 36 A5, 55 O4
Rosewood Qld 115 A5, 117 B12, 123 M9
Roseworthy SA 67 D4, 71 C2, 73 J8
Roslyn NSW 24 G8, 35 E2
Roslynmead Vic. 29 I12, 54 B5, 61 P6
Rosny Tas. xxxiv H10, 1 D6, 137 E8
Rosny Park Tas. 1 E6, 137 F7, 139 J5, 141 K7
Ross Tas. 141 L2, 143 L12
Ross Creek Vic. 42 C4, 49 B11, 63 L4

Rossarden Tas. 143 M10
Rossbridge Vic. 63 I3
Rossi NSW 24 G11, 34 H7, 35 D5, 37 I4
Rosslyn Park SA xxi O5
Rossmore NSW 14 H9
Rossmoyne WA xxiv G10, xxv A11
Rossville Qld 127 L3
Rostrevor SA xxi P2, 66 D6, 67 C8, 68 G1
Rostron Vic. 61 J10
Rothbury NSW 13 E1, 19 A7, 25 L3
Rothwell Qld 114 F3, 115 E2, 117 F9
Rothwell Vic. 44 C1
Roto NSW 29 L3
Round Corner NSW 12 D4, 13 A10, 15 K6
Round Top Island NP Qld 119 G8, 125 K5
Rowella Tas. 143 J6, 145 F7
Rowena NSW 26 D5
Rowland Flat SA 66 H1, 67 E5
Rowsley Vic. 42 F4, 49 G12, 52 A4, 63 O5
Rowville Vic. 40 F7, 41 A9, 43 K6
Roxburgh NSW 25 K2
Roxby Downs SA 74 E4
Royal George Tas. 141 N1, 143 N11
Royal NP NSW 12 C11, 15 K12, 23 H1, 25 K7, 35 H1
Royalla NSW 24 F11, 33 E10, 34 E7, 35 D5, 36 H4
Royston Park SA xxi L2
Rozelle NSW viii C3, x C11
Ruabon WA 86 D6
Rubicon Vic. 41 H3, 43 N2, 52 G2, 54 G12, 56 C11
Ruby Vic. 43 N11, 52 F8
Rubyvale Qld 124 H10
Rudall SA 72 E5
Rudall River NP WA 92 H4, 93 I3, 97 P8
Ruffy Vic. 54 E10, 56 A8
Rufus River NSW 28 C5, 58 D5, 73 P7
Rugby NSW 24 F8, 35 C2
Rukenvale NSW 21 E3, 27 N2
Rules Point NSW 24 E12, 35 B6, 36 D5
Rum Jungle NT 102 E6
Rumula Qld 120 D1, 121 D4
Runaway Bay Qld 116 E4
Runcorn Qld 114 E9, 115 D5, 117 F12
Rundle Range NP Qld 125 N11
Running Creek Vic. 55 L8, 57 J6
Running Stream NSW 24 H4
Runnymede Tas. 139 K2, 141 L6
Rupanyup Vic. 60 H9
Rupanyup North Vic. 60 H8
Rupanyup South Vic. 60 H9
Rushcutters Bay NSW viii H5
Rushworth Vic. 54 D8
Russell ACT 32 G7
Russell Lea NSW viii A2, x A10
Russell River NP Qld 120 E3, 121 G10, 127 M7
Rutherglen Vic. 29 N12, 55 J6, 56 G1
Ryanby Vic. 59 K12, 61 K1
Ryans Creek Vic. 54 H9, 56 E6
Ryanston Vic. 45 P12
Rydal NSW 14 A2, 16 B2
Ryde NSW 12 E6, 13 A12, 15 L8
Rye Vic. 40 B12, 42 H10, 44 G8, 52 B7, 63 P9
Rye Park NSW 24 F8, 35 C2
Rylstone NSW 25 I3
Ryton Vic. 52 H9

Sackville North NSW 15 J3
Saddleworth SA 73 K6
Safety Bay WA 84 C11, 85 B8
Safety Beach NSW 21 E11, 27 N7
Safety Beach Vic. 40 D11, 43 I9, 45 I7, 52 C7
St Albans NSW 13 A6, 25 K5
St Albans Vic. 40 C5, 43 I5, 52 B4, 63 P5
St Albans Park Vic. 44 B4
St Andrews Vic. 40 G3, 41 B5, 43 K4, 52 D3
St Andrews Beach Vic. 44 G9
St Arnaud Vic. 61 K9
St Arnaud Range NP Vic. 61 K10
St Aubyn Qld 123 L8
St Clair NSW 19 A3, 25 L2
St Fillans Vic. 41 F5, 43 M4, 52 F3
St George Qld 122 F9
St Georges SA xxi M8
St Georges Basin NSW 23 C11, 25 I10, 35 G4, 37 O2

St Helena Island NP Qld 114 G6, 115 F4, 117 H11, 123 N9
St Helens Tas. 143 O8
St Helens Vic. 50 A7, 62 F7
St Ives NSW 12 F5, 13 B11, 15 L7
St James Vic. 54 G7, 56 C3
St James WA xxv B9
St Kilda SA 66 B4, 67 B7, 69 H6, 71 B2, 73 J8
St Kilda Vic. xvii K10, 40 D6, 43 I6, 52 C5
St Kilda East Vic. xvii N11
St Kilda West Vic. xvii K9
St Kitts SA 67 F3
St Lawrence Qld 119 H11, 125 K8
St Leonards NSW x F6, 11 A2, 12 F7, 15 L8
St Leonards Tas. 143 K8, 145 H10
St Leonards Vic. 40 B9, 42 H8, 44 F4, 52 B6, 63 P7
St Lucia Qld xxx E10
St Marys NSW 14 H7, 17 O11
St Marys Tas. 143 O9
St Morris SA xxi N4
St Patricks River Tas. 143 L7
St Pauls Qld 128 C1
St Peters NSW viii C10, 13 F1, 19 B7
St Peters SA xxi K3
Sale Vic. 53 K7
Salisbury NSW 19 C2, 20 A9, 25 L2
Salisbury SA 66 D4, 67 C7, 69 H6, 71 B2, 73 J8
Salisbury Vic. 28 C12, 60 E7
Salisbury West Vic. 49 D1, 61 N8
Sallys Flat NSW 24 H4
Salmon Gums WA 91 I8
Salmon Ponds Tas. 138 G3
Salt Ash NSW 19 E8, 20 B12
Salt Creek SA 71 E6
Salter Point WA xxiv G9, xxv A10
Salter Springs SA 67 C1, 69 H4, 71 B1, 73 J7
Saltwater River Tas. 139 L7, 141 L8
Samaria Vic. 54 H9, 56 D7
Samford Qld 114 C5, 115 C3, 117 E10
Samson WA xxiv D12
San Remo Vic. 43 K11, 45 N11, 52 D8
Sanctuary Cove Qld 115 F8, 116 E3, 123 N10
Sanctuary Point NSW 23 D11
Sandalwood SA 71 F3, 73 M9
Sandbanks NP Qld 128 F9
Sandergrove SA 68 H6, 71 C4
Sanderston SA 67 H7, 71 D2, 73 K8
Sandfire Roadhouse WA 94 F10, 97 N1
Sandfly Tas. 138 H6, 141 J8
Sandford Tas. 139 K6, 141 L7
Sandford Vic. 62 D3, 71 H11
Sandgate Qld 114 F5, 115 E3, 117 F10
Sandhill Tas. 145 G3
Sandhill Lake Vic. 28 H11, 61 M4
Sandigo NSW 24 A9, 29 N9
Sandilands SA 69 E5, 72 H8
Sandon Vic. 49 E7, 61 N12, 63 N2
Sandringham Vic. 40 D7, 43 J6, 45 J1, 52 C5
Sandsmere Vic. 28 B12, 60 C7, 71 H7
Sandstone WA 90 F1, 92 F12
Sandy Bay Tas. 1 B10, 136 D10, 137 D9, 139 I6, 141 K7
Sandy Beach NSW 21 E11, 27 N7
Sandy Creek SA 66 F2, 67 D5
Sandy Creek Vic. 55 L7, 57 J4
Sandy Creek Upper Vic. 55 L7, 57 J4
Sandy Flat NSW 21 A6, 27 L4
Sandy Hill NSW 21 B5, 27 L3, 123 L12
Sandy Hollow NSW 25 J2
Sandy Point NSW 12 C9, 15 J10, 24 H10, 35 E4, 37 K2
Sandy Point Vic. 35 A11, 51 A10, 52 G10, 53 P4
Sangar NSW 29 M11, 54 H3
Santa Barbara Qld 115 F8, 116 E3
Santa Teresa (Ltyente Purte) NT 109 J7, 111 L6
Sapphire NSW 27 J5
Sapphire Qld 124 H10
Sapphiretown SA 69 E11, 72 H11
Sarabah NP Qld 21 F1, 27 N1, 115 D10, 123 N10
Saratoga NSW 13 D8, 15 O3
Sarina Qld 119 G8, 125 K6
Sarina Beach Qld 119 G8, 125 K6
Sarsfield Vic. 53 N5

Sassafras NSW 23 A11, 25 I10, 35 F4, 37 M2
Sassafras Tas. 142 H7, 145 B7
Sassafras Vic. 41 B9
Sassafras East Tas. 143 I7, 145 C7
Saunders Islands NP Qld 128 E5
Savage River Tas. 142 C8
Savage River NP Tas. 142 D6, 144 A1
Savenake NSW 29 M11, 54 H4
Sawmill Settlement Vic. 53 I1, 55 I11, 56 F10
Sawpit Creek NSW 36 D9, 51 C3
Sawtell NSW 20 H1, 21 E12, 27 N8
Sawyers Valley WA 84 H5, 85 E4
Sayers Lake NSW 28 G1, 30 F12
Scaddan WA 91 I9
Scamander Tas. 143 O8
Scarborough NSW 23 G3, 25 J8, 35 H2
Scarborough Qld 114 F3, 115 E2, 117 G9
Scarborough WA xxiv A3, 84 C5, 85 B5, 88 B5, 90 B7
Scarsdale Vic. 42 B4, 49 B11, 63 L4
Sceale Bay SA 72 A3, 81 N11
Scheyville Vic. 12 B2, 15 J5
Scheyville NP NSW 12 B2, 15 J4, 25 J6
Schofields NSW 12 A4, 15 I6, 17 P10
School Hill Vic. 45 I9
Scone NSW 25 K1, 26 H12
Scotsburn Vic. 42 D4, 49 C11, 63 M4
Scott NP WA 86 C10, 88 B10, 90 B11
Scotts Creek Vic. 50 G9, 63 J9
Scotts Head NSW 20 G3, 27 M9
Scottsdale Tas. 143 M6
Scottville Qld 119 C5, 125 I4
Sea Elephant Tas. 141 P11
Sea Lake Vic. 28 F10, 61 J3
Seabird WA 88 B3
Seacliff SA 66 B9, 67 B10, 68 E3, 71 B3
Seacombe Vic. 53 L7
Seaford SA 66 A11, 67 A11, 68 E5
Seaford Vic. 40 E9, 43 J8, 45 K3, 52 D6
Seaforth NSW xi K3
Seaforth Qld 119 F7, 125 K5
Seaforth WA 84 F8
Seaham NSW 13 H1, 19 D6, 20 A11, 25 M3
Seahampton NSW 13 F3, 19 C9
Seal Rocks NSW 20 E10, 25 N3
Seaspray Vic. 53 K8
Seaton SA xx C1
Seaton Vic. 53 J6
Seaview Vic. 43 N10, 52 G7
Seawinds Vic. 44 H8
Sebastian Vic. 49 F2, 61 O9
Sebastopol NSW 24 C8, 29 P8
Sebastopol Vic. 42 C3, 47 C12, 49 C10
Second Valley SA 68 B8, 69 G10, 71 A4, 73 I11
Sedan SA 67 H5, 71 D2, 73 L8
Seddon Vic. xiv C9, xvi C1
Sedgwick Vic. 49 G4, 54 A9, 61 O11
Seelands NSW 21 D8, 27 M5
Seisia Qld 128 C3
Selbourne Tas. 143 J8, 145 E10
Selby Vic. 41 B9
Seldom Seen Roadhouse Vic. 35 A10, 51 A8, 53 P2, 55 P12, 57 P11
Sellheim Qld 120 F12, 124 F2
Sellicks Beach SA 68 D6, 69 H9, 71 B4, 73 J10
Semaphore SA 66 B5, 67 A8, 68 E1
Separation Creek Vic. 42 C11, 50 D5, 63 M10
Seppeltsfield SA 67 E4, 73 K8
Serpentine Vic. 61 N8
Serpentine WA 84 F11, 85 D8, 88 C6
Serpentine NP WA 84 F11, 85 D8, 88 C6, 90 C8
Serviceton Vic. 28 B12, 60 B7, 71 H7
Seven Hills Qld xxxi K9
Seven Mile Beach Tas. 139 K5, 141 L7
Seven Mile Beach NP NSW 23 E9, 25 J9, 35 H3, 37 P1
Sevenhill SA 69 H2, 73 J6
Seventeen Seventy Qld 123 M1
Severnlea Qld 21 A3, 27 K2, 123 K11
Seville Vic. 40 H6, 41 C8, 43 L5, 52 E4
Sexton Hill NSW 116 H11
Seymour Tas. 143 O10
Seymour Vic. 54 D10

Shackleton WA 88 F4
Shadforth NSW 24 G5
Shady Creek Vic. 43 O8, 52 G6
Shannon Tas. 141 I2, 143 I11
Shannon WA 87 D3, 88 D11, 90 D11
Shannon NP WA 87 D3, 88 D11, 90 D11
Shannons Flat NSW 24 F12, 34 B12, 35 C6, 36 F7, 51 E1
Shay Gap WA 92 E1, 94 E11, 97 L3
Shays Flat Vic. 61 J11, 63 J1
Sheans Creek Vic. 54 F9, 56 B7
Shearwater Tas. 145 C6
Sheep Hills Vic. 28 E12, 60 H7
Sheffield Tas. 142 H7, 144 H3, 145 A8
Shelbourne Vic. 49 E4, 61 N10
Shelford Vic. 42 D7, 63 M6
Shelley Vic. 55 N7, 57 M3
Shelley WA xxiv H9, xxv B10
Shellharbour NSW 23 F6, 25 J9, 35 H3
Shelly Beach Tas. 139 N2, 141 M5
Shenton Park WA xxiv D6, 84 D6
Sheoaks Vic. 42 E6, 63 N6
Shepherds Flat Vic. 42 E1, 49 E8, 63 N2
Shepparton Vic. 54 E7
Sherbrooke Vic. 41 B9
Sheringa SA 72 C6
Sherlock SA 71 E4, 73 M10
Sherwood Qld xxx C12
Sherwood WA 84 F8
Shipley NSW 14 C5, 16 E7
Shirley Vic. 63 J3
Shoal Bay NSW 19 H8, 20 C12, 25 N4
Shoal Point Qld 119 G7, 125 K5
Shoalhaven Heads NSW 23 E9, 25 J10, 35 H4, 37 P1
Shooters Hill NSW 24 H6
Shoreham Vic. 40 D12, 43 J10, 45 J9, 52 C8
Shorncliffe Qld 114 F5, 115 E3, 117 F10
Shotts WA 86 H3
Shute Harbour Qld 119 F5, 125 K3
Sidmouth Tas. 143 J6, 145 F7
Sidonia Vic. 49 H7, 54 B11, 61 P12, 63 P2
Sierra Gardens NSW 116 D11
Silkwood Qld 120 E5, 127 M8
Silvan Vic. 40 H6, 41 C8, 43 L6
Silver Creek Vic. 55 J7, 56 H4
Silver Sands SA 68 D6, 69 H9
Silverdale NSW 14 F8, 25 J7, 35 H1
Silverleaves Vic. 45 L10
Silverton NSW 30 B10, 75 N8
Silverwater NSW 13 F5, 19 B11
Simmie Vic. 54 C6
Simpson Vic. 50 H9, 63 J9
Simpson Desert NP Qld 76 H1, 77 I1, 109 P9, 130 C12, 132 B1
Simpsons Bay Tas. 139 I10, 141 K9
Single NP NSW 27 J6
Singleton NSW 25 K3
Singleton WA 85 C8, 88 B6, 90 C8
Sir Charles Hardy Group NP Qld 128 F5
Sir James Mitchell NP WA 87 C2, 88 D10, 90 C11
Sisters Beach Tas. 142 E4
Sisters Creek Tas. 142 E4
Skenes Creek Vic. 42 B12, 50 C5, 63 L10
Skenes Creek North Vic. 42 B12, 50 C5, 63 L10
Skipton Vic. 42 A4, 63 K4
Skye SA xxi P5
Slacks Creek Qld 114 F10, 115 E6
Slade Point Qld 119 G7, 125 K5
Slaty Creek Vic. 61 K8
Smeaton Vic. 42 D1, 49 D8, 63 M3
Smiggin Holes NSW 35 B8, 36 D10, 51 B4
Smith Islands NP Qld 119 G6, 125 K4
Smithfield Qld 27 I2, 123 J11
Smithfield SA 66 D3, 67 C6
Smithfield Heights Qld 120 D2, 121 F6, 127 L6
Smiths Beach Estate Vic. 45 L11
Smiths Gully Vic. 41 B6, 43 K4, 52 D3
Smiths Lake NSW 20 E10, 25 N3
Smithton Tas. 142 C4
Smithtown NSW 20 G4, 27 M10
Smithville SA 28 A9, 71 F4, 73 N10
Smoko Vic. 55 L10, 57 J8
Smoky Bay SA 81 M9

Smythesdale Vic. 42 C4, 49 B11, 63 L4
Snake Range NP Qld 124 H12
Snake Valley Vic. 42 B3, 49 A11, 63 L4
Snobs Creek Vic. 41 H2, 43 O2, 52 G2, 54 G12, 56 C11
Snowtown SA 69 G2, 73 I6
Snowy River NP Vic. 35 A10, 51 B8, 53 P3, 55 P12, 57 P11
Snug Tas. 139 I7, 141 K8
Snuggery SA 71 F11
Sodwalls NSW 14 A2, 16 A3
Sofala NSW 24 H4
Somers Vic. 40 E12, 43 J10, 45 K9, 52 D8
Somersby NSW 13 C7, 15 N2
Somerset Tas. 142 F5
Somerset Dam Qld 117 C7
Somerton NSW 26 H9
Somerton Park SA xx C12
Somerville Vic. 40 F10, 43 J9, 45 L6, 52 D7
Sommariva Qld 122 C5, 133 P5
Sorell Tas. 139 K4, 141 L6
Sorrento Vic. 40 B11, 42 H9, 44 F7, 52 B7, 63 P8
South Arm Tas. 139 J7, 141 K8
South Bank Qld 113 C8
South Beach WA 84 C8
South Brisbane Qld xxx F8, 113 A8
South Bruny NP Tas. 138 G12, 139 I11, 141 J11
South Canberra ACT 33 E6
South Coogee NSW ix J12
South Cumberland Islands NP Qld 119 H7, 125 L5
South East Forest NP NSW 35 D10, 36 H12, 37 I11, 51 G6
South Forest Tas. 142 D4
South Fremantle WA xxiv B12
South Grafton NSW 21 D9
South Guildford WA xxv E4
South Gundagai NSW 24 D9, 35 A4, 36 C1, 55 P1
South Hedland WA 92 D1, 94 D12, 96 H3
South Hobart Tas. xxxiv C12 , 137 D9
South Johnstone Qld 120 E5, 121 G12, 127 M7
South Kilkerran SA 69 E5, 72 H7
South Kingsville Vic. xvi A4
South Kumminin WA 88 G5, 90 E7
South Launceston Tas. 145 G2
South Melbourne Vic. xvii J5, 39 C12
South Mission Beach Qld 120 E6, 127 M8
South Mount Cameron Tas. 143 N6
South Nietta Tas. 142 G7, 144 F3
South Norwood Tas. 145 H3
South Perth WA xxiv F7, xxv A8, 83 C12
South Plympton SA xx F10
South Riana Tas. 142 F6, 144 E1
South Springfield Tas. 143 L7
South Stirling WA 87 F8, 88 H10
South Townsville Qld 120 H3
South West Rocks NSW 20 H3, 27 M9
South Yaamba Qld 125 M10
South Yarra Vic. xvii M6, 40 D6
Southbank Vic. xv J12, xvii J3, 39 D9
Southbrook Qld 123 K9
Southend Qld 125 N12
Southend SA 71 E11
Southern Cross Vic. 50 C7, 62 G7
Southern Cross WA 90 F6
Southern Moreton Bay Islands NP Qld 114 H12, 115 G8, 116 F1, 123 N10
Southport Qld 21 G1, 115 G9, 116 F5
Southport Tas. 138 F12, 141 I10
Southwest NP Tas. 138 B5, 140 E7, 141 I10
Southwood NP Qld 122 H9, 123 I9
Spalding SA 69 H1, 73 J5, 75 I12
Spalford Tas. 142 G6, 144 G2
Spargo Creek Vic. 42 E2, 49 E9, 63 N3
Spearwood WA 84 D8, 85 C6
Speed Vic. 28 E9, 58 H12, 60 H2
Speewa Vic. 59 L12, 61 L1
Spencer NSW 13 B8, 15 L3
Spicers Creek NSW 24 G2
Spotswood Vic. xiv B12, xvi B5, 43 I6
Sprent Tas. 142 G6, 144 F2
Spreyton Tas. 142 H6, 144 H2, 145 A7
Spring Beach Tas. 139 N2, 141 M5
Spring Creek Qld 123 L10

Spring Hill NSW 24 G5
Spring Hill Qld xxx G6, 113 E2
Spring Hill Vic. 42 F1, 49 F8, 52 A1, 54 A12, 63 O2
Spring Ridge NSW 24 G1, 26 E12
Springbrook Qld 21 G2, 27 O1, 115 E11, 116 B11, 123 N11
Springbrook NP Qld 21 G2, 27 O1, 115 E11, 116 C10, 123 N11
Springdale NSW 24 C8
Springfield Qld 114 C9, 115 C6
Springfield SA xxi L11
Springfield Tas. 143 L7
Springhurst Vic. 55 I6, 56 G3
Springmount Vic. 42 D2, 49 D9
Springsure Qld 122 F1, 125 I12
Springton SA 67 F6, 71 C2, 73 K8
Springvale Vic. 40 F7, 43 J7, 45 L1, 50 E9, 52 D5, 62 H9
Springvale South Vic. 45 L1
Springwood NSW 14 F5, 17 K9, 25 J6
Springwood Qld 114 F9, 115 E6
Squeaking Point Tas. 145 C6
Staaten River NP Qld 126 F5
Stafford Qld xxx F1, 114 E6, 115 D4, 117 F10
Stafford Heights Qld xxx G1
Staghorn Flat Vic. 55 K7, 57 I3
Stamford Qld 124 A5, 131 M5
Stanage Qld 125 L8
Stanborough NSW 27 I6
Stanhope Vic. 54 D7
Stanley Tas. 142 D3
Stanley Vic. 55 K8, 56 H4
Stanmore NSW viii B7
Stannifer NSW 27 J6
Stannum NSW 27 K4
Stansbury SA 69 E7, 72 H9
Stanthorpe Qld 21 A3, 27 L2, 123 L11
Stanwell Qld 125 M11
Stanwell Park NSW 23 G3, 25 J8, 35 H2
Starcke NP Qld 127 K1, 128 H12
Statham WA 84 F6
Staughton Vale Vic. 42 F5, 63 N6
Stavely Vic. 62 H4
Staverton Tas. 142 G8, 144 F4
Stawell Vic. 61 I11, 63 I1
Steels Creek Vic. 40 H3, 41 C5, 43 L4
Steiglitz Qld 114 H11, 115 F7
Steiglitz Vic. 42 E6, 63 N6
Stenhouse Bay SA 69 B9, 72 G10
Stephens Creek NSW 30 C9, 75 O8
Stepney SA xxi L4
Steppes Tas. 141 J2, 143 J12
Stieglitz Tas. 143 P8
Stirling SA 66 E8, 67 C9, 68 G3
Stirling Vic. 53 N3
Stirling WA xxiv D2, 84 C5, 85 B5
Stirling North SA 73 I2, 74 G9
Stirling Range NP WA 87 C7, 88 G10, 90 E10
Stockdale Vic. 53 L5
Stockinbingal NSW 24 D8, 35 A2
Stockmans Reward Vic. 43 O4, 52 G3
Stockport SA 67 D2
Stockton NSW 13 H3, 18 F1, 19 D9, 20 A12
Stockwell SA 67 F3, 71 C1, 73 K8
Stockyard Hill Vic. 42 A3, 63 K4
Stokers Siding NSW 21 G3, 27 O2
Stokes Bay SA 69 C10, 72 G11
Stokes NP WA 90 H9
Stone Hut SA 73 J4, 74 H11
Stonefield SA 67 H3, 71 D1, 73 L7
Stonehenge NSW 27 K6
Stonehenge Qld 131 L12
Stonehenge Tas. 141 L4
Stoneville WA 84 G4, 85 E4, 91 I5
Stoneyford Vic. 50 A2, 63 K8
Stonor Tas. 141 K4
Stony Creek Vic. 43 O12, 52 G9
Stony Crossing NSW 28 H9, 58 F1, 59 M11, 75 P12
Stony Point Vic. 40 F12, 43 J10, 45 L8, 52 D7
Stony Rise Tas. 145 A3
Stonyfell SA xxi O6
Stoodley Tas. 142 H7, 144 H3, 145 A9
Store Creek NSW 24 G3

Stormlea Tas. 139 M9, 141 M9
Storys Creek Tas. 143 M9
Stotts Creek NSW 116 G12
Stowport Tas. 142 F5
Stradbroke Vic. 53 K8
Stradbroke West Vic. 53 K8
Strahan Tas. 140 C2, 142 C12
Strangways Vic. 49 E7
Stratford NSW 19 F1, 20 C9, 25 M2
Stratford Vic. 53 K6
Strath Creek Vic. 41 B1, 43 K1, 52 D1, 54 D12
Strathalbyn SA 67 E12, 68 H5, 71 C4, 73 K10
Strathallan Vic. 54 C6
Stratham WA 86 D5, 88 C8
Strathblane Tas. 138 F11, 141 I10
Strathbogie Vic. 54 F10, 56 B8
Strathdownie Vic. 62 B4, 71 H11
Strathewen Vic. 41 B5, 43 K3, 52 D3
Strathfieldsaye Vic. 49 G4, 54 A9, 61 O10
Strathgordon Tas. 140 F6
Strathkellar Vic. 62 F4
Strathlea Vic. 49 D6, 61 M12, 63 M1
Strathmerton Vic. 29 K11, 54 F4
Strathpine Qld 114 E5, 115 D3, 117 F10, 123 N9
Stratton WA xxv G1
Streaky Bay SA 72 A3, 81 N10
Streatham Vic. 63 J4
Strickland Tas. 141 I4
Stroud NSW 19 F4, 20 B10, 25 M3
Stroud Road NSW 19 F3, 20 B10, 25 M2
Struan SA 60 A11, 71 G9
Strzelecki Vic. 43 N10, 52 F7
Strzelecki NP Tas. 140 B11, 143 O1
Stuart Mill Vic. 61 K10
Stuart Park NT xxvii C9, 101 F4
Stuart Town NSW 24 G3
Stuarts Point NSW 20 G3, 27 M9
Stuarts Well NT 109 I8
Sturt NP NSW 30 B1, 75 P1, 77 O11, 132 G11
Subiaco WA xxiv E6, 85 C5
Success Harbour WA 84 C8
Sue City NSW 24 D12, 35 B6, 36 D6
Suffolk Park NSW 21 H4, 27 O3, 123 N12
Sugarloaf Qld 119 F5
Suggan Buggan Vic. 35 A9, 51 B7, 53 P1, 55 P11
Sulphur Creek Tas. 142 G5
Summer Hill NSW 13 B12, 15 L9
Summerfield Vic. 49 F1, 54 A7, 61 O9
Summerhill Tas. 145 E4
Summerland Vic. 45 K11
Summerleas Tas. 137 A12
Summertown SA 66 E8, 67 C9, 68 G2
Summervale NSW 31 O9
Sunbury Vic. 40 B3, 42 H3, 52 B3, 63 P4
Sunday Creek Vic. 43 J1, 54 D12
Sunderland Bay Estate Vic. 45 L11
Sundown NP Qld 27 K3, 123 K12
Sunny Cliffs Vic. 28 E6, 58 G6
Sunnybank Qld 114 E9, 115 D5, 117 F12
Sunnyside Tas. 142 H7, 145 B9
Sunnyside Vic. 55 M10, 57 L8
Sunnyvale SA 69 E3
Sunshine Vic. 40 C5, 43 I5
Sunshine Beach Qld 117 H1, 118 F10, 123 N7
Surat Qld 122 G7
Surf Beach NSW 37 L6
Surf Beach Estate Vic. 45 M11
Surfers Paradise Qld 21 G1, 27 O1, 115 G10, 116 F6, 123 N10
Surges Bay Tas. 138 F9, 141 I9
Surry Hills NSW viii G6, 10 E12
Surveyors Bay Tas. 138 G10, 141 J9
Sussex Inlet NSW 23 C12, 25 I10, 35 G4, 37 O3
Sutherland NSW 12 D10, 15 K11, 23 H1
Sutherlands SA 71 D1, 73 K7
Sutton NSW 24 F10, 33 G2, 34 F3, 35 D4, 36 H2
Sutton Vic. 28 F11, 61 J4
Sutton Forest NSW 23 B6, 25 I9, 35 G3
Sutton Grange Vic. 49 G5, 54 A10, 61 O11, 63 O1
Swain Reefs NP Qld 125 O7
Swan Hill Vic. 28 G9, 59 L12, 61 L2
Swan Marsh Vic. 42 A9, 50 A2, 63 K8
Swan Reach SA 71 E2, 73 L8
Swan Reach Vic. 53 N5

Swan View WA xxv H1
Swanbourne WA xxiv B7, 84 C7, 85 B5
Swanhaven NSW 23 C12, 25 I10, 35 G4, 37 O3
Swanpool Vic. 54 G9, 56 D7
Swanport SA 67 H11, 71 D4, 73 L10
Swansea NSW 13 G5, 19 C11, 25 L4
Swansea Tas. 141 N3, 143 N12
Swanwater West Vic. 61 J8
Swanwick Tas. 141 O3, 143 O12
Sweetmans Creek NSW 13 C2
Swifts Creek Vic. 53 N2, 57 M12
Sydenham NSW viii B10
Sydenham Vic. 40 C4, 42 H4, 52 B4, 63 P5
Sydney NSW viii F4, x F12, 10, 12 F7, 13 B12, 15 L9, 25 K7
Sydney Harbour NP NSW viii F2, ix J2, x F10, xi O7, 12 G7, 13 C12, 15 M8, 25 K7
Sylvaterre Vic. 29 I12, 54 A5, 61 O6

Taabinga Qld 118 A10, 123 L7
Tabacum Qld 120 C3, 121 C8, 127 L6
Tabbara Vic. 35 A12, 51 B11
Tabberabbera Vic. 53 L4
Tabbimoble NSW 21 F6, 27 N4
Tabbita NSW 29 M6
Tabilk Vic. 54 D9
Table Top NSW 24 A12, 29 O12, 55 L5, 57 J1
Tabor Vic. 62 F5
Tabourie Lake NSW 25 I11, 35 F5, 37 N4
Tabulam NSW 21 C5, 27 M3, 123 M12
Tacoma NSW 13 E7, 15 P1
Taggerty Vic. 41 F2, 43 N2, 52 F2, 54 F12, 56 B11
Tahara Vic. 62 E4
Tahara Bridge Vic. 62 D4
Tahmoor NSW 23 D2
Tailem Bend SA 71 D4, 73 L10
Takone Tas. 142 E6, 144 B1
Talawa Tas. 143 M7
Talbingo NSW 24 D11, 35 A5, 36 C4
Talbot Vic. 49 B7, 61 L12, 63 L2
Taldra SA 28 B6, 58 B6, 71 G1, 73 O7
Talgai Qld 123 K10
Talgarno Vic. 24 B12, 29 O12, 55 L6, 57 K2
Talia SA 72 B4, 74 A12, 81 O12
Tallaganda NP NSW 24 G12, 34 H10, 35 D5, 37 I6, 51 G1
Tallageira Vic. 60 B10, 71 H9
Tallandoon Vic. 55 L8, 57 K5
Tallangatta Vic. 55 L7, 57 K3
Tallangatta East Vic. 55 M7, 57 K3
Tallangatta Valley Vic. 55 M7, 57 L4
Tallarook Vic. 54 D11
Tallebudgera Qld 115 G11, 116 F9
Tallebung NSW 24 A2, 29 O2
Tallimba NSW 24 B6, 29 O6
Tallong NSW 24 H9, 35 F3
Tallygaroopna Vic. 54 E6, 56 A2
Talmalmo NSW 24 B12, 29 P12, 55 N5, 57 M1
Talwood Qld 26 F1, 122 G10
Tamarama NSW ix L9
Tamarang NSW 26 G10
Tambar Springs NSW 26 F10
Tambaroora NSW 24 G4
Tambellup WA 88 F9, 90 E10
Tambo Qld 122 B2, 133 P2
Tambo Crossing Vic. 53 N4
Tambo Upper Vic. 53 N5
Tamboon Vic. 35 C12, 51 E11
Tamborine Qld 115 E8, 116 A3, 123 N10
Tamborine NP Qld 21 G1, 27 O1, 115 E8, 116 B2, 123 N10
Tamboy NSW 20 D11, 25 N3
Taminick Vic. 54 H7, 56 E4
Tamleugh Vic. 54 F8, 56 B5
Tamleugh North Vic. 54 F8, 56 A5
Tamleugh West Vic. 54 F8, 56 A5
Tammin WA 88 F4, 90 D7
Tamrookum Qld 21 E1, 27 N1, 115 C10
Tandarook Vic. 50 H8, 63 J8
Tandarra Vic. 54 A7, 61 O8
Tangalooma Qld 115 G2, 123 N8
Tangambalanga Vic. 55 L7, 57 J3
Tangmangaroo NSW 24 F8, 35 C2
Tangorin Qld 124 B6, 131 N6

Tanilba Bay NSW 19 F7
Tanja NSW 35 E9, 37 K12
Tanjil Bren Vic. 43 P6, 52 H5
Tanjil South Vic. 43 P8, 52 H6
Tankerton Vic. 40 F12, 43 K10, 45 M9, 52 D8
Tannum Sands Qld 123 L1, 125 N12
Tannymorel Qld 21 C2, 27 L1, 123 L11
Tansey Qld 118 B8, 123 L6
Tantanoola SA 71 F11
Tanunda SA 67 E4, 71 C2, 73 K8
Tanwood Vic. 61 K11, 63 K1
Tanybryn Vic. 42 B11, 50 C5, 63 L10
Taperoo SA 66 B5, 67 A7, 68 E1
Tapin Tops NP NSW 20 D7, 25 N1, 27 K11
Tapitallee NSW 23 C8
Taplan SA 28 B7, 58 B7, 71 H2, 73 O8
Tar Barrel Corner Vic. 45 J8
Tara NT 109 I2
Tara Qld 123 I8
Taradale Vic. 49 G7, 54 A11, 61 O12, 63 O2
Tarago NSW 24 G10, 35 E4, 37 J1
Tarago Vic. 41 G12, 43 N8, 52 G6
Taralga NSW 24 H8, 35 E2
Tarampa Qld 117 B11
Tarana NSW 24 H5
Taranna Tas. 139 M8, 141 M8
Tarcoola SA 81 O4
Tarcoon NSW 31 O6
Tarcowie SA 73 J3, 75 I11
Tarcutta NSW 24 C10, 36 A2, 55 O2
Tardun WA 89 E12, 90 B3
Taree NSW 20 E8, 25 N1, 27 L12
Targa Tas. 143 L7
Tarilta Vic. 49 F7
Tarlee SA 67 D2, 71 C1, 73 J7
Tarlo NSW 24 H8, 35 E3
Tarlo River NP NSW 24 H8, 35 F2
Tarnagulla Vic. 49 C3, 61 M10
Tarneit Vic. 40 A6, 42 H6, 52 B4, 63 P6
Tarnma SA 71 C1
Tarnook Vic. 54 G8, 56 C5
Tarong NP Qld 118 A11, 123 L7
Taroom Qld 123 I4
Taroona Tas. 137 E12, 139 I6, 141 K7
Tarpeena SA 62 A3, 71 G11
Tarra–Bulga NP Vic. 53 I8
Tarragal Vic. 62 C7
Tarraleah Tas. 140 H3
Tarranginnie Vic. 60 D7
Tarrango Vic. 28 D6, 58 E7
Tarranyurk Vic. 28 D12, 60 F6
Tarraville Vic. 53 I9
Tarrawanna NSW 22 D1
Tarrawingee Vic. 55 I7, 56 F4
Tarrayoukyan Vic. 60 D12, 62 D2
Tarrington Vic. 62 F4
Tarrion NSW 31 O5
Tarwin Vic. 43 N12, 52 G9
Tarwin Lower Vic. 52 F10
Tarwin Meadows Vic. 52 F10
Tarwonga WA 88 E7
Tascott NSW 13 D8, 15 N3
Tasman NP Tas. 139 N9, 141 M9
Tatham NSW 21 F5, 27 N4
Tathra NSW 35 E9
Tathra NP WA 90 B4
Tatong Vic. 54 H9, 56 D7
Tatura Vic. 54 E7
Tatyoon Vic. 63 I3
Taunton NP Qld 125 K11
Tawonga Vic. 55 L9, 57 J7
Tawonga South Vic. 55 L9, 57 J7
Tayene Tas. 143 L8
Taylors Arm NSW 20 F3, 27 M9
Taylors Beach Qld 120 F8, 127 M10
Taylors Flat NSW 24 F7, 35 D1
Taylors Lakes Vic. 40 C4, 43 I4, 63 P5
Taylorville SA 73 M7
Tea Gardens NSW 19 H7, 20 C11, 25 N3
Tea Tree Gully SA 66 E5, 67 C7, 68 G1
Tea Tree Tas. 139 I3, 141 K6
Teal Flat SA 71 D3, 73 L9
Tecoma Vic. 40 G7, 41 B9, 43 K6

Teddywaddy Vic. 28 G12, 61 K7
Teesdale Vic. 42 D7, 63 M6
Teewah Qld 118 F9
Telegraph Point NSW 20 F5, 27 M11
Telford Vic. 29 L12, 54 G6, 56 D2
Telita Tas. 143 N6
Telopea NSW 12 D6
Telopea Downs Vic. 28 B11, 60 C6, 71 H7
Temma Tas. 142 A6
Temora NSW 24 C7, 29 P7
Tempe NSW viii B11, 12 E8, 15 L9
Templers SA 67 D4, 71 C1, 73 J8
Templestowe Vic. 40 F5, 43 J5, 52 D4
Templin Qld 115 A8
Tempy Vic. 28 E9, 58 H12, 60 H2
Ten Mile Vic. 43 P3, 52 H2, 56 D12
Tennant Creek NT 107 J9
Tennyson NSW 14 H3, 17 N5
Tennyson Qld xxx D12
Tennyson SA xx A1
Tennyson Vic. 54 B6, 61 P7
Tenterden WA 87 B7, 88 F10
Tenterfield NSW 21 A5, 27 L4, 123 L12
Tepko SA 67 G9, 71 D3, 73 K9
Terang Vic. 50 F7, 63 I7
Teridgerie NSW 26 D8
Teringie SA xxi P4
Terip Terip Vic. 54 F10, 56 A9
Terka SA 73 I2, 74 H10
Termeil NSW 25 I11, 35 F5, 37 M5
Terowie NSW 24 D2
Terowie SA 73 K4, 75 I11
Terranora NSW 21 H2, 27 O2, 115 G12, 116 G12
Terrey Hills NSW 12 F4, 13 B10, 15 M6
Terrick Terrick Vic. 29 I12, 54 A5, 61 O6
Terrick Terrick NP Vic. 54 A5, 61 O6
Terrigal NSW 13 E8, 15 P3, 25 L5
Terry Hie Hie NSW 26 G5
Tesbury Vic. 50 H7, 63 J8
Teviotville Qld 115 A8
Tewantin Qld 115 G1, 118 F10, 123 N7
Tewkesbury Tas. 142 E6, 144 C1
Texas Qld 27 J3, 123 J12
Thallon Qld 26 E1, 122 F11
Thanes Creek Qld 27 K1
Thangool Qld 123 J2
Tharbogang NSW 29 M7
Thargomindah Qld 133 K8
Tharwa ACT 24 F11, 33 C10, 34 D7, 35 C5, 36 G4
The Basin Vic. 40 G6, 41 B9, 43 K6, 53 M4
The Cascade Vic. 55 M7, 57 L3
The Caves Qld 125 M10
The Channon NSW 21 F4, 27 O3
The Cove Vic. 50 E9, 62 H9
The Entrance NSW 13 E7, 15 P2, 25 L5
The Entrance North NSW 13 E7, 15 P2
The Gap NSW 24 B9, 29 P9
The Gap Qld xxx A4, 114 D6, 115 D4, 117 E11, 131 L2
The Gap Vic. 40 B3, 42 H3, 52 B3, 63 P4
The Gardens NT xxvii B9, 101 C3
The Gardens Tas. 143 P7
The Glen Tas. 143 K6, 145 G7
The Gulf NSW 27 J4
The Gums Qld 123 I8
The Gurdies Vic. 43 L10, 45 P9, 52 E8
The Heart Vic. 53 K7
The Highlands Vic. 42 F4, 49 G11, 52 A3, 63 O4
The Hill NSW 18 E6
The Junction NSW 18 B8
The Lakes NP Vic. 53 N6
The Lea Tas. 137 C11
The Monument Qld 130 F5
The Narrows NT xxvii D7
The Oaks NSW 14 F11, 23 D1, 25 J7, 35 G1
The Palms NP Qld 123 L8
The Patch Vic. 41 C9, 43 L6
The Pines SA 69 C7, 72 G9
The Risk NSW 21 E3, 27 N2, 123 M11
The Rock NSW 24 B10, 26 G4, 29 O10, 55 L1
The Rocks NSW viii G3, x G11, 10 E3
The Sisters Vic. 63 I7
The Spit NSW xi K5
The Springs Tas. 137 A9

The Summit Qld 21 A3, 27 L2
The Vale NSW 13 A8
Thebarton SA xx G4
Theodore Qld 123 I3
Theresa Park NSW 14 G10
Thevenard SA 81 M8
Thirlmere NSW 14 F12, 23 D2, 25 J7, 35 G2
Thirlmere Lakes NP NSW 23 D2, 25 J8, 35 G2
Thirlstane Tas. 143 I6, 145 B7
Thirroul NSW 23 G4
Thologolong Vic. 24 B12, 29 P12, 55 M5, 57 L1
Thomas Plains SA 69 F3, 73 I6
Thomastown Vic. 40 E4, 43 J4, 52 C4
Thomson Vic. 42 F8, 44 B4, 46 G9, 50 H1, 53 I6
Thomson Bay WA 84 A7, 85 A6
Thoona Vic. 54 H7, 56 D4
Thora NSW 20 G1, 21 C12, 27 M8
Thornbury Vic. xv O3
Thorneside Qld 114 G8, 115 F5, 117 G11
Thorngate SA 65 D1
Thorngate SA xxi I2
Thornlands Qld 114 H9, 115 F5, 117 H12
Thornlie WA xxv E12
Thornton NSW 13 G2, 19 C8, 20 A12
Thornton Vic. 41 G2, 43 N1, 52 F1, 54 F12, 56 B11
Thorpdale Vic. 43 P10, 52 H7
Thowgla Vic. 36 A8, 55 O7, 57 O4
Thowgla Upper Vic. 36 A9, 55 O8, 57 O4
Thredbo NSW 35 A8, 36 C10, 51 B4
Three Bridges Vic. 41 E9, 43 M6, 52 F5
Three Islands NP Qld 127 L2
Three Springs WA 90 B4
Three Ways Roadhouse NT 107 J9
Thrushton NP Qld 122 D8
Thuddungra NSW 24 D7, 35 A1
Thulimbah Qld 21 A3, 27 L2
Thulloo NSW 24 A5, 29 O5
Thuringowa Qld 120 G10, 124 G1, 127 N11
Thurla Vic. 58 G6
Thursday Island Qld 128 C2
Tia NSW 20 C4, 27 J10
Tiaro Qld 118 D6, 123 M5
Tiberias Tas. 141 K4
Tibooburra NSW 30 D2, 132 H11
Tichborne NSW 24 D4
Tickera SA 69 E2, 72 H6
Tidal River Vic. 52 H12
Tiega Vic. 28 E8, 58 G11
Tieri Qld 125 I9
Tighes Hill NSW 18 A1
Tilba Tilba NSW 35 E8, 37 K10
Tilmouth Well Roadhouse NT 108 G5
Tilpa NSW 31 I7
Timbarra Vic. 53 O3
Timbarra NP NSW 21 B5, 27 L4, 123 L12
Timber Creek NT 104 D10, 106 D2
Timberoo Vic. 28 D9, 58 G11
Timberoo South Vic. 28 D9, 58 G11, 60 G1
Timbertown NSW 20 F6
Timbillica NSW 35 D11, 51 G10
Timboon Vic. 50 F9, 63 I9
Timmering Vic. 54 C7
Timor Vic. 49 B5, 61 M11, 63 M1
Timor West Vic. 49 B5, 61 L11
Tin Can Bay Qld 118 F8, 123 N6
Tinaburra Qld 120 D3, 121 E9, 127 L7
Tinamba Vic. 53 J6
Tinaroo Falls Qld 120 D3, 121 E9, 127 L6
Tincurrin WA 88 F7
Tindal NT 104 G8
Tinderbox Tas. 139 I7, 141 K8
Tingalpa Qld xxxi N9
Tingha NSW 27 I6
Tingoora Qld 118 A9, 123 L6
Tinonee NSW 20 D8, 25 N1, 27 L12
Tintaldra Vic. 24 C12, 36 A7, 55 O6, 57 O2
Tintinara SA 71 E6, 73 M12
Tiona NSW 20 E10, 25 N2
Tiparra West SA 69 E4, 72 H7
Tipton Qld 123 K8
Tirranna Roadhouse Qld 129 D4
Titjikala NT 109 J8
Ti-Tree NT 109 I4
Tittybong Vic. 61 K4

Tiwi NT xxvii E3
Tjukayirla Roadhouse WA 93 K10
Tobermorey NT 109 P4, 130 C6
Tocal Qld 124 A11, 131 M11
Tocumwal NSW 29 L11, 54 F4
Togari Tas. 142 B4
Toiberry Tas. 143 J9, 145 F12
Tolga Qld 120 D3, 121 D9, 127 L7
Tolmans Hill Tas. 137 C10
Tolmie Vic. 54 H10, 56 E8
Tom Groggin NSW 35 A8, 36 B11, 51 A4, 55 P9, 57 P6
Tom Price WA 89 G3, 92 C5, 96 G10
Tomago NSW 13 G2, 19 D8, 20 A12
Tomahawk Tas. 143 N5
Tomahawk Creek Vic. 42 A9, 50 A2, 63 K8
Tomakin NSW 37 L7
Tomaree NP NSW 19 H8, 20 C12, 25 M4
Tombong NSW 35 C9, 51 D7
Tomerong NSW 23 C11, 37 O2
Tomewin Qld 21 G2, 115 F12, 116 D11
Tomingley NSW 24 E2
Tongala Vic. 29 J12, 54 D6
Tonganah Tas. 143 M7
Tonghi Creek Vic. 35 C11, 51 D10
Tongio Vic. 53 N2, 55 N12, 57 M12
Tongio West Vic. 53 N2, 57 M12
Tonimbuk Vic. 41 E11, 43 M7, 52 F6
Tooan Vic. 60 E9
Toobanna Qld 120 E8, 127 M10
Toobeah Qld 26 G1, 122 H10
Tooborac Vic. 54 C10
Toodyay WA 85 F2, 88 D4, 90 C7
Toogong NSW 24 F4
Toogoolawah Qld 117 A7, 123 M8
Toogoom Qld 118 E4, 123 N4
Tookayerta SA 28 A6, 58 A7, 71 G2, 73 N8
Toolamba Vic. 54 E8
Toolangi Vic. 41 D5, 43 L4, 52 E3
Toolern Vale Vic. 40 A3, 42 G4, 49 H11, 52 B3, 63 P4
Tooleybuc NSW 28 G8, 59 L11
Toolibin WA 88 F7
Tooligie SA 72 D6
Toolleen Vic. 54 B9, 61 P10
Toolondo Vic. 60 F11
Toolong Vic. 50 B7, 62 F8
Tooloom NSW 21 C3, 27 M2, 123 L11
Tooloom NP NSW 21 C2, 27 M2, 123 L11
Tooma NSW 24 D12, 35 A6, 36 B7, 51 A1, 55 P6, 57 P2
Toombul Qld 114 E6, 115 E4, 117 F10
Toombullup Vic. 54 H10, 56 E8
Toompine Roadhouse Qld 133 L7
Toongabbie Vic. 53 I6
Toongi NSW 24 F2
Toonumbar NSW 21 D3, 27 M2, 123 M11
Toonumbar NP NSW 21 D3, 27 M2, 123 M11
Tooperang SA 68 G7
Toora Vic. 52 H9
Tooradin Vic. 40 G10, 43 K9, 45 N6, 52 E7
Toorak Vic. xvii P7
Toorak Gardens SA xxi L6
Tooraweenah NSW 26 D10
Toorbul Qld 114 F1, 117 G7
Toorongo Vic. 43 P6, 52 H5
Tootgarook Vic. 44 G8
Tootool NSW 24 B10, 29 O10, 55 L1
Toowong Qld xxx D8, 114 D7, 115 D4, 117 F11
Toowoomba Qld 123 L9
Toowoon Bay NSW 13 E7, 15 P2
Top Springs NT 104 F12, 106 F3
Topaz Qld 120 D4, 121 F10
Topaz Road NP Qld 120 D4, 121 E10, 127 L7
Torbanlea Qld 118 E4, 123 M4
Torndirrup NP WA 87 E12, 88 G11, 90 E11
Toronto NSW 13 F4, 19 C10, 25 L4
Torquay Vic. 42 F9, 44 A7, 50 G2, 63 N8
Torrens Creek Qld 124 D4, 131 P4
Torrens Park SA xxi K12, 67 B9, 68 F2
Torrensville SA xx A4
Torrington NSW 27 K4
Torrita Vic. 28 D9, 58 F11
Torrumbarry Vic. 29 I12, 54 B5, 61 P6
Tostaree Vic. 35 A12, 51 A11, 53 O5

Tottenham NSW 24 C1, 29 P1, 31 P12
Tottington Vic. 61 J10
Toukley NSW 13 F6, 19 B12, 25 L5
Tourello Vic. 42 C1, 49 C8, 63 M3
Towallum NSW 21 D10, 27 M7
Towamba NSW 35 D10, 51 G8
Towaninny Vic. 28 G11, 61 L5
Towarri NP NSW 25 K1, 26 H11
Tower Hill Tas. 143 N9
Tower Hill Vic. 50 B7, 62 G8
Towitta SA 67 H5
Townsville Qld 119 A1, 120 F3, 120 G10, 124 G1, 127 N11
Towong Vic. 35 A7, 36 B8, 51 A2, 55 O7, 57 O3
Towong Upper Vic. 35 A7, 36 B8, 51 A2, 55 P7, 57 P4
Towradgi NSW 22 F3, 23 G4
Towrang NSW 24 H9, 35 E3
Tracy SA 73 K5, 75 J12
Trafalgar Vic. 43 P9, 52 G7
Tragowel Vic. 61 N5
Trangie NSW 26 B11
Tranmere SA xxi N3
Tranmere Tas. 1 H12, 137 H10
Traralgon Vic. 53 I7
Traralgon South Vic. 53 I7
Travancore Vic. xiv G5
Trawalla Vic. 42 B2, 63 K3
Trawool Vic. 54 D11
Trayning WA 88 F2, 90 D6
Traynors Lagoon Vic. 61 J9
Trebonne Qld 120 E8, 127 M10
Tregole NP Qld 122 D6
Trenah Tas. 143 M7
Trentham Vic. 42 F2, 49 F9, 52 A2, 54 A12, 63 O3
Trentham Cliffs NSW 58 H6
Trentham East Vic. 42 F2, 49 G9
Tresco Vic. 28 H10, 61 M3
Tresco West Vic. 61 M3
Trevallyn NSW 19 C5, 20 A10, 25 L3
Trevallyn Tas. 143 K8, 145 G10
Trewalla Vic. 62 D8
Trewilga NSW 24 E3
Triabunna Tas. 139 N1, 141 M5
Trida NSW 29 K3
Trida Vic. 43 N10, 52 G7
Trigg WA xxiv A2
Trinita Vic. 28 E8, 58 H10
Trinity Gardens SA xxi M4
Triunia NP Qld 117 F3, 118 E11, 123 N7
Trowutta Tas. 142 C5
Truganina Vic. 40 B6, 42 H5, 52 B4, 63 P6
Trundle NSW 24 D3
Trunkey NSW 24 G6
Truro SA 67 G3, 71 C1, 73 K7
Tuan Qld 118 F6, 123 N5
Tuart Forest NP WA 86 C6, 88 B8, 90 B10
Tuart Hill WA xxiv E3
Tubbut Vic. 35 B10, 51 C7
Tucabia NSW 21 E9, 27 N6
Tuckanarra WA 89 H9, 92 D11
Tucklan NSW 24 H1, 26 E12
Tuena NSW 24 G7, 35 D1
Tuggerah NSW 13 E7, 15 P1, 25 L5
Tuggeranong ACT 24 F11, 33 D8, 34 D6, 35 C5, 36 G3
Tuggerawong NSW 13 E7, 15 P1, 19 A12
Tugun Qld 21 H2, 115 G11, 116 G9
Tulendeena Tas. 143 M7
Tulkara Vic. 61 J11
Tullah Tas. 142 E9, 144 B7
Tullamore NSW 24 C2
Tullibigeal NSW 24 A4, 29 O4
Tulloh Vic. 42 B9, 50 B2, 63 L8
Tully Qld 120 E6, 127 M8
Tully Gorge NP Qld 120 D5, 121 D12, 127 L8
Tully Heads Qld 120 E6, 127 M8
Tumbarumba NSW 24 D12, 35 A6, 36 B5, 55 P5
Tumbi Umbi NSW 13 E7, 15 P2
Tumblong NSW 24 D10, 35 A4, 36 B1, 55 P1
Tumbulgum NSW 21 G2, 27 O2, 115 G12, 116 F12, 123 N11
Tumby Bay SA 72 E7

Tummaville Qld 123 K10
Tumorrama NSW 24 E10, 35 B4, 36 D1
Tumoulin Qld 120 D4, 121 D11, 127 L7
Tumut NSW 24 D10, 35 A4, 36 C2
Tunart Vic. 28 B6, 58 C7, 71 H2, 73 P8
Tunbridge Tas. 141 L2, 143 L12
Tungamah Vic. 29 L12, 54 G6, 56 C2
Tungamull Qld 125 M11
Tungkillo SA 67 F8, 71 C3, 73 K9
Tunnack Tas. 141 L4
Tunnel Tas. 143 K6, 145 H7
Tunnel Creek NP WA 95 K7, 98 G10
Tura Beach NSW 35 E9
Turallin Qld 123 J9
Turill NSW 25 I1, 26 F12
Turkey Beach 123 L1, 125 O12
Turlinjah NSW 35 F7, 37 L8
Turners Beach Tas. 142 G6, 144 G1
Turners Marsh Tas. 143 K7, 145 H8
Turnip Fields Tas. 137 B10
Turon NP NSW 24 H4, 25 I4
Turondale NSW 24 H4
Tuross Head NSW 35 F7, 37 L8
Turrawan NSW 26 F7
Turriff Vic. 28 E10, 60 H2
Turriff East Vic. 61 I2
Turriff West Vic. 60 H2
Turtle Group NP Qld 127 L1
Turtons Creek Vic. 43 P12, 52 H9
Tusmore SA xxi M6
Tutunup WA 86 D6
Tutye Vic. 28 C9, 58 D11, 60 D1, 73 P10
Tweed Heads NSW 21 H2, 27 O1, 115 G11, 116 H10, 123 N11
Tweed Heads South NSW 116 G11
Tweed Heads West NSW 116 G10
Twelve Apostles Marine NP Vic. 50 G11
Twelve Mile NSW 23 B12, 24 G2, 25 I10, 35 G4, 37 N3
Two Islands NP Qld 127 L2
Two Mile Flat NSW 24 G2
Two Rocks WA 85 A2, 88 B4, 90 B7
Two Wells SA 66 B1, 67 B5, 69 H6, 71 B2, 73 J8
Tyaak Vic. 41 A1, 43 K1, 52 D1, 54 D12
Tyabb Vic. 40 F11, 43 J9, 45 L6, 52 D7
Tyagarah NSW 21 H4, 27 O3
Tyagong NSW 24 E6
Tyalgum NSW 21 F2, 27 O2
Tyenna Tas. 138 D3, 140 H6
Tyers Vic. 53 I7
Tyers Junction Vic. 52 H6
Tylden Vic. 42 G1, 49 G8, 52 A1, 54 A12, 63 O3
Tyndale NSW 21 E8, 27 N5
Tynong Vic. 41 E12, 43 M8, 52 E6
Tyntynder Central Vic. 59 L12, 61 L1
Tyntynder South Vic. 59 L12, 61 L2
Tyrendarra Vic. 62 E7
Tyrendarra East Vic. 62 E7
Tyringham NSW 21 C11, 27 L7
Tyrrell Downs Vic. 28 F9, 59 J12, 61 J2

Uarbry NSW 24 H1, 26 F12
Ubobo Qld 123 K2
Ucolta SA 73 K3, 75 J11
Uki NSW 21 G3, 27 O2, 123 N11
Ulamambri NSW 26 E10
Ulan NSW 24 H2
Ulidarra NP NSW 20 H1, 21 E11, 27 N7
Ulinda NSW 26 E10
Ulladulla NSW 25 I11, 35 G5, 37 N4
Ullina Vic. 42 D1, 49 D8, 63 M2
Ullswater Vic. 60 C10, 71 H9
Ulmarra NSW 21 E8, 27 N6
Ulong NSW 21 D11, 27 M7
Ulooloo SA 73 K4, 75 I12
Ultima Vic. 28 G10, 61 K3
Ultimo NSW viii E6, 10 A11
Ulupna Vic. 29 K11, 54 E4
Uluru–Kata Tjuta NP NT 108 E10, 110 F10
Ulva WA 88 G3
Ulverstone Tas. 142 G6, 144 G1
Umbakumba NT 105 N7
Umina NSW 12 H1, 13 D9, 15 N4, 25 K6

Unanderra NSW 23 F5
Undalya SA 73 J6
Undara Volcanic NP Qld 120 A6, 127 J9
Undera Vic. 54 E6
Undera North Vic. 54 E6
Underbool Vic. 28 D9, 58 F11
Underdale SA xx E4
Underwood Tas. 143 K7, 145 H8
Ungarie NSW 24 B5, 29 O5
Ungarra SA 72 E7
Unley SA xxi J8, 65 D12
Unley Park SA xxi I9, 66 C8, 67 B9, 68 F2
Upper Beaconsfield Vic. 40 H8, 41 C10, 43 L7, 45 O2, 52 E5
Upper Bilambil NSW 116 E11
Upper Bingara NSW 26 H6
Upper Blessington Tas. 143 M8
Upper Bowman NSW 20 B8, 25 M1, 27 J12
Upper Bylong NSW 25 I2
Upper Castra Tas. 142 G7, 144 F3
Upper Cedar Creek Qld 114 C5, 115 C3, 117 D10
Upper Colo NSW 14 H2, 17 O2, 25 J5
Upper Coomera Qld 115 F8, 116 D3
Upper Crystal Creek NSW 116 C12
Upper Dungay NSW 116 D12
Upper Duroby NSW 116 E12
Upper Esk Tas. 143 M8
Upper Ferntree Gully Vic. 41 B9
Upper Freestone Qld 21 B1
Upper Gellibrand Vic. 42 B11, 50 C4, 63 L9
Upper Horton NSW 26 H6
Upper Kedron Qld xxx A1, 114 D6
Upper Laceys Creek Qld 114 B3, 115 B1, 117 D8
Upper Macdonald NSW 13 A6, 25 K5
Upper Mangrove NSW 13 B6, 15 M1
Upper Manilla NSW 26 H8
Upper Mount Hicks Tas. 142 E5
Upper Mudgeeraba Qld 116 D8
Upper Myall NSW 19 H3, 20 C9, 25 N2
Upper Natone Tas. 142 F6, 144 D1
Upper Plenty Vic. 40 E1, 43 J2, 52 D2
Upper Scamander Tas. 143 O8
Upper Stowport Tas. 142 F6, 144 E1
Upper Sturt SA 66 D8, 67 C10, 68 G3
Upper Swan WA 84 F3, 85 D4, 88 C4
Upper Tallebudgera Qld 116 D10
Upper Woodstock Tas. 138 G7
Upper Yarraman Qld 118 A12, 123 L7
Upwey Vic. 40 G7, 41 B9, 43 K6
Uraidla SA 66 E8, 67 C9, 68 G2
Uralla NSW 20 B1, 27 J8
Urana NSW 29 M10, 55 I1
Urandangi Qld 109 P3, 130 C5
Urangeline East NSW 24 A10, 29 N10, 55 K2
Urania SA 69 E5, 72 H8
Uranno SA 72 D7
Uranquinty NSW 24 B10, 29 O10, 55 M1
Urbenville NSW 21 D3, 27 M2, 123 M11
Urliup NSW 116 E12
Urrbrae SA xxi L10
Urunga NSW 20 H2, 21 D12, 27 M8
Uxbridge Tas. 138 F3, 141 I6

Vacy NSW 19 C5, 20 A10, 25 L3
Vale Park SA xxi L1
Valencia Creek Vic. 53 K5
Valla Beach NSW 20 H2, 27 M8
Valley Heights NSW 14 F6, 17 K9
Varley WA 90 F8
Vasey Vic. 62 E2
Vasse WA 86 B6, 88 B9
Vaucluse NSW ix M4, xi M11
Vaughan Vic. 49 F7, 61 N12, 63 N2
Vectis Vic. 60 F9
Veitch SA 28 A7, 58 A8, 71 G2, 73 N8
Venman Bushland NP Qld 114 G10, 115 E6, 123 N9
Ventnor Vic. 43 J11, 45 K10, 52 D8
Venus Bay SA 72 B4, 81 O11
Venus Bay Vic. 52 F9
Veresdale Qld 115 C8
Verona Sands Tas. 138 H10, 141 J9
Verran SA 72 E6
Victor Harbor SA 68 F9, 69 H10, 71 B5, 73 J11

178

Victoria Park WA xxiv H7, xxv A7
Victoria Point Qld 114 H9, 115 F6, 117 H12
Victoria River Roadhouse NT 104 E10, 106 E1
Victoria Valley Tas. 141 I3
Villawood NSW 12 C7, 15 J9
Vincentia NSW 23 D11, 25 J10, 35 G4, 37 O2
Vineyard NSW 12 A3, 15 I5, 17 P8
Vinifera Vic. 59 L12, 61 L1
Violet Town Vic. 52 H4, 54 F8, 56 B6
Virginia Qld 114 E6, 115 E3, 117 F10, 123 L8
Virginia SA 66 C3, 67 B6, 69 H6, 71 B2
Vite Vite Vic. 63 J5
Vite Vite North Vic. 63 J5
Viveash WA xxv E2
Vivonne Bay SA 69 C12, 72 G12
Vulkathunha–Gammon Ranges NP SA 70 G4, 75 J3

W Tree Vic. 35 A10, 51 A9, 53 P3
Waaia Vic. 29 K12, 54 E5
Waarre Vic. 50 G10, 63 I9
Wadbilliga NP NSW 35 D8, 36 H11, 37 I10, 51 G4
Waddamana Tas. 141 I2, 143 I12
Waddi NSW 29 M8
Waddikee SA 72 E4, 74 D12
Waeel WA 88 E4
Wagaman NT xxvii E5
Wagant Vic. 28 E8, 58 H11
Wagerup WA 85 D12, 88 C7
Wagga Wagga NSW 24 B9, 29 P9, 55 M1
Wagin WA 88 F8, 90 D9
Wahgunyah Vic. 29 M12, 55 I5, 56 F1
Wahring Vic. 54 D9
Wahroonga NSW 12 E5
Waikerie SA 71 F1, 73 M7
Waikiki WA 84 C11, 85 B8, 88 B6
Wail Vic. 60 F8
Wairewa Vic. 35 A11, 51 A11, 53 O5
Waitchie Vic. 28 F9, 59 K12, 61 K2
Waitpinga SA 68 E9, 69 H10, 71 B5, 73 J11
Wakerley Qld xxxi P10
Wakool NSW 29 I10, 54 B2, 61 P3
Wal Wal Vic. 60 H10
Walbundrie NSW 24 A11, 29 N11, 55 K4
Walcha NSW 20 B3, 27 J9
Walcha Road NSW 20 A3, 27 J9
Walgett NSW 26 B5
Walgoolan WA 88 G3, 90 E6
Walhalla Vic. 53 I5
Walkamin Qld 120 D3, 121 D8, 127 L6
Walkaway WA 89 D12, 90 A3
Walker Flat SA 71 D2, 73 L9
Walkers Creek Qld 123 K7
Walkers Point Qld 118 E4, 123 M4
Walkerston Qld 119 G8, 125 K5
Walkerville SA xxi K2
Walkerville Vic. 52 G10
Walkerville South Vic. 52 G10
Walla Walla NSW 24 A11, 29 O11, 55 K4
Wallabadah NSW 26 H11
Wallabi Point NSW 20 E8, 25 O1
Wallabrook SA 60 A9, 71 G8
Wallace Vic. 42 E3, 49 D10, 63 N4
Wallace Rockhole NT 108 H7, 110 E6
Wallacedale Vic. 62 E5
Wallacia NSW 14 G8, 25 J7
Wallalong NSW 13 G1, 19 C7
Wallaloo Vic. 61 I9
Wallaloo East Vic. 61 J10
Wallan Vic. 40 E1, 43 J2, 52 C2
Wallangarra Qld 21 A4, 27 K3, 123 K12
Wallangra NSW 27 I4, 123 J12
Wallarah NP NSW 13 G5, 19 C11, 25 L5
Wallarobba NSW 19 D5, 25 M3
Wallaroo Qld 125 K11
Wallaroo SA 69 E3, 72 H6
Wallaville Qld 118 B3, 123 L3
Wallendbeen NSW 24 D8, 35 A2
Wallerawang NSW 14 A1, 25 I5
Walli NSW 24 F5
Wallinduc Vic. 42 B5, 63 K5
Wallingat NP NSW 20 D10, 25 N2
Wallington Vic. 42 G8, 44 C5, 50 H1, 52 A6, 63 O8

Walliston WA 84 F6
Walloon Qld 115 A5, 117 C12
Walloway SA 73 J2, 75 I10
Walls Of Jerusalem NP Tas. 140 G1, 142 G11, 144 F8, 145 A12
Wallsend NSW 13 G3, 19 C9, 20 A12
Wallumbilla Qld 122 G6
Wallup Vic. 28 D12, 60 G7
Walmer NSW 24 F2
Walmer Vic. 49 F5, 61 N11, 63 N1
Walpa Vic. 53 M5
Walpeup Vic. 28 D9, 58 F11
Walpole WA 87 F6, 88 E12, 90 D11
Walpole–Nornalup NP WA 87 F5, 88 E12, 90 D12
Walsall WA 86 C7
Walsh Qld 127 I5
Waltowa SA 71 D5, 73 L11
Walwa Vic. 24 C12, 29 P12, 36 A6, 55 O6, 57 N1
Walyunga NP WA 84 F2, 85 D3, 88 C4, 90 C7
Wamberal NSW 13 E8, 15 P3
Wambidgee NSW 24 D9, 35 A3
Wamboyne NSW 24 C5, 29 P5
Wamoon NSW 29 N7
Wampoony SA 28 A12, 71 G7
Wamuran Basin Qld 114 C1, 117 E7
Wamuran Qld 114 D1, 117 E7, 123 N8
Wanaaring NSW 31 I3, 133 L12
Wanalta Vic. 54 C8
Wanbi SA 71 F2, 73 N9
Wandana Heights Vic. 44 A4
Wandandian NSW 23 C11, 37 N2
Wandangula NT 105 M11, 107 M2
Wandearah SA 73 I4, 74 H12
Wandearah West SA 73 I4, 74 G12
Wandella NSW 35 E8, 37 J10, 51 H4
Wandering WA 85 H9, 88 D6, 90 D8
Wandiligong Vic. 55 K10, 57 I8
Wandilo SA 62 A4, 71 G11
Wandin North Vic. 40 H6, 41 C8, 43 L5, 52 E4
Wando Bridge Vic. 62 D3, 71 H11
Wando Vale Vic. 62 D3, 71 H11
Wandoan Qld 123 I5
Wandong Vic. 43 J2, 52 C2, 54 C12
Wandsworth NSW 27 J6
Wang Wauk NSW 20 D9, 25 N2
Wangara WA 84 C4, 85 B4
Wangarabell Vic. 35 D11, 51 F10
Wangaratta Vic. 55 I7, 56 F4
Wangary SA 72 D8
Wangenella NSW 29 J9
Wangerrip Vic. 50 A5, 63 K10
Wangi Wangi NSW 13 F5, 19 C10
Wangoom Vic. 50 D7, 62 H8
Wanguri NT xxvii E4
Wanilla SA 72 D8
Wanneroo WA 84 C3, 85 B4, 88 B4, 90 B7
Wannon Vic. 62 H3
Wanora Qld 115 A4, 117 C11
Wantabadgery NSW 24 C9, 55 O1
Wanwin Vic. 62 B6, 71 H12
Wapengo NSW 35 E9, 37 K12
Wappinguy NSW 25 J1, 26 G12
Warakurna WA 93 O7, 108 A9
Warakurna Roadhouse WA 93 O7, 108 A9
Warana Qld 117 H4, 118 F12
Waratah Tas. 142 E7, 144 A3
Waratah Bay Vic. 52 G10
Waratah North Vic. 52 G10
Warawarrup WA 86 E1, 88 C7
Warburton Vic. 41 F8, 43 M5, 52 F4
Warburton WA 93 M8
Warburton East Vic. 41 F8, 43 N5
Warburton Roadhouse WA 93 M8
Wardell NSW 21 G5, 27 O4, 123 N12
Wards River NSW 19 F2, 20 B9, 25 M2
Wareek Vic. 49 B5, 61 L11, 63 L1
Warialda NSW 26 H5
Warialda Rail NSW 26 H5
Warilla NSW 23 F6
Warkton NSW 26 E10
Warkworth NSW 25 K3
Warmga Qld 123 K8
Warmun WA 95 N6, 99 M8

Warmun–Turkey Creek Roadhouse WA 95 N6, 99 L8
Warncoort Vic. 42 C9, 50 C2, 63 L8
Warne Vic. 28 F11, 61 K4
Warneet Vic. 40 G10, 43 K9, 45 M6, 52 D7
Warner Qld 114 D5, 115 D3, 117 E10
Warners Bay NSW 13 G4, 19 C10
Warnertown SA 73 I4, 74 H11
Warooka SA 69 D7, 72 H9
Waroona WA 85 D11, 88 C7, 90 C9
Warra Qld 123 J7
Warra NP NSW 21 A9, 27 K6
Warra Yadin Vic. 61 J12, 63 J2
Warrabah NP NSW 27 I8
Warracknabeal Vic. 28 E12, 60 H7
Warradale SA 67 B10, 68 E3, 71 B3
Warraderry NSW 24 E6
Warragamba NSW 14 F8, 25 J7, 35 H1
Warragul Vic. 43 N9, 52 G7
Warrah Creek NSW 26 H11
Warrak Vic. 61 J12, 63 J2
Warralakin WA 88 G2, 90 E6
Warrambine Vic. 42 C6, 63 M6
Warramboo SA 72 D4, 74 B11
Warrandyte Vic. 40 F5, 41 A7, 43 K5, 52 D4
Warrane Tas. 1 F4, 137 G7
Warrawee NSW 13 B11, 15 L7
Warrawong NSW 23 F5
Warrayure Vic. 62 G4
Warrego NT 107 I9
Warrell Creek NSW 20 G3, 27 M9
Warren NSW 26 A10
Warren Qld 125 M11
Warren WA 86 G11, 87 A3, 88 C11, 90 C11
Warrenbayne Vic. 54 G9, 56 C6
Warrenmang Vic. 61 K11, 63 K1
Warrentinna Tas. 143 M6
Warrill View Qld 115 A7, 123 M10
Warrimoo NSW 14 G6, 17 K10
Warringa Tas. 142 G7, 144 F2
Warrion Vic. 42 B8, 50 B1, 63 L7
Warrnambool Vic. 50 C8, 62 G8
Warrong Vic. 62 G7
Warrow SA 72 C7
Warrumbungle NP NSW 26 D9
Warruwi NT 104 H2
Wartook Vic. 60 G11
Warup WA 88 E8
Warwick Qld 21 B1, 27 L1, 123 L10
Warwick WA 84 C5
Warwick Farm NSW 12 B8, 15 J9
Washpool SA 73 J4, 75 I12
Washpool NP NSW 21 B6, 27 L4
Wasleys SA 67 C4, 71 B1
Watagans NP NSW 13 D3, 19 A10, 25 L4
Watarrka NP NT 108 E7
Watchem Vic. 28 F12, 61 I6
Watchman SA 69 H3, 73 J6
Watchupga Vic. 28 F11, 61 I4
Waterfall Gully SA xxi O9, 72 H3, 74 G10
Waterfall NSW 12 B12, 15 J12, 23 H2, 25 K7
Waterford Qld 114 F10, 115 E6
Waterford Vic. 53 L3
Waterford WA xxiv H9, xxv B10
Waterford Park Vic. 43 J2, 52 D1, 54 D12
Waterhouse Tas. 143 M5
Waterloo NSW viii F8
Waterloo SA 73 K6
Waterloo Tas. 138 F9, 141 I9
Waterloo Vic. 42 A1, 63 K3
Waterloo WA 86 E3, 88 C8
Waterman WA xxiv A1
Watervale SA 73 J6
Waterview Heights NSW 21 D9, 27 M6
Watheroo WA 88 B1, 90 B5
Watheroo NP WA 88 B1, 90 B5
Watson SA 80 H3
Watsons Bay NSW ix M2, xi M9
Watsons Creek NSW 27 I8
Watsons Creek Vic. 40 G4, 41 B6, 43 K4
Watsonville Qld 120 C4, 121 C10, 127 L7
Wattamolla NSW 23 D8
Wattamondara NSW 24 E6
Wattle Flat NSW 24 B5, 29 P5, 35 F4, 37 L2

Wattle Glen Vic. 40 F4, 41 A6, 43 K4
Wattle Grove Tas. 138 F8, 141 J9
Wattle Grove WA xxv G8, 84 F7, 85 D5
Wattle Hill Tas. 139 L4, 141 L6
Wattle Hill Vic. 50 H11, 63 J10
Wattle Park SA xxi O6
Wattle Range SA 71 F10
Wattleup WA 84 D9, 85 C7
Waubra Vic. 42 B1, 49 B8, 63 L3
Wauchope NSW 20 F6, 27 L11
Wauchope NT 107 J11, 109 J1
Wauraltee SA 69 D6, 72 H8
Waurn Ponds Vic. 42 F8, 50 G1, 63 N8
Wave Hill NSW 31 N6
Wavell Heights Qld xxxi I1
Waverley NSW ix J9, 12 G8, 15 M9
Waverley Tas. 143 K8, 145 H10
Waverton NSW viii F1, x F8, 11 A6
Wayatinah Tas. 140 H4
Waychinicup NP WA 87 G10, 88 H11, 90 F11
Waygara Vic. 51 A11, 53 P5
Wayville SA xxi I7, 65 B12
Webbs NSW 24 E1, 26 B12
Webbs Creek NSW 15 J1
Wedderburn NSW 14 H12, 23 F2
Wedderburn Vic. 61 L8
Wedderburn Junction Vic. 61 M8
Weddin Mountains NP NSW 24 D6
Wee Jasper NSW 24 E10, 34 A2, 35 B4, 36 F1
Wee Waa NSW 26 E6
Weeaproinah Vic. 42 A11, 50 B4
Weegena Tas. 142 H8, 145 B10
Weemelah NSW 26 E3, 122 G12
Weeragua Vic. 35 C11, 51 E9
Weerite Vic. 50 H7, 63 J7
Weetah Tas. 143 I8, 145 C10
Weetaliba NSW 26 E11
Weethalle NSW 24 A6, 29 N6
Weetulta SA 69 E4, 72 H7
Wehla Vic. 49 B1, 61 L9
Weipa Qld 128 B7
Weismantels NSW 19 F3, 20 B9, 25 M2
Weja NSW 24 B5, 29 O5
Welaregang NSW 24 C12, 36 B7, 51 A1, 55 O6, 57 O2
Weldborough Tas. 143 N7
Welford NP Qld 131 L12, 133 K2
Welland SA xx F3
Wellingrove NSW 27 J5
Wellington NSW 24 F2
Wellington SA 71 D4, 73 L10
Wellington NP WA 86 F3, 88 C8, 90 C9
Wellington Park Tas. xxxiv A11
Wellington Point Qld 114 G8, 115 F5, 117 H11
Wellstead WA 87 H10, 88 H10, 90 F10
Welshmans Reef Vic. 49 E6, 61 N12, 63 N1
Welshpool Vic. 52 H10
Welshpool WA xxv D8, 84 E6, 85 C5
Wembley WA xxiv D4
Wembley Downs WA xxiv C4
Wemen Vic. 28 F8, 59 I9
Wendouree Vic. 42 C3, 47 A2, 49 C10
Wentworth NSW 28 D5, 58 F5
Wentworth Falls NSW 14 D5, 16 G9, 25 I6
Wentworthville NSW 15 J8
Wepowie SA 73 J3, 75 I10
Werakata NP NSW 13 E1, 19 A7, 25 L3
Wereboldera NSW 24 D10, 35 A5, 36 C3
Werneth Vic. 42 B6, 63 L6
Werombi NSW 14 F9, 25 J7, 35 G1
Werona Vic. 42 E1, 49 D7
Werrap Vic. 28 D11, 60 F5
Werri Beach NSW 23 F8
Werribee Vic. 40 A6, 42 H6, 52 B5, 63 P6
Werribee South Vic. 40 B7, 42 H7, 44 F1, 52 B5, 63 P6
Werrikimbe NP NSW 20 D4, 27 K10
Werrimull Vic. 28 C6, 58 E7, 73 P8
Werris Creek NSW 26 H10
Wesburn Vic. 41 E8, 43 M5
Wesley Vale Tas. 142 H6, 145 B6
West Beach SA xx B7
West Burleigh Qld 21 G1, 115 G11, 116 F9
West Cape Howe NP WA 87 C12, 88 G12, 90 E12

West Creek Vic. 45 P12
West Croydon SA xx F1
West End Qld xxx E8, 114 E7
West Footscray Vic. xiv A8
West Frankford Tas. 143 I7, 145 D8
West Hill NP Qld 119 H10, 125 K7
West Hindmarsh SA xx G3
West Hobart Tas. 1 A7, xxxiv D11, 136 C6, 137 D8
West Kentish Tas. 142 G7, 144 G3
West Lakes SA xx A1
West Launceston Tas. 145 F2
West Leederville WA xxiv E5
West MacDonnell NP NT 108 H6, 109 I6, 110 C2, 111 I3
West Melbourne Vic. xiv E10, xvi E2, 39 A4
West Montagu Tas. 142 B3
West Moonah Tas. xxxiv C7, 137 C6
West Perth WA xxiv F5, 83 A1
West Pine Tas. 142 F6, 144 E1
West Richmond SA xx F6
West Ridgley Tas. 142 F6
West Scottsdale Tas. 143 L6
West Swan WA xxv D1
West Takone Tas. 142 E6, 144 B1
West Wallsend NSW 13 F3, 19 C9
West Waterhouse NT 110 E5
West Wollongong NSW 22 B9
West Wyalong NSW 24 B6, 29 P6
Westbourne Park SA xxi I10
Westbury Tas. 143 J8, 145 E11
Westbury Vic. 43 P9, 52 H6
Westby Vic. 28 H10, 61 N4
Westdale NSW 26 H9
Westdale WA 85 G7, 88 D5, 90 C8
Western Creek Tas. 142 H9, 145 B12
Western Flat SA 60 A8, 71 G8
Western Junction Tas. 143 K9, 145 H11
Westerway Tas. 138 E2, 141 I6
Westmar Qld 122 H9
Westmead NSW 12 C6
Westmere Vic. 63 I4
Westminster WA xxiv E1
Weston Creek ACT 33 C6
Weston NSW 13 E2, 19 B8, 25 L4
Westonia WA 88 H3, 90 E6
Westwood Qld 125 L11
Westwood Tas. 143 J8, 145 F10
Weymouth Tas. 143 K5, 145 H5
Wharminda SA 72 E6
Wharparilla Vic. 29 J12, 54 B5, 61 P7
Wharparilla North Vic. 54 B5, 61 P6
Wheatsheaf Vic. 42 F1, 49 F8
Wheeo NSW 24 G8, 35 D2
Whim Creek WA 89 G1, 92 C2, 94 C12, 96 G5
Whiporie NSW 21 E7, 27 N5
Whirily Vic. 61 J5
White Beach Tas. 139 L8, 141 L9
White Cliffs NSW 30 F7
White Flat SA 72 D8
White Gum Valley WA xxiv C12
White Hills Tas. 143 K8, 145 H11
White Mountains NP Qld 124 C3, 131 O3
White Rock Qld 120 E3, 121 F7
Whitefoord Tas. 141 L4
Whiteheads Creek Vic. 54 D10
Whiteman WA xxv B1, 85 C4
Whitemark Tas. 140 B10
Whitemore Tas. 143 J9, 145 F11
Whitewood Qld 124 A5, 131 M5
Whitfield Vic. 55 I9, 56 F7
Whitfords WA 84 C4
Whitlands Vic. 55 I9, 56 F7
Whitsunday Islands NP Qld 119 G5, 125 K3
Whittlesea Vic. 40 F2, 43 J3, 52 D3
Whitton NSW 29 M7
Whitwarta SA 69 G3, 73 J7
Whoorel Vic. 42 C9, 50 D2, 63 M8
Whorouly Vic. 55 J8, 56 G5
Whorouly East Vic. 55 J8, 56 G5
Whorouly South Vic. 55 J8, 56 G5
Whroo Vic. 54 D8
Whyalla SA 72 H3, 74 G11
Whyte Yarcowie SA 73 K4, 75 I11
Wialki WA 88 F1, 90 E5

Wiangaree NSW 21 E3, 27 N2, 123 M11
Wickepin WA 88 F6, 90 D8
Wickham NSW 13 H3, 18 A4, 19 D9
Wickham WA 89 F1, 92 B2, 94 B12, 96 E4
Wickliffe Vic. 62 H4
Widgiemooltha WA 90 H6
Widgiewa NSW 29 M9
Wilberforce NSW 12 A1, 15 I4, 17 P6, 25 J6
Wilburville Tas. 141 J2, 143 J11
Wilby Vic. 29 M12, 54 H6, 56 D2
Wilcannia NSW 30 G9
Wild Cattle Island NP Qld 123 L1, 125 N12
Wild Horse Plains SA 69 G5, 71 B1, 73 I7
Wiley Park NSW 15 K9
Wilga WA 86 H6, 88 D9
Wilgul Vic. 42 B6, 63 L6
Wilkawatt SA 71 F4, 73 N10
Wilkur Vic. 28 E11, 61 I6
Willa Vic. 28 E10, 60 G2
Willagee WA xxiv E11
Willalooka SA 71 F7
Willamulka SA 69 F3
Willandra NP NSW 29 K3
Willare Bridge Roadhouse WA 95 I7, 98 D10
Willatook Vic. 62 G7
Willaura Vic. 63 I3
Willawarrin NSW 20 F3, 27 L9
Willbriggie NSW 29 M7
Willenabrina Vic. 28 D11, 60 G6
Willetton WA xxiv H11, xxv B12
Willi Willi NP NSW 20 E4, 27 L10
William Bay NP WA 87 A12, 88 F12, 90 D11
William Creek SA 76 D10
Williams WA 88 E7, 90 D9
Williamsdale ACT 24 F11, 33 D11, 34 E8, 35 C5, 36 G5
Williamsford Tas. 142 D10, 144 A7
Williamstown SA 66 G3, 67 E6, 71 C2, 73 K8
Williamstown Vic. xvi D10, 40 C6, 43 I6, 52 C4
Williamstown North Vic. xvi A8
Williamtown NSW 19 E8, 20 B12
Williguli WA 89 D12
Willina NSW 20 D9, 25 N2
Willoughby NSW x F4, 12 F6
Willoughby East NSW x G3
Willow Grove Vic. 43 P8, 52 H6
Willow Tree NSW 26 H11
Willowie SA 73 J2, 74 H10
Willowmavin Vic. 43 I1, 52 C1, 54 C12
Willowra NT 106 G12, 108 G2
Willows Qld 124 H11
Willows Gemfields Qld 124 H11
Willowvale Qld 21 B1, 27 L1
Willowvale Vic. 42 A5, 63 K5
Willung Vic. 53 J7
Willung South Vic. 53 J8
Willunga SA 67 B12, 68 E6, 69 H9, 71 B4, 73 J10
Wilmington SA 73 I2, 74 H10
Wilmot Tas. 142 G7, 144 F3
Wilora NT 109 I3
Wilpena SA 70 B10, 75 I6
Wilroy WA 89 E12, 90 B3
Wilson WA xxv C10
Wilsons Promontory NP Vic. 52 H11
Wilsons Valley NSW 36 D9, 51 C3
Wilston Qld xxx G4
Wilton NSW 23 E3, 25 J8, 35 H2
Wiltshire Junction Tas. 142 D4
Wiluna WA 92 F10
Wimba Vic. 42 B11, 50 B4, 63 K9
Wimbleton Heights Estate Vic. 45 L10
Winchelsea Vic. 42 D8, 50 E1, 63 M8
Windang NSW 23 F6, 25 J9, 35 H3
Windarra WA 91 I2, 93 I12
Windellama NSW 24 H10, 35 E4, 37 K1
Windermere Tas. 137 B3, 143 J7, 145 F8
Windermere Vic. 42 C2, 49 B9
Windermere Park NSW 13 F5, 19 B11
Windeyer NSW 24 H3
Windjana Gorge NP WA 95 K7, 98 F9
Windmill Roadhouse WA 88 B3, 90 B6
Windorah Qld 133 I3
Windowie NSW 24 D10, 35 A4, 36 C3, 55 P2
Windsor NSW 12 A2, 15 I5, 17 P7, 25 J6

180

Windsor Qld xxx G4
Windsor SA 69 G5, 71 B1, 73 J7
Windsor Vic. xvii M9
Windy Corner WA 93 K5
Windy Harbour WA 87 B5, 88 D11, 90 C11
Wingeel Vic. 42 C7, 63 M7
Wingello NSW 25 I9, 35 F3
Wingen NSW 25 K1, 26 H12
Wingham NSW 20 D8, 25 N1, 27 K12
Winiam Vic. 28 C12, 60 E7
Winiam East Vic. 60 E7
Winjallok Vic. 61 K10
Winkie SA 58 A6, 73 N7
Winkleigh Tas. 143 J7, 145 E8
Winmalee NSW 14 G5, 17 L8
Winnaleah Tas. 143 N6
Winnambool Vic. 28 F8, 59 I10
Winnap Vic. 62 C5, 71 H12
Winnellie NT xxvii E8, 102 D3
Winnindoo Vic. 53 J6
Winninowie SA 73 I2, 74 G10
Winnunga NSW 24 B5, 29 O5
Winslow Vic. 50 C7, 62 G7
Winthrop WA xxiv F11
Winton Qld 131 L7
Winton Vic. 54 H8, 56 D5
Winton North Vic. 54 H8, 56 E5
Winulta SA 69 F4, 71 A1, 73 I7
Wirha SA 28 A8, 71 G4, 73 N10
Wirlinga NSW 24 A12, 55 L6, 57 J2
Wirrabara SA 73 J3, 74 H11
Wirrega SA 28 A12, 60 A6, 71 G7
Wirrida SA 79 O12, 81 O1
Wirrimah NSW 24 E7, 35 B1
Wirrinya NSW 24 D5
Wirrulla SA 72 B1, 81 O9
Wiseleigh Vic. 53 N5
Wisemans Creek NSW 24 H6
Wisemans Ferry NSW 13 A7, 15 K2, 25 K5
Wishbone WA 88 G7
Wistow SA 66 G10, 67 E11, 68 H4
Witchcliffe WA 86 B9, 88 B10
Withersfield Qld 124 H10
Witjira NP SA 76 C2, 79 P2, 109 L12
Wittenoom WA 89 G3, 92 D4, 96 H8
Wivenhoe Tas. 142 F5
Wivenhoe Pocket Qld 115 A4, 117 C10
Woden Valley ACT 33 D6
Wodonga Vic. 24 A12, 29 N12, 55 K6, 57 I2
Wogyala NT 107 K8
Wokalup WA 86 E2, 88 C8
Woko NP NSW 20 B7, 25 M1, 27 J11
Wokurna SA 69 F2, 73 I5
Wolfe Creek Meteorite Crater NP WA 95 N9
Wollar NSW 25 I2
Wollemi NP NSW 13 A1, 14 G1, 15 I2, 17 M3, 25 J4
Wollert Vic. 40 E3, 43 J4, 52 C3
Wolli Creek NSW viii A11
Wollogorang Roadhouse NT 107 P4, 129 A3
Wollombi NSW 13 C3, 25 K4
Wollomombi NSW 20 D1, 27 K8
Wollongbar NSW 21 G5, 27 O3, 123 N12
Wollongong NSW 22, 23 F5, 25 J8, 35 H2
Wollstonecraft NSW x F8, 11 A4
Wollumbin NP NSW 21 G2, 27 O2, 123 N11
Wollun NSW 20 A2, 27 J9
Wolseley SA 28 B12, 60 B7, 71 G7
Wolumla NSW 35 E9, 51 H7
Womalilla Qld 122 E6
Wombarra NSW 23 G3
Wombat NSW 24 D8, 35 B2
Wombelano Vic. 60 D11
Wombeyan Caves NSW 24 H8, 35 F2
Womboota NSW 29 J11, 54 B4, 61 P5
Won Wron Vic. 53 I9
Wonboyn NSW 35 E11
Wonboyn Lake NSW 51 H9
Wondai Qld 118 A9, 123 L6
Wondalga NSW 24 D10, 35 A5, 36 C3, 55 P3
Wondul Range NP Qld 123 J10
Wonga Qld 121 D3, 127 L5
Wongaling Beach Qld 120 E6, 127 M8
Wongan Hills WA 88 D2, 90 C6
Wongarbon NSW 24 F1, 26 C12

Wongawilli NSW 23 E5
Wongulla SA 71 D2, 73 L8
Wonthaggi Vic. 43 L12, 52 E9
Wonwondah East Vic. 60 G10
Wonwondah North Vic. 60 F10
Wonyip Vic. 52 H9
Wood Wood Vic. 28 G9, 59 L11, 61 L1
Woodanilling WA 88 F8, 90 D9
Woodbridge Tas. 138 H9, 141 J9
Woodbridge WA xxv E2
Woodburn NSW 21 F6, 27 O4
Woodbury Tas. 141 L3
Woodchester SA 66 H12, 67 E12, 71 C4, 73 K10
Woodenbong NSW 21 D2, 27 M2, 123 M11
Woodend Vic. 42 G2, 49 H9, 52 B2, 54 B12, 63 P3
Woodfield Vic. 54 G11, 56 B9
Woodford NSW 14 E6, 17 I9
Woodford Qld 117 E6, 123 M8
Woodford Vic. 50 C7, 62 G8
Woodforde SA xxi P3
Woodgate Qld 118 E3, 123 M4
Woodglen Vic. 53 L5
Woodhill Qld 115 C8
Woodhouselee NSW 24 G8, 35 E2
Woodlands WA xxiv C4, 87 D9, 88 G11
Woodleigh Vic. 43 M10, 52 E8
Woodridge Qld 114 E10, 115 E6
Woods Point SA 71 D4, 73 L10
Woods Point Vic. 43 P4, 52 H3
Woods Reef NSW 26 H7
Woods Well SA 71 D6, 73 L12
Woodsdale Tas. 141 L5
Woodside Beach Vic. 53 J9
Woodside SA 66 G8, 67 E9, 68 H2, 71 C3, 73 K9
Woodside Vic. 53 J9
Woodstock NSW 24 F6
Woodstock Qld 119 A2, 120 G11, 124 G2, 127 N12
Woodstock Tas. 138 G7, 141 J8
Woodstock Vic. 40 E3, 43 J3, 52 C3
Woodvale Vic. 49 F2, 54 A8, 61 O9
Woodville NSW 13 G1, 19 C7, 20 A11, 27 J5
Woodville SA 67 B8, 68 E1, 69 H7
Woodville South SA xx E1
Woodville West SA xx D1
Woody Point Qld 114 F4, 115 E2, 117 G9
Wool Bay SA 69 E7, 72 H9
Wool Wool Vic. 42 A8, 50 A1, 63 K7
Woolamai Vic. 43 L11, 45 O11, 52 E8
Woolamai Waters Vic. 45 M11
Woolaning NT 102 C7, 104 D5
Woolbrook NSW 20 A3, 27 I9
Woolgoolga NSW 21 E11, 27 N7
Wooli NSW 21 F10, 27 N6
Woollahra NSW ix I7
Woolloomooloo NSW viii G5, 10 G8
Woolloongabba Qld xxx H10, 113 G12
Woolner NT xxvii C8
Woolomin NSW 27 I10
Woolooga Qld 118 C8, 123 M6
Woolooware NSW 12 E11, 15 L11
Wooloowin Qld xxxi I2
Woolshed Flat SA 73 I2, 74 G9
Woolshed Vic. 55 J7, 56 H4
Woolsthorpe Vic. 62 G7
Woolwich NSW viii C1, x D8
Woomargama NSW 24 B12, 29 O12, 55 M5
Woomargama NP NSW 24 B12, 29 P12, 55 N5, 57 L1
Woombye Qld 117 F4, 118 E11
Woomelang Vic. 28 E10, 61 I4
Woomera SA 74 E5
Woongoolba Qld 114 H11, 115 F7
Woonona NSW 23 G4
Wooragee Vic. 55 J7, 56 H3
Woorak Vic. 28 C12, 60 E7
Woorak West Vic. 60 E6
Wooramel Roadhouse WA 89 C8
Woorarra Vic. 52 H9
Wooreen Vic. 43 O11, 52 G8
Woori Yallock Vic. 41 D8, 43 M5, 52 E4
Woorim Qld 114 H2, 115 F1, 117 H8
Woorinen Vic. 28 G9, 59 L12, 61 L2
Woorinen North Vic. 59 L12, 61 L1
Woornack Vic. 28 E9, 58 H11, 60 H1

Woorndoo Vic. 63 I5
Wooroloo WA 85 E4, 88 C4
Wooroolin Qld 118 A9, 123 L6
Wooroonook Vic. 28 G12, 61 K7
Wooroonooran NP Qld 120 E4, 121 F9, 127 L7
Woosang Vic. 28 G12, 61 L7
Wootong Vale Vic. 62 E3
Wootton NSW 20 D10, 25 N2
Worongary Qld 116 D7
Woronora NSW 12 C10, 15 K11, 23 H1
Worsley WA 86 F3
Wowan Qld 125 L12
Woy Woy NSW 12 H1, 13 D8, 15 N3, 25 K6
Wrattonbully SA 60 B11, 62 B1, 71 G10
Wrightley Vic. 54 H10, 56 D7
Wroxham Vic. 35 D11, 51 F9
Wubin WA 90 C5
Wudinna SA 72 D3, 74 B11
Wujal Wujal Qld 127 L4
Wuk Wuk Vic. 53 M5
Wulagi NT xxvii F4
Wulgulmerang Vic. 35 A10, 51 A7, 53 P1, 55 P12, 57 P11
Wundowie WA 85 F3
Wunghnu Vic. 29 K12, 54 E6, 56 A2
Wunkar SA 71 F2, 73 N8
Wurankuwu NT 104 C3
Wurdiboluc Vic. 42 D9, 50 E2, 63 M8
Wutul Qld 123 L8
Wutunugurra NT 107 K11
Wy Yung Vic. 53 M5
Wyalkatchem WA 88 E3, 90 D6
Wyalong NSW 24 B6, 29 P6
Wyan NSW 21 E6, 27 N4
Wyandra Qld 122 B7, 133 O7
Wyangala NSW 24 F6
Wybalenna Tas. 140 A10
Wybong NSW 25 J2
Wycarbah Qld 125 L11
Wycheproof Vic. 28 G12, 61 K6
Wychitella Vic. 28 G12, 61 L7
Wycliffe Well Roadhouse NT 107 J11, 109 J1
Wye River Vic. 42 C11, 50 D5, 63 M10
Wyee NSW 13 E6, 19 B11, 25 L5
Wyee Point NSW 13 F5, 19 B11
Wyeebo Vic. 55 M7, 57 L4
Wyelangta Vic. 42 A11, 50 A5
Wyena Tas. 143 L6
Wyening WA 88 C3, 90 C6
Wylie Creek NSW 21 B3, 27 L2, 123 L11
Wymah NSW 24 B12, 55 M6, 57 L2
Wymlet Vic. 28 D8, 58 G10
Wynarka SA 71 E3, 73 L10
Wynbring SA 81 M4
Wyndham NSW 35 D10, 51 G7
Wyndham WA 95 N4, 99 L5
Wynnum Qld 114 G7, 115 E4, 117 G11, 123 N9
Wynnum West Qld xxxi P7
Wynyard Tas. 142 E5
Wyomi SA 71 E9
Wyoming NSW 13 D8, 15 O2, 20 D8, 25 N1, 27 K12
Wyong NSW 13 E7, 15 P1, 19 A12, 25 L5
Wyong Creek NSW 13 D6, 15 O1
Wyperfeld NP Vic. 28 C10, 58 E12, 60 E2, 71 H5, 73 P11
Wyrra NSW 24 B5, 29 P5
Wyrrabalong NP NSW 13 F7, 15 P3, 25 L5
Wyuna Vic. 29 K12, 54 D6

Yaamba Qld 125 M10
Yaapeet Vic. 28 D10, 60 F4
Yabba Vic. 55 L7, 57 K4
Yabba North Vic. 54 F6, 56 B2
Yabbra NP NSW 21 C3, 27 M2, 123 L12
Yabmana SA 69 A1, 72 F5
Yacka SA 69 H1, 73 J5, 74 H12
Yackandandah Vic. 55 K7, 57 I4
Yagoona NSW 12 C8, 13 A12
Yahl SA 62 A5, 71 G12
Yalangur Qld 123 L9
Yalata SA 81 I6
Yalata Roadhouse SA 81 I6
Yalboroo Qld 119 F6, 125 J5
Yalbraith NSW 24 H8, 35 E2

Yalgoo WA 89 F11, 90 C2
Yalgorup NP WA 85 B10, 86 D1, 88 B7, 90 C8
Yallakool NSW 29 I10, 54 B2, 61 P3
Yallaroi NSW 26 H3, 123 I12
Yalleroi Qld 124 D11
Yallingup WA 86 A6, 88 B9, 90 B10
Yallourn North Vic. 52 H7
Yallunda Flat SA 72 D7
Yaloak Vale Vic. 42 F4, 49 F12, 63 N5
Yalwal NSW 23 B9, 25 I10, 35 G4, 37 N1
Yamala Qld 125 I11
Yamanto Qld 114 A9, 115 B6, 117 C12
Yamba NSW 21 F8, 27 O5
Yamba Roadhouse SA 28 B6, 58 B6, 71 G1, 73 O7
Yambacoona Tas. 141 O10
Yambuk Vic. 50 A7, 62 F8
Yambuna Vic. 54 D5
Yan Yean Vic. 40 E3, 43 J4, 52 D3
Yanac Vic. 28 C12, 60 D6
Yanac South Vic. 60 D6
Yanakie Vic. 52 G10
Yanchep WA 84 A1, 85 A2, 88 B4, 90 B7
Yanchep NP WA 84 A1, 85 B2, 88 B4, 90 B7
Yanco NSW 29 N8
Yandaran Qld 118 C1, 123 M3
Yanderra NSW 23 D3, 25 J8, 35 G2
Yandeyarra WA 89 G1, 92 D3, 96 H6
Yandina Qld 117 F3, 118 E11, 123 N7
Yando Vic. 28 H12, 61 M6
Yandoit Vic. 49 E7, 61 N12, 63 N2
Yanerbie Beach SA 72 A3, 81 N10
Yangan Qld 21 B1, 27 L1, 123 L10
Yaninee SA 72 C3, 74 B10, 81 P10
Yanipy Vic. 28 B12, 60 C7, 71 H7
Yankalilla SA 68 D7, 69 G10, 71 B4, 73 J10
Yantabulla NSW 31 K3, 133 M12
Yantanabie SA 72 B2, 81 O9
Yanununbeyan NP NSW 24 G11, 34 G8, 35 D5, 37 I4
Yapeen Vic. 49 E6, 61 N12, 63 N1
Yaraka Qld 133 L2
Yarck Vic. 54 F11, 56 A9
Yarloop WA 85 D12, 86 E1, 88 C7
Yaroomba Qld 117 G3, 118 F11
Yarra NSW 24 G9, 35 E3
Yarra Creek Tas. 141 P12
Yarra Glen Vic. 40 H4, 41 C6, 43 L4, 52 E4
Yarra Junction Vic. 41 E8, 43 M5, 52 F4
Yarra Ranges NP Vic. 41 D6, 43 N5, 52 G4, 56 C12
Yarrabah Qld 120 E2, 121 G7
Yarrabandai NSW 24 C3
Yarrabin NSW 24 G2
Yarraby Vic. 28 G9, 59 K11, 61 K1
Yarragon Vic. 43 O9, 52 G7
Yarrahappini NP NSW 20 G3, 27 M9
Yarralin NT 104 D12, 106 D3

Yarralumla ACT 32 A9
Yarram Vic. 53 I9
Yarramalong NSW 13 D6
Yarraman NSW 26 G4
Yarraman Qld 118 A12, 123 L7
Yarrambat Vic. 52 D3
Yarramony WA 85 G1
Yarrangobilly NSW 24 E11, 35 B5, 36 D5
Yarrangobilly Caves NSW 24 E12, 35 B6, 36 D5
Yarrara Vic. 28 C6, 58 D7, 73 P8
Yarraville Vic. xiv B11, xvi B2
Yarrawalla South Vic. 61 N7
Yarrawarrah NSW 12 C11, 15 J11, 23 H1
Yarrawonga Vic. 29 M12, 54 H5, 56 D1
Yarrawonga Park NSW 13 F5, 19 B11
Yarrock Vic. 28 B12, 60 C7, 71 H7
Yarroweyah Vic. 29 L12, 54 F4
Yarrowitch NSW 20 C5, 27 K10
Yarrowyck NSW 20 A1, 27 J8
Yarto Vic. 28 E10, 60 G2
Yarwun Qld 123 K1, 125 N12
Yass NSW 24 F9, 35 C3
Yatchaw Vic. 62 F5
Yatina SA 73 J3, 75 I11
Yatpool Vic. 28 E6, 58 G7
Yattalunga NSW 13 D8, 15 O3
Yatte Yattah NSW 25 I11, 35 G5, 37 N3
Yaugher Vic. 42 B10, 50 C3
Yea Vic. 41 D1, 43 L1, 52 E1, 54 E12
Yealering WA 88 F6, 90 D8
Yearinan NSW 26 E9
Yearinga Vic. 60 C7, 71 H7
Yednia Qld 117 B4, 118 C12, 123 M7
Yeelanna SA 72 D7
Yeerip Vic. 54 H6, 56 E3
Yeerongpilly Qld xxx F12
Yelarbon Qld 27 I2, 123 J11
Yellangip Vic. 60 G6
Yellingbo Vic. 41 D8, 43 L6
Yellow Rock NSW 14 G6, 17 L9, 23 E6
Yellowdine WA 90 F6
Yelta SA 69 E3, 72 H6
Yelta Vic. 58 G5
Yelverton WA 86 B7
Yenda NSW 29 M7
Yendon Vic. 42 D4, 49 D11, 63 M4
Yengo NP NSW 13 A2, 15 L1, 25 K3
Yennora NSW 15 J8
Yeo Yeo NSW 24 D8, 35 A2
Yeodene Vic. 42 B10, 50 C3, 63 L8
Yeoval NSW 24 F3
Yeppoon Qld 125 M10
Yerecoin WA 88 C2, 90 C6
Yering Vic. 40 H5, 41 C7, 43 L5, 52 E4
Yerong Creek NSW 24 B10, 29 O10, 55 L2
Yeronga Qld xxx E12

Yerranderie NSW 14 B11, 23 A1, 25 I7, 35 F1
Yerrinbool NSW 23 D4, 25 I8, 35 G2
Yetholme NSW 24 H5
Yetman NSW 27 I3, 123 J12
Yeungroon Vic. 61 K8
Yimbun Qld 117 A6
Yin Barun Vic. 54 G9, 56 D6
Yinkanie SA 28 A6, 71 F1, 73 N7
Yinnar Vic. 43 P10, 52 H8
Yirrkala NT 105 N4
Yokine WA xxiv F3
Yolla Tas. 142 E5
Yongala SA 73 K3, 75 I11
Yoogali NSW 29 M7
Yoongarillup WA 86 C6, 88 B9
York WA 85 H4, 88 D4, 90 C7
York Plains Tas. 141 L3
Yorke Valley SA 69 E5, 72 H8
Yorketown SA 69 E8, 72 H9
Yorkeys Knob Qld 120 E2, 121 F6
Yornaning WA 88 E6
Yoting WA 88 F4, 90 D7
Youanmite Vic. 29 L12, 54 F6, 56 B2
Youarang Vic. 54 G6, 56 C2
Youndegin WA 88 E4, 90 D7
Young NSW 24 E7, 35 B1
Younghusband SA 71 D3, 73 L9
Yowah Qld 133 M8
Yowrie NSW 35 E8, 37 J10, 51 H4
Yuelamu NT 108 G4
Yuendumu NT 108 F4
Yugar Qld 114 C5, 115 C3, 117 E10
Yulara NT 108 E10, 110 D9
Yulara Pulka NT 110 C9
Yuleba Qld 122 H6
Yulecart Vic. 62 E4
Yumali SA 71 E5, 73 L11
Yuna WA 89 D12, 90 A3
Yunderup WA 85 C9
Yundi SA 68 F6, 69 H9
Yundool Vic. 54 G6, 56 C3
Yungaburra Qld 120 D3, 121 E9, 127 L7
Yungaburra NP Qld 120 D3, 121 E9, 127 L7
Yungera Vic. 28 G8, 59 K9
Yunta SA 73 L2, 75 K10
Yuraygir NP NSW 21 F9, 27 N6
Yurgo SA 71 F4, 73 M10
Yuroke Vic. 40 D3, 43 I4
Yuulong Vic. 50 H11, 63 J10
Zanthus WA 91 J5
Zeehan Tas. 142 D10
Zeerust Vic. 54 E6, 56 A3
Zetland NSW viii F9
Zillmere Qld 114 E5, 115 D3, 117 F10

Explore Australia Publishing Pty Ltd
85 High Street
Prahran, Victoria 3181, Australia

This edition published by Explore Australia Publishing Pty Ltd, 2007

First published by George Philip & O'Neil Pty Ltd, 1977
New editions and reprints 1981, 1982, 1983, 1984, 1985, 1986
Sixth edition published by Penguin Books Australia Ltd, 1987
New editions 1988, 1989, 1990, 1991, 1992, 1993, 1994, 1995,
1996, 1997, 1998, 1999, 2000, 2001
Twenty-first edition published by Explore Australia Publishing Pty Ltd, 2002
New editions 2003, 2004, 2005, 2006

10 9 8 7 6 5 4 3 2 1

Printed and bound in China by SNP Leefung Printers Limited

ISBN 13 – 978 174117 237 9

Disclaimers: The publisher cannot accept responsibility for any errors or omissions
in this book. While information was correct at the time of research, please be aware
that conditions constantly change, and the representation of any road or track is not
necessarily evidence of public right of way or of safe traveling conditions. It is the
responsibility of the user to obtain permits/permission and check road conditions and
amenities prior to setting out.

Publisher's Note: The publisher welcomes information and suggestions for correction
or improvement to the maps within this book. Write to: Publications Manager, Explore
Australia Publishing, 85 High Street, Prahran, Victoria 3181, Australia.
Email: explore@hardiegrant.com.au

Photographs
Front cover: View of Wilpena Pound from Moralana Drive, Flinders Ranges
National Park, South Australia (Australian Scenics)
Back cover: Lorna Glen Station, near Wiluna, Western Australia (Nick Rains)
Title page: Rainbow Valley, Northern Territory (Jeff Drewitz)
Contents: Avenue of karri trees near Northcliffe, Western Australia
(Australian Scenics)
iv Andrew Gregory; vii Tourism NSW; xiii Andrew Chapman; xix John Baker;
xxiii Len Stewart/Lochman Transparencies; xxix Jeff Drewitz; xxxiii Geoff Murray